Fodor's

HONG KONG

21st Edition

**Where to Stay and Eat
for All Budgets**

**Must-See Sights
and Local Secrets**

Ratings You Can Trust

Fodor's Travel Publications   New York, Toronto, London, Sydney, Auckland
www.fodors.com

FODOR'S HONG KONG

Editors: Joanna G. Cantor, Shannon Kelly, Josh McIlvain

Editorial Contributors: Liana Cafolla, Chris Cottrell, Cherise Fong, Helen Luk, Zoe Mak, Dominique Rowe, Albert Wong

Production Editor: Jennifer DePrima
Maps & Illustrations: David Lindroth, *cartographer;* with additional cartography provided by Henry Colomb, Mark Stroud, Moon Street Cartography; Bob Blake, Rebecca Baer, *map editors;* William Wu, *information graphics*
Design: Fabrizio La Rocca, *creative director*; Guido Caroti, Siobhan O'Hare, *art directors*; Tina Malaney, Chie Ushio, Ann McBride, Jessica Walsh, *designers*; Melanie Marin, *senior picture editor*
Cover Photo (Causeway Bay): So Hing-Keung/Corbis
Production Manager: Amanda Bullock

21st Edition

ISBN 978-1-4000-0810-0

ISSN 1070-6887

SPECIAL SALES
This book is available at special discounts for bulk purchases for sales promotions or premiums. Special editions, including personalized covers, excerpts of existing books, and corporate imprints, can be created in large quantities for special needs. For more information, write to Special Markets/Premium Sales, 1745 Broadway, MD 6-2, New York, New York 10019, or e-mail specialmarkets@randomhouse.com.

AN IMPORTANT TIP & AN INVITATION
Although all prices, opening times, and other details in this book are based on information supplied to us at press time, changes occur all the time in the travel world, and Fodor's cannot accept responsibility for facts that become outdated or for inadvertent errors or omissions. So **always confirm information when it matters,** especially if you're making a detour to visit a specific place. Your experiences—positive and negative—matter to us. If we have missed or misstated something, **please write to us.** We follow up on all suggestions. Contact the Hong Kong editor at editors@fodors.com or c/o Fodor's at 1745 Broadway, New York, NY 10019.

PRINTED IN THE UNITED STATES OF AMERICA

10 9 8 7 6 5 4 3 2 1

Be a Fodor's Correspondent

Your opinion matters. It matters to us. It matters to your fellow Fodor's travelers, too. And we'd like to hear it. In fact, we need to hear it.

When you share your experiences and opinions, you become an active member of the Fodor's community. That means we'll not only use your feedback to make our books better, but we'll publish your names and comments whenever possible. Throughout our guides, look for "Word of Mouth," excerpts of your unvarnished feedback.

Here's how you can help improve Fodor's for all of us.

Tell us when we're right. We rely on local writers to give you an insider's perspective. But our writers and staff editors—who are the best in the business—depend on you. Your positive feedback is a vote to renew our recommendations for the next edition.

Tell us when we're wrong. We're proud that we update most of our guides every year. But we're not perfect. Things change. Hotels cut services. Museums change hours. Charming cafés lose charm. If our writer didn't quite capture the essence of a place, tell us how you'd do it differently. If any of our descriptions are inaccurate or inadequate, we'll incorporate your changes in the next edition and will correct factual errors at fodors.com immediately.

Tell us what to include. You probably have had fantastic travel experiences that aren't yet in Fodor's. Why not share them with a community of like-minded travelers? Maybe you chanced upon a beach or bistro or B&B that you don't want to keep to yourself. Tell us why we should include it. And share your discoveries and experiences with everyone directly at fodors.com. Your input may lead us to add a new listing or highlight a place we cover with a "Highly Recommended" star or with our highest rating, "Fodor's Choice."

Give us your opinion instantly at our feedback center at www.fodors.com/feedback. You may also e-mail editors@fodors.com with the subject line "Hong Kong Editor." Or send your nominations, comments, and complaints by mail to Hong Kong Editor, Fodor's, 1745 Broadway, New York, NY 10019.

You and travelers like you are the heart of the Fodor's community. Make our community richer by sharing your experiences. Be a Fodor's correspondent.

Happy Traveling!

Tim Jarrell, Publisher

CONTENTS

Fodor's Features

ABOUT THIS BOOK

Our Ratings

Sometimes you find terrific travel experiences and sometimes they just find you. But usually the burden is on you to select the right combination of experiences. That's where our ratings come in.

As travelers we've all discovered a place so wonderful that its worthiness is obvious. And sometimes that place is so unique that superlatives don't do it justice: you just have to be there to know. These sights, properties, and experiences get our highest rating, **Fodor's Choice**, indicated by orange stars throughout this book.

Black stars highlight sights and properties we deem **Highly Recommended**, places that our writers, editors, and readers praise again and again for consistency and excellence.

By default, there's another category: any place we include in this book is by definition worth your time, unless we say otherwise. And we will.

Disagree with any of our choices? Care to nominate a place or suggest that we rate one more highly? Visit our feedback center at www.fodors.com/feedback.

Budget Well

Hotel and restaurant price categories from ¢ to $$$$ are defined in the opening pages of each chapter. For attractions, we always give standard adult admission fees; reductions are usually available for children, students, and senior citizens. Want to pay with plastic? **AE, D, DC, MC, V** following restaurant and hotel listings indicate whether American Express, Discover, Diners Club, MasterCard, and Visa are accepted.

Restaurants

Unless we state otherwise, restaurants are open for lunch and dinner daily. We mention dress only when there's a specific requirement and reservations only when they're essential or not accepted—it's always best to book ahead.

Hotels

Hotels have private bath, phone, TV, and air-conditioning and operate on the European Plan (aka EP, meaning without meals), unless we specify that they use the Continental Plan (CP, with a continental breakfast), Breakfast Plan (BP, with a full breakfast), or Modified American Plan (MAP, with breakfast and dinner) or are all-inclusive (including all meals and most activities). We always list facilities but not whether you'll be charged an extra fee to use them, so when pricing accommodations, find out what's included.

Many Listings

★	Fodor's Choice
★	Highly recommended
⊠	Physical address
✛	Directions
⌂	Mailing address
☎	Telephone
🖷	Fax
⊕	On the Web
✉	E-mail
🖻	Admission fee
☉	Open/closed times
Ⓜ	Metro stations
▭	Credit cards

Hotels & Restaurants

🏨	Hotel
🛏	Number of rooms
⟁	Facilities
❮❯	Meal plans
✕	Restaurant
⟳	Reservations
✎	Smoking
🍷	BYOB
✕🏨	Hotel with restaurant that warrants a visit

Outdoors

⚐	Golf
⛺	Camping

Other

☺	Family-friendly
⇨	See also
⊠	Branch address
☞	Take note

Experience Hong Kong

China ferry terminal, Kowloon

WORD OF MOUTH

"I also recommend taking the longest outdoor escalator in the city. No one told us about this and I thought it was one of the most interesting things about the city. It goes and goes and goes and goes. The city is extremely hilly...like San Francisco...and with the high temperatures, the escalator takes you a far distance uphill without the sweat and exertion."

—sueblue

EXPERIENCE HONG KONG PLANNER

Looks Deceive

On the surface it seems that every building is a sculpture of glass and steel and every pedestrian is hurrying to a meeting. But look past the shiny new surfaces to the ancient culture that gives the city its exotic flavor and its citizens their unique outlook.

Wording It Right

Learn a few basic Cantonese expressions like "*lei-ho?*" ("hi, how are you?") and "*mm-goi sai*" ("thanks very much"). The official languages are Chinese and English; most residents speak Cantonese. Mandarin—the "common language" of mainland China—is gaining in popularity here and in Macau, where the official languages are Chinese and Portuguese.

In hotels, major restaurants, and large stores, most people speak English. Many taxi and bus drivers and staffers in small shops, cafés, and market stalls, do not.

Ask for directions from MTR employees or English-speaking policemen, identifiable by the red strips on their epaulets. Get your concierge to write down your destination in Chinese if you're headed off the main trail.

Good for Kids

Put the Zoological & Botanical Gardens, the Symphony of Lights, the Peak Tram, and a skyscraper climb atop your list. The Hong Kong Heritage Museum has a gallery where 4- to 10-year-olds can dress up in Hakka clothes and reconstruct pottery. Colorful, very hands-on main galleries have plenty for teens.

Ocean Park has a balance of toned-down thrills and high-octane rides, so you could take 3- or 4-year-olds right through to teenagers. A massive aquarium and a giant-panda enclosure round out the offerings. Older kids might enjoy seeing candy-pink dolphins in their natural habitat on a Dolphinwatch half-day trip. If you want even more beasties, tropical birds fill the walk-through Edward Youde Aviary in Hong Kong Park.

Mall rats can make plenty of like-minded local friends at Times Square, Pacific Place, and Kowloon Tong's Festival Walk, all of which are safe places to wander.

Visitor Information

Swing by the Hong Kong Tourist Board (HKTB) visitor center before even leaving the airport. It publishes stacks of helpful free exploring booklets, runs a plethora of tours all over the territory (and beyond), and operates a multilingual helpline. Its detailed Web site is a fabulous resource. If you're planning on visiting several museums in a week, pick up an HKTB Museum Tour Pass, which gets you into seven museums and costs HK$50. Buy it at participating museums or at the visitor centers in Causeway Bay or Tsim Sha Tsui.

Hong Kong Tourist Board (*HKTB ⊠ Hong Kong International Airport, Arrivals Level, Lantau ⊘ Daily 7 AM–11 PM ⊠ Causeway Bay MTR Station, near Exit F, Causeway Bay ⊘ Daily 8–8 ⊠ Star Ferry Concourse, Tsim Sha Tsui, Kowloon ⊘ Daily 8–8 ☎ 2508–1234 [hotline daily 9–6] ⊕ www.discoverhongkong.com*).

When to Go

Hong Kong's high season, October through late December, sees sunny, dry days and cool, comfortable nights. January, February, and sometimes early March are cool and dank, with long periods of overcast skies. March and April can be either chilly and miserable or sunny and beautiful. By May the temperature is consistently warm and comfortable.

June through September are the cheapest months for one reason: they coincide with the hot, sticky, and very rainy typhoon (hurricane) season. Hong Kong is prepared for blustery assaults; if a big storm approaches, the airwaves crackle with information, and your hotel will post the appropriate signals (a No. 10 signal indicates the worst of winds, and a black warning is the equivalent for rain). This is serious business—bamboo scaffolding can come hurtling through the streets like spears, ships can sink in the harbor, and large areas of the territory can flood. Museums, shops and transport shut down at signal No. 8.

Navigating

■ Hong Kong's streets seem utterly chaotic, but getting lost in Central is an achievement. If you manage it, get your bearings by looking up: orient yourself using the waterfront Two IFC skyscraper. In Kowloon, remember where you are in relation to Nathan Road, where the MTR (underground railway) stations are.

■ The MTR, which links most of the areas you'll want to visit, is quick, safe, clean, and very user-friendly. The KCR transit system links Kowloon with areas in the New Territories.

■ Pay with a rechargeable Octopus card. You can use it on the MTR, KCR, buses, trams, the Star Ferry, the Peak Tram—even at vending machines, convenience stores, fast-food restaurants, and the racetrack.

■ It's often not worth taking the MTR for one stop, as stations are close. Walk or take a bus or tram.

■ Most MTR stations have multiple exits, so consult the detailed station maps to determine which exit lets you out closest to your destination.

■ If you're crossing Central, use the covered walkways that link its main buildings, thus avoiding stoplights, exhaust fumes, and weather conditions.

■ On Hong Kong Island, Queen's Road changes its suffix every so often, so you get Queen's Road East, Queen's Road Central, and Queen's Road West. These suffixes, however, don't exactly correspond with the districts, so part of Queen's Road Central is actually in Western. As street numbers start again with each new section, be sure you know which part you're headed for, or better still, the intersecting street. The same goes for Des Voeux Road.

HONG KONG TEMPERATURES

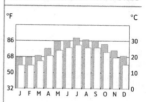

°F · °C · 86 · 68 · 50 · 32 · 30 · 20 · 10 · 0 · J F M A M J J A S O N D

TOP HONG KONG ATTRACTIONS

The Big Buddha

(A) How did a remote Lantau Island plateau make the city's must-do checklist? It's mostly due to the 242-ton Tian Tan Buddha statue, which sits in the lotus position on a hill next to the Po Lin Buddhist Monastery. Nearby is the Wisdom Path, a beautiful religious walk.

Chi Lin Nunnery

(B) Such a peaceful haven seems unlikely amid New Kowloon's grimy sprawl. Yet when you step over the wooden threshold of the Chi Lin Nunnery, the tower blocks fade away. Its stone-flagged courtyards, wooden halls, and unadorned altars invite reflection.

Dim Sum

(C) As you bite into a moist *siu mai* it dawns on you why everyone says you haven't done dim sum until you've done it in Hong Kong. Fresh, innovative ingredients and devout diners make dim sum places here very different from those in Chinatowns worldwide.

Going Green

(D) Hong Kong and its environs are dotted with golf courses: from the popular (and cheap) Kau Sai Chau public course near Sai Kung town to the popular (and luxe) Mission Hills Golf Club & Resort, the world's largest golf facility, near Shenzhen on the mainland.

Harbor Views

(E) The skyline that launched a thousand postcards. . . . See it on a stroll along the Tsim Sha Tsui waterfront, from a Star Ferry crossing the harbor, or from the top of Victoria Peak. By day, the skyscrapers glitter. When the sun sets, Hong Kong puts on its neon party gear.

Hong Kong Heritage Museum

(F) This beautifully planned museum chronicles Hong Kong's changing face, from

scattered fishing and farming communities to booming new towns. An exquisite Chinese art collection and an exhibition on Cantonese opera are two more reasons to head here.

Horse Racing at Happy Valley

(G) Every year, Hong Kongers gamble over US$10 billion, and the Happy Valley Racetrack is one of their favorite places to do it. As the horses pound along, thousands of punters scream themselves into a frenzy—they're more of a spectacle than the races, truth be told.

Jetfoil Getaway

(H) Ask Hong Kongers about Macau, the former Portuguese colony an hour away by jetfoil, and they'll go on about its good food and wine and its casinos. They may forget to tell you about the old town squares paved in elegant patterns and lined with colonial buildings. They may also neglect to mention the gray-sand beaches.

Markets & Malls

(I) Shopping is a religion here, and with so many retail temples, it's easy to see why. At Kowloon's street markets, clothes, electronics, and souvenirs compete for space with food carts. Exquisite antiques fill windows along Hollywood Road, from Central to Sheung Wan, where herbalists peddle strange-looking remedies. Big-name designers monopolize Central's malls. Prices are more down-to-earth in Causeway Bay's Times Square mall.

The Trails

(J) Well-maintained trails crisscross Hong Kong's greenery. Visit the best wilderness areas by tackling part of the MacLehose Trail in Sai Kung Country Park. Crossing the Dragon's Back—a Hong Kong Island ridge—leads to unparalleled Southside sea views and the village of Shek O.

FREE THINGS TO DO

It's easy to spend money in the big city: shopping, entrance fees, food, shows, late-night cocktails. But if you'd like to put your wallet away for a while, here are some of our favorite options.

Art

Works by local prodigies adorn the walls of the tony—but free—private galleries in Central, SoHo, and Sheung Wan. Hanart TZ Gallery, Plum Blossoms, and Grotto Fine Art are stalwarts. There's a leafy backdrop for the Sculpture Walk, a collection of 20 works—including an Eduardo Paolozzi—that winds through Kowloon Park. Contemporary sculpture also dots the waterside promenade near the museum of art in Tsim Sha Tsui.

Bright Lights

During the "Symphony of Lights," held at 8 each night around the harbor, 44 skyscrapers are lit up on cue as a commentator introduces them in time with a musical accompaniment.

Culture Classes

The tourist board runs free classes on feng shui, traditional Chinese medicine, and tea appreciation. A tai ch'i master will put you through the moves in Admiralty's Harcourt Garden every Saturday morning at 8.

Enlightenment

Inner peace is priceless, and though it's customary to make a small donation, all of Hong Kong's temples are free. So are the Tian Tan Buddha and the Wisdom Path on Lantau Island, though you have to pay to get there first.

Bird-watching

See our feathered friends up close and personal, without leaving town—either at the Yuen Po Street Bird Garden, where the caged birds sing on the Kowloon side, or at the Edward Youde Aviary in the heart of Hong Kong Park.

Music

High-quality ensembles perform at "Happy Hour" concerts, Thursdays at 6 PM in the Hong Kong Cultural Centre's foyer. Family variety shows with dance, music, and magic take place on Saturdays at 3 PM. There are also free pipe organ recitals one Saturday a month.

Heritage

Visit the comprehensive Hong Kong Heritage Museum in Sha Tin on a Wednesday, when admission is free of charge for the whole family.

Walkabouts

In town, you can take in colonial architecture during an hour-long stroll through Western between the University of Hong Kong and Western Market. Is the weather bad? Try walking through Central without ever leaving a building—the sign of a true Hong Konger. You can also head for the hills outside of town, hiking along the Dragon's Back or to Lion Rock.

Views

It doesn't cost a cent to ride up to the Bank of China's 43rd-floor observation deck or to visit the Hong Kong Monetary Authority, on the 55th floor of the International Finance Centre, for fabulous harbor views over to Kowloon. Reverse the vista from the Tsim Sha Tsui waterfront promenade, the best place to see the Hong Kong Island skyline.

FEASTS & FÊTES

The loudest and proudest traditional festival, **Chinese New Year** brings Hong Kong to a standstill each year. Shops shut down, and everywhere you look there are red and gold signs, kumquat trees, and pots of yellow chrysanthemums, all considered auspicious. On the first night there's a colorful parade; on the second the crowds ooh and ahh at the no-costs-spared fireworks display over the harbor. (1st day of 1st moon, usually late Jan.–early Feb.)

The Chinese New Year festivities end with the colorful **Spring Lantern Festival.** Hong Kong's green spaces—especially Victoria Park—become a sea of light as people gather with beautifully shaped paper or cellophane lanterns. It's also a day of celebration for couples. (15th day of 1st moon, usually Feb.)

Ancestor-worship is a big part of traditional Chinese religions, and on **Ching Ming** families meet to clean the graves of their departed loved ones. (Apr. 4 or 5)

Thousands make the yearly trip to Cheung Chau Island for the exuberant **Cheung Chau Bun Festival,** a four-day-long Taoist thanksgiving feast. Sixty-foot towers covered in buns quiver outside Pak Tai Temple, and there's a huge procession of children dressed as gods carried atop tall poles. (8th day of 4th moon, usually May)

The **Dragon Boat Festival** pits long, multi-oared dragon-head boats against one another in races across the islands, with the biggest event held at Stanley Beach. It commemorates the hero Qu Yuan, a poet and scholar who drowned himself in the 3rd century BC to protest government corruption. These days, after the races, it's one big beach party. (5th day of 5th moon, usually June)

There are smoldering piles of paper all over the place during **Hungry Ghosts Festival.** Replicas of houses, cars, and Monopoly-style "hell money" are burned as offerings to the ghosts allowed to wander the earth for these two weeks, when the gates of hell are opened. (15th day of 7th moon, usually Aug.–Sept.)

During the **Mid-Autumn Festival,** crowds gather to share *yue bing* or "moon-cakes," which are traditionally stuffed with red-bean or lotus-seed paste. These commemorate a 14th-century revolution, when co-conspirators' notes were baked inside them. Colorful paper lanterns fill Hong Kong's parks, and performers dress up for a huge dragon dance in Causeway Bay. (15th day of 8th moon, usually Sept.–Oct.)

ON THE MOVE

The city's transport options are as varied—old and new, fast and slow, land and sea—as they are comprehensive, safe, and easy to use. There's no train timetable, because they run so frequently. Buses are air-conditioned, have cushioned seating, and are as clean as a whistle. On the seas, enjoy a quick scenic trip across the harbor on the iconic Star Ferries, or take a fast ferry to an outer island or even Macau. For a leisurely ride harking back to the days of old, nothing beats a double-decker tram. So go on: skip taxis and take public transport.

Double-Decker Trams. Tall, thin, and rumbling, the iconic trams have efficiently, albeit *slowly,* moved passengers across Hong Kong Island since 1904. This is the world's largest fleet of double-deckers in operation. The beloved trams, which locals call "ding ding" because of their horns, are a fun and inexpensive way to cruise the island. Enter from the rear, head straight up the narrow staircase, and grab a seat at the very front for the best views. At this height, you can almost reach out and touch the neon signs. One 15-minute journey takes you through Central's forest of skyscrapers east to Wan Chai's wet markets and clothing shops, ending at Southorn Playground, where kids play basketball and soccer and the older folk play chess. All journeys cost HK$2.

Midlevels Escalator. A practical human mover, this is a 1-km-long (½-mi-long) combination of escalators and walkways that provide free, glass-covered transport up or down the steep incline between Central and Midlevels. The trip provides a view of small Chinese shops, a wet market, the Jamia Mosque at Shelley Street, and gleaming residential high-rises. You're often so close to the apartments

FLY THE FRIENDLY SKIES

With 2.9 km (1.8 mi) of moving walkways, 14 acres of glass, and around 30 acres of carpeting, the international terminal at Chek Lap Kok Airport is the world's largest. At $20 billion to build, it's also the world's most expensive. A super-efficient express train runs between the city and this modern marvel in 23 minutes.

that it's impossible to avoid peering in. Starting at Staunton Street, the escalator cuts through the fashionable SoHo area, filled with cafés, bars, and boutiques.

Plan to ride the escalators up between 10:20 AM and midnight. From 6 to 10 AM they move downhill only, so commuters from Midlevels can get to work. After midnight the escalators shut down, and that equates to a long walk on steep steps. You can get off at any point and explore side streets where vendors sell porcelain, clothes, and antiques (not necessarily authentic). Most buildings have tiny makeshift altars to ancestors, usually made of colorful red paper with gold Chinese characters, with offerings of fruit and incense. ⊠ *Enter across from Central Market, at Queen's Rd. Central and Jubilee St., Central* ⊙ *Daily 6 AM–11:30 PM.*

Ngong Ping 360 Skyrail. The breathtaking 5.7-km (3.5-mi) cable-car journey takes you above the Lantau Island's greenery, from Tung Chung to Ngong Ping. During the 25-minute ride, you get a glimpse of the Big Buddha, sitting and smiling on a mountaintop. ☏2109–9898 ⊕*www. np360.com.hk* ⊙ *Weekdays 10–6; Sat. 10–6:30; Sun. and special days 9–6:30* ⊠*HK$58–HK68 one way; HK$-8–HK98 round-trip.*

Peak Tram. Hong Kong is very proud that its funicular railway is the world's steepest. Before it opened in 1880 the only way to get up to Victoria Peak, the highest hill overlooking Hong Kong Harbour, was to walk or take a bumpy ride in a sedan chair on steep steps. On the way up, grab a seat on the right-hand side for the best views of the harbor and mountains. The trams, which look like old-fashioned trolley cars, are hauled the whole way in seven minutes by cables attached to electric motors. En route to the upper terminal, 1,805 feet above sea level, the cars pass five intermediate stations. At times they seem to travel at an impossibly vertical angle.

At the top you enter the Peak Tower, a mall full of restaurants and shops. A viewing platform is on the mall's roof. Outside the Peak Tower, another mall faces you. Well-signed nature walks around the Peak are wonderful respites from the commercialism. Bus 15C, an antique double-decker with an open top, shuttles you to the Peak Tram Terminal from Central Pier 7 or on Connaught Road Central outside City Hall, every 30 minutes. ⊠ *Between Garden Rd. and Cotton Tree Dr., Central* ☎ *2522–0922* ⊕ *www.thepeak.com.hk* 🚋 *HK$22 one way, HK$33 round-trip* ☉ *Daily every 10–15 mins, 7:30 AM–midnight.*

Star Ferry. Since 1898 the ferry pier has been the gateway to the island from Kowloon. If it's your first time in the city, you're all but required to cross the harbor and back on the Star Ferry. It's a beautiful, relaxing trip on antiquated, character-full vessels. An evening ride is even better, when the city's neon and skyscrapers light up the skyline. The distinctive green-and-white vessels are

> ## WELL TRAINED
>
> It's fast, reliable, and spotless. It moves 3.4 million people every weekday. Not many cities have a metro system as efficient and rider-friendly as Hong Kong's MTR. All signs and maps are in Chinese and English, and the eight main train lines take you all across Hong Kong Island and the Kowloon Peninsula.

beloved harbor fixtures. The new Central Star Ferry Terminal is at Piers 7 and 8 of the Outlying Islands Ferry Piers.

On ferries between Central and Tsim Sha Tsui, there are two classes: a first-class ticket (HK$2.20) gives you a seat on the roomier upper deck, with an air-conditioned compartment in front. Second-class seats (HK$1.70) are on the lower deck and tend to be noisy because they're near the engine room. ■ TIP→ **For trips from Central to Tsim Sha Tsui, seats on the eastern side have the best views.**

Across the way, the pier is a convenient starting point for any tour of Kowloon. As you face the bus station, Ocean Terminal, where luxury cruise ships berth, is on your left; inside this terminal, and in adjacent Harbour City, are miles of air-conditioned shopping arcades. ⊠ *Central* ☎ *2767–7065* ⊕ *www.starferry.com.hk* ☉ *Central to/from Tsim Sha Tsui, daily 6:30 AM–11:30 PM.*

FENG SHUI STRUCTURES

There's a battle going on in Central, a battle between good and evil forces. Feng shui (pronounced *foong soy* in Cantonese, *fung shway* in Mandarin, and literally translated as "wind" and "water") is the art of placing objects to bring about yin–yang balance. In the West, feng shui seems like just another interior-design fad; here it's taken very seriously.

One school looks at buildings in relation, say, to mountains or bodies of water. It's ideal, for example, for a building to face out to sea with a mountain behind it. (Is it coincidence that this allows for the best views and breezes?) Another school focuses on shapes in the immediate environment; triangles, for instance, give off bad feng shui. Both schools are concerned with the flow of energy. Entrances are placed to allow positive energy to flow in, and objects such as mirrors are used to deflect negative energy. Cities are often short of such natural feng shui improvers as babbling brooks, but not to worry: a fish tank is a fine alternative.

Case Study 1: Bank of China

Bank of China Tower. In the politics of Hong Kong architecture, the stylish art deco building that served as the old Bank of China headquarters was the first trump: built after World War II, it was 20 feet higher than the adjacent Hongkong & Shanghai Bank (HSBC). In 1985 HSBC finished a steel-and-glass structure that dwarfed the old Bank of China, whose officials in turn commissioned the Chinese-American architect I.M. Pei to build a bigger, better headquarters, which opened in 1990.

Architectural Assessment: Although it's not as innovative as the HSBC skyscraper, the Bank of China Tower is a masterful, twisting spire of replicating triangles (uh

oh). As the first building to break the ridgeline of Victoria Peak, it dominates Hong Kong's landscape and embodies the post-handover balance of power. Its 43rd-floor observation deck also offers panoramic, uncrowded Central views.

Feng Shui Assessment: The tower has some of the worst feng shui in town. Some say that because the building thins at the top, it resembles a screwdriver—one that's drilling the wealth out of Hong Kong; others prefer the metaphor of a knife into the heart of the SAR. The two antennas sticking out of the top are said to resemble the two incense sticks burned for the dead. Circles, which look like coins, bring prosperity. The opposite effect is supposedly caused by the building's triangular angles and sharp edges—indeed, many believe that it has had a negative effect on nearby structures. The Lippo Centre, which faces one of the triangles, was formerly the Bond Centre, owned by disgraced Australian businessman Allen Bond, who was forced to sell the building because of financial troubles. Local gossip has it that Government House—still the residence of colonial governors when the bank was built—was the target of these bad vibes. Indeed, after the handover, Hong Kong's first chief executive,

Tung Chee-Hwa, refused to live there, citing its bad feng shui.

✉ *1 Garden Rd., Central* ☏ *No phone* 🎫 *Free* 🕑 *Observation deck: weekdays 8–6, Sat. 9–1* Ⓜ *Central MTR, Exit J2.*

Case Study 2: HSBC

Hongkong & Shanghai Bank (HSBC) Main Building. Designed by Sir Norman Foster, the headquarters of Hong Kong's premier bank (it's depicted on most of the territory's paper money) was completed in 1985 at a whopping cost of more than US$1 billion. At a time of insecurity vis-à-vis China, it was a powerful statement that the bank had no intention of taking its money out of the territory.

The two bronze lions outside the building also guarded HSBC's previous headquarters, built in 1935. The one with the gaping mouth is named Stephen, after the Hong Kong branch manager at the time; the other's called Stitt, after the manager in Shanghai. If you look closely, you can see bullet marks in them from the 1941 Battle of Hong Kong.

Architectural Assessment: With its distinctive ladder facade, many consider this building a triumph—a landmark of modern architecture, even. It sits on four props that allow you to walk under it and look up through its glass belly into the soaring atrium within. Even more interesting is Foster's sensitive treatment of high-tech details: the mechanics of everything, from the elevators' gears and pulleys to the electric signs' circuit boards, are visible through smoked glass. Because of all these mechanics, irreverent locals call this the Robot Building. ■**TIP→** Computer-controlled glass mirrors—480 of them—change position throughout the day to reflect natural light into the bank. You

can get an insider perspective by taking the escalators through the public banking hall up to the third-floor atrium.

Feng Shui Assessment: Rumor has it that during construction, the escalators were reset from their original straight position so that they would be at an angle to the entrance. Because evil spirits can only travel in a straight line, this realignment was thought to prevent waterborne spirits from flowing in off Victoria Harbor. The escalators are also believed to resemble two whiskers of a powerful dragon, sucking money into the bank. Atop the building and pointing toward the Bank of China Tower are two metal rods that look like a window-washing apparatus. The rods are a classic feng shui technique designed to deflect the negative energy—in this case, of the Bank of China's dreaded triangles—away and back to its source.

✉ *1 Queen's Rd., across from Statue Sq., Central* 🎫 *Free* 🕑 *Weekdays 9–5:30, Sat. 9–12:30* Ⓜ *Central MTR, Exit K.*

THE PEAK EXPERIENCE

Fodor's Choice ☾ **Victoria Peak's** Chinese name, Tai Ping Shan, means Mountain of Great Peace, and it certainly seems to inspire momentary hushed awe in visitors at the viewing point, a few yards left along the road from the tram terminal. Spread below you is a glittering forest of skyscrapers; beyond them the harbor and—on a clear day—Kowloon's eight mountains. On a rainy day wisps of cloud catch on the buildings' pointy tops; at night both sides of the harbor burst into color. Consider having dinner at one of the restaurants near the upper terminus. ■TIP➡ **Forsake all else up here and start your visit with the lookout point: there are a hundred other shopping ops in the world, but few views like this.**

As you step off the Peak Tram, a sharp intake of breath and bout of sighing over the view will cure the feeling that you left your stomach somewhere down in Central. Whatever the time, whatever the weather, be it your first visit or your 50th, this is Hong Kong's one unmissable sight. ■TIP➡ **Before buying a return ticket down on the tram, consider taking one of the beautiful low-impact trails back to Central. There are also buses down.**

There are spectacular views in all directions on the **Peak Circle Walk,** an easy-going 3.5-km (2.2-mi) paved trail that starts at the Upper Tram Terminus. Start by heading north along fern-encroached Lugard Road. There's another stunning view of Central from the lookout, 20 minutes along, after which the road snakes west to an intersection with Hatton and Harlech roads. From here Lantau, Lamma, and—on incredibly clear days—Macau come into view. The longer option from here is to wind your way down Hatton to the University of Hong Kong campus in the Western district. The tacky **Peak Tower** (✉ *128 Peak Rd., Victoria Peak, Central* ☎ *2522–0668* ⊕ *www.thepeak.com.hk* ⊙ *10* AM*–11* PM) is packed with largely forgettable shops and restaurants. Kids might enjoy the free EA Experience virtual gaming room. Local heroes Jackie Chan and Michelle Yeoh are some of the famous faces resisting meltdown at Asia's first branch of London's famous wax works, **Madame Tussaud's** (☎ *2849–6966* ⊕ *www. madame-tussauds.com* ✉ *HK$140* ⊙ *10* AM*–10* PM). The usual celebrity suspects—from Beckham to Marilyn—are here. The **Peak Galleria** mall scores high on nothing else but the cheese scale.

■TIP➡ **Bypass the overpriced tourist traps inside and head straight up the escalators to the rooftop Sky Terrace and Gallery, which looks down over the Pok Fu Lam country park and reservoir, and, on a clear day, Aberdeen.**

> ## PEAK OF EXCLUSIVITY
>
> A trip here puts you within spitting distance of some *very* expensive real estate, though prices have halved since the property boom of the late '90s, when houses fetched up to $130 million. But money couldn't always get you into this club—you needed the governor's permission to have a home on the Peak in the 19th century, because his summer residence was here. Even more preposterously, Chinese people weren't allowed to live here until 1945.

TO YOUR HEALTH

In recent years Traditional Chinese Medicine (TCM) has caused a lot of holistic hype in the West. Round here, though, it's been going strong for a while—more than 2,000 years, to be precise. Although modern Hong Kongers may see western doctors for serious illnesses, for minor complaints and everyday pick-me-ups they still turn to traditional remedies.

To get to the root of your body's disequilibrium, a TCM practitioner takes your pulse in different places and examines your tongue, eyes, and ears, as well as talking to you. Your prescription could include herbal tonics, teas, massage, dietary recommendations, and acupuncture.

Learning to Balance

Taoists believe that the world is made up of two opposing but interdependent forces: negative yin, representing darkness and the female, and positive yang, standing for light and masculinity. Both are essential for good health: when one becomes stronger than the other in the body, we get sick.

Another concept is *qi*, the energy or life force behind most bodily functions. It flows through channels or meridians: if these are blocked, ill health can ensue. Acupuncture along these meridians is a way of putting your qi in order.

It's not all inner peace—to be healthy you have to be in harmony with your environment, too. The Five Elements theory divides up both the universe and the body into different "elemental" categories: water, wood, fire, earth, and metal. Practitioners seek to keep all five elements in balance.

If you don't know your qi from your chin, and you're not sure if you need a dried seahorse or a live snake, head to the **Eu Yan Sang Medical Hall.** Glass cases at this reputable store display reindeer antlers, dried fungi, ginseng, and other medicinal mainstays. Grave but helpful clerks behind hefty wooden counters will happily sell you purported cures for anything from the common cold to impotence (the cure for the latter is usually slices of reindeer antler boiled into tea). ■TIP→ **The Hong Kong Tourism Board runs free introductory classes on Chinese medicine here Wednesday at 2:30** PM. From Sheung Wan MTR, walk left along Wing Lok Street, right into Wing Wo Street, then left onto Queen's Road Central. There are other smaller branches all over Hong Kong; try the one on 18 Russell Street in Causeway Bay for over-the-counter consultations in English. ✉ *152 Queen's Rd. Central, Western* ☎ *2544–3870, hotline 2544–3308* ⊕ *www.euyansang.com* ⊗ *Daily 9–7:30* Ⓜ *Sheung Wan MTR, Exit E2.*

⚠ **Chinese medicines aren't regulated by the Hong Kong government. Anything that sounds dubious or dangerous might be just that.**

Brush up on traditional treatments at the **Hong Kong Museum of Medical Sciences.** The least morbid and most enlightening exhibits compare Chinese and western medical practices, and show Chinese medicines of both animal and plant origin. Elsewhere, dusty displays of old medical equipment send macabre thrills up your spine. Reaching this museum is a healthy experience in itself: you pant up several blocks' worth of stairs to the Edwardian building it's in. ■TIP→ **The cheat's way of getting here is on the Midlevels Escalator: alight at Caine Road and walk west four or five blocks to Ladder Street. The museum is just down the first flight of stairs, on the left.** ✉ *2 Caine*

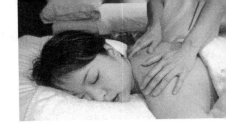

TO YOUR HEALTH

Lane, Western ☎2549–5123 ⊕www.
hkmms.org.hk ✉HK$10 ⊙Tues.–Sat.
10–5, Sun. 1–5.

Taking the Cure

Therapeutic massages are the specialty at
**Charlie's Acupressure and Massage Centre of
the Blind** (✉Canton House, 9th fl., room
903, 54–6 Queen's Rd. Central, Central
☎2877–9999). Ballet dancer Rudolf
Nureyev was one celebrity who relaxed
his overworked muscles here. An hour-
long massage costs around HK$250.

The **Hong Kong University Chinese Medicine
Clinic and Pharmacy** (✉Admiralty Centre,
2nd fl., Unit 50-53, Harcourt Rd., Admiralty ☎3761–1188 Ⓜ Admiralty MTR,
Exit A) is a training clinic run by the most
respected med school in town. It also
has master practitioners of acupuncture
and orthopedics on hand. Consultations
start at HK$100, visits to the masters at
HK$300 (not including medication).

Acupuncture, acupressure, and herbal
medicine are just some of the offerings at
the **Quality Chinese Medical Centre** (✉Jade
Centre, 5th fl., Unit A, 98 Wellington St.,
Central ☎English hotline 2881–8267
⊕www.qualitytcm.com). Consultations

NO GIN, JUST TONIC

Downing a glass of herbal health tonic is
a normal part of many a Hong Konger's
day. There are blends for flu, headaches,
colds, and coughs. Many stores have
English labels; if not, tell the server your
troubles, and he or she will run you off a
glass of whatever works best. Most cost
HK$6–HK$20 a dose.

---

start at HK$70; expect to pay around
HK$250 for an acupuncture session.

Established in 1669, **Tong Ren Tang**
(✉Melbourne Plaza, ground fl., Unit
B, 33 Queen's Rd. Central, Central
☎2868–0609 ⊕www.tongrentang.com)
has long been one of mainland China's
best-respected traditional medicine companies. There are consulting rooms and a
pharmacy at this branch.

Healthy Ways

★ In colonial times **Bonham Strand,** a curving thoroughfare in the Sheung Wan district, was a major commercial hub. Sadly,
its wooden shop fronts are fast falling vic-
tim to real estate development. The few
that remain are medicinal mother lodes:
wood-clad walls are lined with shelves of

SMOOTH MOVES

Tai Chi (A Centuries-Old Art)

Just before dawn you'll see young
businesspeople and retirees alike
practicing tai chi: slow, steady, flowing
movements with moderate postures
designed to improve physical and
mental well-being. There's no better advertising for tai chi than seeing
an octogenarian balance on one leg,
with the other outstretched and held
high for a long moment before grace-
fully swinging into yet another pose.
Although the health and philosophical aspects of tai chi may be common
knowledge, few people know that it's
also a subtle, sophisticated, and scientific method of self-defense.

1

jars filled with pungent ingredients such as fungi, barks, and insects. These are consumed dried and ground up—infused in hot water or tea or taken as powder or pills. West of the intersection with Wing Lok Street, the original facades give way to those with big plate-glass windows displaying bundles of hairy-looking forked yellow roots—this is the heart of the ginseng wholesale trade. Ginseng is a broad-spectrum remedy that's a mainstay of Chinese medicine.

★ A sharp but musty smell fills the air when you turn down **Wing Lok Street** or **Des Voeux Road West,** Sheung Wan streets renowned for their dried-seafood stores. Out of shop fronts spill sacks filled to bursting with dried and salted fish, seahorses, shrimp, and abalone—a shellfish that is to China what oysters are to the West. Foot-wide fungi, gleaming beans, wrinkly red prunes, nuts, and even rosebuds make up the rest of the stock. A grimmer offering lurks behind a few shopwindows: highly prized shark's fins, purported to be an aphrodisiac.

At Possession Street, where Queen's Road Central becomes **Queen's Road West,** shopwindows display what looks like clumps of fine vermicelli noodles, ranging in color from pale gold to rich chestnut. It's not pasta, though; these are birds' nests, another of Sheung Wan's intriguing specialties. They're used to make a highly prized (and correspondingly expensive) soup that tastes rather disappointingly like egg white.

In herb shops on Queen's Road West beyond the intersection with Hollywood Road, it's a tough call as to who's more wizened: the clerks or the dried goods they sell. Either way, these stores convey the longevity benefits of Chinese medicine. Forget the gleaming teak counters of Central's tony TCM boutiques, here the herbs, dried mushrooms, and other more mysterious ingredients are displayed in plastic jars and burlap sacks.

Don't poke your fingers into the grubby cages outside shops on **Hillier Street:** this is the center of the snake trade. A snake's meat is used in winter soups to ward off colds, and its gallbladder reputedly improves vigor and virility.

Tai Chi Masters (AD 1247-New Millennium & Beyond)

Tai chi's founder was Chang San Feng, a Taoist born in AD 1247. One of the greatest masters, however, was Yang Lu Chan (1799–1872), known as Invincible Yang, who served as the chief combat instructor to the Imperial Guard during the Qing Dynasty. To follow in their footsteps you must study under an accomplished master, who can demonstrate techniques, identify faults, and create a calming atmosphere. To try tai chi while you're in town, contact the tourist board, which offers free classes in Admiralty's Harcourt Garden every Saturday morning, and in Tsim Sha Tsui every Monday and Wednesday–Friday at 8 AM.

BEACHES

Surprising as it may seem, Hong Kong has many fantastic beaches with gorgeous views of the sea, dotted with small green islands. In Southside, ever-popular Repulse Bay is a sort of Chinese Coney Island. Just to the south is smaller, less-crowded Deep Water Bay, and farther around is the more intimate South Bay. Turtle Cove is isolated and beautiful, and Shek O's beach has a Mediterranean feel. Day trips to the outlying islands (⇨ Island Hopping) can also include sunbathing time on a clean beach. You can reach most beaches by train, bus, or taxi; the latter will cost HK$150 and up.

The waters off beaches in the New Territories, particularly the Sai Kung Peninsula, are crystal clear. Pollution can be a problem on the Southside, though that doesn't deter the thousands who flock seaside for respite from the heat. ■TIP→ Hong Kong's Environmental Protection Department has set some tough guidelines and goals for cleaning up area waters. For more info, including beach-by-beach pollution ratings, check out the EPD's Web site: www.epd.gov.hk/epd.

Southside

Deep Water Bay. On Island Road, just to the east of Ocean Park and all its amusements, this bay was the setting for the William Holden film *Love Is a Many Splendored Thing* (1955), and its deep coves are still lovely. Near Deep Water Bay are the manicured greens of the Deep Water Bay Golf Course, which is owned by the Hong Kong Golf Club. Not surprisingly, the area has become a multimillionaires' enclave and is home to Hong Kong's richest man, Li Ka-shing, a very private real estate tycoon.

To rent a speedboat, water-skiing equipment, and the services of a driver, contact the **Waterski Club** (⊠ *Pier at Deep Water Bay Beach, Deep Water Bay* ☎ *2812–0391*). The cost is HK$640 per hour for outboard, HK$750 for inboard. *From Exchange Square Bus Terminus in Central, take Bus 6, 64, 260, or 6A.*

■TIP→ For a scenic route to Deep Water Bay, take Bus 70 from Central's Exchange Square to Aberdeen and change to Bus 73, which passes the beach en route to Stanley.

Repulse Bay. It's named after the British warship HMS *Repulse* and not, as some local wags say, after its slightly murky waters. It was home of the now demolished Repulse Bay Hotel, which gained notoriety in December 1941, when Japanese clambered over the hills behind it, entered its gardens, and overtook the British, who were using the hotel as headquarters. Repulse Bay Verandah Restaurant & Bamboo Bar (⊠ *109 Repulse Bay Rd., Southside* ☎ *2292–2822* ⊕ *www.therepulsebay.com*)—a great place for British high tea—is a replica of the eating and drinking establishment that once graced the hotel. High tea is served Tuesday to Saturday from 3 to 5:30 and Sunday from 3:30 to 5:30. You can also grab a bite at one of several Chinese restaurants and snack kiosks that dot the beach. The Lifesaving Club at the beach's east end resembles a Chinese temple, with large statues of Tin Hau, goddess of the sea, and Kwun Yum, goddess of mercy. ⚠ If you opt for a meal in a seafood restaurant here or at any beach, note that physicians caution against eating raw shellfish because of hepatitis outbreaks. *From Exchange Square Bus Terminus in Central, take Bus 6, 6A, 6X, 66, 64, or 260.*

Shek O. This wide beach is almost Mediterranean in appearance with its low-rise houses and shops set prettily on a headland. In Shek O village you can find old mansions, small shops selling inflatable toys and other beach gear, and a few popular Chinese and Thai restaurants. Follow the curving path from the town square across a footbridge to the "island" of Tai Tau Chau, really a large rock with a lookout over the South China Sea. Little more than a century ago, this open water was ruled by pirates. Also near town is the Shek O Golf and Country Club and the superb Shek O Country Park, with great trails and bird-watching: look for Kentish plovers, reef egrets, and black-headed gulls, as well as the colorful rufus-backed shrike and the ubiquitous chatty bulbul. *From Central, take MTR to Shau Kei Wan, then take Bus 9 to last stop (about 30 min).*

Stanley. Notorious during World War II as the home of Japan's largest POW camps in Hong Kong, Stanley is now known primarily for its market, a great place for deals on knickknacks, ceramics, paintings, casual clothing, and sporting goods. The old police station, built in 1859, now houses a restaurant. Past the market, on Stanley Main Street, a strip of restaurants and pubs faces the bay. On the other side of the bay, a temple honoring Tin Hau, goddess of the sea, is wedged between giant modern housing estates.

Stanley's wide main beach is the site of Hong Kong's most popular dragon boat races, usually held in June, in which teams paddle out into the sea, turn around, and, at the sound of the gun, race ferociously back to shore. The beach is popular with the windsurfing, water-skiing, and wakeboarding crowd. **Patrick's Water-skiing** (⊠ *Tai Tam, Stanley* ☎ *2813–2372*) is

> ## WINDSURFING
>
> Windsurfing has grown dramatically in popularity since Hong Kong's Lee Lai-shan sailed off with a women's Olympic gold medal at the 1996 Summer Olympic Games in Atlanta, inspiring a generation of youngsters to take up the sport, which is further popularized on ESPN and MTV. Now windsurfing centers at Tai Tam on Hong Kong Island, Sha Ha beach in Sai Kung, and Tung Wan Beach (Lee's home on Cheung Chau Island) will gladly start you on the path to glory with some lessons.

run by the friendly, laid-back man himself. Patrick will take you to the best area waters and give you pointers on your technique. The fee—HK$700 per hour on weekdays, HK$800 on weekends—includes a range of equipment. *From Exchange Square Bus Terminus in Central, take Bus 6, 6A, 6X, 66, 64, or 260.*

The New Territories

Hap Mun Wan. Half Moon Bay is a brilliant, golden-sand beach on a grassy island near Sai Kung Town. It's one of the many small beaches among dozens of small islands near Sai Kung that are popular and easy to reach. **Bunn's Divers Institute** (⊠ *188 Johnston Rd., Wan Chai* ☎ *2574–7951*) runs outings for qualified divers to areas like Sai Kung. The cost of a day trip runs HK$580 for two sessions, one in the morning and another in the afternoon, and includes lunch, two tanks, and weights. Sampans to Half Moon depart from the Sai Kung waterfront, beside the bus station. If you're sharing a sampan with other passengers, remember the color of the flag on the roof: that's the color you need for your return ferry. Shared sampans cost HK$40. ■ **TIP➔ To**

Hong Kong Beaches

San Tin

Tai Po

Tolo Harbour

KEY

Beaches

Ferry lines

NEW TERRITORIES

Ha Tsuen

Wu Kai Sha

Tai Mong Tsai

Sha Ha

Sai Kung

Hap Mun Wan

Tuen Mun

Sham Tseng

Tsuen Wan

Pak Tin

Ho Chung

Port Shelter

Siu Lam

Ma Wan

Silverstrand

Lung Ha Wan

Hang Hau

KOWLOON

Kowloon Bay

Yau Tong

Tai Chik Sha

Junk Bay

Hong Kong Disneyland

Discovery Bay

Discovery Bay

Kennedy Town

HONG KONG

HONG KONG ISLAND

TUNG LUNG CHAU

Tung Chung

PENG CHAU

HONG KONG ISLAND

Deep Water Bay

Shek O

Mui Wo

Silvermine Bay

HEI LING CHAU

Aberdeen

AP LEI CHAU

LANTAU ISLAND

Silvermine Beach

Repulse Bay

Stanley

Cheung Sha

Pui O Wan

CHI MA WAN PENINSULA

Yung Shue Wan

Stanley Bay

Sheung Sze Mun

PO TOI ISLANDS

CHEUNG CHAU

West Lamma Channel

LAMMA ISLAND

0   4 miles

East Lamma Channel

0   4 kilometers

←TO MACAU

South China Sea

---

cruise around the harbor, rent a *kaido* (pronounced "guy-doe," one of the small boats run by private operators for about HK$130 round-trip), and stop at tiny Yim Tin Tsai Island, which has a rustic Catholic mission church built in 1890. *From Central, take MTR to Choi Hung, then green Minibus 1A to Sai Kung Town.*

Sha Ha. The sand isn't fine and golden, but the main reason people visit this beach is for the windsurfing. Sha Ha's waters are shallow, even far from shore, and ideal for beginning windsurfers. Feeling exhausted after a day out on the water tackling the wind? Grab something to eat at the restaurants and bars that dot the beach. You can take lessons or rent a board or even a kayak at the **Kent Windsurfing Centre** (⊠ *Sha Ha, Sai Kung* ☎ 9733–1228). Ask for Eddy. *From Central take MTR to Choi Hung, then green Minibus 1A to Sai*

Kung Town. It's a 10-min walk along the shore to Sha Ha.

Silverstrand. Though a little rocky in spots, it has soft sand and is crowded on summer weekends. Walk down a steep set of steps to reach the small stretch of beach where families enjoy all manner of floating beds and tubes in the sea. Despite the heat, barbecuing is a popular beach activity here. The local style is to hold long forks laden with sausages, chicken wings, fish balls, or other finger food over the coals. *From Central, take MTR to Diamond Hill, then Bus 91. Alight at big roundabout.*

Lantau Island

An often-overlooked fact is that when visitors arrive, they land on Lantau Island—a large stretch of reclaimed land purposely built for the airport called Chep Lap Kok. Twice the size of Hong

Kong Island, Lantau is also home to the giant Tian Tan Buddha, which sits majestically on a hilltop. The Ngong Ping cable car whisks you here in 25 minutes. Also on Lantau is Disneyland, a small version of its American counterparts, and the charming Tai O Fishing Village.

Cheung Sha. Popular Cheung Sha is only a short taxi or bus ride from the Silvermine Bay ferry pier. Its mile-long expanse is excellent for swimming. The Stoep restaurant on the beach serves great Mediterranean and South African fare. Watching the sunset here is a perfect end to a sun-drenched day. ■TIP→ **There are only 30 taxis on the entire island, so on weekends, when things get busy, make sure you ask the** restaurant to get you one back to the pier. *Take ferry from Central's Pier 6 to Mui Wo. Buses meet ferry every half hour on weekdays and Sat.; on Sun., buses leave when full.*

Silvermine Beach. The stretch of beach can be seen from the ferry as you approach the island, though because of its proximity to the pier and other fishing boats, the waters aren't as clean as those at Cheung Sha. You can rent bikes at the Silvermine Beach Hotel and explore the village of Mui Wo. *Take ferry from Central's Pier 6 to Mui Wo. Buses meet ferry every half hour on weekdays and Sat.; on Sun., buses leave when full.*

REGION/BEACH	Travel Time from Central	Peaceful	Swimmable	Lifeguards	Showers/ Restrooms
Southside					
Deep Water Bay	20 mins.	crowded	often	yes	yes
Repulse Bay	30 mins.	crowded	often	yes	yes
South Bay	30 mins.	crowded	yes	yes	yes
Shek O	60 mins.	crowded	yes	yes	yes
Stanley	40–45 mins.	crowded	yes	yes	yes
New Territories					
Hap Mun Wan	60–75 mins.	often	yes	yes	yes
Sha Ha	60–75 mins.	often	yes	no	no
Silverstrand	60 mins.	crowded	yes	yes	yes
Clear Water Bay	70–80 mins.	crowded	yes	yes	yes
Outer Islands					
Cheung Chau: Tung Wan	60–75 mins.	crowded	yes	yes	yes
Lamma: Hung Shing Ye	60–75 mins.	often	yes	yes	yes
Lamma: Lo So Shing	60–75 mins.	often	yes	yes	yes
Lantau: Cheung Sha Wan	60–75 mins.	often	yes	yes	yes
Tap Mun	90–120 mins.	yes	yes	no	no

ISLAND HOPPING

There are 235 so-called Outer Islands, and several of them are great escapes from the city for the waterfront views, some seafood, and a little peace. Island villages are up to speed (to the regret of many, cell phones work), but they run at a more relaxed pace. Hong Kong ferries travel from Central to many of the islands, where beaches are often a short walk from the pier.

Cheung Chau. This small, carless island southwest of Hong Kong is best known as being the home to windsurfing Olympic gold medalist Lee Lai-shan. At the tip of the beach here is a lovely outdoor restaurant owned by relatives of San-San (as she's affectionately called), who have proudly hung a large framed picture of the athlete in her golden moment. The island community lives mostly on the sandbar that connects the two hilly tips of this dumbbell-shape landmass. It's a one-hour ferry ride from Central's Pier 5 outside Two IFC, and the town harbor is lined with seafood restaurants and shops.

On weekends Tung Wan, Cheung Chau's main beach, is so crowded that its sweep of golden sand is barely visible. At one end of the beach is the Warwick Hotel. Plenty of nearby restaurants offer refreshments, seafood, and shade. There are no private cars allowed on this island, so the air is noticeably cleaner.

Lamma Island. Lamma is as close to a 1960s bohemian scene as Hong Kong gets—full of laid-back expats driven out of Central by high rents. They've spawned a subculture of vegetarian restaurants, health-food shops, and craft stores. The ferry from Central's Pier 4, in front of Two IFC, to the village of

Sok Kwu Wan or to Yung Shue Wan takes about 25 minutes. It doesn't matter which village you go to first—time spent on beaches near them and on the hour-long walk through rolling green hills between them are what a leisurely afternoon on Lamma is all about.

"Beach" overstates the scale of the sandy strip known as Hung Shing Ye. It's also called Power Station Beach because of the massive power plant visible from it. The view doesn't deter the young locals, who materialize whenever the rays shine down. They even swim here—sometimes. Stay on shore if you see plastic bags or other refuse on the water. Or just head to Yung Shue Wan, the former farming and fishing village that's been an expat enclave since the early 1980s. Main Street is lined with handicraft shops, though the smell of the fish markets is a reminder of Lamma's humbler, less cosmopolitan origins.

Popular with families, Lo So Shing beach is an easy 20- to 30-minute hike on a paved path from Sok Kwu Wan, the smaller and grittier of Lamma's two villages and one that's notable mainly for the string of cavernous seafood restaurants that line the path leading from the pier. ■ TIP➔ If you arrive on foot from Yung Shue Wan, your first glimpse of the bay from the hills will be stunning.

Ping Chau. Not to be confused with Peng Chau, this 2½-square-km (1-square-mi) piece of land is in the far northeast of the New Territories, near the mainland coast. It's almost deserted and has a checkered history. Guns and opium were once smuggled from here, and during the Cultural Revolution many mainlanders swam through shark-infested waters

in hopes of reaching Ping Chau and the freedom of Hong Kong.

The island's largest village, Sha Tau, is something of a ghost town, with many cottages boarded up. A large part of the island is country parkland, with footpaths overgrown with orchids, wild mint, and morning glories. At the island's south end are two huge rocks known as the Drum Rocks, or Watchman's Tower Rocks. At the north end is a chunk of land that has broken away from the island; the Chinese say it represents the head of a dragon.

The ferry to Ping Chau departs on weekends at 9 AM and returns only at 5:15 PM. On Saturday there's an extra trip at 3:30 PM. Board the ferry at Ma Liu Shui, near the University KCR stop. Since there's only one daily ferry, be sure to verify the timing with the HKTB before you leave. A round-trip costs HK$80.

Po Toi Island. Three barren little fishing islands, virtually unchanged since medieval times, sit in the extreme southeast of Hong Kong. Only Po Toi Island is inhabited (sort of), with fewer than 100 people. It offers spectacular walks and a fine seafood restaurant. Walk uphill past primitive dwellings, many deserted, to the Tin Hau Temple, or walk east through the hamlet of Wan Tsai, past banana and papaya groves, to some geometric rock carvings, believed to have been carved during the local Bronze Age, about 2,500 years ago.

A trip to the Po Toi Islands is an all-day affair. Ferries leave Aberdeen on Tuesday, Thursday, and weekends at 8:15 AM and from Blake Pier in Stanley at 10 or 11:30 AM. Ferries return at 3 and 4:30 PM directly to Blake Pier, or at 6 PM to

Aberdeen via Blake Pier. A round-trip costs HK$40.

Tap Mun Island. About a 15-minute walk from the Chinese University along Tai Po Road in Sha Tin is the Ma Liu Shui Ferry Pier. This is the starting point for a ferry tour of the harbor and Tap Mun Island, whose east side is home to Tap Mun Cave and some of the territories' best-kept beaches. The ferry makes many stops; if you take the 8:30 AM trip you'll have time to hike around Tap Mun Island and be back in the city by late afternoon. The last ferry returning from the island is at 5:30 PM. A round-trip costs HK$32 on weekdays and HK$50 on weekends.

The New Fisherman's Village, on the island's southern side, is populated mainly by Hakka women. About 1 km (½ mi) north, near the western shore, is the ancient village of Tap Mun, where you'll see old women playing mah-jongg. The Tin Hau Temple, dedicated to the goddess of the sea, is less than ½ km (¼ mi) north of the village. It's atop steps that lead down to the harbor; inside are old model junks and, of course, a veiled figure of the goddess.

SAIL AWAY: SAMPANS & JUNKS

Named after an English lord, not the Scottish city, the Southside town of Aberdeen (30 minutes from Central via Bus 70 or 91) was once a pirate refuge. After World War II it became commercial as the *tanka* (boat people) attracted visitors to their floating restaurants. In the harbor are some 3,000 junks and sampans, still interspersed with floating restaurants, among them the famous Jumbo Kingdom, its faux-Chinese decorations covered in lights. The tanka still live on houseboats, and though the vessels look picturesque, conditions are depressing.

Elderly women with sea- and sun-weathered skin and croaking voices may invite you aboard a sampan for a harbor ride. It's better to go with one of the licensed operators that depart on 20-minute tours daily from 8 to 6 from the seawall opposite Aberdeen Centre. Tickets are HK$40. A tour lets you see how the fishing community lives and works and how sampans are also homes, sometimes with three generations on one small vessel. Ironically, about 110 yards away are the yachts of the Marina Club and the slightly less exclusive Aberdeen Boat Club.

You can also hire a junk to take you to outer islands: Cheung Chau, Lamma, Lantau, Po Toi, or the islands in Port Shelter, Sai Kung. Sailing on a large (up to 80 feet long), well-varnished, plushly appointed, air-conditioned junk—which can serve as a platform for swimmers and water-skiers—is a unique Hong Kong experience. Many local "weekend admirals" command these floating rumpus rooms, which are also known as "gin junks" because so much alcohol is often consumed aboard them.

Ap Lei Chau Island (Duck's Tongue Island), accessible via sampan or Buses 90B or 91 along the bridge that connects it with Aberdeen, has a yard where junks, yachts, and sampans are built, almost all without formal plans. With 86,800 people living on 1.3 square km (½ square mi), Ap Lei Chau is the world's most densely populated island.

■**TIP**➜ Look to your right when crossing the bridge for a superb view of the harbor and its countless junks.

The ritzy bar **aqua luna** (☎2116–8821 ⊕*www.aqua.com.hk*) is on the *Cheung Po Tsai*, an impressive 28-meter junk named for a pirate and created by an 80-year-old local craftsman. It's slow but impressive, with magnificent red sails. A 45-minute cruise through Victoria Harbour costs HK$150 by day and HK$180 at night, which includes one drink. Departures are every afternoon at 1:30 and 2:30, then every hour on the half hour from 5:30 PM to 10:30 PM from Tsim Sha Tsui Pier, near the Cultural Centre, and 15 minutes later from Pier 9 in Central.

The **Duk Ling** (☎2573–5282 ⊕*www.dukling.com.hk*) is a fully restored 50-year-old fishing junk whose large sails are a sight to behold. For HK$50, the HKTB offers visitors aged 3 to 75 one-hour sails from Kowloon Pier (Thursday at 2 PM and 4 PM, Saturday at 10 AM and noon) and from Central's Pier 9 (Thursday at 3 PM and 5 PM, Saturday at 11 AM and 1 PM). Register first at the HKTB Visitor Centres in Causeway Bay or Tsim Sha Tsui; when you do, bring your passport to prove you're from out of town.

HIKING

Most visitors don't come for the lush lowlands, bamboo and pine forests, rugged mountains with panoramas of the sea, and secluded beaches, but nature is never very far from all the skyscrapers. About 40% of Hong Kong is protected in 23 parks, including three marine parks and one marine reserve.

Don't expect unspoiled wilderness, however. Few upland areas escape Hong Kong's plague of hill fires for more than a few years at a time. Some are caused by dried-out vegetation; others erupt from small graveside fires set by locals to clear the land around ancestors' eternal resting spots. Partly because of these fires, most of Hong Kong's forests, except for a few spots in the New Territories, have no obvious wildlife other than birds—and mosquitoes. Bring repellent.

Gear

Necessities include sunglasses or a hat, bottled water, day pack, and sturdy hiking boots. Weather tends to be warm during the day and cold toward nightfall. The cliff sides get quite windy. If you need some basics, there are several options.

Although it doesn't sell the same range of equipment you'd find back home, **Great Outdoor Clothing Company** (⊠*Shop LG48, Silvercord Bldg., 30 Canton Rd., Tsim Sha Tsui, Kowloon* ☎*2730–9009*) will do in a pinch.

Timberland (⊠*Shop 166, Pacific Place, 88 Queensway, Admiralty* ☎*2868–0845*) sells hiking boots, backpacks, and appropriate togs.

World Sports Co. Ltd. (⊠*1st fl., 83 Fa Yuen St., Mong Kok, Kowloon* ☎*2396–9357*) caters to your every outdoor need.

Pick up guides such as *Hong Kong Hikes* from any bookstore.

You can buy trail maps at the **Government Publications Centre** (⊠*Pacific Place, Government Office, ground fl., 66 Queensway, Admiralty* ☎*2537–1910* ⊕*www. bookstore.gov.hk*). Ask for blueprints of the trails and the Countryside Series maps. Note that the HM20C series has handsome four-color maps, but they're not very reliable. The HKTB also provides maps with good walking trails and hikes.

Trails

★ **Fodor's Choice** **Dragon's Back.** One of the most popular trails crosses the "rooftop" of Hong Kong Island. Take the Peak Tram from Central up to Victoria Peak, and tackle as much or as little of the range as you feel like—there are numerous exits "downhill" to public-transport networks. Surprisingly wild country feels a world away from the urban bustle below, and the panoramas—of Victoria Harbour on one side, and South Island and outlying islands on the other—are spectacular. You can follow the trail all the way to the delightful seaside village of Shek O, where you can relax over an evening dinner before returning to the city by minibus or taxi. The most popular route, and shorter, is from Shek O Country Park. Take the MTR from Central to Shau Kei Wan, then Bus 9, alight after the first roundabout, near the crematorium.

Lion Rock. The easiest way to access the trail to Lion Rock, a spectacular summit, is from Kowloon. The hike passes through dense bamboo groves along the Eagle's Nest Nature Trail and up open slopes to Beacon Hill for 360-degree views over hills and the city. The contrasting vistas of green hills and the cityscape

HIKING

are extraordinary. There's a climb up the steep rough track to the top of Lion Rock, a superb vantage point for appreciating Kowloon's setting between hills and sea. The trail ends at Wong Tai Sin Taoist Temple, where you can have your fortune told. To start, catch the MTR to Choi Hung (15 minutes from Tsim Sha Tsui) and a 10-minute taxi ride up Lion Rock. From Wong Tai Sin, return by MTR.

★ **Fodor's Choice** **MacLehose Trail.** Named after a former Hong Kong governor, the 97-km (60-mi) MacLehose is the grueling course for the annual charity event, the MacLehose Trailwalker. Top teams finish the hike in an astonishing 15 hours. Mere mortals should allow three to four days or simply tackle one section or another on a day hike or two.

This isolated trail through the New Territories starts at Tsak Yue Wu, beyond Sai Kung, and circles High Island Reservoir before breaking north. A portion takes you through the Sai Kung Country Park, Hong Kong's most beloved preserve, and up a mountain called Ma On Shan. Turn south for a high-ridge view, and walk through Ma On Shan Country Park. From here walk west along the ridges of the mountains known as the Eight Dragons, which gave Kowloon its name.

After crossing Tai Po Road, the path follows a ridge to the summit of Tai Mo Shan (Big Hat Mountain), which, at 3,140 feet, is Hong Kong's tallest mountain. On a clear day you can even see the spire of the Bank of China building in Central from here. Continuing west, the trail drops to Tai Lam Reservoir and Tuen Mun, where you can catch public transport back to the city. To reach Tsak Yue Wu, take the MTR to Choi Hung and then Bus 92 or

96R, or Minibus 1 to Sai Kung Town. From Sai Kung Town, take Bus 94 to the country park.

■**TIP→** An easier way to access Tai Mo Shan is via an old military road. En route you'll see the old British barracks, now occupied by the People's Liberation Army. Take the MTR to Tsuen Wan and exit the station at Shiu Wo Street, then catch Minibus 82.

Wilson Trail. The 78-km- (48-mi-) long trail runs from Stanley Gap on the south end of Hong Kong Island, through rugged peaks that have a panoramic view of Repulse Bay and the nearby Round and Middle islands, and to Nam Chung in the northeastern New Territories. You have to cross the harbor by MTR at Quarry Bay to complete the entire walk. The trail is smoothed by steps paved with stone, and footbridges aid with steep sections and streams. Clearly marked with signs and information boards, this popular walk is divided into 10 sections, and you can easily take just one or two (figure on three to four hours a section); traversing the whole trail takes about 31 hours.

Section 1, which starts at Stanley Gap Road, is only for the very fit. Much of it requires walking up steep mountain grades. For an easier walk, try Section 7, which begins at Sing Mun Reservoir and takes you along a greenery-filled, fairly level path that winds past the eastern shore of the Sing Mun Reservoir in the New Territories and then descends to Tai Po, where there's a sweeping view of Tolo Harbour. Other sections will take you through the monkey forest at the Kowloon Hill Fitness Trail, over mountains, and past charming Chinese villages.

VERY AMUSING

Given all the malls here, you'd be forgiven for thinking that shopping is all Hong Kongers do for kicks. But a different brand of adrenaline is on offer at the territory's amusement parks, just a short way from the retail strips.

Thrills & Spills

☺ **Hong Kong Disneyland.** If you're expecting an Asian take on the Magic Kingdom, think again—this park on Lantau Island is aimed at mainland Chinese hungry for apple-pie Americana. It's as polished as all the other Disneys, and it has one big advantage: fewer visitors, which means shorter lines. You can go on every ride at least once and see all the attractions in a day. If your kids are theme park-savvy, the tame rides here won't win their respect. That said, there are loads for little kids. Space Mountain is the only attraction with a height restriction. ■ TIP→ **Hong Kong Disneyland operates a Fastpass system, which lets you jump the lines at the most popular attractions.**

You enter right into **Main St., USA,** an area paying tribute to early-20th-century small-town America. Shops—cute though they are—outnumber attractions here, so save lingering for the 3:30 PM parade, which winds up in the Town Square. Sleeping Beauty's castle, with its trademark turrets, is the gateway to faux-medieval **Fantasyland.** Choose from two spin-cycles—the Mad-Hatter's Teacups or Cinderella's Carousel—while you wait for your Winnie-the-Pooh Fastpass time.

Throbbing drums let you know you've hit **Adventureland,** on the park's south side. Landscapers have really run amok at attractions like Tarzan's Treehouse, on an island only accessible by rafts and the Jungle River Cruise. Inspired by the Bog-

art–Hepburn film *The African Queen,* this canopied boat ride takes you past "ancient" ruins, headhunters, and a volcano. Animated beasties—crocs, snakes, hippos, elephants, partying gorillas—will try to scare or squirt you, egged on by the boat's quipping skipper.

In **Tomorrowland** attractions look more like the *Jetsons* than the future. It's home to roller-coaster-in-the-dark Space Mountain, a humbled version of the original. ■ TIP→ **Shade is limited so take the lead from locals and make an umbrella your No. 1 accessory—use it as a parasol if the sun blazes down or the traditional way if it pours.**

If you do one show, make it the *Festival of the Lion King.* Give your feet a rest but get your toes tapping with this energetic live performance of the animated film. The one place where Disney meets the East is at ye olde Corner Café. It may seem surreal, but run with it: the congee, curry, sushi, dim sum, stir fries, and kebabs are excellent, as theme-park food goes. If your kids are suspicious of far-flung fare, the Starliner Diner in Tomorrowland does burgers and fries.

The MTR is the quickest way here: take the Tung Chung line to Sunny Bay Station, then change to the Disneyland Resort Line, whose special trains have royal-blue plush seating and Mickey-shape windows. Check opening hours online or by phone first, as they change monthly. ✉ *Lantau Island* ☎ *3550–3888* ⊕ *www.hongkongdisneyland.com* ✉ *HK$350 weekends, holidays, and July and Aug.; HK$295 other days* ⊗ *Weekdays 10–8, weekends 10 AM–11 PM* Ⓜ *Disneyland Resort Station.*

VERY AMUSING

★ **Ocean Park.** When it comes to amusement parks, there's no question where Hong Kongers' loyalties lie. This marine-theme park embraces both high- and low-octane buzzes and spectacular zoological attractions; they even breed endangered species here. The park stretches out over 170 hilly acres, and you can gaze down at much of it from spookily silent cabins of the mile-long cable car that connects the tamer Lowlands area to the action-packed Headland. ■ **TIP→ If all you fancy is roller-coasting, enter the park at the Tai Shue Wan Middle Kingdom entrance, and head straight up the escalator to Adventure Land. If you're planning to do everything, start at the main entrance.**

The highlights of the **Lowland Gardens** are the giant pandas, particularly the young siblings from China, Le Le and Ying Ying. Paths wind to other enclosures, including a cantilevered butterfly house where rare species are bred, and the traditional Chinese architecture of the Goldfish Pagoda. Cross a rickety bridge to the lush undergrowth of the Amazing Amazon: its inhabitants are richly colored birds like toucans and flamingos.

Hong Kong's biggest roller coaster, the Dragon, is at the **Headland,** where the cable car stops. It might not quite be up to international standards, but it still loops the loops. There's also a Ferris wheel and swinging pirate ship here. If your kids are too small to get past Headland height restrictions, make for the old-school attractions at **Kids World.** There's a carousel as well as kid-size fairground stalls. You can also sneak in some learning at Dolphin University. (The first-ever dolphins born from artificial insemination were born in Ocean Park.)

More than 2,000 fish find their way around the Atoll Reef in **Marine Land,** where the newest exhibits are the Chinese Sturgeon Aquarium and Pacific Pier, which has more than 20 resident seals and sea lions. For sheer visual delight, the Sea Jelly Spectacular offers a colorful display in a dark environment. At the Ocean Theatre, dolphins and sea lions clown around with surprising grace. In **Adventure Land,** the Wild West–theme Mine Train was designed to feel rickety and screw-loose, which is probably why it rates highest on the scream-o-meter. Expect a light spraying or a heavy drenching at the Raging River: it all depends on your seat (and your luck). Rounding up the adrenaline boosts is the Abyss Turbo Drop, consisting, simply, of a 185-foot vertical plunge. It will definitely give you that sinking feeling.

Ocean Park is 30 minutes from Admiralty MTR or Central Star Ferry Pier by Citybus 629. Buses 70, 75, 90, 97, 260, 6A, and 6X also run from Central. ⊠ *Tai Shue Wan Rd., Aberdeen, Southside* ☎ *2552–0291* ⊕ *www.oceanpark.com.hk* ☎ *HK$208* ⊙ *Daily 10–6.*

Quieter Pursuits

★ **Yuen Po Street Bird Garden.** The air fills with warbling and tweeting about a block from this narrow public garden. Around 70 stalls stretch down one side of it, selling all the birds, cages, and accessories a bird owner could need. More gruesome are the heaving bags of creepy-crawlies—old men tending the stalls lift larvae with chopsticks and pop them into the open mouths of baby birds. Birds are a favorite pet in Hong Kong, especially among the elderly, who often take them out for a "walk" in bamboo cages.

Plenty of free birds swoop in to gorge on spilled food and commiserate with imprisoned brethren. The garden was built to replace the old, mazelike Bird Market, which was closed down during the worst bird flu outbreaks. (Government sanitation programs mean the flu is no longer a threat, though all the vendors here ignore signs warning against contact with birds.) From the MTR station walk east along Prince Edward Road for three short blocks, then turn left onto Sai Yee Street, then right onto Flower Market Road, for an aromatic approach. The Bird Garden is at the end of this flower-market street. ✉*Yuen Po St., Prince Edward, Kowloon* ☎*2302–1762* ⊕*www.lcsd.gov.hk/parks/ypsbg* ▣*Free* ⊙*Daily 7 AM–8 PM* Ⓜ*Prince Edward, Exit B1.*

Edward Youde Aviary. Fluttering feathers, caws, chirps, and warbles fill your ears as you enter this aviary that's home to more than 600 birds. You crisscross a rain-forest environment on timber walkways elevated to canopy level (50 feet). Vibrant flashes of color swoop down or settle in nearby branches. The aviary was named for a bird-loving colonial governor and is in the southwest of Hong Kong Park, which you reach by walking up through Pacific Place shopping mall from the Admiralty MTR. ✉*Hong Kong Park, 19 Cotton Tree Dr., Admiralty* ☎*2521–5057* ⊕*www.lcsd.gov.hk/parks/hkp/en/specialties.php* ▣*Free* ⊙*Daily 9–5* Ⓜ*Admiralty MTR, Exit C1.*

☾**Hong Kong Zoological & Botanical Gardens.** The city has grown around the gardens, which opened in 1864, and though they're watched over by skyscrapers, a visit to them is still a delightful escape. Paths lined with semitropical trees, shrubs, and flowers wind through cramped zoo enclo-

sures. Burmese python, Chinese alligator, Bornean orangutan, Bali mynah, ring-tailed lemur, and lion-tailed macaque are among its 500 birds, 70 mammals, and 70 reptiles from some 30 animal species. The Garden houses more than 1,000 species of plants indigenous to tropical and subtropical regions. Albany Road slices the park in half: birds and the greenhouse are on the eastern side, the other animals are to the west. A pedestrian underpass connects the two sides. ✉*Upper Albert Rd. opposite Government House; enter on Garden Rd., Central* ☎*2530–0107* ⊕*www.lcsd.gov.hk/parks/hkzbg* ▣*Free* ⊙*Zoo: daily 6 AM–7 PM. Gardens: daily 6 AM–10 PM. Greenhouse: daily 9–4:30.*

CINEMA HONG KONG

Hong Kong cinema still projects an image of classic martial arts and prolific triad flicks, with a few auteurs capturing the nuanced poetry of life in the former British colony. Inside the territory, however, silly romantic comedies with Cantopop stars, gory/sexy ghost films, cheesy throwaways by Wong Jing, and a handful of thoughtful independent films also populate the screens.

Post-1997

To see what really moves the masses in Hong Kong today, look no further than filmmaker extraordinaire Stephen Chow (of *Shaolin Soccer* and *Kung Fu Hustle* fame), whose movies—localized yet imaginative, at the same time over-the-top in special effects and down-to-earth in situations—are, sadly, increasingly few and far between.

The Hong Kong film industry churned out more than 200 local features a year in the early 1990s; but by 1997 that number had plummeted to 85, and in 2007 Hong Kong released a mere 50 films. This decline in an empire can be credited, not only to changing audience tastes, but to increasing pressure from the "motherland" to target the mainland Chinese market. The result is often big-budget, epic-proportion, crowd-pleasing, censorfriendly co-productions (think Daniel Lee's *Three Kingdoms*).

Among the most popular Hong Kong films expressing post-'97 angst are Fruit Chan's *Made in Hong Kong*, *Durian Durian*, and *Little Cheung*, as well as Johnnie To's *Election* and *Election 2*. For a typical Hong Kong movie about Hong Kong, see Samson Chiu's *Golden Chicken*; for a less typical one, see Toe Yuen's animated *My Life as McDull*.

Other recent local films portraying a less known side of Hong Kong include Wong Ching-po's *My Mother is a Belly Dancer* and Herman Yau's *Whispers and Moans*.

Meanwhile, don't forget to pay tribute to the legend Bruce Lee, whose bronze statue is frozen in stance on the eastern end of Kowloon's Avenue of Stars.

A Night at the Movies

An engaging cinema is an integral part of the Hong Kong moviegoing experience. Except for children's and other niche-market films dubbed in Cantonese, all films have subtitles. Local films are subtitled in both Chinese and English. For show times and theaters, check the Web sites of the movie chains or theaters directly, where you can usually see the seating chart updated in real time, before either booking online by credit card or buying your tickets at the counter later. Prime-time tickets range from HK$–0–HK$80, while most cinemas offer a discount of around 20% on Tuesday and morning matinees. Refreshment kiosks sell two varieties of popcorn—the traditional salty type or a sweet variety. Among the usual candy offerings and hot dogs, you might also find Chinese siu mai or dried squid. ■ TIP➔ **Theaters are notoriously frigid. Bring a sweater, jacket, or, like the locals, borrow a shawl from the cinema.**

★ **Broadway Cinematheque.** The train-station design of this art house has won awards; inside the foyer a departure board displays primarily foreign and independent films. You can read the latest reel-world magazines from around the globe in the mini-library next door. Kubrick also sells film books and other alternative literature in a coffee-shop setting. An oasis of culture in a Kowloon hous-

ing estate, this one shouldn't be missed. To get here, use Yau Ma Tei MTR exit C and browse through the Temple Street trinkets on your way over. ✉ *Prosperous Garden, 3 Public Square St., Yau Ma Tei, Kowloon* ☎ *Ticketing hotline 2388–3188* ⊕ *bc.cinema.com.hk.*

★ **Palace IFC.** Large, sink-into brown leather seats and ushers in tuxedos make this intimate boutique cinema seem more like a Broadway theater than a multiplex. Five screens show new releases, foreign and independent films, and occasionally even celluloid classics such as *Gone With the Wind* and *West Side Story.* The adjoining bookshop and upscale café fit right into IFC's business-posh atmosphere, making it especially popular with the Central after-work jet set. Pricier than most picture houses, but still part of the Broadway circuit, which offers a 10% discount for members. ✉ *IFC Mall, 8 Finance St., level 1, Central* ☎ *2388–6268* ⊕ *www.palaceifc.cinema.com.hk.*

★ **JP Cinema.** When it's good old popcorn action fare you're after, JP treats it patrons right, without the shopping-mall multiplex madness. Past the snack bar you'll enter one of two theaters equipped with panoramic screens, surround sound, and a combined total of 658 red-cushioned seats for your all-round movie experience. Hollywood action thrillers, epic adventures, and blockbuster comedies rule the lineup. Look to your left at the posters as you come up out of Causeway Bay MTR exit E. ✉ *22-36 Paterson St., Causeway Bay* ☎ *2881-5005, booking 3413-6688* ⊕ *www.mclcinema.com.*

★ **President Theatre.** This is one place on the Island where you can still see all the cheesy, vulgar, slapstick, sexy, scary, and silly local romantic comedies, triad films, and Category III (under 18 not allowed) horror flicks. Within walking distance of JP Cinema and UA (*www.cityline.com.hk*) Times Square multiplex in Causeway Bay, it's also another entertaining place to cool down on a hot day. Just point to the poster of the movie you want to watch when you get to the street-level ticket office. ✉ *517 Jaffe Rd., Causeway Bay* ☎ *2836-5581* ⊕ *www.theatre.com.hk.*

★ **Hong Kong Arts Centre agnès b. CINEMA!** For special limited or festival screenings only, often with meet-the-artist Q&A sessions, this cozy auditorium in the basement of the nonprofit Hong Kong Arts Centre has seen many of the territory's independent video and filmmakers' first works. Also popular with students of the adjacent Academy of Performing Arts, it feels almost like a private screening room, where regulars are likely to see a familiar face. ✉ *2 Harbour Rd., Wan Chai* ☎ *2582-0200* ⊕ *www.hkac.org.hk.*

★ **Hong Kong Film Archive.** Still wondering who all those handprints belong to on the Avenue of Stars? This is the place to see the faces behind the names. Not only does the theater screen rare classics from the history of Hong Kong cinema and beyond, but the building houses a genuine, living archive of film reels and documents dating back several decades. Conscientiously curated film programs are accompanied by an exhibition in a separate gallery downstairs. The Archive is a 10-minute walk from Sai Wan Ho MTR exit A. Several open cafés and restaurants overlooking the northeastern waterfront promenade are nearby. ✉ *50 Lei King Rd., Sai Wan Ho, Eastern District* ☎ *2739-2139* ⊕ *www.filmarchive.gov.hk.*

OFF TO THE RACES

Even if you're not a gambler, it's worth going to one of Hong Kong's two tracks just to experience the phenomenon. The "sport of kings" is run under a monopoly by the Hong Kong Jockey Club, one of the territory's most powerful entities. It's a multimillion-dollar-a-year business, employing thousands of people and drawing crowds that approach insanity in their eagerness to rid themselves of their hard-earned money. Profits go to charity and community organizations.

The season runs from September through June. Some 65 races are held at one or the other of the two courses—on Saturday or Sunday afternoon 1 to 6 at Sha Tin and Wednesday night 7:15 to 11 at Happy Valley—which must rank among the world's great horse-racing experiences.

In the public stands the vibe is electric and loud, thanks to feverish gamblers shouting and waving their newspapers madly. Both courses have huge video screens at the finish line, so you can see what's happening every foot of the way. ■ TIP → **The HKTB's Come Horseracing tours begin at HK$690 and include transfers, lunch, and tips on picking a winner.**

Fodor's Choice **Happy Valley Racecourse.** Hong Kong punters are the world's most avid horse-racing fans, and the beloved track in Happy Valley—opened soon after the British first arrived in the territory—is one of their headquarters. The roar of the crowd as the jockeys in bright silk colors race by is a must-see. The joy of the Happy Valley track, even for those who aren't into horses, is that it's smack in the middle of the city and surrounded by towering apartment blocks—indeed, people whose balconies hang over the backstretch often have par-

WORD OF MOUTH

"Happy Valley Racecourse is right in the city. The museum isn't much, but it's definitely a great place for racing. Sha Tin is an excellent easy-to-reach racecourse outside town. If you visit Macau, definitely go to the Macau Jockey Club. I couldn't find any useful handicapping info at Happy Valley. Get the daily paper; the horses' past performances are listed in the sports section."
—mrwunnfl

ties on racing days. The track is a 10-minute walk from Causeway Bay MTR Exit A (Times Square). ⊠ *Hong Kong Jockey Club, 1 Sports Rd., Happy Valley* 🕾 *2966-8111* 🌐 *racecourses.hkjc.com* 🎫 *HK$10.*

★ **Sha Tin Racecourse.** Whether you enter Sha Tin by road or rail, you'll be amazed to find this metropolis in the middle of the New Territories. One of the so-called "new towns," Sha Tin underwent a population explosion starting in the mid-1980s that transformed it from a town of 30,000 to a city of more than a half million. The biggest attraction is the racecourse, which is newer and larger than the one in Happy Valley. In fact, it's one of the world's most modern courses and, as such, is the venue for all championship events, including some equestrian events for the 2008 Olympics. The easiest way to get here is by taxi, or you can catch the MTR to Kowloon Tong and transfer to the KCR train, which stops at the Racecourse Station on race days. A walkway from it takes you directly to the track. ⊠ *Tai Po Rd., next to Racecourse KCR station, Sha Tin* 🕾 *2966-6520* 🌐 *racecourses.hkjc.com* 🎫 *HK$10.*

Hong Kong Neighborhoods

Midlevels

WORD OF MOUTH

"Took the Star Ferry to HK Island and [spent] the day wandering. Walked all through the Western District with its old and picturesque neighborhoods, browsed Hollywood Road (too high-end for us) and Cat Street (interesting, but most items are reproductions), took the Midlevels Escalators, and had a great lunch in Soho. Visited Man Mo Temple, then took the tram to Victoria Peak. The tram was a mob scene, and although the views from Victoria Peak were great, it was sad to see the enormous, tacky complex of tourist shops. . . . I would've rather explored other areas of the city."

—copilot

TO STAND ON THE TIP of Kowloon Peninsula and look across the harbor to the full expanse of the Hong Kong Island skyline is to see the triumph of ambition over fate. Whereas it took Paris and London 10 to 20 generations and New York six to build the spectacular cities seen today, in Hong Kong almost everything you see was built in the time since today's young investment bankers were born.

Hong Kong Island and Kowloon are divided physically and psychologically by Victoria Harbour. On Hong Kong Island, the central city goes only a few kilometers south into the island before mountains rise up, but on the Kowloon side, the city stretches several more kilometers north. In the main districts and neighborhoods, luxury boutiques are a stone's throw from old hawker stalls, and a modern, high-tech horse-racing track isn't far from a temple housing more than 10,000 buddhas.

If you're on Hong Kong Island and feeling disoriented, remember that the water is always north; in Kowloon it's always south. Central, Admiralty, and Wan Chai, the island's main business districts, are opposite Tsim Sha Tsui on the Kowloon Peninsula. West of Central are Sheung Wan and the other (mainly residential) neighborhoods that make up Western. Central backs onto the slopes of Victoria Peak, so the districts south of it—the Midlevels and the Peak—look down on it. Causeway Bay, North Point, Quarry Bay, Shau Kei Wan, and Chai Wan East run east along the shore after Wan Chai. Developments on the south side of Hong Kong Island are scattered: the beach towns of Shek O and Stanley sit on two peninsulas on the southeast; high-tech Cyberport, industrial Aberdeen, and Ap Lei Chau are to the west.

West of Hong Kong Island lie Lamma, Cheung Chau, and Lantau islands. Lantau is connected by a suspension bridge to west Kowloon. More than 200 other islands also belong to Hong Kong.

Kowloon's southern tip is the Tsim Sha Tsui district, which gives way to Jordan, Yau Ma Tei, Mong Kok, and Prince Edward. Northeast are the New Kowloon districts of Kowloon Tong, Kowloon City, and Wong Tai Sin, beyond which lie the eastern New Territories—mostly made up of mountainous country parks and fishing villages. The Sai Kung Peninsula juts out on the east, and massive Sha Tin New Town is north of New Kowloon, over Lion Rock Mountain. The Kowloon-Canton Railway and a highway run north of this to the Chinese border at Lo Wu.

Industrial Sham Shui Po lies west of Prince Edward, and the urban sprawl continues northwest to New Territories New Town Tsuen Wan. The western New Territories is a mixture of country parks and urban areas.

Hong Kong's older areas—the southern side of Central, for example—show erratic street planning, but the newer developments and reclamations follow something closer to a grid system. Streets are usually numbered odd on one side, even on the other. There's no baseline for street numbers and no block-based numbering system.

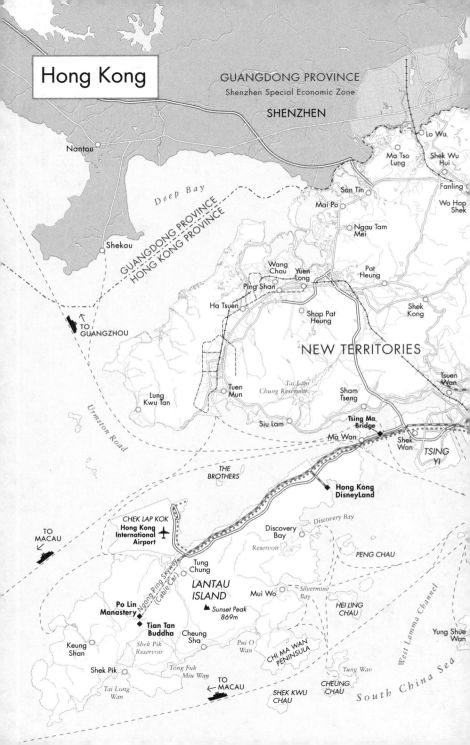

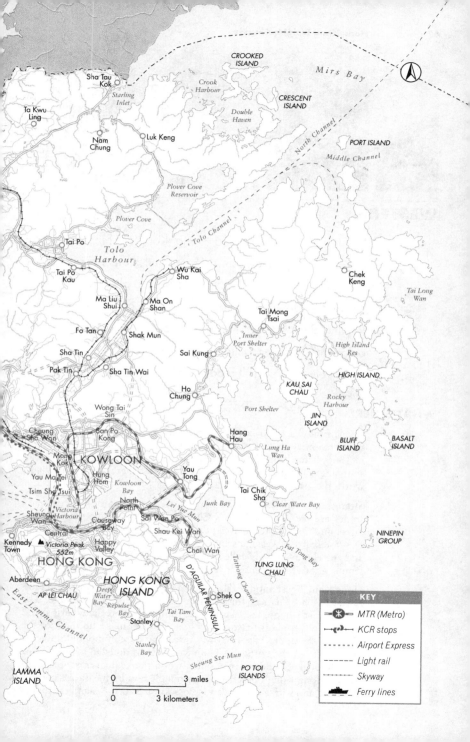

WESTERN

Sightseeing
☆★★★
Dining
☆☆★★
Lodging
☆☆★★
Shopping
☆★★★
Nightlife
☆☆☆★

Western has been called Hong Kong's Chinatown, and though it's a strange-sounding epithet, there's a reason for it. The area is light-years from the dazzle of Central, despite being just down the road. And although developers are making short work of the traditional architecture, Western's colonial buildings, rattling trams, old-world medicine shops, and lively markets still recall bygone times.

WHAT'S HERE

The Sheung Wan district's iconic **Western Market,** a hulking brown-and-white colonial structure, is a good place to get your bearings. Built in 1906, it functioned as a produce market for 83 years. Today it's a shopping center selling trinkets and fabrics—the architecture is what's worth the visit.

Strange smells fill the air in the narrow streets west of the market: many trades are based here. There's Chinese herbal medicine on Ko Shing Street and Queen's Road West; dried seafood on Wing Lok Street and Des Voeux Road West; ginseng and bird's nest on Bonham Strand West; and the engraved seals called chops on Man Wa Lane. Shops selling temple goods like incense are also commonplace.

Hong Kong's best antiques shops and classical-art galleries are on Hollywood Road, named for the holly trees that once grew here. The farther west you go, the less genuine things get. Porcelain, curios, and not-very-old trinkets masquerading as artifacts make up most of the offerings on Upper Lascar Row, a flea market commonly known as Cat Street. At the corner of Hollywood Road and the long flight of stairs known as Ladder Street, sandalwood smoke floats out of **Man Mo Temple.** Hong Kong's oldest Chinese temple honors the Taoist gods of literature and war. Farther west is Possession Street. A sign here marks where Captain Charles Elliott stepped ashore in 1841 to claim Hong Kong for the British empire. This was once the waterfront, but aggressive reclamation has left it several blocks inland.

The maze of streets west of Man Mo Temple is known as Tai Ping Shan (the Chinese name for Victoria Peak, which towers above it). It's a sleepy area filled with small shops. ■**TIP→ Food tourists should duck into Sheung Wan Wet Market, at Sai Ying Pun and Centre streets. Cantonese food demands the freshest ingredients, and serious cooks buy them—often still wriggling—at markets like this.** One of the city's oldest residential districts, Tai Ping Shan was badly hit by plague outbreaks in the 1890s. You can find out all about these and other medical episodes at the **Hong Kong Museum of Medical Sciences,** at the top of Ladder Street.

The unimaginatively named Midlevels is midway up the hill between Victoria Peak and the Western and Central districts. Running through it is the **Midlevels Escalator,** which connects now-defunct Central Market (at the border of Central and Western) with several main residential roads. Free of charge and protected from the elements, this series of moving walkways makes the uphill journey a cinch. Before 10 AM, they move only downward, carrying yuppies bearing coffee to work.

When all you see from the escalator are hip bars and restaurants, you're in SoHo, the area *south* of (i.e., above) Hollywood Road and epicenter of Hong Kong's latest gastro revolution.

The Midlevels Escalator goes right by the gray-and-white **Jamia Mosque** on Shelley Street. The original 1840s structure was rebuilt in 1915, and shows its Indian heritage in the perforated arches and decorative façade work. The mosque isn't open to non-Muslims, but it occupies a small verdant enclosure that's a welcome retreat.

It's worth a trip out to the western end of the Midlevels to see the imposing Edwardian buildings, most along Bonham Road, of Hong Kong University, where competition for a place is fierce. The **Hong Kong University Museum & Art Gallery** has excellent Chinese antiquities.

A PERFECT DAY

A Culinary Adventure. From Sheung Wan's markets to the hip international eateries (and drinkeries) of SoHo, Western is a foodie's heaven. Here's how to make a culinary adventure of it.

There's only one breakfast of champs in Hong Kong, and that's dim sum. Head for the old **Lin Heung Lau Tea House** (➪ *Quick Bites)* any time after 6 AM and fill up on things like *ha gau* (steamed shrimp dumplings) and *cha siu bau* (barbecue pork buns), washed down with lots of tea.

Get to Sheung Wan Wet Market early to watch expert shoppers in action. Earn their respect by examining fish gills for freshness and picking up a bag of lychees or cherries to munch on the go. Take time to browse the dried delicacies—abalone, bird's nest, sea cucumbers, mushrooms—in shops around Wing Lok Street and Des Voeux Road. You might want to invest in an herbal indigestion cure, just in case.

GETTING ORIENTED

SAI YING PUN

Western Park Rd.

Western Harbour Tunnel

H Ferry

Belcher Bay

3

Connaught Rd. West

4

Des Voeux Rd. West

Des Voeux Rd. West

Water St.

Queen's Rd. West

Ko Shing St.

Bon We

Queen's Rd. West

First St.   Yuen Kee
Second   St.
Third St.
High St.

Hospital Rd.

Possession St.

New St.   Tai Pu

Pok Fu Lam Rd.

Westem St.

Centre St.

Eastern St.

SHEK TONG TSUI

South Ln.

Pok Fu Lam Rd.

Park Rd.

Bonham Rd.

Hong Kong University

Babington Path

Pok Fu Lam Rd.

Park Rd.

Hong Kong University Museum & Gallery

Lyttelton Rd.

Robinson Rd.

Hong
Muse
Me
Scie

University Rd.

Kotewall Rd.

Conduit Rd.

MIDLEVELS

Hatton Rd.

Po Shan Rd.

KEY

Hatton Rd.

MTR (Metro)

Airport Express

0   1/4 mile

0   1/4 kilometer

THE TERRITORY

The Midlevels Escalator forms a handy boundary between Western and Central. Several main thoroughfares run parallel to the shore, each farther up the slope: Des Voeux Road (where the trams run), Queen's Road, Hollywood Road (where SoHo starts), and Caine Road (where the Midlevels begin).

As to how far west Western goes, it technically reaches all the way to Kennedy Town, where the tram lines end, but there isn't much worth noting beyond Sheung Wan.

TAKING IT IN

Colonial Architecture. You can see Western's colonial buildings on an hour-long stroll from the University of Hong Kong (take a cab or bus out). East along Bonham Road, which becomes Caine Road, are Victorian apartments. The medical sciences museum is at Ladder Street. Head downstairs, then left onto Hollywood Road to Possession Street. Follow this downhill, doglegging right and left through Bonham Strand, onto Morrison, and to the Western Market.

Traditional Goods. An hour is enough time to wander Sheung Wan's traditional shops. In the morning, when trade's brisk, take the tram to Wilmer Street. Walk a block south and turn left onto Queen's Road West (herbal remedies, temple goods). Walk left for a block at Possession, then loop left through Bonham Strand West (ginseng), right for a block at Des Voeux, then back along Wing Lok (dried seafood). Continue on Bonham Strand (bird's nest), dipping left onto Hillier (snakes) and beyond to Man Wa Lane (chops).

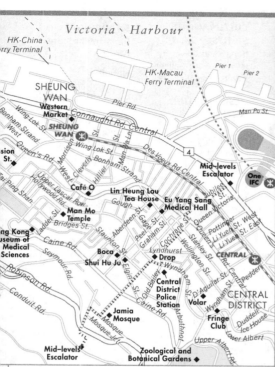

GETTING AROUND

The most scenic way to Sheung Wan is on a tram along Des Voeux Road. From Central or Admiralty, it's probably the quickest, too: no traffic, no subway lines, or endless underground walks. There are stops every two or three blocks. The Sheung Wan MTR station brings you within spitting distance of Western Market.

The Macau Ferry Terminal is behind the MTR (use Exit D).**Turbojet** (☎ *2859–3333* ⊕ *www.turbojet. com.hk*) vessels run every 15 minutes with a reduced schedule from midnight to 7 AM. Crossings take 1 hour. You can usually buy tickets on the spot (from HK$134), but reservations are recommended on weekends (⇨ *Chapter 8, Side Trip to Macau*). ■**TIP**➔ **You need your passport to go to Macau.**

The Midlevels Escalator is fun up as far as SoHo. Buses 3, 40, and 40M run between the university and Jardine House in Central, as does green Minibus 8. Both pass the top of Ladder Street. Expect a taxi from Central to the Midlevels to cost HK$20.

QUICK BITES

Sit on velvet-covered seats at **Boca** (✉ *65 Peel St., Western* ☎ *2548–1717*) and watch trendy SoHo go by. Tapas are the specialty: enjoy classics such as *gambas al ajillo* (prawns sautéed with artichoke hearts, spinach, and paprika) and Hong Kong originals like butterfish in ginger.

Cracked Formica tabletops, cranky waiters, old men reading the newspapers: there's nothing fancy about **Lin Heung Lau Tea House** (✉ *160 Wellington St., Sheung Wan, Western* ☎ *2544–4556*). But it's been doing great dim sum for years, as locals will testify.

Café O (✉ *284 Queen's Rd. Central, Sheung Wan, Western* ☎ *2851–0890*) is a Sheung Wan trailblazer. Pizza by the meter is the signature dish, but the mega-breakfasts (served all day) are fierce competition. Fresher-than-fresh juices and smoothies help you keep your energy up.

Got a sweet tooth? Try a traditional dessert at **Yuen Kee** (✉*32 Centre St., Western* ☎*2548–8687*)—the almond soup is divine.

Walk over to Gage Street for a steaming bowl of wonton noodles at any *dai pai dong* (street-stall restaurant). Wander more stalls on chaotic Graham Street—the meat stalls aren't for the fainthearted—then go for some liquid sustenance. Many SoHo bars along the Midlevels Escalator start happy hour in midafternoon and go until 8 or 9 PM.

Wind up the day with top-notch Shanghainese, Sichuan, or Beijing dishes amid lots of lacquered wood at **Shui Hu Ju** (✉*68 Peel St., SoHo, Western* ☎*2869–6927*).

CENTRAL

Sightseeing
★★★
Dining
☆★★★
Lodging
☆★★★
Shopping
★★★★
Nightlife
★★★★

Shopping, eating, drinking—Central lives up to its name when it comes to all of these. But it's also Hong Kong's historical heart, packed with architectural reminders of the early colonial days. They're in stark contrast to the soaring masterpieces of modern architecture that the city is famous for. Somehow the mishmash works. With the harbor on one side and Victoria Peak on the other, Central's views—once you get high enough to see them—are unrivaled. It's the liveliest district, packed with people, sights, and life.

WHAT'S HERE

One building towers above the rest of Central's skyline: Two IFC, or the second tower of the **International Finance Centre.** The tall, tapering structure has been compared to at least one—unprintable—thing; and is topped with a clawlike structure straight out of Thundercats. Designed by Argentine architect Cesar Pelli (of London's Canary Wharf fame), its 88 floors measure a whopping 1,362 feet. Opposite stands its dinky little brother, the 38-floor One IFC. The massive IFC Mall stretches between the two, and Hong Kong Station is underneath.

Jutting out into the harbor in front of the International Finance Center is the **Central Ferry Pier.** Ferries regularly leave from here to Lantau, Lamma, and Cheung Chau islands.

Just behind the IFC is '60s skyscraper **Jardine House,** recognizable by its many round windows. It's home to Jardine, Matheson & Co., the greatest of the old British *hongs* (trading companies) that dominated trade with imperial China. Once an establishment linked to opium trafficking, it's now a respected investment bank.

GETTING ORIENTED

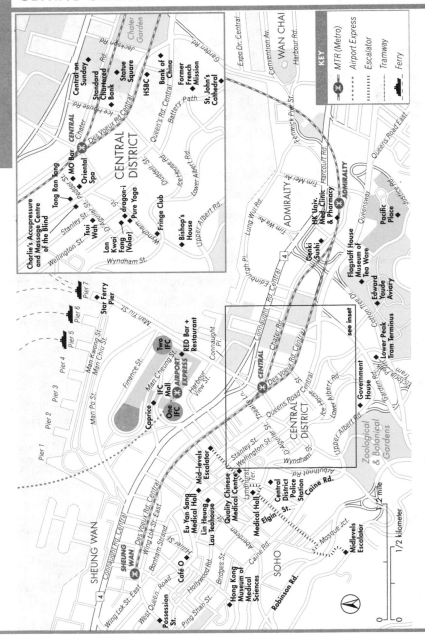

KEY

- ☀ MTR (Metro)
- ∙∙∙∙∙ Airport Express
- ∶∶∶∶∶∶ Escalator
- Tramway
- Ferry

CENTRAL DISTRICT (inset)

Chater Garden
Jackson Rd.
Garden Rd.
Central on Sunday
Standard Chartered Bank
Statue Square
Bank of China
Former French Mission
HSBC
St. John's Cathedral
Chater Rd.
Ice House Rd.
Queen's Rd. Central
Battery Path
MO Bar
Oriental Spa
Duddell St.
Ice House Rd.
Lower Albert Rd.
Charlie's Accupressure and Message Centre of the Blind
Tong Kam Tang
Pottinger St.
Stanley St.
dragon-i
Pure Yoga
Fringe Club
Bishop's House
Tsui Wah
Lan Kwai Fong (Volar)
D'Aguilar St.
Upper Albert Rd.
Wellington St.
Wyndham St.
Wyndham St.

WAN CHAI
Expo Dr. Central
Convention Av.
Harbour Rd.
Fenwick Pier St.
Queens Road East

ADMIRALTY
Tim Mei Av.
Harcourt Rd.
Lung Wui Rd.
Tim Wa Av.
HK Univ. Med. Clinic & Pharmacy
Genki Sushi
Queensway
Flagstaff House
Museum of Tea Ware
Pacific Place
Justice Rd.
Cotton Tree Dr.
Edward Youde Aviary
Edinburgh Pl.
Connaught Rd. Central

Pier 7
Pier 6
Pier 5
Pier 4
Pier 3
Pier 2
Pier 1
Star Ferry Pier
Man Yiu St.
Man Kwong St.
Man Chiu St.
Man Po St.
Finance St.
Man Cheung St.
Two IFC
RED Bar + Restaurant
AIRPORT EXPRESS
IFC Mall
Harbour View St.
Connaught Pl.
Caprice
One IFC
CENTRAL
Des Voeux Rd. Central
Chater Rd.
see inset
Government House
Lower Peak Tram Terminus
Victoria Peak Tram
Garden Rd.
Cotton Tree Dr.
Zoological & Botanical Gardens

CENTRAL DISTRICT
Queens Road Central
Stanley St.
Wellington St.
Ice House Rd.
Lower Albert Rd.
D'Aguilar St.
Wyndham
Upper Albert Rd.
Arbuthnot Rd.

SHEUNG WAN
Connaught Rd. Central
Des Voeux Rd. West
Wing Lok St. East
Des Voeux Rd. Central
Mid-levels Escalator
Quality Chinese Medical Centre
Lyndhurst Ter.
Central District Police Station
Caine Rd.
Eu Yan Sang Medical Hall
Lin Heung Lau Teahouse
Bonham Strand
Hillier St.
Café O
Wing Lok St. East
West Queen Road
Hollywood Rd.
Bridges St.
Caine Rd.
Medical Hall
Elgin St.
Aberdeen St.
SOHO
Mosque Jct.
Mid-levels Escalator
Possession St.
Ping Shan St.
Hong Kong Museum of Medical Sciences
Robinson Rd.

1/2 mile
1/2 kilometer
0

GETTING AROUND

Central MTR station is a mammoth underground warren with a host of far-flung exits. A series of travelators join it with Hong Kong Station, under the IFC Mall, where Tung Chung line and Airport Express trains arrive and depart. Rattling old trams along Des Voeux Road have you at Sheung Wan, Admiralty, and Wan Chai in minutes. They continue to Causeway Bay, Happy Valley, and beyond.

Star Ferry (☎2767–7065 ⊕ www.starferry.com.hk) vessels to Kowloon leave Pier 7 every 6–12 minutes 6:30 AM–11:30 PM; the nine-minute trip costs HK$2.20 (upper deck). Ferries run from the neighboring piers in front of the IFC every half hour 6 AM–midnight.

New World First Ferry (☎2131–8181 ⊕ www.nwff.com.hk) goes to Lantau (from Pier 6) and Cheung Chau (Pier 5). Journeys take 35–55 minutes and cost HK$11.50–HK$32.20.

Discovery Bay Transportation Service (☎2987–7351 ⊕ www.discoverybay.com.hk) has high-speed boats for Lantau every 20–30 minutes from Pier 3 round-the-clock. Trips take 25–30 minutes and cost HK$27.

QUICK BITES

At lunch time people flood the cul-de-sac that is known as Rat Alley (Wing Wah Lane off D'Aguilar Street). Choose from Thai, Malay, Indian, Chinese, or American places.

No visit to Central is complete without a bowl of noodles at **Tsui Wah** (✉ Ground fl., 15–19 Wellington St., Central ☎2525–6338 ⊕ www.tsuiwahrestaurant.com) down the hill from Lan Kwai Fong. It's open 24 hours.

Need an instant sushi fix? Pull up a stool at the conveyor belt at **Genki Sushi** (✉ Ground fl., Far East Finance Centre, 16 Harcourt Rd., Admiralty ☎2865–2933 ⊕ www.genkisushi.com.hk).

THE TERRITORY

The Midlevels Escalator and Cotton Tree Drive form the boundaries of Central with Western and Admiralty districts, respectively. Streets between Queen's Road Central and the harbor are laid out more or less geometrically. On the south side of Queen's Road, however, is a confusion of steep lanes. Overhead walkways connect Central's major buildings, an all-weather alternative to the chaotic streets below.

TAKING IT IN

Colonial Central. *South China Morning Post* columnist Jason Wordie (☎2476–3504 ⊕ www.jasonswalks.com) leads three-hour tours (HK$280 per person) loaded with anecdotes.

The Urban Runway. They say the ability to cross Central without touching street level is the sign of a true Hong Konger. Start in the IFC mall; leave by Pret a Manger on the southeast side, turn right into the walkway, pass the General Post Office and Jardine House and into the Armani floor of the Chater Building. The door between Emporio and Fiori leads to Alexandra House; take the stairs left of Dolce & Gabbana and into the Landmark. Turn right past Jimmy Choo, go downstairs and cross over to the Central Building, turn left, go up the stairs past Clarins, and into the Central Building. Cross to the back right of the elevator lobby, through the bridge into the Entertainment Building, which drops you in Lan Kwai Fong. Time your 15-minute walk to finish at 6 PM—happy hour.

Arguably the best way to take in Central's architecture isn't on land but arriving from Kowloon on one of the sturdy green-and-white Star Ferries. The view of the skyline isn't bad from the **Central Star Ferry Pier,** either. **Statue Square** is directly to the south. The land it's on was gifted to the public by the Hongkong & Shanghai Bank (HSBC, whose head-quarters dominate the southern end), with the proviso that nothing built on it could block the bank's view of the water.

DID YOU KNOW?

Statue Square took its name from bronze figures of British royalty that stood here before the Japanese occupation, when they were removed and melted down. The only figure exempt was stern Sir Thomas Jackson (1841–1915), who looks over the square toward HSBC—he was the chief manager for more than 30 years.

The Victorian–Chinese hybrid building on Statue Square's east side is the Legislative Council Building. Built for the Supreme Court in 1912, it's now home to the 60-member Legislative Council (LegCo). It's often the focus of the demonstrations that have become a fixture of Hong Kong life since 1997. In front of the council building is the Cenotaph, a monument to all who lost their lives in the two World Wars.

Along Statue Square's southern end are the three buildings of Hong Kong's note-issuing banks: the art-deco former headquarters of the **Bank of China,** the rose-color wedge of the **Standard Chartered Bank,** and the spectacular strut-and-ladder façade of the **HSBC.** The latter is one of the most important buildings in 20th-century architecture; walk under it and look up into the atrium through the curved glass floor, or go inside for a view of the building's mechanics.

Hong Kong's answer to New York's 5th Avenue and London's King's Road are the first few blocks of Chater Road, Des Voeux Road Central, and Queen's Road Central (the thoroughfares that stretch west from Statue Square). Few designers do not have—or do not crave—a boutique in priceless über-posh minimalls like the Landmark, Alexandra House, or the Pedder Building. A stone's throw away, but at the other end of the income scale, are Li Yuen Street East and Li Yuen Street West. Known as the Lanes, they're packed with stalls selling cheap *cheongsams* (sexy, slit-skirt, silk dresses with Mandarin collars) and Hello Kitty merchandise. On the south side of Queen's Road is steep Pottinger Street, a haberdasher's dream street.

In Hong Kong, the word "nightlife" is synonymous with **Lan Kwai Fong,** a few narrow lanes filled with bars and clubs just up the hill from the intersection of Queen's Road Central and Pedder Street. Veering right at the top gets you to Wyndham Street and the start of a series of high-caliber antiques and Oriental-rug shops. The colonial building just after the street becomes Hollywood Road is the **Central District Police Station,** a must-have location in any self-respecting Hong Kong cop movie. It was the neighborhood headquarters from 1864—when part of it was built—through 2004.

Several colonial structures are clustered on Lower Albert Road, which starts at the curving eastern end of Wyndham Street. The brown-and-white brick building on the corner is the Old Dairy Farm Building, built in 1898. Once a big glorified fridge housing a meat and dairy shop, it's now home to the **Fringe Club** arts center and the Foreign Correspondents' Club, the haunt of hard-drinking international journalists. The big gray Victorian building across the road is Bishop's House, official residence of the Anglican bishop since 1851. Lower Albert Road forks in two; the lower branch is Ice House Street, which curves down the hill to Queen's Road. Before the bend is a magnificent balustraded stone staircase that becomes Duddell Street; it's adorned with four old-fashioned gas lamps that have been lighting the way since the late 1870s.

Farther uphill on Central's eastern edge are the **Hong Kong Zoological & Botanical Gardens**, a welcome green breathing space.

The handsome white Victorian occupying the land between Upper and Lower Albert roads is **Government House**. Constructed in 1855, it was the official residence of British governors but is shunned by the new chief executives—some say because it has bad feng shui. During the Japanese occupation it was significantly rebuilt, so it exhibits a Japanese influence, particularly in the roof eaves. The gardens are opened to the public once a year in March, when the azaleas bloom.

A peaceful gap in the skyscrapers—on Garden Road and up from Queen's Road Central—accommodates the Anglican **St. John's Cathedral**, a graceful Gothic form. Completed in 1849, it's made of Canton bricks in the shape of a cross. Among the World War II relics it houses are the cathedral doors themselves, made from timber salvaged from British warship HMS *Tamar*.

Victoria Peak soars 1,805 feet above sea level and looks over Central and beyond. Residents here take special pride in the positions to which they have, quite literally, risen; theirs is the island's most exclusive address. The steep tracks up to it starts at the **Peak Tram Terminus**, near St. John's Cathedral on Garden Road.

A narrow tree-lined lane called Battery Path runs uphill parallel to Queen's Road Central behind the HSBC building. The British built it when they arrived in 1841 to move their cannons uphill—hence the name. At the top of Battery Path sits the **Former French Mission Building**, an elegant redbrick building with white stone windows and green shutters. Finished in 1917, it's now home to the Court of Final Appeal.

Central's skyscrapers spill over into Admiralty, the next district east. It's home to **Pacific Place** shopping mall and the 25 green acres of **Hong Kong Park**. Here you'll find the **Flagstaff Museum of Tea Ware**, and the **Edward Youde Aviary**.

A PERFECT DAY (AND NIGHT)

NINE HOURS OF LUXURY

With boutiques, spas, and coffee shops galore, Central has everything you need to be a *tai-tai*—localspeak for ladies who lunch—even if you're a man. There's *so* much more to do than lunch, so take a leaf out of their book and spend some time (and lots of money) on—who else?—yourself.

Start off by harmonizing the inner you with an early-morning yoga class (a trial class is free, or it's HK$800 for a monthlong visitor pass) at **Pure Yoga** (⊠ *The Centrium, 16th fl., 60 Wyndham St., Central* ☎ *2971–0055* ⊕ *www.pure-yoga.com*).

Then head to the **Oriental Spa** (⊠ *Landmark Mandarin Oriental, 15 Queen's Rd., Central* ☎ *2132–0011* ⊕ *www.mandarinoriental. com/landmark*) for the 195-minute Urban Retreat package (HK$2,–60–HK$2,480), which includes a facial, massage, and foot treatment. It's best to make reservations several days ahead.

Relaxing is hungry work. But not just anyone should be allowed to prepare your lunch, so book a table at **Caprice** (⊠ *8 Finance St., Central* ☎ *3196–8888*) in the Four Seasons hotel. It's hard to know whether to gaze at the view of the harbor, the French chandeliers, or the chefs in the open kitchen cooking up some of the best French food in town.

What better way to work off lunch than shopping? The Landmark and Chater House are packed with international designers, but don't neglect the Pedder Building, where local luxury brands such as Shanghai Tang sell made-to-measure Chinese-style suits and cheongsams.

Reflect on your busy day over Bellinis at **MO Bar** (⊠ *15 Queen's Rd. Central, Central* ☎ *2132–0077*) in the Landmark Oriental.

TEN HOURS ON THE TOWN

When the neon lights up, office-Central transforms into party-Central. The nights are long and Hong Kongers play hard, but here's a plan guaranteed to earn local party animals' respect.

Boozing is an expensive pastime, so keep costs down with a happy-hour bar crawl through Lan Kwai Fong. When the sun's about to set, grab a cab over to the IFC Mall and watch the orb descend over the harbor as you sip a quirky cocktail at an open-air table in the **RED Bar + Restaurant** (⊠ *Level 4, Two IFC, 8 Finance St., Central* ☎ *8129–8882*).

Don't worry about losing your momentum by stopping for dinner. Just head to celebrity haunt **dragon-i** (⊠ *Upper ground fl., The Centrium, 60 Wyndham St., Central* ☎ *3110–1222* ⊕ *www.dragon-i.com.hk*), where there's sushi, dim sum, *and* cocktails to nourish you.

Pace yourself at **Drop** (⊠ *On Lok Mansion, 39–43 Hollywood Rd., basement [entrance off Cochrane St.], Central* ☎ *2543–8856* ⊕ *www. drophk.com*), where the fab cocktails are tempting and the funky sounds are mesmerizing. You could easily overindulge. Be sure to hit ultratrendy club **Volar** (⊠ *Basement fl., 38-44 D'Aguilar St., Central* ☎ *2810–1276* ⊕ *www.volar.com.hk*) for dancing.

Central

AT A GLANCE

EXPERIENCES
⇨ CH. 1

On the Move
Midlevels Escalator
Peak Tram
Star Ferry

Feng Shui Structures
Bank of China Tower
Hongkong & Shanghai
Bank

The Peak Experience
Victoria Peak
Peak Circle Walk
Peak Tower
Peak Galleria

To Your Health
Charlie's Acupressure
and Massage Centre of
the Blind
Hong Kong Museum of
Medical Sciences
Hong Kong University
Chinese Medicine Clinic
and Pharmacy
Quality Chinese Medical
Centre
Tong Ren Tang

**Sail Away: Sampans &
Junks**
Duk Ling

Hiking
Dragon's Back

Very Amusing
Edward Youde Aviary
Hong Kong Zoological &
Botanical Gardens

Cinema Hong Kong

Palace IFC
UA Cinemas Pacific Place

ALSO WORTH
NOTING

Central District Police
Station
Flagstaff Museum of Tea
Ware
Fook Ming Tong
Former French Mission
Building
Fringe Club
Government House
Hong Kong Park
International Finance
Centre
Jardine House
Lan Kwai Fong District
Outlying Islands Ferry
Pier
St. John's Cathedral
Standard Charter Bank
Statue Square

Quick Bites
Tsui Wah
Genki Sushi

SHOPPING ⇨ CH. 4

Department Stores
Chinese Arts & Crafts
Harvey Nichols
Lane Crawford
Marks & Spencer
Seibu
Sincere
Yue Hwa Chinese Prod-
ucts Emporium

Malls
IFC Mall
The Landmark
Pacific Place
Pedder Building

RESTAURANTS
⇨ CH. 5

Budget
Good Luck Thai
Heaven on Earth
Mak's Noodles Limited
Tsui Wah Restaurant
Yung Kee

Moderate
Cuisine Cuisine
Dan Ryan's
DiVino
Gaia
Grappa's Ristorante
Hunan Garden
Indochine 1929
Isola
Lumiere
M at the Fringe
Sichuan Garden
Tandoor
Thai Basil
Thai Lemongrass
VEDA
Zen

Expensive
Amber
Bo Innovation
Café Deco Bar & Grill
café TOO
Caprice
dragon-i
Jimmy's Kitchen
JW's California
Lobster Bar
Lung King Heen
Man Ho
Restaurant Pétrus
Shanghai Shanghai
Toscana
Tokio Joe
Yè Shanghai

Stumble out and head to **Tsui Wah** (⇨ *Quick Bites*) for a restorative 3 AM bowl of noodles.

LANTAU ISLAND

Sightseeing
★★★★
Dining
☆☆☆★
Lodging
☆☆☆★
Shopping
☆☆☆★
Nightlife
☆☆☆★

A decade of manic development has seen Lantau become more than just "the place where the Buddha is." There's a mini-theme park at Ngong Ping to keep the Buddha company. Not to be outdone, Disney has opened a park and resort on the northeast coast. And, of course, there's the airport, built on a massive north coast reclamation. At 55 square mi, Lantau is almost twice the size of Hong Kong Island, so there's room for all this development and the laid-back attractions—beaches, fishing villages, and hiking trails—that make the island a great getaway.

WHAT'S HERE

One of Lantau's main ferry hubs, **Mui Wo,** is a sleepy little town with some good waterfront restaurants. Silvermine Bay Beach, a pleasant sandy stretch, is a half-mile northeast of the Mui Wo ferry pier. A gentle uphill trail leads to the Silvermine Caves and Waterfall, the small 19th-century mine that gave the bay its English name. The well-signposted walk takes about an hour from Mui Wo and eventually links with the Lantau Trail. Two miles of golden sand 5 mi southwest of Mui Wo make **Cheung Sha Beach,** Hong Kong's longest. It gets breezy here, but that's why windsurfers love it.

The most glorious views of Lantau—and beyond—are from atop Fung Wong Shan, or **Lantau Peak,** but at 3,064 feet it's not for the faint-hearted. It's a strenuous 7½ mi west from Mui Wo, or you can take the easy way by starting at the Po Lin Monastery—still a good two hours.

Tucked away on the west of Lantau is **Tai O**, a fishing village inhabited largely by the tanka (boat people), whose stilt houses have mostly been replaced by government-funded high-rises. Similarly, an old rope-pulled ferry connecting the village proper with a small island has been replaced with a metal bridge. Aging Hakka women, however, haul the ferry back into action on weekends. You can also see salt pans and a 16th-century temple dedicated to Kwan Tai, god of war.

DID YOU KNOW?

Lantau is connected to the Kowloon Peninsula by the world's longest suspension bridge, the 4,518-foot Tsing Ma Bridge. Airport Express and MTR trains run through its sheltered lower level; a highway runs atop it, with stunning views of the Pearl River Delta to the west.

Lantau's most famous resident is a big guy: the **Tian Tan Buddha** is the world's largest seated outdoor bronze Buddha, a string of qualifiers that's practically a mantra in itself. He sits on the Ngong Ping plateau, beside the **Po Lin Monastery,** a onetime haven of peace. You can still find stillness at the nearby **Wisdom Path,** a short hillside walk lined by massive wooden tablets inscribed with parts of a Buddhist sutra (prayer). Ngong Ping is also home to a religious theme park, **Ngong Ping Village,** with interactive exhibits on the Buddha, as well as gift shops and restaurants.

Lantau's northwest coast looks kind of funny thanks to the curiously geometrical bit of land that was reclaimed for the **Hong Kong International Airport.** You might be too dazed to notice when you arrive, but Sir Norman Foster's Y-shape design is an architectural marvel.

Looking at the tower blocks and perfectly planned avenues of **Tung Chung New Town,** home to around 80,000 people, it's hard to imagine that only 15 years ago this was a small village. Over the MTR station is a mall filled with outlet stores for big local brands. All that remains of the old Tung Chung is the hulking granite **Tung Chung Fort** (⊠ *Tung Chung Rd., Lantau* ⊘ *Wed.–Mon. 10–5*). The first fortification on this spot was built during the Song Dynasty; the current structure dates from 1832.

The latest item on Lantau's laundry list of developments is **Hong Kong Disneyland.** Though it's tame compared to other Magic Kingdoms, it's fast bringing Mai Kei Lo Su—as the world's most famous mouse is known locally—to a mainland audience.

A PERFECT (SUNNY) DAY

Leave Central on the Mui Wo ferry at around 11 AM—bag a window seat for the views. From Mui Wo Ferry Pier catch Bus 1 or a cab to Cheung Sha Beach for an early lunch at The Stoep *(⇨ Quick Bites)* and a stroll on the sands. Bus 2 from here takes you up to Ngong Ping, where you need a good hour or two to visit the Buddha and monastery, more if you plan to tour Ngong Ping Village. Stock up on water here.

There are stunning views from the Wisdom Path. From here, it's an hour's easy hiking to Tung Chung Fort. The well-signposted trail winds

GETTING ORIENTED

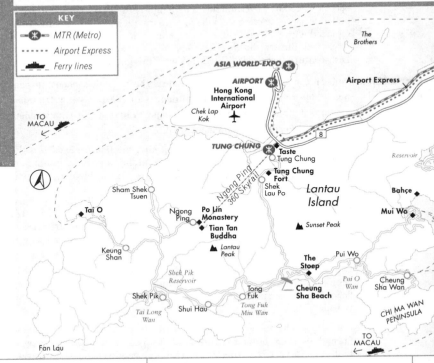

KEY
- ──✷── MTR (Metro)
- - - - - Airport Express
- ⛴ Ferry lines

The Brothers

ASIA WORLD-EXPO ✷

AIRPORT ✷
Hong Kong
International
Airport
Airport Express

Chek Lap Kok ✈

TO MACAU

8

TUNG CHUNG ✷ Taste
Tung Chung

Reservoir

Ngong Ping 360 Skyrail

Tung Chung Fort
Shek Lau Po

Lantau Island

Bahçe

Sham Shek Tsuen

Tai O

Ngong Ping

Po Lin Monastery
Tian Tan Buddha

▲ Sunset Peak

Mui Wo

Keung Shan

▲ Lantau Peak

The Stoep

Pui Wo

Shek Pik Reservoir

Tong Fuk

Pui O Wan

Cheung Sha Wan

Shek Pik

Shui Hau

Tong Fuk Miu Wan

Cheung Sha Beach

CHI MA WAN PENINSULA

Tai Long Wan

Fan Lau

TO MACAU

THE TERRITORY

Most Lantau roads lead to Tung Chung, the north shore new town, close to Hong Kong International Airport. It's connected to Kowloon by the lengthy Tsing Ma Bridge, which starts near Hong Kong Disneyland, on Lantau's northeast tip.

The Tung Chung Road winds through mountains and connects north Lantau with the southern coast. Here, the South Lantau Road stretches from the town of Mui Wo in the east to Tai O in the west, passing Cheung Sha Beach, and Ngong Ping.

TAKING IT IN

Candy-pink dolphins might sound like something Disney cooked up, but Lantau's cutest residents are the endangered species *Sousa chinensis*, native to the Pearl River estuary. Only a few hundred are left, but ecotourism company **Hong Kong Dolphinwatch** (☎ 2984–1414 ⊕ www.hkdolphin watch.com) guarantees you a sighting on their 2½-hour cruises (HK$320)—or a free second trip.

Lantau has some great hiking—friendly guides lead the way at **Walk Hong Kong** (☎ 9187–8641 ⊕ www.walkhongkong. com). Its all-day 12-km (7.5-mi) Lantau trek combines a four-hour hike from the Ngong Ping plateau to Tai O village with sightseeing at each end. The HK$750 cost includes a picnic lunch and transport to and from Central.

To see Lantau's big sights whistle-stop style, try **Splendid Tours** (☎ 2316–2151 ⊕ www.splendid.hk). A daylong trip (HK$580, including lunch) takes in the Tsing Ma Bridge, Cheung Sha Beach, Tai O village and Ngong Ping.

GETTING AROUND

The speediest way to Lantau from Central is the MTR's Tung Chung line (HK$18), which takes about half an hour. A trip by ferry is a 35-minute crossing from Central with great views.

New World First Ferry (☎ *2131–8181* ⊕ *www.nwff.com.hk*) vessels to Mui Wo leave every 30–40 minutes from Central's Pier 6 (HK$13–HK$25.50).

Bus routes are winding, and rides can be heart-stopping. There's service every half hour from Tung Chung and Mui Wo to Ngong Ping, more frequently to Tai O.

The most direct (and daring) way to Ngong Ping is the 25-minute trip on the **Ngong Ping 360 Skyrail** (☎ *2109–9898* ⊕ *www. np360.com.hk* 🚠 *HK$58–68 one way; HK$88–98 round-trip* ☉ *Weekdays 10–6; Sat. 10–6:30; Sun. 9–6:30*).

You can reach Tung Chung by a red taxi from Kowloon or Central, but the long, toll-ridden trip will cost around HK$340 from Central. Blue taxis travel Lantau (but can't leave it)—and hairpin bends make costs add up.

QUICK BITES

If you're hiking, stop off in Tung Chung for provisions. Deli counters in the huge branch of the local supermarket **Taste** (⊠ *Citygate Mall, Basement fl., 20 Tat Tung Rd., Lantau*) have sushi, sandwiches, salads, baked goods, and precut fruit.

For lunch on Cheung Sha Beach—or on Lantau in general—everyone agrees: **The Stoep** (⊠ *32 Lower Cheung Sha Village Rd., Lantau* ☎ *2980–2699*) is the place. Its name means "patio," appropriately: tables are outside, facing the beach. It's run by South Africans, and the food's a mix of Mediterranean standards and South African–style barbecued meat—try the mixed grill.

You're spoiled for choice on the Mui Wo waterfront, but cozy Turkish café **Bahçe** (⊠ *Shop 19, ground fl., Mui Wo Centre, Lantau* ☎ *2984–0222*) is a good bet. You can make a meal out of several *meze* (small snacks)—the flaky filo triangles are delicious—or beef up with a kebab. At night, the place is more like a bar.

Lantau Island

AT A GLANCE

EXPERIENCES
⇨ *CH. 1*
On the Move
Ngong Ping 360 Skyrail

Beaches
Cheung Sha
Silvermine Beach

Hiking
Trail past Shek Pik Reservoir
Wisdom Path

Very Amusing
Hong Kong Disneyland

CULTURAL SIGHTS
⇨ *CH. 3*
Ngong Ping Village
Po Lin Monastery
Tian Tan Buddha
Wisdom Path

ALSO WORTH NOTING
Lantau Peak
Mui Wo (town)

Hong Kong International Airport
Tai O (village)
Tung Chung New Town

Quick Bites
Bahçe
Park 'n' Shop
The Stoep

RESTAURANT ⇨ *CH. 5*
Expensive
Crystal Lotus

down a green valley, passing the occasional stream, several mountains (which you don't have to go up), and the unremarkable Lo Hon Temple. There'll be views of the airport to your left—a reminder of Lantau's changing face.

After a quick visit to the fort, you can walk (or catch a cab) into Tung Chung town center. Refuel with a juice or a coffee at a Citygate Mall café before taking the MTR back to Hong Kong Island.

2

WAN CHAI, CAUSEWAY BAY & BEYOND

Sightseeing
☆★★★
Dining
★★★★
Lodging
☆★★★
Shopping
☆★★★
Nightlife
☆★★★

The Happy Valley races are a vital part of Hong Kong life, so it's only fitting that they're in one of the city's most vital areas. A few blocks back from Wan Chai's new office blocks are crowded alleys where you might stumble across a wet market, a tiny furniture-maker's shop, or an age-old temple. Farther east, Causeway Bay pulses with Hong Kong's best shopping streets and hundreds of restaurants. At night, the whole area comes alive with bars, restaurants, and discos, as well as establishments offering some of Wan Chai's more traditional services (think red lights and photos of seminaked women outside).

WHAT'S HERE

Land is so scarce that developers usually only build skyward, but the **Hong Kong Convention & Exhibition Centre** (✉ *1 Expo Dr., Wan Chai* ☎ *2582–8888*) is an exception. It sits on a spit of reclaimed land jutting into the harbor. Its curved-glass walls and swooping roof make it look like a tortoise lumbering into the sea or a gull taking flight, depending on whom you ask. Of all the international trade fairs, regional conferences, and other events held here, by far the most famous was the 1997 Handover ceremony. An obelisk commemorates it on the waterfront promenade, which also affords great views of Kowloon.

Outside the center stands the *Golden Bauhinia*. This gleaming sculpture of the Bauhinia flower, Hong Kong's symbol, was a gift from China celebrating the establishment of the Hong Kong SAR in 1997. Drop-jawed mainland tourists gather here daily at 7:50 AM, when the police hoist the SAR flag.

GETTING ORIENTED

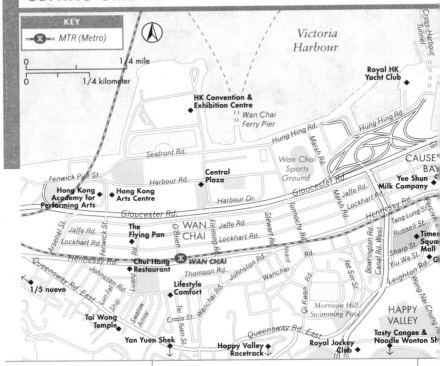

KEY

MTR (Metro)

0   1/4 mile
0   1/4 kilometer

Victoria Harbour

Royal HK Yacht Club

HK Convention & Exhibition Centre

Wan Chai Ferry Pier

Seafront Rd.

Hung Hing Rd.

Hung Hing Rd.

CAUSE BAY

Wan Chai Sports Ground

Fenwick Pier St.

Harbour Rd.

Central Plaza

Gloucester Rd.

Maish Rd.

Jaffe Rd.

Yee Shun Milk Company

Hong Kong Academy for Performing Arts

Hong Kong Arts Centre

Harbour Dr.

Lockhart Rd.

Hennessy Rd.

Gloucester Rd.

Jaffe Rd.

Tang Lung St.

The Flying Pan

WAN CHAI

Jaffe Rd.

Lockhart Rd.

Stewart Rd.

Russell St.

Times Squa Mall

Jaffe Rd.

Lockhart Rd.

Fenwick St.

O'Brien Rd.

Fleming Rd.

Tonnochy Rd.

Sharp St.

Yiu Wa St.

Leighton Rd.

Queensway Rd. East

Johnston Rd.

Luard Rd.

Ship St.

Chui Hang Restaurant

WAN CHAI

Thomson Rd.

Johnston Rd.

Wanchai

Heard Rd.

Yat Sin St.

Bowrington Rd.

Canal Rd. West

Wong Nai Chung Rd.

1/5 nuevo

Lun Fat

Swatow

Amoy

Lifestyle Comfort

Cross St.

Wanchai Rd.

Tai Yuen St.

Qi Kwan Rd.

Morrison Hill Swimming Pool

HAPPY VALLEY

Tai Wong Temple

Yan Yuen Shek

Tai Yuen St.

Queensway Rd. East

Happy Valley Racetrack

Royal Jockey Club

Tasty Congee & Noodle Wonton Sh

Cross-Harbour Tunnel

<table>
<tr><th>THE TERRITORY</th><th>TAKING IT IN</th></tr>
</table>

THE TERRITORY

Wan Chai's trams run mostly along Hennessy Road, with a detour along Johnston Road at the neighborhood's western end. Queen's Road East runs parallel to these two streets to the south, and a maze of lanes connect it with Hennessy.

The thoroughfares north of Hennessy—Lockhart, Jaffe, and Gloucester, which is a freeway—are laid out in a grid. Causeway Bay's diagonal roads make it hard to navigate, but it's small; wander around, and before long you'll hit something familiar.

TAKING IT IN

Once Upon a Time in the East. There were settlements here long before the British arrived, and the area was strategically important after colonization. Find out about it all from local historian Jason Wordie (☎ 2476–3504 ⊕ www.jasonswalks. com), who runs tours through Wan Chai, Causeway Bay, and Shau Kei Wan.

A Wan Chai Wander. Rattle to Wan Chai by tram along roads dense with jutting signs, just like in the movies. Get off at Southorn Playground, and wander the lanes south of Johnston Road before heading up Luard Road and over walkways to the Hong Kong Academy for Performing Arts and Hong Kong Arts Centre, in adjacent seafront buildings. The Hong Kong Convention & Exhibition Centre is a few minutes away—wander its harborside promenade. If you time this part for dusk, Wan Chai's drinking holes will be lighting up as you walk back to the MTR along Fleming Road. Look up at Central Plaza on your right.

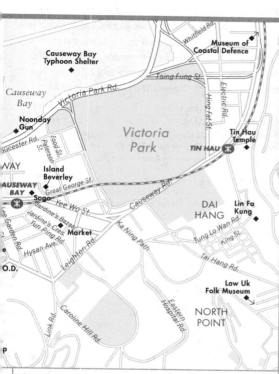

2

GETTING AROUND

Both Wan Chai and Causeway Bay have their own MTR stops, but a pleasant way to arrive from Central is on the tram along Hennessy Road. All the lines go through Wan Chai, but check the sign at the front if you're going beyond. Some continue to North Point and Shau Kei Wan , via Causeway Bay, while others go south to Happy Valley.

The underground stations are small labyrinths, so read the signs carefully to find the best exit. Traffic begins to take its toll on journey times farther east—the MTR is a better option for Shau Kei Wan and Chai Wan.

There are Star Ferries between Tsim Sha Tsui and Wan Chai every 8–20 minutes. They leave from the ferry pier just east of the convention center.

Like all of Hong Kong, Wan Chai isn't really dangerous at night, but single women strolling the streets in the wee hours might get unwanted attention from groups of drunk expats. Taxis are a good idea late at night.

QUICK BITES

In a nightspot-packed district, a café serving breakfast round-the-clock is bound to be a hit. **The Flying Pan Wan Chai** (⊠ *3rd fl., 81–85 Lockhart Rd., Wan Chai* ☎ *2528–9997*) has waffles, blintzes, 16 different omelets, bagels, muffins, grilled sandwiches—the list goes on. Throw in squishy sofas and a jukebox, and it's perfect—be it 3 AM or 3 PM.

Steaming bowls of noodle and dumpling soup are the staple at **Chui Hang Restaurant** (⊠ *80 Hennessy Rd., Wan Chai* ☎ *2186–8522*). If you're only coming once, try a bowl with fish balls; make like other diners and slurp, slurp, slurp.

Yee Shun Milk Company (⊠ *506 Lockhart Rd., Causeway Bay* ☎ *2591–1837*) sounds kooky, but you can't leave Causeway Bay without dessert at this crowded little diner. The signature dish is steamed milk with ginger juice. Alternatively, there's steamed egg, a local custard.

Wan Chai was once one of the five *wan*—areas the British set aside for Chinese residences—but it developed a reputation for vice and attracted sailors on shore leave during the Vietnam War. How times have changed: Wan Chai is still as risqué an area as Hong Kong has to offer, but that says more about the city's overall respectability than it does about the available indulgences. For all its bars and massage parlors, Wan Chai is now so safe that it seems a pale version of the "Wanch" of Richard Mason's novel *The World of Suzie Wong*.

The western end of Wan Chai's waterfront is home to two of Hong Kong's most important arts venues. Dance, classical music, and opera—be it Chinese or Western—make up the lion's share of performances at the massive **Hong Kong Academy for Performing Arts.** On the other side of Fenwick Street is the lower-key **Hong Kong Arts Centre.**

Clad in reflective gold, silver, and copper-color glass, triangular **Central Plaza,** at Harbour and Fleming roads, is glitzy to the point of tastelessness. On completion in 1992 it was briefly the city's tallest building, but then Two IFC beat it by a mere 130 feet. Note the colorful fluorescent tube lights atop the building; they actually make up a clock so complicated that no one knows how to tell time using it.

Trams clatter along Johnston Road, which is choked with traffic day and night. It's also packed with shops selling food, cell phones, herbal tonic, and bargain-basement clothes. Rattan furniture, curtains, picture frames, paper lanterns, and Chinese calligraphic materials make up the more traditional assortment at Queen's Road East, which runs parallel to Johnston Road. The lanes that stretch between the two roads are also lined with stalls, forming a mini-market of clothing and accessories.

Shoppers crowd the streets of Causeway Bay, the area east of Wan Chai, seven days a week. There are also lots of restaurants and the odd sight. The action happens in a five-block radius of the intersection of Hennessy Road and Percival Street. Thirteen-story megamall **Times Square** is here, and a couple of blocks south is trendy hot spot Yiu Wa Street, with designer bars. Also close are Japanese department store **Sogo** and local designer lifestyle specialist G.O.D. Another of the area's specialties are upstairs cafés (non-ground-floor cafés inside combo commercial/residential buildings), often populated by teens and twentysomethings, and mazelike micromalls of independent fashion, jewelry, and gadgets. More upscale Fashion Walk is also on the Sogo side of Hennessy Road.

Opium-smuggler-turned-investment-bank Jardine Matheson once had its warehouses in Causeway Bay. The company moved to Central decades ago, but left a legacy of street names: there's Jardine's Bazaar and Jardine's Crescent, two of Causeway Bay's best shopping streets, and Yee Wo Street with the firm's Chinese name.

Hong Kong's maritime past and present are much in evidence on Causeway Bay's waterfront. Sampan dwellers and old-fashioned junks once gathered during bad weather in the **Causeway Bay Typhoon Shelter.** Most boat-dwellers have moved to dry land, so these days it's mainly yachts and speedboats that moor here. A few traditional sampans, crewed primarily by elderly toothless women, still ferry owners to their sailboats. Nautical expats gather for drinks at the posh **Royal Hong Kong Yacht Club.** A block farther east stands the **Noonday Gun,** which Noël Coward made famous in his song *Mad Dogs and Englishmen*; it's still fired at noon every day.

Victoria Park, Hong Kong Island's largest park, is a welcome breathing space on the edge of Causeway Bay and bounded by Hing Fat, Gloucester, and Causeway roads. It's beautifully landscaped and has recreational facilities for swimming, lawn bowling, tennis, and rollerskating. At dawn every morning hundreds practice tai chi chuan here. It's also the site of midautumn's Lantern Carnival, with the trees a mass of colorful lights. Just before Chinese New Year (late January to early February), the park hosts a huge flower market. On the eve of Chinese New Year, after a traditional family dinner at home, much of Hong Kong happily gathers here to shop and wander until the early hours of the new year.

It's way inland now, but the small **Tin Hau Temple** (⊠ *Tin Hau St., Causeway Bay*) tucked behind Victoria Park once stood on the waterfront: it honors the Taoist goddess of the sea. Its construction date is unknown, but the temple bell was made in 1747.

High above Wan Chai halfway to Victoria Peak, is the suggestively shaped monolith known as **Yan Yuen Shek** (⊠ *South of Bowen Rd. between Wan Chai Gap Rd. and Stubbs Rd.*), or Lovers' Rock. It's a favorite with local Bridget Joneses, who visit it to burn joss sticks and make offerings in hope of finding a husband. The easiest way up is on Minibus 24A from Admiralty.

The biggest attraction east of Causeway Bay for locals and visitors alike is legendary **Happy Valley Racetrack,** where millions of Hong Kong dollars make their way each year. The races make great nights out on the town.

The island's far eastern districts— North Point, Quarry Bay, Shau Kei Wan, and Chai Wan—are all undeniably parts of the "real" Hong Kong, which means they're full of offices, apartment blocks, and factories.

Shau Kei Wan is home to the **Museum of Coastal Defence** (⊠ *175 Tung Hei Rd., Shau Kei Wan, Eastern* 🕾 *2569–1500* ⊕ *hk.coastaldefence. museum* ✆*HK$10; free Wed.* ⊙ *Fri.–Wed. 10–5*) in the converted Lei Yue Mun Fort. The museum is in the redoubt, a high area of land overlooking the narrowest point of the harbor; you take an elevator and cross an aerial walkway to reach it. As well as the fascinating historical displays indoors, there's a historical trail complete with tunnels, cannons, and observation posts.

In the middle of Chai Wan's high-rises is the **Law Uk Folk Museum,** a tiny traditional village house showing what life was like when this part of town was nothing but fields.

A PERFECT DAY (AND NIGHT)

A DAY FOR THOSE WHO CAN'T AGREE

If your group includes both shopaholics and history buffs, there's no need to squabble: Causeway Bay's the perfect place to divide and conquer. Start the day in perfect harmony with midday dim sum at Chung's Cuisine (☎2506–9218) on the 10th floor of Times Square shopping mall. The pickings are top-notch, and the sleek booths and silk cushions seem made for lingering—other diners think likewise, so book a table on weekends.

Time to part company. Retail therapists have a whole afternoon to mall- and stall-trawl. Pickings at Times Square Mall are not particularly unusual, so don't dawdle too long before rifling through the micromall stalls for quirky street wear, followed by Fashion Walk and its surrounding streets, and then bargain-hunt along Jardine's Crescent and Jardine's Bazaar.

Meanwhile, the more studious can take the MTR or a tram to Chai Wan for a brief visit to Law Uk Folk museum. If boats are your bag, take the MTR or a cab to Shau Kei Wan, where the Museum of Coastal Defence will keep you busy for a good couple of hours. Then a waterfront cab ride brings you to the Royal Hong Kong Yacht Club to check out the rich boys' toys and the Noonday Gun and Typhoon Shelter.

Rendezvous near Times Square, and sweeten things up with a dessert at Hui Lau Shan—nothing beats the sago in mango juice with extra mango. Hours on your feet will have taken their toll, so counter the effects together with a foot massage and back rub at one of the massage places *without* a red light outside—there are lots in the Bartlock Centre at 3 Yiu Wa Street in Causeway Bay.

A NIGHT IN THE EAST

When the sun goes down, all kinds of other lights fill the sky: in Wan Chai, the neon signs of bars (both reputable and otherwise); on the waterfront, the beams illuminating skyscrapers in the Symphony of Lights; and in Happy Valley, the floodlighting at the racetrack.

If it's race night, grab an early, stabilizing meal around the corner at the **Tasty Congee and Noodle Wonton Shop** (⊠*21 King Kwong St., Happy Valley, Wan Chai* ☎*2838–3922*), a Cantonese restaurant with a retro décor. Then, dressed comfortably but chicly, be at the track by 8 for turf 'n' tippling. Take some throat lozenges if you plan to bet—you'll want to scream as loudly as the thousands around you. Wait for the crowds to ease, and then get a cab over to Wan Chai for drinking and dancing. There are plenty of feel-good beery boozers where you know the words to every song—Carnegie's, Delaneys, Joe Banana's, and From Dusk Till Dawn, to name a few.

If you fancy something sophisticated, look the part and make your way to **1/5 nuevo** (⊠*9 Star St., Wan Chai* ☎*2529–2515*), pronounced "one-fifth," where martinis are shaken to house music. When you're done? Why, breakfast at the **Flying Pan** *(⇨ Quick Bites)*, no matter the hour.

Wan Chai, Causeway Bay & Beyond

2

EXPERIENCES
⇨ *CH. 1*
To Your Health
Lifestyle.Comfort

Cinema Hong Kong
Cine-Art House
Hong Kong Arts Centre
Theatre

Off to the Races
Happy Valley Racetrack

CULTURAL SIGHTS
⇨ *CH. 3*
Law Uk Folk Museum

ALSO WORTH NOTING
Causeway Bay Typhoon
Shelter
Central Plaza
Hong Kong Academy for
Performing Arts
Hong Kong Arts Centre
Hong Kong Convention &
Exhibition Centre
Museum of Coastal
Defence
Noonday Gun

Royal Hong Kong Yacht
Club
Tin Hau Temple
Victoria Park
Yan Yuen Sheck (Lovers'
Rock)

Quick Bites
Chui Hang Restaurant
The Flying Pan Wan Chai
Tasty Congee and Noo-
dle Wonton Shop
Yee Shun Milk Company

SHOPPING ⇨ *CH. 4*
Department Stores
Lane Crawford
Seibu
Sogo
Wing On

Malls
Cityplaza
Island Beverly
Lee Gardens One and
Two
Times Square

Markets
Jardine's Bazaar &
Jardine's Crescent

RESTAURANTS
⇨ *CH. 5*
Budget
Hay Hay
Xiao Nan Guo

Moderate
Bebek Bengil 3
Che's Cantonese Res-
taurant
Dim Sum
Gitone Fine Arts
Island Seafood &
Oyster Bar
Sushi Hiro
Water Margin
W's Entrecote
Wu Kong

Expensive
Dynasty
JJ's
One Harbour Road
Opia
ToTT's Asian Grill & Bar
Victoria City Seafood
Wasabi Sabi

SOUTHSIDE

Sightseeing
☆★★★

Dining
☆☆★★

Lodging
☆☆☆★

Shopping
☆☆☆★

Nightlife
☆☆☆★

For all the unrelenting urbanity of Hong Kong Island's north coast, its south side consists largely of green hills and a few residential areas around picturesque bays. With beautiful sea views, real estate is at a premium; some of Hong Kong's wealthiest residents live in beautiful houses and luxurious apartments here. Southside is a breath of fresh air—literally and figuratively. The people are more relaxed, the pace is slower, and there are lots of sea breezes.

WHAT'S HERE

On side streets in the town of **Aberdeen** you'll find outdoor barbers at work and any number of dim sum restaurants. You'll also see traditional sights like the Aberdeen Cemetery with its enormous gravestones, and yet another shrine to the goddess of the sea: the Tin Hau Temple. During the Tin Hau Festival in April and May, hundreds of boats converge along the shore here.

Aberdeen's harbor contains about 3,000 junks and sampans. Several generations of one family can live on each junk (you may recall when Angelina Jolie's character, Lara Croft, stepped aboard such a boat in *Tomb Raider 2*). This area is also home to the **Jumbo Kingdom** floating restaurant—a riot of neon lights and color (⇨ *Quick Bites)*. A bridge connects Aberdeen with **Ap Lei Chau Island** (Duck's Tongue Island), where boat-builders work in the old way. Unspoiled just a decade ago, Ap Lei Chau is now covered with public housing, private estates, and shopping malls.

Most Hong Kongers have fond childhood memories of **Ocean Park.** It was built by the omnipresent Hong Kong Jockey Club on 170 hilly acres overlooking the sea just east of Aberdeen. Highlights include the four resident giant pandas; Marine Land's enormous aquarium; Ocean Theatre, where dolphins and seals perform; and such thrill rides as the gravity-defying Abyss Turbo Drop. Just east of Ocean Park, and the first beach you reach after leaving Central, is the lovely **Deep Water Bay.**

Repulse Bay is home to a landmark apartment building with a hole in it. Following the principles of feng shui, the opening was incorporated into the design so the dragon that lives in the mountains behind can readily drink from the bay. The popular Repulse Bay Verandah Restaurant and Bamboo Bar (⇨ *Quick Bites*) is a great place for a meal with majestic bay views. The beach is large and wide, but be warned: it's the first stop for most visitors. At the beach's east end, huge statues of Tin Hau—Goddess of the Sea and Goddess of Mercy—border on gaudy. In the 1970s, when worshippers were planning to erect just one statue, they worried she'd be lonely, so an additional statue was created to keep her company.

Beyond Deep Water and Repulse bays is the town of **Stanley.** There's great shopping in the renowned at Stanley Market, whether you want casual clothes, sneakers, cheap souvenirs, cheerful bric-a-brac—even snow gear. Stanley's popular beach is the site of the Dragon Boat Races held every June.

DID YOU KNOW?   The Chinese name for Stanley translates as "Red Pole." Depending on who you talk to, it refers to the red flowers on two silk-cotton trees here or to a nearby hill that turns red at sunset, acting as a beacon for sailors. The English name comes from Lord Stanley, a 19th-century British official.

Seaside **Shek O** is Southside's easternmost village. Weekend beachgoers and hikers crowd the Thai restaurant on the left as you enter town. Every shop here sells the same inflatable beach toys—the bigger the better, it seems. Cut through town to a windy road that takes you to the "island" of Tai Tau Chau, really a large rock with a lookout over the South China Sea. Little more than a century ago, this open water was ruled by pirates. You can hike through nearby Shek O Country Park, where the bird-watching is great, in less than two hours.

A PERFECT DAY (OR SO)

Grab breakfast at your hotel, and get off from Central to Aberdeen for a sampan ride. Be prepared for the strong smell of drying fish and the noise of boat women shouting over engine noise. Afterward hop a cab or bus for a 10-minute ride to Repulse Bay beach for a swim and some sunbathing.

Refuel on the terrace of the Repulse Bay Verandah Restaurant (⇨ *Quick Bites*), before taking a cab or bus to Stanley Market, 10 to 15 minutes away. Enjoy sundowners at a restaurant or bar on Stanley's Main Street overlooking the bay. Take a taxi or bus back to Aberdeen for dinner at the Top Deck at the Jumbo Kingdom floating restaurant (⇨ *Quick Bites*).

GETTING ORIENTED

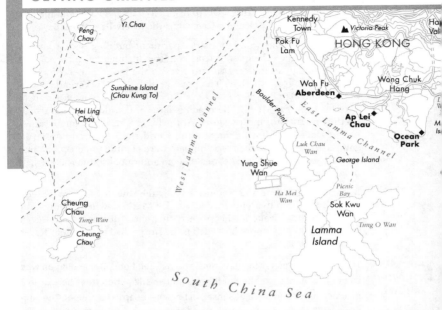

TAKING IT IN

If you travel independently, pick one hub and explore in and around it: Aberdeen with its junks and sampans on the southwest coast; Stanley and its market on the south central coast; or, perhaps, Shek O with its beaches and parkland far to the southeast.

Gray Line Tours (☎ 2368–7111 ⊕ www.grayline.com.hk) has seven-hour day trips of Hong Kong Island including Man Mo Temple, the Peak, Aberdeen, Repulse Bay, Stanley Market, and dim sum lunch at Jumbo Kingdom for HK$460 per adult.

TRANSPORTATION FROM CENTRAL TO …

Aberdeen: 30 minutes via Bus 70 or 91. (Ap Lei Chau is 15 minutes from Aberdeen on Bus 90B or 91; 10 minutes by sampan).

Deep Water Bay: 20 minutes via Bus 6, 64, 260, or 6A.

Ocean Park: 30 minutes via Star Ferry Pier and Bus 629.

Repulse Bay: 30 minutes via Bus 6, 6A, 6X, 66, 64, or 260.

Shek O: 50 minutes via MTR to Shau Kei Wan and then Bus 9 to the last stop.

Stanley: 40 minutes via Bus 6, 6A, 6X, 66, 64, or 260.

Note that express buses skip Aberdeen and Deep Water Bay, heading directly to Repulse Bay and Stanley. Buses run less frequently in the evening, so it's more convenient to grab a taxi (they're everywhere).

2

QUICK BITES

In **Stanley Market** there are dozens of cheap local and international eateries. For more upscale yet still casual joints, head to Stanley Main Road, where restaurants overlook the bay.

Treat yourself to British high tea at the **Repulse Bay Verandah Restaurant & Bamboo Bar** (⊠ *109 Repulse Bay Rd., Southside* ☎ *2292–2822* ⊕ *www.therepulsebay.com*). Tea is served Tuesday to Saturday from 3 to 5:30 and Sunday from 3:30 to 5:30.

A favorite place for lunch, drinks, or just alfresco lounging is Shek O's **Black Sheep Restaurant** (⊠ *Ground fl., 330, Southside, Shek O* ☎ *2809–2021*), a small place with an eclectic menu and a relaxed vibe that makes you wonder if you're still in Hong Kong.

The **Top Deck at the Jumbo** (⊠ *Jumbo Aberdeen Pier, Shum Wan Pier Dr., Wong Chuk Hang, Southside* ☎ *2552–3331* ⊕ *www. cafedecogroup.com*) was built on the previously unused upper deck of the Jumbo Kingdom floating restaurant. It's a fantastic alfresco spot on the water, serving international cuisine.

GOLFERS TAKE NOTE

Deep Water Bay is flanked to the north by the **Deep Water Bay Golf Club** (⊠ *19 Island Rd., Deep Water Bay* ☎ *2812–7070* ⊕ *www.hkgolfclub.org*), which is owned by the Hong Kong Golf Club. The most convenient course to play if you're staying on Hong Kong Island has nine challenging holes. It's a members' club (some of Hong Kong's richest businessmen play here), but it's casual, and visitors with handicap certificates are admitted on weekdays from 9 to 2 (walk-in only).

Greens fees are HK$500 for 18 holes. Club rental will cost you another HK$300; a caddy, still another HK$150. The club also has two restaurants (one serving Chinese fare, the other western dishes), plus a members-only fitness center and swimming pool.

Southside

EXPERIENCES
⇨ *CH. 1*

Beaches
Deep Water Bay
Repulse Bay
Shek O
Stanley

Island Hopping
Cheung Chau
Lamma Island
Po Toi Island

Sail Away: Sampans &
Junks
aqua luna
Jumbo Kingdom Floating
Restaurant

Hiking
Dragon's Back
Wilson Trail

Very Amusing
Ocean Park

ALSO WORTH
NOTING
Aberdeen (town)
Ap Lei Chau (Duck's
Tongue Island)

Quick Bites
Black Sheep Restaurant
Repulse Bay Verandah
Restaurant

SHOPPING ⇨ *CH. 4*
Market
Stanley Village Market

RESTAURANTS
⇨ *CH. 5*
Budget
Shek O Chinese & Thai-
land Seafood Restaurant

Moderate
The Boathouse
El Cid
Han Lok Yuen (Lamma
Island)
Jumbo Floating Res-
taurant
Lucy's
Spices
The Verandah

Expensive
Top Deck (at the Jumbo)

If you have kids, spend the whole day at Ocean Park. Afterward high tea at the Repulse Bay Verandah Restaurant is a must.

If you only have a half day, take a sampan ride around Aberdeen, followed by a dim sum lunch at the Jumbo Kingdom floating restaurant. Take a taxi to Stanley Market.

KOWLOON

Sightseeing
☆★★★
Dining
★★★★
Lodging
★★★★
Shopping
★★★★
Nightlife
☆★★★

There's much more to the Kowloon Peninsula than rock-bottom prices and goods of dubious provenance. Just across the harbor from Central, this piece of Chinese mainland takes its name from the string of mountains that bound it in the north: *gau lung*, "nine dragons" (there are actually eight mountains, the ninth represented the emperor who named them). Although less sophisticated and more wild than its island-side counterpart, Kowloon's dense, gritty urban fabric is the backdrop for Hong Kong's best museums and most interesting spiritual sights. And there's street upon street of hard-core consumerism in every imaginable guise.

WHAT'S HERE

One of the best things to see in Tsim Sha Tsui (TST) is, well, Central. There are fabulous cross-harbor views from the **Star Ferry Pier** as well as from the ferries themselves. The sweeping pink-tile **Hong Kong Cultural Centre** and the Former KCR (Kowloon–Canton Railway) Clock Tower are a stone's throw away, the first stop along the breezy pedestrian **TST East Promenade,** which starts at the Avenue of Stars and stretches a couple of miles east. ■TIP→ **Try to visit the promenade once in the daytime and once at 8 PM for the "Symphony of Lights," a nightly show in which 44 skyscrapers light up on cue as a commentator introduces them in time with a musical accompaniment.**

One of the world's best Chinese art collections is inside the tiled cube that is the **Hong Kong Museum of Art** (⇨ *Chapter 3, Cultural Sights*).

GETTING ORIENTED

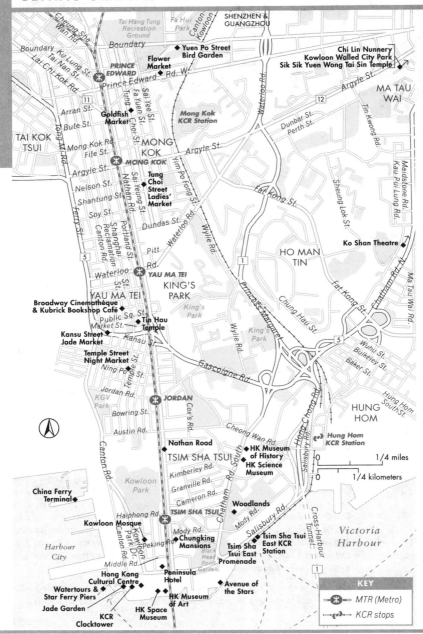

KEY

⊛ ⟶ MTR (Metro)

⟶⟶ KCR stops

GETTING AROUND

The most romantic way from Hong Kong Island to southern Tsim Sha Tsui (TST) is by Star Ferry. There are crossings from Central every 6–12 minutes and a little less often from Wan Chai.

TST is also accessible by MTR. Underground walkways connect the station with Kowloon-Canton Railway's Tsim Sha Tsui East terminus, where KCR East Rail trains depart every 10–15 minutes for the eastern New Territories. The Kowloon Airport Express station is amid a construction wasteland west of TST. One day it will connect with KCR West Rail; for now hotel shuttles link it to the rest of Kowloon.

The MTR is your best bet for Jordan, Yau Ma Tei, Mong Kok, Kowloon Tong, Lok Fu, and Wong Tai Sin. But you'll need a bus or cab to reach Kowloon Tong from Wong Tai Sin or TST East.

QUICK BITES

Woodlands (⊠ *1st fl., Wing On Plaza, 62 Mody Rd., Tsim Sha Tsui East, Kowloon* ☎ *2369–3718*) is a find. Expect fabulous south Indian food—all vegetarian—and fantastic mango lassi. The HK$65/75/85 *thalis* (10 tiny curry dishes served with rice and chapatis) are perfect for the indecisive, uninitiated, or just plain greedy.

Arty tomes surround the tables at the **Kubrick Bookshop Café** (⊠ *Broadway Cinemathèque, 3 Public Square St., Yau Ma Tei, Kowloon* ☎ *2384–8929*). It's attached to the city's best art-house cinema. Tuck into sandwiches, pasta dishes, and cakes. The coffee's great, too.

Jade Garden (⊠ *4th fl., Star House, opposite Star Ferry Concourse, Tsim Sha Tsui, Kowloon* ☎ *2730–6888*) is a popular dim sum chain. Come early on weekends.

THE TERRITORY

Kowloon's southernmost district is Tsim Sha Tsui (TST), home to the Star Ferry Pier. The waterfront extends a few miles to TST East. Shops and hotels line Nathan Road, which runs north from the waterfront through the market districts of Jordan, Yau Ma Tei, and Mong Kok.

New Kowloon is the unofficial name for the sprawl beyond Boundary Street. The district just north is Kowloon Tong. Two spiritual sights—Wong Tai Sin and Lok Fu—are a little farther east. The tongue sticking out into the sea to the south was the runway of the old Kai Tak Airport. Kowloon City is a stone's throw west.

TAKING IT IN

Walk the Talk (⊠ *HKTB Office, TST Star Ferry Concourse* ⊕ *www. walkthetalk.hk*) tours use your mobile phone as an audio guide. The TST tour is packed with serious history and kooky anecdotes.

Kowloon looks great from the harbor, and the **Hong Kong Tourist Board** (*HKTB* ⊠ *TST Star Ferry Concourse* ☎ *2508–1234* ⊕ *www.discoverhongkong.com*) runs cruise combos. The Harbour Lights Cruise leaves before sunset and winds up at Lei Yue Mun, a fishing community in east Kowloon, for a seafood dinner. The Top of the Town tour starts at a revolving restaurant in Wan Chai before heading to Temple Street Market and a nighttime harbor trip. Plain old cruises depart morning, afternoon, and evening.

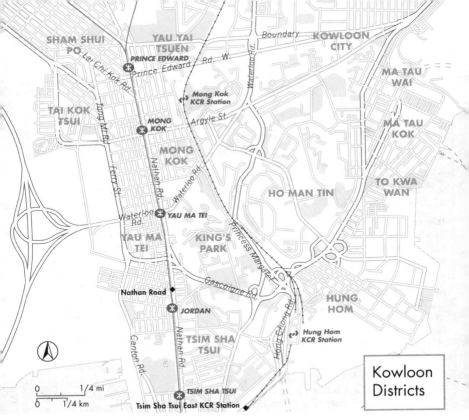

Looking like an oversize golf ball sliced in half, the **Hong Kong Space Museum** (⊠*10 Salisbury Rd., Tsim Sha Tsui, Kowloon* ☎*2734–2722* ⊕ *hk.space.museum*) stands behind the art museum. Despite many attractions—a planetarium, a solar telescope, an Omnimax theater— it's fairly unremarkable, and children under 3 aren't allowed. Admission is HK$10, excluding special exhibitions; hours are Monday and Wednesday–Friday 1–9, weekends and holidays 10–9.

The grand building on the other side of Salisbury Road is the famed **Peninsula Hotel.** The fleet of Rolls-Royce taxis outside indicate the heights of luxury here. You can have tea in the colonnaded lobby and stroll through the shopping arcade.

You have to look down to appreciate the **Avenue of Stars** (⊠*TST East Promenade outside New World Renaissance Hotel, Tsim Sha Tsui, Kowloon*). Over the past several decades countless local film stars have pawed the wet concrete—you won't recognize their names unless you're a fan, but it goes to show how old Hong Kong's film industry is.

The area beyond Chatham Road South is known as TST East, reclaimed land that's still taking form and is home to the fascinating **Hong Kong Museum of History** (⇨ *Chapter 3, Cultural Sights).*

The **Hong Kong Science Museum** (✉2 *Science Museum Rd., corner of Cheong Wan Rd. and Chatham Rd., Tsim Sha Tsui East, Kowloon* ☎*2732–3232* ⊕ *hk.science.museum*) has kid-friendly hands-on exhibits, including an energy machine, a miniature submarine, and cognitive and memory tests. That said, it's more of a rainy-day time-killer than a must-see. Admission is HK$25 or HK$35 for special exhibitions; hours are Monday to Wednesday and Friday 1–9, weekends 10–9.

Kowloon's famous Nathan Road runs several miles north from Salisbury Road in TST. It's filled with hotels, restaurants, and shops—indeed, retail space is so costly that the southern end is dubbed the Golden Mile. The mile's most famous tower block is ramshackle **Chungking Mansions,** packed with cheap hotels and Indian restaurants. It was the setting for arty local director Wong Kar-Wai's film *Chungking Express.* To the left and right are mazes of narrow streets with even more shops selling jewelry, electronics, clothes, souvenirs, and cosmetics. Skulking individuals chanting "copy watch" and "copy suit" are on every street corner—at least they're honest about the "Rolexes" they sell.

Just behind Nathan Road, at TST's north end, are the 33 acres of **Kowloon Park.** It's crisscrossed by paths and landscaped to within an inch of its life but is still refreshing after all those shops.

Hong Kong's largest Islamic worship center, **Kowloon Mosque,** stands in front of the park.

The heart of Yau Ma Tei, north of TST, is **Temple Street,** home to Hong Kong's biggest night market. Stalls selling kitsch of all kinds set up in the late afternoon in the blocks north of Public Square Street. Fortune-tellers, prostitutes, and street doctors also offer their services here.

Traditional trades are plied on Shanghai Street. There are blocks dominated by tailors or by shops selling Chinese cookware or everything you need to set up a household shrine. Nearby Ning Po Street is known for its paper kites and for the colorful paper and bamboo models of worldly possessions (boats, cars, houses) that are burned at Chinese funerals.

From priceless ornaments to fake pendants, if it's green and shiny, it's at the **Kansu Street Jade Market.** Quality and prices at the stalls vary hugely, so if you're not with a jade connoisseur, stick with the cheap and cheerful. Chaotic street markets continue in Mong Kok, technically the last Kowloon district (Boundary Street marks the beginning of the New Territories, though these days the urbanized areas are known as New Kowloon). It's one of the best places to see gritty Hong Kong.

As you head north it's mostly tourists browsing the **Tung Choi Street Ladies' Market.** It runs the entire length of the street but is best between Dundas and Argyle. Despite its name, stalls are filled with no-brand clothes and accessories for both sexes. Parallel **Fa Yuen Street** is sneaker central; its sports shops sell some brands you know and lots you don't.

East of Nathan Road, things get back to nature. The few blocks between Prince Edward Road West and Boundary Street are home to a **Flower Market, Goldfish Market,** and the twittering, fluttering **Yuen Po Street Bird Garden.** The vastly varying prices of the flora and fauna on offer are defined not just by their rarity but by how lucky they're thought to be. Arguably Hong Kong's most beautiful park, **Kowloon Walled City Park,** designed in Qing Dynasty style, is near the old Kai Tak Airport, between Tung Tau Tsuen and Tung Tsing roads. Hong Kong's Thai community is based in the streets south of the park, and there are countless hole-in-the-wall Thai restaurants.

DID YOU KNOW?

Only the occasional patch of daylight was visible from the labyrinthine alleys of the Kowloon Walled City, Hong Kong's most notorious slum. Originally a 19th-century Chinese fortress, the city wasn't included in the British lease of the New Territories, thus it remained part of China and out-of-bounds to the Hong Kong Police. The Triads ruled its unlicensed doctors and dentists, opium dens, brothels, gambling houses, and worse.

Two spiritual sights dominate New Kowloon. Exuberant **Sik Sik Yuen Wong Tai Sin Temple** is a Taoist-Buddhist-Confucianist complex filled with noisy worshippers. In Diamond Hill, peace pervades the all-wood **Chi Lin Nunnery,** built in Tang Dynasty style without nails.

PERFECT HOURS IN KOWLOON

Only got a couple of hours between meetings? Your kids—or you—haven't got the stamina to keep going all day? Kowloon's fragmented layout means it's perfect for breaking up into short-tour-size chunks. Hard-core sightseeing masochists can lump them all into one tourist feast.

A FEW HOURS OF . . .

. . . the Movies. Start at Chungking Mansions, which starred in the art-house classic *Chungking Express*. It's a short walk to the Avenue of Stars and the handprints of Jackie Chan and company. From here you'll have a great view of the harbor, which Pierce Brosnan appeared out of in *Die Another Day* (not to be tried on your own; the water is very polluted). On the other side is the IFC building that La Jolie jumped from in *Tomb Raider 2*, as well as The Centre and the Hong Kong Exhibition & Convention Centre that had Batman cameos in *The Dark Knight*. Catch the MTR to the Broadway Cinemathèque in Yau Ma Tei for an art flick and a bite at Kubrick Café.

. . . Indulgence. When it comes to luxury, the **Peninsula Hotel** (✉ *Salisbury Rd., Tsim Sha Tsui, Kowloon* ☎ *2366–6251* ⊕ *www.peninsula.com*) is your one-stop shop. Start with afternoon tea in the lobby (HK$398 for two); have a 50-minute body massage (HK$990) at the spa; buy a dinner outfit at Chanel or Shanghai Tang; take the elevator to 28th-floor Felix for harbor-view cocktails; then book a table downstairs at Gaddi's for a fabulous French dinner. A suite here would be a fitting finish.

. . . Spiritual Stuff. Only one MTR stop apart, Wong Tai Sin Temple and Chi Lin Nunnery are two of Hong Kong's must-do spiritual sights. One's a clattering, chaotic temple-turned-spiritual-mall, the other a peaceful haven.

Kowloon

EXPERIENCES
⇨ *CH. 1*

On the Move
Star Ferry

Hiking
Lion Rock

Very Amusing
Bird Garden
Hong Kong Science
Museum
Hong Kong Space
Museum

Cinema Hong Kong
Broadway Cinemathèque

CULTURAL SIGHTS
⇨ *CH. 3*
Chi Lin Nunnery
Hong Kong Museum
of Art
Hong Kong Museum of
History
Sik Sik Yuen Wong Tai
Sin Temple
Tin Hau Temple

**ALSO WORTH
NOTING**
Avenue of the Stars
Chungking Mansions
Hong Kong Cultural
Centre
Kowloon Park
Kowloon Mosque

Kowloon Walled City
Park
Peninsula Hotel
TST East Promenade

Quick Bites
Jade Garden
Joyful Vegetarian
Kubrick Bookshop Café
Woodlands

SHOPPING ⇨ *CH. 4*

Department Stores
Chinese Arts & Crafts
Lane Crawford
Marks & Spencer
Seibu
Sincere
Sogo
Yue Hwa Chinese Prod-
ucts Emporium

Malls
Festival Walk
Harbour City (Ocean
Terminal, Ocean Centre,
Gateway Arcade)
Langham Place
Rise Commercial Building

Markets
Arts & Crafts Fair
Flower Market
Goldfish Market
Kansu Street Jade Market
Ladies' Market

Temple Street Night
Market

RESTAURANTS
⇨ *CH. 5*
Budget
Best Noodle Restaurant
Guangdong Barbecue
Restaurant
Happy Garden Noodle &
Congee Kitchen
Hing Fat Restaurant
Kung Tak Lam
Tao Shanghai Noodle
Tso Choi Koon

Moderate
Aqua
Avenue
Café Kool
Great Shanghai Res-
taurant
Hutong
Lo Chiu Vietnamese Res-
taurant
Main Street Deli
Spring Deer
Tapas Bar

Expensive
Felix
Morton's of Chicago
Oyster & Wine Bar
Sabatini
SPOON by Alain Ducasse
Steak House
Yan Toh Heen

If your soul's still hungry, there's the Tin Hau Temple in Yau Ma Tei;
the Shanghai Street altar shops are just up the road.

. . . the Old Days. Start at the top by taking a cab or bus to Kowloon
City Park, where the old walled city stood: there's a model inside the
renovated almshouse. Then take a couple of hours to wise up at the
History Museum in TST East, before strolling to the old KCR Clock
Tower (built in 1915) near the Star Ferry, which has run since 1888.

THE NEW TERRITORIES

Sightseeing
☆★★★

Dining
☆☆☆★

Lodging
☆☆☆★

Shopping
☆☆☆★

Nightlife
☆☆☆★

Rustic villages, incense-filled temples, green hiking trails, pristine beaches—the New Territories have a lot to offer. Until a generation ago, the region was mostly farmland with the occasional walled village. Today, thanks to a government housing program that created "new towns" like Sha Tin and Tuen Mun with up to 500,000 residents, parts of the region are more like the rest of Hong Kong. Within its expansive 518 square km (200 square mi), however, you'll still feel far removed from urban congestion and rigor. Here you can visit the area's most lush parks and sneak glimpses into traditional rural life in the restored walled villages and ancestral clan halls.

WHAT'S HERE

Head to Tsuen Wan in the western New Territories to visit **Sam Tung Uk Museum**, which translates to "Three Rows of Dwelling Museum." It's the restoration of a walled Hakka village built in 1786. The large front door faces west–southwest, and follows the feng shui principles of placement between mountain and water. In line with the traditional village architecture, rooms extend from a central courtyard. There's also an ancestral hall and an exhibition space with displays of period furniture, handicrafts, and agricultural equipment.

DID YOU KNOW?

The New Territories got their name when the British acquired this area. Whereas Hong Kong Island and Kowloon were taken outright following the Opium War of 1841, the land that now constitutes the New Territories was

handed over much later on a 99-year lease. It was this lease that expired in 1997 and was the catalyst for the return of the entire colony to China.

The **Yuen Yuen Institute** (⊠ *Lo Wai Village, Tsuen Wan* ☎ *2492–2220*) is made up of pavilions and prayer halls built in the 1950s to bring together the three streams of Chinese thought: Buddhism (which emphasizes nirvana and physical purity), Taoism (nature and inner peace), and Confucianism (following the practical and philosophical beliefs of Confucius). The main three-tier red pagoda is a copy of the Temple of Heaven in Beijing, and houses 60 statues representing the full cycle of the Chinese calendar—you can look for the one that corresponds to your birth year and make an incense offering. To reach the institute, take the MTR to Tsuen Wan and exit the station at Shiu Wo Street, then catch a green minibus to To Lo Wai. Admission is free, and hours are daily 9 to 5.

Made of volcanic rock, **Tai Mo Shan**—which means Big Hat Mountain—is Hong Kong's highest point at 3,140 feet. It's in Tai Mo Shan Country Park, north of Tsuen Wan, and is also known as Foggy Mountain, as it's covered in clouds almost daily. When the mist—and pollution—clears, the view stretches all the way to Hong Kong Island.

The huge **Ching Chung Koon Taoist Temple,** adjacent to the Ching Chung LRT station near the town of Tuen Mun in the far western New Territories, has room after room of altars filled with the heady scent of incense burning in bronze holders. On one side of the main entrance is a cast-iron bell with a circumference of about 5 feet—all large monasteries in ancient China rang such bells at daybreak to wake the monks and nuns for a day of work in the rice fields. On the other side of the entrance is a huge drum that was used to call the workers back in the evening. Inside, some rooms are papered with small pictures; people pay the temple to have these photos displayed so they can see their dearly departed as they pray. Colorful plants and flowers, hundreds of dwarf shrubs, ornamental fishponds, and pagodas bedeck the grounds. Take the MTR to Tsuen Wan station and then Bus 66M or 66P to Tuen Mun. Alternatively, you can take the MTR to Kwai Fong Station, then board Bus 58M, alighting at the Tuen Mun Catholic Secondary School. The temple is nearby, but the entrance isn't obvious, so ask for directions.

In the far northern New Territories—just south of Shenzhen—a small unmarked path in the village of Sheung Shui leads to the ancestral hall **Liu Man Shek Tong.** It was built in 1751 and was one of few such halls that survived the Cultural Revolution. A restoration preserved the spectacular original roofs and ornamentation, but substituted concrete walls to take the weight off rickety pillars—at some cost to the site's aesthetic unity, unfortunately. The Liu clan, for whom this hall was built, was obsessed with education: the wood panels hung in the rear hall indicate the education levels achieved by various clan members under the old imperial civil-service-exam system of the Qing Dynasty. Take the KCR to Sheung Shui, then Bus 73K and alight at Sheung Shui

GETTING ORIENTED

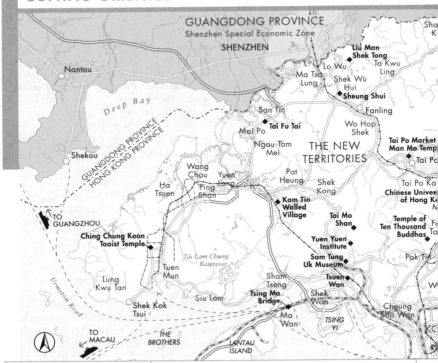

THE TERRITORY	QUICK BITES
The New Territories borders mainland China to the north and Sai Kung Peninsula to the east. Places worth visiting are a fair distance from each other, so day trips here take some planning—and some patience. You're definitely on "the other side," where few people speak English. It's best to choose two or three sights to visit in a day, allowing 15–30 minutes of travel time between each, depending on whether you're going by bus or taxi.	Sai Kung Town's waterfront has a plethora of outdoor seafood restaurants. If you have a sweet tooth, drop by the famous **Honeymoon Dessert Shop** (⊠ *Ground fl., 10C Po Tung Rd., Sai Kung*) for such saccharine delights as mango pudding, chilled sago coconut soup, and banana crepes. Go on, you deserve it. On Castle Peak Road near Tuen Mun, the **Miu Fat Buddhist Monastery** is a popular place for a vegetarian lunch. Dishes have lots of greens, mushrooms, and "meat," which is actually made from rice flour. Lunch is served between noon and 3:30. Take the MTR to Tsuen Wan, then a taxi to the monastery. Alternatively, take the Airport Railway train to Tsing Yi Station and then take Bus 53, 63M, 63X, or 68A.

2

TAKING IT IN

Even if you don't think of yourself as a tour type, the best way to see some of the smaller villages is on one of the Hong Kong Tourist Board's organized tours that loop through the region. The guides are extremely knowledgeable and helpful.

Gray Line Tours (☎ 2207–7235 ⊕ www.grayline.com.hk) has full- and half-day tours that stop at the Yuen Yuen Institute and Tai Mo Shan lookout, among other places. Full-day tours (HK$420, including lunch) depart from City Hall in Central at 8:30 AM and from the YMCA in Tsim Sha Tsui in Kowloon at 9 AM. Half-day tours (HK$320) depart from the same places and return one hour earlier, without lunch.

Gray Line's five-hour Heritage Tour (HK$320) takes you to the Man Mo Temple, Lam Tsuen Wishing Trees, and other cultural sights. Tours depart from the Kowloon Hotel in Tsim Sha Tsui at 8:45 AM Monday, Wednesday, Friday, and Saturday.

GETTING AROUND

Between the bus, MTR, and the Kowloon–Canton Railway (KCR), you can get close to many sights. Set off on the MTR from Central to Tsuen Wan; from there, taxis, buses, and minibuses will take you to places such as the Yuen Yuen Institute and Tai Mo Shan. For Sha Tin and other spots in the east, take the MTR to Kowloon Tong; transfer to the KCR to Sha Tin station. To reach the Sai Kung Peninsula, take the MTR from Central to Choi Hung, then the green Minibus 1A to Sai Kung Town.

To tour at your own pace consider hiring a car and driver.

Ace Hire Car (☎ 2893–0541) charges HK$220 per hour (three-hour minimum).

For a HK$5 call charge, you can hire a cab from the **Hong Kong Kowloon Taxi Knowledge Association** (☎ 2574–7311) to pick you up and take you anywhere in Hong Kong.

Wai on Jockey Club Road. The hall is open Wednesday, Thursday, and weekends 9 to 1 and 2 to 5. Admission is free.

Tai Po, which means "shopping place," more than lives up to its name. In the heart of the region's breadbasket, the town is fast becoming a utilitarian "new town," but its main open-air market is a feast for the eyes, with baskets of lush green vegetables, freshly cut meat hanging from great racks overhead, fish swimming in tanks awaiting selection, and all types of baked and steamed treats. To reach the village, take the KCR to the Tai Po Market stop.

Adjacent to the Tai Po market is the 100-year-old **Man Mo Temple;** you'll smell the incense offered by worshippers. The temple is open daily from 9 to 6.

The **Lam Tsuen Wishing Trees,** which were featured in Hong Kong's chapter of *The Amazing Race* TV show, are an important Chinese New Year pilgrimage site. People from throughout Hong Kong come to the two banyan trees to make wishes and offerings. Some people burn joss sticks and incense; others throw an orange—tied to a wish written on a piece of paper—up into a tree (if it catches on a branch the wish will come true). Unfortunately, the weight of the oranges has caused several branches to fall off. People also visit the trees during exam time or when their health or that of a loved one is in jeopardy. Take the KCR train to Tai Po Market train station, then take Bus 64K or 65K, or Minibus 25K.

Whether you enter **Sha Tin** by road or rail, you'll be amazed to find this new town metropolis smack dab in the middle of the New Territories. It's home to the popular **Sha Tin Racecourse,** Hong Kong's largest and a spectacular place to watch a race. Racing season is from September through June. The racecourse has its own stop on the KCR (called "Racecourse"). Sha Tin is also home to the fantastic **Hong Kong Heritage Museum** (⇨ *Chapter 3, Cultural Sights*), devoted to Chinese history, art, and culture. Exhibitions are housed in a five-story building surrounded by a traditional Chinese courtyard.

The **Chinese University of Hong Kong Art Museum** (✉ *Tai Po Rd., Sha Tin* ☎ *2609–7416* ⊕ *www.cuhk.edu.hk/ics/amm* 🎫 *Free*), in the Institute of Chinese Studies Building, has paintings and calligraphy from the Qing period to modern times. There are also collections of bronze seals, carved jade flowers, and ceramics from South China. Take the KCR to University station, then a campus bus or taxi. The museum is open daily 10 to 5, closed on holidays.

The **Temple of Ten Thousand Buddhas** houses, in fact, nearly 13,000 Buddha statues, each in a slightly different pose. It's an impressive feat, which took Shanghai craftsmen 10 years to complete. There are some 500 steps leading to the temple, so bring water.

To the east of Sha Tin, **Sai Kung Peninsula** has a few small towns and Hong Kong's most beloved nature preserve. The hikes through the hills surrounding High Island Reservoir are spectacular, and the beaches are among the territory's cleanest. Seafood restaurants dot the waterfront at Sai Kung town as well as the tiny fishing village of Po Toi O in Clear Water Bay. Take the MTR to Choi Hung and then Bus 92 or 96R, or Minibus 1 to Sai Kung Town. Instead of taking the bus, you can also catch a taxi along Clearwater Bay Road, which will take you into forested areas and land that's only partially developed with Spanish-style villas overlooking the sea. At Sai Kung Town, you can rent a sampan that will take you to one of the many islands in the area for a day at the beach. Sai Kung Country Park has several hiking trails that wind through majestic hills overlooking the water. This excursion will take a full day, and you should only go if it's sunny.

Tap Mun Island, also known as Grass Island, makes a great day trip. Most people have a seafood lunch at the restaurant run by Loi Lam, a stocky, vivacious fellow who speaks fluent English with a fantastic accent from Manchester, England. There are a couple of temples and shrines dotting the island, as well as beautiful beaches. A sampan from Wong Shek Pier in Sai Kung Country Park will speed you here.

TWO-AND-A-HALF PERFECT DAYS

Catch the MTR from Central to Tsuen Wan, then take Minibus 81 to Lo Wai Village to reach the Yuen Yuen Institute, the only temple in Hong Kong devoted to all three Chinese religions: Buddhism, Confucianism, and Taoism. For lunch, take a taxi to the Miu Fat Buddhist Monastery, a popular restaurant serving vegetarian dishes. Take a break from the history and culture and walk off the lunch by heading to Tai Mo Shan by taxi, and hike through the country park, experiencing the greener side of Hong Kong.

Alternatively head to Tap Mun Island for a day of sunbathing on a pristine beach, punctuated only by a delicious seafood lunch. You can take the MTR from Central to the Chinese University Station and then walk 15 minutes along Tai Po Road in Sha Tin to the Ma Liu Shui Ferry Pier, where a vessel will take you to the island. Or you can take the MTR from Central to Choi Hung, then Bus 92 or 96R or Minibus 1 to Sai Kung Town. From there, jump in a taxi to Wong Shek Pier in Sai Kung Country Park and then board a sampan for the island.

If you only have half a day to spend in the New Territories, then Sha Tin is the place to be. Take the MTR to Kowloon Tong, then the KCR to Tai Wai to visit the Hong Kong Heritage Museum, dedicated to Chinese history, art, and culture. From here, take a taxi to the Sha Tin KCR station and follow the signs to the Temple of 10,000 Buddhas. Hike up the steps to reach the temple where thousands of gold statues sit in various poses. End the day at Sha Tin Racecourse (via taxi or the KCR to Racecourse Station).

AT A GLANCE

New Territories

EXPERIENCES
⇨ *CH. 1*

Beaches
Hap Mun Wan
Sha Ha
Silverstrand

Island Hopping
Ping Chau
Tap Mun Island

Hiking
MacLehose Trail

Off to the Races
Sha Tin Racecourse

CULTURAL SIGHTS
⇨ *CH. 3*

Hong Kong Heritage
Museum
Pak Tai Temple
Sam Tung Uk Museum

Tai Fu Tai
Temple of Ten Thousand
Buddhas

**ALSO WORTH
NOTING**
Chinese University of
Hong Kong Art Museum
Ching Chung Koon Taoist
Temple
Lam Tusen Wishing Trees
Liu Man Shek Tong
(ancestral hall)
Man Mo Temple
Sai Kung Peninsula
(nature preserve)
Tai Mo Shan (Big Hat
Mountain)
Tai Po (town)
Yuen Yuen Institute
(prayer halls)

Quick Bites
Honeymoon Dessert
Shop
Miu Fat Buddhist
Monastery

SHOPPING ⇨ *CH. 4*

Mall
New Town Plaza

RESTAURANTS
⇨ *CH. 5*

Budget
Chung Thai Food
Restaurant & Sea Food

Moderate
Jaspa's
Tung Kee Seafood
Restaurant

Cultural Sights

Entrance to Wong Tai Sin Temple, Kowloon

WORD OF MOUTH

"There are several beautiful old clan halls which you can visit here, they are still active with clan association activities. There are several "walled villages" in the New Territories which are hundreds of years old but are still lived in and have been adapted, in some cases kind of bizarrely, to modern life, that are very interesting to visit."

—Cicerone

Updated by
Cherise Fong

You hear so much about the material wealth, but Hong Kong has cultural riches as well. Locals may worship the dollar, but they also pay respects to a host of deities in colorful temples. Hong Kong's intriguing history and Chinese art are the strengths of the city's well-curated museums. And though continual redevelopment means most old buildings were demolished years ago, some exquisite traditional constructions—notably temples and villages—remain.

LIFE AS IT WAS

Urban Hong Kong may be a concrete jungle, but the territory actually has a large proportion of green space. Having trouble envisioning life before skyscrapers? Preserved Hakka villages can help, as do several museums tracing Hong Kong from rural backwater to pulsating hub.

ART IMMERSION

Hong Kong is often maligned as a cultural desert. Keep your expectations reasonable, and stick to the exhibits the city does best. Several excellent collections make this one of the best places in the world to see Chinese art, especially since the Cultural Revolution wreaked havoc with such things on the other side of the border.

SACRED SPACES

Hong Kongers are intensely superstitious. Most homes have some kind of household god, and people regularly consult fortune-tellers or astrologers. When clinching deals and building skyscrapers, businessmen and architects take numerology and feng shui into account. That said, spirituality is a very down-to-earth affair here. Buddhism, Taoism, and Confucianism are the territory's major religions, and some temples roll them together for worshipping ease. Clattering temple courtyards are the best place to see up close how nothing—and everything—is sacred in Hong Kong.

CHI LIN NUNNERY

5 Chi Lin Dr., Diamond Hill, Kowloon

☎ 2354–1789

💲 Free

🕓 Nunnery daily 9–4:30, lotus-pond garden daily 7–7

Ⓜ Diamond Hill, Exit C2.

TIPS

■ Left of the Main Hall is a don't-miss hall dedicated to Avalokitesvra, better known in Hong Kong as Kwun Yum, goddess of mercy and child-bearing, among other things. She's one of the few exceptions to the rule that bodhi-sattvas are represented as asexual beings.

■ Be sure to keep looking up—the latticework ceilings and complicated beam systems are among the most beautiful parts of the building.

■ Combine Chi Lin Nunnery with a visit to Sik Sik Yuen Wong Tai Sin Temple, only one MTR stop or a short taxi ride away.

★ **Fodor's Choice** Not a single nail was used to build this nunnery, which dates from 1934. Instead, traditional Tang Dynasty architectural techniques involving wooden dowels and bracket work hold its 228,000 pieces of timber together. Most of the 15 cedar halls house altars to bodhisattvas (those who have reached enlightenment)—bronze plaques explain each one.

HIGHLIGHTS

Feng shui principles governed construction. The buildings face south toward the sea, to bring abundance; their backs are to the mountain, provider of strength and good energy. The temple's clean lines are a vast departure from most of Hong Kong's colorful religious buildings—here, polished wood and gleaming Buddha statues are the only adornments.

The Main Hall is the most imposing—and inspiring—part of the monastery. Overlooking the smaller second courtyard, it honors the first Buddha, known as Sakyamuni. The soaring ceilings are held up by 28 cedar columns, measuring 18 feet each. They also support the roof—no mean feat, given that its traditionally made clay tiles make it weigh 176 tons.

Courtyards and gardens, where frangipani flowers scent the air, run beside the nunnery. The gardens are filled with bonsai trees and artful rockeries. Nature is also present inside: the various halls and galleries all look onto two courtyards filled with geometric lotus ponds and manicured bushes.

HONG KONG HERITAGE MUSEUM

1 Man Lam Rd., New Territories, Sha Tin

☎ 2180–8188

⊕ hk.heritage.museum

🎫 HK$20; HK$10 Wed.

🕙 Mon., Wed.–Sat. 10–6, Sun., holidays 10–7

Ⓜ Che Kung or Sha Tin KCR

TIPS

■ Look for the audio tours in English, which are available for special exhibitions.

■ There's lots of ground to cover: prioritize the New Territories Heritage, the T. T. Tsui Gallery, and the Cantonese Opera Halls, all permanent displays, and do the temporary history and art exhibitions if energy levels permit.

■ Don't miss the opera hall's virtual makeup display, where you get your on-screen face painted like an opera character.

■ The museum is a five-minute signposted walk from Che Kung Temple KCR Station. If the weather's good, walk back along the leafy riverside path that links the museum with the Sha Tin KCR Station, in New Town Plaza mall, 15 minutes away.

★ **Fodor's Choice** This fabulous museum is Hong Kong's largest, yet it still seems a well-kept secret: chances are you'll have most of its 10 massive galleries to yourself. They ring an inner courtyard, which pours light into the lofty entrance hall.

HIGHLIGHTS

The New Territories Heritage Hall is packed with local history—6,000 years of it. See life as it was in beautiful dioramas of traditional villages—one on land, the other on water (with houses on stilts). The last gallery documents the rise of massive urban New Towns. There's even a computer game where you can design your own.

In the T. T. Tsui Gallery of Chinese Art, exquisite antique Chinese glass, ceramics, and bronzes fill nine hushed second-floor rooms. The curators have gone for quality over quantity. Look for the 4-foot-tall terra-cotta *Horse and Rider*, a beautiful example of the figures enclosed in tombs in the Han Dynasty (206 BC–AD 220). The Tibetan religious statues and *thankga* paintings are unique in Hong Kong.

The Cantonese Opera Hall is all singing, all dancing, and utterly hands-on. The symbolic costumes, tradition-bound stories, and stylized acting of Cantonese opera can be impenetrable: the museum provides simple explanations and stacks of artifacts, including century-old sequined costumes that put Vegas to shame.

Kids love the Children's Discovery Gallery, where hands-on activities for 4- to 10-year-olds include putting a broken "archaeological find" together. The Hong Kong Toy Story charts more than a century of local toys.

HONG KONG MUSEUM OF ART

10 Salisbury Rd., Tsim Sha Tsui, Kowloon

☎ 2721–0116

🌐 hk.art.museum

💳 HK$10

🕐 Fri. and Sun.–Wed. 10–6, Sat. 10–8

Ⓜ Tsim Sha Tsui MTR, Exit E

TIPS

■ Traditional Chinese landscape paintings are visual records of real or imagined journeys—a kind of travelogue. Pick a starting point and try to travel through the picture, imagining the journey the artist is trying to convey.

■ There are educational rooms tucked away on the eastern side of every floor. Kids can emboss traditional motifs on paper or do brass rubbings; there are also free gallery worksheets in English. A good selection of reference books makes them useful learning centers for adults, too.

■ Guided tours can help you to understand art forms you're not familiar with. There are general museum tours in English Tuesday through Sunday at 11 AM. Check the Web site for the schedule of more detailed visits to specific galleries—they change every month.

■ If you prefer to tour alone, consider an English-language audio guide: it's informative, if a little dry, and it costs only HK$10.

★Fodor's Choice An extensive collection of Chinese art is packed inside this boxy tiled building on the Tsim Sha Tsui waterfront in Kowloon. The collections here contain a heady mix of things that make Hong Kong what it is: Qing ceramics, 2,000-year-old calligraphic scrolls, kooky contemporary canvases. Thankfully it's organized into thematic galleries with clear, if uninspired, explanations. Hong Kong's biggest visiting exhibitions are usually held here too. The museum is a few minutes' walk from either the Star Ferry or Tsim Sha Tsui MTR stop.

HIGHLIGHTS

The Chinese Antiquities Gallery is the place to head if Ming's your thing. A series of low-lit rooms on the third floor houses ceramics from Neolithic times through the Qing dynasty. Unusually, they're displayed by motif rather than by period: dragons, phoenixes, lotus flowers, and bats are some of the auspicious designs. Bronzes, jade, lacquerware, textiles, enamel, and glassware complete this collection of decorative art.

In the Chinese Fine Art Gallery you get a great introduction to Chinese brush painting, often difficult for the Western eye to appreciate. Landscape paintings from the 20th-century Guangdong and Lingnan schools form the bulk of the collection, and modern calligraphy also gets a nod.

The Contemporary Hong Kong Art Gallery showcases a mix of traditional Chinese and western techniques—often in the same work. Paintings account for most of the pieces from the first half of the 20th century, when local artists used the traditional mediums of brush and ink in innovative ways. Western techniques dominate later work, the result of Hong Kong artists spending more time abroad.

TIAN TAN BUDDHA

Ngong Ping, Lantau Island

☎ 2109—9898 Ngong Ping hotline

🌐 www.plm.org.hk/blcs/en/index.asp

💳 Monastery and path free. Walking with Buddha: HK$35.

🕙 Buddha daily 9:30–6:30. Monastery and path daily 9–6.

TIPS

■ You can get here on the Ngong Ping 360 Skyrail or via Buses 2 and 23 from Mui Wo and Tung Chung, respectively. To reach Lantau Island from Central take the MTR to Tung Chung or the New World First Ferry from Pier 6 to Mui Wo.

■ The only way to the upper level, right under the Buddha, is through an underwhelming museum inside the podium. You only get a couple of feet higher up.

■ The booth at the base of the stairs is only for tickets for lunch—wandering around the Buddha is free.

■ The monastery's vegetarian restaurant is a clattering canteen with uninspiring fare. Pick up sandwiches at the Citygate Mall, Tung Chung, or eat at a restaurant in Ngong Ping Village.

★ **Fodor's Choice** Hong Kongers love superlatives, even if making them true requires strings of qualifiers. So the Tian Tan Buddha is the world's largest Buddha—that's seated, located outdoors, and made of bronze. Just know its vast silhouette is impressive. Steep stairs lead to the lower podium, essentially forcing you to stare up at all 202 tons of Buddha as you ascend. At the top, cool breezes and fantastic views over Lantau Island await.

HIGHLIGHTS

Po Lin Monastery. It's hard to believe today, but from its foundation in 1927 through the early '90s, this monastery was virtually inaccessible by road. These days, it's at the heart of Lantau's biggest attraction. The monastery proper has a gaudy, commercial, orange temple complex. Still, it's the Buddha people come for.

Wisdom Path. This peaceful path runs beside 38 halved tree trunks arranged in an infinity shape on a hillside. Each is carved with Chinese characters that make up the Heart Sutra, a 5th-century Buddhist prayer that expresses the doctrine of emptiness. The idea is to walk around the path—which takes five minutes—and reflect. Follow the signposted trail to the left of the Buddha.

Ngong Ping Village. People were fussing about this attraction before its first stone was laid. Ngong Ping Village is a moneymaking add-on to the Tian Tan Buddha. Walking With Buddha is intended to be an educational stroll through the life of Siddhartha Gautama, the first Buddha, but it's more of a multimedia extravaganza that shuns good taste with such kitsch as a self-illuminating Bodhi tree and piped-in incense. No cost has been spared in the dioramas that fill the seven galleries—ironic, given that each represents a stage of the Buddha's path to enlightenment and the eschewing of material wealth.

MORE ON LIFE AS IT WAS

3

★ **Hong Kong Museum of History.** A whopping HK$156 million went into making this museum engaging and educational. The permanent Hong Kong Story re-creates life as it was rather than simply displaying relics of it: indeed, actual artifacts are few. The museum's forte is clear explanations of spectacular life-size dioramas, which include village houses and a Central shopping street in colonial times. The ground-floor Folk Culture section is a Technicolor introduction to the history and customs of Hong Kong's main ethnic groups: the Punti, Hakka, and Hoklo. Upstairs, gracious stone-walled galleries whirl you through the Opium Wars and the beginnings of colonial Hong Kong. ■ TIP→ **Unless you're with kids who dig models of cavemen and bears, skip the prehistory and dynastic galleries. Reserve energy for the last two galleries: a chilling account of life under Japanese occupation and a colorful look at Hong Kong life in the '60s.**

Budget at least two hours to stroll through—more if you linger in each and every gallery. Pick your way through the gift shop's clutter to find local designer Alan Chan's T-shirts, shot glasses, and notebooks. His retro-kitsch aesthetic is based on 1940s cigarette-girl images. To get here from the Tsim Sha Tsui MTR walk along Cameron Road, then left for a block along Chatham Road South. A signposted overpass takes you to the museum. ⊠ *100 Chatham Rd. South, Tsim Sha Tsui, Kowloon* ☎ *2724–9042* ⊕ *hk.history.museum* ☜ *HK$10; free Wed.* ⊘ *Mon. and Wed.–Sat. 10–6, Sun., holidays 10–7* Ⓜ *Tsim Sha Tsui MTR, Exit B2.*

Law Uk Folk Museum. This restored Hakka house was once the home of the Law family, who arrived here from Guangdong in the mid-18th century. It's the perfect example of a triple-*jian,* double-*lang* residence. Jian are enclosed rooms—here, the bedroom, living room, and workroom at the back. The front storeroom and kitchen are the *lang,* where the walls don't reach up to the roof, and thus allow air in. Although the museum is small, informative texts outside and displays of rural furniture and farm implements inside give a powerful idea of what rural Hong Kong was like. It's definitely worth a trip to bustling industrial Chai Wan, at the eastern end of the MTR, to see it. Photos show what the area looked like in the 1930s—these days a leafy square is the only reminder of the woodlands and fields that once surrounded this buttermilk-color dwelling. ⊠ *14 Kut Shing St., Chai Wan, Eastern* ☎ *2896–7006* ⊕ *www.lcsd.gov.hk/CE/Museum/History/en/luf.php* ☜ *Free* ⊘ *Mon.–Wed., Fri. and Sat. 10–6, Sun., holidays 1–6* Ⓜ *Chai Wan, Exit B.*

Sam Tung Uk Museum. A walled Hakka village from 1786 was saved from demolition to create this museum. It's in the middle of industrial Tsuen Wan, in the western New Territories, so its quiet whitewashed courtyards and small interlocking chambers contrast greatly with the nearby residential towers. Hakka villages were built with security in mind, and this one looks more like a single large house than a village. Indeed, most Hakka village names end in *uk,* which literally means "house"—Sam Tung Uk translates as "Three Beam House." Rigid symmetry dictated the village's construction: the ancestral hall and two common chambers form the central axis, which is flanked by the more private areas. The front door is angled to face west–south-west, in keeping with feng shui principles of alignment between mountain and water. Traditional furniture and farm tools are displayed in each room. ■TIP➡**Head through the courtyards and start your visit in the exhibition hall at the back, where a display gives helpful background on Hakka culture and pre-industrial Tsuen Wan—explanations are sparse elsewhere. You can also try on a Hakka hat.** ✉*2 Kwu Uk Lane, Tsuen Wan, New Territories* ☎*2411–2001* ✇*www.heritagemuseum.gov.hk/english/branch_sel_stu.htm* ✉*Free* ☉*Wed.–Mon. 9–5* Ⓜ*Tsuen Wan, Exit B3.*

THE HAKKA

The Hakka, or "guest," people from northeast China arrived in Hong Kong during a late-17th-century government effort to populate the coast. They fiercely held onto their language and traditions, were dealt the worst lands, and were scorned by the local Punti community. Their farming lifestyle was notoriously tough; women worked the fields as hard as men (leading to a happy side effect of unbound feet). In the New Territories you still might see traditionally dressed women in open-crown, broad-brimmed hats, circled by a curtain of black cloth.

★ **Tai Fu Tai.** It's worth the trek almost to the Chinese border to visit this preserved 1865 home of New Territories merchant and philanthropist Man Ching-luen. The surefire path to becoming a big shot in Imperial China was passing civil service examinations, but few people from Hong Kong—which was hicksville at the time—made the grade. Man Ching-luen proved the exception in 1875. Congratulatory tablets from the emperor hang in the house's entrance hall. The room layout, beautifully decorated doors, and roof ridges are all characteristic of Qing Dynasty architecture. Stained-glass and rococo moldings reflect European influences, a result of the British victory over China in the Opium War of 1841. Women could watch guests unobserved from an upper gallery here, which also has an enclosed courtyard for stargazing, charmingly called a "moon playing chamber." To reach the house, cross over the road outside Sheung Shui KCR station and take Bus 76K toward Yuen Long—alight at San Tin, 5½ km (3½ mi) away. The five-minute walk to the mansion is signposted from there. Alternatively, get a taxi from the station—one-way costs HK$35; for under HK$100 the taxi will wait for you and take you back, too. ✉*Wing Ping Tsuen, San Tin, New Territories* ✇*www.lcsd.gov.hk/CE/Museum/Monument/en/monuments_32.php* ✉*Free* ☉*Wed.–Mon. 9–1 and 2–5.*

MORE ART IMMERSION

★ **Hong Kong University Museum Art Gallery.** Chinese harp music and a faint smell of incense float through its peaceful rooms. The small but excellent collection of Chinese antiquities includes ceramics and bronzes, some dating from 3,000 BC; fine paintings; lacquerware; and carvings in jade, stone, and wood. There are some superb ancient pieces: ritual vessels, decorative mirrors, and painted pottery. The museum has the world's largest collection of Nestorian crosses, dating from the Mongol Period (1280–1368). These belonged to a heretical Christian sect who came to China from the Middle East during the Tang Dynasty (618–907).

There are usually two or three well-curated temporary exhibitions on: contemporary artists who work with traditional media are often featured. ■TIP→ **Don't miss part of the museum: the collection is spread between the T. T. Tsui Building and the Fung Ping Shan Building, which you access via a first-floor footbridge.** The museum is out-of-the-way—20 minutes from Central via Buses 3A or 40 M, or a 15-minute uphill walk from Sheung Wan MTR—but it's a must for the true Chinese-art lover. ⊠ *94 Bonham Rd., Pokfulam, Western* ☎ *2241–5500* ⊕ *www.hku.hk/hkumag* ⊡ *Free* ⊗ *Mon.–Sat. 9:30–6, Sun. 1–6.*

> ### MINI-MUSEUMS
>
> In Central, the antiques stores and galleries that pack the curving block of Wyndham Street from, roughly, Lower Albert Road to where Wyndham becomes Hollywood Road, are more like miniature museums than shops. Their showrooms—generally open daily 10 to 7—have furniture, art, and artifacts; prices aren't low but they're less than elsewhere. Shops farther west along Hollywood sell curios masquerading as artifacts. Still farther west, shops and stalls collectively known as Cat Street sell a mix of fake antiques and genuine communist kitsch. Cat Street is Upper Lascar Row in Sheung Wan.

MORE SACRED SPACES

Man Mo Temple. It's believed to be Hong Kong Island's oldest temple, though no one knows exactly when it was built—the consensus is sometime around the arrival of the British in 1841. It's dedicated to the Taoist gods of literature and of war: Man, who wears green, and Mo, dressed in red. A haze of incense fills the small building—you first catch the fragrance a block away. Huge spirals of the stuff coil down from the ceiling as food for the ancestors. The temple bell, cast in Canton in 1847, and the drum next to it are sounded to attract the gods' attention when a prayer is being offered—give it a ring to make sure yours are heard. ■TIP→ **To check your fortune, stand in front of the altar, ask a question, select a small bamboo cylinder, and shake it until a stick falls out. The number on the stick corresponds to a written fortune. Then go next door, where an English-speaking fortune-teller can tell you what it means for HK$20.** ⊠ *Hollywood Rd. at Ladder St., Western* ⊗ *Daily 8–6* Ⓜ *Sheung Wan, Exit A2.*

Pak Tai Temple. In the 19th century, Cheung Chau Island was a haven for pirates like the notorious Cheung Po Tsai, whose name translates as Cheung Po the Kid and whose treasure cave is reportedly on the island's southwest tip. The temple here is dedicated to Pak Tai, the god of the

Continued on page 100

SPIRITUALITY IN CHINA

Even though it's officially an atheist nation, China has a vibrant religious life. But what are the differences between China's big three faiths of Buddhism, Taoism, and Confucianism? Like much else in the Middle Kingdom, the lines are often blurred.

Walking around the streets of any city in China in the early 21st century, it's hard to believe that only three decades ago the bulk of the Middle Kingdom's centuries-old religious culture was destroyed by revolutionary zealots, and that the few temples, mosques, monasteries, and churches that escaped outright destruction were desecrated and turned into warehouses and factories, or put to other ignoble uses. Those days are long over, and religion in China has sprung back to life. Even though the official line of the Chinese Communist Party is that the nation is atheist, China is rife with religious diversity.

Perhaps the faith most commonly associated with China is Confucianism, an ethical and philosophical system developed from the teachings of the sage Confucius. Confucianism stresses the importance of relationships in society and of maintaining proper etiquette. These aspects of Confucian thought are associated not merely with China (where its modern-day influence is dubious at best, especially in a crowded subway car), but also with East Asian culture as a whole. Confucianism also places great emphasis on filial piety, the respect that a child should show an elder (or subjects to their ruler). This may account for

(left) Offering up joss sticks.
(below) The Yong he Gong Lama temple in Beijing.

Confucianism's status as the most officially tolerated of modern China's faiths.

Taoism is based on the teachings of the *Tao Te Ching*, a treatise written in the 6th century BC, and blends an emphasis on spiritual harmony with that of the individual's duty to society. Taoism and Confucianism are complementary, though to the outsider, the former might seem more steeped in ritual and mysticism. Think of it this way: Taoism is to Confucianism as Catholicism is to Protestantism. Taoism's mystic quality may be why so many westerners come to China to study "the way," as Taoism is sometimes called.

Buddhism came to China from India in the first century AD and quickly became a major force in the Middle Kingdom. The faith is so ingrained here that many Chinese openly scoff at the idea that the Buddha wasn't Chinese. In a nutshell, Buddhism teaches that attachment leads to suffering, and that the best way to alleviate the world's suffering is to purify one's mind, to

Tian Tan, The Temple of Heaven in Beijing.

abstain from evil, and to cultivate good. In China, there are three major schools: the Chinese school, embraced mainly by Han Chinese; the Tibetan school (or Lamaism) as practiced by Tibetans and Mongolians; and Theravada, practiced by the Dai and other ethnic minority groups in the southwest of the country.

TEMPLE FAUX PAS

Chinese worshippers are easygoing. Even at the smallest temple or shrine, they understand that some people will be visitors and not devotees. Temples in China have relaxed dress codes, but you should follow certain rules of decorum.

■ You're welcome to burn incense, but it's not required. If you do decide to burn a few joss sticks, take them from the communal pile and be sure to make a small donation. This usually goes to temple upkeep or local charities.

The Buddha

■ When burning incense, two sticks signify marriage, and four signify death.

■ Respect signs reading NO PHOTO in front of altars and statues. Taoist temples seem particularly sensitive about photo taking. When in doubt, ask.

■ Avoid stepping in front of a worshipper at an altar or censer (where incense is burned).

■ Speak quietly and silence mobile phones inside of temple grounds.

■ Don't touch Buddhist monks of the opposite sex.

■ Avoid entering a temple during a ceremony.

TEMPLE OBJECTS

For many, temple visits are among the most culturally edifying parts of a China trip. Large or small, Chinese temples incorporate a variety of objects significant to religious practice.

INCENSE

Incense is the most common item in any Chinese temple. In antiquity, Chinese people burned sacrifices both as an offering and as a way of communicating with spirits through the smoke. This later evolved into a way of showing respect for one's ancestors by burning fragrances that the dearly departed might find particularly pleasing.

CENSER

Every Chinese temple will have a censer in which to place joss sticks, either inside the hall or out front. Larger temples often have a number of them. These large stone or bronze bowls are filled with incense ash from hundreds of joss sticks placed by worshippers. Some incense censers are ornate, with sculpted bronze rising above the bowls.

BAGUA

Taoist temples will have a bagua: an octagonal diagram pointing toward the eight cardinal directions, each representing different points on the compass, elements in nature, family members, and more esoteric meanings. The bagua is often used in conjunction with a compass to make placement decisions in architectural design and in fortune-telling.

STATUES

Chinese temples are known for being flexible, and statues of various deities and mythical figures abound. Confucius is usually rendered as a wizened man with a long beard, and Taoist temples have an array of demons deities.

PRAYER WHEEL

Used primarily by Tibetan Buddhists, the prayer wheel is a beautifully embossed hollow metal cylinder mounted on a wooden handle. Inside the cylinder is a tightly wound scroll printed with a mantra. Devotees believe that the spinning of a prayer wheel is a form of prayer that's just as effective as reciting the sacred texts aloud.

"GHOST MONEY"

Sometimes the spirits need more than sweet-smelling smoke, and this is why many Taoists burn "ghost money" (also known as "hell money"), a scented paper resembling cash. Though once more popular in Taiwan and Hong Kong (and looked upon as a particularly capitalist superstition on the mainland), the burning of ghost money is now gaining ground throughout the country.

CHINESE ASTROLOGY

According to legend, the King of Jade invited 12 animals to visit him in heaven. As the animals rushed to be the first to arrive, the rat snuck a ride on the ox's back. Just as the ox was about to cross the threshold, the rat jumped past him and arrived first. This is why the rat was given first place in the astrological chart. Find the year you were born to determine what your astrological animal is.

RAT
1924 · 1936 · 1948 · 1960 · 1972 · 1984 · 1996 · 2008
Charming and hardworking, Rats are goal setters and perfectionists. Rats are quick to anger, ambitious, and lovers of gossip.

OX
1925 · 1937 · 1949 · 1961 · 1973 · 1985 · 1997 · 2009
Patient and soft-spoken, Oxen inspire confidence in others. Generally easygoing, they can be remarkably stubborn, and they hate to fail or be opposed.

TIGER
1926 · 1938 · 1950 · 1962 · 1974 · 1986 · 1998 · 2010
Sensitive, and thoughtful, Tigers are capable of great sympathy. Tigers can be short-tempered, and are prone to conflict and indecisiveness.

RABBIT
1927 · 1939 · 1951 · 1963 · 1975 · 1987 · 1999 · 2011
Talented and articulate, Rabbits are virtuous, reserved, and have excellent taste. Though fond of gossip, Rabbits tend to be generally kind and even-tempered.

DRAGON
1928 · 1940 · 1952 · 1964 · 1976 · 1988 · 2000 · 2012
Energetic and excitable, short-tempered and stubborn, Dragons are known for their honesty, bravery, and ability to inspire confidence and trust.

SNAKE

1929 · 1941 · 1953 · 1965 · 1977 · 1989 · 2001 · 2013

Snakes are deep, possessing great wisdom and saying little. Snakes can often be vain and selfish while retaining sympathy for those less fortunate.

HORSE

1930 · 1942 · 1954 · 1966 · 1978 · 1990 · 2002 · 2014

Horses are thought to be cheerful and perceptive, impatient and hot-blooded. Horses are independent and rarely listen to advice.

GOAT

1931 · 1943 · 1955 · 1967 · 1979 · 1991 · 2003 · 2015

Wise, gentle, and compassionate, Goats are elegant and highly accomplished in the arts. Goats can also be shy and pessimistic, and often tend toward timidity.

MONKEY

1932 · 1944 · 1956 · 1968 · 1980 · 1992 · 2004 · 2016

Clever, skillful, and flexible, Monkeys are thought to be erratic geniuses, able to solve problems with ease. Monkeys are also thought of as impatient and easily discouraged.

ROOSTER

1933 · 1945 · 1957 · 1969 · 1981 · 1993 · 2005 · 2017

Roosters are capable and talented, and tend to like to keep busy. Roosters are known as overachievers, and are frequently loners.

DOG

1934 · 1946 · 1958 · 1970 · 1982 · 1994 · 2006 · 2018

Dogs are loyal and honest and know how to keep secrets. They can also be selfish and stubborn.

PIG

1935 · 1947 · 1959 · 1971 · 1983 · 1995 · 2007 · 2019

Gallant and energetic, Pigs have a tendency to be single-minded and determined. Pigs have great fortitude and honesty, and tend to make friends for life.

sea, who is supposed to have rid the island of pirates. He's thanked during the weeklong, springtime Bun Festival. Expect parades of the island's deities, huge towers of buns, and lots of color. The renovated temple originally dates to 1783, when an image of Pak Tai was brought to appease the spirits of people killed by pirates, thought to be the source of bubonic plague outbreaks. Apparently he did the trick: he remains the island's favorite deity. Beside the main altar are four whalebones from the nearby sea. ■TIP➜ **Make a full day of your trip to Cheung Chau. It's a gorgeous island with several temples. Kwan Yu Pavilion, the biggest, is dedicated to war god Kwan Tai. There's also a Kwun Yum temple and four shrines honoring sea goddess Tin Hau. A walk takes in most places of worship as well as the pirate cave.**

New World First Ferry sails to Cheung Chau twice hourly from Central Ferry Pier 5. Normal ferries take 50 minutes, fast ones 30. Turn left from Cheung Chau ferry pier and walk ½ km (¼ mi) along waterfront Praya Street, until you see the temple to your right, over a playground. ⊠*Pak She St., Cheung Chau Island, New Territories* ⊕*www.ctc.org. hk/en/directcontrol/temple23.asp* ⊡*Free* ☉*Daily 7–5.*

★ **Sik Sik Yuen Wong Tai Sin Temple.** There's a very practical approach to prayer at one of Hong Kong's most exuberant places of worship. Here the territory's three major religions—Taoism, Confucianism, and Buddhism—are all celebrated under the same roof. You'd think that highly ornamental religious buildings would look strange with highly visible vending machines and LCD displays in front of them, but Wong Tai Sin pulls it off in cacophonic style. The temple was established in the early 20th century, on a different site, when two Taoist masters arrived from Guangzhou with the portrait of Wong Tai Sin—a famous monk who was born around AD 328—that still graces the main altar. In the '30s the temple was moved here; continuous renovations make it impossible to distinguish old from new.

Start at the incense-wreathed main courtyard, where the noise of many people shaking out *chim* (sticks with fortunes written on them) forms a constant rhythmic background. After wandering the halls, take time out in the Good Wish Garden—a peaceful riot of rockery—at the back of the complex. At the base of the complex is a small arcade where soothsayers and palm readers are happy to interpret Wong Tai Sin's predictions for a small fee. At the base of the ramp to the Confucian Hall, look up behind the temple for a view of Lion Rock, a mountain in the shape of a sleeping lion. ■TIP➜ **If you feel like acquiring a household altar of your own, head for Shanghai Street in Yau Ma Tei, the Kowloon district north of Tsim Sha Tsui, where religious shops abound.** ⊠*Wong Tai Sin Rd., Wong Tai Sin, Kowloon* ☎*2327–8141* ⊡*Donations*

expected. Good Wish Garden:
HK$2 ⊙ *Daily 7–5:30* Ⓜ *Wong*
Tai Sin, Exit B2 or B3.

★ **Temple of Ten Thousand Buddhas.**
You climb some 400 steps to reach
this temple: but look on the bright
side, for each step you get about 32
Buddhas. The uphill path through
dense vegetation is lined with life-
size golden Buddhas in all kinds of
positions. If you're dragging bored
kids along, get them to play "Spot
the Celebrity Lookalike" on the
way. ■ TIP➡ **In summer bring water
and insect repellent.** Prepare to be
dazzled inside the main temple:
its walls are stacked with gilded
ceramic statuettes. There are actually nearly 13,000 Buddhas here,
a few more than the name suggests. They were made by Shang-
hai craftsmen and have been donated by worshippers since the temple
was built in the 1950s. Kwun Yum, goddess of mercy, is one of several
deities honored in the crimson-walled courtyard.

> ### GODS OF WORK & WAR
>
> Different gods often watch over
> various professions. Man Cheung
> (Man for short) protects civil ser-
> vants and those taking exams, for
> example. Strangely, one of the
> territory's most popular deities is
> the patron of both policemen and
> their mafia enemies, the Triads.
> Kwan Tai is a deified 3rd-century
> warlord recognized by Buddhists,
> Taoists, and Confucianists. He's
> known as the God of War, but he
> actually promotes the values of
> brotherhood and loyalty rather
> than bloodthirstiness. His other
> names include Guan Yu, Kwan Yu,
> and Mo.

Look southwest on a clear day and you can see nearby **Amah Rock,**
which resembles a woman with a child on her back. Legend has it that
this formation was once a faithful fisherman's wife who climbed the
mountain every day to wait for her husband's return, not knowing
he'd been drowned. Tin Hau, goddess of the sea, took pity on her and
turned her to stone.

The temple is in the foothills of Sha Tin, in the central New Territories.
Take Exit B out of the Sha Tin KCR station, walk down the pedestrian
ramp, and take the first left onto Pai Tau Street. Keep to the right-hand
side of the road and follow it around to the gate where the signposted
path starts. ■ TIP➡ **Don't be confused by the big white buildings on the
left of Pai Tau Road. They are ancestral halls, not the temple.** ⊠ *Off Pai
Tau St., Sha Tin, New Territories* 🎫 *Free* ⊙ *Daily 9–5:30* Ⓜ *KCR East
Rail: Sha Tin.*

Tin Hau Temple. This incense-filled site is dedicated to Taoist sea goddess
Tin Hau, queen of heaven and protector of seafarers. The crowds here
testify to her being one of Hong Kong's favorite divine beings—indeed,
this is one of around 40 temples dedicated to her. Like all Tin Hau
temples, this one once stood on the shore. Kowloon reclamation started
in the late 19th century, and now the site is more than 3 km (2 mi)
from the harbor.

The main altar is hung with gold-embroidered red cloth and usually
piled high with offerings. There are also two smaller shrines inside the
temple honoring earth god Tou Tei and city god Shing Wong. Both the

temple and stalls in the eponymous market outside are fortune-telling hot spots: you may well be encouraged to have a try with the chim. Each stick is numbered, and you shake them in a cardboard tube until one falls out. A fortune-teller asks you your date of birth and makes predictions from the stick based on numerology. Alternatively, you could have a mystically minded bird pick out some fortune cards for you. ■TIP➡ **It's a good idea to agree on prices first; bargaining with fortune-tellers is common.** ✉ *Market St., Yau Ma Tei, Kowloon* ◷ *Daily 7–5:30* Ⓜ *Yau Ma Tei, Exit C.*

SEA GODS

Tin Hau, the Taoist Queen of Heaven, is also the goddess of the sea and patroness of seafarers. Her birthday is celebrated at Joss House Bay in Sai Kung in late April or early May. She's also known as Mazu (in Mandarin) and A-ma (in Macau). Pak Tai, the Supreme Emperor of Dark Heaven and the Taoist sea god, is thanked for ridding Cheung Chau Island of pirates during the Bun Festival (usually in May). He's known as Bei Di in Mandarin. Kwun Yum (Guan Yin in Mandarin) is the Buddhist goddess of mercy; she rivals Tin Hau as the protector of sailors and fisherfolk.

Shopping

WORD OF MOUTH

"I would go to the Temple Street night market. It's more interesting, with one area you may see people doing small-scale Cantonese opera, and food stalls."

—rkkwan

"We loved the bird market, also the jade market . . . shopping in TST is fantastic . . . the peddler building on the HK side has many good discount shops . . . the chinese craft store near to the star ferry in TST is quite a fantastic place to shop."

—rhkkmk

SHOPPING PLANNER

Pace Yourself

Shopping streets and malls are packed with people. In summer, pounding the streets weighed down by bags quickly starts to feel like an exercise from *Survivor.* Then, the minute you step into a mall, arctic a/c blasts have you shivering. Dress comfortably, carry a water bottle and light sweater, and stop frequently to rest and refuel.

Way Up

With space at a premium, shops and small businesses are tucked into all sorts of places—up the back staircase of a scruffy building, down an alleyway, or on an office tower's 13th floor.

Shopping Tours

Asian Cajun (☎2817–3687 ⊕ www.asiancajun.com) runs tours to choice shops, including little-known stores and private dealers.

Malls, markets, and outlets are a part of tailor-made tours led by **Shopping 4 U.** Book through **Concorde Travel** (☎2526–3391 ⊕ www.concordetravel.com). Costs range from HK$350 to HK$500 per person for daylong tours (8- to 10-person minimum).

Best Buys

Brushing Up. Granted, becoming a master brush painter takes years. But calligraphy equipment makes a wonderful display, even if your brushwork doesn't. Boxed sets of bamboo-handled brushes, porcelain inkwells, and smooth inkstones start at HK$200 at Yue Hwa.

Kung-Fu Fighting. You've seen *Enter the Dragon* a hundred times, you've visited all the Bruce Lee locations, you practice your karate chops daily. Time to get the drum cymbal, leather boots, sword, whip, double dagger, studded bracelet, and *kempo* gloves. **Kung Fu Supplies Co.** (✉192 *Johnston Rd., Wan Chai 2891–1912 www.kungfu.com. hk*) can kit you out.

On the Table. Remind yourself of all those dim sum meals by dressing up your dining room. Black-lacquer chopsticks and brocade place mats are in street stalls all over. Stanley Market has beautiful appliqué table linen. Department stores like Wing On sell cheap bamboo dim sum baskets— good for cooking or storage.

Opium Den Chic. Silk dressing gowns and basic *cheongsams* (silk dresses with Mandarin collars) are a bargain in markets and at Yue Hwa or Chinese Arts & Crafts. For more luxurious versions, try Shanghai Tang or Blanc de Chine, who also do men's Mao jackets. Get some brocade cushion covers for a matching bedroom.

Seal of Approval. Have your name engraved in Chinese, English, or both on traditional chops (seals). Made of wood, stone, or even jade, they're usually ornately carved, often with animals of the Chinese zodiac. Sets come with a tub of sticky red ink. Man Wa Lane in Sheung Wan is a great place to find them.

Tea for Two. Yixing teapots like those at Fook Ming Tong will melt even coffee-guzzlers' hearts. For the best brews head to Lock Cha Tea Shop. Standard leaves come in pretty tins at local supermarkets like Park 'n' Shop. Yue Hwa does cheap porcelain tea sets. *For more information, see All the Tea in China in chapter 5.*

Shop Around

Prices vary hugely. For big items, do research before the trip and then comparison shop in different districts. Ask clerks to record prices on store business cards: it helps you to keep track and ensures you get the quoted rate if you return to buy. Keep expectations realistic. A US$5 (about HK$40) pure silk shirt probably isn't pure silk. That said, it may still be a good shirt at a great price.

Sales

Hong Kongers look forward to the sales like other people look forward to summer vacation. From late December through February and July through September, prices plummet. It may be retail heaven, but it isn't therapy—shoppers all but wrestle bargains from each other at hot sales like Lane Crawford's or Joyce's. Many shops frown on trying things on during sales. Stand your ground, and you'll probably swing a fitting room.

The Perfect Fit

There's no two ways about it: most Americans stand a few inches taller (and wider) than the average Hong Konger. Finding bigger sizes, particularly at cheap shops, can be frustrating. Tailoring—thank goodness it's affordable here—may be the only way to go.

Tricks of the Trade

Be wary of absurd discounts, designed purely to get you in the door. Product switches are also common—after you've paid, they pack a cheaper model. Avoid electronics shops in Tsim Sha Tsui, whose fearsome reputation is well earned. Check purchases carefully, ensuring clothes are the size you wanted, jewelry is what you picked, and electronics come with the accessories you paid for. *Always* get an itemized receipt. Without one, forget about getting refunds. Shops displaying the Hong Kong Tourism Board's (HKTB) QUALITY TOURISM SERVICE sticker (an easily recognizable junk boat) are good bets. You can complain about prices or treatment at them to the **HKTB** (☎2508–1234). For complaints about all other shops, call the **Hong Kong Consumer Council** (☎2929–2222).

Bargaining Power

Prices are always negotiable at markets, and you can expect discounts in small shops, too, especially for electronics or if you buy several things at once. The norm ranges from 10% to 50% off. Be firm and decisive—walking away from a stall can often produce a radical price drop.

Don't let anyone guilt-trip you; no Hong Kong salesperson will sell you anything that doesn't cut them a profit.

Faking It

The Hong Kong government has seriously cracked down on designer fakes. Depending on how strict the police are being when you visit, you may not find the choice of knockoffs you were hoping for.

Bear in mind that designer fakes are illegal, and as such you could get into trouble if you get caught with them going through customs.

Cash or Plastic

In spite of the credit-card decals on shop doors (every card you could possibly imagine and more), many smaller stores will insist on cash or add 3% to 5% to the total if you pay by credit card.

If you plan to use plastic, ask if there's a charge before gloating over your "bargain."

By Victoria Patience and Sofia Suárez Updated by Zoe Mak and Dominique Rowe

They say the only way to get to know a place is to do what the locals do. When in Rome, scoot around on a Vespa and drink espresso. When in Hong Kong, shop. For most people in this city, shopping is a leisure activity, whether that means picking out a four-figure party dress, rifling through bins at an outlet, upgrading a cell phone, or choosing the freshest fish for dinner.

Shopping is so sacred that sales periods are calendar events, and most stores close on just three days a year—Christmas Day and the first two days of Chinese New Year. Imagine that: 362 days of unbridled purchasing. Opening hours are equally conducive to whiling your life away browsing the racks: all shops are open until 7 or 8 PM; many don't close their doors until midnight.

It's true that the days when everything in Hong Kong was mind-bogglingly cheap are over. It *is* still a tax-free port, so you can get some good deals. But it isn't just about the savings. Sharp contrasts and the sheer variety of experiences available make shopping here very different from back home.

You might find a bargain or two elbowing your way through a chaotic open-air market filled with haggling vendors selling designer knockoffs, the air reeking of the *chou tofu* ("stinky" tofu) bubbling at a nearby food stand. But then you could find a designer number going for half the usual price in a hushed marble-floor mall, the air scented by designer fragrances worn by fellow shoppers. What's more, in Hong Kong, the two extremes are often within spitting distance of each other.

Needless to say, thanks to travelers like you running out of space in their suitcases, Hong Kong does a roaring trade in luggage. No need to feel guilty, though—shopping here is practically cultural research. All you're doing is seeing what local life is really like.

MAJOR SHOPPING AREAS

HONG KONG ISLAND

WESTERN

The past is very much alive in Western, Hong Kong Island's most traditional neighborhood, and nowhere more than in its shops. Different streets are known as centers for particular trades. Along Hollywood Road, between Sheung Wan and Central, antique Chinese furniture and collectibles fetch high prices in upscale showrooms. You can get similar-looking items half their price (and less than half their age) in Upper Lascar Row, which also does a brisk trade in Communist retro paraphernalia, mah-jongg tiles, and fans.

Man Wa Lane is the place for chops (seals carved in stone with engraved initials). Traditional Chinese medicine is the commercial lifeblood of Sheung Wan proper: ginseng, snake musk, birds' nests, and shark's fins are some of the delicacies available. *(For more information, see To Your Health in chapter 1.)* Locals stock up on less exotic household goods at Sincere and Wing On, two of Hong Kong's largest department stores.

CENTRAL

New York, London, Paris, Milan . . . Central. When it comes to designer labels, the district's name says it all. Where else can you find a mall with a whole floor dedicated to Armani or calculate the Pradas per square mile? Spacious, golden-hue centers like the IFC Mall, the Landmark, Prince's Building, and the Galleria are the fashion hunting grounds of Hong Kong's well-to-do, and all places to head if your shopping list reads like *Vogue's* directory pages.

Platinum taste but no platinum card? Cut-price designer outlets fill the Pedder Building, also home to iconic local store Shanghai Tang. There's offbeat urban attire—jeans, in particular—at the hip boutiques scattered through Lan Kwai Fong and SoHo. Hong Kong's coolest art galleries are also here, if it's your walls you're looking to dress.

Central may be fashion heaven, but there's an earthier side to it, too. Head out of the air-conditioned malls and down to the stalls on Li Yuen streets East and West for cheap souvenirs like silk dressing gowns. Ribbons, buttons, and sequins come in colors you didn't know existed on steep Pottinger Street, a haberdasher's dream.

ADMIRALTY

Shopping in Admiralty is synonymous with one thing—glitzy Pacific Place Mall. Locals come here for the designer labels, and visitors to stock up on souvenirs at Chinese Arts & Crafts. Elevated walkways connect it to three lesser shopping centers: the Admiralty Centre, Queensway Plaza, and United Centre.

WAN CHAI

No malls, no air-conditioning, no Prada—Wan Chai has all these things in its favor when shopping in Central starts to feel a bit samey. Tourists don't shop here much, so you can try out your Cantonese at the rock-bottom no-name outlets on the lanes between Johnston Road and Queen's Road East. Everything from underwear to evening wear is on offer. On Johnston Road shops selling bamboo birdcages and kung fu gear pay homage to Wan Chai's traditional side; the Suzy Wong stereotype lives on in the marine-filled tattoo parlors lining Lockhart Road. Rosewood furniture and camphor-wood chests are two of the specialties of the furniture shops on Queen's Road East and Wan Chai Road, near Admiralty. If this all sounds too traditional, don't despair: techno-happy modern Hong Kong is alive and well at the Wan Chai Computer Centre on Hennessy Road, a collection of dozens of computing outlets.

CAUSEWAY BAY

Hong Kong fashionistas hungry for new labels choose Causeway Bay over Central any day. Quirky-but-cool Asian brands that won't arrive stateside for years are the pull at Japanese department store Sogo and micromalls like the Island Beverley. The low-profile storefronts on Yiu Wa Street belie its being *the* hottest address for homegrown clothing and housewares. Similar up-and-coming boutiques are scattered along Vogue Alley, at the intersection of Paterson and Kingston streets. Local shops that have already made their name around here include lifestyle specialists G.O.D., which has a big branch on Leighton Street.

Ten-story megamall Times Square soars behind all this—its mix of designer and midrange gear makes it a good one-stop shop destination. Other good bets for clothing are the big branches of local chains like Giordano on Kai Chui Road. Prices in the stalls and poky shops along Jardine's Crescent and Jardine's Bazaar are unbeatable. Cheap souvenir stalls here are another boon. You can see how real Hong Kongers do their food shopping at the "wet market" (so called because the vendors are perpetually hosing down their produce), at the end of these streets. Locals also head to Hennessy Road for jewelry, watches, luggage, stereos, cameras, and electronic goods.

SOUTHSIDE

Stanley Village Market is the reason most visitors come south. Trawling its crowded lanes for clothes, sportswear, and table linen can take half a day—more if you stop to eat. Classy reproductions of traditional Chinese furniture (with price tags to match) are the main draw at the Repulse Bay's shopping arcade, nearby. Farther west is Ap Lei Chau, a small island known for its designer outlets—the most famous is Joyce. A bridge connects it to Hong Kong Island proper.

KOWLOON

Kowloon is home to the famous Nathan Road, where bright neon lights adorn every building. Locals usually don't shop on Nathan Road, and tourists usually get ripped off there. But when it comes to outdoor markets, Kowloon draws locals and in-the-know visitors who are willing to bargain for their bargains. In addition to good sales at outdoor vending areas such as the Temple Street Night Market and the Ladies' Market, cultural shopping experiences abound in places such as the Bird Garden or the Jade Market.

■ T.I.P → Visiting all the outdoor markets in Kowloon in one day may be exhausting. You're better off picking three sites you want to spend some time in rather than rushing through them all.

TSIM SHA TSUI

Lighted up in neon and jam-packed with shops, garish Nathan Road is Tsim Sha Tsui's main drag, usually crammed with tourists and sketchy salespeople alike. "What a drag" is the phrase that often comes to mind when shopping here: sky-high prices and shop assistants bent on ripping you off leave you wishing you'd gone elsewhere. Slip down the side streets, though, and things get better. Granville and Cameron roads are home to cheap clothing outlets, while Japanese imports and young designers fill the boutiques at the funky minimall called Rise. Chinese emporiums Yue Hwa and Chinese Arts & Crafts have big branches here—both are great places to stock up on cheap souvenirs.

Although Tsim Sha Tsui is known for its low-end shopping, that doesn't mean luxury goods are out of the picture. The Peninsula Arcade, Joyce, and the vast Harbour City shopping center all have a big-name count fit to rival Central's. One contrast are the shoppers, who tend to be a bit lower key. Bespoke tailoring is another Tsim Sha Tsui specialty—quality varies enormously, so try to choose somewhere well established, like Sam's. *(For tips on tailoring, see It Suits You, below.)*

JORDAN, YAU MA TEI & MONG KOK

The bright-lights-big-city look of Tsim Sha Tsui gives way to housing blocks and tenements hung with aging signs north of Jordan Road. Streets are crowded and traffic is manic, but this down-to-earth chaos is what makes shopping in these north Kowloon neighborhoods rewarding. Well, that and all the bargains at the area's markets. Yau Ma Tei has jade and pearls at Kansu Street; and bric-a-brac and domestic appliances fill atmospheric Temple Street nightly. Farther north are blocks and blocks of brandless clothes and accessories at the Fa Yuen Street Ladies' Market. Parallel Tung Choi Street has cut-price sporting goods. Goldfish, flowers, and birds each have their own dedicated market in Prince Edward, north of Mong Kok. Yue Hwa's five-story Jordan shop is one of the best places in Hong Kong for cheap gifts. The new kid on this particular block is Langham Place shopping mall, slated to transform Mong Kok shopping. So far it's certainly changed the landscape—the tall glass-and-steel building is like nothing else in the neighborhood.

SHAM SHUI PO

Two stops from Mong Kok on the MTR is Sham Shui Po, a labyrinth of small streets teeming with flea markets and wholesale shops, where you can buy anything from electronics to computers to clothing. The Golden Computer Arcade, stuffed with small computer hardware shops, is favored by local mouse potatoes. Prices are competitive, but parts usually come without a warranty.

NEW KOWLOON & NEW TERRITORIES

The best shopping to be had beyond Boundary Street—the official start of the New Territories—is in malls. Luminous, spacious, and with an excellent selection of shops, Kowloon Tong's Festival Walk is one of the most pleasant such places in town. New Town Plaza in Sha Tin is easily reached by KCR and has some local brands hard to get in Central or Kowloon.

THE STORES

DEPARTMENT STORES

Hong Kong's many Chinese-product stores offer some of the territory's most unusual and spectacular buys—sometimes at better prices than in the rest of China. Whether you're looking for pearls, gold, jade, silk jackets, fur hats, Chinese stationery, or just a pair of chopsticks, you can't go wrong with these stores. Most are open seven days a week but are crowded on sale days and at lunchtime on weekdays. The clerks are expert at packing, shipping, and mailing goods abroad, if not so well schooled in the finer art of pleasant service.

★ **Chinese Arts & Crafts.** Head to this long-established mainland company to blitz through that tiresome list of presents in one fell swoop. It stocks a huge variety of well-priced brocades, silk clothing, carpets, and cheap porcelain. Incongruously scattered throughout the shops are specialty items like large globes with lapis oceans and landmasses inlaid with semiprecious stones for a mere HK$70,000. Other more accessible—and more packable—gifts include appliqué tablecloths and cushion covers or silk dressing gowns. ⊠ *Pacific Place, Admiralty* ☎ *2827–6667* ⊕ *www.chineseartsandcrafts.com.hk* Ⓜ *Admiralty, Exit F* ⊠ *Asia Standard Tower, 59 Queen's Rd., Central* Ⓜ *Central, Exit D2* ⊠ *China Resources Bldg., 26 Harbour Rd., Wan Chai* Ⓜ *Wan Chai, Exit A5* ⊠ *Star House, 3 Salisbury Rd., Tsim Sha Tsui, Kowloon* Ⓜ *Tsim Sha Tsui, Exit F* ⊠ *JD Mall, 233 Nathan Rd., Jordan, Kowloon* Ⓜ *Jordan, Exit A.*

★ **City'super.** Wherever you're from and whatever you're missing, whether it's fresh oysters from France or Japanese cosmetics, this gourmet supermarket and international variety store is the place to begin your search. Locals and tourists looking for gadgets, inexpensive jewelry and accessories, and quirky products like bottled water for pets often find what they're looking for here, and this store will never bore you. The Times Square location often has international-themed food festivals. Be sure to check out the Japanese imported sweets like Royce Chocolate's unusual chocolate chips. ⊠ *IFC Mall, 8 Finance St., Central* ☎ *2234–7128* ⊕ *www.citysuper.com.hk* Ⓜ *Hong Kong, Exit A1* ⊠ *Times Square, 1 Matheson St., Causeway Bay* Ⓜ *Causeway Bay, Exit A* ⊠ *Harbour City, 3 Canton Rd., Tsim Sha Tsui, Kowloon* Ⓜ *Tsim Sha Tsui, Exit A1.*

Harvey Nichols. When this legendary British retailer announced its Hong Kong opening, locals were skeptical, saying nothing would ever live up to the original London store. But Harvey Nicks quickly had them eating their (Phillip Treacy) hats with the sheer volume of hyper-cool labels they stock. The menswear section has been a particularly big hit with local celebs, while local *tai-tais* (ladies who lunch) have declared the fourth-floor restaurant *the* place for mid-shopping-spree coffee breaks. ⊠ *The Landmark, 15 Queen's Rd., Central* ☎ *3695–3388* ⊕ *www.harveynichols.com* Ⓜ *Central, Exit G.*

TOP SHOPS
Best Upscale Mall: Festival Walk
Biggest Selection Under One Roof: Harbour City
Chinese Chic: Shanghai Tang
Gifts Galore: Yue Hwa
Best Custom Suit: Sam's Tailor
Best Designer Outlet: Joyce Warehouse

★ **Lane Crawford.** This prestigious western-style department store has been the favorite of local label-lovers for years—not bad for a brand that started out as a makeshift provisions shop back in 1850. The massive new flagship store in the IFC mall feels like a monument to fashion's biggest names, with exquisitely designed acres divided up into small gallery-like spaces for each designer. The phenomenal brand list includes everything from haute couture through designer denim to Agent Provocateur lingerie. Sales here are more like fashionista wrestling matches, with everyone pushing and shoving to find bargains. ⊠ *Podium 3, IFC Mall, 8 Finance St., Central* ☎ *2118–3388, 2118–7777 Lane Crawford concierge* ⊕ *www.lanecrawford.com* Ⓜ *Hong Kong, Exit A1* ⊠ *Pacific Place, 88 Queensway, Admiralty* Ⓜ *Admiralty, Exit F* ⊠ *Gateway Mall, 3 Canton Rd., Tsim Sha Tsui, Kowloon* Ⓜ *Tsim Sha Tsui, Exit E* ⊠ *Times Square, 1 Matheson St., Causeway Bay* Ⓜ *Causeway Bay, Exit A.*

LCX. This spacious store combines local and international fashion, beauty products, and dining under one roof. Clothing brands like BCB-Girls, GAS, and Killah all have their own areas here, along with Apivita, Phytomer, and other cosmetics lines, and TechnoMarine and ToyWatch watches for men and women. The Harbour city store also has restaurants and cafés including the California Pizza Kitchen, Iccho Japanese Restaurant, and Suzuki Cafe. ⊠ *9 Kingston, Causeway Bay* ☎ *2890–5200* ⊕ *www.lcx-group.com* Ⓜ *Causeway Bay, Exit E* ⊠ *Harbour City, 3 Canton Rd., Tsim Sha Tsui Kowloon* Ⓜ *Tsim Sha Tsui, Exit E.*

Marks & Spencer. Classic, good-quality clothing is what this British retailer has built an empire on—its underwear, in particular, is viewed as a national treasure. Although basics are on the staid side, the newer Per Una, Autograph, and Limited collections are decidedly trendier. This is one of the few stores in town to stock a full range of sizes. There are branches in many of Hong Kong's malls—most of the shops have a British specialty food section, too. ⊠ *28 Queen's Rd., Central* ☎ *2921–8321* Ⓜ *Central, Exit D1* ⊠ *Times Square, 1 Matheson St., Causeway Bay* Ⓜ *Causeway Bay, Exit A* ⊠ *Harbour City, 5 Canton Rd., Tsim Sha Tsui, Kowloon* Ⓜ *Tsim Sha Tsui, Exit E.*

4

Seibu. This Japanese department store is actually owned by local tycoon Dickson Poon, who counts Harvey Nichols among his other possessions. Western ready-to-wear labels make up the bulk of its offerings: expect hip street wear at Langham Place and more professional looks at the Pacific Place branch. This is also home to Japanese housewares shop Loft, and the aptly named Great Food Hall, where homesick expat foodies stock up on imported delicacies. ✉ *Pacific Place, 88 Queensway, Admiralty* ☎ *2971–3333* Ⓜ *Admiralty, Exit F* ✉ *Kowloon Hotel, 19–21 Nathan Rd., Tsim Sha Tsui Kowloon* Ⓜ *Tsim Sha Tsui, Exit F* ✉ *Langham Place, 8 Argyle St., Mong Kok, Kowloon* Ⓜ *Mong Kok, Exit C3.*

Sincere. Hong Kong's most eclectic department store stocks everything from frying pans to jelly beans. Run by the same family for more than a century, Sincere has several local claims to fame: it was the first store in Hong Kong to give paid days off to employees, the first to hire women in sales positions—beginning with the founder's wife and sister-in-law—and the first to establish a fixed-price policy backed up by the regionally novel idea of issuing receipts. Although you probably won't have heard of its clothes or cosmetic brands, you might come across a bargain. ✉ *173 Des Voeux Rd., Central* ☎ *2544–2688* ⊕ *www.sincere. com.hk* Ⓜ *Sheung Wan, Exit E3.*

Sogo. A lynchpin of the Causeway Bay shopping scene, Japanese brand Sogo's main branch has 10 floors of clothing, cosmetics, and housewares. There's a dazzling variety of Chinese, Japanese, and international brands—the store is particularly strong on street wear, makeup, and accessories. The downside is that it's all squeezed into a tiny retail space, which can make shopping here cramped work. The considerably smaller Tsim Sha Tsui branch is in the basement shopping arcade under the Space Museum. ✉ *555 Hennessy Rd., Causeway Bay* ☎ *2833–8338* ⊕ *www.sogo.com.hk* Ⓜ *Causeway Bay, Exit D* ✉ *12 Salisbury Rd., Tsim Sha Tsui, Kowloon* Ⓜ *East Tsim Sha Tsui, Exit J.*

Wing On. Great values on household appliances, kitchenware, and crockery have made Wing On a favorite with locals on a budget since it opened in 1907. It also stocks clothes, cosmetics, and sportswear, but don't expect to find big brands (or even brands you know). You *can* count on rock-bottom prices and an-off-the-tourist-trail experience, though. ✉ *211 Des Voeux Rd. Central, Sheung Wan, Western* ☎ *2852–1888* ⊕ *www.wingonet. com* Ⓜ *Sheung Wan, Exit E3* ✉ *Cityplaza, 18 Tai Koo Shing Rd., Tai Koo, Eastern* Ⓜ *Tai Koo, Exit D2* ✉ *Wing On Kowloon Centre, 345 Nathan Rd., Jordan, Kowloon* Ⓜ *Jordan, Exit A.*

Fodor'sChoice **Yue Hwa Chinese Products Emporium.** Its five floors contain Chinese goods, ★ ranging from clothing and housewares through tea and traditional medicine. The logic behind the store's layout is hard to fathom, so go with time to rifle around. As well as the predictable tablecloths, silk pajamas, and chopstick sets, there are cheap and colorful porcelain sets and offbeat local favorites like mini-massage chairs. The top floor is entirely given over to tea—you can pick up a HK$50 packet of leaves or an antique Yixing teapot stretching into the thousands. ✉ *301–309 Nathan Rd., Jordan, Kowloon* ☎ *3511–2222* ⊕ *www.yuehwa.com* Ⓜ *Jordan, Exit A* ✉ *55 Des Voeux Rd., Central* Ⓜ *Central, Exit B* ✉ *1 Kowloon Park Dr., Tsim Sha Tsui, Kowloon* Ⓜ *Tsim Sha Tsui, Exit E.*

MALLS & CENTERS

Cityplaza. An ice-skating rink, a bowling alley, and a multiplex theater are some of the reasons Cityplaza is the city's most popular family mall. So popular, in fact, that it's best to steer clear on weekends, when you have to fight through the crowds. Toys and children's clothing labels are well represented, as are low- to midrange local and international adult brands. There are also branches of Marks & Spencer, local department store Wing On, Japanese supermarket Apita, and Japanese stationery and accessory shop Muji. ✉ *18 Tai Koo Shing Rd., Tai Koo, Eastern* ⊕ *www.cityplaza.com.hk* Ⓜ *Tai Koo, Exit D2.*

★ **Elements.** This upscale shopping mall, which opened in 2007, is located in the newly developed Kowloon West residential and commercial district. The mall is beautifully designed and is divided into five different zones based on the elements: metal, wood, water, earth, and fire. This is one-stop shopping as far as international luxury brands are concerned, with Valentino, Paule Ka, Mulberry, Lanvin, Prada, and Gucci, just to name a few. A complimentary shuttle bus is available every 20 minutes from 12:30 PM to 9:30 PM outside of the duty-free shop on Peking Road, Tsim Sha Tsui. ✉ *1 Austin Rd. W, Tsim Sha Tsui, Kowloon* ⊕ *www.elementshk.com* Ⓜ *Kowloon, Exit D1.*

Fodor'sChoice ★ **Festival Walk.** Don't be put off by Festival Walk's location in residential Kowloon Tong—it's 20 minutes from Central on the MTR. Make the effort to get here: Festival Walk has everything from Giordano (Hong Kong's answer to the Gap) to Vivienne Tam. By day the six floors sparkle with sunlight, which filters through the glass roof. Marks & Spencer and Esprit serve as anchors; Armani Exchange and Calvin Klein draw the elite crowds; while Camper and Agnès b. keep the trend spotters happy. Hong Kong's best bookstore, Page One, has a big branch downstairs. The mall also has one of the city's largest ice rinks as well as a multiplex cinema, perfect if you're shopping with kids who want a respite from the sometimes scorching-hot weather. ✉ *80 Tat Chee Ave., Kowloon Tong, Kowloon* ⊕ *www.festivalwalk.com.hk* Ⓜ *Kowloon Tong, Exit C2.*

Fodor'sChoice ★ **Harbour City.** The four interconnected complexes that make up Harbour City contain almost 700 shops between them—if you can't find it here, it probably doesn't exist. Pick up a map on your way in as it's easy to get lost. **Ocean Terminal,** the largest section, runs along the harbor and is divided thematically, with kids' wear and toys on the ground floor, and sports and cosmetics on the first. The top floor is home to white-hot street-wear store LCX (⇨ *above*). Near the Star Ferry pier, the **Marco Polo Hong Kong Hotel Arcade** has branches of the department store Lane Crawford. Louis Vuitton, Prada, and Burberry are some of the posher boutiques that fill the **Ocean Centre** and **Gateway Arcade,** parallel to Canton Road. Most of the complex's restaurants are here, too. A cinema and three hotels round up Harbour City's offerings. Free Wi-Fi is available. ✉ *Canton Rd., Tsim Sha Tsui, Kowloon* ⊕ *www. harbourcity.com.hk* Ⓜ *Tsim Sha Tsui, Exit E.*

★ **IFC Mall.** The people at the International Finance Centre love superlatives: having made Hong Kong's tallest skyscraper (Two IFC), they built the city's poshest mall under it. A quick glance at the directory—Tiffany, Kate Spade, Prada, Gieves & Hawkes—lets you know that the IFC isn't for the faint of pocket. Designer department store Lane Crawford also has its flagship store here. Even the mall's cinema multiplex is special: the deluxe theaters have super-comfy seats with extra legroom. If you finish your spending spree at sunset, go for a cocktail at RED or Isola, two rooftop bars with fabulous harbor views. The Hong Kong Airport Express station (with in-town check-in service) is under the mall, and the Four Seasons Hotel connects to it. Avoid the mall between 12:30 and 2, when it's flooded with lunching office workers from the two IFC towers. ⊠*8 Finance St., Central* ⊕*www.ifc.com.hk* Ⓜ*Hong Kong, Exit A1.*

The Landmark. If you haven't got a boutique in the Landmark, you clearly haven't made it in the fashion world, darling. Central's most prestigious shopping site houses Celine, Loewe, Gucci, Joyce Boutique, Hermès, and Harvey Nichols, among others. Even if your credit-card limit isn't up to a spree here, the hushed atrium café is the best place in town to watch well-coiffed tai-tais on the prowl. A pedestrian bridge links the Landmark with shopping arcades in Jardine House, the Prince's Building, the Mandarin Oriental Hotel, and 9 Queen's Road. ⊠*Pedder St. and Des Voeux Rd., Central* Ⓜ*Central, Exit G.*

Langham Place. This mall's rich brown sandstone stands in stark contrast to the pulsating neon signs and crumbling residential blocks around it. Yet Langham Place has fast become a fixture of Mong Kok's chaotic shopping scene, with nearly 300 shops packed into 15 floors. It's especially popular with hipsters, who come for the local and Japanese labels in offbeat boutiques ranged around a spiral walkway on the 11th and 12th floors. Extra-long escalators—dubbed "Xpresscalators"—whisk you quickly up four levels at a time. The elegant glass-and-steel skyscraper atop the mall is the Langham Place Hotel. ⊠*8 Argyle St., Mong Kok, Kowloon* ⊕*www.langhamplace.com.hk* Ⓜ*Mong Kok, Exit C3.*

Lee Gardens One and Two. These two adjacent malls are a firm favorite with local celebrities. They come as much for the mall's low-key atmosphere—a world away from the bustle of Central—as for the clothes. And with so many big names under one small roof—Gucci, Ralph Lauren, Y's Yohji Yamamoto, Jean-Paul Gaultier, and Hermès, to name but a few—who can blame them? The second floor of Lee Gardens Two is taken up with designer kiddie wear. The two buildings, one on either side of Hysan Avenue, are linked by a second-floor footbridge. ⊠*33 Hysan Ave., Causeway Bay* ⊕*www.leegardens.com.hk* Ⓜ*Causeway Bay, Exit F.*

Mega Box. This 18-story mall is a great option for family shopping expeditions: those with minimal shopping stamina can amuse themselves at the video arcade, the IMAX theater, or the skating rink, and there are also numerous eateries. Shops include B&Q, a U.K.-based company that is equivalent to Home Depot in the United States. However, unlike other malls that are walking distance from MTR stations, visitors need to take its free shuttle from the Kowloon Bay MTR Station. To catch the shuttle, exit the MTR station at Exit A and go through Telford Plaza; you can always ask the Plaza concierge if you're confused. Shuttles run about every 10 minutes. ⊠*38 Wang Chiu Rd., Kowloon Bay, Kowloon* ☎*2989–3000* ⊕*www.megabox.com.hk/tc* Ⓜ*Kowloon Bay, Exit A.*

New Town Plaza. If you're looking to come down to fashion earth after the designer heaven that is Central, Sha Tin's New Town Plaza is a great bet. Decidedly off the tourist trail, the New Territories' best mall has more than 350 midrange shops and restaurants anchored by Marks & Spencer and Japanese department store Seibu. The usual local suspects abound, but lesser known local brands like Pedder Red also have stores. International names like Miss Sixty, French Connection, and Kookai make up the pickings. A huge multiplex cinema draws crowds on weekends. New Town Plaza is also home to two of Hong Kong's kitscher attractions: a musical fountain and Snoopy World, celebrating Schultz's hound. The mall is connected to several other smaller malls and a hotel via a series of walkways and is adjacent to the Sha Tin station. ⊠*18 Sha Tin Centre St., Sha Tin* ☎*2699–5992* ⊕*www. newtownplaza.com.hk* Ⓜ*Sha Tin.*

Pacific Place. Once Hong Kong islands' classiest mall, Pacific Place has since been upstaged by the IFC. Yet it remains popular with well-to-do Hong Kongers, perhaps because it's quieter and more exclusive than most malls. High-end international prêt-à-porter fills most of its four floors, and two department stores, Seibu and Lane Crawford, also have branches here. When your bags are weighing you down, sandwiches, sushi, and Starbucks are on hand, as is a multiplex cinema. The Marriott, the Island Shangri-La, and the Conrad hotels are all connected to this plaza. Elevated walkways join Pacific Place with three lesser arcades: the **Admiralty Centre**, **United Centre**, and **Queensway Plaza.** ⊠*88 Queensway, Admiralty* ⊕*www.pacificplace.com.hk* Ⓜ*Admiralty, Exit F.*

★ **Pedder Building.** Although dwarfed by flashy skyscrapers, the Pedder Building is an elegant stone construction housing a mix of outlets and shops with local luxury brands. Shanghai Tang's flagship store takes up the ground floor and basement. Upstairs, Blanc de Chine does clothes in similar styles to Shanghai Tang but in subtler colors. Floors 4, 5, and 6 are packed with small designer outlets, with 30% or more off retail prices. Labels Plus has some men's fashions as well as women's daytime separates. La Place has Prada bags and a large selection of Chanel jackets at about 20% off retail. Many discounted items are actually seconds, so look carefully for defects. ⊠*12 Pedder St., Central* Ⓜ*Central, Exit D1.*

Rise Commercial Building. Many a quirky Hong Kong street-wear trend is born in this fabulous micromall. Don't let its grubby exterior put you off: this arcade is a haven of Asian cool. Japanese designers are particularly well represented—look out for überhip brand A Bathing Ape, which does some of the funkiest T-shirts around. Handmade shoes and oversized retro jewelry are other fixtures—and all at bargain prices. ⊠*5–11 Granville Circuit, off Granville Rd., Tsim Sha Tsui, Kowloon* Ⓜ*Tsim Sha Tsui, Exit B2.*

★ **Times Square.** This gleaming mall packs in most of Hong Kong's best-known stores into 12 frenzied floors, organized thematically. Lane Crawford and Marks & Spencer both have big branches here, as does favored local deli City'Super. Many restaurants are located in the basement, giving way to designers like Anna Sui on the second floor, and midrange options like Zara higher up. The electronics, sports, and outdoors selection is particularly good. An indoor atrium hosts everything from heavy-metal bands to fashion shows to local movie stars; there's also a cinema complex and a dozen or so eateries. The huge Page One bookshop is on the ninth floor. ✉*1 Matheson St., Causeway Bay* ⊕*www.timessquare.com.hk* Ⓜ*Causeway Bay, Exit A.*

MARKETS

Markets embody some of the best things about Hong Kong shopping—bargains, local color, and buzz. Bargaining is the norm, so take initial asking prices with a grain of salt, and stand your ground. Leave all guilt at home—however low you get the salesperson to go, they'll always come out with a profit.

Famous Cat Street—the curio haunt in Upper Lascar Row, running behind Central and Western—is now full of small, high-quality Chinese antiques shops, but in the street outside you'll still see plenty of hawkers selling inexpensive jewelry, opium pipes, Mao buttons, and assorted paraphernalia.

Cutesy characters like Hello Kitty are plastered over wallets, pencil cases, and a hundred other products in the stalls on Li Yuen Streets East and West, two parallel lanes in Central. Embroidered dressing gowns and cheap watches are also specialties here. Similar goods fill the stands on Wan Chai's Spring Garden Lane, where you can sometimes pick up wicker items, too. Rock-bottom clothing outlets fill the surrounding streets. Over in Mong Kok entire streets have been given over to stalls selling imitation clothing, accessories, and souvenirs.

Each Hong Kong district has an Urban Council–run market selling fruit, vegetables, meat, seafood, and live chickens (squeamish people take note: chickens are slaughtered out in the open here). Surrounding the markets are small stores with every imaginable kitchen and bathroom appliance, as well as clothes and electronics.

Around heavy pedestrian areas you'll find illegal hawkers with a wide variety of cheap goods, but beware—vendors are constantly on the lookout for the police and may literally run off with their goods. If they do, get out of their way! In summer they often materialize in Tsim Sha Tsui in front of the Hyatt, around Granville and Mody roads, and at the Star Ferry Terminal.

Arts & Crafts Fair. Small stalls from local cottage industries sell handicrafts each Sunday and on public holidays outside the Cultural Centre on the Tsim Sha Tsui waterfront. Portrait artists are at hand to capture your likeness, and there's other artwork, jewelry, clothing, and knickknacks. Each stall holder is chosen by a panel of judges who look to promote Hong Kong artists and small businesses. ✉*Hong Kong Cultural Centre Piazza, Salisbury Rd., Tsim Sha Tsui, Kowloon* ☉*Sun. and public holidays 2–7* Ⓜ*Tsim Sha Tsui, Exit E.*

Flower Market. Huge bucketfuls of roses and gerbera spill out onto the sidewalk along Flower Market Road, a collection of street stalls selling cut flowers and potted plants. Delicate orchids and vivid birds of par-

Continued on page 122

MARKETS
A GUIDE TO BUYING SILK, PEARLS & POTTERY

Chinese markets are hectic and crowded, but great fun for the savvy shopper. The intensity of the bargaining and the sheer number of goods available are pretty much unsurpassed anywhere else in the world.

Nowadays wealthier Chinese may prefer to flash their cash in department stores and designer boutiques, but generally, markets are still the best places to shop. Teens spend their pocket money at cheap clothing markets. Grandparents, often toting their grandchildren, go to their local neighborhood food market almost daily to pick up fresh items such as tofu, fish, meat, fruit, and vegetables. Markets are also great places to mix with the locals, see the drama of bargaining take place, and watch as the Chinese banter, play with their children, challenge each other to cards, debate, or just lounge.

Some markets have a mishmash of items, whereas others are more specialized, dealing in one particular ware. Markets play an essential part in the everyday life of the Chinese and prices paid are always a great topic of conversation. A compliment on a choice article will often elicit the price paid in reply and a discussion may ensue on where to get the same thing at an even lower cost.

GREAT FINDS

The prices we list below are meant to give you an idea of what you can pay for certain items. Actual post-bargaining prices will of course depend on how well you haggle, while pre-bargaining prices are often based on how much the vendor thinks he or she can get out of you.

PEARLS

Many freshwater pearls are grown in Taihu; seawater pearls come from Japan or the South Seas. Some have been dyed and others mixed with semiprecious stones. Designs can be pretty wild and the clasps are not of very high quality, but necklaces and bracelets are cheap. Post-bargaining, a plain, short strand of pearls should cost around HK$40.

MAOMORABILIA

The Chairman's image is readily available on badges, bags, lighters, watches, ad infinitum. Pop-art–like figurines of Mao and his Red Guards clutching red books are kitschy but iconic. For soundbites and quotes from the Great Helmsman, buy the Little Red Book itself. Pre-bargaining, a badge costs HK$25, a bag HK$50, and a ceramic figurine HK$370. Just keep in mind that many posters are fakes.

ETHNIC-MINORITY HANDICRAFTS

Brightly colored skirts from the Miao minority and embroidered jackets from the Yunnan area are great boho souvenirs. The heavy, elaborate jewelry could decorate a side table or hang on a wall. Colorful children's shoes are embellished with animal faces and bells. After bargaining, a skirt in the markets should go for between HK$215 to HK$295, and a pair of children's shoes for HK$40 to HK$60.

CERAMICS

Most ceramics you'll find in markets are factory-made, so you probably won't stumble upon a bargain Ming dynasty vase, but ceramics in a variety of colors can be picked up at reasonable prices. Opt for pretty pieces decorated with butterflies, or for the more risqué, copulating couples. A bowl-and-plate set goes for around HK$25, a larger serving plate HK$50.

RETRO

Odd items from the hedonistic '20s to the revolutionary '60s and '70s include treasures like old light fixtures and tin advertising signs. A rare sign such as one banning foreigners from entry may cost as much as HK$9,700, but small items such as teapots can be bought for around HK$240. Retro items are harder to bargain down for than mass-produced items.

BIRDCAGES

Wooden birdcages with domed roofs make charming decorations, with or without occupants. They are often seen being carried by old men as they promenade their feathered friends. A pre-bargaining price for a medium-sized wooden cage is around HK$175.

PROPAGANDA AND COMIC BOOKS

Follow the actions of Chinese revolutionary hero, Lei Feng, or look for scenes from Chinese history and lots of *gongfu* (Chinese martial arts) stories. Most titles are in Chinese and often in black and white, but look out for titles like *Tintin and the Blue Lotus*, set in Shanghai and translated into Chinese. You can bargain down to around HK$15 for less popular titles.

SILK

Bolts and bolts of silk brocade with blossoms, butterflies, bamboo, and other patterns dazzle the eye. An enormous range of items made from silk, from purses to slippers to traditional dresses, are available at most markets. Silk brocade costs around HK$35 per meter, a price that is generally only negotiable if you buy large quantities.

JADE

A symbol of purity and beauty for the Chinese, jade comes in a range of colors. Subtle and simple bangles vie for attention with large sculptures on market stalls. A lavender jade Guanyin (Goddess of Mercy) pendant runs at HK$250 and a green jade bangle about HK$275 before bargaining.

MAH-JONGG SETS

The clack-clack of mah-jongg tiles can be heard late into the night on the streets of most cities in summer. Cheap plastic sets go for about HK$50. Far more aesthetically pleasing are ceramic sets in slender drawers of painted cases. These run about HK$245 after bargaining, from a starting price of HK$440. Some sets come with instructions, but if not, instructions for the "game of four winds" can be downloaded in English at www.mahjongg.com.

SHOPPING KNOW-HOW

When to Go

Avoid weekends if you can and try to go early in the morning, from 8AM to 10AM, or at the end of the day just before 6PM. Rainy days are also good bets for avoiding the crowds and getting better prices.

Bringin' Home the Goods

Although that faux-Gucci handbag is tempting, remember that some countries have heavy penalties for the import of counterfeit goods. Likewise, that animal fur may be cheap, but you may get fined a lot more at your home airport than what you paid for it. Counterfeit goods are generally prohibited in the United States, but there's some gray area regarding goods with a "confusingly similar" trademark. Each person is allowed to bring in one such item, as long as it's for personal use and not for resale. For more details, go to the travel section of www.cbp.gov. The HM and Revenue Customs Web site, www.hmrc.gov.uk, has a list of banned and prohibited goods for the United Kingdom.

⚠ The Chinese government has regular and very public crackdowns on fake goods, so that store you went to today may have different items tomorrow. In Shanghai, for example, pressure from the Chinese government and other countries to protect intellectual property rights led to the demise of one of the city's largest and most popular markets, Xiangyang.

BEFORE YOU GO

■ Be prepared to be grabbed, pushed, followed, stared at, and even to have people whispering offers of items to buy in your ear. In China, personal space and privacy are not valued in the same way as in the West, so the invasion of it is common. Move away but remain calm and polite. No one will understand if you get upset anyway.

■ Many Chinese love to touch foreign children, so if you have kids, make sure they're aware of and prepared for this.

■ Keep money and valuables in a safe place. Pickpockets and bag-slashers are becoming common.

■ Pick up a cheap infrared laser pointer to detect counterfeit bills. The light illuminates the hidden anti-counterfeit ultraviolet mark in the real notes.

■ Check for fake items, like silk and pearls.

■ Learn some basic greetings and numbers in Chinese. The local people will really appreciate it.

HOW TO BARGAIN

Successful bargaining requires the dramatic skills of a Hollywood actor. Here's a step-by-step guide to getting the price you want and having fun at the same time.

DO'S	DONT'S

Browsing in a silk shop

Chinese slippers at a ladies' market

DO'S

■ Start by deciding what you're willing to pay for an item.

■ Look at the vendor and point to the item to indicate your interest.

■ The vendor will quote you a price, usually by punching numbers into a calculator and showing it to you.

■ Here, expressions of shock are required from you, which will never be as great as those of the vendor, who will put in an Oscar-worthy performance at your prices.

■ Next it's up to you to punch in a number that's around 25% of the original price—or lower if you feel daring.

■ Pass the calculator back and forth until you meet somewhere in the middle, probably at up to (and sometimes less than) 50% of the original quote.

DONT'S

■ Don't enter into negotiations if you aren't seriously considering the purchase.

■ Don't haggle over small sums of money.

■ If the vendor isn't budging, walk away; he'll likely call you back.

■ It's better to bargain if the vendor is alone. He's unlikely to come down on the price if there's an audience.

■ Saving face is everything in China. Don't belittle or make the vendor angry, and don't get angry yourself.

■ Remain pleasant and smile often.

■ Buying more than one of something gets you a better deal.

■ Dress down and leave your jewelry and watches in the hotel safe on the day you go marketing. You'll get a lower starting price if you don't flash your wealth.

adise are some of the more exotic blooms. During Chinese New Year there's a roaring trade in narcissi, poinsettias, and bright yellow chrysanthemums, all auspicious flowers. ✉ *Flower Market Rd., off Prince Edward Rd. W, Mong Kok, Kowloon* ◷ *Daily 7 AM–7:30 PM* Ⓜ *Prince Edward, Exit B1.*

☺ **Goldfish Market.** Goldfish are considered auspicious in Hong Kong (though aquariums have to be positioned in the right place to bring good luck to the family), and this small collection of shops is a favorite local source. Shop fronts are decorated with bag upon bag of glistening, pop-eyed creatures, waiting for someone to take them home. Some of the fishes inside shops are serious rarities and fetch unbelievable prices. ✉ *Tung Choi St., Mong Kok, Kowloon* ◷ *Daily 10–6* Ⓜ *Mong Kok, Exit B2.*

Jardine's Bazaar and Jardine's Crescent. These two small parallel streets are so crammed with clothing stalls it's difficult to make your way through. Most offer bargains on the usual clothes, children's gear, bags, and cheap souvenirs like chopstick sets. The surrounding boutiques are also worth a look for local and Japanese fashions, though the sizes are small. ✉ *Jardine's Bazaar, Causeway Bay* ◷ *Daily noon–10 PM* Ⓜ *Causeway Bay, Exit F.*

Kansu Street Jade Market. Jade in every imaginable shade of green, from the milkiest apple tone to the richest emerald, fills the stalls of this Kowloon market. If you know your stuff and haggle insistently, you can get fabulous bargains. Otherwise, stick to cheap trinkets. Some of the so-called "jade" sold here is actually aventurine, bowenite, soapstone, serpentine, and Australian jade—all inferior to the real thing. ✉ *Kansu St. off Nathan Rd., Yau Ma Tei, Kowloon* ◷ *Daily 10–4* Ⓜ *Yau Ma Tei, Exit C.*

★ **Ladies' Market.** Block upon block of tightly packed stalls overflow with clothes, bags, and knickknacks along Tung Choi Street in Mong Kok. Despite the name there are clothes for women, men, and children here. Most offerings are imitations or no-name brands; rifle around enough and you can often pick up some cheap and cheerful basics. Haggling is the rule here: a poker face and a little insistence can get you dramatic discounts. At the corner of each block and behind the market are stands and shops selling the street snacks Hong Kongers can't live without. Pick a place where locals are munching and point at whatever takes your fancy. Parallel **Fa Yuen Street** is Mong Kok's unofficial sportswear market. It's lined with small shops selling cut-price sneakers—some real, others not so real. To reach the market, walk two blocks east along Nelson Street from the Mong Kok MTR station. ✉ *Tung Choi St., Mong Kok, Kowloon* ◷ *Daily noon–11 PM* Ⓜ *Mong Kok, Exit E.*

★ **Stanley Village Market.** This was once Hong Kong's most famed bargain trove, but its ever-growing popularity means that Stanley Village Market no longer has the best prices around. Still, you can pick up some good buys in sportswear and casual clothing if you comb through the stalls. Good value linens—especially appliqué tablecloths—also abound. Dozens and dozens of shops line a main street so narrow that awnings from each side meet in the middle, and on busy days your elbows will come in handy. Weekdays are a little more relaxed. One of the best things about Stanley Market is getting here: the winding bus ride from Central (routes 6, 6X, 6A, or 260) or Tsim Sha Tsui (route 973) takes you over the top of Hong Kong Island, with fabulous views on the way. ⊠*Stanley Village, Southside* ⊘*Daily 11–6.*

★ **Temple Street Night Market.** Each night, as it gets dark, the lamps strung between the stalls of this Yau Ma Tei street market slowly light up, and the air fills with the smells wafting from myriad food carts. Hawkers try to catch your eye by flinging clothes up from their stalls. Cantonese opera competes with pop music, and vendors' cries and shoppers' haggling fills the air. Adding to the color here are the fortune-tellers and the odd magician or acrobat who has set up shop in the street. Granted, neither the clothes nor cheap gadgets on sale here are much to get excited about, but it's the atmosphere people come for—any purchases are a bonus. The market stretches for almost a mile and is one of Hong Kong's liveliest nighttime shopping experiences. ⊠*Temple St., Mong Kok, Kowloon* ⊘*Daily 5* PM–*midnight; best after 8* PM Ⓜ*Jordan, Exit A.*

Western Market. This redbrick Victorian in the Sheung Wan district was built in 1906 and was originally used as a produce market. These days the first floor is filled with unmemorable shops selling crafts, toys, jewelry, and collectibles; second-floor shops sell a remarkable selection of fabric. A more surreal experience is lunch, dinner, or high tea in the Grand Stage Chinese restaurant and ballroom on the top floor. After a great Chinese meal you can while away the afternoon with the old-timers trotting around the room to a live band belting out the cha-cha and tango. ⊠*Des Voeux Rd., Western* Ⓜ*Sheung Wan.*

SPECIALTY SHOPS

ANTIQUES

What could be a better souvenir than an exquisite antique to pass down through the generations? Hong Kong has many reputable dealers with covetable collections of genuine antiques. Still, you'll need to be careful lest that "Ming" vase you bought was actually made in a factory yesterday.

Inspect the piece from every angle, even if it means getting on your hands and knees. Antique furniture fans have no qualms about opening up a piece and asking to see its back side to compare the patina and quality of the woods. Factors that determine value include condition, age, rarity, workmanship, and materials. In-depth knowledge of the item and its history not only safeguards your investment, it also deepens your enjoyment of it for the long term. You'll also be in a better position to buy once you've read up on items that interest you. For example, doing research on Tang horses and camels will reveal that such pieces were damaged in the tombs and rarely come with the original legs.

Be sure to request not only receipts but also certificates of authenticity. For major investments, consider having tests done to verify age. At the end of the day, if something seems too good to be true, it prob-

> **LAW ON YOUR SIDE**
>
> Although mainland law forbids that any item more than 120 years old leave China, the SAR isn't held to this rule. It's perfectly legal to ship your antique treasures home.

ably is. The best defense is to buy from a reputable dealer. Look for the QUALITY SERVICES TOURISM logo at the door, check the Hong Kong Tourist Board's *A Guide to Quality Shops* or download it from the HKTB Web site for your PDA. *Arts of Asia,* published six times a year, has been a wonderful resource for Asian antiquities collectors since 1970. Its charismatic publisher and editor, Tuyet Nguyet, brings together experts from around the world and shares her unique insights. You can read past articles, buy a subscription, or purchase back issues through the Web site www.artsofasianet.com.

AUCTION HOUSES

The auction scene is filled with record-breaking sales and some of the planet's finest Asian art and antiques. Major houses usually host sales at the Hong Kong Convention and Exhibition Centre in spring and fall. Call them or check their Web sites for full schedules and lot references.

Christie's. Christie's entered the market in 1985. Its respected specialists focus on Asian art and jewelry such as jadeite pieces and watches. Among the art auctions are those devoted to Chinese ceramics, Chinese calligraphy, and classical, modern, and contemporary paintings from China and elsewhere in Asia. ✉*22nd fl., Alexandra House, 18 Chater Rd., Central* ☎*2521–5396* ⊕*www.christies.com* Ⓜ*Central.*

Sotheby's. The respected auction house opened here in 1973. Its teams work with Chinese ceramics, jade carvings, snuff bottles, and classical and contemporary paintings. The auction house also deals in watches and jewelry, including jadeite and western pieces. ✉*31st fl., Pacific Place, 88 Queensway, Admiralty* ☎*2524–8121* ⊕*www.sothebys.com* Ⓜ*Admiralty.*

DEALERS

Altfield Gallery. If only your entire home could be outfitted by Altfield. Established in 1980, the elegant gallery carries exquisite antique Chinese furniture, Asia-related maps and topographical prints, Southeast Asian sculpture, and decorative arts from around Asia, including silver artifacts and rugs. ✉*2nd fl., Prince's Bldg., 10 Chater Rd., Central* ☎*2537–6370* ⊕*www.altfield.com.hk* Ⓜ*Central.*

Arch Angel Antiques. Ask for Bonnie Groot, who will enthusiastically and knowledgeably guide you through the three floors of fine ceramics, furniture, ancestor portraits, and more. Across the road, the Groots have opened Arch Angel Art and Arch Angel Galerie, which specializes in contemporary Vietnamese and Southeast Asian art. ✉*Ground fl., 53–55*

Hollywood Rd., Central ☎*2851–6848* ⊕*www.archangelgalleries.com* Ⓜ*Central* ✉*58 Hollywood Rd., Central* Ⓜ*Central.*

Chine Gallery. Dealing in antique furniture and rugs from China, and furniture from Japan, this dark, stylish gallery accommodates international clients by coordinating its major exhibitions with the spring and fall auction schedules of Christie's and Sotheby's. ✉*42A Hollywood Rd., Central* ☎*2543–0023* ⊕*www.chinegallery.com* Ⓜ*Central.*

The Green Lantern. Irish expat Olive Forrest has cleverly retained original elements of the former print shop in which her store is housed. With her unique sense of style, Forrest brings together Chinese and Tibetan antiques, contemporary lighting designed in-house, silk soft furnishings, high-quality OM Living bed linens, and home accessories. ✉*72 Peel St., SoHo, Central* ☎*2526–0277* Ⓜ*Central*

Hanlin Gallery. For Japanese works of art and woodblocks, visit this refined, calm gallery run by specialist Carlos Prata since 1986. His collection and expertise extend to furniture, textiles, silver, and European glass. ✉*Ground fl., Wilson House, 19–27 Wyndham St., Central* ☎*2522–4479* ⊕*www.hanlingallery.com* Ⓜ*Central.*

Honeychurch Antiques. Highly respected dealers Lucille and Glenn Vessa (one of the few accredited appraisers here) were the first to set up shop on Hollywood Road. The landscape has changed, but this shop still provides fine Chinese, Japanese, and Southeast Asian antique silver, porcelain, and unaltered furniture. ✉*Ground fl., 29 Hollywood Rd., Central* ☎*2543–2433* Ⓜ*Central.*

Lok Man Rare Books. This shop's wooden shelves and cases are packed with an impressive collection of rare books that are still in very good condition. Browse around for first- and second-edition copy of books, including children's favorites, or ask the owner to show you around. The collection includes some rare pre-1900 finds, like a first edition of *Oliver Twist*. Also check out vintage board games and antique chess sets. ✉*129A Hollywood Rd., Sheung Wan* ☎*2868–1056* ⊕*www.lokmanbooks.com.*

Manks Ltd. Inside a historic house surrounded by skyscrapers and highways you'll not only find 20th-century decorative arts, European antiques, and Scandinavian furniture, but also the delightful Susan Man. Visits to her shop are by appointment only. ✉*Shop House, 2 Kennedy Terrace, above Kennedy Rd., Midlevels, Western* ☎*2522–2115* ⊕*www.manks.com.*

Oi Ling Fine Chinese Antique. This beautiful showroom displays Chinese antique furniture, scholar's items, and archaeological stone works. Owner Oi Ling Chiang gives frequent talks. Succinct books on collecting by type are also sold here. A second branch (✉*Ground fl., 85 Hollywood Rd., Central* ☎*2964–0554* Ⓜ*Central*), just down the road, sells terra-cotta, pottery, and bronze antiques. ✉*Ground fl., 52 Hollywood Rd., Central* ☎*2815–9422* ⊕*www.oilingantiques.com* Ⓜ*Central.*

Picture This Gallery. It's a one-of-a-kind source for vintage posters—mainly with travel and movie themes—early photography of Hong Kong and elsewhere in China, antique maps, prints and engravings, antiquarian books, and limited-edition reproductions or works by artists such as Dong Kingman. You might imagine a dusty library, but

Christopher Bailey's welcoming gallery is spacious, bright, and organized. ⊠ *13th fl., 9 Queen's Rd., Central* ☎*2525–2820* ⊕*www.picture thiscollection.com* Ⓜ*Central* ⊠*2nd fl., Prince Bldg., 10 Chater Rd., Central* Ⓜ*Central.*

Tào Evolution. Here, old and new objects are among the unusual finds of a pair of designers whose work takes them around the globe. Look for contemporary and tribal art as well as furniture that conveys an eclectic Asian spirit. ⊠*Ground fl., 58 Peel St., SoHo, Central* ☎*2530–2102* Ⓜ*Central.*

Teresa Coleman Fine Arts Ltd. You can't miss the spectacular textiles hanging in the window of this busy corner shop. Specialist Teresa Coleman sells embroidered costumes from the Imperial Court, antique textiles, painted and carved fans, jewelry, lacquered boxes, and engravings and prints. ⊠*79 Wyndham St., Central* ☎*2526–2450* ⊕*www.teresacoleman. com* Ⓜ*Central.*

The Tibetan Gallery. At this extension of Teresa Coleman Fine Arts you'll find antique Tibetan *thangkas* (Buddhist paintings), bronzes, textiles, and exquisite rugs. Manager Josephine Chan is also a restoration expert. ⊠*55 Wyndham St., Central* ☎*2530–4863* ⊕*www.teresacoleman. com* Ⓜ*Central.*

Wattis Fine Art. Run by affable expert Jonathan Wattis and his wife, Vicky, for over 20 years, Wattis Fine Art specializes in antique maps and prints and photographs of Hong Kong, China, and Southeast Asia. ⊠*2nd fl., 20 Hollywood Rd., Central* ☎*2524–5302* ⊕*www.wattis.com.hk.*

Wing Tei. Helpful owner Peter Lee and his family sell wonderful porcelain plates as well as curios, furniture, and wood carvings. ⊠*190–F Hollywood Rd., Central* ☎*2547–4755* Ⓜ*Central.*

Yue Po Chai Antique Co. One of Hollywood Road's oldest shops is at the Cat Street end, next to Man Mo Temple. Its vast and varied stock includes porcelain, stone carvings, and ceramics. ⊠*Ground fl., 132–136 Hollywood Rd., Central* ☎*2540–4374* Ⓜ*Central.*

ART

Hong Kong is a hub for contemporary Asian art, particularly that from Hong Kong and mainland China, Indonesia, Vietnam, Thailand, and the Philippines. Although concentrated around the antiques dealers on Hollywood Road, art spaces stretch east to Wan Chai, west to Sheung Wan, and well beyond into the New Territories.

Openings take place weekly. A quick reference for what's on, *ArtMap* (⊕*www.artmap.com.hk*), is a free monthly distributed in most coffee shops and countless other outlets. *Asian Art News* is a bimonthly magazine with a good guide to what's happening in galleries around the region. It's sold at bigger newsstands for HK$65.

GALLERIES

Alisan Fine Arts. In a quiet corner of the sleek Prince's Building shopping arcade is this established authority on contemporary Chinese artists. Styles range from traditional to modern abstract, and media include oil, acrylic, and Chinese ink. Founded in 1981 by Alice King, this was one of the first galleries in Hong Kong to promote the genre. ⊠*3rd fl., Prince's Bldg., 10 Chater Rd., Central* ☎*2526–1091* ⊕*www.alisan.com.hk* Ⓜ*Central.*

■ **TIP**→ Galleries can arrange to have your work of art framed or can recommend a reputable framer.

Galerie La Vong. The works of today's leading Vietnamese artists, many of whose creations reveal an intriguing combination of French impressionist and traditional Chinese influences, are the focus here. ✉ *13th fl., 1 Lan Kwai Fong, Central* ☎ *2869–6863* Ⓜ *Central.*

Gallery on Old Bailey. Gallery director Ma Choi attracts prominent and innovative contemporary artists to display their work at this well-established gallery, which draws an appreciative crowd of local and international patrons. ✉ *Basement fl. and ground fl., 17 Old Bailey St., Central* ☎ *2869–7122* Ⓜ *Central.*

Grotto Fine Art. Director and chief curator Henry Au-yeung writes, curates, and gives lectures on 20th-century Chinese art. His hidden gallery (hence the "grotto" in the name) focuses exclusively on local Chinese artists, with an interest in the newest and most avant-garde works. Look for paintings, sculptures, prints, photography, mixed-media pieces, and conceptual installations. ✉ *2nd fl., 31C–D Wyndham St., Central* ☎ *2121–2270* ⊕ *www.grottofineart.com* Ⓜ *Central.*

Hanart TZ Gallery. This is a rare opportunity to compare and contrast cutting-edge and experimental art from mainland China, Taiwan, and Hong Kong selected by one of the field's most respected authorities. Unassuming curatorial director Johnson Chang Tsong-zung also cofounded the Asia Art Archive, and has curated exhibitions at the São Paolo and Venice biennials. ✉ *2nd fl., Henley Bldg., 5 Queen's Rd., Central* ☎ *2526–9019* ⊕ *www.hanart.com* Ⓜ *Central.*

Plum Blossoms Gallery. You can't miss this gallery's unique, asymmetrical window. The airy, New York–style space displays groundbreaking contemporary Chinese art alongside ancient Asian textiles and rugs. Ask the refreshingly knowledgeable staff to escort you upstairs to see more. ✉ *1 Hollywood Rd., Central* ☎ *2521–2189* ⊕ *www.plumblossoms. com* Ⓜ *Central.*

Sandra Walters Consultancy Ltd. Sandra Walters, a longtime figure on the art scene, represents a stable of Asian and international artists encompassing a variety of periods and styles. Make an appointment for her or one of her team to advise you on small to significant investments. ✉ *501 Hoseinee House, 69 Wyndham St., Central* ☎ *2522–1137* Ⓜ *Central.*

Schoeni Art Gallery. Known for vigorously promoting Chinese art on a global scale, this gallery, founded by Manfred Schoeni in 1992, has represented and supported various artists from mainland China with styles ranging from neorealism to postmodernism. Manfred's daughter Nicole now pinpoints exciting new artists for her prominent clientele. Informative past exhibition catalogs are placed atop Chinese antiques,

---

ART SCOOP

The **Asia Art Archive** saw it before the rest of us: contemporary Asian art is big. In 2000 the AAA set out to address the lack of information on the emerging field and to record its growth. It provides comprehensive research resources through its Web site, library, and reading facilities, which are open to the public. ✉ *11th fl., Hollywood Centre, 233 Hollywood Rd., Sheung Wan, Western* ☎ *2815–1112* ⊕ *www.aaa.org.hk* Ⓜ *Central.*

4

SOHO & NOHO

When it comes to big malls, big labels, and big spenders, Central is true to its name. However, ride three minutes uphill on the Midlevels Escalator, step off at Hollywood Road, and you'll find a different world. This century-old antiques hub bisects the districts known as SoHo (South of Hollywood Road) and NoHo (North of Hollywood Road).

On SoHo's winding, low-rise streets, independent designers, hole-in-the-wall boutiques, and international restaurants coexist with traditional paper lantern shops, antiques shops, incense-heady shrines, and Chinese doctors.

NoHo runs from Gage Street's outdoor food market at the Central end, with its photogenic charm and olfactory assault, through Gough Street's boutiques and interior design stores, down to Cat Street Market, a more affordable alternative to the five-figure antiques on Hollywood Road, in Sheung Wan.

BEST TIME TO GO

Shops here open and close late, operating from around 11 AM to 11 PM, seven days a week.

BEST GIFT FOR YOUR SIBLING

Your earth-friendliest relation will love a stylish reusable shopping bag from the retro-chic **G.O.D.** Made of canvas and synthetic leather, the totes are printed with classic Hong Kong images.

For late sleepers, "Clocky," a best seller at design shop **Homeless**, puts the *alarm* back into alarm clock. An extra tap on the snooze button sends the clock's monster-truck wheels bumping around the room.

Taking the tram, Victoria Peak.

(top) Star Ferry views are among the best. (bottom) Cantonese opera performers, Hong Kong Heritage Museum.

(top) Tai chi practitioners William Ng and Pandora Wu Ng, Hong Kong Park. (bottom) Real life in the city, Wan Chai shopping street.

One of the world's largest bronze Buddhas sits on a lotus flower at Po Lin Monastery, Lantau Island.

(top left) The Chinese introduced tea to the world; learn all about it at the Flagstaff House Museum of Tea Ware. (top right) *Manpower* sculpture by Rosanna Li, Grotto Fine Art gallery. (bottom) Energy = trams + taxis + neon.

(top) A promenade and lanterns frame the Hong Kong skyline, Avenue of the Stars, Kowloon waterfront.
(bottom left) Hakka woman in traditional garb. (bottom right) Shopping is a religion in Hong Kong, and the
Pacific Place mall is just one of its many temples.

(top) Po Lin Monastery, Lantau Island. (bottom) Women drumming at a Chinese New Year's parade.

(top) Who knew there were such beaches here? Sai Kung Peninsula, New Territories. (bottom left) Native son Chow Yun-Fat in *Crouching Tiger, Hidden Dragon*. (bottom right) Rides on the restored *Duk Ling* junk are compliments of the tourist board.

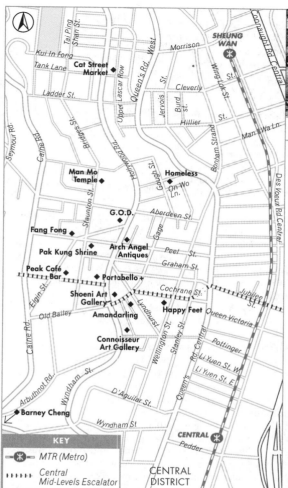

WHAT YOU'LL WANT

ART & ANTIQUES

Connoisseur Art Gallery. Past the ubiquitous bazooka-wielding nymphs is a superlative collection of Chinese artwork. Seek out future stars at sister gallery **Connoisseur Contemporary**, next door.

Schoeni Art Gallery. Here you'll find the big names in Chinese avant-garde, including Yu Chen, Chen Yu, and Zhang Lin Hai. The Hollywood Road site is a showcase; the main gallery is a minute's walk away.

Arch Angel Antiques. This shop specializes in Chinese rarities, from pocket-sized marvels to multistory statues of horses and warriors.

BEST BOUTIQUES

Amandarling. Locally designed beachwear for Bali, Capri, or your super-yacht. Collections include printed cotton beach dresses and sexy Bond-girl bikinis.

Fang Fong. Small but perfectly formed collection of affordable, sophisticated vintage and Asian-influenced designs, including silk day dresses, sequined cocktail attire, and whimsical wedding gowns.

REFUELING & REJUVENATING

Step off the world's longest outdoor covered escalator, and take a colonial-style time out with some delicious tea and cake at **Portobello+**. If it's a stiff one you're after, make like a fashionista and mainline G&Ts as you recline and watch the world float uphill at decadent **Peak Café Bar**.

A foot massage is the ultimate post-shopping treat. Sit back and feel the pressure melt away at **Happy Foot**, next to the escalator. Don't be put off by the NO SCREAMING signs; while traditional Chinese wisdom propagates the "no pain, no gain" school of thought, a lighter touch can be applied on request.

which are also presented in this huge space. You're likely to pass the Hollywood Road branch first, but Old Baily Street gallery is the better of the two. ⊠*Upper ground fl., 21–31 Old Bailey St., Central* ☎*2525–5225* ⊕*www.schoeni. com.hk* Ⓜ*Central.*

Sin Sin Fine Art. Take the escalator up to Prince's Terrace, where you can't miss this corner gallery's large windows or the arresting human-form sculpture installed on an outer wall. Inside, works by diverse emerging and established artists from Indonesia, Thailand, mainland China, Hong Kong, and France reveal the aesthetic individuality of the lively Hong Kong designer and entrepreneur, Sin Sin. There are also regular exhibitions and artist talks. The Sin Sin Annex extension, near Cat Street in Sheung Wan, is a space for more progressive installations, objets, and performance art. ⊠*Ground fl., 1 Prince's Terr., Midlevels, Western* ☎*2858–5072* ⊕*www.sinsin.com.hk.* **Sin Sin Annex** ⊠*Ground fl., 52 Sai St., Sheung Wan, Western.*

10 Chancery Lane Gallery. A visit here takes you behind the historic Central Police Station, where walls facing the gallery's distinctive red door are still topped by broken glass, a common security measure. Since it opened in 2000, the clean, white-walled gallery has focused on emerging artists from all over the world, as well as more established names. Owner-curator Katie de Tilly has a particularly keen eye for photography. ⊠*Ground fl., 10 Chancery La., SoHo, Central* ☎*2810–0065* ⊕*www.10chancerylanegallery.com* Ⓜ*Central.*

Yan Gallery. This is the place for Hong Kong–based artist Hu Yongkai's charming, slightly cartoonish depictions of Chinese women in traditional settings (you've almost certainly seen fakes in a Stanley Market stall). The gallery, which isn't as stuffy as some and more commercial than others, also represents Bob Yan, whose extremely popular and colorful dog portraits are commissioned by private clients. ⊠*1st fl., Oriental Crystal Commercial Bldg., 46 Lyndhurst Terr., Central* ☎*2139–2345* ⊕*www.yangallery.com* Ⓜ*Central.*

Zee Stone Gallery. Massive street-level windows display the decorative kind of paintings we've come to expect from Vietnam, Burma, and China—from photorealistic portraits to abstract landscapes. A visit here provides a view into what's popular with casual collectors. ⊠*Ground fl., Yu Yuet Bldg., 43–55 Wyndham St., Central* ☎*2810–5895* ⊕*www. zeestone.com* Ⓜ*Central.*

BEAUTY & COSMETICS

World-class shrines to cosmetics have brought almost every European, American, and Japanese beauty line you can think of—from drugstore makeup to niche skin-care systems—to Hong Kong. For an overview of what's on offer, just visit a department store like Harvey Nichols or Seibu.

At Lane Crawford, customer service—not always Hong Kong's strongest suit—is taken to new levels with a personalized "cosmetic concierge service." Although questionable regulation and typically poor quality make it best to avoid cheap mainland cosmetics, a few local brands do stand out. Discount chains have become so popular, there's at least one in every shopping district. And if all this shopping is tiring you out, retail therapy of another kind is within reach at Hong Kong's pampering spas.

DISCOUNT SHOPS

Lung Shing Dispensary. This small pharmacy and cosmetics shop does not look as fancy as Sa Sa but there's more here than might initially meet the eye, including all sorts of international beauty products, from La Prairie to Korean brands like Laneige, at excellent prices. The Dispensary's wide selection of sample-size products is particularly handy for travelers who've left something behind. ⊠*28 Granville Rd., Tsim Sha Tsui, Kowloon* ☎*2367–9274* Ⓜ*Tsim Sha Tsui.*

Sa Sa Cosmetics. The fuchsia-pink signs that announce Hong Kong's best and largest cosmetic discounter will become familiar sights on any shopping expedition. Look for deals on everything from cheap glittery makeup to sleek designer lines. Fragrances are a particularly good buy; prices are usually even lower than those at airport duty-free shops. ⊠*Shop G01, Hang Lung Centre, 2–20 Paterson St., Causeway Bay* ☎*2577–2286, 2505–5023 customer service and branch info* ⊕*www. sasa.com* Ⓜ*Causeway Bay* ⊠*1st fl., Chung King Express 36–44 Nathan Rd., Tsim Sha Tsui , Kowloon* Ⓜ*Tsim Sha Tsui.*

DRUGSTORES

Mannings. Like Watsons, this chain can be found throughout the city. It sells everything from shampoo and lotions to emery boards and cough medicine (western and Chinese brands). Some stores have pharmacies. ⊠*IFC Mall, 8 Finance St., Central* ☎*2523–8326, 2299–3381 customer service and branch information* Ⓜ*Central.*

Watsons. Spread over city, this chain—the CVS of Hong Kong—sells western medicines and health and beauty products, as well as some traditional Chinese products. Some branches also have pharmacies. ⊠*Festival Walk, 80 Tat Chee Ave., Kowloon Tong, Kowloon* ☎*2608–8383* Ⓜ*Kowloon Tong.*

HONG KONG GOODIES

Eu Yan Sang. The Sheung Wan area is a quaint and pungent place to shop for traditional Chinese herbs and medicines. But this reliable source—in operation since 1879—is a more straightforward option. ⊠*152–156 Queens Rd., Western* ☎*2544–3870, 2544–3308 customer service and branch information* ⊕*www.euyansang.com* ⊠*Ground fl., 18 Russell St., Causeway Bay* ☎*2573–2038* Ⓜ*Causeway Bay* ⊠*Ground fl., 11–15 Chatham Rd. S, Tsim Sha Tsui, Kowloon* Ⓜ*Tsim Sha Tsui.*

Kwong Sang Hong. This shop carries Hong Kong's first local cosmetics line, also known as Two Girls Brand. The colorful, old-fashioned packaging, which is reminiscent of traditional Chinese medicines, is more remarkable than the products. That said, the line's classics—including hair oil, talcum powder, and face cream—do make lovely gifts. ⊠*Causeway Place, Hong*

Kong Mansion, 2–10 Great George St., Causeway Bay ☎2504–1811 ⊕*www.ksh.com.hk* Ⓜ*Causeway Bay.*

Skin Nursery by menthoderm. The unisex skin care line sold here is known for deep-pore cleansing, which tends to be more aggressive in Asia than elsewhere. So what if its natural, concentrated ingredients come from Europe and are blended in a U.S. laboratory? The line's cosmopolitan approach makes it quintessentially Hong Kong. Its spacious Skin Nursery also provides facial and body treatments for women and men. ✉*3rd fl., CNAC Group Bldg., 10 Queen's Rd. Central, Central* ☎2147–3803 ⊕*www.menthoderm.com* Ⓜ*Central.*

INTERNATIONAL LINES

FACES. FACES is a sprawling one-stop shop carrying a long list of high-profile and niche beauty brands. It also hosts regular product launches and special presentations by international beauty experts. ✉*Ocean Terminal, Canton Rd., Tsim Sha Tsui, Kowloon* ☎2118–5622 Ⓜ*Tsim Sha Tsui.*

Pure Beauty by Watsons. Developed by one of Hong Kong's oldest drugstores, this slick, well-lighted store focuses on "masstige" (mass—as in the masses—plus prestige, i.e. obtainable luxuries for the ordinary shmo) cosmetics and skin care. Like ordinary Watsons stores, Pure Beauty also carries health supplements, professional hair-care products, and fragrances. ✉*Basement 2, Times Square, 1 Matheson St., Causeway Bay* ☎2506–1521 Ⓜ*Causeway Bay.*

SPAS

Hong Kong's mix of western and eastern treatments is unrivaled. You can have a quick manicure or an extravagant spa day. With treatments for men and treatment rooms for couples, the boys don't need to feel left out, either. Warning: you'll be spoiled for life.

■TIP➔ Hotel spas stay open until 10 or 11 pm, a few hours later than the stand-alone establishments, so you can leave your day open for shopping.

Acupressure and Massage Centre of the Blind. Looking for a good massage without all the glitz? Visit these skilled and affordable blind masseurs trained in acupressure, reflexology, and Chinese massage. ✉*2nd fl., Tung Ming Bldg., 40–42 Des Voeux Rd., Central* ☎2810–6666 Ⓜ*Central.*

The Feel Good Factor. It's the perfect place to unwind after antiquing on nearby Hollywood Road. During your pedicure or express manicure, you can sit by the window and watch the world go by or you can choose a cozier, more secluded spot. For facials, massages, waxing, and airbrush tanning, you'll be escorted to inner rooms. ✉ *2nd fl., Winsome House, 73 Wyndham St., Central* ☎2530–0610 ⊕*www. feelgoodfactor.com.hk* Ⓜ*Central.*

Four Seasons. Enter via a light-wood and stark white hallway into treatment rooms that ooze modern cool. The two-hour, signature Pure Indulgence treatment uses organic products—it's head-to-toe pampering for your body and your soul. Harbor views and a Japanese garden also help to alter your mood. ✉*8 Finance St., Central* ☎3196–8888 ⊕*www.fourseasons.com* Ⓜ*Central.*

★ **Happy Foot Reflexology Center.** Who knew pressure on your big toe could help clear your sinuses? Reflexology is Hong Kong's cheap way to relax, and Happy Foot is the legendary place to have it done. The armchairs are comfortable, and the therapists are experts, but don't expect a luxe experience. Interiors are basic, and you'll share a room with other customers. ⊠*6th fl., 11th fl., and 13th fl., Jade Centre, 98–102 Wellington St., Central* ☎*2544–1010* Ⓜ*Central* ⊠*19th fl., Century Square, 1–13 D'Aguilar St., Central* Ⓜ*Central* ⊠*1st fl., Elegance Court, 2–4 Tsoi Tak St., Happy Valley.*

Indulgence. Enter at street level via the calm, white, Provençal-style boutique filled with hard-to-find brands for the true beauty addict. Ascend the stairs to check in. You'll be guided farther into the 5,700-square-foot space with rooms for manicures and pedicures, facial and body treatments, and hair styling for men and women. The terrace café has spa cuisine. ⊠*Ground fl., 33 Lyndhurst Terrace, Central* ☎*2815–6600* Ⓜ*Central.*

Fodor'sChoice ★ **The Mandarin Spa & the Oriental Spa.** If you indulge in just one Hong Kong spa treatment, have it at one of these sister spas, located at The Mandarin Oriental and the Landmark Mandarin Oriental hotels. Designed as a journey from the outer into the inner world, the experience begins on the check-in and fitness floor. You're taken up to the next level and offered a welcome tea, then guided deeper into this haven, where treatments are administered by excellent therapists in serene rooms. Try the signature Time Ritual, a holistic combination of therapies adapted to your specific needs on the day. Treatments here get you access to the vitality pool, the amethyst-crystal steam room, the authentic Turkish hammam, and more. Next door to the Mandarin, the legendary **Mandarin Beauty Salon and Barber Shop** (⊠*Mandarin Oriental, 5 Connaught Rd., Central* ☎*2825–4888* Ⓜ*Central*) offers traditional favorites. Ask for a famous Shanghainese pedicure with Samuel and his knives (yes, knives!), or see Betty for eyebrow threading. ⊠*Landmark Mandarin Oriental, 15 Queen's Rd. Central, Central* ☎*2132–0011* ⊕*www.mandarinoriental.com* Ⓜ*Central.*

★ **More Than Skin Urban Spa.** Located in a small building on Gilmann's Bazaar between Sheung Wan and Central, this petite spa creates a feeling of warmth with its unique Victorian design, green wooden furniture, and earth tones. Owner Annie Fung has incorporated craft objects collected on her travels into the decor, like a small waterbuck (an African antelope) modified to become a sink in one of the bathrooms. The spa offers typical treatments, including excellent massage, and is also equipped with a Vichy shower, and an infrared sauna. We recommend the Vichy shower and the Valmont facial. ⊠*1st fl., 8–12 Gilmann's Bazaar, Central* ☎*2815–5590* ⊕*www.morethanskin.hk* Ⓜ*Sheung Wan.*

Paul Gerrard Hair and Beauty. Up the copper-gilt stairwell of this old Chinese building on an old Hong Kong–style stepped street, this sophisticated little spa has got it just right. When respected hair stylist Paul Gerrard took on an extra floor for facial and body treatments he considered every detail—even the wheels on his carts are soundproof. Sink into a massage chair for a manicure or pedicure, and just relax. ⊠*1st fl., Wah Hing House, 35 Pottinger St., Central* ☎*2869–4200* ⊕*www. paulgerrard.com* Ⓜ*Central.*

The Peninsula Spa. Here's another excuse to visit Hong Kong's grande dame hotel—as if you needed one. Even the aromatic hand soaps in the bathrooms soothe the senses at this lavish east-meets-west sanctuary, which has separate facilities for men and women. You'll enjoy Orien-

4

tal, ayurvedic, and other therapies in rooms overlooking the harbor. Consider booking a Peninsula Ceremony, a series of holistic treatments chosen for you by a skilled therapist. ✉ *7th fl., The Peninsula, Salisbury Rd., Tsim Sha Tsui, Kowloon* ☎ *2315–3322* ⊕ *www.peninsula.com* Ⓜ *Tsim Sha Tsui.*

Quality Chinese Medical Centre. Acupuncture looks alarming but is painless. Where better to try it than in China? This reputable center is also a good place to learn more about traditional Chinese medicine and herbal remedies. ✉ *5th fl., Jade Centre, 98 Wellington St., Central* ☎ *2881–8267* ⊕ *www.qualitytcm.com* Ⓜ *Central.*

WAX FIGURES

No one likes to contemplate hair removal, especially the dreaded Brazilian wax, but Hong Kong has some true experts in the field. No-nonsense Betty at the **Mandarin Beauty Salon and Barber Shop** (✉ *Mandarin Oriental, 5 Connaught Rd., Central* Ⓜ *Central*) has hair-removal techniques that are whispered about in the best of circles. The gentle Helena at the hidden **Beautiful Skin Centre** (✉ *Pacific Place, 88 Queensway, Admiralty* ☎ *2877–8911* ⊕ *www.paua.com.hk* Ⓜ *Admiralty*) uses an ultrasoothing coconut wax to get you bare.

CLOTHING

You've come at a good time. Creativity is on the rise, and new designers and shops are cropping up across the territory. There are countless opportunities to visit out-of-the-way ateliers, meet designers, and even commission one-off pieces that will never go out of style. Brands from around the world converge in this shopping mecca. Some lines, especially those from Japan, might be new discoveries. Others are luxury brands you have at home (you'd be hard-pressed to find a brand that isn't distributed here).

Whether you get a better deal on designer labels is debatable. For now, Hong Kong has no sales tax, which certainly makes a difference on big-ticket items. It also means that prices are the best in Asia and generally lower than in North America (though not necessarily than in Europe). Look for good deals on cashmere, custom-made clothing and accessories, and jewelry.

CASHMERE

In the SAR, you can drape yourself in soft, sumptuous cashmere for a lot less than in other cities around the world. Chinese department stores carry basic, square-cut cashmere sweaters for men and women at decent prices. That said, cashmere is sold at every price point, so comparison shopping is a must.

■ TIP➡ **Remember that pure cashmere comes from a Kashmir goat. If the knit includes wool, silk, or any other material, it's a blend. Also inspect weight (a big price determinate), texture, and weave.**

Dorfit. A longtime cashmere manufacturer and retailer, Dorfit caters to a variety of men's, women's, and children's tastes. Knitwear here comes in pure cashmere as well as blends, so be sure to ask which is which.
■ TIP➡ **After visiting the Pedder Building branch of Dorfit be sure to duck into other on-site discount cashmere shops, such as Aptitude Clothing**

International and Fabel. ✉*6th fl., Mary Bldg., 71–77 Peking Rd., Tsim Sha Tsui, Kowloon* ☎*2312–1013* ⊕*www.dorfit.com.hk* Ⓜ*Tsim Sha Tsui* ✉*6th fl., Pedder Bldg., 12 Pedder St., Central* Ⓜ*Central.*

Lung Sang Hong. It's easy to miss this little shop, quite literally set up in a staircase. Although it doesn't sell the cheapest cashmere scarves in town (about HK$1,245–HK$1,400), it has some of the finest, with the quality, diamond weave, and lightness of the fabled "ring pashmina." Men's and women's cashmere knits are also sold here. Ask to go up to the first-floor showroom for more. ✉*Ground fl., 45–47 Stanley Main St., Stanley Market, Stanley, South Side* ☎*2577–6802 or 9323–2360.*

★ **Pearls & Cashmere.** Warehouse prices in chic shopping arcades? It's true. This old Hong Kong favorite is elegantly housed in hotels on both sides of the harbor. In addition to quality men's and women's cashmere sweaters in classic designs and in every color under the sun, they also sell reasonably priced pashminas, gloves, and socks, which make great gifts for men and women. In recent years the brand has developed the more fashion-focused line, BYPAC. ✉*Mezzanine, Peninsula Hotel Shopping Arcade, Salisbury Rd., Tsim Sha Tsui, Kowloon* ☎*2723–8698* Ⓜ*Tsim Sha Tsui* ✉*Mezzanine, Mandarin Oriental, 5 Connaught Rd., Central* Ⓜ*Central* ✉*Ground fl., New World Centre, 18–24 Salisbury Rd., Tsim Sha Tsui, Kowloon* Ⓜ*Tsim Sha Tsui.*

CHILDREN'S CLOTHES

Several malls have dedicated special sections to western-style children's clothing, accessories, and toys, including: Ocean Terminal in Tsim Sha Tsui, Times Square and Windsor House in Causeway Bay, and Prince's Building in Central. The famous labels are here, but they aren't necessarily priced lower than you'd find at home. Stanley Market and similar shopping streets, however, sell recognizable brands at generous discounts.

For Chinese-style kids' clothing, nothing beats the collection by Shanghai Tang, where the luxury and the prices are both high. Look for acceptable, cheaper alternatives in Chinese department stores or markets such as the Lanes on Li Yuen streets East and West.

Bumps to Babes. It has everything you could possibly need for babies and children, all in one place. In addition to familiar brands of clothing, diapers, toiletries, food, and toys, look for strollers, books, maternity wear, furniture, and more. ✉*5th fl., Pedder Bldg., 12 Pedder St., Central* ☎*2522–7112* ⊕*www.bumpstobabes.com* Ⓜ*Central* ✉*21st fl., Horizon Plaza, 2 Lee Wing St., Southside* ✈*Ap Lei Chau.*

★ **Hoi Yuen Emporium Co.** Of all the cheaper alternatives to Shanghai Tang, this is the best. It has a fantastic selection of Mao collared jackets for boys and girls. Chinese-style onesies come in muted, noncartoonish colors, and cost less than HK$80. ✉*Stanley Market, 64 Stanley Main St., Southside, Stanley* ☎*2813–0470.*

Lace Department Store. You might head straight for the embroidered linens, but back up and review the children's clothing by the door. You've seen these beautiful, traditional, hand-smocked cotton dresses and baby overalls in elegant European stores, sold at prices to make you faint. Here expect to pay as little as HK$195 to HK$230. As you tour the city, keep an eye out for embroidered-linens specialists who

The Choice Is Joyce

Local socialites and couture addicts still thank Joyce Ma, the fairy godmother of luxury retail in Hong Kong, for bringing must-have labels to the city. Others may be catching up, but her Joyce boutiques are still ultrachic havens outfitted with a *Vogue*-worthy wish list of designers and beauty brands.

Joyce Beauty. Love finding unique beauty products from around the world? Then this is the place for you, with cult perfumes, luxurious skin solutions, and new discoveries to be made. Bring your credit card—"bargain" isn't in the vocabulary here. ⊠ *Times Square, 1 Matheson St., Causeway Bay* ☎ *2970–2319* Ⓜ *Causeway Bay* ✉ *Ground fl., New World Tower, 16–18 Queen's Rd. Central, Central* Ⓜ *Central* ✉ *The Gateway, 3–27 Canton Rd., Tsim Sha Tsui, Kowloon* Ⓜ *Tsim Sha Tsui* ✉ *Festival Walk, 80 Tat Chee Ave., Kowloon Tong, Kowloon* Ⓜ *Kowloon Tong.*

Joyce Boutique. Not so much a shop as a fashion institution, Joyce Boutique's hushed interior houses the worship-worthy creations of fashion's

greatest gods and goddesses. McCartney, Galliano, Dolce & Gabbana, Prada, Miyake: the stock list is practically a mantra. Joyce sells unique household items, too, so your home can live up to your wardrobe. ⊠ *New World Tower, 16 Queen's Rd., Central* ☎ *2810–1120* ⊕ *www.joyce.com* Ⓜ *Central, Exit G* ✉ *Pacific Place, 88 Queensway, Admiralty* Ⓜ *Admiralty, Exit F* ✉ *Harbour City, Tsim Sha Tsui, Kowloon* Ⓜ *Tsim Sha Tsui, Exit F.*

Joyce Warehouse. Fashionistas who've fallen on hard times can breathe a sigh of relief. Joyce's outlet on Ap Lei Chau, the island offshore from Aberdeen in Southside, stocks last season's duds from the likes of Jil Sander, Armani, Ann Demeulemeester, Costume National, and Missoni. Prices for each garment are reduced by about 10% each month, so the longer the piece stays on the rack, the less it costs. Bus 90B gets you from Exchange Square to Ap Lei Chau in 25 minutes; then hop a taxi for the four-minute taxi ride to Horizon Plaza. ⊠ *21st fl., Horizon Plaza, 2 Lee Wing St., Southside* ☎ *2814–8313* ⊙ *Tues.– Sat. 10-6, Sun. noon-6.*

carry similar dresses. ⊠*6th fl., Pedder Bldg., 12 Pedder St., Central* ☎*2523–8162* Ⓜ*Central.*

Marleen Molenaar Sleepwear. When Hong Kong–based Dutch designer and mother Marleen Molenaar discovered how limited her choices were for children's pajamas and sleepwear, she founded her own label. The gorgeous 100% cotton, high-quality classic European collections are sold around the world and through her showroom, by appointment. ⊠*10th fl., Winner Bldg., 27–39 D'Aguilar St., Central* ☎*2525–9872 or 9162–0350* ⊕*www.marleenmolenaar.com* Ⓜ*Central.*

HONG KONG COUTURE

Hong Kong has a surprising number of talented designers. Although labels like Shanghai Tang and Blanc de Chine have achieved worldwide attention, others are still in the exciting chrysalis stage—which means you can still say you knew them when.

Azalea by i'sis. A fantastic place for hip yet understated dresses and separates that will have everyone asking, "Ooh, where'd you get that?" At first glance, this looks like all the other trendy little boutiques in Causeway Bay, but everything here is just that much better made—and better looking—with a fit that accounts for curves. You can find the same items at select U.S. boutiques, but prices may be twice what they are here. ⊠ *Ground fl., Po Foo Bldg., 3–5 Foo Ming St., Causeway Bay* ☎ *2808–4183* Ⓜ *Causeway Bay.*

Barney Cheng. One of Hong Kong's best-known, locally based designers, Barney Cheng creates haute couture designs and prêt-à-porter collections, infusing his glam, often sequined, pieces with wit. When the Kennedy Center in Washington, D.C., hosted an exhibition titled "The New China Chic," Cheng was invited to display his works alongside those by the likes of Vera Wang and Anna Sui. ⊠ *12th fl., World Wide Commercial Bldg., 34 Wyndham St., Central* ☎ *2530–2829* ⊕ *www. barneycheng.com* Ⓜ *Central.*

DaDa. This boutique, popular with local hipsters, is owned and "curated" by a woman known as Celia, who's a stylist for stars such as local singer and actress Kelly Chen. She's handpicked each piece of this international clothing collection, so the chances of selecting a wrong outfit here are minimal. ⊠ *2nd fl., Silvercord, 30 Canton Rd., Tsim Sha Tsui, Kowloon* ☎ *3105–2225* Ⓜ *Tsim Sha Tsui.*

Episode. Locally owned and designed Episode collections focus on accessories and suiting and other elegant clothing for working women and ladies who lunch. Look also for the younger Jessica, the trendy Colour, and the casual Weekend Workshop and Oxygen collections. Though distinct, each collection pays close attention to current trends in the fashion world. ⊠ *Basement fl., Entertainment Bldg., 30 Queen's Rd., Central* ☎ *2943–2115 customer service* ⊕ *www.toppy.com.hk* Ⓜ *Central* ⊠ *Gateway Arcade, Harbour City, Canton Rd., Tsim Sha Tsui, Kowloon* Ⓜ *Tsim Sha Tsui.*

Initial. This brand makes simple but unique women's wear in comfy earth tones. The store's design matches the back-to-basics feeling of the collection, making it a pleasant place to shop. ⊠ *Ground fl., China Insurance Bldg, 48 Cameron Rd., Tsim Sha Tsui, Kowloon* ☎ *3402–4499* ⊕ *www.initialfashion.com* Ⓜ *Tsim Sha Tsui* ⊠ *Ground fl., Style House, 310 Gloucester Rd. Causeway Bay* Ⓜ *Causeway Bay.*

Lu Lu Cheung. A fixture on the Hong Kong fashion scene for more than a decade, Lu Lu Cheung's designs ooze comfort and warmth. In both daytime and evening wear, natural fabrics and forms are represented in practical yet imaginative ways. ⊠ *The Landmark, Central* ☎ *2537–7515* ⊕ *www.lulucheung.com.hk* Ⓜ *Central* ⊠ *New Town Plaza, Shatin Centre St., New Territories, Shatin* Ⓜ *Shatin.*

Boutique Alert: Hip

For years, fashion cognoscenti and victims alike have relied on **D-mop** (⊕ www.d-mop.com for info and locations) to bring out new generation talent, whatever the cost. **Ztampz** (⊕ www.ztampz.com for info and locations) mixes cartoonish and avant-garde fashion from all over, including up-and-coming designers from Thailand and Japan. Limited-edition T-shirts printed with slick simians are what cult Japanese brand **A Bath-** ing Ape (⊕ www.bape.com for info and locations) built their empire on. True devotees call it "Bape." **Sistyr Moon** (⊠ Lee Garden Two, 33 Hysan Ave., Causeway Bay Ⓜ Causeway Bay ⊕ www.sistyrmoon.com) shops, including Soul Sistyr and Hysteric Glamour, offer a distinct blend of cute, sexy, rock-chick fashion from Brazil to Australia. When their cool customers become mothers, they can dress the kids at Hysteric Mini.

Moussy. This midrange Japanese brand arrived in town in 2006. The tight-fitting tees and vintage-wash jeans are a big hit among young local women who are going for the rock-star look. ⊠ 3rd fl., Ocean Terminal, 5 Canton Rd., Tsim Sha Tsui, Kowloon ☎ 2736–8261 Ⓜ Tsim Sha Tsui.

Olivia Couture. The surroundings are functional, but the gowns, wedding dresses, and cheongsams by local designer Olivia Yip are lavish. With a growing clientele, including socialites looking to stand out, Yip is quietly making a name for herself and her Parisian-influenced pieces. ⊠ Ground fl., Bartlock Centre, 3 Yiu Wah St., Causeway Bay ☎ 2838–6636 ⊕ www.oliviacouture.com Ⓜ Causeway Bay.

Pocket Venus. Hong Kong–based English designer Jane Troughton creates spirited, youthful women's wear with a vintage touch—think exclusive prints and beautiful beading. This charming, by-appointment-only atelier provides the opportunity to not only view the latest collections, seen on countless London celebrities, but also to meet the friendly designer. Her fashions are also sold at Seibu department store, but a trip there is far less entertaining. Following her marriage in a dress of own her own design, Troughton launched a bespoke wedding-gown service. ⊠ Ground fl., Koon Nam House, 14 Shing Wong St., SoHo, Central ☎ 2548–8086 ⊕ www.pocket-venus.net Ⓜ Central.

Ranee K. Designer Ranee Kok Chui-Wah's showrooms are scarlet dens cluttered with her one-off dresses and eclectic women's wear that bring new meanings to "when East meets West." Known for her quirky cheongsams and dresses, she has also collaborated with brands such as Furla and Shanghai Tang. Special clients and local celebrities enjoy her custom tailoring, too. ⊠ Ground fl., 16 Gough St., Central ☎ 2108–4068 ⊕ www.raneek.com Ⓜ Central.

Sabina Swims. A few minutes' walk from Central, Sabina Swims is in a quaint old building, formerly an art gallery. One of the pioneers in the now burgeoning NoHo area, Hong Kong girl Sabina Wong Sutc first opened the boutique as a showroom for her pretty bikinis. Other unique swimwear, accessories, and resort-wear brands have since chosen the airy yet discreet space to show their wares. The Sabina Swims collection is cleverly sold as separates because the designer knows that women aren't always the same size on top and on the bottom. There are also matching swimsuits for mother-and-daughter outings and reversible sun hats in the same materials. ⊠*1st fl., 99F Wellington St., NoHo, Central* ☎*2115–9975* ⊕*www.sabinaswims.com.*

Fodor's Choice
★ **Shanghai Tang.** In addition to the brilliantly hued—and expensive—displays of silk and cashmere clothing, you'll find custom-made suits starting at around HK$5,000, including fabric from a large selection of Chinese silks. You can also have a cheongsam (a sexy slit-skirt silk dress with a Mandarin collar) made for HK$2,500–HK$3,500, including fabric (⇨*also Tailoring, below*). Ready-to-wear Mandarin suits and unisex kimonos are all in the HK$1,500–HK$2,000 range. Among the Chinese souvenirs are novelty watches with mah-jongg tiles or dim sum instead of numbers. There's a second location inside the Peninsula Hong Kong. ⊠*12 Pedder St., Central* ☎*2525–7333* ⊕*www.shanghaitang. com* Ⓜ*Central* ⊠*Peninsula Hong Kong, Salisbury Rd., Tsim Sha Tsui, Kowloon* Ⓜ*Tsim Sha Tsui.*

Siberian Fur Store Ltd. In general, furs sold by reputable Hong Kong dealers are the ideal combination of superior quality and low prices. This shop, owned and operated by a prominent local family, is famous for its high-quality furs and special attention to design. ⊠*Ground fl., 29 Des Voeux Rd. Central, Central* ☎*2522–1380* Ⓜ*Central* ⊠*Ground fl., 21 Chatham Rd. S, Tsim Sha Tsui, Kowloon* Ⓜ*Tsim Sha Tsui.*

★ **Sin Sin Atelier.** Sin Sin represents the best of Hong Kong design. Her conceptual, minimalist clothes, jewelry, and accessories retain a Hong Kong character, while drawing from other influences—especially Japanese. Yet the pieces are ultimately a unique expression of her ebullient spirit. A regular performer in Hong Kong community theater, Sin Sin prefers to introduce her collections via unusual presentations such as modern dance performances rather than catwalk shows. She also has an art space directly across the road and a fine art gallery up the hill in SoHo. ⊠*Ground fl., 52 Sai St., off Hollywood Rd. at Cat St. end, Western* ☎*2521–0308* ⊕*www.sinsin.com.hk.*

Sonjia by Sonjia Norman. Walk past a local garage and snoozing dogs in this old-style Hong Kong area to find the low-key atelier of Korean-English ex-lawyer Sonjia Norman. The designer, known for her active-wear brand, Chibi, has quietly crafted luxurious, one-of-a-kind pieces and modified vintage clothing for years under the Sonjia label. Her clothes are the epitome of understated stealth wealth. A new adjacent store houses Norman's home and living collection, including tableware, linens, and all sorts of pillows and cushions. ⊠*Ground fl., 1A–2 Sun St., Wan Chai* ☎*2529–6223* ⊕*www.sonjiaonline.com* Ⓜ*Wan Chai.*

Spy Henry Lau. Local bad boy Henry Lau brings an edgy attitude to his fashion for men and women. Bold and often dark, his clothing and accessories lines are not for the fainthearted. ⊠*1st fl., Cleveland Mansion, 5 Cleveland St., Causeway Bay* ☎*2317–6928* ⊕*www.spyhenrylau. com* Ⓜ*Causeway Bay* ⊠*Shop C, ground fl., 11 Sharp St., Causeway Bay* Ⓜ*Causeway Bay.*

Vivienne Tam. You know it when you walk into a Vivienne Tam boutique—the strong Chinese-motif prints and modern updates of traditional women's clothing are truly distinct. Don't let the bold,

CAUSEWAY BAY

From local celebrities to mall rats, shoppers flowing through the streets of Causeway Bay are from all walks of life, but they're united by a common mission: to drop some cash on the three Rs (retail, restaurants, and recreation).

If Hong Kong is the gateway to China, then Causeway Bay is the shortcut to her cash-filled wallet. Retail skyscrapers tower over micromalls and scruffy low-rises bursting with independent boutiques and restaurants. High-end flagships occupy the malls of Hysan Avenue, often called Hong Kong's Rodeo Drive. Times Square is a 16-floor midrange mall and includes the sleek, western-style Lane Crawford department store. Japanese department store Sogo carries many big brands, and Fashion Island is the place to go for lines like Armani Exchange and DKNY.

The adjacent streets are lined with painfully hip concept malls such as LCX and Delay No Mall, and midrange boutiques such as Ztampz and Pink Martini. And if all this label talk is hurting your wallet, head to the stalls at Jardine's Crescent for budget fashion.

BEST TIME TO GO

Opening times vary but noon is the most common. Shoppers are still going strong at 10 PM on weekdays and till 11 PM on weekends. Sale seasons run from December to February and July to September.

BEST SOUVENIR

Milan Station is the city's largest, most discerning chain for pre-owned designer handbags. Look for the world's most coveted handbag, the Hermès Birkin, which occasionally shows up on the shelves for close to the original price (thousands of U.S. dollars) but without the waiting list.

Hipster magnet **D-mop** showcases items from the hottest international alternative fashion lines.

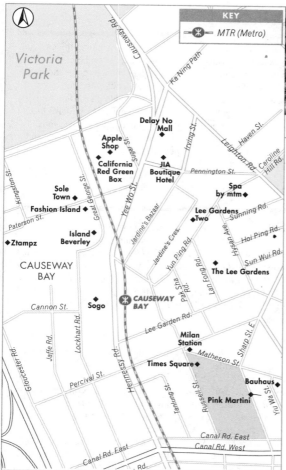

WHAT YOU'LL WANT

HIGH-END HEAVEN

Lee Gardens & Lee Gardens Two. Lee Gardens houses classic blueblood labels including Hermès, Chanel, and Christian Dior, while Lee Gardens Two features funkier brands such as Miu Miu, Joseph, and Agnès b.

ROCK-STAR STYLE

Bauhaus. For the best rock-star duds in town, this multistory fashion gallery is a favorite of former Jane's Addiction front man Perry Farrell.

Pink Martini. This tiny boudoir gets more ink in fashion magazines than its size would dictate, thanks to its affordable tea dresses, shoes, and vintage jewelry.

Sole Town. Imagine a gigantic space-age sweet shop, but replace the candy with colorful shoes and bags for every occasion.

BARGAINS

Aroma Natural Skin Care. Housed in mazelike minimall **Island Beverly**, this tiny store sells cult skin-care products at low direct-import prices.

REJUVENATING

Spa by mtm, a Japanese spa, is a sanctuary, where products are custom-blended on-site. The aesthetic is as important as the physical treatments, and each room has a specific identity. Follow a shiatsu massage in the "wisdom" room with a pensive soak in a Japanese-style bamboo sake bath. The "energy" room features a psychedelic starry sky on the ceiling.

Let off some steam with a couple of drinks and a blowout sing-along in your own private karaoke room. As a home-away-from-home for Japanese nationals, Causeway Bay is also the spiritual center of karaoke in Hong Kong. **California Red Green Box** is among the most popular places to belt out a tune.

Boutique Alert: Jeans

A crop of fun boutiques, many with several locations, capitalizes on the world's fascination with high-end denim and contemporary clothing. **Bauhaus** (⊕ www.bauhaus.com.hk for info and locations) sheds light on local youth fashion with an especially strong selection of jeans from around the world. **Indigo** (⊕ www. indigohongkong.com for info and locations) was one of the first shops to introduce a denim bar, with "Jeanuine Experts" to help you find the best fit. They have a good range of sizes, too. Hong Kong's younger generations create their looks with contemporary-casual and denim pieces from the immensely popular **I.T** (⊕ www.ithk. com for info and locations) shops, which include I.T, i.t, izzue, b+ab, and double-park.

ready-to-wear collections distract you from the very pretty accessories, which include footwear with Asian embellishments such as jade. Tam is one of the best-known Hong Kong designers and, even though she's now based outside the SAR, the city still claims her as its own. ⊠ *Pacific Place, 88 Queensway, Admiralty* ☎ *2918–0238* ⊕ *www.viviennetam. com* Ⓜ *Admiralty* ⊠ *Harbour City, Canton Rd., Tsim Sha Tsui, Kowloon* Ⓜ *Tsim Sha Tsui* ⊠ *Festival Walk, 80 Tat Chee Ave., Kowloon Tong, Kowloon* Ⓜ *Central.*

HONG KONG CASUAL

Bossini. A Giordano competitor, Bossini takes a very similar approach to casual clothing, with collections for women, men, and children. Its brand philosophy, "Color Our World," is an indication of the variety on offer. ⊠ *6–12A Sai Yeung Choi St., Mong Kok, Kowloon* ☎ *2710–8466* ⊕ *www.bossini.com* Ⓜ *Mong Kok* ⊠ *Ground fl., On Lok Yuen Bldg., 27A Des Voeux Rd., Central* Ⓜ *Central* ⊠ *Cityplaza, 18 Tai Koo Shing Rd., Tai Koo* Ⓜ *Tai Koo.*

F.C.K. (Fashion Community Kitterick). One of the trendiest local chains sells several brands including Kitterick, Z by Kitterick, indu homme, K-2, a.y.k, and the Lab. These are clothes that Hong Kong's brand-conscious youth is happy to wear. ⊠ *1st fl., Hong Kong Pacific Centre, 28 Hankow Rd., Tsim Sha Tsui, Kowloon* ☎ *2721–0836* ⊕ *www.kitterick. com.hk* Ⓜ *Tsim Sha Tsui.*

G2000. This inexpensive chain carries men's and women's business wear in Asian sizes. It's a great place to look for suits with matching shirts (and ties) for a good price, and it's an especially good find for anyone petit. G2000 also has a few diffusion lines, including G2000 Pink for a city-chic look, a casual line called **G2 Blu,** and **G2 Black Label,** an urban-wear collection. ⊠ *Ground fl., Lin Fook House, Jardine Crescent, Causeway Bay* ☎ *2527–8604* ⊕ *www.g2000.com.hk/region/hk* Ⓜ *Causeway Bay* ⊠ *88 Nathan Rd., Tsim Sha Tsui, Kowloon* Ⓜ *Tsim Sha Tsui.*

Giordano. Hong Kong's version of the Gap is the most established and ubiquitous local source of basic T-shirts, jeans, and casual wear. Like its U.S. counterpart, the brand now has a bit more fashion sense and slick ad campaigns, but still offers reasonable prices. A few of its hundreds of stores are listed here, but you'll have no problem finding one on almost every major street. A new line, **Giordano Concepts,** offers more stylish (and pricier) urban wear in neutral colors like black, gray, and white. Customer service is generally good, even if the young, energetic staff screeches "hello" then "bye-bye" at every customer in a particularly jarring way. ⊠ *Ground fl., Capitol Centre, 5–19 Jardine's Crescent, Causeway Bay* ☎*2923–7110* ⊕*www.giordano.com.hk* Ⓜ*Causeway Bay* ⊠*Ground fl., Yu To Sang Bldg., 37 Queen's Rd., Central* Ⓜ*Central* ⊠*Ground fl., 74–76 Nathan Rd., Tsim Sha Tsui, Kowloon* Ⓜ*Tsim Sha Tsui.*

Giordano Ladies. If Giordano is the Gap, Giordano Ladies is the Banana Republic, albeit with a more Zen approach. It's clean-line modern classics in neutral black, gray, white, and beige; each collection is brightened by a single highlight color, red one season, blue the next, and so on. Everything is elegant enough for the office and comfortable enough for the plane. ⊠ *1st fl., Capitol Centre, 5–19 Jardine's Crescent, Causeway Bay* ☎*2923–7118* ⊕*www.giordanoladies.com* Ⓜ*Causeway Bay* ⊠*Man Yee Bldg., 60–68 Des Voeux Rd., Central* Ⓜ*Central* ⊠*1st fl., Manson House, 74–78 Nathan Rd., Tsim Sha Tsui, Kowloon* Ⓜ*Tsim Sha Tsui.*

Uniqlo. If you are a Giordano or Bossini fan, don't miss this Japanese chain, which opened its first U.S. branch in New York in 2006. Uniqlo carries a wide variety of inexpensive, fashionable casual wear for women, men, and children. New locations have been opening rapidly throughout the city since 2007. Popular items include T-shirts, jeans, and pajamas. ⊠*2nd fl., LeeTheatre Plaza, 99 Percival St., Causeway Bay* ☎*2577–5811* ⊕*www.uniqlo.com.hk* Ⓜ*Causeway Bay* ⊠*2nd fl., Miramar Shopping Centre, 132 Nathan Rd., Tsim Sha Tsui, Kowloon* Ⓜ*Tsim Sha Tsui.*

CRAFTS & CURIOS

China's traditional crafts include lanterns, temple rubbings, screen paintings, paper cuttings (still sold in most stationery shops), bamboo-stemmed brushes and calligraphy accoutrements, and engravings on stone. Although finding them all in one place seems like cheating, Chinese department stores make it easy with entire departments dedicated to Chinese crafts.

Upper Lascar Row, better known as Cat Street, comes at the western end of Hollywood Road, just below Man Mo Temple. Colorful stalls outside small antiques shops sell reproduction ceramics, giant paintbrushes, Communist little red books, and various other old (or old-looking) curios.

Custom-made chops, or carved Chinese seals, have been ordered on Ma Wa Lane in Sheung Wan since the 1920s. The experts here will give you a Chinese name (be warned, they sometimes have fun with this), and carve it onto your choice of soapstone, ivory, stone, jade, etc., in as little as one hour, giving you time to wander past this interesting area's herbal, snake, and birds' nest shops. These stalls will also print name cards with a bit more lead time (one to seven days).

Good Laque. These elegant lacquerwares make wonderful gifts. The reasonably priced decorative home accessories, tabletop items, and photo albums come in classic red, black, and metallic colors as well as silver or gold. ⊠ *Ground fl., Stanley Market, 40–42D Stanley Main St., Southside, Stanley* ☎ *2899–0632* ⊕ *www.goodlaque.com* ⊠ *16th fl., Horizon Plaza, 2 Lee Wing St., Southside* ⊹ *Ap Lei Chau.*

★ **Mountain Folkcraft.** A little old-fashioned bell chimes as you open the door to this fantastic old shop filled with handicrafts and antiques from around China. Amid the old treasures, carved woodwork, rugs, and curios, are stunning folk-print fabrics. To reach the store from Queen's Road Central, walk up D'Aguilar Street toward Lan Kwai Fong, then turn right onto Wo On Lane. ⊠ *Ground fl., 12 Wo On La., Central* ☎ *2525–3199* Ⓜ *Central.*

The Pottery Workshop. The small gallery in the entrance of this workshop—which holds pottery classes and shows—sells works by local artists, many of whom are also instructors here. Enter on Wyndham Street or through a door inside the Fringe Club. ⊠ *Ground fl., 2 Lower Albert Rd., Central* ☎ *2525–7949* ⊕ *http://ceramics.com.hk* Ⓜ *Central.*

Sang Woo Loong. At more than 90 years old, Mr. Leung Yau Kam is Hong Kong's oldest lantern maker and he has refused to move his workshop across the border like all the others. These intricate, handmade works in paper take fantastical forms such as bright-orange goldfish. Their role has changed over his long career from functional to purely decorative, but lanterns are still important in Chinese society. This is especially true during the Mid-Autumn Festival, when children carry their special lanterns outdoors to view the full moon. Ask for one that can pack flat. ⊠ *Ground fl., 28 Western St., Sai Ying Pun, Western* ☎ *2540–1369.*

Tittot. Glass works here are made using the laborious lost-wax casting technique, used by artists for centuries to create a bronze replica of an original wax or clay sculpture. The collection includes tableware, paperweights and decorative pieces, glass Buddhas, and jewelry. ⊠ *Harbour City, 5 Canton Rd., Tsim Sha Tsui, Kowloon* ☎ *2175–5992* ⊕ *www. tittot.com* Ⓜ *Tsim Sha Tsui.*

GIZMOS, GADGETS & ACCESSORIES

Variety and novelty—not prices—are the reasons to buy electronic goods and accessories in Hong Kong these days. Products are often launched in this keen, active electronics market before they are in the United States and Europe. The street sweepers may wear old-fashioned rattan Hakka hats, but even they carry cutting-edge, almost impossibly tiny phones. Indeed, cell phones are status symbols—often they're changed seasonally, like fashion accessories.

Broadway. Like its more famous competitor, Fortress, Broadway is a large electronic-goods chain. It caters primarily to the local market, so some staff members speak better English than others. Look for familiar-name-brand cameras, computers, sound systems, home appliances, and mobile phones. Just a few of the many shops are listed here. ⊠ *7th fl., Times Square, 1 Matheson St., Causeway Bay* ☎ *2506–0228* ⊕ *www. ibroadway.com.hk* Ⓜ *Causeway Bay* ⊠ *3rd fl., Ocean Centre, Harbour City, Canton Rd., Tsim Sha Tsui, Kowloon* Ⓜ *Tsim Sha Tsui* ⊠ *Ground* *fl., 78 Sai Yeung Choi St. S, Mong Kok, Kowloon* Ⓜ *Mong Kok.*

★ **Fortress.** Part of billionaire Li Ka-shing's empire, this extensive chain of shops sells electronics with warranties—a safety precaution that draws the crowds. It also has good deals on printers and accessories, although selection varies by shop.

You can spot a Fortress by looking for the big orange sign. For the full list of shops, visit the Web site. ✉ *Times Square, 7th fl., 1 Matheson St., Causeway Bay* ☎ *2506–0031* ⊕ *www.fortress.com.hk* Ⓜ *Causeway Bay* ✉ *3rd fl., Ocean Centre, Harbour City, Canton Rd., Tsim Sha Tsui, Kowloon* Ⓜ *Tsim Sha Tsui* ✉ *Chung Kiu Commercial Bldg., 47–51 Shan Tung St., Mong Kok, Kowloon* Ⓜ *Mong Kok* ✉ *Lower ground fl., Melbourne Plaza, 33 Queen's Rd. Central, Central* Ⓜ *Central.*

CAMERAS

Many of Hong Kong's thousands of camera shops are clustered in the back streets around Nathan Road in Tsim Sha Tsui, and around Stanley Street in Central. (Just remember to follow the guidelines in the "Shop Smart" box, particularly in Tsim Sha Tsui.) There are also secondhand sellers in the market on Ap Liu Street (take the MTR to Sham Shui Po, and exit at Ap Liu Street) and the warren of little shops in Champagne Court (16 Kimberley Road, Tsim Sha Tsui). True aficionados will be able to sort the vintage Hasselblads from the junk.

Delon Photo & Hi-Fi Centre. Longtime residents ask for popular salesman Elmen Sit when they come to Delon. He'll take you through the range carried here. Sit also demystifies various bits of equipment for novices—he'll even tell you what you *don't* need. Prices are good, but not amazingly cheap. ✉ *Ocean Centre, Harbour City, Canton Rd., Tsim Sha Tsui, Kowloon* ☎ *2730–0214* Ⓜ *Tsim Sha Tsui.*

Digitalrev Ltd. This simply designed showroom has a good selection of digital cameras, from amateur to professional, on display. Shoppers are free to take their time, trying cameras and asking technicians questions, before making a decision. Camera accessories are also available here. ✉ *2nd fl., Star House, 3 Salisbury Rd. Tsim Sha Tsui, Kowloon* ☎ *2375–1303* Ⓜ *Tsim Sha Tsui.*

Photo Scientific Appliances. This is where local photographers come for their equipment. Expect good prices on both new and used cameras, lenses, video cameras, and accessories. While you're here, pump the regular customers for insider tips. ✉ *Ground fl., 6 Stanley St., Central* ☎ *2522–1903* Ⓜ *Central.*

William's Photo Supply. For those who prefer to shop in air-conditioned comfort, this reliable dealer is discreetly positioned on an upper floor of the elegant Prince's Building. The selection here caters to both amateur and professional photographers. ✉ *341 Prince's Bldg., 10 Chater Rd., Central* ☎ *2522–8437* Ⓜ *Central.*

Shop Smart

Do some research beforehand and know what you want. Then ask lots of questions and compare prices before making a purchase. Stick to shops listed in the HKTB's free *Guide to Quality Shops*. Featured shops usually have the QTS logo on their door or window. Here are a few other considerations:

■ **Be aware of regional differences.** Although technology is moving toward multisystem capabilities, it's not quite there yet. DVDs and players might work in only a specific region. Some recording equipment still works on only NTSC (United States), PAL (Hong Kong, Australia, Great Britain, most of continental Europe), or SECAM (France, Russia). Whenever possible, ask for "region-free." Also, although most electronics now automatically convert between 110 and 220 volts, it's best to ask before you buy.

■ **Check the paperwork.** Reputable dealers should give you a one-year *worldwide* guarantee; however, not all guarantees and warranties cross borders. Make sure you'll have the customer service and assistance you require when you take it back home. Some of the cheapest electronics in Hong Kong are parallel imports, which

rarely have international warranties. Also, make sure the instructions are in English.

■ **Never be rushed.** Don't be afraid to walk away, even if a clerk claims an item is the last one in stock. This will give you more bargaining power, as will buying several items at once.

■ **Be wary of "great" deals.** A common ploy is to lure customers in with the promise of a great deal, only to "discover" that item is suddenly out of stock. When you're offered a more expensive alternative, walk away.

■ **Test the equipment.** Be sure that the picture or sound quality is truly good. If a shopkeeper cannot oblige a test-run request, ask him or her to direct you to the manufacturer's showroom.

■ **Watch for hidden fees.** Paying by credit card may increase the final bill by 3% to 5%, even though most card companies prohibit the practice.

■ **Don't fall for the old bait and switch.** Before you leave the store, double-check that you've been given the model you selected and that everything it comes with is there, including all parts, accessories, the warranty card, and your invoice.

CDS, DVDS & VCDS

If you'd like to stock up on Hong Kong and Asian movies, from the Kung Fu classics of the Shaw Brothers to the latest art-house works from mainland China, then you've come to the right place. Love Canto-Pop and Mando-Pop music? It's here in abundance. If you're hoping to find prices slashed, though, you'll be disappointed.

Small stores in Sham Shui Po, Mong Kok, and Causeway Bay seem promising and cheap, but rarely offer prices much lower than the established shops listed below. They're also known to carry poor quality, pirated copies that look and sound like they were captured by a novice with the family video camera.

Be aware of regional designations for DVDs and players. The United States and Canada are Region 1; the United Kingdom is Region 2. Newer players might be region-free or multiregion, but double-check before you buy. VCDs don't have the picture quality or added features of DVDs, but they're usually region-free and significantly cheaper (about HK$15–HK$45). Just be sure the foreign-language movies have subtitles in English.

CD Warehouse. Though not quite warehouse level, prices here are low enough to compete with the cheap outlets around Causeway Bay and Sham Shiu Po, especially for DVDs and VCDs of the latest movies and TV shows. Music CDs also cost less than at major retailers in Hong Kong, but are not cheaper than in the United States. The catalog includes releases from around Asia and abroad. ✉ *Basement 2, Times Square, 1 Matheson St., Causeway Bay* ☎ *2506–0621* Ⓜ *Causeway Bay* ✉ *New Town Plaza, Shatin Centre St., New Territories, Shatin* Ⓜ *Shatin.*

HMV. This U.K.-based chain has a wide selection of local and international music covering everything from rap to classical and Canto-Pop to Japanese music. A huge selection of DVDs and VCDs are here as well, ranging from U.S. and international movies and television shows to local movies. VCDs are a lot cheaper than DVDs. International magazines are sold here at the best prices in town, but they still cost a lot more than in their countries of origin. For more locations, check the Web site. ✉ *Ground fl. and 1st fl., HK Pacific Centre, 28 Hankow Rd., Tsim Sha Tsui, Kowloon* ☎ *2302–0122* ⊕ *www.hmv.com.hk* Ⓜ *Tsim Sha Tsui* ✉ *1st fl., Central Bldg., 1–3 Pedder St., Central* Ⓜ *Central.*

Hong Kong Records. Although this company from way back hasn't updated its look in years, you'll find a good selection of current local and international CDs and DVDs. The lower profile also means prices are sometimes lower than in flashier retailers. ✉ *Gateway Arcade, Harbour City, 3 Canton Rd., Tsim Sha Tsui, Kowloon* ☎ *2175–5700* Ⓜ *Tsim Sha Tsui* ✉ *Festival Walk, 80 Tat Chee Ave., Kowloon Tong, Kowloon* Ⓜ *Kowloon Tong.*

COMPUTERS

Several malls specialize in computers and peripherals. Each mall contains hundreds of shops, ranging from small local enterprises to branches of international brands. Legitimate products sit beside blatant fakes, and the individual shops rarely give out retail phone numbers. The real computer bargains are the generic brands from Asia.

Computer games, which are immensely popular here, average HK$195 to HK$230, and the variety is wide due to the selection of Sony Playstation and Dreamcast imports from Japan. Not all games, however, are compatible with U.S. systems.

■ TIP→ **Because they couldn't possibly keep the stock in these miniscule spaces, staffers usually have to fetch the product once you've confirmed interest. They'll ask you to pay beforehand, but don't hand over any money until you've inspected the product.**

DG Lifestyle Store. An appointed Apple Center, DG carries Macintosh and iPod products. High-design gadgets, accessories, and software by other brands are add-ons that meld with the sleek Apple design philosophy. ✉*Times Square, 1 Matheson St., Causeway Bay* ☎*2506–1338* ⊕*www. dg-lifestyle.com* Ⓜ*Causeway Bay* ✉*IFC Mall, 8 Finance St., Central* Ⓜ*Central* ✉*Mega Box, Kowloon Bay, Kowloon* Ⓜ*Kowloon Bay.*

Golden Computer Arcade. It's the most famous—some would say infamous—computer arcade in town. Know what you want before you go to avoid being dazed by the volume of computer equipment and software. ✉*146–152 Fuk Wa St., Sham Shui Po, Kowloon* ☎*2729–7399* ⊕*www.goldenarcade.org* Ⓜ*Sham Shui Po.*

Star Computer City. Right next to the Star Ferry and the Harbour City megamall complex, Star Computer City has one whole floor dedicated to computers. The 2C Software Collection offers a variety of software. Look carefully, and you'll find bargains. ✉*2nd fl., Star House, Salisbury Rd., Tsim Sha Tsui, Kowloon* ☎*2730–4382* Ⓜ*Tsim Sha Tsui.*

★ **Wanchai Computer Centre.** You'll find honest-to-goodness bargains on computer goods and accessories in the labyrinth of shops here. And you can negotiate prices. Your computer can be put together by a computer technician in less than a day if you're rushed; otherwise, two days is normal. The starting price is HK$5,000 depending on the hardware, processor, and peripherals you choose. This is a great resource, whether you're a techno-buff who's interested in assembling your own computer (a popular pastime with locals), or a technophobe looking for discounted earphones. ✉*130 Hennessy Rd., Wan Chai* ☎*No phone* Ⓜ*Wan Chai.*

HOME FURNISHINGS

ASIAN-LIFESTYLE STORES

Over the last decade, Hong Kongers have woken up to the joys of home decor, and they're doing it with pieces inspired by and produced in Asia. Enlightened lifestyle retailers range from cheeky to aloof, affordable to exorbitant—but all have a modern Asian approach.

Franc Franc. This home and living store is sort of like a higher-end IKEA, with everything you'd need to equip your downtown apartment, from bookshelves to bubble bath. The funky designs and intriguing gadgets will keep both male and female shoppers entertained, and it's quite a feat to leave the store with empty hands. ✉*2nd fl., Hang Lung Centre, 2–20 Paterson St., Causeway Bay* ☎*3427–3366* ⊕*www.francfranc. com* Ⓜ*Causeway Bay.*

G.O.D. This lifestyle pioneer plays with ideas, designs, and words with wonderfully imaginative yet functional results. Its huge product range consists mostly of home furnishings and tableware, though there are some fashion items. Affordable creations, such as red rubber trays for making "double happiness" character ice cubes, Buddha statues irreverently painted in Day-Glo tones, and old-fashioned Chinese textiles reimagined in modern settings, are both nostalgic and contemporary. ✉*Ground fl. and 1st fl., Leighton Centre, 77 Leighton Rd., entrance on Sharp St. E, Causeway Bay* ☎*2890–5555* ⊕*www.god.com.hk* Ⓜ*Causeway Bay* ✉*Ground fl. and 1st fl., 48 Hollywood Rd., Central* Ⓜ*Central* ✉*Basement fl., Silvercord, 30 Canton Rd., Tsim Sha Tsui, Kowloon* Ⓜ*Tsim Sha Tsui.*

Inside. Inside takes Asian concepts and motifs and transforms them into its own fresh, contemporary home accessories, soft furnishings, table linens, gifts, and select clothing for adults and children. Made from natural materials and fibers, the products come in signature white and sun-bleached tones with a few well-placed highlights and discreet flashes of sparkle. There's a nice balance of luxury and casual items, with prices to match. ⊠*Prince's Bldg., 10 Chater Rd., Central* ☎*2537–6298* ⊕*www.inside.com.hk* Ⓜ*Central* ⊠*The Repulse Bay, 109 Repulse Bay Rd., South Side* ⊠*Horizon Plaza, 2 Lee Wing St., South Side* ⊕*Ap Lei Chau.*

Kou. Socialite and interior designer Louise Kou's lifestyle boutique is a moody mix of dark jewel tones and silver on two floors connected by an internal staircase. Different rooms allow her to showcase chinaware, silverware, lamps, linens, fashion accessories, clothes, lingerie, and unique household items. When Kou can't find what she desires somewhere in the world, she simply has it custom-made. ⊠*22nd fl., Fung House, 19–20 Connaught Rd., Central* ☎*2530–2234* ⊕*www. kouconcept.com* Ⓜ*Central.*

Muji. Those familiar with this Japanese brand are often delighted to find one of its stores, and Hong Kong now has a number of branches (seven at this writing, including one at the airport). The full name is Mujirishi Ryohin (meaning, "no-brand quality goods"), which only partly describes the sleek minimalism of everything from household items and stationery to clothing and simply packaged snacks. ⊠*3rd fl., Lee Theatre Plaza, 99 Percival St., Causeway Bay* ☎*2808–0622* ⊕*www.muji.com.hk* ⊠*Level 7, Langham Place, 8 Argyle St., Mong Kok, Kowloon* Ⓜ*Mong Kok* ⊠*3rd fl., Miramar Shopping Centre, 132 Nathan Rd., Tsim Sha Tsui, Kowloon* Ⓜ*Tsim Sha Tsui.*

OVO. Push past heavy, giant doors to enter this atmospheric, high-ceiling showroom, which feels like a cross between a museum and a temple. The fusion and contrasts of east and west permeates every surface of the minimalist furniture, home furnishings, and accessories designed by the in-house team. Items are smart and rarely fussy. Beautiful, unvarnished blocks of wood, for example, are proposed as side tables. ⊠*Ground fl., 16 Queen's Rd. E, Wan Chai* ☎*2526–7226* ⊕*www.ovo.com.hk* Ⓜ*Admiralty.*

CARPETS & RUGS

You might walk in looking for a carpet, but ask the right questions and you're sure to leave with much more. Many of these merchants share the origins of their stock, especially Pakistan, and some have been here for generations. Consummate salespeople, they're happy to run through the history and different types of old and new rugs from Persia, China, India, Pakistan, and elsewhere. Contemporary designs are a newer category with price tags to rival designer versions sold abroad. Overall, though prices have increased since the late 1990s, carpets are still cheaper in Hong Kong than in Europe and the United States. Note: Americans *are* allowed to import Persian rugs into the United States.

CarpetBuyer. With a modern approach to an age-old business, a son of the Oriental Carpet Trading House family sells high-quality carpets from

China, India, and Pakistan at warehouse prices. ⊠ *Ground fl., Horizon Plaza, 2 Lee Wing St., Southside* ⚓ *Ap Lei Chau* ☏ *2850–5508* ⊕ *www.carpetbuyer.com.*

Tai Ping Carpets. Headquartered in Hong Kong, Tai Ping is highly regarded for its custom-made rugs and wall-to-wall carpets. It takes 2½ to 3 months to make specially ordered carpets; you can specify color, thickness, and even the direction of the weave. Tai Ping's occasional sales are well worth attending; check the classified section of the *South China Morning Post* for dates. ⊠ *Prince's Bldg, 10 Chater Rd., Central* ☏ *2522–7138* ⊕ *www.taipingcarpets.com* Ⓜ *Central.*

CERAMICS

Before you try to board the plane with the new 24-person dinner set or massive planter that you bought for a song, consider all your options. You'll begin to recognize classic Chinese colors and motifs such as blue and white, famille rose, dragons, goldfish, flowers, and even bats—a lucky symbol in the culture. Be sure to ask if any intended tableware is microwave-safe and can be put in the dishwasher, and find out if staffers can arrange shipping for you.

For a full selection of ceramic Chinese tableware, visit the various Chinese department stores, which also have bargains on attractively designed vases, bowls, and table lamps. Inexpensive buys can also be had in the streets of Tsim Sha Tsui, the shopping centers of Tsim Sha Tsui East and Harbour City, the side streets of Western, and the shops along Queen's Road East in Wan Chai.

Lee Fung China Ware Co., Ltd. Friendly service and a decent selection of Chinese and western-style dinnerware make this a good one-stop shop, uniquely situated just off the Midlevels Escalator. It also carries vases and antique reproductions. ⊠ *Ground fl., 18 Shelley St., SoHo, Central* ☏ *2524–0630* ⊕ *www.leefungchina.biz.com.hk.*

Wah Tung Ceramic Arts. It's a slightly slick but reliable manufacturer and retailer of predominantly handcrafted ceramics that has been in operation since the early days of trade with the West (1863). The overwhelmingly large product line includes antique replicas, vases, dinnerware, figurines, and more—all in classic Chinese motifs. ⊠ *7th fl., 57–59 Hollywood Rd., Central* ☏ *2543–2823* ⊕ *www.wahtungchina. com* Ⓜ *Central* ⊠ *14th fl.–17th fl., Grand Marine Ind. Bldg., 3 Yue Fung St., Southside, Aberdeen.*

JEWELRY

Visitors from all walks of life come to Hong Kong, and the one thing they all want to buy is jewelry. It is, in fact, the most popular item with foreign shoppers, as evidenced by entire tour buses you'll see idling outside large jewelry chains. Jewelry is not subject to any local tax or duty, which helps keep prices down. Settings for diamonds and other gems also cost less here than in most western cities, though quality engraving services are hard to find. Hong Kong is known as a center for jade jewelry, and has become a trading and distribution center for pearls, too, thanks in part to growth in the Chinese and South Sea pearl

That's a Wrap

Wander into the pretty Edwardian-style Western Market in Sheung Wan, and you'll find the entire second floor bursting with pure silk shantung, cotton-piqué shirting, French lace, silk brocade, velvet, damask, and printed crepe de chine—just some of the exquisite, reasonably priced fabrics available in Hong Kong. Although professional sourcing agents spend most of their time in Sham Shui Po on Kowloon side, Western Market's vast selection is more than adequate. Thai silk costs a bit more here than in Bangkok but is still much cheaper than in the United States or Europe.

Chinese Arts & Crafts and Yue Hwa Chinese Products Emporium have great selections of Chinese brocades and other fabrics. Look also for Chinese hand-embroidered and -appliquéd linen and cotton in Stanley Market. ■TIP→ **When buying a hand-embroidered item, check that the edges are properly over-**cast; if not, it's probably machine made. You'll be looking for reasons to buy lots of the blue-and-white, patterned Chinese country fabrics at Mountain Folkcraft. Just check that you can bring your bolts on the plane; shipping costs may cancel out any discount.

The **Textile Society of Hong Kong** (⊕ *www.textilesocietyofhk.org*) hosts talks, expeditions, and events to explore all aspects of traditional and contemporary textiles. It counts as its members design professionals, museum curators, collectors, historians, textile conservators, dealers, and craftspeople. Textile Society member Edith Cheung's atelier, **Cloth Haven** (✉ *Ground fl., 7 Upper Station St., Central* ☎ *2546–0378 www.cloth haven.com*), hosts weaving classes on looms right on the shop floor—amid a mix of textiles, vintage clothing, and design inspirations.

4

industry and the decline of Tahitian pearls. Turnover is fast, competition is fierce, and the selection is fantastic.

■TIP→ **Some countries charge a great deal more for imported set jewelry than for unset gems, so do check your country's customs regulations to avoid a nasty surprise.**

The city is also a leading pure-gold item producer. Hong Kong law requires all jewelers to indicate both the number of carats and the identity of the shop or manufacturer on every gold item displayed or proffered for sale. Make sure these marks are present and that you receive an invoice listing specifics, such as the weight and price of each item. Also, check current gold prices, which many stores display, against the price of the gold item you're thinking of buying.

Main areas for gold jewelry include Yee Wo Street and Hennessy Road (take the MTR to Causeway Bay and use Exit D2) and Nathan Road from Mong Kok to Tsim Sha Tsui (take the MTR to Mong Kok, Yau Ma Tei, Jordan, Tsim Sha Tsui stations). For factory outlets, see the HKTB's *Factory Outlets for Locally Made Fashion and Jewellery*. Consult the **Hong Kong Jewellers' & Goldsmiths' Association** (☎ *2543–9633* ⊕ *www.jewelrynet. com/hkjga*) for information on the gold jewelry scene.

Carat. Forget the cheesy cubic zirconium of the past. One look at its stark white showrooms, and you'll see that Carat has mastered the creation and presentation of synthetic gemstones. Hand-assembled in precious-metal settings, the large collection spans various eras of jewelry styles. The second line, Carat Emporium, is inspired by far-flung cultures and made with colorful semiprecious stones. ⊠ *Ground fl., 23 D'Aguilar St., Central* ☎*2526–9688* ⊕*www.carat.cc* Ⓜ *Central* ⊠*IFC Mall, 8 Finance St., Central* Ⓜ*Central.*

Chocolate Rain. The collections—dreamed up by a Hong Kong fine arts graduate—consist of pieces handcrafted of recycled materials, jade, crystals, precious stones, and mother-of-pearl. The showroom also displays works by the designer's friends, and it doubles as a classroom for jewelry-making courses. ⊠ *Ground fl., 34 Staunton St., SoHo, Central* ☎*2975–8318* ⊕*www.chocolaterain.com* Ⓜ *Central.*

Kai-Yin Lo. Kai-Yin Lo is famous for her Asian-inspired jewelry, combining contemporary style with ancient Chinese designs and materials such as jade. The *International Herald Tribune* has credited her with bridging the gap between fine and fashion jewelry. Lo acts as a consultant, lecturer, and writer on heritage, art, culture, and philanthropy; sales of her jewelry continue by appointment. ⊠*55 Garden Rd., Central* ☎*2773–6009* ⊕*www.kaiyinlo-design.com.*

Karen Jewel Co. Designer Karen Lee studied jewelry making in Florence before creating her own brand in 2003. She uses a variety of precious stones, including rubies, sapphires, and emeralds, in her one-of-a-kind custom-made jewelry, which tends to have an antique look. Her showroom, where you can check out some sample pieces, is worth a visit; appointments are required, so call ahead. ⊠*17A, 128 Wellington St., Central* ☎*2151–9622* ⊕*www.karenjewel.com* Ⓜ *Central.*

Jan Logan. This Australian designer has celebrities wearing her youthful yet elegant designs. Pieces contrast cultured, South Sea, and Tahitian pearls with onyx, diamonds, quartz, and other stones. ⊠*IFC Mall, 8 Finance St., Central* ☎*2918–4212* ⊕*www.janlogan.com* Ⓜ*Central.*

Qeelin. With ancient Chinese culture for inspiration and *In The Mood for Love* actress Maggie Cheung as the muse, something extraordinary was bound to come from Qeelin. Its name was cleverly derived from the Chinese characters for male ("qi") and female ("lin"), and symbolizes harmony, balance, and peace. The restrained beauty and meaningful creations of designer Dennis Chan are exemplified in two main collections: Wulu, a minimalist form representing the mythical gourd as well as the lucky number eight; and Tien Di, literally "Heaven and Earth," symbolizing everlasting love. Classic gold, platinum, and diamonds mix with colored jades, black diamonds, and unusual materials for a truly unique effect. A sweeter addendum to the collection was added recently in the form of Bo Bo, the panda bear. ⊠*IFC Mall, 8 Finance St., Central* ☎*2389–8863* ⊕*www.qeelin.com* Ⓜ*Central* ⊠*Peninsula Shopping Arcade, Salisbury Rd., Tsim Sha Tsui, Kowloon* Ⓜ*Tsim Sha Tsui.*

Saturn Essentials. If you're looking for a local artisan, a reasonably priced piece of silver, semiprecious stones, and sometimes even gold jewelry—or you just want a chat with a nice lady—visit Maureen "Mo" Gerrard. Her shop is opposite the wonderful salon of her son, Paul Gerrard (⇨*Spas,* *above).* ✉*11th fl., 51 Wellington St., Central* ☎*2537–9335 www. saturnessentials.com* Ⓜ*Central.*

Tayma Fine Jewellery. Unusual colored "connoisseur" gemstones are set by hand in custom designs by Hong Kong–based jeweler Tayma Page Allies. The collection is designed to bring out the personality of the individual wearer, and includes oversize cocktail rings, distinctive bracelets, pretty earrings, and more. ✉*Prince's Bldg., 10 Chater Rd., Central* ☎*2525–5280* ⊕*www.taymajewellery.com* Ⓜ*Central.*

★ **Sin Sin Atelier.** Everything Sin Sin does is dynamic, exciting, and unique. Her shop is at the far end of Hollywood Road, near the Cat Street Bazaar, where you can glimpse old Hong Kong. Displayed beside clothing inspired by innovative Japanese fashion is her silver jewelry done in bold, beautiful geometric designs—what she calls "artsy yet wearable." The multitalented Sin Sin also performs Cantonese opera in venues such as City Hall. ✉*Ground fl., 52–53 Sai St., Central* ☎*2521–0308* ⊕*www.sinsin.com.hk.*

DIAMONDS

Hong Kong is one of the world's largest diamond-trading centers, and prices are often at least 10% lower than world-market levels. For information or advice contact the **Diamond Federation of Hong Kong, China Ltd.** (☎*2524–5081* ⊕*www.dfhk.com.hk*).

▉**TIP→** When buying diamonds, remember the four Cs: color, clarity, carat (size), and cut. Shop only in reputable outlets—those recommended by a local or listed in the HKTB's shopping guide.

King Fook Jewellery. When considering jewelry stores, longevity is a good thing. King Fook has been around since 1949, promising stringent quality control, quality craftsmanship, and professional service. **Masterpiece by King Fook,** the higher-end King Fook line, sells first-grade diamonds and precious jewelry. ✉*Ground fl., 1 Yee Wo St., Causeway Bay* ☎*2576–1032* ⊕*www.kingfook.com* Ⓜ*Causeway Bay* ✉*Ground fl., 30–32 Des Voeux Rd. Central, Central* Ⓜ*Central* ✉*Ground fl., Hotel Miramar Shopping Arcade, 118–130 Nathan Rd., Tsim Sha Tsui Kowloon* Ⓜ*Tsim Sha Tsui.*

Larry Jewellery. This is a long-established source for handcrafted jewelry made from high-grade precious stones. Catering to local tastes since 1967, the traditional company has a new push to attract younger customers. That said, there really is a wide enough range to please most tastes. ✉*Ground fl., 72 Queens Rd. Central, Central* ☎*2521–1268* ⊕*www.larryjewelry.com* Ⓜ*Central* ✉*The Landmark, Pedder St. and Des Voeux Rd., Central* Ⓜ*Central* ✉*Pacific Place, 88 Queensway, Admiralty* Ⓜ*Admiralty* ✉*Ground fl., 33 Nathan Rd., Tsim Sha Tsui, Kowloon* Ⓜ*Tsim Sha Tsui.*

Ronald Abram Jewellers. Looking at the rocks in these windows can feel like a visit to a natural history museum. Large white- and rare-color diamonds sourced from all over the world are a specialty here, but the shop also deals in emeralds, sapphires, and rubies. With years of expertise, Abrams dispenses advice on both the aesthetic merits and the investment potential of each stone or piece of jewelry. ✉ *Mezzanine, Mandarin Oriental, 5 Connaught Rd., Central* ☎ *2810–7677* ⊕ *www. ronaldabram.com* Ⓜ *Central.*

TSL Jewellery. One of the big Hong Kong chains, TSL (Tse Sui Luen), specializes in diamond jewelry and manufactures, retails, and exports its designs. Its range of 100-facet stones includes the Estrella cut, which reflects nine symmetrical hearts and comes with international certification. Although its contemporary designs use platinum settings, TSL also sells pure, bright, yellow-gold items targeted at Chinese customers. ✉ *G9–10, Park Lane Shopper's Blvd., Nathan Rd., Tsim Sha Tsui, Kowloon* ☎ *2332–4618* ⊕ *www.tsljewellery.com* Ⓜ *Tsim Sha Tsui* ✉ *Ground fl., 35 Queen's Rd. Central, Central* Ⓜ *Central* ✉ *Ground fl., 1 Yee Woo St., Causeway Bay* Ⓜ *Causeway Bay.*

JADE

The days of romantic, ocean-crossing quests for treasure may seem long gone (especially when your local store stocks items from Bangkok to Bologna). Yet jade, a wonderful Hong Kong buy, has retained its exoticism. It comes not only in green but also in shades of purple, orange, yellow, brown, white, and violet.

Buying jade is tricky and best done with an expert or trusted merchant. Translucency and evenness of color and texture determine jade's value. Top-quality jade is pure green and very expensive. Yellow-tinged pieces are acceptable, but those with brown or gray are not.

Be careful not to pay jade prices for green stones such as aventurine, bowenite, soapstone, or serpentine, which can be bleached and impregnated with polymers or dyed to look like rare jade. Many of the pieces for sale at the Kansu Street Jade Market are made of these impostors. That said, there are wonderful finds in the endless sea of stalls brimming with trinkets of every size, shape, and color.

Chinese Arts & Crafts. In direct contrast to the thrill of digging through dusty piles at the open-air Jade Market, the trustworthy Chinese Arts & Crafts department stores provide a clean, air-conditioned environment in which to shop for classic jade jewelry—the prices reflect that but aren't too outrageous. ✉ *Ground fl., Star House, 3 Salisbury Rd., Tsim Sha Tsui, Kowloon* ☎ *2735–4061* ⊕ *www.chineseartsandcrafts. com.hk* Ⓜ *Tsim Sha Tsui.*

Chow Sang Sang. Chow Sang Sang has more than 100 shops in China. In addition to its contemporary gold, diamond, jade, and wedding collections for the local market, the manufacturer and retailer also sources international brands. ✉ *Ground fl., Park Lane Shopper's Blvd., 111–139 Nathan Rd., Tsim Sha Tsui, Kowloon* ☎ *3105–9708, 2192–3123 customer service and branch information* ⊕ *www. chowsangsang.com* Ⓜ *Tsim Sha Tsui* ✉ *LG2, Festival Walk, 80 Tat*

Chee Ave., Kowloon Tong, Kow-loon Ⓜ *Kowloon Tong* ✉ *Ground fl., 525 Hennessy Rd., Causeway Bay* Ⓜ *Causeway Bay.*

Chow Tai Fook. Jade is not the only thing you'll see from this local chain founded in 1929. It also has fine jewelry in diamond, jadeite, ruby, sapphire, emerald, pearl, 18K gold, and more-traditional pure gold.

✉ *Ground fl., AON China Bldg., 29 Queen's Rd. Central, Central* ☏ *2523–7128, 2526–8649* ⊕ *www.chowtaifook.com* Ⓜ *Central* ✉ *Park Lane Shopper's Boulevard, 123 Nathan Rd., Tsim Sha Tsui, Kowloon* Ⓜ *Tsim Sha Tsui* ✉ *Ground fl., Chow Tai Fook Centre, 580A Nathan Rd., Mong Kok, Kowloon* Ⓜ *Mong Kok.*

Edward Chiu. Everything about Edward Chiu is *fabulous*, from the flamboyant way he dresses to his high-end jade jewelry. The minimalist, geometric pieces use the entire jade spectrum, from deep greens to surprising lavenders. He's also famous for contrasting black-and-white jade, setting it in precious metals and adding diamond or pearl touches. ✉ *IFC Mall, 8 Finance St., Central* ☏ *2525–2618* ⊕ *www.edwardchiu.com* Ⓜ *Central.*

Wing On Jewelry Ltd. There's a nostalgic charm to the butterflies, birds, and natural forms fashioned from jade, pearls, precious stones, and gold here. Everything looks like an heirloom inherited from your grandmother. With on-site gemologists and artisans, and a commitment to post-sale service, this store has a long list of repeat customers. If, however, you lean toward Scandinavian aesthetics and clean lines, this probably isn't the place for you. ✉ *146 Johnston Rd., Wan Chai* ☏ *2572–2332* ⊕ *www.wingonjewelry.com.hk* Ⓜ *Wan Chai* ✉ *459 Hennessy Rd., Causeway Bay* Ⓜ *Causeway Bay.*

PEARLS

From lifelong investments handed down for generations to affordable fashion jewelry, pearls are still a good buy in Hong Kong. A symbol of purity and one of the eight jewels in Chinese culture, pearls come in a variety of shades including white, silver white, light pink, darker pink, cream, and yellow. The most coveted are perfectly round, though baroque (asymmetrical), semi-baroque, drop, and oval are also popular.

Cultured pearls are grown in mollusks with a surgically implanted tissue or bead nucleus. Freshwater pearls (grown in a freshwater mollusk) tend to look like rough grains of rice. The larger cultured types grown in the white-lip oyster, about 8 mm to 22 mm in diameter, are known as South Sea pearls and come in hues from white to darker gold. Tahitian pearls are produced by the black-lip oyster; they come in shades of black and gray, as well as blue, purple, green, orange, and gold.

When shopping for pearls, look at luster, size, color, and surface—judgments that are properly made against a white background in daylight.

(Biting them to test for that authentic gritty texture will not help your chances of a discount.)

■ TIP→ **For a better understanding of pearls, consult an expert or take the HKTB's Secrets of Pearl Shopping class, in which you'll learn how to use a pearl grading chart and how to shop with confidence.**

Gallery One. This is the next-best option for midrange pearls if you can't make it to the Jade Market. Gallery One blends into Hollywood Road's backdrop of trinket-filled storefronts, but its selection of freshwater pearls stands out. Prices are reasonable, and they will string together whichever combination of pearls and semiprecious stones you choose. Gallery One also carries Tibetan and Buddhist beads in wood and amber as well as bronze sculptures. ⊠*Ground fl., 31–33 Hollywood Rd., Central* ☎*2545–6436* ⊕*www.gallery-one.com.hk* Ⓜ*Central.*

K.S. Sze & Sons. More salon than store, powdered elderly ladies who lunch and casually dressed tourists all come here for the same thing: quality pearls, fine jewelry, and excellent service. In addition to classic styles, K.S. Sze works closely with clients on custom orders. ⊠*Prince's Building, 10 Chater Rd., Central* ☎*2524–2803* ⊕*www.kssze.com* Ⓜ*Central.*

Mandarin Australia. These are not your grandmother's pearls. The story goes something like this: a Hong Kong resident and an Australian woman met in a Chinese language course in Beijing and became fast friends. They shared an idea to create young, funky pearl bracelets and necklaces to sell at low prices, and, unlike so many of us would-be entrepreneurs, they actually did it. Now sold to retailers on several continents, the collections feature baroque pearls with accents picked up on trips: antique buttons from Shanghai, Murano glass from Venice, turquoise and gold from Istanbul, and silver beads from Mexico. You'll need to make an appointment; ask for Joanna when you call. ☎*9670–8253.*

Po Kwong Jewellery Ltd. Specializing in strung pearls from Australia and the South Seas, Po Kwong will add clasps to your specifications. They also carry pearl earrings, rings, and pendants. ⊠*18th fl., HK Diamond Exchange Bldg., 8–10 Duddell St., Central* ☎*2521–4686.*

Sandra Pearls. Without a recommendation like this, you might be wary of the lustrous pearls hanging at this little Jade Market stall. The charming owner, Sandra, does, in fact, sell genuine and reasonably priced cultured and freshwater pearl necklaces and earrings. Some pieces are made from shell, which Sandra is always quick to point out, and could pass muster among the snobbiest collectors. ⊠*Stalls 381 and 447, Jade Market, Kansu St., Yau Ma Tei, Kowloon* ☎*9485–2895* Ⓜ*Yau Ma Tei.*

Super Star Jewellery. Discreetly tucked in a corner of Central, Super Star looks like any other small Hong Kong jewelry shop—with walls lined by display cases filled with the usual classic designs (old-fashioned to some) in predominantly gold and precious stones. What makes them stand out are the good prices and personalized service. The cultured pearls and mixed strands of colored freshwater pearls are not all shown, so ask Lily or one of her colleagues to bring them out. ⊠*The Galleria, 9 Queen's Rd. Central, Central* ☎*2521–0507* Ⓜ*Central.*

WATCHES

Street stalls, department stores, and jewelry shops overflow with every variety, style, and brand imaginable, many with irresistible gadgets. Just remember Hong Kong's remarkable talent for imitation. A super-bargain gold "Rolex" may have hidden flaws—cheap local mechanisms, for instance, or "gold" that rusts. Stick to officially appointed dealers carrying the manufacturers' signs if you want to be sure you're getting the real thing.

When buying an expensive watch, check the serial number against the manufacturer's guarantee certificate and ask the salesperson to open the case to check the movement serial number. If the watch has an expensive band, find out whether it comes from the original manufacturer or is locally made, as this will dramatically affect the price (originals are much more expensive). Always obtain a detailed receipt, the manufacturer's guarantee, and a worldwide warranty.

Artland Watch Co Ltd. Elegant but uncomplicated, the interior of this established watch retailer is like its service. The informed staff will guide you through the countless luxury brands on show and in the catalogs from which you can also order. Prices here aren't the best in Hong Kong, but they're still lower than at home. ⊠*Ground fl., Mirador Mansion, 54–64B Nathan Rd., Tsim Sha Tsui, Kowloon* ☎*2366–1074* Ⓜ*Tsim Sha Tsui* ⊠*Ground fl., New Henry House, 10 Ice House St., Central* Ⓜ*Central.*

City Chain Co. Ltd. With more than 200 shops in Asia and locations all over Hong Kong, City Chain has a wide selection of watches for various budgets, including Swatch, Cyma, and Solvil & Titus. ⊠*Times Square, 1 Matheson St., Causeway Bay* ☎*2506–4217* ⊕*www.citychain.com* Ⓜ*Causeway Bay* ⊠*Ground fl., Yat Fat Bldg., 44–46 Des Voeux Rd. Central, Central* Ⓜ*Central* ⊠*L2, Festival Walk, 80 Tat Chee Ave., Kowloon Tong, Kowloon* Ⓜ*Kowloon Tong.*

Eldorado Watch Co Ltd. At this deep emporium of watch brands, seek the advice of one of the older staffers who look like they've been there since the British landed. Brands include: Rolex, Patek Philippe, Girard-Perregaux, etc. ⊠*Ground fl., Peter Bldg., 60 Queen's Rd., Central* ☎*2522–7155* Ⓜ*Central.*

Elegant Watch & Jewellery Company Limited. With luxury watch collectors in mind, Elegant Watch is an authorized dealer of more than 35 top brands such as Tag Heuer, Breitling, Vacheron Constantin, Seiko, Franck Muller, and more. ⊠*Times Square, 1 Matheson St., Causeway Bay* ☎*2506–3663* ⊕*www.elegantwatch.net* Ⓜ*Causeway Bay* ⊠*Ocean Terminal, Harbour City, Canton Rd., Tsim Sha Tsui, Kowloon* Ⓜ*Tsim Sha Tsui.*

Prince Jewellery And Watch Company. This shop carries timepieces made by more than 50 international brands such as Franck Muller, Omega, Chopard, and Piaget, in addition to other jewelry which may entertain those accompanying the avid watch-shopper. ⊠*Ground fl., Bo Yip Bldg, 10 Peking Rd., Tsim Sha Tsui, Kowloon* ☎*2369–2123.*

SHOES & BAGS

Shoes: they fit even when your skinny jeans don't; they're among the first things you look at when sizing someone up; and they captivate people the world over, from dictators' consorts to humble housewives. Hong Kongers are just as obsessed with footwear as the rest of the world. Add to that an obsession with brands and the next "it" bag, and you have the makings for an amazing shoe and bag marketplace.

In opulent malls and department stores, designer must-haves seem to have leapt from the pages of fashion magazines onto the shelves. You'd be hard-pressed to name an international label not represented here. Hong Kong also has a growing number of local brands that fill the gap between high fashion and cheap market products. Out of Asia, they become exotic objects that only you possess. That said, prices are rarely better than back home, and it's often hard to find shoes larger than size 8.

The best buys are custom-made. Wong Nai Chung Road, near the race-course where Causeway Bay meets Happy Valley, has long been the destination for reasonably priced, medium-quality shoes. Some shops can whip up an order in five days, though more complicated designs could take three weeks or more. A few stores will arrange delivery by mail, but it's always best to receive orders in person in case of problems.

■ TIP➜ Your feet swell as the day goes on (especially true in Hong Kong, thanks to heat and humidity). It may seem counterintuitive, but try shoes in the afternoon, when your feet are swollen. It's better to have shoes that are loose early in the day and just right later on than to have shoes that are just right early in the day and tight later on.

Brand Off. This Japanese chain hit town in June 2008; like Milan Station, it carries secondhand goods from luxury brands like Louis Vuitton, Hermès, Chanel, Gucci, Prada, and Dior. The shop is also a member of the Association Against Counterfeit Product Distribution, a Japanese organization that uses scientific evidence to determine whether products are genuine or knockoffs. ✉ *1st fl., Cityplaza, 18 Tai Koo Shing Rd., Tai Koo* Ⓜ *Tai Koo.*

Fodor's Choice ★ **The Green Lantern.** Previously known as Tef Tef, this shop has exquisite, statement-making bags by Hong Kong–based designer Tomoko Oka-mura. The collection is handmade with Chinese metalwork, vintage Japanese fabrics, Thai silks, and bamboo. Of all the artisanal Asian fabric bags, these are the best. They're sold in various locations, including the Green Lantern (but you'll get the best prices here). ✉ *Ground fl., 72 Peel St., SoHo, Central* ☎ *2526–0277.*

Hop's Handbag Co. Ltd. Uh-oh. You've over-shopped, and now packing is a problem. Hop over to Hop's for cheap luggage, from generic to name brands such as Samsonite. It also sells lots of handbags: some nameless but acceptable; others, amazing throwbacks to the '80s (and now back in fashion). ✉ *Ground fl., 19 Li Yuen St. E, Central* ☎ *2523–3888* Ⓜ *Central.*

J. J. Partners. You won't see the men who manage this store flipping through the pages of *Vogue,* but the selection of ready-made and cus-tom shoes and bags at this sophisticated choice in Happy Valley suggests they're up on fashion. Even better, prices are comparable with neighboring shops. ⊠ *Ground fl., 173 Wong Nai Chung Rd., Happy Valley* ☎ *2577–2383* Ⓜ *Causeway Bay.*

Kow Hoo Shoe Company. If you like shoes made the old-fashioned way, then Kow Hoo, one of Hong Kong's oldest (circa 1946), is for you. It also does great cowboy boots—there's nothing like knee-high calfskin. ⊠ *2nd fl., Prince's Bldg., 10 Chater Rd., Central* ☎ *2523–0489* Ⓜ *Central.*

Kwanpen. Famous for its crocodile bags and shoes, Kwanpen has acted as a manufacturer for famous brands since 1938, as well as being a stand-alone retailer. It also uses ostrich and leather. ⊠ *Pacific Place, 88 Queensway, Admiralty* ☎ *2918–9199* ⊕ *www.kwanpen.com* Ⓜ *Admiralty.*

Ladyplace. The prices on French Sole brand ballerinas will have you doing pirouettes. In the United States, the ballet flats by British designer Jane Winkworth sell for about US$160. At Ladyplace, they're HK$—95—or about US$115—a pair. While you're here, browse through the secondhand shoes and apparel by famous fashion labels, all at discounted prices. ⊠ *1st fl., World Trust Tower, 50 Stanley St., Central* ☎ *2854–2321* ⊕ *www.ladyplace.com* Ⓜ *Central.*

Lianca. This is one of those unique places that makes you want to buy something even if there's nothing you need. Lianca, first and foremost a manufacturer, sells well-made leather bags, wallets, frames, key chains, and home accessories in timeless, simple designs. It's an unbranded way to be stylish. ⊠ *Basement fl., 27 Staunton St., entrance on Graham St., SoHo, Central* ☎ *2139–2989* ⊕ *www.lianca.com.hk* Ⓜ *Central.*

★ **Lili Lili Shoes.** Possibly the best and most fashionable custom shoemakers in Hong Kong, the Chan brothers have also become the most arrogant. Prices have tripled over the last few years (to between HK$1,300 and HK$2,300 for high heels), but the excellent shoes and good bags keep pulling customers back. Despite the attitude, they will remake your shoes if you're unhappy with the results. ⊠ *Admiralty Centre, 18 Harcourt Rd., Wan Chai* ☎ *2136–9739* Ⓜ *Admiralty.*

Mayer Shoes. Since the 1960s, Mayer has been making excellent custom-order shoes and accessories in leather, lizard, crocodile, and ostrich. Go to them for the classic pieces for which they became famous rather than this season's "it" bag. Prices start at about US$200. ⊠ *Mandarin Oriental, 5 Connaught Rd., Central* ☎ *2524–3317* Ⓜ *Central.*

Milan Station. Even if you're willing to shell out for an Hermès Kelly bag, how can anyone expect you to survive the waitlist? Milan Station resells the "it" bags of yesterday that have been retrieved from Hong Kong's fickle fashionistas. Inexplicably, the shop entrances were designed to look like MTR stations. The concept has been so successful, unimaginatively named copycats have sprung up, such as Paris Station. Discounts vary according to brand and trends, but the merchandise is in good condition. ⊠ *Ground fl., Percival House, 77–83 Percival St., Causeway Bay* ☎ *2504–0128, 2730–8037 customer service* ⊕ *www. milanstation.net* Ⓜ *Causeway Bay* ⊠ *Ground fl., 26 Wellington St., Central* ⊠ *Ground fl., Pakpolee Commercial Centre, 1A–1K Sai Yeung Choi St., Mong Kok, Kowloon* Ⓜ *Mong Kok* ⊠ *Ground fl., 81 Chatham Rd., Tsim Sha Tsui, Kowloon* Ⓜ *Tsim Sha Tsui.*

NATHAN ROAD

With its frenetic forest of clashing neon signs, Nathan Road is a postcard image of a busy Hong Kong street. It's also the main artery through a throbbing cluster of markets and shopping streets.

If it's a rarified shopping experience you're after, forget it: this 'hood is all about bargains, and it's a different world from the organized chaos of Central's covered walkways. Once you step off poker-straight Nathan Road, you can become lost in the perpetual stream of humanity weaving through the streets. But focus on all the amazing finds, and it's easier to fend off claustrophobia. Whether you're after classic Chinese souvenirs, jewelry, gadgets, clothes, shoes, or brand-name rip-offs (naughty you), it's all here. Keep your valuables tucked away safely, and keep that map in your hand. Nathan Road itself is the best landmark. Chinese street names are totally different from the anglicized versions, and many local people don't speak English.

BEST TIME TO GO

Arrive early to see communes of old men hanging their birdcages and chatting in the morning sunlight as the Bird, Goldfish, and Jade Markets gather momentum at around 9 AM. Mong Kok's clothing markets open at midday and specialize in cheap bags, jeans, and toys. Temple Street's Night Market comes alive after dark.

BEST GIFT FOR MOTHER-IN-LAW

Just because it looks like antique jade doesn't mean it is. Keep her having happy thoughts for years to come with a carved soapstone coaster or trivet, around HK$90, from **Kansu Street Jade Market**.

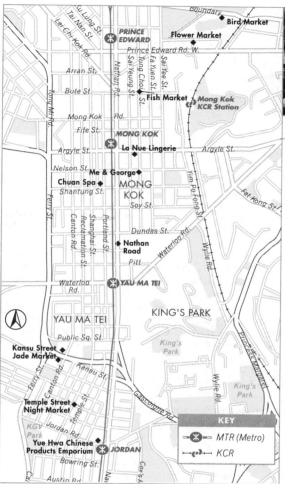

WHAT YOU'LL WANT

BARGAINS

Fa Yuen Street. Also known as Sneaker Street, here you'll feast your eyes on all the kicks you've ever wanted.

La Nue Lingerie. Despite the shabby exterior, La Nue is a chic boutique with gorgeous, inexpensive lingerie.

Me & George. Rummage for vintage treasures including tea dresses and men's leather jackets amid racks of junk starting at only HK$10.

Yuen Po Street Bird Garden. Forget Tweety—these delicate birdcages make perfect planters to hang outside your window.

SOUVENIRS

Yue Hwa Chinese Products Emporium. If haggling isn't your thing, this long-standing institution, which offers all manner of "Made in China" items at set prices, is for you.

Temple Street Night Market. Although Temple Street stalls peddle a lot of stuff you probably won't want—touristy souvenirs and knockoffs—this market is worth a visit for the atmosphere alone.

REJUVENATING

If it's a quiet moment you're after, skip fast-food joints, dai pai dong (cheap outdoor eateries), and noisy yum cha (dim sum) halls at street level. Your best bet is **Chuan Spa**, which overlooks the city from the top floor of arctic oasis Langham Place Mall and Hotel. In five-star spa surroundings, consult with a Traditional Chinese Medicine (TCM) practitioner: you'll likely be prescribed cupping (an ancient Chinese acupressure technique), acupuncture, or myofascial therapy (a gentle massage and stretching technique), all of which aim to distribute chi (energy) throughout the body and promote health and balance. (Or you could just have a massage.)

Mischa Designs. Designer Michelle Lai's bags are handmade from Japanese brocade obis (sashes) and kimonos from the 1920s to the 1950s. Clutch bags such as the Dumpling or any of the reversible styles could make even the most unremarkable outfit look noteworthy. Keep an eye out for bigger totes made of obis paired with leather. The designs are sold by appointment or at Sharon Rocks fashion jewelry showroom. ⊠ *11th fl., Yu Yuet Lai Bldg., 43–55 Wyndham St., Central* ☎*2523–9333 or 6199–4145* ⊕*www.mischadesigns.com.*

> **FIX IT & FORGET IT**
>
> Shoe troubles? For basic services the shoe-repair chains in MTR stations or hotels can help. But for special cases (mauled Manolos, for instance) head to the **Top Shoes Repair & Lock Centre** (⊠ *Ground fl., 35 Queen's Rd. Central, Central* ☎*2530–0978* Ⓜ *Central*).

Noven Shoes & Handbags. At this reliable shoe- and bag maker in the valley, styles range from gaudy to good, all for about HK$400 per pair. Custom-made boots take three weeks—longer than shoes and bags. ⊠*Ground fl., 163 Wong Nai Chung Rd., Happy Valley* ☎*2577–8323* ⊕*www.noven.com.hk.*

On Pedder. The art installation–style window displays will draw you into this stunning boutique. Designed as a giant jewel box, the store's brand directory reads like a fashion editor's wish list of world-famous shoe, bag, accessory, and jewelry designers. You might see the same brands at Lane Crawford—that's because they're sister companies. For the same aesthetics at lower prices, check out trendy younger sibling **Pedder Red** (⊠*The Gateway, Harbour City, Canton Rd., Tsim Sha Tsui, Kowloon* Ⓜ *Tsim Sha Tsui*). ⊠*Ground fl., Wheelock House, 20 Pedder St., Central* ☎*2118–3388, 2118–0130 for branch information* ⊕ *www.onpedder.com* Ⓜ *Central.*

Prestige Shoe Co. Ltd. Like the Happy Valley shoemakers, Prestige does fashion-forward, acceptable-quality, reasonably priced shoes. Unlike its valley brethren it's more convenient, with several locations around town. ⊠*Ground fl., 4 Queen Victoria St., Central* ☎*2869–9033* Ⓜ *Central* ⊠ *World Wide House, 19 Des Voeux Rd. Central, Central* Ⓜ *Central.*

★ **Rabeanco.** Hong Kong–based Rabeanco has a reasonably priced line of beautiful, quality leather bags in contemporary but never flashy or absurd designs. Buy yours now before the world discovers them. ⊠*Ground fl., 33 Sharp St. E, Causeway Bay* ☎*2577–9221, 2245–5085 customer service and branch information* ⊕*www.rabeanco.com* Ⓜ *Causeway Bay* ⊠*L1, Man Yee Arcade, 68 Des Voeux Rd., Central* Ⓜ *Central* ⊠ *Ground fl., Hong Kong Pacific Centre, 28 Hankow Rd., Tsim Sha Tsui, Kowloon* Ⓜ *Tsim Sha Tsui.*

Right Choice Export Fashion Co. Take a moment to look past the plastic stilettos worthy of an exotic dancer, and you might just discover unfathomably cheap yet stylish shoes (if they'll only last one season). The sandals are especially pretty and can cost as little as HK$60. Look for shops like this near most market streets. ⊠*Ground fl., 187 Fa Yuen St., Mong Kok, Kowloon* ☎*2394–6953* Ⓜ *Prince Edward.*

Sam Wo. A veteran of this area, Sam Wo sells fashion-inspired leather bags at low prices and without the branding. You'll need a keen eye to spot the must-haves amid all the must-nots. See neighboring stalls for closer interpretations of branded bags. ⊠*Basement, 41–47 Queen's Rd. Central, Central* ☎*2524–0970* Ⓜ*Central.*

Sportshouse. Come here for trendy sneakers and other casual footwear by brands like Nike, Adidas, Crocs, Converse, Havaianas, Playboy, Red Wing, and Birkenstock. The shop also offers athletic and casual apparel, and bags. C.P.U. and Match Box, two other chains, are under the same management and carry similar goods. ⊠*Ground fl., 61 Fa Yuen St., Mong Kok, Kowloon* ☎*2332–3099* ⊕*www.sportshouse. com* Ⓜ*Mong Kok* ⊠*Ground fl., Silvercord, 30 Canton Rd., Tsim Sha Tsui, Kowloon* Ⓜ*Tsim Sha Tsui* ⊠*3rd fl., New Town Plaza Phase 1, 18 Sha Tin Centre St., Shatin* Ⓜ*Shatin.*

TAILOR-MADE CLOTHING

CHINESE CLOTHING TAILORS

Chinese clothing has the potential to look incredibly chic or embarrassingly trashy. At the street level, it's easy to find a bargain cheongsam, though standard cuts don't allow for western hips and curves. Similarly, the market variety of men's jackets with Mandarin collars (lower) or Mao collars (higher) can look cheap. Rely on these experts for classic, tailor-made Chinese clothing.

Blanc de Chine. Blanc de Chine has catered to high society and celebrities, such as actor Jackie Chan, for years. That's easy when you're housed on the second floor of an old colonial building (just upstairs from Shanghai Tang) and you rely on word of mouth. The small, refined tailoring shop neatly displays exquisite fabrics. Next door is the Blanc de Chine boutique filled with lovely ready-made women's wear, menswear, and home accessories. With newer stores in New York and Beijing, it appears the word is getting out. Items here are extravagances, but they're worth every penny. ⊠*Pedder Bldg., 12 Pedder St., Central* ☎*2104–7934* ⊕*www.blancdechine.com* Ⓜ*Central.*

Linva Tailors. It's one of the best of the old-fashioned cheongsam tailors, in operation since the 1960s. Master tailor Mr. Leung takes clients through the entire process and reveals a surprising number of variations in style. Prices are affordable, but vary according to fabric, which ranges from basics to special brocades and beautifully embroidered silks. ⊠*38 Cochrane St., Central* ☎*2544–2456* Ⓜ*Central.*

★ **Shanghai Tang—Imperial Tailors.** Upscale Chinese lifestyle brand Shanghai Tang has the Imperial Tailors service in select stores, including the Central flagship. A fabulous interior evokes the charm of 1930s Shanghai, and gives an indication of what to expect in terms of craftsmanship and price. From silk to velvet, brocade to voile, fabrics are displayed on the side walls, along with examples of fine tailoring. The expert tailors here can make conservative or contemporary versions of the cheongsam. Men can also have a Chinese *tang* suit made to order. ⊠*Ground fl., 12 Pedder St., Central* ☎*2525–7333* ⊕*www.shanghaitang.com* Ⓜ*Central.*

MEN'S TAILORS

A-Man Hing Cheong Co., Ltd. People often gasp at the very mention of A-Man Hing Cheong in the Mandarin Oriental Hotel. For some it symbolizes the ultimate in fine tailoring with a reputation that extends back to its founding in 1898. For others it's the lofty prices that elicit a reaction. Regardless, this is a trustworthy source of European-cut suits, custom shirts, and excellent service. ⊠ *Mezzanine, Mandarin Oriental, 5 Connaught Rd., Central* ☎ *2522–3336* Ⓜ *Central.*

Ascot Chang. This self-titled "gentleman's shirtmaker" makes it easy to find the perfect shirt, even if you could get a better deal in a less prominent shop. Ascot Chang has upheld exacting Shanghainese tailoring traditions in Hong Kong since 1955, and now has stores in New York, Beverly Hills, Manila, and Shanghai, in addition to offering online ordering and regular American tours. The focus here is on the fit and details, from 22 stitches per inch to collar linings crafted to maintain their shape. Among the countless fabrics, Swiss 200s two-ply Egyptian cotton by Alumo is one of the most coveted and expensive. Like many shirtmakers, Ascot Chang does pajamas, robes, boxer shorts, and women's blouses, too. It also has developed ready-made lines of shirts, T-shirts, neckties, and other accessories. ⊠ *Prince's Bldg., 10 Chater Rd., Central* ☎ *2523–3663* ⊕ *www.ascotchang.com* Ⓜ *Central* ⊠ *IFC Mall, 8 Finance St., Central* Ⓜ *Central* ⊠ *Peninsula Hong Kong, Salisbury Rd., Tsim Sha Tsui, Kowloon* Ⓜ *Tsim Sha Tsui* ⊠ *New World Centre, InterContinental Hong Kong, 18–24 Salisbury Rd., Tsim Sha Tsui, Kowloon* Ⓜ *Tsim Sha Tsui.*

David's Shirts Ltd. Like so many of its competitors, the popular David's Shirts has global reach and even a branch in New York City. But customers still enjoy the personalized service of a smaller business supervised by David Chu himself since 1961. All the work is done in-house by Shanghainese tailors with at least 20 years' experience each. There are more than 6,000 imported European fabrics to choose from, each prewashed. Examples of shirts, suits, and accessories—including 30 collar styles, 12 cuff styles, and 10 pocket styles—help you choose. Single-needle tailoring, French seams, 22 stitches per inch, handpicked, double-stitched shell buttons, German interling—it's all here. Your details, down to on which side you wear your wristwatch, are kept on file should you wish to use its mail-order service in the future. ⊠ *Ground fl., Wing Lee Bldg., 33 Kimberley Rd., Tsim Sha Tsui, Kowloon* ☎ *2367–9556* ⊕ *www.davidsshirts.com* ⊠ *Mezzanine, Mandarin Oriental, 5 Connaught Rd., Central* Ⓜ *Central.*

Jantzen Tailor. You'll have to push past a lively crowd and eclectic shops in a mall preferred by Filipina domestic helpers to get to Jantzen. Catering to expatriate bankers since 1972, this reputable yet reasonable tailor specializes in classic shirts; it also makes suits and women's garments. The comprehensive Web site displays its commitment to quality, such as hand-sewn button shanks, Gygil interling, and Coats brand thread. ⊠ *2nd fl., United Chinese Bank Bldg, 31–37 Des Voeux Rd., Central* ☎ *2570–5901 or 2810–8080* ⊕ *www.jantzentailor.com* Ⓜ *Central.*

Maxwell's Clothiers Ltd. After you've found a handful of reputable, high-quality tailors, one way to choose between them is price. Maxwell's is known for its competitive rates. It's also a wonderful place to have favorite shirts and suits copied and for straightforward, structured women's shirts and suits. It was founded by third-generation tailor Ken Maxwell in 1961 and follows Shanghai tailoring traditions while also providing the fabled 24-hour suit upon request. The showroom and workshop are in Kowloon, but son Andy and his team take appointments in the United States, Canada, and Europe twice annually. The motto of this family business is, "Simply let the garment do the talking." ✉ *7th fl., Han Hing Mansion, 38–40 Hankow Rd., Tsim Sha Tsui, Kowloon* ☎ *2366–6705* ⊕ *www.maxwellsclothiers.com* Ⓜ *Tsim Sha Tsui.*

Fodor's Choice
★ **Sam's Tailor.** Unlike many famous Hong Kong tailors, you won't find the legendary Sam's in a chic hotel or sleek mall. But don't be fooled. These digs in humble Burlington House, a tailoring hub, have hosted everyone from U.S. presidents (back as far as Richard Nixon) to performers such as the Black Eyed Peas, Kylie Minogue, and Blondie. This former uniform tailor to the British troops once even made a suit for Prince Charles in a record hour and 52 minutes. The men's and women's tailor does accept 24-hour suit or shirt orders, but will take about two days if you're not in a hurry. Founded by Naraindas Melwani in the 1950s, "Sam" is now his son, Manu Melwani, who runs the show with the help of his own son, Roshan, and about 55 tailors behind the scenes. In 2004 Sam's introduced a computerized bodysuit that takes measurements without a tape measure. (It uses both methods, however.) These tailors also make annual trips to Europe and North America. (Schedule updates are listed on the Web site.) ✉ *Burlington House, 90–94 Nathan Rd., Tsim Sha Tsui, Kowloon* ☎ *2367–9423* ⊕ *www. samstailor.com* Ⓜ *Tsim Sha Tsui.*

W. W. Chan & Sons Tailors Ltd. Chan is known for excellent-quality suits and shirts, classic cuts, and has an array of fine European fabrics. It's comforting to know that you'll be measured and fitted by the same master tailor from start to finish. The Kowloon headquarters features a mirrored, hexagonal changing room so you can check every angle. Tailors from here travel to the United States several times a year to fill orders for its customers; if you have a suit made here and leave your address, they'll let you know when they plan to visit. ✉ *2nd fl., Burlington House, 92–94 Nathan Rd., Tsim Sha Tsui, Kowloon* ☎ *2366–9738* ⊕ *www.wwchan.com* Ⓜ *Tsim Sha Tsui.*

Yuen's Tailor. Need a kilt? This is where the Hong Kong Highlanders Reel Club comes for custom-made kilts. The Yuen repertoire, however, extends to well-made suits and shirts. The tiny shop is on an unimpressive gray walkway and is filled from floor to ceiling with sumptuous European fabrics. It's a good place to have clothes copied; prices are competitive. ✉ *2nd fl., Escalator Link Alley, 80 Des Voeux Rd., Central* ☎ *2815–5388* Ⓜ *Central.*

WOMEN'S TAILORS

Irene Fashions. In 1987 the women's division of noted men's tailor, W. W. Chan, branched off and was renamed Irene Fashions. You can expect the same level of expertise and a large selection of fine fabrics. Experienced at translating ideas and pictures into clothing, in-house designers will sketch and help you develop concepts. Like its parent company,

Irene promises the same tailor will take you through the entire process, and most of the work is done on-site. ⊠ *Burlington House, 92–94 Nathan Rd., Tsim Sha Tsui, Kowloon* ☎*2367–5588* ⊕*www.wwchan. com* Ⓜ*Tsim Sha Tsui.*

Irene Fashions. In addition to having the same name as the W. W. Chan women's division, this Irene Fashions promises much of the same guidance and workmanship. But don't confuse this popular Central tailoress with her Kowloon-side counterpart; the two are *not* related. Slightly more well known, this tailor attracts many expatriate women in search of everything from suits to evening wear. Service in the cluttered atmosphere may be brusque, but it's only because they know what they're talking about. ⊠*3rd fl., Tung Chai Bldg., 86–90 Wellington St., Central* ☎*2850–5635* Ⓜ*Central.*

Margaret Court Tailoress. A name frequently passed on by expert Hong Kong shoppers, Margaret Wong's tailoring services span women's daywear to bridal gowns to Chinese cheongsam. Prices tend to be midrange. ⊠*8th fl., Block A, Winner Bldg., 27–37 D'Aguilar St., Central* ☎*2525–5596* ⊕*www.margaret-court.com.hk* Ⓜ*Central.*

Mode Elegante. Don't be deterred by the somewhat dated mannequins in the windows. Mode Elegante is a favorite source for custom-made suits among women and men in the know. Tailors here specialize in European cuts. You'll have your choice of fabrics from the United Kingdom, Italy, and elsewhere. Your records are put on file so you can place orders from abroad. It'll even ship the completed garment to you almost anywhere on the planet. Alternatively, you can make an appointment with director Gary Zee, one of Hong Kong's traveling tailors who make regular visits to North America, Europe, and Japan. ⊠*11th fl., Star House3 Salisbury Rd., Tsim Sha Tsui, Kowloon* ☎*2366–8153* ⊕*www.modeelegante.com* Ⓜ*Tsim Sha Tsui.*

Perfect Dress Alteration (aka Ann & Bon). Hong Kong's tai tais bring their couture here for adjustments, as evidenced by the Chanel, Escada, and Versace bags hanging overhead in this cluttered little workshop buzzing with the sound of sewing machines. Although primarily known for alterations, it also offers tailoring services for women. ⊠*2nd fl., Melbourne Plaza, 33 Queen's Rd., Central* ☎*2522–8838* Ⓜ*Central.*

Siriporn. Visible from the Midlevels Escalator and one of the most highly recommended Thai tailors in town, Siriporn is known for an acute sense of aesthetics, reasonable prices, and brightly colored Thai silks. It's also capable of crafting subtle garments to please minimalists. ⊠*1st fl., Merlin Bldg., 28 Cochrane St., Central* ☎*2866–6668* Ⓜ*Central.*

Teneel. The fume-filled thoroughfare that leads to Teneel, also known as Made to Measure, doesn't exactly put you in the mood to talk about evening wear, but you should persist. Teneel Chan is experienced in women's wear, particularly gowns. Although some of her creations are on the garish side (think T-shirts adorned with expletives in Swarovski crystals), clear direction will put her on the right track. Even better, her prices are low. Remember to ask about delivery times as more complicated work could take two or more weeks. ⊠*Ground fl., 28C Canal Rd. E, Causeway Bay* ☎*2892–2465* Ⓜ*Causeway Bay.*

IT SUITS YOU

No trip to Hong Kong would be complete without a visit to one of its world-famous tailors, as many celebrities and dignitaries can attest. In often humble, fabric-cluttered settings, customer records contain the measurements of notables such as George Clooney, Kate Moss, David Bowie, David Beckham, and Queen Elizabeth II.

Prince Charles, who has his pick of Savile Row craftsmen, placed a few orders while in the territory for the 1997 handover. When Bill Clinton passed through, word has it that tailors were up until 4 AM to accommodate him.

Like some of their international clientele, who often make up a third of their total business, a handful of tailors are famous themselves. They even go on world tours for their fans. Picking the right tailor can be daunting in a city where the phone book lists about 500 of them. A good suit will last for 20 years if cared for correctly. A bad one will probably leave your closet only for its trip to the thrift store. All the more reason to make thoughtful, educated choices.

TIP

The special economic zone of Shenzhen on the mainland, just a train ride away, is known for competitively priced and speedy tailoring. Quality doesn't always measure up, though, so buyer beware.

5 STEPS TO SIZING THINGS UP

If you've ever owned a custom-made garment, you understand the joy of clothes crafted to fit your every measurement. In Hong Kong, prices rival exclusive ready-to-wear brands.

Hong Kong is best known for men's tailoring, but whether you're looking for a classic men's business suit or an evening gown, these steps will help you size things up.

1. SET YOUR STYLE

Be clear about what you want. Bring samples—a favorite piece of clothing or magazine photos. Also, Hong Kong tailors are trained in classic, structured garments. Straying from these could lead to disappointment. There are three basic suit styles. Experienced tailors can advise on the best one for your shape.

The **American cut** is considered traditional by some, shapeless by others. Its jacket has notched lapels, a center vent, and two or three buttons. The trousers are lean, with flat fronts. The **British cut** also has notched lapels and two- or three-button jackets, but it features side vents and pleated trousers. The double-breasted **Italian cut** has wide lapels and pleated trousers—a look in remission these days.

2. CHOOSE YOUR FABRIC

You're getting a deal on workmanship, so consider splurging on, say, a luxurious blend of cashmere, mink, and wool. When having something copied, though, choose a fabric similar to the original. And buy for the climate you live in, not the climate of your tailor. (How often will you wear seersucker in Alaska?) Take your time selecting: fabric is the main factor affecting cost.

Examine fabric on a large scale. Small swatches are deceiving. Those strong pinstripes might be elegant on a tiny card, but a full suit of them could make you look like an extra from *The Godfather*.

3. MEASURE UP

Meticulous measuring is the mark of a superior craftsman, so be patient. And for accuracy, stand as you normally would (you can't suck in that gut forever). Tailors often record your information, so you can have more garments sent to you without returning to Hong Kong. Still, double check measurements at home before each order.

4. PLACE YOUR ORDER

Consider ordering two pairs of trousers per suit. They wear faster than jackets, and alternating between two will help them last longer.

Most tailors require a deposit of 30%–50% of the total cost. Request a receipt detailing price, fabric, style, measurements, fittings, and production schedule. Also ask for a swatch to compare with the final product.

5. GET FIT

There should be at least two fittings. The first is usually for major alterations. Subsequent fittings are supposed to be for minor adjustments, but don't settle for less than perfect: keep sending it back until they get it right.

Bring the right clothes, such as a dress shirt and appropriate shoes, to try on a suit. Having someone you trust at the final fitting helps ensure you haven't overlooked anything.

Try jackets buttoned and unbuttoned. Examine every detail. Are shoulder seams puckered or smooth? Do patterns meet? Is the collar too loose or tight? (About two fingers' space is right.)

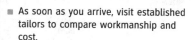

FINDING A TAILOR

- As soon as you arrive, visit established tailors to compare workmanship and cost.

- Ask if the work is bespoke (made from scratch) or made-to-measure (based on existing patterns but handmade according to your measurements).

- You get what you pay for. Assume the workmanship and fabric will match the price.

- A fine suit requires six or more days to create. That said, be wary but not dismissive of "24-hour tailors." Hong Kong's most famous craftsmen have turned out suits in a day.

MEN'S TAILORING

Although most tailors can accommodate women—and a few even focus on womenswear (see listings)—Hong Kong tailors are best known for men's suits and shirts. Many shirtmakers also do pajamas, boxer shorts, and women's shirts. To help you with all the options, here are some basics.

JACKETS

Buttons: Plastic buttons can make exquisite tailoring look cheap. Select natural materials like horn. (No two natural buttons will be exactly alike.) Ask for extras, too.

Cuffs: The rule is the number of buttons on each cuff should match the total number on the front of the jacket.

Double- or Single-Breasted: Single-breasted jackets are more versatile: you can dress them up or down and wear them open or buttoned. Two buttons are most popular, but single-breasted jackets can have from one to four.

Lining: The interior (sleeves and pockets, too) should be lined with a beautifully stitched, high-quality fabric like silk. The lining affects both how the jacket falls and how readily it glides on and off.

Pockets: Standard jackets have straight pockets; modern designs have slanted ones. Both can be a slot style or have flaps, which may add girth. A small ticket pocket above a standard pocket is a nice touch.

Stitching: Handstitched lapels subtly show off fine tailoring; the discerning request handstitched buttonholes as well. At the first fitting, stitches should be snug and free of any fraying.

Vent: The vent was created to allow cavalry officers to sit in their saddles comfortably. Although you probably won't go riding in your suit, don't skip the vent. Unvented jackets simply aren't flattering.

SHIRTS

Back: The back can be plain or have a box, side, or inverted pleat.

Collars: Some are straight (pointed), others are rounded. Ask for removable stays; cleaning with them inside a collar causes points to fray. The English collar has a semi-cutaway style; a tab collar has a strip of fabric holding it in place. Button-down collars are more casual.

Cuffs: Cuffs should just show from beneath jacket sleeves. Styles include rounded, square, or angled with one or two buttons. The elegant French (or double) cuff is worn with cufflinks.

Fit: Tailors can make shirts snug or baggy, depending on your taste, and still avoid the ballooned look of mass-produced garments.

Front: You can choose a plain front or one with a placket. Pockets (optional) can go on the left or right and be monogrammed.

TROUSERS

Hems: Some argue cuffless or flat hems are formal; others consider them casual—even costume-like. It's your call. To accommodate shoes, hems are slightly shorter at the front.

Length: Prescribed lengths differ by style, but socks should remain hidden, and trousers should cover half to two-thirds of the shoe.

Pleats: Younger generations prefer flat-front trousers. Traditionalists like single or double pleats, which are roomier in the hips and thighs.

Pockets: Pockets cut on the diagonal are standard, but you can opt for horizontal or vertical designs. One or two (more casual) back pockets, with or without flaps, are also options.

Waist Details: You can request waist adjusters (internal buttons and straps that let you adjust the waist by about 2 inches) or waistband buttons for suspenders.

	Save	Splurge	Break the Bank
SUITS	HK$2,800 (Yuen's Tailor and Jantzen Tailor); HK$3,000 (Sam's Tailor)	HK$4,500 (Mode Elegante); HK$7,000 (Ascot Chang)	HK$8,000–HK$17,000 (A-Man Hing Cheong)
SHIRTS	HK$300 (Yuen's Tailor); HK$350 (Sam's Tailor).	HK$500 (Mode Elegante)	HK$700–HK$6,000 (Ascot Chang, HK$1,000 is average); HK$-00–HK$1,800 (A-Man Hing Cheong).

Where to Eat

WORD OF MOUTH

"Best 'cha chan teng' food in Central [is Tsui Wah] and I'm Chinese! Avoid the over-priced beer and you can't go wrong."

—drlam

"The prices of food vary greatly depending on where you eat. One can get at bowl of fish ball noodle soup for HK$16. Or one can have a piece of cake for 4 times that amount."

—yk

WHERE TO EAT PLANNER

Dining Strategy

With thousands of Hong Kong eateries competing for your attention, it may seem daunting. But fret not—the 90-plus selections here represent the best the region has to offer. Search "Best Bets" for top recommendations by price, cuisine, and experience. Sample local flavor in the neighborhood features. Or find a review in the alphabetical listings. Delve in, and enjoy!

Reservations

Book ahead during Chinese holidays and the eves of public holidays, or at high-end hotel restaurants like Alain Ducasse's SPOON or Caprice. Certain classic Hong Kong preparations (e.g., beggar's chicken, whose preparation in a clay pot takes hours) require reserving not just a table but the dish itself. Do so at least 24 hours in advance.

You'll also need reservations for a meal at one of the so-called private kitchens—unlicensed culinary speakeasies, which are often the city's hottest tickets. Book several days ahead, and be prepared to pay a deposit. Reservations are virtually unheard of at small, local restaurants.

Share & Share Alike

In China food is meant to be shared. Instead of ordering individual main dishes, it's usual for those around a table—whether two or 12 people—to share several. Four people eating together, for example, might order a whole or half chicken, another type of meat, a fish dish, a vegetable, and fried noodles—all of which would be placed on the table's lazy Susan. Restaurants may adjust portions and prices according to the number of diners.

Western-style cutlery is common in many—but not all—up-market restaurants in Hong Kong, but what better place to practice your chopstick skills? Serving chopsticks are usually provided for each dish. You should use these to serve yourself and others. If no serving chopsticks are provided, serve yourself using your own chopsticks; just be sure to use the ends that you haven't put into your mouth.

Hours

A typical Hong Kong breakfast is often congee (a rice porridge) or noodles. Most hotels serve western-style breakfasts, however, and coffee, pastries, and sandwiches are readily available at Delifrance, Starbucks, and local coffee-shop chains. Lunchtime is between noon and 1:30 PM; normal dinner hours are from 7 until 10 PM, but Hong Kong is a 24-hour city and you'll be able to find a meal here at any hour. Dim sum begins as early as 10 AM, but it's unusual to find it served in the evenings.

What to Wear

Casual dress—sports shirts, T-shirts, clean jeans, and the like—is acceptable almost everywhere in Hong Kong, although shorts and sneakers or flip-flops will feel out of place at trendy venues and five-star restaurants where people dress to impress. Generally, the dress code in Hong Kong is stylish but quite conservative; most office workers, both male and female, wear suits to work and favor dark colors.

Cru or Brew?

Traditionally, markups on wine have been high here, and wine lists uninspired. In 2008, Hong Kong scrapped import duties on wines, but at the time of writing, the impact had yet to trickle down to most restaurants. French reds have long had a cachet in Hong Kong but wine lists increasingly include selections from Australia, New Zealand, and South America that are often better suited to the local cuisine and the climate. Many midrange restaurants and private kitchens allow you to bring your own wine for a corkage fee.

For Cantonese food, tea is traditional, but Hong Kong likes its beer—before, during, or after dinner. It's generally light stuff, like Heineken, the locally brewed San Miguel, or a Chinese lager such as immensely popular Tsing Tao. Several English and Irish pubs have Guinness and Harp on tap. When it's time to hit the karaoke bars or discotheques, though, people switch to whiskey. It's generally drunk on the rocks or mixed with sweetened, iced, green tea. Beware: this local concoction goes down very easily.

Prices, Tipping & Tax

The ranges in our chart reflect actual prices of main courses on dinner menus (unless dinner isn't served). That said, the custom of sharing dishes affects the ultimate cost of your dinner. Further, we exclude outrageously expensive dishes—abalone, bird's nest soup, shark's fin soup.

Don't be shocked that you've been charged for everything, including tea, rice, and those side dishes placed automatically on your table. At upmarket and western-style restaurants, tips are appreciated (10% is generous); the service charge on your bill doesn't go to the waitstaff.

WHAT IT COSTS IN HK$

¢	$	$$	$$$	$$$$
AT DINNER				
under HK$50	HK$50–HK$100	HK$100–HK$200	HK$200–HK$300	over HK$300

Prices are per person for a main course at dinner and exclude the customary 10% service charge.

5

Ancient Secrets

If you keep an open mind about food, you can lose yourself in the magic of a cuisine whose traditions have been braising for millennia. It has its roots in Guangdong (Canton) Province. Cantonese cooks believe that the secret to bringing out the natural flavors of food is to cook fresh ingredients quickly at very high temperatures. The resulting dishes are then served and eaten immediately.

BEST BETS FOR HONG KONG DINING

Fodor's writers and editors have listed their favorite restaurants by price, cuisine, and experience below. In the first column the Fodor's Choice properties represent the "best of the best" across price categories. You can also search by area in the following pages.

FODOR'S CHOICE

L'Atelier de Joël Robuchon, $$$$, p.187
Cinecittà, $$$, p.195
H One, $$$-$$$$, p.186
Hutong, $$$-$$$$, p.216
Ko Lau Wan Hotspot and Seafood Restaurant, $$, p.216
Lucy's, $$$, p.202
Lung King Heen, $$$, p.188
Shek O Chinese Thai Seafood Restaurant, $, p.202
The Verandah, $$$$, p.203

By Price

¢

Mak's Noodles Limited, p.189
Tsui Wah Restaurant, p.190

$

Good Luck Thai, p.183
Jing Cheng Xiao Chu, p.179

$$

Grappa's, p.192
Jaspa's, p.220
The Press Room, p.189
Spices, p.202
Tandoor, p.190

$$$

M at the Fringe, p.188
Tokio Joe, p.190
Yung Kee, p.191

$$$$

Dynasty, p.195
Spoon by Alain Ducasse, p.218
Caprice, p.182

By Cuisine

CANTONESE & DIM SUM

Dynasty, $$$$
Gitone Fine Arts, $$$, p.195
Ko Lau Wan Hotspot and Seafood Restaurant, $$
Lung King Heen, $$$
OVOlogue, $$, p.197
Yung Kee, $$-$$$
Zen, $$-$$$, p.194

ASIAN

Bo Innovation, $$$$, p.181
Good Luck Thai, $
Spices, $$

JAPANESE

Sushi Hiro, $$$, p.198
Tokio Joe, $$

INTERNATIONAL

Grappa's, $$
H One, $$$-$$$$
Lucy's, $$$
Malouf's Modern Middle Eastern, $$$, p.217

EUROPEAN

Amber, $$$$
L'Atelier de Joël Robuchon, $$$$
Caprice, $$$$
Cinecittà, $$$
M at the Fringe, $$$-$$$$
The Press Room, $$
Restaurant Pétrus, $$$$, p.193

By Experience

GREAT VIEW

Café Deco, $$, p.182
Felix, $$$$, p.214
Pearl on the Peak, $$$, p.189
Restaurant Pétrus, $$$$
Spoon by Alain Ducasse, $$$$

BUSINESS DINING

Dynasty, $$$$
Grappa's, $$
H One, $$$-$$$$
Lung King Heen, $$$
Zen, $$-$$$

CHILD-FRIENDLY

Café Kool, $$$, p.219
Dan Ryan's, $$$, p.192
Jaspa's, $$
Shek O Chinese Thai Seafood Restaurant, $
Top Deck, $$$-$$$$, p.202
Zak's, $$, p.206

HOT SPOTS

L'Atelier de Joël Robuchon, $$$$
Zuma, $$$$, p.191

MOST ROMANTIC

Caprice, $$$$
Lucy's, $$$
OVOlogue, $$
Pearl on the Peak, $$$
The Verandah, $$$

Updated by
Liana Cafolla
& Helen Luk

Stand your ground when faced with a barrage of 16-stroke Chinese characters. Don't wince at the steaming cauldron of innards or the rows of webbed duck feet that announce the corner restaurant's offerings. Be bold at the sight of a vicious cleaver beheading a roast suckling pig.

If you do, you'll find that the resulting crackles of pork fat and tender slices of meat—served with rice and some glistening greens—taste better than anything at the western-theme restaurant or pan-Chinese chain down the street. You know the one. It has the English-language menu and the empty tables.

At small, local restaurants specializing in Cantonese food, don't expect an English menu or knives and forks. (Tip: if you struggle with chopsticks, keep a plastic fork or spoon in your bag). The best advice is to follow the crowds. Choose a restaurant that's full, and don't be shy about pointing to an interesting dish at your neighbor's table. This is often the best way to order, since even when there is an English menu, local specialties may not be on it.

The pointing method of ordering will come in handy when you visit the plethora of small, brightly lit dives, many open into the wee hours, that specialize either in noodle soups or roast meats. At noodle-centric restaurants, fish-ball soup with ramen noodles is an excellent choice, and the goose, suckling pig, honeyed pork, and soy-sauce chicken are good bets at the roast-meat shops. A combination plate, with a sampling of meats and some greens on a bed of white rice, is a foolproof way to go.

Other than being adventurous, what's the best way to enjoy a memorable meal in Hong Kong? Remember that many fine-dining restaurants are located in five-star hotels and shopping malls. Several of these restaurants, such as Dynasty and Caprice, offer seasonal menus or special chef's selections along with their standard à la carte options, and these are often the best bets.

Finally, remember that Hong Kong is the world's epicenter of dim sum. While you're here you must have at least one dim sum breakfast or lunch in a teahouse. Those steaming bamboo baskets you see conceal delicious dumplings, buns, and pastries—all as comforting as they are exotic.

HONG KONG ISLAND

WESTERN

The restaurants listed in this section (the Western district) are all in a neighborhood known as SoHo (the area *south of Hollywood* Road), which is a few minutes' walk uphill from Central. SoHo spreads mainly along Elgin Street, Staunton Street, and Old Bailey Street, and is accessible by the long, outdoor Midlevels Escalator. The emphasis in SoHo is generally on foreign cuisines, including Spanish, Italian, Indian, Argentinean, Cuban, French, Portuguese, and Russian. Quality and authenticity of the food varies, and (as seems to be the case in every SoHo in the world) trendiness can get the better of some of these joints—but the area is worth a visit to experience the SoHo atmosphere.

$$–$$$
SICHUAN
✕ **Da Ping Huo.** If you can find the semi-hidden door to this restaurant speakeasy, one of Hong Kong's famed private kitchens, the rewards are great indeed. It begins with a 14-course meal that takes you on a spicy tour of the Sichuan province, and ends with live Chinese opera, courtesy of the chef. The menu varies day to day—it's whatever the chef feels like preparing—so leave your food phobias and quirks at the door, especially if those phobias include a burning mouth: this is some of the spiciest food in town. ⊠ *49 Hollywood Rd., SoHo, Western* ☎ *2559–1317* ☐ *AE, MC, V* ⊙ *No lunch* Ⓜ *Central.*

$
CANTONESE
✕ **Jing Cheng Xiao Chu.** You'll have to take a taxi to the quiet Sai Ying Pun residential neighborhood to sample the delights of this private kitchen, which, unlike most of Hong Kong's many so-called "speakeasy restaurants," is actually licensed. The chef, who goes by "Master Law," takes orders in advance for dishes from all over China, which might include chicken in a farmer's bucket, jumbo shrimp in sweet sauce, or Ningbo pine-nut fish. The restaurant also pitches a health-food angle, but as is generally the case in Hong Kong, it's dubious. This will take you well off the tourist track, and delightfully so. ⊠ *92 High St., Sai Ying Pun, Western* ☎ *2291–0289* ☐ *No credit cards.*

¢–$
MALAYSIAN
✕ **Katong Laksa.** Not many tourists wind up spending much time in Sheung Wan, but if you do, it's worth trying one of the many new Malaysian noodle shops in the area. This bright little Singaporean-Malaysian restaurant is one such place, and it makes a great lunch stop. Try the Straits noodle dishes such as laksa, a seafood noodle soup and the restaurant's namesake, or anything including shrimp. Service is more than welcoming. ⊠ *8 Mercer St., Sheung Wan, Western* ☎ *2543–4008* ☐ *No credit cards* Ⓜ *Sheung Wan.*

$$
NORTHERN CHINESE

✕**Shui Hu Ju.** It's hard to characterize the cuisine of this evocative and romantic theme restaurant whose influence comes from the north of China. You'll find Shanghainese, Cantonese, and Sichuan dishes on the menu; perhaps the epicenter of inspiration is the last of those, with successful versions of dishes such as deep-fried chicken with hot chilies. Good, too, is crispy mutton. Ultimately, though, Shui Hu Ju's atmosphere is an even greater draw than the food: heavy antique doors welcome you into an intimate, lacquered-wood space that makes you feel as though you've just walked into a Zhang Yimou movie. It's expensive, but it's a Hong Kong experience not to be missed. ⊠*68 Peel St., SoHo, Western* ☎*2869–6927* ⊕*www.aqua.com.hk* ⊟ *DC, MC, V* ⊙*No lunch* Ⓜ*Central.*

> **SPICY SICHUAN**
>
> Also known as Szechuan, this cooking style features an eye-watering array of chilies and the ingredients are cooked slowly for an integrated flavor—the opposite of Cantonese food. Sichuan rice, bamboo, wheat, river fish, shell-fish, chicken, and pork dishes are all prepared with plenty of salt, anise, fennel seed, chili, and coriander.

CENTRAL

One of Hong Kong's busiest areas is particularly crazy at lunchtime, when office workers crowd the streets and eateries. Most restaurants have set lunches—generally good values—with speedy service, so everyone gets in and out within an hour. At night the norm is either a formal dinner or a quick bite followed by many drinks, especially in Central's nightlife center, a warren of cobbled backstreets called Lan Kwai Fong. If you want to sample the expat party scene, you might want to eat elsewhere and head to LKF after dinner; restaurants in this district tend to have a contrived quality, with stylized themes and menus along with relatively steep prices. They remind us more of places in Las Vegas or Times Square rather than in the gateway to China.

$$$$
FRENCH

✕**Amber.** When the Landmark Mandarin Oriental hotel opened in 2005 its aim was to be seen as the preeminent hotel on Hong Kong Island. It made sense that it would contain a flagship power-lunch restaurant that aspires to a similar level of impeccable, modern style. Chef Richard Ekkebus's tasting menu includes creative dishes such as Dungeness crab served in five different forms—jelly, salad, foam, bisque, and ice cream—and New Zealand langoustine with seared pork belly and purple artichokes. ⊠*Landmark Mandarin Oriental Hotel, 15 Queen's Rd., Central* ☎*2132–0066* ⊟*AE, DC, MC, V* Ⓜ*Central.*

$$$$
CONTEMPORARY

✕**Bo Innovation.** The mastermind behind this deservedly renowned and upscale "private kitchen" is Alvin Leung, who dubbed himself the "demon chef" and had that moniker tattooed on his arm. Leung set up Bo Innovation in Central in 2005 to serve what he calls "extreme Chinese" cuisine, applying molecular gastronomy, French, and Japanese cooking techniques to traditional Cantonese dishes. Three years later, the restaurant has moved to a bigger spot in Wan Chai with outdoor seating, but Leung's cooking remains quirky and hard to define. Some of

CHINA'S CUISINES

To help you navigate China's many cuisines we have used the following terms in our restaurant reviews.

Cantonese: A diverse cuisine that roasts and fries, braises and steams. Spices are used in moderation. Notable dishes include fried rice, sweet-and-sour pork, and roasted goose.

Chinese: Catch-all term used for restaurants that serve cuisine from multiple regions of China; pan-Chinese.

Chinese Fusion: Any type of Chinese cuisine with international influences.

Chiu Chow: Known for its vegetarian and seafood dishes, which are mostly poached, steamed, or braised. Signature dishes include *popiah* (non-fried spring rolls), baby oyster congee, and fish ball noodle soup.

Hunan: Stewing, frying, braising, and smoking are featured cooking methods. Flavors are spicy, incorporating chili peppers, shallots, and garlic, along with dried and preserved condiments. Signature dishes are Mao's braised pork, steamed fish head with shredded chilies, and spicy eggplant in garlic sauce.

Macanese: An eclectic blend of southern Chinese and Portuguese cooking, featuring the use of salted dried fish, coconut milk, turmeric, and other spices. Common dishes are "African" barbecued chicken with spicy piri piri sauce, pork buns, and curried baked chicken.

Mandarin (Beijing): China's capital city, Beijing, features cuisine from all over the country. Dishes from the city typically are snack sized, featuring ingredients like dark soy paste, sesame paste, and sesame oil. Regional specialties include Peking duck, moo shu pork, and quick-fried tripe.

Northern Chinese (inner Mongolia and environs): Staples are lamb and mutton, preserved vegetables, and noodles, steamed breads, pancakes, stuffed buns, and dumplings. Common dishes are cumin-scented lamb, congee porridge with pickles, and Mongolian hotpot.

Sichuan (central province): Famed for bold flavors and spiciness resulting from liberal use of chilies and Sichuan peppercorns. Regional dishes include "dan dan" spicy rice noodles, twice-cooked pork, and tea-smoked duck.

Shanghainese: Cuisine characterized by rich flavors produced by braising and stewing, and the use of alcohol in cooking. Dumplings, noodles, and bread are served more than rice. Signature dishes are baby hairy crabs stir-fried with rice cake slices, steamed buns and dumplings, and "drunken chicken."

Taiwanese: Diverse cuisine owing to its history and subtropical location. Seafood, pork, rice, soy, and fruit form the backbone of the cuisine. Specialties include "three cups chicken" with a sauce made of soya, rice wine, and sugar; oyster omelets; cuttlefish soup; and dried tofu.

Tibetan: A cuisine reliant on foodstuffs that grow at high altitudes, including barley flour; yak meat, milk, butter, and cheese; and mustard seed used for seasoning. Salted black tea with yak butter is a staple beverage.

Yunnan (southernmost province): This region is known as the "kingdom of plants and animals." Its cuisine is noted for its use of vegetables, fruit, bamboo shoots, and flowers in its spicy preparations. Signature dishes include rice noodle soup with chicken, pork, and fish; steamed chicken with ginseng and herbs; and the cured Yunnan ham.

5

his recent creations include an egg-tart martini, which turns the classic Hong Kong pastry into an eggnog-like drink with a crust around the rim in place of salt. The toro (tuna belly) sashimi topped with foie gras powder blends two rich flavors into one. The Australian Wagyu strip-loin with black-truffle *cheung fan*,

or rice roll, is a winner. At dinner, choose between the eight-course tasting menu (HK$680) or the 12-course chef's menu (HK$1,080); it's not possible to dine à la carte. Tables are often full on Friday and Saturday, so book in advance. ⊠*Shop No. 13, 2nd fl., J Residence, 60 Johnston Rd., Wan Chai* ☎*2850–8371* ⊕*www.boinnovation.com* ⌕*Reservations essential* ⊟*AE, DC, MC, V* ⊘*Closed Sun. No lunch Sat.* Ⓜ *Wan Chai.*

$$
ECLECTIC
✕**Café Deco Bar & Grill.** As is often the case where there's a captive audience, dining up at the Peak Galleria mall is a crapshoot. This huge eatery is no exception: you come for the views, not the food. The best strategy might be to come here in time for sunset, hit Café Deco just for drinks and appetizers, and enjoy the vistas; then head down to the city for dinner. Dishes on the overly ambitious menu traverse five or six continents, and are dramatically prepared by chefs in open kitchens (which will, at least, amuse the kids). Oysters are good and the pizza is okay, but you should avoid the insipid Southeast Asian fare and overpriced steaks. When you book (and you must), be sure to request a table with a view, as many tables in the place have none, which defeats the purpose of coming. ⊠*1st fl., Peak Galleria, 118 Peak Rd., The Peak, Central* ☎*2849–5111* ⊕*www.cafedecogroup.com* ⌕*Reservations essential* ⊟*AE, DC, MC, V.*

$$$$
FRENCH
✕**Caprice.** The Four Seasons spared no expense in creating this stunning space, bringing in well-known designers and feng shui masters, which has resulted in a private dining room that is quite possibly one of the most spectacular in the world: you sit next to an indoor garden, looking through the entire open kitchen, floor-to-ceiling glass, and the great harbor beyond. Crystal chandeliers sparkle in the main dining hall with two Mucha replicas lining the wall. Chef Vincent Thierry sets himself apart with the details: the lobster carpaccio is mixed perfectly with the caviar and yuzu blanc manger, while the slow-cooked lamb fillet topped with black truffle is heavenly. The talented sommelier seems to be able to pick the best wine to go with any dish. Don't forget to sample the wide selection of cheese, including a Comté cheese that took four years to age—Caprice is the only restaurant in Hong Kong that serves this. Reserve well in advance. ⊠*Four Seasons Hotel, 8 Finance St., Central* ☎*3196–8888* ⊕*www.fourseasons.com* ⌕*Reservations essential* ⊟*AE, DC, MC, V* Ⓜ*Central.*

$$$$
CANTONESE
✕**Cuisine Cuisine.** The dramatic structures that make up the International Finance Centre complex, dominated by IFC One, Hong Kong's tallest skyscraper, have become a hotbed of ambitious new restaurants—almost all of which have harbor views. This Cantonese res-

taurant is one of the best, already gaining praise for its traditional menu (albeit with some nouvelle liberties) such as sautéed fresh lobster with scrambled egg white and almond sauce. Other winners are chicken baked with rock salt in an age-old method, and roasted crispy duck breast with Chinese-style blini. ✉*3101–3107, podium level 3, International Finance Center Mall, Central* ☎*2393–3933* ⊕*www.cuisinecuisine.hk* 🖃*AE, DC, MC, V* Ⓜ*Central.*

WORD OF MOUTH

"Quite popular with the after-work crowd, DiVino makes for an energizing start to a big night out in Hong Kong."   –Nicole

$$$ | **ITALIAN** ✕**DiVino.** This ultracool wine bar feels like something straight out of Milan, bringing with it small plates for casual snacking and mixed platters ideal for sharing. Not surprisingly, it's popular with the drinks-after-work crowd—and you get complimentary savory treats with your wine from 6 to 8 PM. But don't underestimate the cuisine: the tailor-made cold-cut platters, for starters, are superb. The cheese board is served with crusty, oven-warm bread. Pasta main courses include Gorgonzola and black-truffle penne and pumpkin gnocchi with sage and ricotta cheese. The place also stays open for revelry late into the evening. ✉*Shop 1, 73 Wyndham St., Central* ☎*2167–8883* ⊕*www. divino.com.hk* 🖃*AE, DC, MC, V* ⊘*No lunch Sun.* Ⓜ*Central.*

$$–$$$ | **PAN-ASIAN** ✕**dragon-i.** If you can stomach the scene at this scenester hangout, an evening at dragon-i can be a memorable experience. The hip interior is a window into the world of Hong Kong's beautiful people. A velvet rope shows up at some point each evening, and the models all put in an appearance on Wednesday nights (and along follows everyone else). Happily, the Japanese and traditional Cantonese cuisines generally keep up—just don't come with lofty expectations, and be prepared to spend a lot for small portions. Dim sum lunch on the terrace is a lower-impact way to go. ✉*Basement fl., The Centrium, 60 Wyndham St., Central* ☎*3110–1222* ⊕*www.dragon-i.com.hk* ⚘*Reservations essential* 🖃*AE, DC, MC, V* ⊘*Closed Sun.* Ⓜ*Central.*

$$$ | **ITALIAN** ✕**Gaia.** Even if you find the concept here—a re-creation of Rome's Spanish steps—cheesy, it's hard to argue with the alfresco seating at this trendy wine bar and restaurant. You should venture indoors only if you can put up with the loud investment bankers. The authentic pan-Italian fare includes pappardelle (wide pasta noodles) in a Sangiovese-marinated rabbit ragout, and a simple *fritto misto*, the classic combination of fried fish, calamari, and shrimp. ✉*Ground fl., The Piazza, Grand Millennium Plaza, 181 Queen's Rd., Central* ☎*2167–8200* ⊕*www. gaiaristorante.com* 🖃*AE, DC, MC, V* Ⓜ*Sheung Wan.*

$ | **THAI** ⟳ ✕**Good Luck Thai.** Located in a lane off the nightlife frenzy of Lan Kwai Fong, Good Luck Thai offers two menus—one Thai and one Malaysian, each with a very wide selection. Come here for authentic, tasty, no-frills food with friendly prices and smiling service. The restaurant has expanded and now has a second dining room; the larger has more atmosphere, while the smaller one to the left of the lane is quieter and slightly smarter, but you don't come here for the decor.

5

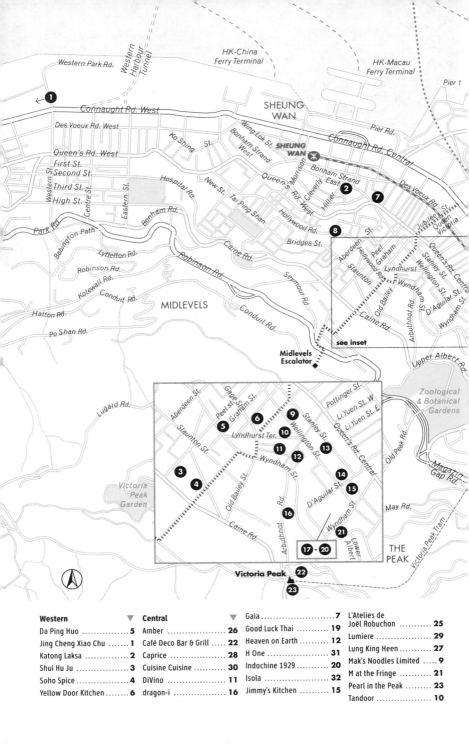

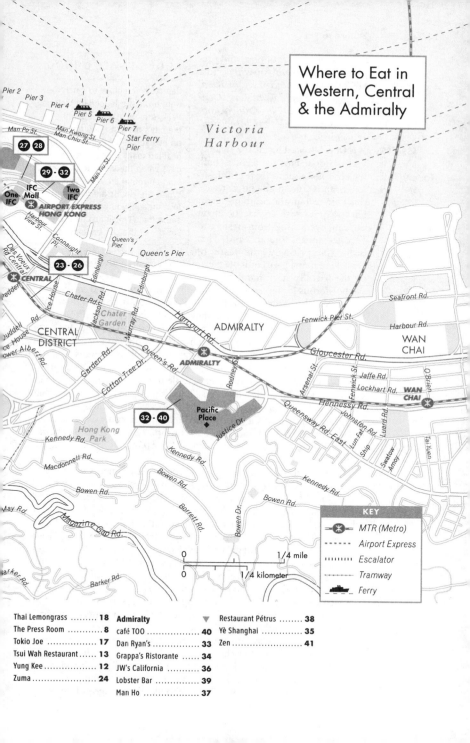

Where to Eat in Western, Central & the Admiralty

Pier 2
Pier 3
Pier 4
Pier 5
Pier 6
Pier 7
Star Ferry Pier

Man Po St.
Man Kwong St.
Man Chiu St.
Man Yiu St.

27 28

29 - 32

One IFC
IFC Mall
Two IFC

AIRPORT EXPRESS
HONG KONG

Harbour View St.

Des Voeux Rd Central

Connaught Pl.

Queen's Pier

Queen's Pier

23 - 26

Ice House

Edinburgh

Edinburgh

CENTRAL

Pedden

Chater Rd.

Jackson Rd.

Murray Rd.

Harcourt Rd.

Chater Garden

Victoria Harbour

ADMIRALTY

Fenwick Pier St.

Seafront Rd.

Harbour Rd.

WAN CHAI

Juddell

ce House

ower Albert Rd.

CENTRAL DISTRICT

Garden Rd.

Cotton Tree Dr.

Queen's Rd.

Rodney St.

ADMIRALTY

Gloucester Rd.

Arsenal St.

Fenwick St.

Jaffe Rd.

Lockhart Rd.

WAN CHAI

O'Brien

32 - 40

Pacific Place

Justice Dr.

Hennessy Rd.

Queensway Rd. East

Johnston Rd.

Lun Fat

Ship St.

Luard Rd.

Swatow

Amoy

Tai Yuen

Hong Kong Park

Kennedy Rd.

Macdonnell Rd.

Bowen Rd.

Kennedy Rd.

Bowen Rd.

Bowen Rd.

Kennedy Rd.

May Rd.

Magazine Gap Rd.

Borrett Rd.

Bowen Dr.

arker Rd.

Barker Rd.

0   1/4 mile

0   1/4 kilometer

KEY

MTR (Metro)
Airport Express
Escalator
Tramway
Ferry

It's great for kids, couples, and pre-party fuel. Corkage for wine is just HK$50. ⊠*Ground fl., Lan Kwai Fong, 13 Wing Wah La., Central* ☎*2877–2971* ⊕*www.lank waifong.com* ⊟*V* ⊗*Closed Sun.* Ⓜ*Central.*

ABOVE-IT-ALL DINING

Central is the place to catch the tram up to the legendary Victoria Peak. A meal in a restaurant at the city's highest point has to be on everyone's itinerary. The trip is justified many times over on clear days when the views from the top (and en route) are unparalleled. When the clouds are thick and low, though, you won't be able to see a thing–you'll just hear the sounds of the city beneath you.

$$$–$$$$
ECLECTIC
Fodor'sChoice
★
✕**H One.** Situated inside the swanky International Finance Centre mall, which houses more than 200 fashion brands and high-end eateries, this chic restaurant combines great harbor views with an eclectic menu offering everything from oysters to Mediterranean, Indian, and Thai dishes. Surprisingly, the team of chefs here manages to pull off the ambitious menu with great skill, aided by the friendly staff: handmade pastas concocted by Alberto Boccelli, the boisterous Italian executive chef, the Italian marinated sardines, and the Indian chicken makhani (a dish of peanutty, buttery, Indian spiced chicken goodness) are all exceptional. The charcoal-grilled sirloin is done to perfection and one of the best in town. Diners can also opt for tasting menus of five to eight courses, which cost HK$680 and up, and include dishes such as sautéed Venetian baby clams, white asparagus soup with Dungeness crab meat and truffle, herb-braised Italian baby goat, and baby scampi spinosini (square egg-noodle pasta). Tip: the tasting menus do not typically include Indian or Thai dishes unless you request them. Reservations are recommended for window seats. Nearby G Bar and The Box (which offers a good-value lunch buffet and private parties at night), are run by the same restaurant group. ⊠*Shop 4008–10, podium level 4, IFC Mall 8 Finance St., Central* ☎*2805–0638* ⊟*AE, DC, MC, V* Ⓜ*Central.*

$–$$
SHANGHAINESE
✕**Heaven on Earth.** There are some Hong Kong moments when all you feel like eating is a simple bowl of spicy noodles, but you aren't in the mood for the sensory barrage and language-barrier antics associated with the neighborhood noodle shops. That's where Heaven on Earth, which used to be just a bar and still feels like a sleek cocktail lounge, comes in. It's a modern, dimly lighted, but relatively inexpensive place for Shanghainese noodle and dumpling dishes that nudge toward originality but don't cross familiar bounds. Lunch specials at HK$50 are a particular bargain. ⊠*Century Square, basement, 1–13 D'Aguilar St., Central* ☎*2537–8083* ⊕*www.kingparrot.com* ⊟*AE, MC, V* Ⓜ*Central.*

$$
HUNAN
✕**Hunan Garden.** Run by Hong Kong's largest restaurant chain, Maxim's, this eatery serves Hunan cuisine that has been watered down for Hong Kongers' mild palates. The elegant black-and-white decor resembles a European restaurant more than a typical Chinese joint. Dishes may not be spicy-hot but the signature dish—codfish fillet with fried minced beans, a chewy and nutty bean paste—is well worth trying. So is the smooth Hunan chicken soup with minced chicken and pork, served in a small porcelain container. Those who like the orange-colored sweet-

and-sour sauce may want to try the Beijing-style deep-fried prawns in chili sauce. ⊠*Shop 1302, 13th fl., Food Forum, Times Square, Causeway Bay* ☎*2506–9288* ⊟*AE, DC, MC, V* Ⓜ*Causeway Bay.*

$$
VIETNAMESE ✕**Indochine 1929.** It's touristy and it caters to westerners, but this second-floor Vietnamese restaurant

in the heart of the Lan Kwai Fong nightlife strip is fun, too, transporting you to a French plantation veranda in colonial Indochina, surrounded by old maps, antique fans, and lamps. Most of the spices used are imported from Vietnam, even if they're employed less liberally than they would be over there. Highlights include soft-shell crabs, grilled beef salad, and fried fish Hanoi style (using northern spices). Unfortunately, in classic LKF form, service is distracted, sometimes even rude—maybe they're sick of listening to all the raucous foreigners. ⊠*2nd fl., California Tower, 30–32 D'Aguilar St., Lan Kwai Fong, Central* ☎*2869–7399* ⊕*www.lankwaifong.com* ⊟*AE, DC, MC, V* ☉*No lunch Sun.* Ⓜ*Central.*

$$$
ITALIAN ✕**Isola.** In the shadow of the world's sixth-tallest building, flowing Isola is everything that the new Hong Kong is all about, especially the outdoor seats amid an urban jungle of concrete, manicured glass, and potted trees, in front of the open harbor. But Isola's regional Italian cuisine is authentic, with selections like chestnut pappardelle with wild-duck ragout, simple and well-executed stone-baked pizzas, or roasted king prawns wrapped in *lardo di collonnata,* a delicious cured ham. Even so, Isola is as much of a nighttime bar scene as anything else, and it's worth coming just to sample cocktails and take in the soaring room. ⊠*Levels 3 & 4, International Finance Center Mall, Central* ☎*2383–8765* ⊕*www.isolabarandgrill.com* ⊟*AE, DC, MC, V* Ⓜ*Central.*

$$$
ECLECTIC ✕**Jimmy's Kitchen.** One of the oldest restaurants in Hong Kong, Jimmy's opened in 1928 and serves comfort food from around the world to a loyal clientele in a private-club atmosphere. Neither the food nor the decor has changed much in the last 30 years. Its handy location just off Queen's Road in Central and a menu that offers a wide selection of both western and Asian dishes including borscht, goulash, bangers and mash, curry, and burgers have made Jimmy's a favorite with both Chinese and western locals as well as tourists looking for a taste of home. It's not cheap, but it's a good choice for a night out with friends, especially if your group's cravings are pulling you in different directions. ⊠*Basement, South China Bldg., 1–3 Wyndham St., Central* ☎*2526–5293* ⊟*AE, DC, MC, V* Ⓜ*Central.*

$$$$
FRENCH ✕ **L'Atelier de Joël Robuchon.** Robuchon is one of the best celebrity chefs to have opened shop in Hong Kong in the past two years. Though
Fodor'sChoice his creations do come at an astronomical price, Robuchon, who has
★ 18 Michelin stars under his belt, claims that his atelier (or "artist's workshop") is for casual dining, not haute cuisine. Diners sit on red-leather-and-chrome barstools around a square, black marble counter, designed like a Japanese sushi bar so that everyone can watch the

5

chef and his staff painstakingly preparing the food in the open kitchen. Though entrées are available, diners typically order several small plates designed for sharing. Everything from the freshly baked bread, stacked in a coral-shaped basket, to desserts like the delectable Le Chocolate Sensation, a

creamy dark Valrhona chocolate sorbet on an Oreo biscuit, topped with raspberry–mango sauce is immaculately presented. The scallop savarin topped with truffle spaghetti coiled into a bowl shape, the tête de veau (crispy veal head), and the deservedly famous mashed potatoes are all standouts. The restaurant also has a fine-dining section, Le Jardin, overlooking a well-groomed lawn and Central high-rises. Reservations are recommended for Friday and Saturday. For those who do not want to splurge on a full meal, try the superb croissants, cakes, and coffee at the tea salon one floor down from the restaurant. ⊠*Shop 315 (salon) & 401(restaurant), The Landmark, 15 Queen's Rd., Central* ☎*2166–9000* ⊕*www.robuchon.hk* ⊟*AE, DC, MC, V* Ⓜ*Central.*

$$$
ECLECTIC

✕**Lumiere.** Modern, sexy Lumiere, in the IFC Mall, bills itself as a "Szechuan Bistro and Bar," and its menu blends Sichuan and South American cuisines. Although main courses are Sichuan in inspiration, like spicy jumbo crab claws, the starters include ceviche. Another signature dish is seared Chilean sea bass in Sichuan style. Also getting high marks is the unique cocktail list at the long bar, which overlooks the harbor. Drinks are classified into "fruity," "creamy," "dry," and "sweet-and-sour," and also categorized by strength. Here, too, there's South America to thank, as in a "Caipiritini" (a mix of caipirinha and martini)—or, if you prefer, there's always the 1970 Pétrus. ⊠*3101–3107, podium level 3, International Finance Center Mall, Central* ☎*2393–3933* ⊕*www.cuisinecuisine.hk* ⊟*AE, DC, MC, V* Ⓜ*Central.*

$$$
CANTONESE
Fodor's Choice
★

✕**Lung King Heen.** It's made a serious case for being the best Cantonese restaurant in Hong Kong—and consequently, the world. Where other contenders tend to get too caught up in prestige dishes, and hotel restaurants in name-brand chefs, here there's a complete focus on taste. When you try a little lobster-and-scallop dumpling, or a dish of housemade XO sauce that is this divine, you will be forced to reevaluate your entire conception of Chinese cuisine. ⊠*Podium 4, Four Seasons Hotel, 8 Finance St., Central* ☎*3196–8880* ⊕*www.fourseasons.com* ⌂*Reservations essential* ⊟*AE, DC, MC, V* Ⓜ*Central.*

$$$–$$$$
ECLECTIC

✕**M at the Fringe.** When Michelle Garnaut opened M at the Fringe in 1989, the idea of a high-end restaurant that offered dishes from several cuisines and was not affiliated with any hotel was completely novel to Hong Kong. Although the concept is no longer unusual, the restaurant continues to delight diners with signature dishes such as crispy suckling pig and tender slow-cooked lamb. The ajo blanco, a white gazpacho made with almond paste, is truly original. The menu also serves Middle Eastern dishes such as couscous and an Iranian stew of chicken and pomegranate, in addition to traditional French and Italian cuisines such as foie gras terrine and beef carpaccio. The common denominator, says Garnaut, is "simple, good, down-to-earth food that I like to eat and cook." Her pavlova is legendary; try it on the grand platter of eight bite-size desserts. ⊠ *1st fl., South Block, 2 Lower Albert Rd., Central* ☎ *2877–4000* ⊕ *www.m-restaurantgroup.com* ⚑ *Reservations essential* ⊟ *AE, MC, V* ⊗ *No lunch weekends* Ⓜ *Central.*

¢
CANTONESE
✕ **Mak's Noodles Limited.** Mak's looks like any other Hong Kong noodle shop, but it's one of the best known in town, with a reputation that belies its humble decor. The staff is attentive, and the menu includes some particularly inventive dishes, such as tasty pork-chutney noodles. The real test of a good noodle shop, however, is its wontons, and here they're fresh, delicate, and filled with whole shrimp. And don't miss the *sui kau,* filled with minced chicken and shrimp. ⊠ *77 Wellington St., Central* ☎ *2854–3810* ⊟ *No credit cards* Ⓜ *Central.*

$$$
AUSTRALIAN
✕ **Pearl on the Peak.** Sitting atop the Peak, one of Hong Kong's must-see attractions, this Australian restaurant offers you a 270-degree view of the glittering city far below through its floor-to-ceiling windows. Though the stunning view alone is reason to come, this lofty place has more than a sensational view—it serves good modern Australian cuisine. The restaurant is a collaboration by Hong Kong restaurant chain Maxim Group and award-winning Australian chef Geoff Lindsay and is fashioned after his Melbourne restaurant, Pearl. For starters, try the mother-of-pearl meat fried with shiitake mushroom or the refreshing gazpacho topped with crab salad and avocado. The signature entrée—tiger prawn with scampi custard—is heavenly. The Wagyu beef tenderloin, however, was quite bland and a disappointment at HK$480. For desserts, try the aromatic rose-petal and Turkish delight ice cream. The menu changes seasonally. Book well in advance for tables next to the windows as there are only 11 of them. For those who just want to enjoy the view, the restaurant has a 10-seat bar area on the terrace. ⊠ *Shop 2, level 1, The Peak Tower, 128 Peak Rd., Central* ☎ *2849–5123* ⊟ *AE, DC, MC, V* Ⓜ *Admiralty or Central.*

$$–$$$
FRENCH
✕ **The Press Room.** Light and airy with a high ceiling and open windows overlooking Hollywood Road, the Press Room is an unexpected soupçon of Paris in this arts and antiques district—come here for mouthwatering seafood platters, steak, sandwiches, and more. Try "Le Grand" seafood platter for a beautifully presented array of oysters, crab, mussels, prawns, and ceviche. Fans of authentic French desserts should not miss the sticky, light, and sensational "Tarte Tatin aux Poires" (pear tart). Large blackboards with daily specials and staff decked out in long aprons complete the picture. This chic, lively eatery is great for business lunches but relaxed enough to bring the whole family. It's also perfectly located if you're visiting Man Mo Temple. Brunch is served from 10 to 4 on weekends. ⊠ *108 Hollywood Rd., Central* ☎ *2525–3444* ⊟ *AE, DC, MC, V* Ⓜ *Central.*

$$
THAI
✕ **Soho Spice.** As with a lot of restaurants in SoHo, the foremost emphasis here is on design: a stone-walled garden out back with tables and trees just oozes with feng shui—it's an excellent alfresco choice—and floor-to-ceiling glass doors allow the light and greenery to enliven the

5

minimalist indoor room as well. The Thai-Vietnamese fare isn't the most impressive in town, but it's a good choice if you're in the area; try the green papaya and mango salad, or red curry duck. ⊠*47B Elgin St., SoHo, Central* ☎*2521–1600* ⊕*www.diningconcepts.com.hk* ⊟*AE, DC, MC, V.*

$$
INDIAN ✕**Tandoor.** A hidden gem of an Indian restaurant, Tandoor's location slightly away from the main nightlife areas means it risks being over-looked by all but Indian regulars in the know. Look no further for excellent food from a classic, wide-ranging menu and gentle, efficient service. Appetizers and tandoori dishes are particularly good. The large screen showing Bollywood movies and music is the one odd aspect of an otherwise elegant interior, but the effect is not overbearing. There's a lunch buffet on weekdays and a great value dinner buffet Monday through Thursday. Live classical Indian music plays here every night except Sunday. ⊠*1st fl., Lyndhurst Tower, Lan Kwai Fong, 1 Lyndhurst Terr., Central* ☎*2845–2262* ⊕*www.hktandoor.com* ⊟*AE, DC, MC, V.* Ⓜ*Central.*

$$
THAI ✕**Thai Lemongrass.** This relaxed restaurant serves regional Thai cuisine adjusted for palates not accustomed to spicy tastes. Large windows overlook the bustling nightlife in Lan Kwai Fong. For a refreshing drink, try the lychee and jasmine mojito. The menu highlights dishes from three different regions of Thailand, including grilled, whole fresh-water fish and herbs cooked in banana leaves with coriander-chili-lime sauce (north and northeast); sizzling seafood mousse with light red curry and coconut milk; roast duck in red curry (Central Plains); or Thai barbecued lamb cutlets (south). ⊠*30–32 D'Aguilar St., California Tower, Lan Kwai Fong, Central* ☎*2905–1688* ⊕*www.lankwaifong.com* ⊟*AE, DC, MC, V* ⊙*No lunch Sun.* Ⓜ*Central.*

$$–$$$
JAPANESE ✕**Tokio Joe.** This funky, casual joint in Lan Kwai Fong serves Japanese food with attentive and courteous finesse. The interior blends modern decoration with a touch of Japanese style—there are lanterns and a Japanese drum hanging from the ceiling. Chefs work in a central bar area and lend a wonderfully contemporary twist to some classic dishes. Start off with Chuhai, a delicious cocktail made with lemon juice, lychee liqueur, and sake, before moving onto sushi rolls and a sashimi platter. Other delightful dishes include spicy toro tartare, kelp-grilled sea bass topped with miso sauce and the Kobe beef tempura. For those who want a more intimate service directly from the chef, ask for omakase, an eight-course chef's menu that costs between HK$400 and HK$600. ⊠*16 Lan Kwai Fong, Lan Kwai Fong, Central* ☎*2525–1889* ⊕*www.lankwaifong.com* ⊲*Reservations essential* ⊟*AE, DC, MC, V* ⊙*No dinner Sun.* Ⓜ*Central.*

¢
ASIAN ✕**Tsui Wah Restaurant.** Finding a hearty meal in Central doesn't mean you have to spend a fortune—especially not if you head here first. Join the locals and order milk tea, and then move on to the extensive menu, which ranges from toasted sandwiches to noodles, fried rice, and Malaysian curries. Although it's not quite what typical Hong Kongers

would make at home, it's as close as you can come to Chinese comfort food. Noodles and fried rice are some of the safest bets for timid palates. There's also a wide range of set meals with very reasonable prices. ✉ *15D–19 Wellington St., Central* ☎ *2525–6338* ⊕ *www.tsuiwah restaurant.com* ▭ *No credit cards* Ⓜ *Central.*

$$$
SICHUAN
✕ **Yellow Door Kitchen.** A sunny, casual Sichuan private kitchen (unlicensed restaurant), the Yellow Door is still one of the most talked-about places to eat in SoHo, even though it's been open since 2002. The space is downhome and personal, with good food and good feelings. Many of the spices and ingredients are shipped in from Sichuan province to create such wonders as bean curd and meat cooked in spicy Sichuan sauce and a memorable stuffed Hangzhou-style "8-treasure duck," which is stuffed with sticky rice and braised. The HK$288 set dinner is great value. ✉ *6th fl., 37 Cochrane St., SoHo, Central* ☎ *2858–6555* ⊕ *www.yellowdoorkitchen.com.hk* ⌂ *Reservations essential* ▭ *AE, DC, MC, V* ⊘ *Closed Sun. No lunch Sat.* Ⓜ *Central.*

$$–$$$
CANTONESE
✕ **Yung Kee.** Close to Hong Kong's famous bar and dining district of Lan Kwai Fong, Yung Kee has turned into a local institution since it first opened shop as a street-food stall in 1942. It serves authentic Cantonese cuisine amid riotous decor and writhing gold dragons. Locals come here for roast goose with beautifully crisp skin and tender meat, as well as dim sum. Other award-winning dishes include the "cloudy tea" smoked pork, which needs to be reserved a day in advance, and deep-fried prawn with mini crab roe. More adventurous palates may wish to check out the thousand-year-old preserved eggs. ✉ *32–40 Wellington St., Central* ☎ *2522–1624* ⊕ *www.yungkee.com.hk* ▭ *AE, DC, MC, V* Ⓜ *Central.*

$$$$
JAPANESE
✕ **Zuma.** This funky izakaya (something like a Japanese bistro) has been serving good (though pricey) Japanese food since it opened here in 2007 following the huge success of its London restaurant. Located in the heart of Hong Kong's financial district, Zuma's Hong Kong branch makes abundant use of wood and stone in its design, creating a hip but relaxing atmosphere. Chefs concoct primarily Japanese food with a creative twist in an open kitchen. The daikoku (one of Japan's seven gods of fortune) tasting menu includes chu toro (medium-fatty tuna), thinly sliced sea bass with yuzu (a Japanese grapefruit), truffle oil, and salmon roe, and the perfectly grilled, massive Hokkaido scallops. The sushi and sashimi are fresh and beautifully presented on a slab of ice with chrysanthemum flower petals sprinkled on top. The dessert platter, which includes a chocolate cake that has a melted chocolate center and exotic Asian fruits, is equally stunning. An outdoor balcony allows diners to take in the surrounding Central night view. ✉ *Levels 5 and 6, The Landmark Atrium, 15 Queen's Rd., Central* ☎ *3657–6388* ⊕ *www.zumarestaurant.com* ▭ *AE, DC, MC, V* Ⓜ *Central.*

ADMIRALTY

Since this is essentially an office area, wedged between Central and Wan Chai and made up of a series of large shopping malls, much of the food is aimed at meeting the lunch needs of workers and shoppers. A major cinema and several good restaurants in the Pacific Place mall, however, make it a convenient destination for dinner as well. Admiralty is also home to several large hotels, which is part of why the area, along with Lan Kwai Fong and Tsim Sha Tsui, has one of Hong Kong's highest concentrations of western restaurants. Not that that's necessarily a good thing.

$$$$
ECLECTIC

✕ **café TOO.** It'll amuse the buffet-loving kids, at least: the innovative café TOO introduces all-day dining and drama with seven separate cooking "theaters" and a brigade of 30 chefs. The liveliness and bustle make it a good place to stop for breakfast or lunch. Take your pick from seafood, sushi, and sashimi; Peking duck and dim sum; a carving station for roasts, poultry, and game; noodles and pastas; and pizzas, curries, tandoori, antipasto, cured meats, salads, or sandwiches. You can even have a late-night snack here from 10:30 PM to midnight. ⊠*7th fl., Island Shangri-La hotel, Pacific Place, Supreme Court Rd., Admiralty* ☎*2820–8571* ⊕*www.shangri-la.com* ▭*AE, DC, MC, V* Ⓜ*Admiralty.*

$$$
AMERICAN
☽

✕ **Dan Ryan's.** If, after a few days of goose web and thousand-year egg, you have a sudden burger craving, this is the place. You'll find good approximations of the kind expats dream about when they think of the States. The popular bar and grill is often standing room only, so call ahead for a table. Apart from burgers, steaks, and ribs, the menu offers a smattering of international dishes—pasta and the like—but we recommend that you stay away from anything complicated (and certainly anything with fish) and stick to the simple, rib-sticking fare, served up without fuss or formality. ⊠*114 Pacific Place, 88 Queensway, Admiralty* ☎*2845–4600* ⊕*www.danryans.com* ⬧*Reservations essential* ▭*AE, DC, MC, V* Ⓜ*Admiralty.*

$$
ITALIAN

✕ **Grappa's Ristorante.** Don't let this restaurant's banal location put you off. It may be inside a shopping mall, but Grappa's lively atmosphere will make you forget your surroundings as soon as you're inside. The menu offers a wide selection of tasty Italian fare: pizzas, pastas, seafood antipasti, and plenty of meat dishes, all served in generous portions on oversized plates. Choose from inventive dishes like porcini mushroom and goose-liver risotto or *salsiccia lunganega*—homemade savory Italian sausage served with polenta and stewed vegetables. The decor is light and modern, with jazz playing in the background, and service is smart and efficient. Book a booth table for more privacy, or a terrace-style table if you want to watch the shoppers and strollers and pretend you're on a city sidewalk. Hip, talkative, international types like it here, which means you could happily dine alone and people-watch. ⊠*Shop*

132, Pacific Place, 88 Queensway, Admiralty ☎*2868–0086* ⊕*www. elgrande.com.hk* ⊟*AE, DC, MC, V* Ⓜ*Admiralty.*

$$$$
INTERNATIONAL
✕**JW's California.** Lobster and raw fish are the draw at this sleek, trendy flagship of the JW Marriott Hotel. Slide up to the sushi bar and leave your fate in the hands of the virtuoso sushi chef, who serves up pricey but artistic plates of sushi and sashimi made with incredibly fresh fish. You might also try salmon with artichokes and chorizo, spring lamb done three ways (cutlet, confit, and liver), and finish with the Napa Valley dessert sampler of chocolate Napoleon, peanut butter mousse, and a raspberry tart. ⊠*5th fl., JW Marriott Hotel, Pacific Place, 88 Queensway, Admiralty* ☎*2841–3899* ⊕*www.jwmarriotthk.com* ⊟*AE, DC, MC, V* Ⓜ*Admiralty.*

$$$$
SEAFOOD
✕**Lobster Bar & Grill.** The giant tropical-fish tank at the entrance sets the scene here. As the name suggests, lobster is the featured ingredient, whipped into soups, stuffed into appetizers, and presented in full glory in numerous entrées. Lobster bisque is creamy yet light, with great chunks of meat at the bottom. The seafood platter—half a lobster thermidor, whole grilled langoustine, shrimps, baked oysters, creamy scallops, crab cakes, black cod—doesn't disappoint. Decorated in blue and gold, with mahogany timbers, leather upholstery, and the sparkle of stained glass, the restaurant has a vibe that is at once formal and cozy—and as such, the place is also great for before- or after-dinner drinks at the bar. ⊠*Lobby level, Island Shangri-La hotel, Pacific Place, Supreme Court Rd., Admiralty* ☎*2820–8560* ⊕*www.shangri-la.com* ⚐*Reservations essential* ⊟*AE, DC, MC, V* Ⓜ*Admiralty.*

$$$
CANTONESE
✕**Man Ho.** The big, open, banquet-style room with rows of round tables is the most authentic format for Cantonese high dining, and it's nice to see the JW Marriott's flagship Chinese dining room still wedded to tradition. The same can be said for the food: it's high-end and well executed, but you won't find fusion here. This is a good place to try abalone (in dishes such as a casserole with braised chicken with fresh abalone), fresh fish (pan-fried garoupa [grouper] in soy sauce has a wonderfully delicate flavor), and Cantonese classics like the impossibly light, roast crispy suckling pig, with its skin the consistency of a wafer—it's one of the best in the city. ⊠*JW Marriott Hotel, Pacific Place, 88 Queensway, Admiralty* ☎*2841–3853* ⊕*www.jwmarriotthk.com* ⊟*AE, DC, MC, V* Ⓜ*Admiralty.*

$$$$
FRENCH
✕**Restaurant Pétrus.** Commanding breathtaking views atop the Island Shangri-La, Restaurant Pétrus scales the upper Hong Kong heights of prestige, formality, and price. This is one of the city's few flagship hotel restaurants that have not attempted to reinvent themselves as fusion; sometimes, traditional French haute cuisine is what you want. Likewise, the design of the place is in the old-school restaurant-as-ballroom mode. The kitchen has a particularly good way with (surprise!) foie gras, and the wine list is memorable, with verticals of Chateau Pétrus among the roughly 1,000 celebrated vintages. The dress here is business casual—no jeans or sneakers. ⊠*56th fl., Island Shangri-La, Pacific Place, Supreme Court Rd., Admiralty* ☎*2820–8590* ⊕*www.shangri-la.com* ⚐*Reservations essential* ⊟*AE, DC, MC, V* Ⓜ*Admiralty.*

5

$$$–$$$$
SHANGHAINESE

✕ **Yè Shanghai.** This nostalgic replica of old Shanghai is part of a chain expanding across Asia. The old-fashioned setting includes 1950s furnishings and ceiling fans. First there are the dumplings: an exemplary version of steamed pork soup dumplings, for instance; then, entrées like pork knuckle braised in sweet soy sauce, or braised meatballs ("lion's head"). For dessert, try the Shanghai staple, deep-fried egg white stuffed with banana and mashed red-bean paste. Reserve early for comfortable booth seats or window tables. ⊠ *Shop 332, level 3, Pacific Place, 88 Queensway, Admiralty* ☎ *2918–9833* ⊕ *www.elite-concepts.com* ⊟ *AE, DC, MC, V* Ⓜ *Admiralty.*

$$–$$$
CANTONESE

✕ **Zen.** Located in the ground-floor food area of one of the city's most popular malls, Zen is a perfect pit stop for shoppers who want tasty, accessible Cantonese food. With its almost all-white decor, it looks like an oasis of otherworldliness amid this frenzy of consumerism, but step inside and you'll find a spacious and lively (though not raucous) restaurant that serves delicious dim sum and an extensive selection of Cantonese dishes from an English menu. The roast pork dim sum and dumplings in soup with mushrooms are house specialties. Bring the family, a business contact, or a crowd. ⊠ *Lower Level, The Mall, One Pacific Place, 88 Queensway, Admiralty* ☎ *2845–4555* ⊟ *AE, DC, MC, V* Ⓜ *Admiralty.*

WAN CHAI

At lunchtime Wan Chai is just another jumble of people, but after dark it comes into its own. This is Hong Kong's prime nightlife district, its long roads lined with fluorescent lights and jam-packed with taxis and lively crowds of people. The range of dining options is extreme—from five-star luxury to noodle-shop dives open into the wee hours. On the ground-floor level along main drags, in part because of the western nightlife influence, you're far more likely to find a mediocre pan-European tapas bar hawking happy-hour specials than a brilliant, innovative Asian restaurant. To find the best local places you have to head to the upper floors or hit the side streets.

$$
INDONESIAN

✕ **Bebek Bengil 3** *(Dirty Duck Diner).* Inspired by a tiny but legendary institution in Bali, this re-creation in the heart of Wan Chai similarly specializes in crispy duck, marinated for 36 hours in an age-old recipe of spices. The seating is *sala*-style (at a low table, sitting on pillows on the floor), on an outside terrace overlooking bustling Lockhart Road. Familiar Indonesian dishes like *nasi goreng* (spicy noodles) and beef *rendang* (a spicy concoction with ginger, lemongrass, and coconut milk) are on the menu. Finish with drinks at BB's lively sister establishment on the ground floor, the Klong Bar & Grill. ⊠ *5th fl., The Broadway, 54–62 Lockhart Rd., Wan Chai* ☎ *2217–8000* ⊕ *www.elite-concepts. com* ⊟ *AE, DC, MC, V* Ⓜ *Wan Chai.*

$-$$ ✕ **Che's Cantonese Restaurant.** Smartly dressed locals in the know head
CANTONESE for this casually elegant dim sum specialist, which is in the middle
of the downtown bustle yet well concealed on the fourth floor of an
office building. From the elevator, you'll step into a classy Cantonese
world. It's hard to find a single better dim sum dish than Che's crispy
pork buns, whose sugary baked pastry conceals the brilliant saltiness of
stewed pork within. Other dim sum to try include panfried turnip cake;
rich, tender braised duck web (foot) in abalone sauce; and a refreshing
dessert of cold pomelo and sago with mango juice for a calming end to
an exciting meal. ⊠*4th fl., The Broadway, 54–62 Lockhart Rd., Wan
Chai* ☎*2528–1123* ▤*AE, DC, MC, V* Ⓜ*Wan Chai.*

$$$ ✕**Cinecittà.** Come here for fine Roman cuisine in this up-and-coming
ITALIAN foodie enclave just around the corner from Pacific Place. As the name
Fodor's Choice suggests, the theme is Italia cinema, centered on Fellini and his works.
★ The interior is mostly white and glass, the atmosphere trendy and elegant,
and the food always top-notch. Order from the menu or ask the chef to
compose a tasting selection for you. Pastas are homemade and are excel-
lent. Come to admire the fashionistas, show off your glad rags, or just
to focus on the fabulous food. ⊠ *9 Star St., Wan Chai* ☎*2529–0199*
⊕*www.elite-concepts.com* ▤*AE, DC, MC, V* Ⓜ*Wan Chai.*

$$$$ ✕**Dynasty.** Dining on haute Cantonese cuisine at the highest Chinese
CANTONESE restaurant in Hong Kong, with panoramic views over Victoria Harbor,
☾ is indeed a memorable experience. The chef, Tam Sek Lun, is famed for
adapting family-style recipes into works of art, and the service here is
impeccable yet friendly. The menu changes with the seasons and leans
heavily toward fresh seafood, plus luxurious temptations like bird's
nest and shark's fin. With its high ceilings, old-world charm, and laid-
back tempo, Dynasty is one of the rare top-notch restaurants where
you can comfortably linger over a meal. Ask for a table with a view of
the harbor. ⊠*3rd fl., Renaissance Harbour View, 1 Harbour Rd., Wan
Chai* ☎*2802–8888 Ext. 6971* ▤*AE, DC, MC, V* Ⓜ*Wan Chai.*

$$$ ✕**Gitone Fine Arts.** Highly recommended by locals, this pottery-studio-
SHANGHAINESE cum-restaurant-speakeasy has acquired quite a following since its 1995
opening. An artistic couple runs the studio and gallery, and turn it into
a cozy, unlicensed "private dining" restaurant at night. The menu varies
completely from day to day, but there are generally both Shanghainese
and Cantonese options. Go for the Shanghai-style meal, as this is the
specialty—it will include up to 16 small courses making up a long night
of adventurous tasting. The pork leg braised in sweet soy, when available, is outstanding; it's a Shanghainese classic. Booking is absolutely
essential, and unless you get lucky on a particular night, you must have
at least a group of four. ⊠*Ground fl., shop GB, 27–28, Site B, Lei King
Wan, 45–47 Tai Hong St., Sai Wan Hoi* ☎*2527–3448 or 2525–6077*
⌂*Reservations essential* ▤*AE, DC, MC, V* Ⓜ*Sai Wan Ho.*

¢   ✕**Hay Hay.** The best food in Hong Kong can hide out in the dingiest
CANTONESE storefronts, and nowhere is this more true than at Hay Hay, a restaurant whose business card contains not a word of English. Surprisingly, though, an English menu lurks somewhere in the back office,
but you shouldn't bother with it. Instead, just point to what looks
good on other tables—it's likely to be a delicious plate of rice, sweet,

Shark's Fin Soup

It makes sense that soup made from shark's fin—said to be an aphrodisiac—costs so much. Only the promise of increased virility would lead someone to pay HK$1,000 or more for a bowl of the stuff. It actually consists of cartilage from the great beast's pectal, dorsal, and lower tail fins that has been skinned, dried, and reconstituted in a rich stock form. This cartilage has almost no taste on its own and is virtually indistinguishable from *tun fun* (cellophane) noodles that are used to create "mock shark's fin soup."

Selling shark's fins is a big business, and Hong Kong is said to be responsible for 50% of the global trade. The soup is a fixture at banquets, weddings, and state dinners here. Love potion, elixir, vitality booster, or not, at the very least the dish is high in protein. Recently, however, conservation groups have pointed out that it's also high in mercury. But of even greater concern is the practice of "finning." Since shark meat as a whole isn't valuable, fishermen often clip the fins and dump the rest of the animal back into the sea.

So, is eating shark's fin soup a not-to-be-missed Hong Kong experience or a morally reprehensible act? Well, we don't need to take sides in the debate to warn you away from it. Let us repeat: the shark's fin cartilage *has no taste*. This makes it—and bird's nest soup, that other tasteless Cantonese delicacy—one of the biggest wastes of money in the culinary universe.

tender roast goose or pork, and greens; or an exemplary noodle soup with slices of roast meat resting on top. Apply the hot sauce liberally, and don't expect the staff to speak English. ⊠ *72–86 Lockhart Rd., corner of Ward St., Wan Chai* ☎ *2143–6183* ⊟ *No credit cards* Ⓜ *Wan Chai.*

$$$$ ✕ **JJ's.** For years, JJ's was one of the hottest tickets in town for live
THAI music and revelry, with a particular following among expats. Then, after Hong Kong's economic downturn, it closed, but has since reopened and is as good as ever. A visit here is first and foremost about the atmosphere and the music; with nooks, crannies, dark wood, and twisting staircases, the place feels akin to a dim Parisian artists' haunt, but with live bands. There's a Thai menu that's more creative than the norm, and a large cocktail list. ⊠ *Grand Hyatt Hotel, 1 Harbour Rd., Wan Chai* ☎ *2584–7662* ⊕ *www.hongkong.grand.hyatt.com* ⊟ *AE, DC, MC, V* Ⓜ *Wan Chai.*

$$$$ ✕ **One Harbour Road.** It's hard to say what's more impressive at the
CANTONESE Grand Hyatt's Cantonese showpiece—the interior design (two terraced indoor levels, the sound of rushing water, and an incredible sense of space and motion), or the view over the harbor from the restaurant's floor-to-ceiling windows, which dominates the experience of every table on both levels of the restaurant. Unlike many harborside establishments, you don't need a window seat to catch the view. And the Cantonese cuisine is traditional but excellent—for best results, order from among the rotating seasonal dishes. ⊠ *8th fl., Grand Hyatt Hotel, 1 Harbour Rd., Wan Chai* ☎ *2584–7938* ⊕ *www.hongkong.grand. hyatt.com* ⊟ *AE, DC, MC, V* Ⓜ *Wan Chai.*

$$ ✕**OVOlogue.** Located in one of Hong Kong's last remaining colonial buildings, this stylish and innovative Cantonese restaurant offers an elegant respite from the hectic shopping streets of Wan Chai. The menu includes dim sum with a few novel additions, as well as a selection of popular Cantonese dishes. The decor—1920s Shanghai style—is exquisitely executed and evokes a bygone Chinese era. This is a good choice for diners who want to try Cantonese cuisine and dim sum in beautiful surroundings. ⊠*3rd fl., Renaissance Harbour View, 1 Harbour Rd., Wan Chai* ☎*2802–8888 Ext. 6971* ☲*AE, DC, MC, V* Ⓜ *Wan Chai.*

CANTONESE

> ### SHANGHAI STYLE
>
> Shanghai's culinary traditions favor seafood, but the city is also famous for its great varieties of buns and dumplings. Rich-flavored Shanghainese hairy crabs are winter favorites; sautéed freshwater shrimp are also a staple. Many dishes are fried and can be a bit greasy.

$$$ ✕**Victoria City Seafood.** This perennially popular restaurant excels at Cantonese dim sum, Shanghainese, and seafood. It's a big, bright, banquet-style space, generally packed with large groups. Not to be missed are the spectacular soup dumplings with hairy-crab roe; steamed blood with leek and egg tarts; and stir-fried rice rolls with XO sauce. Seafood, which you select live from the tank, might include whitebait in chili sauce, steamed prawns in vinegar sauce, whole local garoupa with ginger, or crab cooked with fried garlic. There's an Admiralty branch, too. ⊠*Sun Hung Kai Center, 30 Harbour Rd., Wan Chai* ☎*2827–9938* ⊠*5th fl. Citic Tower, 1 Tim Mei Ave., Admiralty* ☎*2877–2211* ☲*AE, DC, MC, V* Ⓜ *Wan Chai.*

SEAFOOD

CAUSEWAY BAY

With a series of large Japanese department stores and numerous shopping malls, Causeway Bay is one of Hong Kong's busiest shopping districts, and becomes a real cultural phenomenon on Saturday afternoons. Adjoining Causeway Bay on its southern edge is Happy Valley, where the density of the population can be overwhelming. Several pubs are in the vicinity, but they're not concentrated on one strip; likewise, there are several good restaurants, but they can be hard for the uninitiated to find. Times Square, a huge, modern shopping mall, has four floors of restaurants in one of its towers, serving international cuisines including Korean, French, steak, and regional Chinese.

$–$$ ✕**Dim Sum.** This elegant jewel breaks with tradition and serves dim sum all day and night. The original menu goes beyond common Cantonese morsels like *har gau* (steamed shrimp dumplings), embracing dishes more popular in the north, including chili prawn dumplings, Beijing onion cakes, and steamed buns. Lobster bisque and abalone dumplings are also popular. Lunch reservations are not taken on weekends, so there's always a long line. Arrive early, or admire the antique telephones and old Chinese posters while you wait. Even if it feels somewhat contrived, it's worth it. ⊠*63 Sing Woo Rd., Happy Valley* ☎*2834–8893* ☲*AE, MC, V* Ⓜ*Happy Valley.*

CANTONESE

5

$$$
JAPANESE

✕ **Sushi Hiro.** Uni (sea urchin). Shirako (blowfish sperm). O-toro (the fattiest of fatty tuna). If these words make you drool, then you should make a beeline for Sushi Hiro, buried within an office building, and quite possibly the best place for raw fish in Hong Kong. The minimalist interior stays faithful to Japanese style, unlike some more opulent Hong Kong restaurants. But what really draws in the Japanese crowd is the freshness of the fish, which you can watch being filleted in front of you at the sushi bar. And by high-end sushi standards, Hiro is relatively inexpensive. ✉ *10th fl. Henry House, 42 Yun Ping Rd., Causeway Bay* ☎*2882–8752* ▭*AE, DC, MC, V* Ⓜ*Causeway Bay.*

> **WORD OF MOUTH**
>
> "Located on the 34th floor of the Excelsior with window views of Causeway Bay and Admiralty, ToTT's is an experience for all the senses." —cjbryant

$$$$
INTERNATIONAL

✕ **ToTT's Asian Grill & Bar.** The funky interior—zebra-stripe chairs, a central oval bar, and designer tableware—is matched by the East-meets-West cuisine at this restaurant on top of the Excelsior hotel, which looks down on Causeway Bay and the marina. It's one of the very best dinner views in town, with a fun, lively vibe to boot. Best on the menu are steaks, with excellent imported meat cooked properly to order; there's also an extensive wine list. Live music kicks in late during the evening, offering a chance to burn a few calories on the dance floor. ✉*Excelsior Hotel, 281 Gloucester Rd., Causeway Bay* ☎*2837–6786* ▭*AE, DC, MC, V* Ⓜ*Causeway Bay.*

$$$$
JAPANESE

✕ **Wasabi Sabi.** Panes of glass glowing in shades of red escort you into a world of columns of golden light draped from the ceiling, round black banquettes, and swiveling red sofas—the interior of Wasabi Sabi transports you far away from the shopping mall outside. The Japanese creations served here seem also to come from another realm: from the carpaccio of sea bream with wasabi–red-tea jelly, to a sea urchin custard, they are delightfully original, reaching far beyond sushi and sashimi. ✉*13th fl. Times Sq., 1 Matheson Rd., Causeway Bay* ☎*2506–0009* ⊕*www.aqua.com.hk* ▭*AE, DC, MC, V* Ⓜ*Causeway Bay.*

$$$
NORTHERN
CHINESE

✕ **Water Margin.** Care to spend an evening along the ancient Silk Road? Water Margin, a beautiful, immensely popular restaurant done up in dark wood, stone, and red hanging lanterns—is as close as you'll get to it in Hong Kong. The meal begins with kimchi—the north of China is close to Korea—and continues with daring preparations of pig's throat, jellyfish, and braised lotus root. Steamed scallops in pumpkin puree would be a great winter dish if only Hong Kong had winter. ✉*Food Forum, 12th fl. fl. Times Sq., 1 Matheson Rd., Causeway Bay* ☎*3102–0088* ⊕*www.aqua.com.hk* ▭*AE, DC, MC, V* Ⓜ*Causeway Bay.*

$$
SHANGHAINESE

✕ **Wu Kong.** This chain restaurant right next to Hunan Garden serves good Shanghainese fare at reasonable prices. Pigeon in wine sauce is an excellent appetizer and the honey ham and crispy bean curd skin wrapped in soft bread is delicious and authentic. The Shanghai-style doughnut on the dessert menu is a deep-fried sweet ball whipped up with fluffy egg whites and stuffed with red bean and banana. The

HK$75 set lunch, which includes an appetizer, a main dish, dim sum of your choice and free dessert, is great value. ⊠*13th fl., Food Forum, Times Square, 1 Matheson St., Causeway Bay* ☎*2506–1018* ⊕*www.shangri-la.com* ⊟*AE, DC, MC, V* Ⓜ *Causeway Bay.*

WORD OF MOUTH

"I spent 12 days in Hong Kong and went to Wu Kong 4 times. No matter what we ordered, it was terrific." —Susan

$$
SHANGHAINESE ✕**Xiao Nan Guo.** First, a disclosure: this is a chain restaurant. But in this case it's not a bad thing, since it's part of a Shanghai chain, and you want your Shanghainese food to be authentic. In the years since it came to Hong Kong, Xiao Nan Guo has developed a serious following, particularly for dim sum. The feeling is casual and unpretentious, with a bright, expansive, bustling dining room lined with round tables. The focus is really on the food: soup dumplings are excellent, as you'd expect, but don't forget about the fatty "Lion's Head" meatballs, or the pork belly. ⊠*Shop 1301, 13th fl. Times Sq., 1 Matheson Rd., Causeway Bay* ☎*2506–0009* ⊠*Shop 1201, 12th fl. fl. Times Sq., 1 Matheson Rd., Causeway Bay* ⊟*AE, DC, MC, V* Ⓜ*Causeway Bay.*

SOUTHSIDE

The south side of Hong Kong Island is a string of beaches, rocky coves, and luxury developments; and Repulse Bay, 20 minutes away by bus from Central, is comprised of all three. Popular on weekends and in summer, the beach here is one of the best on the island. The Repulse Bay complex also has some good restaurants and shops, along with corporate apartments (housing for business travelers). The fastest way to get to this area is by taxi, though taking a bus is much cheaper.

A visit to Stanley Village reveals another side of Hong Kong, with a much slower pace of life than the one you see in the city. After exploring the market, historical sights, and beaches, take a leisurely meal at one of the top-notch restaurants scattered around, some of which have harbor views. Stanley is 30 minutes by bus or taxi from Central.

Also on the south side, Shek O is a tiny seaside village with a few decent open-air restaurants. Once you've made the trek—the longest overland trip possible from Central—you'll need some sustenance. You can reach the village by bus or minibus from the Chai Wan MTR stop.

$$$-$$$$
MEDITERRANEAN ✕**The Boathouse.** The cozy Boathouse has a lovely view of the seafront, making it the perfect spot to hang out with friends and family. A bucket of mussels, served with nicely toasted garlic bread, goes down well with a glass of chilled white wine. Sandwiches and pastas are good bets for casual dining. And the delicious cobbler with wild berries will send you home happy. ⊠*86–88 Stanley Main St., Southside, Stanley* ☎*2813–4467* ⊟*AE, DC, MC, V.*

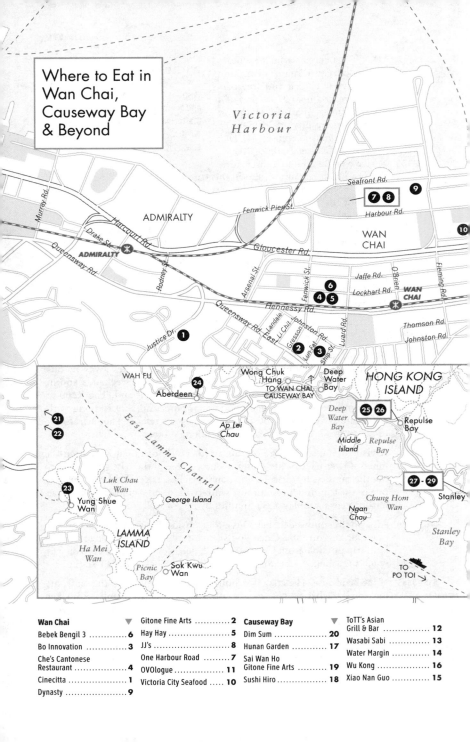

Where to Eat in Wan Chai, Causeway Bay & Beyond

Victoria Harbour

ADMIRALTY

WAN CHAI

7 **8** **9**

10

Seafront Rd.

Fenwick Pier St.

Harbour Rd.

Gloucester Rd.

Jaffe Rd.

Lockhart Rd.

6

4 **5**

WAN CHAI

Hennessy Rd.

Thomson Rd.

Johnston Rd.

1

2 **3**

Murray Rd.

Harcourt Rd.

Drake St.

ADMIRALTY

Queensway Rd.

Rodney St.

Queensway Rd. East

Arsenal St.

Tonnochy Rd.

Gresson St.

Lun Fat St.

Li Chit St.

Johnston Rd.

Luard Rd.

Ship St.

Fleming Rd.

O'Brien Rd.

Justice Dr.

WAH FU

Aberdeen

24

Wong Chuk Hang

TO WAN CHAI, CAUSEWAY BAY

Deep Water Bay

HONG KONG ISLAND

21

22

Ap Lei Chau

Deep Water Bay

Middle Island

Repulse Bay

25 **26**

Repulse Bay

27 - **29**

Stanley

East Lamma Channel

Luk Chau Wan

George Island

23

Yung Shue Wan

Chung Hom Wan

Ngan Chau

Stanley Bay

LAMMA ISLAND

Ha Mei Wan

Picnic Bay

Sok Kwu Wan

TO PO TOI

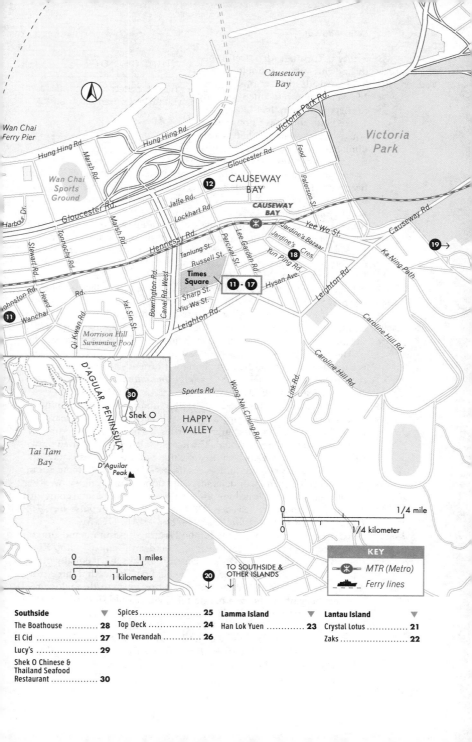

$$$
MEDITERRANEAN
Fodor'sChoice
★

✕**Lucy's.** Turn left after Delifrance to find this warm, intimate eatery, hidden inside the famous Stanley Market and rarely uncovered by tourists. You may feel like you've walked into someone's house when you enter the small, shabby-chic dining room, but Lucy's is a professionally run restaurant offering excellent, home-cooked food. Try the delicious homemade chicken liver pate. The daily specials are a very safe bet and often include risottos and grilled or roasted meat; there are also plenty of fresh fruits and veggies on the menu. Desserts, especially the pecan pudding with toffee cream sauce, are not to be missed. More upscale than most of the beachside restaurants here and with oodles more character, Lucy's is a perfect end to a relaxed day browsing in the market, and easily your best bet in Stanley. ⊠ *Ground fl., 64 Stanley Main St., Southside, Stanley* ☎*2813–9055* ⊟*MC, V.*

$
ASIAN
☺
Fodor'sChoice
★

✕**Shek O Chinese Thai Seafood Restaurant.** The seaside village of Shek O lies past Stanley, and is worth a trip for the large sandy beach and fresh local seafood. For the quality and variety of food, this casual eatery is an all-time favorite. Come here for simple seaside dining at its best—the menu is extensive and everything's good and fresh—but prepare for plastic tables and toilets that are best approached with caution. This is a great spot for relaxing and dining with friends or family for a very reasonable price. ⊠*303 Shek O Village, main intersection, next to bus stop, Southside, Shek O* ☎*2809–4426* ⊟*AE, DC, MC, V.*

$$
ASIAN

✕**Spices.** Located inside the Repulse Bay luxury residential complex, Spices is a staunch favorite among well-heeled locals in search of relaxed dining. The menu offers favorites from throughout Asia. Service is friendly and professional. The mango salad and deep-fried prawn cakes are excellent. Other choices include tandoori dishes, satay, and fried noodles; everything here is a safe bet. The indoor dining room, with high ceilings and wooden tables and floors, can get noisy. Weather permitting, reserve an outdoor table in the evocative colonial courtyard for the full tropical experience. ⊠ *Ground fl., The Repulse Bay, 109 Repulse Bay Rd., Southside* ☎*2292–2821* ⊟*AE, DC, MC, V.*

$$$–$$$$
ECLECTIC
☺

✕**Top Deck.** For a long time, the Jumbo Floating Restaurant and Dragon Court were the only places to eat at Aberdeen's famed Jumbo Kingdom. But now there's Top Deck, a classier, less kitschy, if equally pricey alfresco option on the roof deck of the big boat, beneath a three-story pagoda. It has a vastly better view (and breeze) than the indoor restaurants beneath. If the weather permits, you should sit outdoors. The menu is somewhat haphazard (Thai, Japanese, Indian, Italian, steak . . .) but generally good. The raw bar is the best option, if you like seafood. A jazz band plays on Wednesday, and there's a Sunday brunch every week. ⊠*Shum Wan Pier Path, Wong Chuk Hang, Southside, Aberdeen* ☎*2552–3331* ⊕*www.cafedecogroup.com* ⊟*AE, DC, MC, V* ☺*Closed Mon.*

$$$$\
CONTINENTAL\
Fodor'sChoice\
★

✕**The Verandah.** You will not forget an evening at The Verandah. From the well-spaced, candlelit tables overlooking the bay to the menu of delicious classics (French onion soup, baked milk-fed veal, slow-cooked duck breast) and excellent, unobtrusive service, this is an unabashedly colonial experience that delivers with finesse at every turn. A live pianist sets the scene for romance, while slow-moving ceiling fans add to that hazy feeling that time is standing still. The food doesn't disappoint and the wine list is more reasonably priced than you might expect. If you can't make it for dinner, visit for the traditional afternoon tea (Tuesday– Sunday, HK$178), or try Sunday brunch (11–2:30, HK$398). ⊠*1st fl., The Repulse Bay, 109 Repulse Bay Rd., Southside* ☎*2292–2882* ⊕*www.hongkong.peninsula.com* ▭*AE, DC, MC, V.*

OUTER ISLANDS

5

LAMMA ISLAND

Lamma Island is relatively easy to get to, with ferries leaving Central's pier almost hourly. Yung Shue Wan, where you disembark, has several local seafood restaurants, one or two western ones, and an odd assortment of shops.

$\
CANTONESE

✕**Han Lok Yuen.** Roast pigeon is the star at Han Lok Yuen. Everyone in Hong Kong makes a pilgrimage here at one time or another to try it, usually during a boat trip. Don't arrive too late, or you might miss out: the pigeon can be sold out by 8 PM on busy weekend nights, when booking in advance is usually essential. The kitchen also turns out an array of typical Chinese dishes to accompany the pigeon. Beautiful sea views make this institution popular with locals and visitors alike. ⊠*16–17 Hung Shing Ye, Yung Shue Wan* ☎*2982–0680* ▭*AE, MC, V.*

LANTAU ISLAND

You'll wind up on Lantau Island if you're visiting Disneyland Hong Kong. There are several restaurants within the Disneyland park itself, none of them distinguished. The best restaurants are in the hotels.

$$$\
CANTONESE

✕**Crystal Lotus.** The first thing you'll notice in the Disneyland Hotel's flagship restaurant is also the most Disney-ish touch: a computer-animated koi pond, where electronic fish deftly avoid your feet, darting out of the way as you walk across. Once inside the glittering, crystal-studded yet warm and inviting space, you'll choose from a well-thought-out menu that's really more pan-Chinese than Cantonese, with careful preparations of dishes like barbecue fillets of eel glazed with Osmanthus honey, gently stewed king prawn with spicy Sichuan sauce, and perfectly executed XO seafood fried rice. If you wind up in Disneyland—perhaps on your way to or from the airport—this is by far the best way to dine (unless the kids demand a character meal at the **Enchanted Garden** in the hotel's lower level). ⊠*Hong Kong Disneyland Hotel, Hong Kong Dis-*

The Dim Sum Experience

Dim sum restaurants have always been associated with noise, so don't be dissuaded by the boisterous throngs of locals gathered around large round tables. At one time, big metal carts filled with bamboo baskets were pushed around the restaurant by ladies who would shout out the names of the dishes and stamp a mark onto a table's check when it ordered a basket of this or that. This is still the typical dim sum experience outside of China, but in Hong Kong, most restaurants require you to order off a form, creating a more sedate dining experience. Thankfully, many places offer English-translated order forms or menus, although you should ask your waiter about daily specials that might not appear in translation, as those are often some of the most exciting dim sum options. And never forget that most basic principle of Hong Kong ordering: simply point to something you see at a nearby table.

Although dim sum comes in small portions, it's still intended for sharing between three or four people. When all is said and done, a group can expect to try about 10 or 12 dishes, but don't order more than one of any single item. Most dim sum restaurants prepare between 15 and 100 varieties of the more than 2,000 kinds of dim sum in the Cantonese repertoire, daily. These can be buns, crepes, cakes, pastries, or rice; they can be filled with beef, shrimp, pork, chicken, bean paste, or vegetables; and they can be bamboo-steamed, panfried, baked, or deep-fried. More esoteric offerings vary vastly from place to place. Abandon any squeamish tendencies and try at least one or two unusual plates, like duck web (foot) in abalone sauce, liver dumplings, or dried pork bellies.

You'll be able to find dim sum from before dawn to around 5 or 6 PM, but it's most popular for breakfast (from about 7:30 to 10 AM) and lunch (from about 11:30 AM to 2:30 PM). Dim sum is served everywhere from local teahouses to high-concept restaurants, but it's often best at casually elegant, blandly decorated midrange spots that cater to Chinese families.

The following is a guide to some of our favorite common dim sum items, but don't let it narrow your mind. It's almost impossible to find a bite of dim sum that's anything less than delicious, and the more unique house specialties can often be the best.

BUNS

■ **Cha siu so:** baked barbecued pork pastry buns; they're less common than the steamed cha siu bao, but arguably even better.

■ **Cha siu bao:** steamed barbecued pork buns are an absolute must. With the combination of soft and chewy textures and sweet and salty tastes, you might forget to remove the paper underneath before eating.

DUMPLINGS

■ **Ha gow:** steamed dumplings with a light translucent wrap that conceals shrimp and bamboo shoots.

■ **Siu mai:** steamed pork dumplings are the most common dumplings and you'll find them everywhere; some are stuffed with shrimp.

MEATS

■ **Ngau yuk:** steamed beef balls, like meatballs, placed on top of thin bean-curd skins; not the most flavorful option, but a good one for kids or picky eaters.

5

■ **Pie gwat:** bite-sized pieces of succulent pork spare ribs in a black bean and chili pepper sauce.

RICE CREATIONS

■ **Ha cheong fun:** shrimp-filled rice rolls, whose dough is made in a rice-noodle style; the thick, flat rice rolls are drowned in soy sauce. Other versions include ngau yuk cheong fun (beef filled) and cha siu cheong fun (barbecued pork filled; if available, these are not to be missed).

■ **Ho yip fan:** delicious sticky rice, which is usually cooked with chopped Chinese mushrooms, Chinese preserved sausage, and dried shrimp, and wrapped and steamed in a lotus leaf to keep it moist (don't eat the leaf).

DON'T BE AFRAID OF . . .

■ **Woo tao go:** a glutinous panfried taro cake, sweet enough for dessert but eaten as a savory dish, with delicate undertones that come from preserved Chinese sausage, preserved pork belly, and dried shrimp. Another version of this is lau bak go, which is made with turnip instead of taro.

■ **Foong jow:** marinated chicken feet, whose smooth, soft texture is unlike any other. Once you get past the idea that you're sucking the cartilage off a foot, the sensation is wonderful.

SWEETS

■ **Dan taht:** tarts with a custard filling, generally served for dessert. These sweet pastries are a Macau specialty.

■ **Mong gwor bo deen:** mango pudding that has a consistently glassy texture and is not too sweet.

neyland, Lantau Island ☎3510–6000 ⊕http://park.hongkongdisney-land.com ⊟AE, DC, MC, V ⓂDisneyland Resort.

$$ ✗**Zak's.** A large, laid-back, beachfront dining terrace and an extensive
INTERNATIONAL   international menu make this one of the best outdoor restaurants in
Hong Kong. Perched on the Discovery Bay promenade a 25-minute
ferry ride from Central, Zak's sea and beach views alone easily worth
the trip. Signature dishes are surf and turf and baby back ribs, and
there's a wide choice of lightly prepared fresh seafood as well as pizzas
and Asian and Mexican favorites, all served in generous portions. Come
early to enjoy the great beach, and stay to catch a free view of nearby
Disneyland's nightly fireworks display at 8 PM. If you spend more than
HK$100, you get a free ticket back to Central. ✉ *Water Margin Com-
plex, Discovery Bay Plaza, Discovery Bay, Lantau Island* ☎2987–6232
⊕ *www.zaks.com.hk* ⊟*AE, DC, MC, V* Ⓜ*Disneyland Resort.*

KOWLOON

Parts of Kowloon are among the most densely populated areas on the
planet, and support a corresponding abundance of restaurants. Many
hotels, planted here for the view of Hong Kong Island (spectacular at
night), also have excellent restaurants, though they're uniformly expen-
sive. Some of the best food in Kowloon is served in backstreet eateries,
where immigrants from Vietnam, Thailand, and elsewhere in Asia keep
their native cooking skills sharp.

Tsim Sha Tsui, on Kowloon's tip, is crammed with shops and restau-
rants, from spots in luxury hotels to holes-in-the-wall. Starting from
the Kowloon-side Star Ferry Terminal, the district embraces the most
glittering end of the famous Nathan Road's "Golden Mile," snakes
around the harbor front to Tsim Sha Tsui East, and extends to the end
of Kowloon Park at Austin Road, marking the boundary of Jordan.
The restaurants here are easily accessible from either the Tsim Sha Tsui
MTR stop or Kowloon's Star Ferry Terminal. Beyond Chatham Road
and south toward the Cross-Harbour Tunnel, Tsim Sha Tsui East is
packed with high-end hotels with exquisite restaurants. The closest
MTR stop is the Tsim Sha Tsui stop.

Locals go to Kowloon City, a 10-minute taxi ride north from Tsim Sha
Tsui, adjoining Hong Kong's former international airport at Kai Tak,
for casual, authentic, tasty meals at affordable prices. Renowned for its
seafood restaurants and neighborhood hill-walking tracks, Sai Kung is
off most tourist itineraries. Yet it's a town worth investigation, and it's
really only a 20-minute taxi ride north of Tsim Sha Tsui (or you can
take Minibus 1 from Choi Hung MTR). Many restaurants run adjoin-
ing seafood shops, so you can select a fresh catch from tanks and have
it cooked to order—steamed, fried, sautéed, or deep-fried with salt and
pepper. There are also lots of intimate, laid-back western restaurants
serving delicious food.

Continued on page 214

FOR ALL THE TEA IN CHINA

Legend has it that the first cup dates from 2737 BC, when Camellia sinensis leaves fell into water being boiled for Emperor Shenong. He loved the result, tea was born, and so were many traditions.

Historically, when a girl accepted a marriage proposal she drank tea, a gesture symbolizing fidelity (tea plants die if uprooted). Betrothal gifts were known as "tea gifts," engagements as "accepting tea," and marriages as "eating tea." Today the bride and groom kneel before their parents, offering cups of tea in thanks.

Serving tea is a sign of respect. Young people proffer it to their parents or grandparents; subordinates do the same for their bosses. Pouring tea also signifies submission, so it's a way to say you're sorry. When you're served tea, show your thanks by tapping the table with your index and middle fingers.

And forget about adding milk or sugar. Not only is most Chinese tea best without it, but why dilute and sweeten a beverage long known by herbalists to be good for you? Even modern medicine acknowledges that tea's powerful antioxidants reduce the risk of cancer and heart disease. It's also thought to be such a good source of fluoride that Mao Zedong eschewed toothpaste for a green-tea rinse. Smiles, everyone.

DRINKING IN THE CULTURE

The way tea was prepared historically bears little resemblance to the steep-a-teabag method many westerners employ today. Tea originally came in bricks of compressed leaves bound with sheep's blood or manure. Chunks were broken, ground into a powder, and whisked into hot water. In the first tea manual, *Cha Jing (The Way of Tea)*, Tang-dynasty writer Lu Yu describes preparing powdered tea using 28 pieces of teaware, including big brewing pans and shallow drinking bowls.

The potters of Yixing (near Shanghai) gradually transformed wine vessels into small pots for steeping tea. Yixing pottery is ideal for brewing: its fine unglazed clay is highly porous, and if you always use the same kind of tea, the pot will take on its flavor.

Today the most elaborate Chinese tea service—which requires only two pots and enough cups for all involved—is called *gong fu cha* (skilled tea method). Although you can experience it at many teahouses, most people consider it too involved for every day. They simply brew their leaf tea in three-piece lidded cups, called *gaiwan*, tilting the lid as they drink so that it acts as a strainer.

THE CEREMONY

1 Rinse teapot with hot water.

2 Fill with black or oolong to one third of its height.

3 Half-fill teapot with hot water and empty immediately to rinse leaves.

4 Fill pot with hot water, let leaves steep for a minute; no bubbles should form.

5 Pour tea into small cups, moving the spout continuously over each, so all have the same strength of tea.

6 Pour the excess into a second teapot.

7 Using the same leaves, repeat the process up to five times, extending the steeping time slightly.

Gaiwan

TEA TIMELINE

Yunnan Pu-erh Tea Bricks

350 AD	"Tea" appears in Chinese dictionary.
618–1644	Tea falls into and out of favor at Chinese court.
7th c.	Tea introduced to Japan.
1610–1650	Dutch and Portuguese traders bring tea to Europe.
1662	British King Charles II marries Portugal's Catherine of Braganza, a tea addict. Tea craze sweeps the court.
1689	Tea taxation starts in Britain; peaks at 119%.
1773	Boston Tea Party: Americans dump 342 chests of tea into Boston Harbor, protesting British taxes.

HOW TEA IS MADE

Chinese tea is grown on large plantations and nearly always picked by hand. Pluckers remove only the top two leaves. A skilled plucker can collect up to 35 kg (77 lbs) of leaves in a day; that's 9 kg (almost 20 lbs) of tea, or 3,500 cups. After a week, new top leaves will have grown, and bushes can be plucked again. Climate and soil play an important role on a tea plantation, much as they do in a vineyard. But what really differentiates black, green, and oolong teas is the way leaves are processed.

Plucked leaves arrive at factory

Leaves left to wilt in warm, humid environment

STEAM
GREEN TEA: Steam leaves to prevent oxidation

OXIDATION
Leaves broken to encourage oxidation.
BLACK TEA: 4 hrs
OOLONG: 1–2 hrs

FIRING
(dried in warm ovens or large woks)

GREEN TEA
Curled, packed flat, or rolled into pellets

OOLONG TEA
Formed/packed like green tea

BLACK TEA

WHITE TEA
Only new buds; processed like green tea

PU-ERH TEA
Green, black, and oolong are fermented and compressed

FLAVORED TEA
Flavorings added to black or oolong

5

IN FOCUS FOR ALL THE TEA IN CHINA

1784	British tea taxes slashed; consumption soars.
1835	Tea cultivation starts in Assam, India.
1880s	India and Ceylon produce more tea than China.
1904	Englishman Richard Blechynden creates iced tea at St. Louis World's Fair.
1908	New York importer Thomas Sullivan sends clients samples in silk bags—the first tea bags.
2004	Chinese tea exports overtake India's for the first time since the 1880s.

TYPES OF TEA

 Some teas are simply named for the region that produces them (Yunnan or Assam); others are evocatively named to reflect a particular blend. Some are transliterated (like Keemun); others translated (Iron Goddess of Mercy). Confused? Keep two things in mind. First, the universal word for tea comes from *one* Chinese character—pronounced either "te" (Xiamen dialect) or "cha" (Cantonese and Mandarin). Second, all types of tea come from *one* plant.

	BLACK	PU-ERH	GREEN
Overview	It's popular in the West so it makes up the bulk of China's tea exports. It has a stronger flavor than green tea, though this varies according to type.	Pu-erh tea is green, black, or oolong fermented from a few months to 50 years and formed into balls. Pu-erh is popular in Hong Kong, where it's called Bo Le.	Most tea grown and consumed in China is green. It's delicate, so allow the boiling water to cool for a minute before brewing to prevent "cooking" the tea.
Flavor	From light and fresh to rich and chocolatey	Rich, earthy	Light, aromatic
Color	Golden dark brown	Reddish brown	Light straw-yellow to bright green
Caffeine per Serving	40 mg	20–40 mg	20 mg
Ideal Water Temperature	203°F	203°F	160°F
Steeping Time	3–5 mins.	3–5 mins.	1–2 mins.
Examples	Dian Hong (chocolatey aftertaste; unlike other Chinese teas, can take milk). Keemun (Qi Men; mild, smoky; once used in English breakfast blends). Lapsang Souchong (dried over smoking pine; strong flavor). Yunnan Golden (full bodied, malty).	Buying Pu-erh is like buying wine: there are different producers and different vintages, and prices vary greatly.	Bi Luo Chun (Green Snail Spring; rich, fragrant). Chun Mee (Eyebrow; pale yellow; floral). Hou Kui (Monkey Tea; nutty; sweet; floral aftertaste). Long Ding (Dragon Mountain; sweet, minty). Long Jing (Dragon's Well; bright green; nutty).

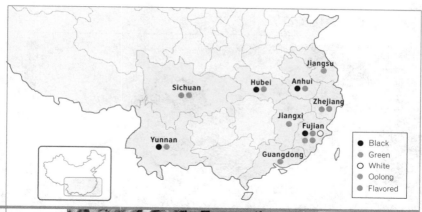

- ● Black
- ● Green
- ○ White
- ● Oolong
- ● Flavored

	WHITE	OOLONG	FLAVORED
Overview	The rare white tea is made from the newest buds, picked unopened at daybreak and processed like green tea. Small batches mean high prices. It's a tea for refined palates.	Halfway between green and black tea, this tea is more popular in China than elsewhere. The gong fu cha ceremony best reveals its complexities.	Petals, bark, and other natural ingredients are added to black or green tea to create these brews. Earl Grey is black tea scented with bergamot (a recipe supposedly given to the tea's 18th-century namesake by a Mandarin). Jasmine tea is green tea dried with jasmine petals. Others include lychee congou and rose congou: black tea dried with lychee juice or rose petals. Flavor, color, caffeine content, and ideal preparation depend on the tea component of the blend. Don't confuse flavored teas with the caffeine-free herbal teas made from herbs, roots, and blossoms (e.g., chamomile, peppermint, rosehips, licorice, ginger).
Flavor	Very subtle	Aromatic, lighter than black tea	
Color	Very pale yellow	Pale green to pale brown	
Caffeine per Serving	15 mg	30 mg	
Ideal Water Temperature	185°F	203°F	
Steeping Time	4–15 mins	1–9 mins.	
Examples	Bai Hao Yin Zhen (Silver Needle; finest white tea; sweet and very delicate, anti-toxin qualities). Bai Mu Dan (White Peony; smooth and refreshing).	Da Hong Pao (Scarlet Robe; comes from only 4 bushes; full bodied, floral). Tie Guan Yin (Iron Goddess of Mercy; legend has it a farmer repaired statue of the goddess, who rewarded him with the tea bush shoot; golden yellow; floral).	

LEAVES OF THE CITY

Tea in the morning; tea in the evening, tea at suppertime...

Get up early in Hong Kong, and you'll see old men shuffling along the streets with their pet birds in tow. The destination? A teahouse for some warm brew and chat with pals while their birds chirp away from cages hung nearby.

But tea isn't just for old-timers. Hot black tea comes free—usually in glass beakers that are constantly refilled—with all meals in Chinese restaurants. Pu-erh tea, which is known here as Bo Lei, is the beverage of choice at dim sum places. In fact, another way to say dim sum is *yum cha*, meaning "drink tea."

Afternoon tea is another local fixation. Forget cucumber sandwiches and petit fours. Here we're talking neighborhood joints with Formica tables, grumpy waiters, and menus only in Chinese. Most people go for *nai cha* made with evaporated milk. A really good cup is smooth, sweet, and hung with drops of fat. An even richer version, *cha chow*, is made with condensed milk. If *yuen yueng* (yin yang, half milk tea and half

instant coffee) sounds a bit much, *ling-mun cha* (lemon tea) is also on hand. Don't forget to order buttered toast or *daan-ta* (custard tarts).

The bubble (or boba) tea craze is strong. These cold brews contain pearly balls of tapioca or coconut jelly. There's also been a return to traditional teas. Chains such as Chinese Urban Healing Tea serve healthy blends in MTR stations all over town—giving Starbucks a run for its money.

FLAGSTAFF HOUSE
MUSEUM OF TEA WARE

All that's good about British colonial architecture is exemplified in the simple white facade, wooden monsoon shutters, and colonnaded verandas of Flagstaff House. Over 600 pieces of delicate antique teaware from the Tang (618–907) through the Qing (1644–1911) dynasties fill rooms that once housed the commander of the British forces. ■TIP→ **Skip the lengthy, confusing tea-ceremony descriptions; con-**

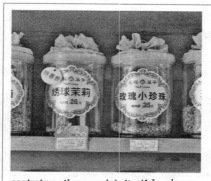

centrate on the porcelain itself. Look out for the unadorned brownish-purple clay of the Yixing pots: unglazed, their beauty hinges on perfect form. There's a carved wooden booth on the first floor where you can listen to Chinese tea songs.

The best place to put your tea theory into practice is the Lock Cha Tea Shop (☎2801–7177 ⊕www.lockcha.com), in the K.S. Lo Gallery annex of Flagstaff House. It's half shop, half teahouse, so you can sample brews before you buy. Friendly staffers prepare the tea gong-fu style at carved rosewood tables. Try the Tie Guan Yin, a highly aromatic green tea. ⊠ *Hong Kong Park, 10 Cotton Tree Dr., Admiralty* ☎*2801–7177* ⊕*www.lcsd.gov.hk* 🖅*Free* ⊗ *Wed.–Mon. 10–5* Ⓜ*Admiralty MTR, Exit C1.* ■TIP➜The Hong Kong Tourist Board runs tea appreciation classes at Lock Cha Tea Shop—phone the shop to book a place.

FOOK MING TONG

Staffers will brew you any of their range of teas at this classy store inside the IFC Mall. Look for books about tea, tea caddies and sets, and Yixing pots (some with hefty price tags). ⊠ *IFC Mall, shop 3006, 8 Finance St., Central* ☎*2295–0368* ⊕*www.fookmingtong.com* Ⓜ*Hong Kong Station MTR, Exit F.*

PENINSULA HOTEL

The British haven't been in the tea business as long as the Chinese, but they know a thing or two about it. Afternoon tea in the soaring grand lobby of this icon is all very Noël Coward. A string quartet plays as liveried waiters pour from silver pots. Three tiers' worth of salmon sandwiches, petit fours, and Valrhona truffles will keep you munching for a while. There's clotted Devonshire cream for the airy scones—so popular the Pen makes 1,000 a day. All this comes to a snip of what a suite here costs: HK$268 per person or HK$398 for two. ⊠*Salisbury Rd., Tsim Sha Tsui, Kowloon* ☎*2920–2888* ⊕*www.peninsula.com* 🖃*AE, DC, MC, V* ⊗*Tea served daily 2–7* Ⓜ*Tsim Sha Tsui MTR, Exit E.*

■TIP➜ You can't make reservations for tea at the Peninsula; to avoid lines come at 2 on the dot or after 5:30.

TEA ALTERNATIVES

Green Tea Ice Cream. It's the dessert of choice at Genki, a popular local sushi chain. ⊠World Trade Centre, 280 Gloucester Rd., Causeway Bay ☎2506–9366 ⓂCauseway Bay MTR, Exit D.

Green Tea Dumplings. In a tranquil white setting 15 minutes from Central's crowds, Green T. House serves green tea fennel dumplings, in addition to green tea ice cream and delicious tea-flavored chocolates. ⊠No. 208, The Arcade, 100 Cyberport Road, Pok Fu Lam ☎2989–6036.

Green Tea Frappuccino. The Starbucks take on green tea is everything the stuff normally isn't: creamy, sugary, and icy.

Green Tea Bread. It looks like something Shrek made, but tastes surprisingly wholesome. German-style bakery Das Gute might be on to something. ⊠Times Square Mall, Shop B301, 1 Matheson St., Causeway Bay ☎2506–9488 ⓂCauseway Bay MTR, Exit A.

TSIM SHA TSUI

$$$
ECLECTIC

✕**Aqua.** Perhaps in reference to Hong Kong's many yoga studios, Tsim Sha Tsui's gracefully arching One Peking Road building seems to be doing a giant steel back bend. This trendy restaurant and bar is in the penthouse, and goes by many names (Aqua Tokyo, Aqua Roma, Aqua Spirit). Similarly, the chefs here wear many hats, combining sashimi, crab tempura with crab roe miso, and a heavy risotto into one meal. The raw fish, flown in from Japan, is a better choice than the uninspired pasta, but the only thing really worth going to Aqua for is the superb view from the windows of the Hong Kong skyline. You might just stop in for a drink—the bar stays open until 2 AM, 3 AM on weekends. ✉*Penthouse, 1 Peking Rd., Tsim Sha Tsui, Kowloon* ☎*3427–2288* ⊕*www.aqua.com.hk* ▤*AE, DC, MC, V* Ⓜ*Tsim Sha Tsui.*

¢–$
SHANGHAINESE

✕**Best Noodle Restaurant.** Just beyond the northern boundary of Tsim Sha Tsui, on a side street off Nathan Road, near the Jordan MTR station, this humble place is popular among locals seeking a quick bowl of noodles or a simple, tasty Shanghainese dish. Try a dish of Shanghainese rice with vegetables, topped with your choice of meat, or the fried noodles, soup noodles, and sweet spareribs. ✉*105 Austin Rd., Jordan, Kowloon* ☎*2369–0086* ▤*No credit cards* Ⓜ*Tsim Sha Tsui.*

$$$$
INTERNATIONAL

✕**Felix.** It's not for the faint of stomach, this Philippe Starck–designed, preposterously fashionable scene atop the Peninsula. The floor-to-ceiling walls do have breathtaking views of Hong Kong though, unless the blinds are drawn, as they sometimes are. The dinner menu, which might include Asian-influenced items such as miso-marinated Atlantic cod or honeyed tempura prawns, is good but certainly overpriced. Most people come just for cocktails—or to try out the most celebrated pissoir in Asia, whose views across Tsim Sha Tsui are superior to those in the restaurant itself. ✉*28th fl., Peninsula Hong Kong, Salisbury Rd., Tsim Sha Tsui, Kowloon* ☎*2315–3188* ⊕*www.hongkong.peninsula. com* ⌖*Reservations essential* ▤*AE, DC, MC, V* Ⓜ*Tsim Sha Tsui.*

¢
CANTONESE

✕**Guangdong Barbecue Restaurant.** Of the many typical roast meat (Chinese barbecue) shops that line the streets of Tsim Sha Tsui, this is one of the most popular. Between the two rooms, the clanking plates, and the shouting in Cantonese, it can be bewildering at first; don't be put off if you're pushed out of the way by a server before being seated. Once seated, you can order from an English menu (you have to ask for it). The roast goose is delicious, as is the crispy roasted pig, soy sauce chicken, and honeyed roast pork. All are served with rice and greens. You might want to just order by pointing to someone else's plate if it looks appealing; and don't forget to pile on the chili sauce and other condiments. ✉*Ground fl., Hankow Bldg., 43 Hankow Rd., Tsim Sha Tsui, Kowloon* ☎*2735–5151* ▤*No credit cards* Ⓜ*Tsim Sha Tsui.*

¢–$
CANTONESE

✕**Hing Fat Restaurant.** So many simple roast meat and noodle soup shops are around lower Nathan Road that it can be hard to choose one. The popular Hing Fat is a reliable choice both for soup dumplings and for Cantonese-style roast meats—and the place is open all night, which is a definite plus. If you've made a long night of it, plop down here among the locals for late-night refueling within easy reach of the big Tsim Sha Tsui hotels. ✉*Ground fl., 8–10 Ashley Rd., Tsim Sha Tsui, Kowloon*

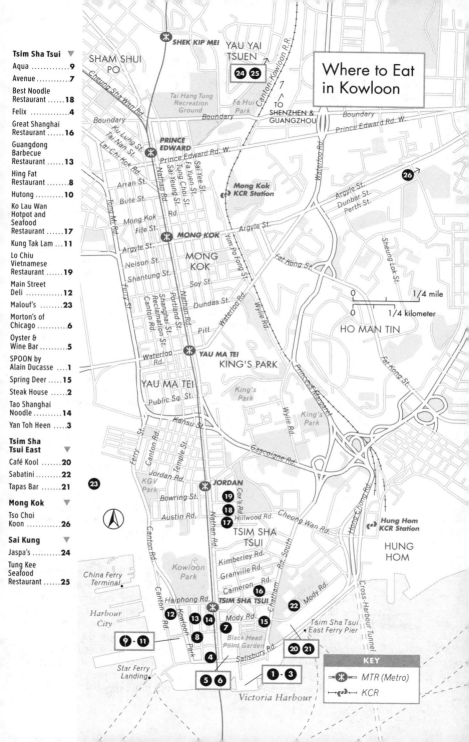

Where to Eat in Kowloon

KEY

🔀 *MTR (Metro)*

⊷⊷ *KCR*

☎2736–7788 ▭No credit cards
Ⓜ*Tsim Sha Tsui.*

$$$–$$$$
NORTHERN
CHINESE
Fodor'sChoice
★

✕**Hutong.** It's not hard to see why Hutong is one of the hottest tables in Hong Kong: it has some of the most imaginative food in town, yet it's completely Chinese. Meanwhile, its spot at the top of the dramatic One Peking Road tower overlooks the entire festival of lights that is the Island skyline. Best among a sensa-

> **MANDARIN CUISINE**
>
> This hearty fare is designed for the chilly climate of northern China—noodles, dumplings, and breads are more evident than rice. Peking duck is a perennial favorite. Firm flavors—such as garlic, ginger, and leek—are popular.

tional selection of northern Chinese creations are crispy, deboned lamb ribs, whose crackling skin conceals a deep, tender gaminess within. More subtle is Chinese spinach in a well-developed herbal ginseng broth, and delicate scallops with fresh pomelo. If you have just one meal in Hong Kong, make certain it's here. And remember to reserve well in advance. ⊠*28th fl., 1 Peking Rd., Tsim Sha Tsui, Kowloon* ☎*3428–8342* ⊕*www.aqua.com.hk* ⚓*Reservations essential* ▭*AE, DC, MC, V* Ⓜ*Tsim Sha Tsui.*

$$
CANTONESE
Fodor'sChoice
★

✕**Ko Lau Wan Hotpot and Seafood Restaurant.** Those seeking authentic Cantonese hotpot need not look further. Locals flock here for the tender beef and a wide selection of seafood, served in small slices that you cook at your table in a piping-hot soup (the satay broth and the coconut broth with pork are particularly tasty.) The owner runs his own fish farm in the seaside district of Sai Kung—no wonder the cuttlefish or shrimp balls and the yellow tail, amberjack, and abalone sashimi are all so tantalizingly fresh. The adventurous should try the geoduck, a giant clam, popular among Hong Kongers, which can be eaten raw with soy sauce and wasabi or slightly cooked in a soup. ⊠*1st fl., Vincent Commercial Building, 21–23 Hillwood Rd., Tsim Sha Tsui, Kowloon* ☎*3520–3800* ⊕*www.hotpotexpress.com* ▭*MC, V* ☽*No lunch; open from 6 PM to 3 AM daily* Ⓜ*Jordan.*

$
VEGETARIAN

✕**Kung Tak Lam.** Health-conscious diners will appreciate this simple Shanghainese vegetarian food. The interior is light and airy, in keeping with the ultramodern One Peking Road tower feel. Still, it's the food that makes this place so popular. The menu revels in its vegetarianism, rather than trying to emulate meat; highlights include the Golden Treasure Cold Platter, which includes delicious sweet gluten with mushrooms; the Shanghai-style cold noodles with seven different sauces; and gentle bean curd dumplings. Good, too, are the sweet panfried cakes. Set-price meals are incredibly cheap, but beware the high prices on the à la carte menu, which can add up. ⊠*7th fl., 1 Peking Rd., Tsim Sha Tsui, Kowloon* ☎*2312–7800* ▭*AE, DC, MC, V* Ⓜ*Tsim Sha Tsui.*

$–$$
VIETNAMESE

✕**Lo Chiu Vietnamese Restaurant.** The spartan interior may not impress, but pay no heed since what you're here for is the hearty authentic food. Take your time and try not to burn your tongue on the sizzling-hot and wonderfully flavorsome lemongrass chicken wings. Deep-fried sugarcane with minced shrimp is sweet and juicy. There is also a good variety of noodles and vermicelli served in soup or with fish sauce. A bottle of imported French beer is just the thing to wash it all down.

✉ *Ground fl., shop 1, Diamond Court, 10–12 Hillwood Rd., Tsim Sha Tsui, Kowloon* ☎*2314–7966* ▤*MC, V* Ⓜ*Tsim Sha Tsui.*

$$–$$$ ✕**Main Street Deli.** Inspired by New
AMERICAN York's (now closed) Second Avenue Deli, with a tiled interior to match, Main Street Deli introduced traditional Big Apple neighborhood favorites to Hong Kong and found

immediate popularity with visitors and locals alike. The chef even trained at the Second Avenue Deli, and continues to make lunch favorites such as hot dogs, bagels, and pastrami on rye and hot corned beef sandwiches. Brisket, meat loaf, and matzo-ball soup satisfy homesick New Yorkers. Lemon meringue pie makes an ideal accompaniment to afternoon coffee. ✉*Ground fl., Langham Hong Kong, 8 Peking Rd., Tsim Sha Tsui, Kowloon* ☎*2375–1133* ⊕*http://hongkong.langham hotels.com* ▤*AE, DC, MC, V* Ⓜ*Tsim Sha Tsui.*

$$$ ✕**Malouf's Modern Middle Eastern.** Modern Middle Eastern cuisine in a
MIDDLE small, luxurious setting makes Malouf's a great choice for a roman-
EASTERN tic dinner à deux or an indulgent meal after emptying your pockets in the adjacent Elements mall. The menu does not overwhelm with options but offers more than enough to intrigue even discerning palates. Choices include pigeon pie served with minted cabbage salad, and prawn-and-mussel tagine with caramelized fennel and couscous. Generous portions of hearty fare mean two starters could be plenty for some. Velvet banquettes and a beautiful mosaic ceiling add a touch of the Middle East, while views from the floor-to-ceiling windows are pure 21st-century Hong Kong. ✉*Shop R008, Civic Square, 3rd fl., Elements, 1 Austin Rd. West, Tsim Sha Tsui, Kowloon* ☎*2810–8585* ▤*AE, MC, V* Ⓜ*Tsim Sha Tsui.*

$$$$ ✕**Morton's of Chicago.** Some might argue that the outpost of an Ameri-
STEAK can steak-house chain would not be the appropriate place for a break-the-bank meal in Hong Kong. And in many ways they'd be right. On the other hand, Morton's does what it does so well—and so consistently—that it can well satisfy the steak craving that can sometimes arise when you're in faraway places. The meat is world-class: most flavorful is the New York strip; the filet mignon is juicy and tender; and the porterhouse, for sharing, combines the best of both worlds. ✉*3rd fl. and 4th fl., Sheraton Hotel, 20 Nathan Rd., Tsim Sha Tsui* ☎*2732–2343* ⊕*www.mortons.com* ▤*AE, DC, MC, V* Ⓜ*Central.*

$$$$ ✕**Oyster & Wine Bar.** Atop the Sheraton Hong Kong Hotel & Towers,
SEAFOOD against the romantic backdrop of Hong Kong's twinkling harbor, this is the top spot in town for oyster lovers. More than 30 varieties are flown in daily and kept alive on ice around the horseshoe oyster bar, ready for shucking. Staff cheerfully explain the characteristics of the available oysters and guide you to ones to suit your taste. Also on the aphrodisiac menu is the San Francisco fisherman's stew, as well as clams, mussels, crab, and black cod. An extensive wine selection lines the walls. ✉*Sheraton Hong Kong Hotel & Towers, 20 Nathan Rd., Tsim Sha*

5

Tsui, Kowloon ☎*2369–1111 Ext. 3145* 🖃*AE, DC, MC, V* ⊘*No lunch* Ⓜ*Tsim Sha Tsui.*

$$$$ ✕**SPOON by Alain Ducasse.** Even
FRENCH if culinary legend Alain Ducasse is not exactly presiding over this kitchen, his inspiration is felt at this sleek restaurant, especially in preparations such as steamed foie

gras, which balances the richness of seared foie gras with the resilience of a cold terrine de foie gras. Despite the occasional Asian flavor (seaweed pesto and shiitake mushrooms), the menu is contemporary French, liberally employing lobster, truffle, and other luxury ingredients with a keen sense of balance. The best, if priciest, way to go is the multicourse tasting menu. The tables overlooking the harbor provide a romantic setting—or reserve the kitchen-side chef's table for a completely different experience. ⊠*Lobby level, Hotel InterContinental Hong Kong, 18 Salisbury Rd., Tsim Sha Tsui, Kowloon* ☎*2313–2256* ⊕*http://hongkong-ic.intercontinental.com* ⚏*Reservations essential* 🖃*AE, DC, MC, V* Ⓜ*Tsim Sha Tsui.*

$$ ✕**Spring Deer.** With shades of pastel blue and green in a somber interior,
MANDARIN and waiters in bland uniforms, this Peking duck specialist looks like something out of 1950s communist Beijing. The crowd, too, is hilariously old-school, which only adds to your duck experience. You'll see locals with noodle dishes, stir-fried wok meat dishes, and so forth, and they're good, but the Peking duck is the showstopper—it might be the best in town. Even the peanuts for snacking, which are boiled to a delectable softness, go above and beyond the call of duty. ⊠*1st fl., 42 Mody Rd., Tsim Sha Tsui, Kowloon* ☎*2366–401 or 2366–5839* 🖃*AE, DC, MC, V* Ⓜ*Tsim Tsa Shui.*

$$$$ ✕**Steak House.** This restaurant with its lively, informal din, salad buffet,
STEAK and gleaming harbor views, serves the best steak in the city. After being seated, you are made to choose from among 10 steak knives, 12 mustards, and eight kinds of rock salt—gimmicky, but fun. But the main event is of course the meat: Wagyu steaks from Japan and Australia are aged for more than a year, and the results are shockingly tender, buttery, and flavorful. Other delicious cuts are flown in from the United States; and all of it is lovingly seared on a charcoal grill. There isn't a jacket-and-tie policy but note that shorts are not allowed. ⊠ *Lower level, Hotel InterContinental Hong Kong, 18 Salisbury Rd., Tsim Sha Tsui, Kowloon* ☎*2313–2405* ⊕*http://hongkong-ic.intercontinental. com* ⚏*Reservations essential* 🖃*AE, DC, MC, V* Ⓜ*Tsim Sha Tsui.*

$$$$ ✕**Yan Toh Heen.** This Cantonese restaurant in the Hotel InterContinen-
CANTONESE tal sets formal elegance against expansive harbor views, and its food
Fodor'sChoice is at the top of its class in town. Exquisite is hardly the word for the
★ place settings, all handcrafted with green jade. Equally successful are dim sum, sautéed Wagyu beef with mushrooms and shishito pepper (a mild green chili pepper), and exemplary braised whole abalone in oyster sauce. The vast selection of seafood—the largest range in Hong Kong—transcends the usual tank to offer such exotic fishes as maori

and green wrasse and shellfish like red coral crab, cherrystone clam, and sea whelk. Shorts are not allowed. ✉*Lower level, Hotel Inter-Continental Hong Kong, 18 Salisbury Rd., Tsim Sha Tsui, Kowloon* ☎*2313-2243* ⊕*http://hongkong-ic.intercontinental.com* ⚓*Reservations essential* ☰*AE, DC, MC, V* Ⓜ*Tsim Sha Tsui.*

TSIM SHA TSUI EAST

$$$$ ✕**Café Kool.** This 300-seat international food court has something
INTERNATIONAL fun for the whole family, with entertainment provided by chefs in six
ⓒ "show kitchens" focusing on cuisines from around the world. Pick from the salad counter; a seafood station serving oysters and sashimi; pasta and meat-carving stations from the western kitchen; dim sum, Mongolian stir-fry, and other Asian dishes; tandoori and curries from the Indian counter; and fresh soufflés, crepes, and a chocolate fountain at the dessert station. Good-value, all-you-can-eat buffets are served until 9:30 PM on weekdays and till 11 PM on Saturday. The à la carte menu includes good pizzas and a deli sells take-out food. ✉*Kowloon Shangri-La, 64 Mody Rd., Tsim Sha Shui East, Kowloon* ☎*2733–8753* ⊕*www.shangri-la.com* ☰*AE, DC, MC, V* Ⓜ*Tsim Sha Tsui.*

$$$$ ✕**Sabatini.** Run by the Sabatini family, who have restaurants in Rome,
ITALIAN Japan, and Singapore, this small corner of Italy with sponge-painted walls and wooden furnishings is in the Royal Garden's atrium. It has a cult following among those who crave authentic Italian cuisine. Linguine Sabatini, the house specialty, is prepared according to the original Roman recipe in a fresh-tomato-and-garlic marinara sauce, served with an array of seafood. For dessert, try homemade tiramisu or refreshing wild-berry pudding. ✉*3rd fl., Royal Garden, 69 Mody Rd., Tsim Sha Tsui East, Kowloon* ☎*2733–2000* ⊕*www.rghk.com.hk* ⚓*Reservations essential* ☰*AE, DC, MC, V* Ⓜ*Tsim Sha Tsui.*

$–$$ ✕**Tapas Bar.** International tapas meet New World wines at this upbeat
SPANISH venue in the Kowloon Shangri-La Hotel. Chefs work in an open kitchen, where a tandoor oven regularly produces freshly baked bread to go with the little dishes. Typical Spanish tapas like whitebait, sardines, and chorizo are served, but there are also dips from around the world, a smorgasbord of olives, sushi-style tuna, and potato-wrapped shrimp—plus a global oyster selection. ✉*1st fl., Kowloon Shangri-La, 64 Mody Rd., Tsim Sha Tsui East, Kowloon* ☎*2733–8756* ⊕*www. shangri-la.com* ☰*AE, DC, MC, V* Ⓜ*Tsim Sha Tsui.*

MONG KOK

¢–$ ✕**Tso Choi Koon.** If you have a delicate constitution, or prefer fine food,
CANTONESE take a pass on this home-style Cantonese restaurant. Tso Choi (which translates as "rough dishes") is not everyone's cup of tea. Tripe lovers and haggis fans, however, might like to try the Chinese versions of some of their favorites: fried pig tripe, fried pig brain (served as an omelet), double-boiled pig brain—you get the idea. The older Hong Kong generation still likes this stuff; younger folks may demur. The wary can still opt for creamy congee, fried chicken, or a fish fillet. ✉*17–19A Nga*

Tsin Wai Rd., Kowloon City, Kowloon ☎*2383–7170* ▭*No credit cards* Ⓜ*Kowloon City.*

SAI KUNG

$$ ✕**Jaspa's.** What could be better
ECLECTIC than heading straight to a cozy res-
Ⓒ taurant after a day out in the coun-
tryside? The food here is delicious
and filling, perfect after a day walk-
ing in the hills or enjoying the water
and sun. Sit out on the terrace or
indoors. The chicken fajitas arrive

on your table sizzling hot; bay bugs
(large crayfish, available in season) and lamb chops are also delicious.
✉*13 Sha Tsui Path, Sai Kung, Kowloon* ☎*2792–6388* ▭*AE, MC,
V* Ⓜ*Hung Hau.*

$$$ ✕**Tung Kee Seafood Restaurant.** Lobsters, slipper lobsters, clams, aba-
SEAFOOD lone, crabs, prawns, fish, and everything else from the deep blue sea is
here for the tasting on Sai Kung's picturesque harbor. Crustaceans and
fish are quickly cooked by steaming and wok-frying and are presented
whole, leaving no doubt as to the freshness of your food. A quick look
inside the tank is like a lesson in marine biology. Pick your favorites,
and leave the rest to the chef. Then just prepare yourself for a feast *de la
mer.* ✉*96–102 Man Nin St., Sai Kung, Kowloon* ☎*2792–7453* ▭*AE,
DC, MC, V* Ⓜ*Hang Hau.*

Where to Stay

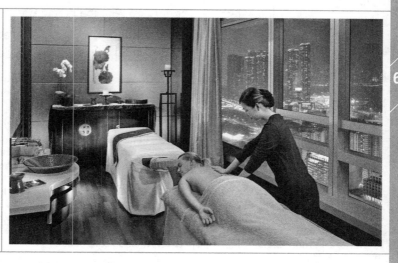

Langham Place Hotel

WORD OF MOUTH

"So for me, in a nutshell it comes down to this: unless you have a harbor view room on the Kowloon side, I would not stay on the Kowloon side. . . . I would take the Hong Kong side over anything on the Kowloon side. And remember that even with a harbor view room, you will end up spending a good bit of time on the Hong Kong side anyway."

—Cicerone

Updated by
Albert Wong

Whether you are a business traveler or a casual tourist, you will inevitably be caught up with the manic pace of life here. Luckily, Hong Kong's hotels are constantly increasing their efforts to make you feel at home, so you can enjoy wonderful views of either city life or the world-famous harbor free from stress.

The conventions and exhibitions industry is booming in Hong Kong at the moment, and it's rare to find a hotel without the latest technologies, be they iPod docks, Wi-Fi, or the latest ayurvedic spa treatments. Yet these days Hong Kong hotels are overrun by vacationing upper-middle-class mainland Chinese as much as by the international business set. Space is at a premium, so rooms are smaller than what you may be used to at home, but the better hotels use innovative design to ward off any feelings of claustrophobia. Reserve well in advance, and plan to pay dearly. Room shortages mean that the age of the under-US$100 hotel room is vanishing; top spots run US$500–US$600.

The rock stars of Hong Kong's hotel industry are perfectly situated on either side of the harbor. In addition to the established Grand Hyatt, InterContinental, and the Peninsula, a Four Seasons has recently opened on the Central harbor front. But with space around the harbor running out, new luxury hotels are having to make some new inroads. Low-profile boutique hotels are now springing up farther into the city, where exclusivity and attention to detail make up for the lack of massive pools and unhindered harbor views. However, hipness hardly guarantees quality service, so don't ignore the formidable reputation of a hotel such as the Mandarin Oriental for the sake of trying something new.

WHERE SHOULD I STAY?

	Neighborhood Vibe	Pros	Cons
Western & Southern	A sprawling area with hidden alleyways, antiques shops, and temples, Western is the area of choice for artists and designers. In Southern you'll find beaches and outdoor dining (but no bargains).	Western has an East-meets-West atmosphere; Southern feels almost like a tropical island, with great views on clear days. Lower building density here means a more laid-back feel than in the city.	Not the easiest area to access since the MTR cannot take you up the hills, and driving is complicated on narrow one-way roads. On a hot day, walking up the slopes can be quite an effort.
Central	An international finance center, Central is full of businesspeople in sharp suits for whom a wasted second means millions squandered.	The major luxury brands have their flagship stores here; luxury hotels here house some fine restaurants. Near famous nightlife area Lan Kwai Fong.	Congested; even crossing the road during the business day is a struggle. For some, proximity to rowdy drinkers in Lan Kwai Fong is an annoyance.
The Admiralty	Another business district, the Admiralty is dominated by lawyers because of its proximity to the courthouses. Hotels here cater to business clientele.	Convenient to all public transit. Pacific Place shopping mall has everything from luxury brands to chain stores with all the basics.	Tourists will find little to explore here. Shops and restaurants are mostly inside shopping malls and thus close relatively early.
Lantau Island	Hong Kong's largest island is home to a strange combination: convention facilities, unspoiled natural scenery, and Hong Kong Disneyland.	If you need to be near the airport or are visiting Disneyland, the Tung Chung neighborhood of Lantau is the place to be.	Inconvenient for exploring Hong Kong Island: it's a 45-minute metro ride to the city center from here.
Wan Chai	Lockhart Road's hostess bars have given the area a seedy reputation. But Wan Chai is also home to the Hong Kong Exhibition and Convention Center and a number of decent restaurants.	Dining here tends to be more affordable than in Central, with a distinctly local taste. Cheaper, more laid-back nightlife than in Lan Kwai Fong, if you can see past the seedy spots.	In this large district, a short tram ride to the nearest metro station may be required. Caucasian men walking down Lockhart Road alone may be targeted by hostess-bar staff.
Causeway Bay & Eastern	Causeway Bay is where young locals gather on the weekends to eat, shop, and hang out. Eastern is a quieter but relatively more affordable area.	Causeway Bay is a great neighborhood for shopping, dining, and people-watching, with a good of hotels in all price ranges. There's easy access to public transit.	Causeway Bay is extremely crowded on the weekends. There's not much of interest east of Victoria Park.
Kowloon	Home to the Kowloon Mosque, the "other side," as Kowloon is sometimes called, is truly multicultural. Many South Asians conduct business here.	The harborside promenade has the best views of Hong Kong's famous skyline. A variety international cuisines, like Korean and Indian, are available.	Kowloon side is not everyone's idea of a holiday—it's generally even more hectic than the island.

6

HONG KONG LODGING PLANNER

Lodging Strategy

With hundreds of hotels, it may seem daunting to choose. But fret not—our expert writers and editors have done most of the legwork. The 60-plus selections here represent the best this city has to offer. Scan "Best Bets" on the following pages for top recommendations by price and experience. Reviews are arranged alphabetically by neighborhood. Happy hunting!

Reservations

Book well in advance, especially for March or September to early December, high seasons for conventions. Most hotels have reliable Internet booking systems; phone reservations are also accepted, and receptionists speak English.

Specify arrival and departure dates; room size (single or double), type (standard, deluxe, or suite); the number of guests; and whether you want a bathroom with a shower or bathtub (or both). Ask if a deposit is required and what happens if you cancel.

Flights from the United States often arrive in the evening. It's a good idea to tell your hotel when you'll be checking in so they don't give away your room.

Rooms with a View

Hotels in Tsim Sha Tsui (TST), on the Kowloon side, generally have the best views because it's across the harbor from the most distinctive area of skyline. Because of the curvature of the bay, hotels in Causeway Bay can also have an equally exhilarating view down the coast of HK Island as well as Kowloon. Remember that silence speaks loudly; if your room (or hotel) isn't advertised as "harbor view," it's almost certainly not. And be wary of the nomenclature: rooms described as "peak view" have exactly the views you *don't* want—that is, back toward the hills rather than over the beautiful harbor.

Executive Privilege

Most high-end hotels have a restricted-access executive floor or club. Free breakfast and cocktails are generally served in these clubs, which can range from modest rooms with a few tables, newspapers, and a fridge full of drinks, to lavish halls with daylong buffets. The business facilities tend to include faxes, laser printing, special dedicated concierges, and sometimes a mini conference room.

Entry to these clubs and lounges is based on what category of room you book, although some hotels allow guests staying in less expensive rooms to pay an additional fee for executive privileges. The InterContinental, for example, charges an extra HK$900 per day for the use of all executive facilities, which club members may use for free.

Children

Many hotels allow children under a certain age to stay in their parents' room at no extra charge, but find out the cutoff age. The Marco Polo has lots of kid-friendly amenities including miniature bathrobes, mild shampoos, and rubber duckies. Hotels with large pools and rec facilities—the Peninsula, Grand Hyatt, Renaissance Harbour View, Salisbury YMCA, and Holiday Inn—are good. And hotels at Hong Kong Disneyland are the definition of kid-friendly.

Hotel Features

Unless stated in the review, hotels are equipped with elevators, and all guest rooms have air-conditioning, TV, telephone, and private bathroom. It's rare to find places that expect guests to share toilets or bathrooms in Hong Kong. However, bathrooms with showers but no bathtubs are common, so be sure to ask if this is a concern.

Note that we use "Internet" to designate the presence of genuine high-speed broadband lines and mention wireless access where available. Most moderately priced hotels will come with the state-of-the-art technologies; dial-up Internet access is virtually extinct. However, Wi-Fi access usually costs extra, unless you are staying in an "executive room" with free use of an executive lounge with Wi-Fi access.

Prices

Prices vary dramatically depending on season. During the convention months (Sept.–Dec.), even budget hostels usually catering to student backpackers double their prices. However, many Hong Kong hotels offer packages which cater to families, couples, and business travelers.

Most hotels operate on the European plan (no meals included). All rooms have private baths unless indicated otherwise.

WHAT IT COSTS FOR TWO PEOPLE IN HK$

¢	$	$$	$$$	$$$$
under HK$700	HK$700–HK$1,100	HK$1,100–HK$2,100	HK$2,100–HK$3,000	over HK$3,000

Prices are for two people in a standard double room in high season, excluding 10% service charge and a 3% government tax.

In this Chapter

Checking In

Typical check-in and check-out times are 2 PM and noon, respectively, although most hotels will be flexible if they are not fully booked. Large hotel chains such as the Regal and the Marco Polo have privilege clubs which allow their members to extend their check-out times until the evening.

BEST BETS FOR HONG KONG LODGING

Fodor's offers a selective listing of quality lodgings at every price range, from the city's best budget motel to its most sophisticated luxury hotels. We've compiled our top recommendations by price and experience. The best properties are designated in the listings with a Fodor's Choice logo.

HONG KONG ISLAND

WESTERN

The Western district has several hotels in the lower Midlevels and Sheung Wan areas. The steep, narrow streets also make the area ripe for a growing number of boutique hotels catering to those who favor style over opulence. These places are conveniently located near the Peak Tram, as well as SoHo (South of Hollywood Road), one of Hong Kong's top nightlife areas. It also has that eclectic mix of international restaurants, boutiques, and bourgeois-bohemian development that seems common to areas dubbed "SoHo" around the world.

$ **Bishop Lei International House.** Owned and operated by the Catholic diocese of Hong Kong, this guesthouse is up the Midlevels Escalator at the top of SoHo. Rooms are quite small but functional, and half have harbor views. Although it's economically priced, there is a fully equipped business center, a workout room, a pool, and a restaurant serving Chinese and western meals. **Pros:** walking distance to SoHo and Lan Kwai Fong, good value. **Cons:** starting to show age. ⊠ *4 Robinson Rd., Midlevels, Western* ☎ *2868–0828* ⊕ *www.bishopleihtl.com.hk* ☞ *104 rooms, 101 suites* △ *In-room: safe, refrigerator, Internet. In-hotel: restaurant, pool, gym, laundry service, no-smoking rooms.* ⊟ *AE, DC, MC, V* Ⓜ *Central.*

FodorsChoice ★

$$ **Garden View YWCA.** Don't be put off by the name: this attractive cylindrical guesthouse on a hill overlooks the botanical gardens and harbor, and its well-designed rooms make excellent use of small irregular shapes and emphasize each room's picture windows. If you want to do your own cooking, ask for a room with a kitchenette (which will include a microwave oven); if not, the coffee shop serves European and Asian food. You can also use the swimming pool and gymnasium in the adjacent YWCA. Garden View is a five-minute drive (Bus 12A or Minibus 1A) from Central and a few minutes from the Peak tram station. **Pros:** excellent price for convenient location, walking distance to city center. **Cons:** traffic can get pretty bad in the morning and early evenings due to a nearby school. ⊠ *1 MacDonnell Rd., Midlevels, Western* ☎ *2877–3737* ⊕ *www.ywca.org.hk* ☞ *136 rooms* △ *In-room: kitchen (some), refrigerator, Internet. In-hotel: restaurant, pool, gym, laundry service, no-smoking rooms.* ⊟ *AE, DC, MC, V* Ⓜ *Central.*

$–$$ **Hotel Jen.** This new hotel, which opened in early 2008 on the site of an old Novotel, has a sleek, Zen-like atmosphere, with lots of white and other calming neutral colors, beige wood, and plenty of natural light. Guest rooms have daybeds in front of their large windows, which are perfect for reading during the day as well as accommodating an extra person at night. Long desks accommodate those with work to get done,

FodorsChoice ★

6

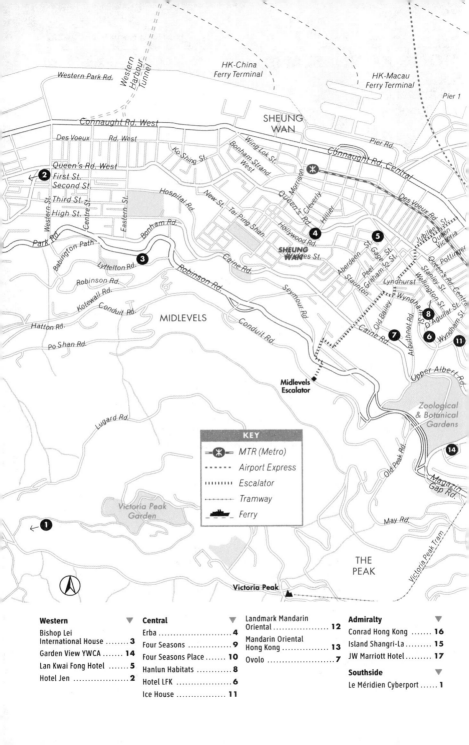

Where to Stay in
Western, Central
& the Admiralty

Pier 2 Pier 3 Pier 4 Pier 5 Pier 6 Pier 7

Man Po St. Man Kwong St. Man Chiu St. Star Ferry Pier

9 **10**

One IFC IFC Mall Two IFC

Victoria Harbour

Harbour View St.

Des Voeux Rd Central

Pedder St.

Connaught Pl.

Queen's Pier Queen's Pier

Edinburgh

Edinburgh

Chater House

Jackson Rd.

Murray Rd.

Harcourt Rd.

AIRPORT EXPRESS HONG KONG **13**

Chater Garden

CENTRAL DISTRICT

Ice House

Duddell

Lower Albert Rd.

CENTRAL

Garden Rd.

Cotton Tree Dr.

Queensway Rd.

ADMIRALTY

Rodney St.

Gloucester Rd.

Seafront Rd.

Fenwick Pier St.

Harbour Rd.

WAN CHAI

Arsenal St.

Fenwick St.

Jaffe Rd.

Lockhart Rd.

Hennessy Rd.

15 **17** **16**

Pacific Place

Justice Dr.

Queensway Rd. East

Johnston Rd.

Lun Fat

Ship

Luard Rd.

Swatow

Amoy

Tai Yuen

O'Brien

WAN CHAI

Hong Kong Park

Kennedy Rd.

Macdonnell Rd.

ADMIRALTY

Kennedy Rd.

Bowen Rd.

Bowen Rd.

Borrett Rd.

Bowen Dr.

Kennedy Rd.

Bowen Rd.

May Rd.

Magazine Gap Rd.

Barker Rd.

Barker Rd.

Wan Chai Gap Rd.

0 — 1/4 mile
0 — 1/4 kilometer

though Korean and Japanese tourists comprise a significant portion of the clientele here. The bright and uncluttered Sky Lounge, a lounge and bar area on the 28th floor for hotel guests, is generally not crowded and makes a nice place to relax with a magazine. If visiting Western's antiques stores is high on your itinerary, this is a great alternative to pricier boutique hotels. **Pros:** unbeatable value, relaxing atmosphere. **Cons:** no easy access to an MTR station, so not convenient for visiting other parts of Hong Kong; not for those seeking raucous nightlife. ⊠*508 Queen's Rd. W, Western* ☎*2974–1234* ⊕*www.hoteljen.com* ☏*280 rooms, 5 suites* ⌂*In-room: safe, kitchen (some), refrigerator, DVD (some), Internet, Wi-Fi. In-hotel: restaurant, room service, bar, pool, gym, laundry service, Wi-Fi, parking (paid), no-smoking rooms.* ▭*AE, D, DC, MC, V.*

$$$

Fodor's Choice

. ★

Lan Kwai Fong Hotel. This boutique hotel, which opened in 2006, is popular with journalists and designers who appreciate its contemporary Chinese decor and SoHo location. Rooms are decorated with Asian accents but avoid an overdone, theme-park look, and bathrooms are outfitted with rain showerheads. The hotel's location in the middle of the Western SoHo area, which is full of art galleries, antiques shops, and boutiques, is another major selling point; an open-air breakfast lounge capitalizes on these colorful surroundings. Pricier rooms have unobstructed harbor views, although avid people-watchers may prefer "city-view" rooms, which look onto the vibrant street life below. **Pros:** hotel and neighborhood have lots of character. **Cons:** narrow roads surrounding hotel are often congested. ⊠*3 Kau U Fong, Western* ☎*3650–0000* ⊕*www.lankwaifonghotel.com.hk* ☏*162 rooms, 5 suites* ⌂*In-room: safe, kitchen (some), refrigerator, Internet, Wi-Fi. In-hotel: 2 restaurants, room service, bar, gym, laundry service, no-smoking rooms.* ▭*AE, D, DC, MC, V.*

CENTRAL

While it's by no means the center of Hong Kong geographically, Central is Hong Kong's financial hub and it's full of top restaurants. The hotels here are arenas in which deals are hatched, closed, and celebrated; prepare to pay a lot for top-notch service and marvelous skyline views. If you want a departure from the sobriety of business, there's always the Lan Kwai Fong nightlife district up the hill.

$$$$

Four Seasons. When the Four Seasons opened, in the shadow of the world's sixth-tallest building, there was a collective intake of breath: with the elegantly colorful Chinese-theme rooms and their more muted western counterparts, the place displays equal levels of effortless modern style, yet they're not about trendy minimalism; the *smallest* of them is a roomy 500 square feet. World-class linens, feng shui elevator banks, heated infinity pools, 42-inch plasma TVs, skyline-view hot-rock massages in the city's most cutting-edge spa, clairvoyant service, fantastic restaurants—and this list doesn't even include the holistic effect of staying in a place that's redefining the world's very notion of an urban luxury hotel. **Pros:** spacious rooms, great views, no luxury overlooked. **Cons:** having everything comes at a price. ⊠*Interna-*

tional Finance Center, 8 Finance Rd., Central ☎*3196–8888* ⊕*www. fourseasons.com* ⏎*399 rooms, 54 suites* Ⅲ*In-room: refrigerator, safe, DVD, Wi-Fi. In-hotel: 5 restaurants, room service, bars, pools, gym, spa, laundry service, Wi-Fi, no-smoking rooms.* ☰*AE, DC, MC, V* Ⓜ*Sheung Wan.*

$$$$ Ⓣ**Hotel LKF.** Easily confused with Lan Kwai Fong Hotel farther west, this newer boutique hotel opened in 2006 and has been building quite a reputation for itself. Its obvious advantage is its location—in the center of the Lan Kwai Fong entertainment district—but there's more to it than convenience for partygoers. Don't be fooled by the small lobby with its dizzying array of wavy and circular patterns; the guest rooms themselves are decorated in deep, soothing colors and are surprisingly spacious given the small size of the building itself. Expect the most high-tech facilities, including 42-inch plasma screen and ergonomic Aeron chairs. The staff will make arrangements for pets and young children upon request, and all rooms are equipped with Illy coffee machines. The spectacular rooftop bar, Azure, lets you literally tower over Lan Kwai Fong. **Pros:** hippest hotel in town, Azure bar. **Cons:** rowdy neighborhood streets may not be the best environment for young children. ✉*33 Wyndham St., Central* ☎*3518–9333* ⊕*www.hotel-lkf.com. hk* ⏎*95 rooms* Ⅲ*In-room: safe, kitchen (some), refrigerator, DVD (some), Internet, Wi-Fi (some). In-hotel: restaurant, room service, bar, gym, laundry service, some pets allowed, no-smoking rooms.* ☰*AE, D, DC, MC, V.*

$ Ⓣ**Ice House.** Consider yourself lucky to be alive at the right time: the apart-hotel accommodation concept has finally hit Hong Kong, and at the Ice House, it's done right. These chic, modern studio apartments are available to rent by the day or week, not just by the month (which, by the way, is quite reasonable at around HK$14,000). Sunlight is plentiful, and the glass-cube showers are an amusing touch. The location is excellent, next to the Foreign Correspondents' Club and Lan Kwai Fong, and studios come with free unlimited broadband, direct phone line, and other business amenities. There's housekeeping service every day but Sunday. If you want to feel like you have a place of your own in town, the Ice House is a unique option. **Pros:** free broadband, great value if your needs are basic. **Cons:** no hotel-style pampering here. ✉*38 Ice House St., Central* ☎*2836–7333* ⊕*www.icehouse.com.hk* ⏎*30 rooms* Ⅲ*In-room: kitchen, Internet. In-hotel: laundry service, no-smoking rooms.* ☰*AE, DC, MC, V.*

$$$$ Ⓣ**Landmark Mandarin Oriental.** Hong Kong hotels are like computers: every year, the new technology outdoes the old by such a staggering margin that you're left wondering why anyone would stick by their old models. The design of this boutique-size hotel is dazzling, and a complete departure from the Mandarin's standard MO. The three room types are named for their square footage; the midrange L600 is the most interesting, with a round bathroom fascinatingly placed at the center of the space. Everything from iPod docks to surround-sound speakers are controlled through your TV remote, and the 21,000-square-foot spa has Turkish baths and "rain forest" steam room. And all of this is implausibly concealed within the financial mitochondrion of the city.

6

Pros: you can't get more central in Central. **Cons:** even more expensive than other high-end hotels in Central. ✉ *15 Queen's Rd. Central, Central* ☎ *2132–0188* ⊕ *www.mandarinoriental.com/landmark* ⟿ *113 rooms* ♿ *In-room: refrigerator, DVD, Wi-Fi. In-hotel: 3 restaurants, room service, bar, pool, gym, spa, laundry service, Wi-Fi, no-smoking rooms.* ▭ *AE, DC, MC, V* Ⓜ *Central.*

$$$$ ▦ **Mandarin Oriental Hong Kong.** In September 2006, the legendary Mandarin, which has served the international elite since 1963, completed a top-to-bottom renovation that included the installation of one of the city's most elaborate spas. The hotel is such a symbol of Hong Kong's colonial and financial history that rumors of the renovations sparked fierce debate amongst the business elite. However, the Mandarin has not lost its characteristic charm in the face of modernization; sumptuous materials and furnishings, like silky cognac drapes and leather armchairs in guest rooms, are the norm here, but now so are flat-panel LCDs and iPod docks. Everything you see, you want to touch. Five new categories of rooms, from "study" to "harbour," span a wider price range than ever before. On the 25th floor, rising high above the Central skyline, are renowned chef Pierre Gagnaire's French restaurant Pierre and the panoramic M Bar. Walking around the new spa area is a delight in itself, as every corridor, alleyway and room feels like a classic Oriental boudoir, concealing hidden delights. **Pros:** staying here is a classic Hong Kong experience, rooms have wonderful study areas. **Cons:** standard rooms are relatively small for a luxury hotel. ✉ *5 Connaught Rd., Central* ☎ *2522–0111* ⊕ *www.mandarin-oriental.com/hongkong* ⟿ *434 rooms, 68 suites* ♿ *In-room: safe, Internet, Wi-Fi. In-hotel: 6 restaurants, room service, bars, pool, gym, spa, laundry service, Wi-Fi, no-smoking rooms.* ▭ *AE, DC, MC, V* Ⓜ *Central.*

ADMIRALTY

You might think that because Admiralty is not in the center of the city's financial nerve, you'd save a few cents on a hotel here. You'd be wrong. Admiralty hotels, particularly those in Pacific Place, are every bit as classy and expensive as the big names in Central, and they soar just as proudly. You get great skyline, Victoria Peak, and harbor views as well as myriad (although westernized) shopping and dining options. However, what were once the primogenitors of the modern all-inclusive hotel are starting to look outdated in the current trend towards designer boutique lodgings.

$$$$ ▦ **Conrad Hong Kong.** This luxurious hotel occupies part of a gleaming-white, oval-shape tower rising from Pacific Place, an upscale complex with a multistory mall at the edge of Central. Along with the nearby Shangri-La and Marriott, the Conrad enjoys a reputation for reliable, high-quality service. Rooms are spacious, have dramatic views of the harbor and city, and have recently been installed with the latest gadgets such as flat-screen TVs; all have irons and ironing boards, coffee and tea facilities, and high-speed Internet access. Five executive floors have their own private elevator, lounge, and gym. The pool, tucked beneath an apocalyptic skyscraper-scape, is legendary, and Nicholini's, the top-floor Italian restaurant, is popular with city executives. **Pros:** reputation for excellent service, good location in Admiralty. **Cons:** doesn't have a lot of personality. ✉*Pacific Place, 88 Queensway, Admiralty* ☎*2521--3838* ⊕*www.conradhotels.com* ⌥*513 rooms, 46 suites* ♨*In-room: safe, refrigerator, Internet, Wi-Fi (some). In-hotel: 4 restaurants, room service, bar, pool, gym, laundry service, Wi-Fi, parking (paid), no-smoking rooms.* ▤*AE, DC, MC, V* Ⓜ*Admiralty.*

$$$$ ⌨**Island Shangri-La.** This trademark elliptical building has become an icon of Hong Kong, as has *The Great Motherland of China,* the world's largest Chinese landscape painting, which is housed in its glass atrium. The painting, which spans 16 stories, can be viewed from elevators soaring up and down through the atrium, carrying guests to their rooms. The lobby of the deluxe hotel, affectionately known to locals as the "Island Shang," sparkles with more than 780 dazzling Austrian crystal chandeliers hanging from high ceilings and huge, sunlit windows. Take the elevator up from the 39th floor and see the mainland's misty mountains drift by. Rooms are some of the largest on Hong Kong Island and have magnificent views; all have large desks and all-in-one bedside control panels. For very upscale dining there's the scenic, formal French eatery Pétrus on the top floor, or for Chinese food, the classy Summer Palace. **Pros:** *The Great Motherland,* spectacular reputation for quality service, large rooms. **Cons:** it costs to be fabulous. ✉*Two Pacific Place, Supreme Court Rd., Admiralty* ☎*2877–3838, 800/942–5050 in U.S.* ⊕*www.shangri-la.com* ⌥*531 rooms, 34 suites* ♨*In-room: safe, refrigerator, DVD, Wi-Fi. In-hotel: 4 restaurants, room service, pool, gym, laundry service, Wi-Fi, parking (paid), no-smoking rooms.* ▤*AE, DC, MC, V* Ⓜ*Admiralty.*

LANTAU ISLAND

The main advantage of staying on Lantau Island is its proximity to the airport. It's a good choice if you arrive late at night and don't want to put up with the chaos of the city on your first night, or on the back end of your trip if you have an early-morning flight. Most come to Lantau only to seek a beach escape or to finally satisfy the kids' Disney dreams, but public transportation to and from the city has been improving in recent years with some new development near the airport.

$$ ⌨**Disney's Hollywood Hotel.** Like its pricier sister, the Disneyland Hotel, ☺ Disney's Hollywood Hotel could theoretically be viewed simply as one of Asia's best airport hotels. But that would hardly do justice to the creativity and attention to detail that so brightly color every aspect of your stay here. The theme is the golden age of Hollywood, and if you're from the United States you'll smile at the loving display of Americana here, from the New York–theme restaurant to the art-deco frontage of the cocktail lounge. Of course, this is Disneyland, and there are the Chef Mickey restaurants, too. There's a playroom, Malibu Toy Shop, as well as a number of activities for kids. Rooms are on the smaller side, and a bit more "Goofy" than they are at the Disneyland Hotel, with perhaps even greater appeal for the children. **Pros:** great value. **Cons:** cut off from Hong Kong attractions, which is not great if you get

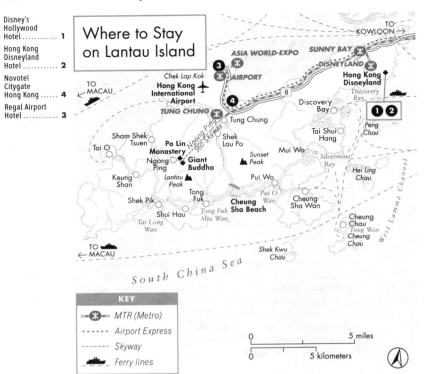

Where to Stay on Lantau Island

KEY

- ━✳━ MTR (Metro)
- ----- Airport Express
- .... Skyway
- ━━⛴━ Ferry lines

sick of Disneyland. ✉*Hong Kong Disneyland Resort, Lantau Island* ☎*1–830–830* ⊕*www.hongkongdisneyland.com* ⌘*600 rooms* ⌂*In-room: safe, refrigerator, Internet. In-hotel: 3 restaurants, room service, bars, tennis court, pool, gym, spa, children's programs (ages 2–12), laundry service, no-smoking rooms.* ▤*AE, DC, MC, V.*

$$$ 🏨 **Hong Kong Disneyland Hotel.** Modeled in Victorian style after the ⟳ Grand Floridian in Florida's Walt Disney World Resort, this top-flight hotel is beautifully executed on every level, from the spacious rooms with balconies overlooking the sea to the topiary of Mickey's Maze, and grand, imposing ballrooms that wouldn't be out of place in a fairy-tale secret castle. There's a full daily schedule of activities, many aimed at children although adults may enjoy the horticulture tours; and downstairs, Disney characters meet and greet guests during the enormous buffet breakfast—a good way to get your kids to forgive you for the three days you spent sampling geese hanging from their necks in Mong Kok. Don't overlook Disneyland as a place to stay before or after your early-morning or late-night flight—it's minutes from the airport. **Pros:** great for kids. **Cons:** overpriced compared to Disney's Hollywood. ✉*Hong Kong Disneyland Resort, Lantau Island* ☎*1–830–830* ⊕*www.hongkongdisneyland.com* ⌘*400 rooms* ⌂*In-room: safe, refrigerator, Internet. In-hotel: 3 restaurants,* *room service, bars, tennis court, pool, gym, spa, children's programs (ages 2–12), laundry service, parking (free), no-smoking rooms.* ▤*AE, DC, MC, V.*

$$$ 🖥 **Novotel Citygate Hong Kong.** This hotel's out-of-the-way location on
🕒 Lantau Island may not immediately strike you as desirable: it's not next to either the airport (though it's only a five-minute bus ride away) or Disneyland, and it's quite a way from the city center. However, Lantau has been developing as a tourist attraction in its own right, and the island's natural beauty is finally getting the publicity it deserves. The Novotel is perfectly situated for exploring Lantau's sights. Buses to Tai O, a remote fishing village on the other side of the island, leave just five minutes from here on foot; the Ngong Ping 360 cable car is also close by. Experienced trekkers can even try walking the Lantau hills from here, although there aren't designated, easy trails yet. The concierge can organize white dolphin sightseeing trips, which depart from the nearby pier. Guest rooms are spacious and bright, with large windows and open bathroom, and have spectacular views of either the sea or the Lantau hills and cable cars. Should the weather not hold up, there is an outlet mall adjoining the hotel that can keep you occupied for a day. A metro ride from the nearby Tung Chung Center will take you into the city in 30 minutes. **Pros:** great for families interested in outdoor activities. **Cons:** not convenient for city pursuits. ✉*51 Man Tung Rd. , Tung Chung, Lantau Island* ☎*3602–8888* ⊕*www.novotel.com* 🛏*440, 14 suites* �029*In-room: safe, kitchen (some), Internet, Wi-Fi. In-hotel: 4 restaurants, room service, bar, pool, gym, laundry service, Wi-Fi, parking (paid), no-smoking rooms.* ▤*AE, D, DC, MC, V.*

$$$ 🖥 **Regal Airport Hotel.** Ideal for passengers in transit, this is one of the largest airport hotels in the world. It's some distance from the city, but the efficient high-speed rail system can have you on Hong Kong Island in around 25 minutes, and a free shuttle bus can take you to Tsimshatsui, for a little longer depending on traffic. It's also connected directly to the passenger terminal by an air-conditioned, moving walkway. Consistently voted one of the best airport hotels in the world, it has a spa, opened in 2006, with an impressive range of treatments and private spa suites that allow guests to receive treatments in their own rooms. Some rooms have terrific views of planes landing from afar; those with balconies overlook the hotel's two swimming pools and make you feel like you're staying in a resort. **Pros:** can't get any closer to the airport than this, great amenities for an airport hotel. **Cons:** not convenient to Hong Kong sights. ✉*9 Cheong Ted Rd., Lantau Island* ☎*2286–8888* ⊕*www.regalhotel.com* 🛏*1,171 rooms, 32 suites* �029*In-room: safe, refrigerator, kitchen (some), Wi-Fi. In-hotel: 7 restaurants, room service, bar, pool, gym, laundry service, parking (paid), no-smoking rooms.* ▤*AE, DC, MC, V.*

WAN CHAI

Wan Chai, east of Central and Admiralty, was once a boozy sailor's dream. It still has plenty of nightlife (and the red-light activity to go with it) and everything from 24-hour noodle joints to hip new wine bars.

At the same time, office high-rises and the Hong Kong Convention & Exhibition Centre, a Sydney Opera House–wannabe structure and the territory's most popular venue for large-scale conferences, draw businesspeople to the area. Thus Wan Chai has some prestigious business hotels: the Grand Hyatt rivals the shining stars of the IFC, Pacific Place, and Tsim Sha Tsui for CEO appeal; the Renaissance Harbour View isn't far behind. Surprisingly the area has also more budget hotels than neighboring districts.

$$$$ ☐ **Grand Hyatt.** A ceiling painted by Italian artist Paola Dindo tops the Hyatt's art-deco-style lobby, and black-and-white photographs of classic Chinese scenes hang on the walls. The elegant guest rooms have sweeping harbor views, many with interesting zigzag window frames; amenities include large interactive TVs with cordless keyboards. The One Harbour Road Cantonese restaurant is notable—as is JJ's nightclub and Thai restaurant—and the ground-floor breakfast buffet is a decadent feast. The Plateau spa has a Zen-like calm and there are extensive outdoor facilities. The hotel is especially convenient if you're spending time at the Hong Kong Convention & Exhibition Centre, which is connected to the building. **Pros:** excellent sports facilities, including tennis and squash courts and a driving range. **Cons:** no space in the minibar for your own items. ⊠ *1 Harbour Rd., Wan Chai* ☎ *2588–1234* ⊕ *www.hongkong.grand.hyatt.com* ⟿ *512 rooms, 37 suites* ⚐ *In-room: safe, Wi-Fi. In-hotel: 8 restaurants, room service, bars, tennis courts, pool, gym, spa, laundry service, Wi-Fi, parking (paid), no-smoking rooms.* ⊟ *AE, DC, MC, V* Ⓜ *Wan Chai.*

$$ ☐ **The Harbourview.** This waterfront YMCA property has small but relatively inexpensive rooms near the Wan Chai Star Ferry Pier. Rooms are not luxurious but have recently been renovated and now have new TVs, curtains, and carpets; some have harbor views. However, the final stage of renovations, set to begin in 2009, will temporarily reduce the number of available rooms. The hotel is well placed if you want to attend cultural events in the evening: both the Arts Centre and the Academy for Performing Arts are next door. It's also just opposite the Hong Kong Convention & Exhibition Centre. The 16-story building provides free shuttle service to Causeway Bay and the Central Star Ferry. You can use the superb YMCA Kowloon facilities, just a short ferry ride away, for a small fee. **Pros:** use of YMCA facilities across the harbor, affordable rates for reliable service and decent rooms. **Cons:** not close to a metro station. ⊠ *4 Harbour Rd., Wan Chai* ☎ *2802–0111* ⊕ *www.theharbourview.com.hk* ⟿ *320 rooms* ⚐ *In-room: refrigerator, Internet, Wi-Fi. In-hotel: restaurant, room service, laundry service, Wi-Fi, no-smoking rooms.* ⊟ *AE, DC, MC, V* Ⓜ *Wan Chai.*

$$ ☐ **Luk Kwok.** This contemporary hotel and office tower designed by Hong Kong's leading architect, Remo Riva, replaced the Wan Chai

landmark of the same name immortalized in Richard Mason's novel *The World of Suzie Wong.* The Luk Kwok's appeal, aside from its slightly kitschy classic Asian feel, is its proximity to the Hong Kong Convention & Exhibition Centre, the Academy for Performing Arts, and the Arts Centre. Guest rooms, in the building's 19th to 29th floors, are simply furnished; higher floors have mountain or city views. **Pros:** landmark sight, has a popular Chinese restaurant. **Cons:** Wan Chai's rowdy nightlife district not great for children. ⊠*72 Gloucester Rd., Wan Chai* ☎*2866–2166* ⊕*www.lukkwokhotel.com* ⌑*196 rooms, 4 suites* ⌕*In-room: safe, refrigerator, Internet, Wi-Fi. In-hotel: 2 restaurant, room service, bar, gym, laundry service, Wi-Fi, no-smoking rooms.* ⊟*AE, DC, MC, V* Ⓜ*Wan Chai.*

$$ ⊡**Novotel Century Hong Kong.** This hotel was redesigned to suit the needs of business travelers, but vacationers will also appreciate the modern facilities and reasonable price tag. Rooms have dark woods and a boardroom feel, with large desks for work and adaptors for electrical equipment. Although situated in the heart of Wan Chai, it's just a five-minute walk by covered overpass (a lifesaver in the steamy summer heat) from the Hong Kong Convention Center. For a city hotel, the gym is particularly impressive and has an outdoor pool and a sauna. Buffet meals in the restaurant have won praise around town for being great value. **Pros:** modern, many useful amenities, oyster buffet. **Cons:** difficult to book rooms during convention season. ⊠*238 Jaffe Rd., Wan Chai* ☎*2598–8888* ⊕*www.novotel.com* ⌑*511 rooms, 23 suites* ⌕*In-room: safe, refrigerator, Internet, Wi-Fi (some). In-hotel: 2 restaurants, room service, bars, pool, gym, laundry service, Wi-Fi, no-smoking rooms.* ⊟*AE, DC, MC, V* Ⓜ*Wan Chai.*

$$$$ ⊡**Renaissance Harbour View.** Sharing the Hong Kong Convention & Exhibition Centre complex with the Grand Hyatt is this more-modest but attractive hotel. Guest rooms are medium size with plenty of beveled-glass mirrors that reflect the modern decor. Many rooms have good harbor views and all have high-speed Internet access. Grounds are extensive and include a large outdoor pool, gardens, a playground, and jogging trails, which makes this a good place to stay if you are with children. The wonderfully scenic, soaring lobby lounge has a live jazz band in the evening and is a popular rendezvous spot for locals and visiting businesspeople. **Pros:** you can't get any closer to the Convention Centre, excellent facilities. **Cons:** flanked by office buildings, so it can feel rather dead at night; no Wi-Fi in guest rooms. ⊠*1 Harbour Rd., Wan Chai* ☎*2802–8888* ⊕*www.renaissancehotels.com/hkghv* ⌑*862 rooms, 53 suites* ⌕*In-room: safe, refrigerator, Internet. In-hotel: 3 restaurants, room service, bars, tennis courts, pool, gym, laundry service, Wi-Fi, parking (paid), no-smoking rooms.* ⊟*AE, DC, MC, V* Ⓜ*Wan Chai.*

CAUSEWAY BAY

If Central is the heart of finance, Causeway Bay is the heart of commerce. The brightly lighted district, whose 24-hour crowds defy all logic with their relentless energy, teems with restaurants, cinemas, shopping, and street life—especially in the area around Times Square.

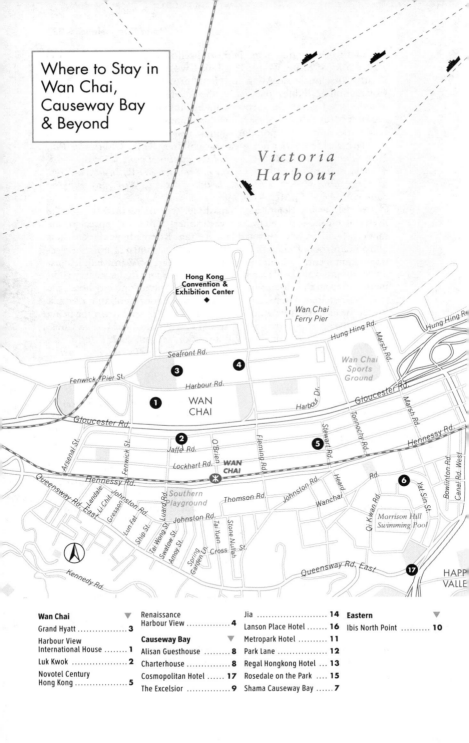

Where to Stay in Wan Chai, Causeway Bay & Beyond

Victoria Harbour

Hong Kong Convention & Exhibition Center

Wan Chai Ferry Pier

Wan Chai Sports Ground

WAN CHAI

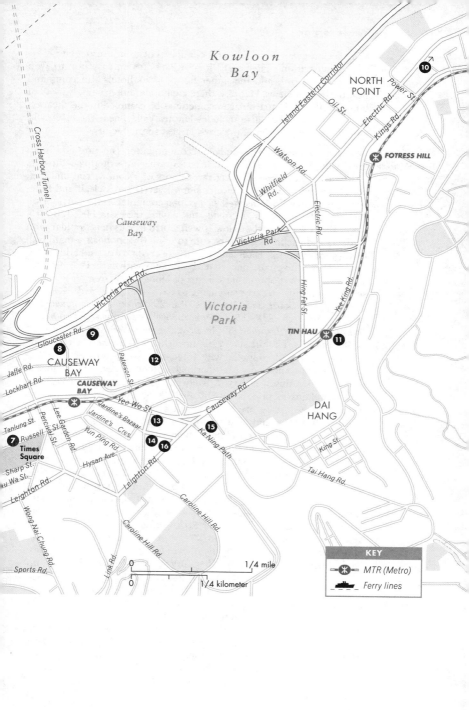

Why is Causeway Bay so up-and-coming? Location, for one: it's close to the convention center and Victoria Park, it's an easy hop to Wan Chai and Central, and the upper floors of its hotels still command beautiful water views. Happily, there are hotels here to suit a variety of budgets, although quarters can sometimes be cramped in the cheapest spots. Causeway Bay also includes Happy Valley, near the racetrack, and Hong Kong Stadium, the city's largest sports facility.

¢

Fodor'sChoice

★

Alisan Guesthouse. This budget accommodation is a rare find in an area with mostly luxury hotels. It has a rather unorthodox setup—its 21 rooms are dispersed among three floors of a commercial building, with a reception area on the fifth floor. Everything is clean and functional, with free Wi-Fi as well as a public computer in the corridor on each floor. Basic rooms are small, and paying the extra HK$120 for a larger room with a harbor view is well worth it. Alisan is popular with students and backpackers, so be sure to book (by phone or e-mail) well in advance. The staff is reluctant to accept credit cards and adds a 7% service charge if you use one, so it's best to pay with cash. **Pros:** friendly staff, great budget option in the heart of Hong Kong, free Wi-Fi. **Cons:** small rooms, fills up early, surcharge to pay with credit card. ⊠ *Flat A, 5th fl., Hoi To Court, 275 Gloucester Rd., 23 Cannon St, Causeway Bay* ☎ *2574–8068 or 2838–0762* ⌂ *alisangh@hkstar.com* ⌨ *21 rooms* ♿ *In-hotel: Internet terminal, Wi-Fi, no-smoking rooms.* ▭ *MC, V.*

$$$

The Excelsior. Despite its 1970s furnishings and interior, this hotel remains perennially popular with travelers, mainly because its prices are moderate compared with other high-end hotels, especially those in the center of Causeway Bay. A lively English pub is in the basement, which explains its popularity with British business types and British Airways crews. Some rooms are spacious with splendid views of the sea and the yachts and boats moored at the Hong Kong Yacht Club; other rooms are smaller and have street views. The location, adjacent to Victoria Park, is ideal for shopping and dining. ToTT's Asian Grill & Bar, on the top floor, has Asian fusion cuisine and live music. On a historical note, the hotel sits on the first plot of land auctioned by the British government when Hong Kong became a colony in 1841. **Pros:** friendly staff in the basement pub, close to metro, convenient for late-night shopping. **Cons:** building looks dated compared to many Hong Kong hotels. ⊠ *281 Gloucester Rd., Causeway Bay* ☎ *2894–8888* ⊕ *www.excelsiorhongkong.com* ⌨ *886 rooms, 22 suites* ♿ *In-room: safe, refrigerator, Internet, Wi-Fi. In-hotel: 7 restaurants, room service, bars, tennis courts, gym, laundry service, Wi-Fi, parking (paid), no-smoking rooms.* ▭ *AE, DC, MC, V* Ⓜ *Causeway Bay.*

$$$

Fodor'sChoice

★

Jia. The first boutique hotel designed by Philippe Starck in Asia is a wonder to behold, beginning with the (see-and-be) scene in the lobby, bar, and restaurant—one of the hippest places to drink or dine in town. Although the sculptural furniture and accompanying trendiness won't be everyone's cup of tea, this is still a groundbreaking concept that is helping to redefine the modern Hong Kong hotel landscape. It doesn't have rooms; rather, it has "apartments," with mini-kitchens, dining tables, and cookware. You can choose between smaller studios or the larger one-bedroom suites, which have separate bedrooms. At this writing, a new restaurant and bar are due to open by the end of 2009. **Pros:** trendy yet reasonably priced for the area. **Cons:** no on-site gym, only one dining option. ✉ *1–5 Irving St., Causeway Bay* ☎ *3196–9000* ⊕ *www.jiahongkong.com* ⤳ *34 studios, 24 suites* ⌂ *In-room: kitchen, DVD, Internet. In-hotel: restaurant, room service, bar, laundry service, Wi-Fi, no-smoking rooms.* ☰ *AE, DC, MC, V* Ⓜ *Causeway Bay.*

$$$ 🏨 **Lanson Place Hotel.** The European facade doesn't give away the paradise of exclusive luxury that awaits you inside this hotel, nor does the deceptive ground-floor reception area. The real lobby and concierge are on the first floor, along with a lounge, dining area, and library, all designed in a neoclassical-meets-retro style that somehow works. Lanson Place feels like an upscale apartment building, and every room has different decor. All rooms besides the penthouses are called suites and have small kitchens and living areas, although it's clever use of space that has made this design possible, since they aren't particularly large. There's no restaurant, although Continental breakfast and cocktails and snacks at night are available. Long-term guests like it here, so be sure to book as early as you can. **Pros:** free use of lending library with books and DVDs. **Cons:** no harbor views, no substantial dining. ✉ *133 Leighton Rd., Causeway Bay* ☎ *3477–6888* ⊕ *www.lansonplace.com* ⤳ *188 suites, 6 penthouses* ⌂ *In-room: safe, kitchen, DVD, Wi-Fi. In-hotel: bar, gym, laundry facilities, laundry service, Wi-Fi, no-smoking rooms.* ☰ *AE, D, DC, MC, V.*

$$ 🏨 **Metropark Hotel.** At this contemporary hotel you'll get a prime location and unobstructed views for a lower cost than at many others. Most rooms, though not strikingly designed, have extensive views of either Victoria Park or the harbor through the floor-to-ceiling windows. The tiny lobby leads into Vic's bar; the Café du Parc serves French-Japanese fusion cuisine. The rooftop pool may be too small for those seeking their daily exercise, but has a spectacular view of Victoria Park and the harbor. Free shuttle buses to and from the Hong Kong Convention & Exhibition Centre and the hub of Causeway Bay run throughout the day. **Pros:** spectacular views at an affordable price, next door to Victoria Park. **Cons:** boring interior design. ✉ *148 Tung Lo Wan Rd., Causeway Bay* ☎ *2600–1000* ⊕ *www.metroparkhotel.com* ⤳ *266 rooms, 56 suites* ⌂ *In-room: safe, refrigerator, Internet, Wi-Fi (some). In-hotel: restaurant, room service, bar, pool, gym, spa, laundry service, Wi-Fi, no-smoking rooms.* ☰ *AE, DC, MC, V* Ⓜ *Causeway Bay.*

$$ 🏨 **Park Lane.** With an imposing facade that wouldn't look out of place in London, this elegant hotel overlooks Victoria Park and backs onto one of Hong Kong Island's busiest shopping, entertainment, and business areas, Causeway Bay. There's a spacious and grand lobby and rooms have luxurious marble bathrooms, elegant handcrafted furniture, and marvelous views of the harbor, Victoria Park, or the city. The rooftop restaurant has a panoramic view and serves international cuisine with a touch of Asian flavor. **Pros:** in the central shopping district. **Cons:** always crowded. ✉ *310 Gloucester Rd., Causeway Bay* ☎ *2293–8888* ⊕ *www.parklane.com.hk* ⤳ *810 rooms, 33 suites* ⌂ *In-room: safe, refrigerator, Internet. In-hotel: 4 restaurants, room service, bar, gym,* *laundry service, Wi-Fi, parking (paid), no-smoking rooms.* ⊟*AE, DC, MC, V* Ⓜ*Causeway Bay.*

$$$ ⌨**Regal Hongkong Hotel.** This hotel recently went through major renovations, adding four floors on top of the existing structure and significantly enlarging its executive area. The reception area is quite small, but gilded elevators take you up to guest rooms with brightly colored bedspreads, furniture handcrafted by local artisans, and spacious bathrooms with triangular tubs. Restaurants include the Mediterranean Zeffirino's, which has a great view of Victoria Park and its own patisserie with a good selection of breads. The peaceful rooftop pool and terrace also have impressive views, although the pool is too small for an energetic swim. The hotel is close to the Hong Kong Stadium and the Happy Valley Racetrack, as well as the city's most popular shopping area, Causeway Bay. **Pros:** location, great view from suites. **Cons:** distinct decor with lots of gold and mirrors won't appeal to everyone. ⊠*88 Yee Wo St., Causeway Bay* ☎*2890–6633, 800/222–8888 in U.S.* ⊕*www.regalhongkong.com* ⇆*475 rooms, 30 suites* ⌂*In-room: safe, refrigerator, DVD (some), Internet, Wi-Fi (some). In-hotel: 3 restaurants, room service, pool, gym, laundry service, Wi-Fi, parking (paid), no-smoking rooms.* ⊟*AE, DC, MC, V* Ⓜ*Causeway Bay.*

$$ ⌨**Rosedale on the Park.** This "cyber boutique hotel," the first of its kind in Hong Kong, has lots of high-tech extras. All public areas have computers, and you can rent a printer, computer, or fax for use in your room, where you also have broadband Internet access and a cordless telephone that can be used anywhere on the property. Mobile phones are also available for rent during your stay. You're in Hong Kong, after all, so why not take advantage of all that technology? Although only the top few floors have park or stadium views, all rooms are bright and comfortable. Next to Victoria Park and only a five-minute walk to the MTR subway, it's a great location for shopping—and the price is one of the best values for a hotel in the middle of Causeway Bay. Cheena, the Rosedale's contemporary Chinese restaurant, is a popular lunch spot which promises not to use MSG. **Pros:** free broadband access in guest rooms. **Cons:** not all rooms have Wi-Fi access. ⊠*8 Shelter St., Causeway Bay* ☎*2127–8888* ⊕*www.rosedale.com.hk* ⇆*274 rooms, 45 suites* ⌂*In-room: safe, refrigerator, Internet, Wi-Fi (some). In-hotel: 2 restaurants, room service, bar, laundry service, no-smoking rooms.* ⊟*AE, DC, MC, V* Ⓜ*Causeway Bay.*

EASTERN

Eastern is not the most popular hotel location in Hong Kong. Though connected by MTR, North Point lacks the energy of Hong Kong's bigger districts. It's notable, however, for its relatively reasonable prices,

Apartment Rentals

If you're in town for a month or more, consider staying in a serviced apartment. It's expensive but you'll save about 50% compared with a month at a hotel.

■ **Erba.** Given the location (near SoHo), its ultramodern apartments are described as New York–style. Think "feng shui." Then think browns and greens and wood and metal. ⊠ *284 Queen's Rd., Central* ☎ *2910–0700* ⊕ *www.erba.hk* ⌂ *Kitchen, Internet, Wi-Fi, laundry facilities, laundry service* ⊟ *AE, MC, V* Ⓜ *Central.*

■ **Four Seasons Place.** These apartments are some of Hong Kong's most modern and beautiful, with prices to match. They're managed by the world-class Four Seasons Hong Kong, so renting here gets you access to the hotel's spa and gym facilities—and what facilities they are. ⊠ *International Finance Centre, 8 Finance St., Central* ☎ *3196–8228* ⊕ *www.fsphk.com* ⌂ *Kitchen, Wi-Fi, 5 restaurants, room service, bars, pools, gym, spa, laundry service* ⊟ *AE, DC, MC, V* Ⓜ *Central.*

■ **Hanlun Habitats.** These economical studios and one-bedrooms have well-equipped kitchens and TVs just about everywhere you turn. A stay here gets you access to a nearby gym and puts you close to SoHo and Lan Kwai Fong. ⊠ *284 Queen's Rd., Central* ☎ *2868–0168* ⊕ *www.hanlunhabitats.com* ⌂ *Gym, laundry service* ⊟ *AE, DC, MC, V* Ⓜ *Central.*

■ **Ovolo.** Thanks to bold design elements and primary colors, these bedroom apartments look like bachelor pads. The location could hardly be more convenient in terms of Hong Kong Island's nightlife and business areas. ⊠ *2 Arbuthnot Rd., Central* ☎ *3105–2600* ⊕ *www.home2home.hk* ⌂ *Kitchen, Internet, Wi-Fi, laundry facilities, laundry service* ⊟ *AE, DC, MC, V* Ⓜ *Central.*

■ **Shama Causeway Bay.** It's in Causeway Bay's centrally located Times Square complex. Its modern apartments have stereo systems and original Asian artwork. The roof deck is done up with ponds and barbecues. ⊠ *8 Russell St., Causeway Bay* ☎ *2522–3082* ⊕ *www.shama.com* ⌂ *Kitchen, DVD, Internet, Wi-Fi, laundry facilities, laundry service* ⊟ *AE, DC, MC, V* Ⓜ *Causeway Bay.*

especially if you prefer to stay on the Hong Kong Island side of things rather than heading up to the farther-out areas of Kowloon, where budget hotels generally proliferate.

$ 🖵 **Ibis North Point.** In the increasingly developed eastern harbor-front area, this hotel is well located for business travelers who are working around Quarry Bay, but it's somewhat out of the way for vacationers. The prices might also be attractive to the budget-minded who want to stay on the Hong Kong side. Many rooms have harbor views, compensating for their small size, and have a full range of functional amenities. But don't expect plush linens or high-end service; this is bare-bones. **Pros:** inexpensive, reliable service. **Cons:** uninteresting neighborhood, no frills. ⊠ *138 Java Rd., North Point, Eastern* ☎ *2204–6618* ⊕ *www.accorhotels-asia.com* ⇋ *275 rooms, 3 suites* ⌂ *In-room: safe, Internet,*

Wi-Fi. In-hotel: restaurant, room service, bar, laundry service, Wi-Fi, no-smoking rooms. ▭*AE, DC, MC, V* Ⓜ*Quarry Bay.*

SOUTHSIDE

The Southside of Hong Kong Island finally has a hotel, the Le Méridien Cyberport, which is on the waterfront of Telegraph Bay. Built as a high-tech business hub, Cyberport also has residential and leisure facilities, including the hotel and a commercial complex. More hotel and retail development is planned in the area, one of the many districts of Hong Kong that is enjoying an unprecedented boom.

$$$ 🏨**Le Méridien Cyberport.** This relatively small, boutique-style hotel is the first high-profile hotel to open in Hong Kong's Southside. Though business travelers are a large portion of the clientele, this hotel has a retreat feel to it and may appeal to families interested in exploring the area. It comes with high-tech amenities such as 42-inch plasma TVs and wireless Internet in all rooms, as well as hip bars, restaurants, and a decent-sized outdoor pool. Rooms are spacious and bright, with big windows mostly facing out to the sea; bathrooms have so-called "rain" showers, which have extra-large showerheads with many spouts that rain water down onto you. Each room also has a "soothing corner," where you'll find a stone bowl filled with fresh flower petals, essential oils, and floating candles. Some of the suites on the corner of the building have incredible 270-degree panoramic views of the sea, perfect for watching the sunset. You can also request for a private boat to take you onto Lamma Island for seafood. **Pros:** a successful combination of business and resort facilities, popular with local celebrities and others who want to escape attention. **Cons:** feels quite removed from main Hong Kong attractions, even those in Southside, considering how small the island is. ✉*100 Cyberport Rd., Cyberport, Southside* ☎*2980–7778* ⊕*www.lemeridien.com/hongkong* 🛏*170 rooms, 4 suites* &*In-room: safe, refrigerator, Wi-Fi. In-hotel: 3 restaurants, room service, bars, pool, laundry service, no-smoking rooms.* ▭*AE, DC, MC, V.*

KOWLOON

HUNG HOM

Hung Hom, adjacent to Tsim Sha Tsui East, includes a noisy old residential area and a private-housing complex with cinemas, shops, and hotels. Its hotels are relatively new and tend to have lower prices than those in Tsim Sha Tsui and other better-known areas.

$$ 🏨**Harbour Plaza Hong Kong.** Harbour Plaza is famous for housing Chinese leaders who are visiting Hong Kong, although the great majority of tourists will not be staying in the presidential suite. The atrium lobby is spacious with lounges on two levels. Rooms are large, comfortable, and contemporary, with the option of harbor views, although they do not look out towards the most exciting part of Hong Kong Island.

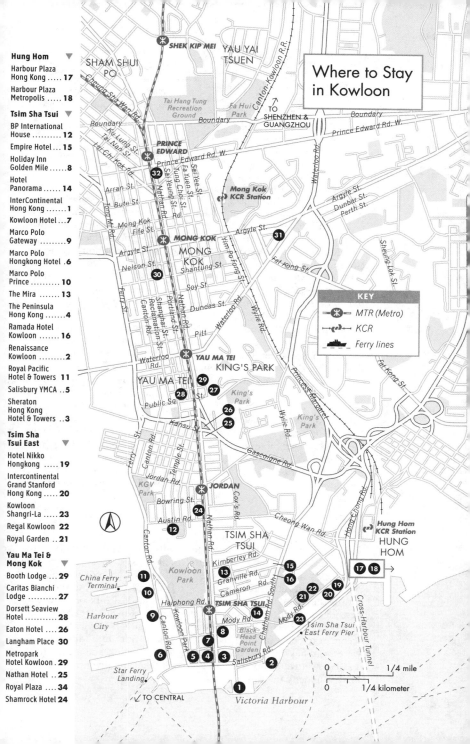

Where to Stay in Kowloon

Hung Hom ▼
Harbour Plaza Hong Kong **17**
Harbour Plaza Metropolis **18**

Tsim Sha Tsui ▼
BP International House **12**
Empire Hotel ...**15**
Holiday Inn Golden Mile **8**
Hotel Panorama **14**
InterContinental Hong Kong **1**
Kowloon Hotel ...**7**
Marco Polo Gateway **9**
Marco Polo Hongkong Hotel .**6**
Marco Polo Prince **10**
The Mira **13**
The Peninsula Hong Kong **4**
Ramada Hotel Kowloon **16**
Renaissance Kowloon **2**
Royal Pacific Hotel & Towers **11**
Salisbury YMCA ..**5**
Sheraton Hong Kong Hotel & Towers ..**3**

Tsim Sha Tsui East ▼
Hotel Nikko Hongkong **19**
Intercontinental Grand Stanford Hong Kong **20**
Kowloon Shangri-La ..**23**
Regal Kowloon ..**22**
Royal Garden ..**21**

Yau Ma Tei & Mong Kok ▼
Booth Lodge ...**29**
Caritas Bianchi Lodge **27**
Dorsett Seaview Hotel **28**
Eaton Hotel **26**
Langham Place **30**
Metropark Hotel Kowloon .**29**
Nathan Hotel ..**25**
Royal Plaza **34**
Shamrock Hotel **24**

KEY
✳ MTR (Metro)
KCR
Ferry lines

Dining options include a Japanese *robatayaki* grill restaurant, where seats surround a grill, and a lively pub called the Pit Stop. A scenic rooftop pool, a fitness center, and a spa are also on-site. Although it's in the residential area of Whampoa Gardens, which is out of the way of most of what you'll probably be up to, hotel shuttles run the 10- to

15-minute trip to Tsim Sha Tsui all day—and you'll get more bang for the buck because of the location. Close by is the railway station, with trains to China, and a ferry terminal for Hong Kong Island. You'll be relying on the ferry to get to Hong Kong Island, which is a nice way to travel, but you'll be pretty isolated if the ferries suspend their service due to bad weather. **Pros:** nice range of dining options. **Cons:** not close to a metro station. ⊠*20 Tak Fung St., Hung Hom, Kowloon* 🕾*2621–3188* ⊕*www.harbour-plaza.com* 🛏*554 rooms, 48 suites* ⟁*In-room: safe, Internet, Wi-Fi. In-hotel: 4 restaurants, room service, bar, pool, gym, spa, laundry service, public Wi-Fi, parking (paid), no-smoking rooms.* ▭*AE, DC, MC, V.*

$$ 🏨 **Harbour Plaza Metropolis.** The Harbour Plaza Metropolis is an ideal place to stay if you're planning to travel by train into China. It's next to the Kowloon–Canton Hung Hom Railway Station, which has a direct link to Shenzhen and Guangzhou. It's also next to the Coliseum, where concerts and sports events take place. A shuttle bus to nearby Tsim Sha Tsui leaves every 20 minutes. Rooms are small and have showers only; most have harbor views. Restaurants include the Patio, which serves Thai food alfresco along with panoramic harbor views. **Pros:** perfectly located for catching early trains into mainland China. **Cons:** not convenient for visiting Hong Kong Island. ⊠*7 Metropolis Dr., Hung Hom, Kowloon* 🕾*3160–6888* ⊕*www.harbour-plaza.com* 🛏*617 rooms, 202 suites* ⟁*In-room: safe, refrigerator, Internet, Wi-Fi. In-hotel: 5 restaurants, bar, pool, gym, laundry service, Wi-Fi, parking (paid), no-smoking rooms.* ▭*AE, DC, MC, V.*

TSIM SHA TSUI

This is Hong Kong's hotel heartland, with many of the city's best (the InterContinental Hong Kong, for instance) and most famous (the Peninsula) accommodations. The fabled Golden Mile of shopping on Nathan Road runs through Tsim Sha Tsui, and restaurants and stores fill the surrounding backstreets, striking an ideal mix of local Chinese joints and high-concept western malls. Meanwhile, the area could hardly be more convenient to Central or Wan Chai, whether on the scenic Star Ferry or on a five-minute MTR ride. In addition, TST's waterfront has the best views of Hong Kong's skyline and nightly light-and-laser show. Many TST hotel rooms take full advantage of these Blade Runner panoramas.

$$ 🏨 **BP International House.** Built by the Boy Scouts Association, this hotel next to Kowloon Park offers an excellent value for the money. A portrait of association founder Baron Robert Baden-Powell, hangs in the spacious modern lobby. The hostel-like rooms are small and spartan but have regular hotel amenities and panoramic views of Victoria Harbour and clear views of the busiest part of Kowloon. Ask to see your room before settling in, as some rooms are better than others. A multipurpose hall hosts exhibitions, conventions, and concerts, and the health club is one of the biggest in town. Another attraction for budget travelers is the self-service coin laundry. There are Internet terminals available for use. **Pros:** efficient reception service, very good value. **Cons:** can get crowded with tour groups, rooms vary significantly. ✉*8 Austin Rd., Jordan, Kowloon* ☎*2376–1111* ⊕*www.bpih.com.hk* 🛏*529 rooms, 4 suites* ⚂*In-room: safe, refrigerator, Internet, Wi-Fi. In-hotel: 2 restaurants, gym, laundry facilities, laundry service, Wi-Fi, parking (paid), no-smoking rooms.* ⊟*AE, DC, MC, V* Ⓜ*Jordan.*

$$ 🏨 **Empire Hotel.** This midrange hotel in a round, modern skyscraper has a glittery Asian feel to it. The indoor swimming pool is in a giant atrium. Standard rooms are small but posh, decked out in that futuristic Hong Kong way; many of the windows look out onto the beautiful skyline. Ask for a room on an upper floor. The Kimberley Road location is in the middle of things, and prices are moderate given the upscale feel of the place and the extensive facilities. Renovations, due to conclude in 2009, include technological updates and the addition of spa rooms with easy access to the new spa. The Empire also has a branch in Wan Chai. **Pros:** great value. **Cons:** small rooms. ✉*62 Kimberley Rd., Tsim Sha Tsui* ☎*2685–3000* ⊕*www.empirehotel.com.hk* 🛏*292 rooms, 23 suites* ⚂*In-room: safe, refrigerator, Internet. In-hotel: restaurant, room service, bar, pool, gym, spa, laundry service, parking (paid), no-smoking rooms.* ⊟*AE, DC, MC, V* Ⓜ*Tsim Sha Tsui.*

$$$ 🏨 **Holiday Inn Golden Mile.** On the Golden Mile of Nathan Road, the hub of Kowloon's business and shopping area, is this business-style hotel whose friendly service has ensured its popularity with tourists, business travelers, and locals for more than two decades. The cozy lobby lounge, from which an elegant staircase leads up to the lounge bar, has an East-meets-West theme. The medium-size rooms are designed for comfort and have a sofa and coffee table; the views, however, are not the best in town. The Avenue restaurant serves delicious contemporary European cuisine overlooking the neon sights and sounds of Tsim Sha Tsui's main artery. **Pros:** great location for shopping, friendly service. **Cons:** can get crowded. ✉*50 Nathan Rd., Tsim Sha Tsui, Kowloon* ☎*2369–3111* ⊕ *www.holidayinn.com/hongkong-gldn* 🛏*594 rooms, 9 suites* ⚂*In-room: safe, refrigerator, DVD (some), Internet, Wi-Fi. In-hotel: 3 restaurants, room service, bar, pool, gym, spa, laundry service, Wi-Fi, no-smoking rooms.* ⊟*AE, DC, MC, V* Ⓜ*Tsim Sha Tsui.*

$$$ 🏨 **Hotel Panorama.** Don't be fooled by the tiny ground-floor reception at this new boutique hotel; the first-floor lobby has a large café and is already bustling with guests, though it just opened in 2008. The Panorama is under the same ownership as Hotel LKF, and the guest rooms here have similarly modern designs though they are slightly more

6

down-to-earth. About two-thirds of rooms face the harbor, while the others have still-interesting views of the long, crowded, and neon-lit streets of Kowloon. Restaurant Santa Lucia, on the top floor, offers fancy international dining, but the neighborhood is full of local cheap eats as well. The MTR station is literally just round the corner. **Pros:** an injection of ultramodern in an old neighborhood, convenient to MTR. **Cons:** guests must pay to use a public gym in a nearby mall. ⊠ *8A Hart Ave., Tsim Sha Tsui, Kowloon* ☎ *3550–0388* ⊕ *www.hotelpanorama. com.hk* ⌨ *324 rooms, 12 suites* ⏃ *In-room: safe, refrigerator, Internet, Wi-Fi (some). In-hotel: 2 restaurants, room service, bar, laundry service, no-smoking rooms.* ⊟ *AE, D, DC, MC, V* Ⓜ *Tsim Sha Tsui.*

$$$$ 🏨**InterContinental Hong Kong.** Don't be fooled by its aging exterior; perhaps one of the most attractive hotels in Asia, the InterContinental Hong Kong is opulent inside and offers a panoramic view of the whole coast of Hong Kong Island. Coming here for a spectacularly conceived cocktail at 8 PM to take in the skyline light show, perhaps equivalent to tea at the Peninsula, should be on your must-do list. The lobby has a delicious airy quality, and the impeccably modern rooms are just as exciting, with luxuriously large beds, desks with ergonomically designed chairs, and superlative showers in the bathrooms. Corner suites have 180-degree harbor views as well as spacious outdoor terraces. The restaurant lineup includes Nobu and SPOON by Alain Ducasse. **Pros:** sets the standard for luxury, executive lounge open to nonexecutive guests for an extra fee, exceptional spa. **Cons:** all this luxury has a high price tag. ⊠ *18 Salisbury Rd., Tsim Sha Tsui, Kowloon* ☎ *2721–1211, 800/327–0200 in U.S.* ⊕ *www.hongkong-ic.inter continental.com* ⌨ *495 rooms, 92 suites* ⏃ *In-room: safe, refrigerator, Wi-Fi. In-hotel: 5 restaurants, room service, pool, gym, spa, laundry service, parking (paid), no-smoking rooms.* ⊟ *AE, DC, MC, V* Ⓜ *Tsim Sha Tsui.*

$$ 🏨**Kowloon Hotel.** The mirrored exterior and the chrome, glass, and marble lobby reflect the hotel's high-tech orientation. Kowloon means "nine dragons" in Cantonese, and is the theme here. Triangular windows and a pointed lobby ceiling, made from hundreds of handblown Venetian-glass pyramids, represent dragons' teeth. The Kowloon is the lesser sibling to the adjacent Peninsula hotel, so you can sign up for services at the Pen and charge them to your room account here; similarly, all the facilities at the Peninsula are open to you. Rooms are small, but each has a computer with free Internet service and fax. Airline information is displayed in the lobby *and* in each room. **Pros:** in-room fax and Wi-Fi, access to Peninsula facilities. **Cons:** Internet access only free for the first 15 minutes even in executive club, small rooms. ⊠ *19–21 Nathan Rd., Tsim Sha Tsui, Kowloon* ☎ *2929–2888* ⊕ *www.harbour-plaza. com/klnh* ⌨ *733 rooms, 7 suites* ⏃ *In-room: safe, refrigerator, Wi-Fi. In-hotel: 3 restaurants, room service, laundry service, no-smoking rooms.* ⊟ *AE, DC, MC, V* Ⓜ *Tsim Sha Tsui.*

$$$ 🏨**Marco Polo Gateway.** This 16-story hotel, popular with Japanese tour groups and corporate clients, is in the shopping and commercial area along Canton Road and close to the Tsim Sha Tsui MTR station. Rooms here are showing their age and feel positively antiquated compared to other Hong Kong hotels in this price range. However, some rooms have a unique view of Kowloon Mosque dome rising above the trees on Nathan Road. The Gateway's greatest asset is its restaurant, La Brasserie, which serves French provincial cuisine in typical brasserie style (dark wood, long bar, leather seats, red-checkered tablecloths). The business center is well supplied, and the staff is helpful. You can use the pool, gym, and spa at the nearby Marco Polo Hongkong Hotel. **Pros:** French restaurant. **Cons:** rooms here are showing their age. ⊠*Harbour City, Canton Rd., Tsim Sha Tsui, Kowloon* ☎*2113–0888* ⊕*www.marcopolohotels.com* ⚡ *433 rooms, 55 suites* ⚷*In-room: safe, refrigerator, Internet. In-hotel: 3 restaurants, room service, bar, laundry service, public Wi-Fi, parking (paid), no-smoking rooms.* ☐*AE, DC, MC, V* Ⓜ*Tsim Sha Tsui.*

$$$ ☷**Marco Polo Hongkong Hotel.** Next to the Cultural Centre and part ♻ of the wharf-side Harbour City complex, this is the largest and best of three Marco Polo hotels along the same street (the other two share the pool, gym, and spa at this location). Spacious rooms have special touches such as a choice of 11 types of pillows and, for children, miniature bathrobes, mild shampoos, and rubber ducks. The hotel's location on the edge of Tsim Sha Tsui means that most rooms have sweeping views of Hong Kong Island, the sea, and Kowloon West, including the new ICC tower. The Marco Polo Hongkong enjoys a long-standing reputation among European and American travelers and is the official hotel for the Hong Kong Sevens' rugby players. The largest Oktoberfest in town takes place here, with more than 1,000 thigh-slapping, beer-swilling, fun-loving participants. **Pros:** the most affordable of the grand, harbor-view hotels. **Cons:** difficult or impossible to get a room here in late March during the Hong Kong Sevens tournament, boisterous crowds during Oktoberfest. ⊠*Harbour City, Canton Rd., Tsim Sha Tsui, Kowloon* ☎*2113–0088* ⊕*www.marcopolohotels.com* ⚡*664 rooms, 49 suites* ⚷*In-room: safe, refrigerator, Internet. In-hotel: 7 restaurants, room service, bar, pool, gym, spa, laundry service, parking (paid), no-smoking rooms.* ☐*AE, DC, MC, V* Ⓜ*Tsim Sha Tsui.*

$$$ ☷**Marco Polo Prince.** Like its neighboring Marco Polo namesakes in the Harbour City complex (the Hongkong and Gateway), the Prince is convenient to upscale shops, cinemas, and the restaurants and shops of Tsim Sha Tsui. It's also near the China Hong Kong Terminal, where ferries, boats, and buses depart for mainland China. Most of the small but comfortable rooms overlook expansive Kowloon Park, and some suites have views of Victoria Harbour. By the end of 2009, all guest rooms should be refurbished with updated technology such as flat-screen TVs and cordless phones, making this the second choice of the three Marco Polos. The Spice Market restaurant has a Southeast Asian buffet and an international menu. You can use the pool, gym, and spa at the Marco Polo Hongkong, a five-minute walk away. **Pros:** easy access to other Marco Polo hotels, Harbour City shopping complex, and China Ferry Terminal. **Cons:** no harbor views, not convenient to leave the building for gym and spa access. ⊠*Harbour City, Canton Rd., Tsim Sha Tsui, Kowloon* ☎*2113–1888* ⊕*www.marcopolohotels.com* ⚡*393 rooms,*

49 suites △ *In-room: safe, refrigerator, Internet. In-hotel: 4 restaurants, room service, bar, laundry service, Wi-Fi, parking (paid), no-smoking rooms.* ⊟*AE, DC, MC, V* Ⓜ *Tsim Sha Tsui.*

$$ **The Mira.** When it opened in 1948, this building, formerly known as the Miramar, was owned by the Spanish Catholic Mission, which intended to use the structure to shelter missionaries expelled from China. As tourism blossomed here, the priests changed their plan and turned the premises into a hotel. In 2008, the Miramar underwent a comprehensive renovation and rebranding (all guest rooms and the new spa should be complete by early 2009). Now known as the Mira, the hotel has a thoroughly contemporary feel, including a stunning new lobby with flowing wave patterns running from the walls to the ceiling. White and gray are used throughout, and, with the lighting, they create an iceberg effect. Rooms have an impressive array of new gadgets such Bose entertainment systems, electrical outlets inside safes so you can charge your laptop while you're out, and a mobile phone with free local service to use during your stay. Additional renovations scheduled for 2009 include a new rooftop restaurant. **Pros:** along the shopping route known as the Golden Mile, convenient to metro station, free cell phone for local calls. **Cons:** no real retreat from the hustle and bustle. ✉*118–130 Nathan Rd., Tsim Sha Tsui, Kowloon* ☎*2368–1111* ⊕*www.themirahotel. com* ↙*493 rooms, 30 suites* △*In-room: safe, refrigerator, Internet. In-hotel: 4 restaurants, bar, pool, laundry service, parking (paid), no-smoking rooms.* ⊟*AE, DC, MC, V* Ⓜ*Tsim Sha Tsui.*

$$$$ **The Peninsula Hong Kong.** Established in 1928, the Peninsula has long been synonymous with impeccable taste and colonial glamour. And many people adore this hotel. Rooms have been updated recently with the flat-screen TVs and DVD players, and the hotel's renowned Rolls-Royces were replaced with newer models in 2006, but don't expect a high-tech feel here—this hotel is for those with old-world tastes. The spa is decked out with faux-Roman statues that are all show without a sense of style. But at about US$600 for the cheapest harbor-view room, it seems the Peninsula's most modern feature is its price. However, views at the popular Philippe Starck–designed Felix restaurant on the rooftop are unrivaled and there is still the famous high tea in the lobby bar. **Pros:** old-world glamour. **Cons:** may just seem old to those with a more modern aesthetic. ✉*Salisbury Rd., Tsim Sha Tsui, Kowloon* ☎*2366–6251* ⊕*www.peninsula.com* ↙*300 rooms, 54 suites* △*In-room: safe, kitchen (some), refrigerator, DVD, Internet, Wi-Fi. In-hotel: 8 restaurants, room service, bar, pool, gym, spa, laundry service, parking (free), no-smoking rooms.* ⊟*AE, DC, MC, V* Ⓜ*Tsim Sha Tsui.*

$$ **Ramada Hotel Kowloon.** The Ramada is relatively small by Hong Kong standards, and tries to use its size to create a cozy, home-away-from-home feeling. There's a decorative fireplace in the lobby and comfortable rooms with natural-wood furniture. The bar attracts young locals for drinks and karaoke. Rooms are small and do not have spectacular views, but are well maintained. **Pros:** located in an area full of small boutiques and clothing stores popular with young locals. **Cons:** shops stay open late, so not the quietest area. ✉*73–75 Chatham Rd. S, Tsim*

Sha Tsui, Kowloon ☎2311–1100 ⊕*http://ramadahongkong.com* ↩ *205 rooms, 10 suites* ♿*In-room: safe, refrigerator, Internet, Wi-Fi. In-hotel: restaurant, room service, laundry service, Wi-Fi, no-smoking rooms.* ▤*AE, DC, MC, V* Ⓜ*Tsim Sha Tsui.*

$$$ ▦**Renaissance Kowloon.** Part of a large shopping complex, and now a member of the Marriott chain, this popular hotel on the Tsim Sha Tsui waterfront has perfect views of Hong Kong Island from its upper club floors, rivaled only by the adjacent hotel InterContinental Hong Kong, part of the same complex. Long escalators lead from the shopping area to the hotel's large second-floor lobby. The comfortable, modern guest rooms are homey and have plenty of space for working and relaxing. Greenery surrounds the outdoor pool, which stays open throughout the year. The Panorama restaurant, one of three in the hotel, has one of the best harbor views in town. **Pros:** reasonably priced considering views and facilities. **Cons:** you'll have to walk through a maze of shopping malls to get to the metro station which can be frustrating during peak shopping hours. ⊠*22 Salisbury Rd., Tsim Sha Tsui, Kowloon* ☎2369–4111 ⊕*www.marriott.com* ↩*492 rooms, 53 suites* ♿*In-room: safe, refrigerator, Wi-Fi (some). In-hotel: 3 restaurants, room service, bar, pool, gym, spa, laundry service, Wi-Fi, parking (paid), no-smoking rooms.* ▤*AE, DC, MC, V* Ⓜ*Tsim Sha Tsui.*

$$ ▦**Royal Pacific Hotel & Towers.** On the Tsim Sha Tsui waterfront, the Royal Pacific is part of the Hong Kong China City complex, which includes the terminal for ferries to mainland China. Guest rooms are arranged in two blocks, the hotel and tower wings. Tower-wing rooms have harbor views and are luxuriously furnished, while more inexpensive hotel-wing rooms have Kowloon street and park views and are smaller but just as attractive. The hotel connects to Kowloon Park by a footbridge and is close to shops and cinemas. It doesn't have an executive floor, but a club lounge providing a similar service. **Pros:** good location. **Cons:** not distinctive. ⊠*33 Canton Rd., Tsim Sha Tsui, Kowloon* ☎2736–1188 ⊕*www.royalpacific.com.hk* ↩*673 rooms, 34 suites* ♿*In-room: safe, Internet. In-hotel: 4 restaurants, room service, bar, gym, laundry service, Wi-Fi, parking (paid), no-smoking rooms.* ▤*AE, DC, MC, V* Ⓜ*Tsim Sha Tsui.*

$$ ▦**Salisbury YMCA.** This upscale YMCA is Hong Kong's most popular and is great value for your money. Next to the Peninsula and opposite the Cultural Centre, Space Museum, and Art Museum, it's in an excellent location for theater, art, and concert crawls. The pastel-color rooms have harbor views and broadband Internet access. The Y also has a chapel, a garden, dance halls, a children's library, and excellent health and fitness facilities including squash courts and two climbing

6

walls. Neighborhood restaurants are cheap and good, and the shopping is great. **Pros:** same view as Peninsula guests for a quarter the price, enough indoor activities to occupy you for days should a tropical storm hit. **Cons:** lobby sometimes feels more like a student center. ☒*41 Salisbury Rd., Tsim Sha Tsui, Kowloon* ☏*2369–2211* ⊕*www.ymcahk. org.hk* ⟿*301 rooms, 62 suites* ☐*In-room: safe, Internet. In-hotel: 2 restaurants, room service, bar, pool, gym, laundry facilities, Wi-Fi, no-smoking rooms.* ⊟*AE, DC, MC, V* Ⓜ*Tsim Sha Tsui.*

$$$ 🏨**Sheraton Hong Kong Hotel & Towers.** Across the street from the InterContinental at the southern end of the fabled Golden Mile, the Sheraton is somewhat packed in on Nathan Road and so doesn't get as much light as some of its competition. But the lobby is filled with artwork and feels airy and expansive. Guest rooms are comfortable yet modern with flat-screen televisions, slick glass desktops, and glass-bowl sinks in the bathrooms. There are harbor, city, or courtyard views from the rooms. Make your way to the rooftop pool and terrace via the exterior glass elevator. The sky lounge has a fantastic harbor view, and Someplace Else is a popular hangout at happy hour; the Oyster & Wine Bar is on the top floor. **Pros:** modern and comfortable facilities. **Cons:** congested area once you set foot out the door. ☒*20 Nathan Rd., Tsim Sha Tsui, Kowloon* ☏*2369–1111* ⊕*www.sheraton.com* ⟿*782 rooms, 91 suites* ☐*In-room: safe, Wi-Fi (some), DVD (some). In-hotel: 5 restaurants, room service, pool, gym, laundry service, Wi-Fi, parking (paid), no-smoking rooms.* ⊟*AE, DC, MC, V* Ⓜ*Tsim Sha Tsui.*

TSIM SHA TSUI EAST

Tsim Sha Tsui East is a grid of modern office blocks—many with restaurants or nightclubs—and luxury hotels. The neighborhood has little character, and the wide roads mean the hotels are popular with tour groups traveling by bus. The Tsim Sha Tsui and Tsim Sha Tsui East metro stations are walking distance away, but it's quite a hike through a ho-hum area. However, the hotels are large and convenient for anyone traveling to mainland China by train from the nearby Hung Hom station.

$$$ 🏨**Hotel Nikko Hongkong.** Part of the Japanese chain, this luxury harborfront hotel at the far end of Tsim Sha Tsui East attracts mostly Japanese travelers. The large, split-level atrium mimics a Japanese garden with water trickling between the greenery. The rooms and bathrooms are comfortable and spacious; nearly 200 rooms have harbor views; those on the executive floors have additional facilities such as tea- and coffeemakers. The Kyoto-inspired restaurant Sagano uses ingredients imported from Japan. **Pros:** clean, efficient, nice views from rooftop pool. **Cons:** not a very exciting neighborhood. ☒*72 Mody Rd., Tsim Sha Tsui East, Kowloon* ☏*2739–1111* ⊕*www.hotelnikko.com.hk* ⟿*463 rooms, 18 suites* ☐*In-room: safe, refrigerator, Internet, Wi-Fi (some). In-hotel: 4 restaurants, room service, bars, pool, gym, parking (paid), no-smoking rooms.* ⊟*AE, DC, MC, V* Ⓜ*Tsim Sha Tsui.*

$$$$ 🏨**InterContinental Grand Stanford Hong Kong.** More than half the rooms in this luxury hotel, the sibling of the larger InterContinental Hong

Kong in downtown Tsim Sha Tsui, have an unobstructed harbor view. The elegant lobby is spacious, the staff is helpful and friendly, and the comfortable, modern rooms are decorated in warm earth tones with wood trim and large desks. Executive rooms have a direct-line fax machine and amenities include trouser presses. There isn't quite an executive floor, but the club lounge serves the same purpose. The restaurants, which are well known locally, include Mistral (Italian), Belvedere (regional French), and Tiffany's New York Bar, which celebrates the Roaring 1920s with antique furniture, Tiffany-style glass ceilings, and a live band. **Pros:** same quality service as the downtown Inter-Continental for a little less. **Cons:** not in the center of Tsim Sha Tsui, lacks the prestige of the downtown branch. ✉ *70 Mody Rd., Tsim Sha Tsui East, Kowloon* ☎ *2721–5161* ⊕ *www.hongkong.intercontinental. com* ☎ *554 rooms, 25 suites* ⚤ *In-room: safe, Wi-Fi. In-hotel: 4 restaurants, room service, bar, pool, gym, spa, laundry service, parking (paid), no-smoking rooms.* ☐ *AE, DC, MC, V* Ⓜ *Tsim Sha Tsui.*

$$$ ⊞ **Kowloon Shangri-La.** Catering mainly to business travelers, this upscale hotel has a 24-hour business center with teleconferencing facilities as well as some strange features, such as the elevator carpets that are changed at midnight to indicate the day of the week. You'll feel like a tycoon in the posh lobby; the guest rooms all have magnificent harbor or city views, and although it doesn't have quite the glamour or services (or the accompanying sky-high prices) of the Island Shangri-La, it's still a wonderful place to stay. Complimentary newspapers are delivered daily to your room; club rooms have combination fax/printer/copier/scanners, as well as in-room DVD players and even TVs in the bathroom. A wireless telephone system allows guests to receive calls throughout the hotel. Attention to detail and outstanding service, in a city where service is already tops, set this hotel apart. **Pros:** outstanding service, many amenities. **Cons:** no easy access to public transit. ✉ *64 Mody Rd., Tsim Sha Tsui East, Kowloon* ☎ *2721–2111, 866-565-5050–in U.S.* ⊕ *www.shangri-la.com/kowloon* ☎ *700 rooms, 30 suites* ⚤ *In-room: safe, refrigerator, DVD (some), Wi-Fi. In-hotel: 5 restaurants, room service, bar, pool, gym, laundry service, Wi-Fi, no-smoking rooms.* ☐ *AE, DC, MC, V* Ⓜ *Tsim Sha Tsui East.*

$$ ⊞ **Regal Kowloon.** If you're in the mood for a French experience, check in at the Regal. The lobby has an impressive tapestry, and Louis XVI–style furniture graces the guest rooms and one of the lounges. Rooms on the club floors have a more minimalist, modern, two-tone appeal than the rest of the hotel would suggest. The French restaurant Maman serves home-style French cooking in a relaxed setting. Still, the hotel is starting to show its age, and it's a bit far from the lively and busy area of Tsim Sha Tsui. **Pros:** reliable hotel will meet your expectations. **Cons:** remote location. ✉ *71 Mody Rd., Tsim Sha Tsui East* ☎ *2722–1818* ⊕ *www.regalkowloon.com* ☎ *600 rooms, 38 suites* ⚤ *In-room: safe, refrigerator, Internet, Wi-Fi. In-hotel: 6 restaurants, room service, bars, gym, laundry service, Wi-Fi, no-smoking rooms.* ☐ *AE, DC, MC, V* Ⓜ *Tsim Sha Tsui.*

$$$$ ⊞ **Royal Garden.** A garden atrium with lush greenery and whispering running water rises from the ground floor to the Royal Garden's rooftop. Glass elevators, live classical music, trailing greenery, and trickling streams create a sense of serenity. The spacious, comfortable rooms surround the atrium. Rooftop health facilities include an indoor-outdoor pool fashioned after an ancient Roman bath with fountains, a colorful sun mosaic, and underwater music. Its Sabatini restaurant is a sister establishment to the popular restaurant by the same name in Rome. **Pros:** illuminated rooftop tennis court, good facilities, good restaurant. **Cons:** relatively pricy, especially in the high season. ✉ *69 Mody Rd., Tsim Sha Tsui East, Kowloon* ☎ *2721–5215* ⊕ *www.rghk.com. hk* ⇦ *419 rooms, 18 suites* ⇦ *In-room: safe, refrigerator, Internet. In-hotel: 6 restaurants, room service, bar, tennis court, pool, gym, spa, laundry service, Wi-Fi, parking (paid), no-smoking rooms.* ⊟ *AE, DC, MC, V* Ⓜ *Tsim Sha Tsui.*

YAU MA TEI & MONG KOK

Yau Ma Tei and Mong Kok are known for their noisy street life, bargain shopping, night markets, and cheap and cheerful dining. They also have older, smaller, more moderately priced hotels than Tsim Sha Tsui, often with small, less-than-peaceful rooms. Most of these hotels are on or near Nathan Road and many are good for travelers on budgets. This is an exciting part of Kowloon if you can handle the crowds, which don't seem to dwindle until about 10 PM. But although Hong Kong is one of the safest cities in the world, this is the one area where you may run into some trouble due to local mafia activity. Tourists are unlikely to be hassled, but you should keep your wits about you and avoid inadvertently walking into a bad situation. Use common sense: stay out of alleyways, and avoid shops that serve no visible purpose other than allowing a group of men to gather. Excellent bus service and the MTR connect both Yau Ma Tei and Mong Kok to the center of Tsim Sha Tsui.

¢ 🏨**Booth Lodge.** This pleasant retreat, which is down a dead-end side street near the Jade Market, is operated by the Salvation Army. But contrary to the image that might conjure up for you, everything in this lodge looks bright and fresh, from the walls to the starched sheets on the double beds. The lobby may resemble an office, but the Booth is a good value overall. The coffee shop serves mainly buffets, with a small outdoor balcony offering nice views. The Yau Ma Tei MTR is nearby. **Pros:** clean lodgings at a bargain price. **Cons:** not a particularly pleasant location. ✉ *11 Wing Sing La., Yau Ma Tei, Kowloon* ☎ *2771–9266* ⊕ *http://boothlodge.salvation.org.hk* ⇦ *60 rooms* ⇦ *In-room: refrigerator, Wi-Fi. In-hotel: restaurant, laundry service, Wi-Fi, no-smoking rooms.* ⊟ *AE, MC, V* Ⓜ *Yau Ma Tei.*

$ 🏨**Caritas Bianchi Lodge.** Rooms at this friendly hostel, operated by the Catholic Diocese of Hong Kong, are simple and modern and have basic facilities including TVs, minibars, air-conditioning, and private bathrooms. Just around the corner from busy Nathan Road, the lodge is also close to the Jade Market and the nightly Temple Street Market, but it offers peace and quiet due to its dead-end location. **Pros:** friendly service. **Cons:** not that cheap given its bare-bones facilities. ✉ *4 Cliff Rd., Yau Ma Tei, Kowloon* ☎ *2388–1111* ⊕ *www.caritas-chs.org.hk* ⇦ *88* *rooms, 2 suites* ♿*In-room: refrigerator, Internet (some). In-hotel: restaurant, laundry service.* ▤*AE, DC, MC, V* Ⓜ*Yau Ma Tei.*

$ 🏨**Dorsett Seaview Hotel.** High-rise buildings now block the Dorsett's sea view, but the location is still a good one if you want to see traditional Hong Kong. Guest rooms are very small; staff are friendly and efficient. The hotel is close to the Yau Ma Tei MTR as well as decent shopping; Shanghai Street is filled with shops selling everything from handmade kitchenware to temple offerings. The restaurant has bargain-priced buffets, especially for lunch. The hotel often gets very busy with tour groups and checkout can be chaotic. **Pros:** good value, helpful staff. **Cons:** small rooms, very busy. ✉*268 Shanghai St., Yau Ma Tei, Kowloon* 🕾*2782–0882* ⊕*www.dorsettseaview.com.hk* ☞*255 rooms, 3 suites* ♿ *In-room: safe, refrigerator, Internet, Wi-Fi. In-hotel: restaurant, room service, bar, laundry service, no-smoking rooms.* ▤*AE, DC, MC, V* Ⓜ*Yau Ma Tei.*

$$ 🏨**Eaton Hotel.** In a brick-red shopping and cinema complex in the middle of Nathan Road, the Eaton provides quick access to Hong Kong's bustling after-dark street scene: it's a stone's throw from the Temple Street Night Market. The modern rooms have all the necessities, including fast Internet access and business services. The top floor has a swimming pool and a gym. The hotel completed a substantial makeover in 2008 and now has a more contemporary style and high-tech facilities. **Pros:** convenient location **Cons:** Nathan Road can be overwhelming with the traffic and the noise, made worse by the stifling heat in the summer. ✉*380 Nathan Rd., Yau Ma Tei, Kowloon* 🕾*2782–1818* ⊕*http://hongkong.eatonhotels.com* ☞*465 rooms, 26 suites* ♿*In-room: safe, refrigerator, Internet. In-hotel: 6 restaurants, room service, bar, pool, gym, laundry service, Wi-Fi, parking (paid), no-smoking rooms.* ▤*AE, DC, MC, V* Ⓜ*Jordan.*

$$$ 🏨**Langham Place.** When the Langham opened in March 2005 as part of the new Langham Place Shopping Center, it ushered in an era of prestige and prominence for its once seedy, but still refreshingly unwesternized Mong Kok neighborhood, full of bustling markets, characteristic noodle shops, and, yes, the occasional prostitute. Mao's Red Guards stand at attention at the entrance to this sleek, cyber-age hotel full of glass and steel; it's a great exemplar of that specific science-fiction feel that defines much of modern Hong Kong. The hotel's top three stories are consumed by the Chuan (Chinese spa), with panoramic city views to accompany treatments. The price is significantly lower than what you'd pay for such luxury elsewhere in town. **Pros:** free Wi-Fi throughout. **Cons:** no sense of retreat from the mall. ✉*555 Shanghai St., Mong Kok* 🕾*3552–3388* ⊕*www.langhamhotels.com* ☞*665 rooms* ♿*In-room: safe, refrigerator, DVD, Wi-Fi. In-hotel: 3 restaurants, room service, bar, pool, gym, spa, laundry service, Wi-Fi, parking (paid), no-smoking rooms.* ▤*AE, DC, MC, V* Ⓜ*Mong Kok.*

$$ 🏨**Metropark Hotel Kowloon.** Just north of Nathan Road's major shopping area, the Metropark (formerly known as the Metropole) is a diner's delight. The on-site Chinese restaurant, House of Tang, is locally renowned for its Sichuanese resident master chefs, who serve authentic Sichuan and Cantonese food. The modern rooms are small and

feel slightly dated, but they have a harmonious mélange of East and West furnishings, and the Mong Kok area, nearby, is a fun Chinese section of the city. The rooftop pool is a relaxing space to unwind. **Pros:** free Wi-Fi throughout, great restaurant. **Cons:** no special facilities for children, small rooms. ⊠*75 Waterloo Rd., Yau Ma Tei, Kowloon* ☎*2761–1711* ⊕*www.metroparkhotelkowloon.com* ⇙*479 rooms, 8 suites* ⌂*In-room: safe, refrigerator, Internet, Wi-Fi. In-hotel: 3 restaurants, room service, bar, pool, gym, laundry service, parking (paid), no-smoking rooms.* ⊟*AE, DC, MC, V* Ⓜ*Yau Ma Tei.*

$ 🏨**Nathan Hotel.** Popular with tour groups from both the East and the West, this busy hotel is near the Jordan MTR and just a stone's throw away from the street-market attractions of Mong Kok and Yau Ma Tei. Rooms are moderately sized and colorful, and include all the basic necessities. Keep in mind that if you stay here, you'll have to stomach the incredibly crowded streets and noise level in the area. The hotel did some renovating and now offers new executive-floor rooms with large flat-screen TVs and free Wi-Fi access. **Pros:** affordable and clean. **Cons:** very popular with tour groups, noisy area. ⊠*378 Nathan Rd., Yau Ma Tei, Kowloon* ☎*2388–5141* ⊕*www.nathanhotel.com* ⇙*189 rooms 13 suites* ⌂*In-room: safe, refrigerator, DVD (some), Internet, Wi-Fi (some). In-hotel: restaurant, room service, bar, laundry service, gym, no-smoking rooms.* ⊟*AE, DC, MC, V* Ⓜ*Jordan.*

$$ 🏨**Royal Plaza.** The Royal Plaza is easily accessible from either the adjacent Kowloon-Canton Railway station or the nearby Mong Kok MTR station. As part of the massive Grand Century Place complex, it's a shopper's delight. Rooms, which have views of Lion Rock and Kowloon, are elegant and modern and surprisingly quiet considering the busy location. The hotel itself offers a mix of restaurants, bars, and leisure facilities, including a ballroom and a large pool with underwater music. The garden allows seekers of solitude to contemplate the true meaning of Mong Kok in peace and quiet. **Pros:** easy access to various transportation, great for shoppers. **Cons:** shopping overload for some. ⊠*193 Prince Edward Rd. W, Mong Kok, Kowloon* ☎*2928–8822* ⊕*www.royalplaza.com.hk* ⇙*693 rooms, 35 suites* ⌂*In-room: safe, Internet, Wi-Fi (some). In-hotel: 3 restaurants, room service, bar, pool, gym, laundry service, Wi-Fi, parking (paid), no-smoking rooms* ⊟*AE, DC, MC, V* Ⓜ*Mong Kok.*

$$ 🏨**Shamrock Hotel.** One of the oldest budget hotels on Nathan Road, the Shamrock opened its doors in the early 1960s. It's just north of Kowloon Park and steps from the Jordan MTR, putting it in the middle of all the 24-hour-a-day Yau Ma Tei action. Still, the northern location translates to better value than Tsim Sha Tsui, and rooms are a decent size for the price. The hotel also offers buffet-style dining from its in-house restaurant. **Pros:** good value for the location. **Cons:** could use updating. ⊠*223 Nathan Rd., Yau Ma Tei, Kowloon* ☎*2735–2271* ⊕*www.shamrockhotel.com.hk* ⇙*157 rooms, 2 suites* ⌂*In-room: safe, refrigerator, Internet. In-hotel: restaurant, room service, laundry service, no-smoking rooms.* ⊟*AE, DC, MC, V* Ⓜ*Jordan.*

After Dark

Carnegie's Pub, Wan Chai

WORD OF MOUTH

"[At Red Bar] I just love the deck/terrace with the gorgeous panoramic view of the city. You go and order, grab your drink and find a table. The servers won't come to you. I had one of the best drinks here. It's a cosmopolitan but mixed with tequila instead of vodka. Amazing! My sister ordered the same and declared it a 'perfect 10.'"

—Kooba

AFTER DARK PLANNER

Mug or Martini Glass

From champagne decadence to sports bars lined with peanut shells, each of Hong Kong's districts has its own distinct night-time personality. Even on one street, dress codes and drink prices can vacillate wildly. The bar- and pub-lined streets of Lan Kwai Fong, Wan Chai, and Kowloon are a fairly casual affair, though shorts and flip-flops will limit your options. A beer or a mixed drink will cost from HK$50 to HK$80.

The Central, SoHo, and Wyndham Street environs are home to world-class bars and glamorous nightclubs where a cosmopolitan mix of high rollers and partiers comes out to play. Drinks are expensive; a fresh-fruit martini will set you back more than HK$100. If you're prepared to pay a steep minimum for bottle service (HK$1,000 to HK$10,000 depending on the club), you can reserve a table for your party at some of these swanky establishments. Door trolls abound, so dress up to get in and blend in—shorts, flip-flops, and sneakers are definite no-nos.

Members Only

Many bars and clubs have a "members-only" policy, but don't let this deter you. It's mostly a way of prioritizing the guest list on busy nights. It can also mean that you're required to pay a cover charge, usually in the region of HK$150 to HK$200 and including a drink on the house.

Hot Picks

Best Neighborhood to Let Loose: Lan Kwai Fong, 262
Best Drink with a View: Aqua, 271
Best Disco Room: JJ's, 269
Best Irish Export: Delaney's, 272
Best Live Music Venue: Fringe Club, 266
Best Gay Club: Propaganda, 266
Hostesses with the Mostest: Club BBoss, 272

Nightlife Savvy

HK Magazine and *Beats* magazine are distributed free each Thursday. Another good source of nightlife and cultural information is daily English-language newspaper, the *South China Morning Post.* The free newspaper *City News* lists City Hall performances and events.

Tickets for most big cultural events are on sale through city-wide branches of **URBTIX** (☎2111–5999 ⊕ *www.urbtix. hk*). **HK Ticketing** (☎3128–8288 ⊕ *www.hkticketing.com*) sells tickets to many shows.

Hours

Twenty-four-hour liquor licenses are common, so strict closing times are not. Bars start closing around 2 AM, clubs around 4 AM, with some seeing in the sunrise. Happy hours are from midafternoon to 8 or 9 PM on weekdays. Closing times listed refer to Friday, Saturday, and the eves of public holidays; you can expect things to wind down an hour or two earlier midweek. Bars are typically open nightly, but nightclubs are closed or quiet on Sunday and Monday.

Disco Dancing

Discos and nightclubs range from boisterous cover bands in down-to-earth settings to hermetically sealed hip-hop dungeons packed with models and millionaires. The venues listed here tend to be smaller and more intimate than their high-octane megaplex cousins. Cover charges, if levied, can be steep, from HK$120 to HK$250, but often include a drink or two. Information and tickets for international DJ events can be found on posters around the streets of Central, or at ⊕ www.hkclubbing.com. Some bars and restaurants also hold weekly or monthly club nights, where music ranges from drum-and-bass to deep house.

Hostess Clubs

Many hostess clubs found in Hong Kong are clubs in name only. Some of these are multimillion-dollar operations with plush interiors and hundreds of hostess-companions working for them. Hostess clubs are a stage for showgirls and tycoons, designed to sweeten lucrative deals and lubricate business relationships. Expect to see exhibitions of arguably tasteless extravagance as patrons pay up to HK$1,000 per hour for the privilege of drinking in the company of attractive women. Between minimum drink charges, drinks for the hostesses, tips, and the possibility of spending upwards of five figures on a bottle of wine, you're looking at an HK$100,000-plus tab, which does not faze the regulars. Indeed, legend has it that the biggest security problem faced by bouncers is breaking up fights over who gets to pay the bill.

The better clubs are on a par with music lounges in deluxe hotels, though they cost a little more. Dance floors are often large, with live bands and a lineup of both pop and cabaret singers. Their happy hours start in the afternoon, when many have a sort of tea-dance ambience, and continue through to mid-evening. Peak hours are 10 PM to 4 AM.

Many so-called hostess clubs, however, are in fact fronts for prostitution. In Wan Chai, for instance, hostess clubs—too many to mention by name—are dotted among regular bars. Most if not all of them are sad little places full of leering men watching girls with vacant expressions, dressed in leotards, performing halfhearted pole dances. These houses of prostitution are not the same as establishments such as the upmarket Club BBoss in Tsim Sha Tsui.

Better Safe than Sorry

All premises licensed to serve alcohol are supposedly subject to stringent fire, safety, and sanitary controls, although at times this is hard to believe, given the overcrowding at the hippest places. Think twice before succumbing to the city's raunchier hideaways. If you stumble into one, check out cover and hostess charges *before* you get too comfortable, and pay for each round of drinks as it's served (by cash rather than credit card).

Hong Kong is a surprisingly safe place, but as in many tourist destination the art of the tourist rip-off has been perfected. If you're unsure, visit places signposted as members of the Hong Kong Tourist Board (HKTB).

After the Party

The ever-reliable MTR shuts down at around 1 AM, depending on your location. Taxis are your only way home after that. They can easily be flagged down on the street; when the light on the car roof is on, it's available for hire. If the cab has an OUT OF SERVICE sign over its round FOR HIRE neon sign on the dashboard, it means it's a cross-harbor taxi.

7

By Eva Chui
Loiterton
Updated by
Dominique
Rowe

A riot of neon, heralding frenetic after-hours action, announces Hong Kong's nightlife districts. Clubs and bars fill to capacity, evening markets pack in shoppers looking for bargains, restaurants welcome diners, cinemas pop corn as fast as they can, and theaters and concert halls prepare for full houses.

The neighborhoods of Wan Chai, Lan Kwai Fong, and SoHo are packed with bars, pubs, and nightclubs that cater to everyone from the hippest trendsetters, to bankers ready to spend their bonuses, and more laid-back crowds out for a pint. Partying in Hong Kong is a way of life; it starts at the beginning of the week with a drink or two after work, progressing to serious barhopping, and clubbing if it's the weekend. Work hard, play harder is the motto here and people follow it seriously.

Because each district has so much to offer, and since they're all quite close to each other, it's perfectly normal to pop into two or three bars before heading to a nightclub. At the other end of the spectrum, the city's arts and culture is equally lively, with innovative music, dance, and theater. Small independent productions as well as large-scale concerts take to the stage across the territory every weekend. You simply cannot go home without a Hong Kong nightlife story to tell!

HONG KONG ISLAND

CENTRAL

On weekends, the streets of Lan Kwai Fong are liberated from traffic, and the swilling hordes from both sides of the street merge into one heaving organism. A five-minute walk uphill is SoHo. Back in the '90s, it took local businesses some effort to convince district councillors that the sometimes vice-associated moniker (which in this case stands for South of Hollywood Road) was a good idea, but Hong Kong is now proud of this *très* chic area, a warren of streets stuffed with commensurately priced restaurants, bars, and late-night boutiques. Midway between Lan Kwai Fong's madness and SoHo's glamour is the newly regenerated Wyndham Street, home to a sophisticated array of bars, nightclubs, and restaurants.

BARS

Barco. Had enough of the crowds and looking for a quiet drink and conversation that you can actually hear? Barco is the place. It's cozy, with a small lounge area and an even smaller courtyard in the back, and an assortment of board games if you're feeling playful. ✉*42 Staunton St., SoHo, Central* ☎*2857–4478* ⊘*Closes 1 AM.*

★ **California.** Set in a semi-basement, but with large open windows at the top so the crowds in Lan Kwai Fong can easily peer inside, California is a slice of the West Coast for homesick expats or western visitors looking for a more familiar environment. It's almost an institution, having survived the notoriously high turnover rate in the area, and remains one of the busiest bars in the neighborhood. ✉*32–34 D'Aguilar St., Lan Kwai Fong, Central* ☎*2521–1345* ⊘*Closes 3 AM.*

Club 71. This bohemian diamond-in-the-rough was named in tribute to July 1, 2003, when half a million Hong Kongers successfully rallied against looming threats to their freedom of speech. Tucked away on a terrace down a market side street, the quirky, unpretentious bar is a mainstay of artists, journalists, and left-wing politicians. ✉*B/F, 67 Hollywood Rd., Sheung Wan* ☎*2858–7071* ⊘*Closes 2 AM.*

F.I.N.D.S. The name of this supercool restaurant and bar is an acronym of Finland, Iceland, Norway, Denmark, and Sweden. The striking decor is pale blue and white, with sparkling granite walls. There's a large outdoor terrace, with comfortable seating. About 30 premium vodkas are served. You can also try one of the many tasty themed cocktails with corny names such as the Edvard Munch, made with lime aquavit and ginger wine. ✉*2nd fl., LKF Tower, 33 Wyndham St., entrance of D'Aguilar St., Central* ☎*2522–9318* ⊘*Closes 3 AM.*

Goccia. Beautiful people both young and not-so-young flock to this Italian bar (with a restaurant upstairs) and it's packed wall-to-wall most nights. *Goccia*—which means "drop" in Italian—occupies a long room on the ground floor, and if it had a VIP table, it would have to be one by the window facing the street where you can see and be seen. ✉*73 Wyndham St., Central* ☎*2167–8181* ⊘*Closes 3 am.*

Insomnia. It's *almost* open 24/7 (closing for only three hours from 6 to 9 AM), hence the name. Live music is what really draws people here; there's a small stage and a dance floor at the back, but you'll have to fight your way there on weekends through the perfumed women and suited men. You might have more breathing room if you stay near the front bar, by the arched windows. ✉*38–44 D'Aguilar St., Lan Kwai Fong, Central* ☎*2525–0957.*

Le Jardin. For an otherworldly, cosmopolitan vibe, check out this casual bar with a lovely outdoor terrace overlooking the gregarious al fresco dining lane known locally as "Rat Alley." Walk through the dining area, and up a flight of steps. It's a little tricky to find, but the leafy, fairy-lit setting is worth it. ✉*1st fl., 10 Wing Wah La., Central* ☎*2526–2717* ⊘*Closes 3 AM.*

7

Lan Kwai Fong

A curious, L-shape cobblestone lane in Central is the pulsating center of nightlife and dining in Hong Kong. Lan Kwai Fong, or just "the Fong," is a spot that really shines after the sun sets. You can start with a predinner drink at any number of bars, then enjoy some of the territory's finest dining, before stopping at a nightclub to boogie the night away.

For such a small warren, Lan Kwai Fong has an incredibly broad range of nightlife to offer, with more than 20 bars, restaurants, and clubs within just a few blocks. Since most of the ground-floor establishments spill out onto the pavement, there's an audible buzz about the place, lending it a festive air that's unmatched elsewhere in Hong Kong. Whether it's corporate financiers celebrating their latest million-dollar deals at California, or more humble office workers having drinks with their buddies at Le Jardin or Insomnia, there's a place here to suit everyone.

The same "something for everyone" motto extends to the plethora of upmarket restaurants in Lan Kwai Fong. From Asia, there are Chinese, Thai, Japanese, and Vietnamese restaurants, while European food can be found at French and Italian establishments. If your wallet's feeling a little light from your latest shopping expedition, take heed of the excited waiters waving to potential customers along Wing Wah Lane. Here you'll find rowdy Indian, Thai, and Malaysian restaurants that serve piping-hot dishes at reasonable prices.

Lan Kwai Fong used to be a hawkers' neighborhood before World War II. Its modern success is largely due to Canadian expatriate Allan Zeman, an eccentric figure who has been dubbed the "King of Lan Kwai Fong" by the local media. He opened his first North American–style restaurant here 20 years ago; today he not only owns dozens of other restaurants and bars, but also the buildings they're in. He claims to have about 100 restaurants, and although he doesn't actually own them all, he acts as the landlord for most of them. The Fong restaurants are now simply a hobby for Zeman whose business empire includes everything from property development to fashion.

New Year's Eve (December 31) is undoubtedly the busiest time for Lan Kwai Fong. Thousands of people line the tiny area to celebrate and party. You'll notice a strong police presence moving the human traffic through the streets and keeping an eye out for any troublemakers. This is mainly to prevent another tragedy such as the one in the early 1990s when 21 people were crushed to death as a massive throng went out of control as they ushered in a new year. Now when large crowds are anticipated—usually New Year's Eve, Christmas Eve, and also Halloween—the police carefully monitor the number of people entering the area.

Call it progress or a type of survival-of-the-strongest evolution, but this trendy neighborhood has seen as many establishments open as those that have closed down. New spots are constantly in development, or old places under refurbishment. Regardless of the changes, Lan Kwai Fong is always alive with scores of people and places to be merry.

–Eva Chui Loiterton

Lei Dou. Meaning simply "here" in Cantonese, this otherworldly spot, hidden away in the heart of the action, is where those in the know (and those seeking discretion) come to wind down in style. Lei Dou's fans love it for its decadent, candlelit decor, down-tempo jazz, and comfortable seating. ✉ *Ground fl., 20–22 D'Aguilar St., Central* ☎*2526–6628* ◷ *Closes 3* AM.

Lux. The well-heeled drink martinis and designer beers at this swanky corner spot. It has a prime location in Lan Kwai Fong and is another great bar to people-watch; it also serves excellent food in booths at the back. ✉ *California Tower, 30–32 D'Aguilar St., Lan Kwai Fong, Central* ☎*2868–9538* ◷*Closes 4* AM.

MO Bar. This plush bar in the Landmark Mandarin Oriental is where the banking set goes to relax. You'll pay top dollar for the martinis (up to HK$150), but the striking interior makes it worthwhile. A huge, red-light circle dominates an entire wall, the "O" being a Chinese symbol of shared experience. ✉*The Landmark Mandarin Oriental, 15 Queen's Road Central, The Landmark, Central* ☎*2132–0077* ◷*Closes 2* AM.

RED Bar. Although its shopping mall location, outdoor terrace self-service policy, and incongruous affiliation with the next-door gym may not seem appealing, once you arrive, you'll throw all your preconceived notions into the harbor. On the roof of IFC Mall, RED has breathtaking views of the city, making it a great place to grab an early dinner, and relax with a cocktail while watching the sunset. ✉*Level 4, Two IFC, 8 Finance St., Central* ☎*8129–8882* ◷*Closes 2* AM.

Staunton's Wine Bar & Cafe. Adjacent to Hong Kong's famous outdoor escalator is this popular bistro-style café and bar. Partly alfresco, it's the perfect place to people-watch. You can come for a drink at night, or for coffee or a meal during the day. It's also a Sunday-morning favorite for nursing hangovers over brunch. ✉*10–12 Staunton St., SoHo, Central* ☎*2973–6611* ◷*Closes 3* AM.

DISCOS & NIGHTCLUBS

Azure. If Lan Kwai Fong's masses are wigging you out, head skywards to this fabulous and spacious club at the top of the 30-story Hotel LKF. With its 270-degree panorama of the harbor, pool table, DJ booth, dance space, and smokers' terrace, the venue manages to balance coolness with good, old-fashioned fun. ✉ *29th fl., Hotel LKF, 33 Wyndham St., Central* ☎*3518–9330* ◷*Closes 3* AM.

Cliq. Cliq has garnered plaudits as one of the city's top clubbing venues. Its 6,000 square feet comprise an unusually spacious dance floor, a wall of TV screens, black chandeliers, polished concrete surfaces, and a large platform for visiting DJs. ✉*2nd fl., On Hing Building, On Hing Terrace, Central* ☎*2868–3111* ⊕ ◷*Closes 3* AM.

Club 97. As the first glitzy Lan Kwai Fong nightspot, Club 97 draws mobs of beautiful people. It started off life as a members-only club, but that rule has since been disregarded. The space is dominated by a circular bar in the center of the room, and has a small dance floor surrounded by cozy nooks. ✉*9–11 Lan Kwai Fong, Central* ☎*2186–1897* ◷*Closes 4* AM.

★ **dragon-i.** A place to prance, pose, and preen, dragon-i is owned by local party-boy socialite Gilbert Yeung. The entrance is marked by an

Art Spaces

Fringe Club. The pioneer of Hong Kong's alternative arts scene has been staging excellent independent theater, music, and art productions since opening in 1983. The distinctive brown-and-white striped structure that houses it was built as a cold-storage warehouse in 1892. It was derelict when the Fringe took over; the painstaking renovation has earned awards. Light pours through huge windows into the street-level Economist Gallery, with its small, well-curated exhibitions.

The über-cool Fotogalerie, upstairs, is Hong Kong's only photographic space. Downstairs, meat and cheese were once sold in the space that now houses the Fringe Theatre. The lighting box of the smaller Studio Theatre was once a refrigeration unit, built to preserve not food but colonials' winter clothes from summer mildew. (Fringe productions are sometimes in Cantonese, so check the program carefully.) ⊠ *2 Lower Albert Rd., Central* ☎ *2521–7251 general inquiries, 3128–8288 box office* ⊕ *www.hkfringe.com.hk* ✉ *Galleries free* ⊘ *Art galleries and box office: Mon.–Sat. noon–10* PM. *Fotogalerie: Mon.–Thurs. noon–midnight, Fri. and Sat. noon–3 am. Fringe Gallery Bar: Mon.–Thurs. 3 pm–midnight, Fri. and Sat. 3* PM*–3* AM Ⓜ *Central MTR, Exit D2.*

Hong Kong Arts Centre. A hodge-podge of activities takes place in this deceptively bleak concrete tower, financed with horse-racing profits donated by the Hong Kong Jockey Club. Intriguing contemporary art exhibitions are held in the 14th-floor Goethe Gallery, a white-cube space. Thematic cycles of art-house flicks run in the basement Agnès b. CINEMA! Community theater groups are behind much of the fare at the Shouson Theatre and smaller McAulay Studio, though international drama and dance troupes sometimes appear. Quality is hit-and-miss so check newspaper reviews for advice. From Wan Chai MTR, cross the footbridge to Immigration Tower, then dogleg left through the open plaza until you hit Harbour Road: the center is on the left. ⊠ *2 Harbour Road, Wan Chai* ☎ *2582–0200, 2802–0088 Goethe Gallery* ⊕ *www.hkac.org.hk* ✉ *Free* ⊘ *Center: daily 10–8. Goethe Gallery: weekdays 9–9, Sat. 2–6* Ⓜ *Wan Chai MTR, Exit C.*

Ma Tau Kok Cattle Depot. A former slaughterhouse in industrial To Kwa Wan—aka the middle of nowhere—has become a happening hub of independent art. The century-old brown-brick building looks like it would be more at home in northern England than Hong Kong. It's divvied up into spaces run by different groups. In July 1997—handover month—a group of young local artists formed the **Artists' Commune** (⊠ *Unit 12* ☎ *2104–3322* ⊕ *www.artist-commune.com* ✉ *Free* ⊘ *Tues.–Sun. 2–8*), whose massive loftlike premises showcase offbeat works. Expect funky, well-curated pickings at **1aspace** (⊠ *Unit 14* ☎ *2529–0087* ⊕ *www.oneaspace. org.hk* ✉ *Free* ⊘ *Tues.–Sun 2–8*), a cool, sleek gallery. The easiest way to get here is by taxi from Tsim Sha Tsui (around HK$50) or from Lok Fu MTR (around HK$35). ⊠ *63 Ma Tau Kok Rd., To Kwa Wan, Kowloon.*

–Victoria Patience

Late-Night Bites

Nix that looming hangover with a greasy fry-up *before* you hit the sack. **The Flying Pan** (✉ *Ground fl., 9 Old Bailey St., Central* ☎ *2140–6333* ✉ *3rd fl., 81–85 Lockhart Rd., Wan Chai* ☎ *2528–9997*), is a popular 24-hour breakfast diner, equally busy at 3 AM and 3 PM on weekends. Eggs any style come with your two picks from a huge list of sides including grits, blintzes, baked beans, and fruit salad. The truly greedy can order a Kitchen Sink, which is a taste of everything.

A perennial late-supper favorite is **Post 97** (✉ *1st fl., 9 Lan Kwai Fong, Lan Kwai Fong* ☎ *2810–9333*), where the kitchen is open until 2 AM on Friday and Saturday. The all-day menu has consistently good grub from focaccia and salads to chicken wings

and hearty breakfasts. Grab a window seat to peer down at the other late-night revelers of Lan Kwai Fong.

While locals head to **Tsui Wah** (✉ *15–19 Wellington St., Central* ☎ *2525–6338*), a large, three-story Chinese restaurant, at any time of the day, the late-night crowds are the happiest. Service is quick, there's a huge menu of typical Chinese fare such as fried rice and noodles, as well as western dishes such as steak. It's noisy, smoky, has bright fluorescent lighting, and the crowds just keep on coming. You may even find the odd celebrity chowing down on beef brisket noodles at 2 AM. The place closes at 4 AM.

–Eva Chui Loiterton

7

enormous birdcage (filled with real budgies and canaries) made entirely of bamboo poles. Have a drink on the wonderful alfresco deck by the doorway or step inside the rich, red playroom, which doubles as a restaurant in the early evening. Take a trip to the bathroom to see arguably the biggest cubicles in Hong Kong, with floor-to-ceiling silver tiles and double-height mirrored ceilings. ✉ *The Centrium, 60 Wyndham St., Central* ☎ *3110–1222* ✆ *Closes 5* AM.

★ **Drop.** This pint-sized gem is where celebrities party—usually until sunrise when they're in town. Hidden down an alley beside a hot dog stand, its location only adds an air of exclusivity to the speakeasy-like feel. Excellent fresh-fruit martinis are its forte. Drop has two incarnations: after-dinner cocktail lounge before midnight, and impenetrable fortress later on, so arrive early to avoid disappointment. ✉ *Basement, On Lok Mansion, 39–43 Hollywood Rd., entrance off Cochrine St., Central* ☎ *2543–8856* ✆ *Closes 6* AM.

Volar. By midnight, the line outside this club is more like a scrimmage as die-hard clubbers claw through the Darwinian fray to face the meanest door staff in town. The maze of low-ceilinged basement rooms features a so-hip-it-hurts crowd, and a genuinely eclectic mix of music, from electro-house to hip-hop, to rock n roll mash-ups. ✉ *Basement, 39–44 D'Aguilar St., Lan Kwai Fong, Central* ☎ *2810–1272.*

Yumla. This diminutive music bar features consistently good DJs playing to a tiny, explosive dance-floor crowd of locals and expats, and an adjacent "beer garden," which is actually a conveniently located public park. ✉ *Lower basement, 79 Wyndham St., Central* ☎ *2147–2382* ✆ *Closes 4* AM.

GAY & LESBIAN SPOTS

Propaganda. Off a quaint but steep cobblestone street, this is *the* most popular gay club in Hong Kong; its near-monopoly on the late-night scene is reflected in its steep cover charge (HK$180 Friday, HK$220 Saturday, including one drink). The art deco bar area is a pleasant schmooze-fest, with elegant booths and soft lighting, while the dance floor has lap poles on either side for go-go boys to flaunt their wares. It's pretty empty during the week; the crowds arrive well after midnight on weekends. The entrance is in an alleyway, Ezra Lane, which runs parallel to Hollywood Road. ⊠ *1 Hollywood Rd., Central* ☎*2868–1316* ⊙*Closes 5:30* AM.

Virus. Girls come here in groups to play drinking games, drink cheap beer, and sing along to Canto-pop—not a great scene for a foreigner looking to meet people, but typical of Hong Kong's under-the-radar lesbian scene. For something more inviting, check out Les Peches (⇨ *box, above*). ⊠*6th fl., 268 Jaffe Rd., Causeway Bay* ☎*6108–6255* ⊙*Closes 5* AM.

Volume. Nestled down a leafy residential staircase off Hollywood Road, Volume hosts a friendly, mixed crowd of gays, lesbians, and their friends, thanks to free entry and an open-door policy. New Arrivals Wednesdays are a staple of the scene, welcoming tourists and newbies, and attracting locals with free vodka between 7 and 9 pm. The entrance is just below street level, around the corner from the main road. ⊠ *83–85 Hollywood R., Sheung Wan* ☎*2857–7683* ⊙*Closes late.*

LES PECHES

Though Central has a relatively open gay scene, Hong Kong's lesbians are notoriously low profile. For newcomers, Les Peches Lounge is an oasis of sorts: a monthly get-together, open to lesbians, bisexual women, and their friends, with a good mix of ages and ethnic backgrounds. Les Peches takes place on the first Tuesday of every month at Fong Underground (⊠ *34–35 D'Aguilar St., Lan Kwai Fong);* the HK$80 cover includes one drink. Past themes have included wine tasting, belly dancing, fashion shows, drag kings, and palm reading. For more information, contact *lespechesinfo@yahoo.com.*

MUSIC CLUBS

The Cavern. This large bar at the top of Lan Kwai Fong is a laid-back space where locals and tourists alike come to drink beer, eat peanuts, tap their feet to the lively cover bands, and watch the swelling streets from the pavement tables. ⊠*Shop 1, ground fl., LKF Tower, 33 Wyndham St., entrance on D'Aguliar St., Central* ☎*2121–8969* ⊙*Closes 4* AM.

★ **Fringe Club.** The arts-minded mingle in this historic redbrick building that also houses the members-only Foreign Correspondents' Club, next door. The Fringe is the headquarters for Hong Kong's alternative arts scene and normally stages live music twice a week. ⊠*2 Lower Albert Rd., Central* ☎*2521–7251* ⊙*Closes 3* AM.

PUBS

Globe. Between Lan Kwai Fong and SoHo, the Globe is one of the few laid-back places in the area to knock back a beer or two with down-to-earth folks. It's the local pub for homesick expats who live in the area, and does a great Sunday roast. ⊠*39 Hollywood Rd., Central* ☎*2543–1941* ⊙*Closes 2* AM.

Chinese Opera

There are 10 **Cantonese opera** troupes headquartered in Hong Kong, as well as many amateur singing groups. Some put on performances of "street opera" in, for example, the Temple Street Night Market almost every night, while others perform at temple fairs, in City Hall, or in playgrounds under the auspices of the Urban Council. Those unfamiliar with Chinese opera might find the sights and sounds of this highly complex and sophisticated art form a little strange. Every gesture has its own meaning; in fact, there are 50 gestures for the hand alone.

Props attached to the costumes are similarly intricate and are used in exceptional ways. For example, the principal female often has 5-foot-long pheasant-feather tails attached to her headdress; she shows anger by dropping the head and shaking it in a circular fashion so that the feathers move in a perfect circle. Surprise is shown by what's called "nodding the feathers." You can also "dance with the feathers" to show a mixture of anger and determination. Orchestral music punctuates the singing. It's best to attend with someone who can translate the gestures for you; or you can learn more at the Cantonese Opera Halls in the Hong Kong Heritage Museum.

The highly stylized **Peking opera** employs higher-pitched voices than Cantonese opera. Peking opera is an older form, more respected for its classical traditions; the meticulous training of the several troupes visiting Hong Kong from the People's Republic of China each year is well regarded. They perform in City Hall or at special temple ceremonies. You can get the latest programs from the Hong Kong Cultural Centre.

—Eva Chui Loiterton

The Keg. As its name implies, beer and more beer is the beverage of choice at this small pub. Large wooden barrels serve as tables and the floors are covered with discarded peanut shells. All manner of sports coverage reigns on the TV screens. ⊠ *52 D'Aguilar St., Lan Kwai Fong, Central* ☎ *2810–0369* ☽ *Closes 3* AM.

WINE BARS

Boca Tapas and Wine Bar. What better combination than mouthwatering tapas accompanied by a 140-bottle globally sourced wine list? Boca—"mouth" in Spanish—has a diverse tapas menu, too, ranging from traditional chorizo and stuffed olives to Asian bites such as spicy spring rolls and satay sticks. ⊠ *64 Peel St., SoHo, Central* ☎ *2548–1717* ☽ *Closes 2* AM.

Le Tire Bouchon. If you're planning a romantic encounter, try this restaurant and wine bar, where fine wines by the glass accompany traditional French cuisine, and warm, friendly service. ⊠ *45A Graham St., Central* ☎ *2523–5459* ☽ *Closes 12:30* AM.

WAN CHAI

Wan Chai is the pungent night flower of the nocturnal scene, where the way of life served as inspiration for the novel *The World of Suzie Wong*. It now shares the streets with hip wine bars, salsa nights, old men's pubs, and after-parties that continue past sunrise. The seedy "hostess bars" in this neighborhood are easy to spot and avoid, with curtained entrances guarded by old ladies on stools and suggestive names in neon. But some things never change: the busiest nights are still when there's a navy ship in the harbor, on an R&R stopover. Wednesday's ladies' night, with half-price drinks, is also a big draw.

ARTFUL DATES

Hong Kong City Fringe Festival (January): Theater, dance, comedy, film, visual arts, new media take place in venues across town. ⊕ *www.hkfringe.com.hk.*

Hong Kong Arts Festival (February and March): Past visitors have included Mikhail Baryshnikov, Pina Bausch, and José Carreras. The focus is on performing arts. ⊕ *www.hk.artsfestival.org.*

Hong Kong International Film Festival (April): Asian cinema accounts for many of the 200 new films shown in this festival. ⊕ *www.hkiff.org.hk.*

BARS

★ **Mes Amis.** In the heart of Wan Chai, on the corner of Lockhart and Luard roads, Mes Amis is a friendly bar that also serves good food. Its corner setting and open bi-fold doors mean that none of the action outside is missed, and vice versa—the perpetual crowd of patrons inside are on display to those on the street. ⊠ *83 Lockhart Rd., Wan Chai* ☎2527–6680 ⊙ *Closes 6 AM.*

★ **1/5 nuevo.** Once one of Hong Kong's slickest nightspots, 1/5 moved down to street level in 2007 and morphed into a tapas lounge and cocktail bar, hence the addition of "nuevo" to its name. High-flyers, financiers, and expats populate this dark, sophisticated Star Street hangout. ⊠ *9 Star St., Wan Chai* ☎2529–2300 ⊙ *Closes midnight.*

The Pawn. In a district plagued by controversial redevelopment, this attractive historic building, a former pawnshop, has been preserved with minimal fuss. The stylish interior is decorated with retro furniture, while a cranky old foosball table lends a fun, youth-club feel. The long balcony overlooking the iconic Hong Kong tramway is a great place for curious tourists to spy on bustling everyday life below. ⊠ *62 Johnston Rd., Wan Chai* ☎2866–3444 ⊙ *Closes 2 AM.*

Vertigo Lounge. Situated a few streets away from Wan Chai's seedy neon strip, closer to Admiralty and fashionable, upmarket Star Street, this skyscraping bar has a DJ booth in the main arena, and three private party rooms, one with a full-size American pool table, another with a karaoke setup. ⊠ *26th fl. 202 Queen's Rd. East, Wan Chai* ☎2575–8980 ⊙ *Closes 3 AM.*

DISCOS & NIGHTCLUBS

Dusk Till Dawn. Loud, energetic cover bands get the dance floor jumping on Wednesday to Saturday nights. Popular with expats, it can be seedy, but patrons are usually having too much fun to notice or care. ⊠ *76–84 Jaffe Rd., Wan Chai* ☎2528–4689 ⊙ *Closes 7 AM.*

Joe Bananas. This disco and bar's reputation for all-night partying and general good times remains unchallenged. People dressed too casually are strictly excluded: no shorts, sneakers, or T-shirts (the only exception is the Rugby Sevens weekend when even Joe can't turn away the thirsty swarm). Arrive before 11 PM to avoid the line. ✉ *23 Luard Rd., Wan Chai* ☎ *2529–1811* ⊘ *Closes 5* AM.

Tribeca. A self-proclaimed "New York–style nightclub," Tribeca occupies the space that formerly housed Manhattan and more recently Club Ing. Unlike many other nightclubs in Hong Kong, it has a huge space—one of the largest in the city—full of dance floors, bars, lounges, and the requisite VIP areas. The plush interior attempts to emulate a swanky nightclub in the Big Apple, and judging by the crowds who flock here, it's doing a good job. ✉ *4th fl., Convention Plaza, 1 Harbour Rd., Wan Chai* ☎ *2836–3690* ⊘ *Closes 4* AM.

MUSIC CLUB

JJ's. Dark wood decor and vintage photographs give this famous nightspot in the Grand Hyatt a comforting, old-school feel. The Music Room is renowned for having the best in-house hotel bands in town as well as a large dedicated dance floor space. Since its inception in 1989, it's been a notorious pickup joint. We're not ones to judge, but fellas, watch out for the lonely lady at the bar—she's working. ✉ *Grand Hyatt Hotel, 1 Harbour Rd., Wan Chai* ☎ *2584–7662* ⊘ *Closes 3* AM.

PUBS

Carnegie's. Named after the Scotsman and steel baron Andrew Carnegie, whose family sailed to America in the late 1800s, this rock-and-roll bar lives up to its name. Although Carnegie himself probably didn't imagine bar-top dancing to classic rock tunes at an establishment bearing his name, the Scottish owners feel that the spirit of his love of music lives on regardless. ✉ *53–55 Lockhart Rd., Wan Chai* ☎ *2866–6289* ⊘ *Closes 4* AM.

Horse & Groom. This friendly pub has a lot of charm, and plenty of regulars who come here to unwind after a day's work. ✉ *161 Lockhart Rd., Wan Chai* ☎ *2507–2517* ⊘ *Closes 3* AM.

Old China Hand. Once full of gritty booths and stark lighting, this pub now has a facade that opens onto the street, absorbing all the hustle and bustle of Lockhart Road. It's open 24/7, and has been here from time immemorial (as have some of its patrons, by the looks of it). The kitchen serves typical pub fare and is something of an institution for those wishing to sober up with greasy grub after a long night out. ✉ *104 Lockhart Rd., Wan Chai* ☎ *2865–4378*.

CAUSEWAY BAY

BAR

ToTT's Asian Bar and Grill. Also known as Talk of the Town, this full-floor restaurant and bar was once more famous for its weird and wacky decor than the 270-degree vista, but has recently undergone a major makeover, becoming sleeker, and more sophisticated with neutral tones that complement, rather than distract from, the skyline. ✉ *34th fl., The Excelsior, 281 Gloucester Rd., Causeway Bay* ☎ *2837–6786* ⊘ *Closes 2* AM.

Performance Places

City Hall. From Isaac Stern, Yo-Yo Ma, and the New York Phil to the Bee Gees; from the Royal Danish Ballet to the People's Liberation Army Comrade Dance Troupe, the offerings here are varied, but consistently excellent. Two buildings make up the chunky '60s complex, divided by a World War II memorial garden and shrine. The 1,500-seat concert hall and a smaller theater are in the low-rise block, as is Maxim's City Palace, a massive clattering restaurant with really good dim sum. The high-rise building has an exhibition space and a smaller recital hall as well as a public library and marriage registry office. Performances are usually held Friday and Saturday at 8 PM. ✉ *5 Edinburgh Pl., Central* ☎ *2921—2840, 2734–9009 box office* ⊕ *www.lcsd.gov.hk* ⊗ *Daily 9–9; box office daily 10–8* Ⓜ *Central MTR, Exit K.*

Hong Kong Academy for Performing Arts. Many of Hong Kong's most talented performers studied at this academy's schools of drama, music, dance, television, and film. It also has five theaters and a gallery. Large-scale productions are staged in the huge Lyric Theatre and the smaller Drama Theatre; offerings are often in-the-round at the dinky Studio Theatre. The two concert halls host choice classical or traditional Chinese music performances. ∎**TIP**➔ **When the weather's good, inquire about shows in the garden amphitheater.** ✉ *1 Gloucester Rd., Wan Chai* ☎ *2584–8580* ⊕ *www.hkapa.edu* ⊗ *Box office Mon.–Sat. noon–6 PM* Ⓜ *Wan Chai MTR, Exit C.*

Hong Kong Cultural Centre. Superlatives abound here: the massive oval concert hall, which seats 2,000, is Asia's biggest; its 8,000-pipe Austrian organ is one of the world's largest. Only slightly smaller, the tiered Grand Theatre often hosts visiting Broadway musicals and opera and ballet productions. Cozier plays take place in the Studio Theatre. Look out for performances by the world-class **Hong Kong Philharmonic Orchestra** (☎ *2721–2030* ⊕ *www.hkpo.com*), which performs everything from classical to avant-garde to contemporary music by Chinese composers. Past soloists have included Vladimir Ashkenazy, Rudolf Firkusny, and Maureen Forrester. Exhibits are occasionally mounted in the atrium. ✉ *10 Salisbury Rd., Tsim Sha Tsui, Kowloon* ☎ *2734–2010, 2734–9009 box office* ⊕ *www.lcsd.gov.hk* ⊗ *Daily 11–11; box office daily 10–9:30* Ⓜ *Tsim Sha Tsui MTR, Exit E.*

Kwai Tsing Theatre. It might be in the sticks, but it's a major player in the cultural scene. Sunlight pours into the atrium through a curving glass facade that looks onto a plaza where performances are often held. Inside, the 900-seat theater provides a much-needed middle ground between the massive spaces and tiny studio theaters at other venues. And if the likes of Phillip Glass and the Royal Shakespeare Company can schlep out here, 20 minutes from Central, to perform, you can certainly get out here to watch. ✉ *12 Hing Ning Rd., Kwai Chung, New Territories* ☎ *2408–0128, 2406–7505 box office* ⊕ *www.lcsd. gov.hk* ⊗ *Daily 9 AM–11 PM* Ⓜ *Kwai Fong MTR, Exit C.*

–Victoria Patience

PUB

East End Brewery. Deep in the veritable beer desert of Hysan Avenue lies a pub with the refreshing motto "Let No Man Thirst For Want Of Real Ale" displayed on its wall. Here, you will find dozens of brews, accompanied by live sports coverage and a reassuring ocean of peanut shells underfoot. ☒ *Sunning Plaza, 10 Hysan Ave., Causeway Bay* ☎*2577–9119* ☉*Closes 1:30* AM.

KOWLOON

Central and Wan Chai are undoubtedly the king and queen of nightlife in Hong Kong. If you're staying in a hotel, however, or having dinner across the water in Kowloon, Ashley Road and an out-of-the-way strip called Knutsford Terrace still make for a fun night out.

BARS

Aqua. Felix at the Peninsula Hotel has had a stronghold on the sophisticated bar-with-a-view competition for years, but now its crown has been handed over to Aqua. Inside One Peking, an impressive curvaceous skyscraper dominating the Kowloon skyline, this very cool bar is on the mezzanine level of the top floor. The high ceilings and raking glass walls offer up unrivaled views of Hong Kong Island and of the harbor filled with ferries and ships. ☒*29th fl. and 30th fl., One Peking, 1 Peking Rd., Tsim Sha Tsui, Kowloon* ☎*3427–2288* ☉*Closes 2* AM.

Bahama Mama's. You'll find tropical rhythms at the Caribbean-inspired bar, where world music plays and the kitsch props include a surfboard over the bar and the silhouette of a curvaceous woman showering behind a screen over the restroom entrance. ☒*4–5 Knutsford Terr., Tsim Sha Tsui, Kowloon* ☎*2368–2121* ☉*Closes 4* AM.

Balalaika. Vodka is served in a –20°C (–36°F) room at this Russian-theme bar, but don't be alarmed at the freezing temperature—it provides fur coats and traditional Russian fur hats. Take your pick from the 15 varieties of vodka from five different countries. ☒*2nd fl., 10 Knutsford Terr., Tsim Sha Tsui, Kowloon* ☎*2312–6222* ☉*Closes 1* AM.

The Lobby. You'll feel well taken care of at the Peninsula's classically colonial lobby bar. Society watchers linger here; sit to the right of the hotel entrance to observe the crème de la crème. ☒*Peninsula Hotel, Salisbury Rd., Tsim Sha Tsui, Kowloon* ☎*2920–2888* ☉*Closes 1* AM.

Fodor'sChoice **Felix.** High up in the Peninsula Hotel, this bar is immensely popular ★ with visitors; it not only has a brilliant view of the island, but the interior was designed by the visionary Philippe Starck. Don't forget to check out the padded mini-disco room. Another memorable feature is the male urinals, situated right by glass windows overlooking the city. ☒*28th fl., Peninsula Hong Kong, Salisbury Rd., Tsim Sha Tsui, Kowloon* ☎*2920–2888* ☉*Closes 2* AM.

Gripps. With spectacular harbor views from the ocean-liner level and a central bar modeled after a high-class London pub, this bar in the Marco Polo draws the executive set, and, more recently, businessmen from mainland China and some tourists who stay at this hotel in the heart of

Kowloon. ⊠*6th fl., Marco Polo Hongkong Hotel, Harbour City, Canton Rd., Tsim Sha Tsui, Kowloon* ☎*2113–0088* ⊘*Closes 1* AM.

Sky Lounge. Ride the bubble elevator to this bar high up in the Sheraton in time for sunset, and you won't be disappointed. Once you're there, try one of the frozen fruit cocktails or the signature lychee martinis. ⊠*18th fl., Sheraton Hong Kong Hotel & Towers, 20 Nathan Rd., Tsim Sha Tsui, Kowloon* ☎*2369–1111* ⊘*Closes 2* AM.

Spasso. For the best sundowner in town, try this modern Italian restaurant and bar's west-facing terrace, which overlooks a fine slice of the skyline. Complimentary hors d'oeuvres and a choice of 50 wines by the glass can only add to the experience. But who needs glasses when you're on vacation—go on, get a bottle. ⊠*Shop 403, 4th fl., Ocean Centre, Tsim Sha Tsui* ☎*2730–8027* ⊘*Closes 1:30* AM.

HOSTESS CLUBS

Fodor'sChoice **Club BBoss.** It's hard to fathom the size of a club that can accommodate
★ 3,000 people, but with over 60,000 square feet of space, more than a thousand staff, a rotating stage, and three nightly cabaret shows to entertain a crowd of moneyed execs, Club BBoss is hostess paradise. Women are welcome, provided they are accompanying male customers. ⊠*Mandarin Plaza, Tsim Sha Tsui East, Kowloon* ☎*2369–2883* ⊘*Closes 4* AM.

Club Kokusai. As its name implies, this place appeals to visitors from the Land of the Rising Yen. Interestingly, there's no karaoke here, just the shows—and girls, of course. ⊠*81 Nathan Rd., Tsim Sha Tsui, Kowloon* ☎*2367–6969* ⊘*Closes 3* AM.

SOMETHING DIFFERENT

Aqua Luna. As the city's last traditionally crafted vessel, or junk, Aqua Luna's dramatic appearance and red sails make her easy to spot. Step off dry land from either pier, in Kowloon or Central, order a G&T, and take in the shimmering harbor sights for 45 minutes, with snack menus, and plush seating. The HK$180 price tag includes one drink. ⊠*Cultural Centre Pier, Tsim Sha Tsui* ⊠*Pier No. 9, Central* ☎*2116–8821* ⊘*Last sail 10:30* PM *Tsim Sha Tsui; 10:45* PM *Central.*

PUBS

★ **Delaney's.** Both branches of Hong Kong's pioneer Irish pub have Irish interiors that were shipped here, and the mood is as authentic as the furnishings. Guinness and Delaney's ale (a specialty microbrew) are on tap, and there are corner snugs (small private rooms) and an Irish menu. The crowd includes some genuine Irish regulars; get ready for spontaneous outbursts of fiddling and other Emerald Isle traditions. Happy hour runs from 5 to 9 PM daily. ⊠*Basement fl., 71–77 Peking Rd., Tsim Sha Tsui, Kowloon* ☎*2301–3980* ⊠*Ground fl., One Capital Place, 18 Luard Rd., Wan Chai* ☎*2804–2880* ⊘*Closes 3* AM.

Ned Kelly's Last Stand. Come to this boisterous Aussie-managed haven on this lively nighttime strip for pub meals and, oddly enough, an exuberant six-piece Dixieland jazz outfit, who play from 9:30 pm to 1 am nightly. Arrive early for decent seats. ⊠*11A Ashley Rd., Tsim Sha Tsui, Kowloon* ☎*2376–0562* ⊘*Closes 2* AM.

Side Trip to Macau

Largo do Senado, the main square, central Macau

8

WORD OF MOUTH

"Include a trip down to Coloane to see what Macau used to be like. Very few tourists go there, and you will be able to enjoy this area at a much slower pace. There are beaches all along the southern coast, from Hác Sá to the village of Coloane. . . . You can take the #25 bus down to Coloane from Senado Square in about 30 minutes."

—Cicerone

WELCOME TO MACAU

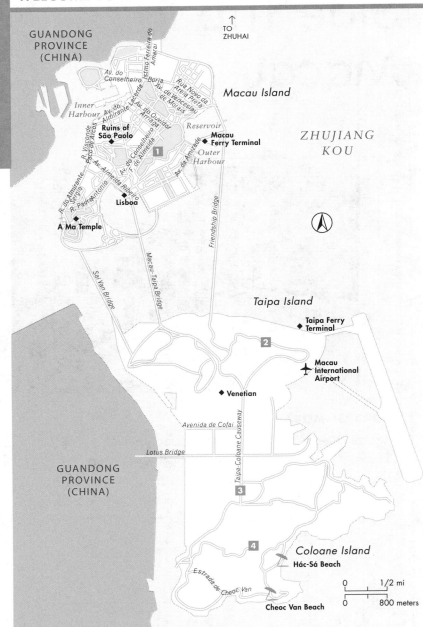

GUANDONG PROVINCE (CHINA)

TO ZHUHAI

Inner Harbour

Av. do Conselheiro

Rua Novo da Areia Preta

Istmo Ferreira do Amaral

Av. de Venceslau de Morais

Rua Novo da Areia Preta

Macau Island

Av. do Almirante Laverda

Av. do Ouvidor Arriaga

Ruins of São Paolo

Reservoir

R. Visconde Paço do Arcos

Av. do Conselheiro F. de Almeida

Av. Almirante Ribeiro

Macau Ferry Terminal

Outer Harbour

ZHUJIANG KOU

Av. de Amizade

R. do Almirante Sérgio

R. Padre Antonio

Lisboa

A Ma Temple

1

Friendship Bridge

Sai Van Bridge

Macau-Taipa Bridge

Taipa Island

Taipa Ferry Terminal

2

Macau International Airport

Venetian

Avenida de Cofai

Taipa-Coloane Causeway

Lotus Bridge

3

GUANDONG PROVINCE (CHINA)

4

Coloane Island

Hác-Sá Beach

Estrada de Cheoc Van

Cheoc Van Beach

0		1/2 mi
0		800 meters

GETTING ORIENTED

Macau, a Special Administrative Region (SAR) of the People's Republic of China, is on the western bank of the Pearl River Delta, about an hour from Hong Kong by hydrofoil. It consists of the Macau Peninsula and Taipa and Coloane islands. The Cotai area, a glitzy, Vegas-like strip of hotels and casinos that began development in 2006, lies between Taipa and Coloane and virtually merges the two.

Most people visit Macau to gamble, eat cheap seafood, and shop without crowds. But don't overlook its timeless charms and unique culture, born from centuries of both Portuguese and Chinese influence.

1 Downtown Macau. You'll experience authentic Macau in a downtown square, with its European-style paving and sidewalk cafés, as well as in a Buddhist temple, with its red lanterns and fragrant joss sticks. But perhaps even more authentic is that pink colonial Portuguese building that houses a Chinese herbal medicine shop.

2 Taipa Island. Although the Portuguese presence on Macau dates from the mid-1500s, Taipa wasn't occupied until the mid-1800s. The island remained a garrison and a pastoral retreat until the 1970s, when it was linked to Macau by bridge. Today, some parts retain a village feel, while other parts are crowded with soul-less high-rises.

3 Cotai. The 3-km (2-mi) causeway that once separated Coloane from Taipa has been bridged by a massive land-reclamation and development project that includes casinos and casino hotels, resorts, and shopping malls.

4 Coloane Island. The larger island remains less populated and more intimate than Taipa, and few tourists venture this far south. It's also known for its parks, beaches, and golf club, as well as its unchanged Portuguese architecture and cobblestone streets.

TOP REASONS TO GO

Ruins of São Paulo. The church facade is a symbol of Macau. En route to it, sample regional cuisine and experience local charm in Senado Square.

A-Ma Temple. It's steeped in Macau's culture and history. Search for the Lucky Money Pool, then wash your hands in the blessed water before heading to the casinos.

Place Your Bets. Even if you don't gamble, take a peek inside the Lisboa, a classic Macau landmark, or the much newer Venetian, whose sprawling complex includes singing gondoliers on indoor canals and high-luxury shopping.

Relax on Hác-Sá Beach. Sunbathe on charcoal-gray sands before taking a stroll, heading out on Jet Skis, or feasting on seafood.

Spaaahhh. Macau's spas have ultra-indulgent treatments and world-class facilities—with prices to match. But who cares? You're on vacation.

8

MACAU PLANNER

The Basics

The Macau Government Tourist Office (MGTO) is well managed.

Macau Government Tourist Office (*MGTO;* ✉ *Macau Ferry Terminal, Macau* ☎ *853/2833–3000* ⊕ *www.macautourism.gov.mo* ✉ *Shun Tak Centre, 200 Connaught Rd., Central, Hong Kong* ☎ *2857–2287*).

PASSPORTS & VISAS

To enter Macau, Americans, Canadians, and EU citizens need only a valid passport for stays of up to 90 days.

CURRENCY

The Macanese pataca (MOP) has a fixed exchange rate of MOP$1.032 to HK$1—roughly MOP$7 to US$1. Patacas come in 10, 20, 50, 100, 500, and 1,000 MOP banknotes plus 1, 5, and 10 MOP coins. A pataca is divided into 100 avos, which come in 10-, 20-, and 50-avo coins. Hong Kong dollars are accepted in Macau on a 1:1 basis.

LANGUAGE

Chinese and Portuguese are Macau's official languages. Cantonese and Mandarin are widely spoken. English is unreliable outside tourist areas. It's best to print your destination in Chinese characters for taxi drivers.

Getting to Macau

BY AIR

International flights (from Asia) come into Macau, but there are no planes from Hong Kong. Sixteen-minute helicopter flights fly between Hong Kong's Shun Tak Centre and the Macau Ferry Terminal on East Asia Airlines; they leave every 30 minutes from 9:30 AM to 10:30 PM daily. Prices are HK$1,925 Monday to Thursday with a HK$200 surcharge on Friday, Saturday, Sunday, and holidays. Reservations are essential.

East Asia Airlines (☎ *853/2872–7288 Macau Terminal, 2108–9898 Shun Tak Centre* ⊕ *www.helihongkong.com*).

Macau International Airport (☎ *853/2886–1111* ⊕ *www.macau-airport.gov.mo*).

BY FERRY

Ferries run every 15 minutes with a reduced schedule from midnight to 7 AM. Prices for economy/ordinary and super/deluxe run HK$133–HK$275. VIP cabins cost HK$944 (four seats) to HK$2,136 (eight seats). Weekday traffic is usually light, so you can buy tickets right before departure. Weekend tickets often sell out, so make reservations. You can book tickets up to 90 days in advance with China Travel Service (⊕ *www.ctshk.com*) agencies or directly with CotaiJet or TurboJET by phone or online. Booking by phone requires a Visa card. You must pick tickets up at the terminal at least a half hour before departure.

Most ferries leave from Hong Kong's Shun Tak Centre Sheung Wan MTR Station in Central, though limited service is available from First Ferry at Kowloon's Tsim Sha Tsui Terminal. In Macau most ferries disembark from the main Macau Ferry Terminal, but CotaiJet services the terminal on Taipa Island. The trip takes one hour one way. Buses, taxis, and free shuttles to most casinos and hotels await on the Macau side.

CotaiJet (☎ *853/2885–0595 in Macau, 2359–9990 in Hong Kong* ⊕ *cotaijet.com.mo*). **First Ferry** (☎ *2131–8181* ⊕ *www.nwff.com.hk*). **TurboJET** (☎ *2859–3333 information, 2921–6688 reservations* ⊕ *www.turbojet.com.hk*).

Getting Around Macau

BY BUS

Public buses are clean and affordable; trips to anywhere in the Macau peninsula cost MOP$2.50. Service to Taipa Island is MOP$3.30, and service to Coloane is MOP$5. Buses run 6:30–midnight and require exact change upon boarding. But you can get downtown for free, via casino shuttles, from the official Border Gate crossing just outside mainland China, from the airport, and from the Macau Ferry Terminal.

BY CAR

Like in Hong Kong, Macau motorists drive on the left-hand side of the road. Road signs are in Chinese and Portuguese only. Rental cars with Avis are available at the Mandarin Oriental Hotel. Regular cars go for MOP$900 on weekdays and MOP$1,200 on weekends. Book three to four days in advance for weekend rentals.

Avis (☎ *853/2833–6789 in Macau, 2926–1126 in Hong Kong* ⊕ *www.avis.com*).

BY TAXI

Taxis are inexpensive, but not plentiful in Macau. The best places to catch a cab are the major casinos—the Wynn, Sands, and Venetian. Carry a bilingual map or ask the concierge at your hotel to write the name of your destination in Chinese. All taxis are metered, air-conditioned, and reasonably comfortable. The base charge is MOP$13 for the first 1½ km (1 mi) and MOP$1 per additional 600 feet. Trips between Coloane and either the Macau Peninsula or Taipa incur respective surcharges of MOP$5 or MOP$2. Drivers don't expect a tip.

WHAT IT COSTS IN MOP$

Restaurants				
under MOP$50	MOP$50–$100	MOP$100–$200	MOP$200–$300	over MOP$300

Hotels				
under MOP$700	MOP$700–$1,000	MOP$1,100–$2,100	MOP$2,100–$3,000	over MOP$3,000

Restaurant prices are per person for a main course at dinner and exclude the customary 10% service charge. Hotel prices are for two people in a standard double room in high season, excluding 10% service charge and 3% government tax.

Tours

Depending on your mindset, tours of Macau can either be spontaneously joined or meticulously made-to-order. If you're just debarking for the day at the main ferry terminal, find the **Kamlon Travel** (⊠ *Macau Ferry Terminal, Av. da Amizade* ☎ *853/2833–6611 or 853/2872–5813*) counter, where you can join a four- to five-hour tour of the peninsula's top attractions, departing daily at 11 AM and 12:45 PM.

For a tour of the islands, the **Venetian Travel Shop** (⊠ *Shop 1028, Venetian Macao-Resort-Hotel* ☎ *853/8118–2930 or 853/8118–2833*) hosts daily tours from 9:15 to 1 that include the Taipa Houses Museum and the A-Ma Cultural Village on Coloane for MOP$250 per person.

Book at least one day in advance from one of many travel agents in Hong Kong. Browse your options at the travel counters of the main ferry terminals in either Macau or Hong Kong, or check ⊕ *www. macautourism.gov.mo* for a list of authorized travel agencies in Macau; some offer tours in multiple languages.

Estoril Tours (⊠ *Shop 3711, 3rd fl., Shun Tak Centre, 200 Connaught Rd., Central, Hong Kong* ☎ *2559–1028* ⊕ *www. estoril.com.mo*) will customize a private group tour, from bungee-jumping off the Macau Tower to wandering through Coloane Village or a day visiting museums.

8

By Hiram Chu
Updated by
Chris Cottrell
& Cherise
Fong

Enter the desperate, smoky atmosphere of a Chinese casino, where frumpy players bet an average of five times more than the typical Vegas gambler. Sit down next to grandmothers who smoke like chimneys while playing baccarat—the local game of choice—with visiting high rollers. Then step out of the climate-controlled chill and into tropical air that embraces you like a warm, balmy hug. Welcome to Macau.

The many contrasts in this tiny enclave of 552,000 people serve as reminders of how very different cultures have embraced one another's traditions for hundreds of years. Though Macau's population is 95% ethnic Chinese, there are still vibrant pockets of Portuguese and Filipino expats. And some of the thousands of Eurasians—who consider themselves neither Portuguese nor Chinese, but something in between—can trace the intermarriage of their ancestors back a century or two.

Macau's old town, while dominated by the buildings, squares, and cobblestone alleyways of colonial Portugal, is tinged with eastern influences as well, as in the Buddhist temple at the intersection of the Travessa de Dom Quixote and Travessa de Sancho Panca. In Macau you can spend an afternoon strolling the black sands of Hác-Sá Beach before feasting on a dinner of *bacalhau com natas* (dried codfish with a cream sauce), grilled African chicken (spicy chicken in a coconut-peanut broth—a classic Macanese dish), Chinese lobster with scallions, or fiery prawns infused with Indian and Malaysian flavors. Wash everything down with *Vinho Verde,* the crisp young wine from northern Portugal, and top it all off with a traditional Portuguese *pastel de nata* (egg-custard tart) and dark, thick espresso.

SIGHTS & EXPERIENCES

Macau is a small place where, on a good day, you could drive from one end to the other in 30 minutes. This makes walking and bicycling ideal ways to explore winding city streets, nature trails, and long stretches of beach. Most of Macau's population lives on the peninsula attached to mainland China. The region's most famous sights are here—Senado Square, the Ruins of St. Paul's, A-Ma Temple—as are most of the luxury hotels and casinos. As in the older sections of Hong Kong, cramped older buildings stand comfortably next to gleaming new structures.

> ## THE BIG BOSS
>
> Many mixed-blood Macanese are from old, established families, including that of Dr. Stanley Ho, Macau's biggest *taipan* (Chinese for "big boss"). Dr. Ho—and his gambling and tourism empire under the Sociedade de Jogos de Macau (SJM) umbrella—kept the region afloat for four decades, providing more than 70% of the government's tax revenues until the gambling monopoly officially came to an end in 2002. His interests could include the boat that speeds you from Hong Kong to Macau, the hotel you stay at, the casino you lose money in, the one TV station you watch, and the electricity you use.

DOWNTOWN MACAU

Chances are you'll arrive at the Macau Ferry Terminal after sailing from Hong Kong. There's not much to see around the terminal itself, so hop into one of the many waiting casino or hotel shuttles and head straight downtown, less than 10 minutes away. From there it's a short walk to the city's historic center, along the short stretch of road named Avenida Almeida Ribeiro, more commonly known as San Ma Lo, which is Macau's commercial and cultural heart.

GET FORTIFIED

Fodor's Choice **Fortaleza da Guia.** The Guia Fortress, built between 1622 and 1638
★ on Macau's highest hill, was key to protecting the Portuguese from invaders. You can walk the steep, winding road up to the fortress or take a five-minute cable-car ride from the entrance of Flora Garden on Avenida Sidónio Pais. Once inside the fort, notice the gleaming white Guia Lighthouse (you can't go inside, but you can get a good look at the exterior) that's lit every night. Next to it is the Guia Chapel, built by Clarist nuns to provide soldiers with religious services. The chapel is no longer used for services, but restoration work in 1998 uncovered elaborate frescoes mixing western and Chinese themes. They're best seen when the morning or afternoon sun floods the chapel. ⊠ *Guia Hill, Downtown* ☎ *853/8399–6699* ✉*Free* ☉ *Daily 9–5:30.*

> ## WORLD HERITAGE
>
> In 2005 "The Historic Centre of Macau" was listed as China's 31st UNESCO World Heritage Site. The term "center" is misleading, as the site is really a collection of churches, buildings, and neighborhoods that colorfully illustrate Macau's 400-year history. Included in it are China's oldest examples of western architecture and the region's most extensive concentration of missionary churches.

8

Fortaleza do Monte (*Mount Fortress*). On the hill overlooking the ruins of São Paulo and affording great peninsular views, this renovated fort was built by the Jesuits in the early 17th century. In 1622 it was the site of Macau's most legendary battle, where a priest's lucky cannon shot hit an invading Dutch ship's powder supply, saving the day. The interior buildings were destroyed by fire in 1835, but the outer walls remain, along with several large cannons and artillery pieces. Next to the fort, exhibits at the **Macau Museum** (✉112 *Praceta do Museu de Macau, Monte Hill, Downtown* ☎853/2835–7911 ✆*MOP$15 [free on the 15th of each month]* ⊗*Tues.–Sun. 10–6*) take you through Macau's history, from its origins to modern development. ✉*Monte Hill, Downtown* ☎853/2833–5141 ✆*Free* ⊗ *Tues.–Sun. 10–7.*

SAY A LITTLE PRAYER
Admission to all churches and temples is free, though donations are suggested.

Igreja de São Lourenço. One of Macau's three oldest churches, the Church of St. Lawrence was founded by Jesuits in 1560 and has been lovingly rebuilt several times. Its present appearance dates to 1846. It overlooks the South China Sea amid pleasant, palm-shaded gardens. Families of Portuguese sailors used to gather on the front steps to pray for the sailors' safe return; hence its Chinese name, Feng Shun Tang (Hall of the Soothing Winds). Focal points of its breathtaking interior are the elegant wood carvings, a baroque altar, and crystal chandeliers. ✉*Rua de São Lourenço, Downtown* ☎*No phone* ⊗*Daily 10–4.*

Lin Fung Miu. Built in 1592, the Temple of the Lotus honors several Buddhist and Taoist deities, including Tin Hau (goddess of the sea), Kun Iam (goddess of mercy), and Kwan Tai (god of war and wealth). The front of the temple has awesome clay bas-reliefs of renowned figures from Chinese history and mythology. Inside are several halls, shrines, and courtyards. The temple is best known as a lodging place for Mandarins traveling from Guangzhou. Its most famous guest was Commissioner Lin Zexu, whose confiscation and destruction of British opium was largely responsible for the First Opium War. ✉*Av. do Almirante Lacerda, Downtown* ☎*No phone* ⊗*Daily dawn–dusk.*

Fodor's Choice ★ **Ruínas de São Paulo** (*Ruins of St. Paul's Church*). Only the magnificent, towering facade, with its intricate carvings and bronze statues, remains from the original Church of Mater Dei, built between 1602 and 1640 and destroyed by fire in 1835. The church, an adjacent college, and Mount Fortress, all Jesuit constructions, once formed East Asia's first western-style university. Now the widely adopted symbol of Macau,

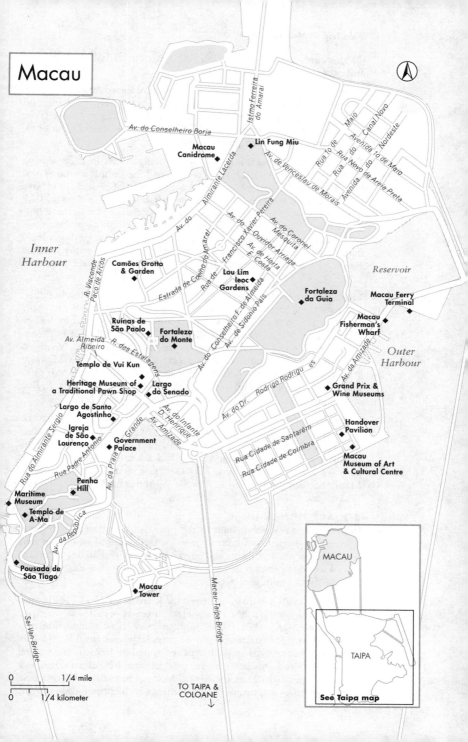

Macau

Inner Harbour

Av. do Conselheiro Borja

Macau Canidrome

Lin Fung Miu

Av. de Venceslau de Morais

Almirante Lacerda

Istmo Ferreira do Amarial

Maio

Canal Novo

Avenida 10 de Maio

Rua 1o de

Rua Novo da Areia Preta

Avenida

Av. do Coronel Mesquita

Av. do Francisco Xavier Pereira

Av. do Ouvidor Arriaga

Av. de Horta e Costa

Av. do Coelho do Amaral

Estrada de Coelho do Amaral

Rua dos Estalagens

R. Visconde Paço de Alcos

Camões Grotto & Garden

Lou Lim leoc Gardens

Av. do Conselheiro f. de Almeida

Av. de Sidónio Pais

Fortaleza da Guia

Reservoir

Macau Ferry Terminal

Macau Fisherman's Wharf

Ruínas de São Paolo

Fortaleza do Monte

Templo de Vui Kun

Av. Almeida Ribeiro

R. das Estalagens

Heritage Museum of a Traditional Pawn Shop

Largo do Senado

Largo de Santo Agostinho

Av. do Infante D. Henrique

Av. Amizade

Igreja de São Lourenço

Government Palace

Av. do Dr. Rodrigo Rodrigues

Av. da Amizade

Outer Harbour

Grand Prix & Wine Museums

Handover Pavilion

Rua Cidade de Santarém

Rua Cidade de Coimbra

Macau Museum of Art & Cultural Centre

Rua do Almirante Sergio

Rua Padre Antonio

Av. da Praia Grande

Penha Hill

Maritime Museum

Templo de A-Ma

Av. da República

Pousada de São Tiago

Macau Tower

San Van Bridge

Macau-Taipa Bridge

0 ———— 1/4 mile
0 ———— 1/4 kilometer

TO TAIPA & COLOANE
↓

MACAU

TAIPA

See Taipa map

the ruins are a primary tourist attraction, with snack bars and antiques and other shops at the foot of the site.

Behind the facade of São Paulo is the **Museum of Sacred Art and Crypt** (☎ *No phone* ☜ *Free* ☉ *Daily 9–6*), which holds statues, crucifixes, and the bones of Japanese and Vietnamese martyrs. There are also some intriguing Asian interpretations of Christian images, including samurai angels and a Chinese Virgin and child.

The **Templo de Na Tcha** is a small Chinese temple built in 1888, during the Macauan plague. The hope was that Na Tcha Temple would appeal to a mythical Chinese character who granted wishes and could save lives. The **Troco das Antigas Muralhas de Defesa** (Section of the Old City Walls) is all that remains of Macau's original defensive barrier, and borders the left side of the Na Tcha Temple. These crumbling yellow walls were built in 1569 and illustrate the durability of *chunambo,* a local material made from compacted layers of clay, soil, sand, straw, crushed rocks, and oyster shells. ⊠ *Top end of Rua de São Paulo, Downtown* ☎ *853/8399–6699* ☉ *Daily 8–5.*

Fodor's Choice ★ **Templo de A-Ma** *(A-Ma Temple).* Thought to be Macau's oldest building, this temple, properly Ma Kok Temple but known to locals as simply A-Ma, is also one of Macau's most picturesque. The structure has its origins in the Ming Dynasty (1368–1644), and was influenced by Confucianism, Taoism, and Buddhism, as well as local religions. Vivid-red calligraphy on large boulders tells the story of the goddess A-Ma (also known as Tin Hau), the patron of fishermen. A small gate opens onto prayer halls, pavilions, and caves carved directly into the hillside. ⊠ *Rua de São Tiago da Barra, Largo da Barra, Downtown* ☉ *Daily 7–6.*

Templo de Sam Kai Vui Kun. Built in 1750, this temple is dedicated to Kuan Tai, the bearded, fierce-looking god of war and wealth in Chinese mythology. Statues of him and his two sons sit on an altar. A steady stream of people come to pray and ask for support before they go wage battle in the casinos. May and June see festivals throughout Macau honoring Kuan Tai. ⊠ *Rua Sui do Mercado de São Domingos, Downtown* ☉ *Daily 8–6.*

SQUARE THINGS UP

Largo de Santo Agostinho. Built in the image of traditional Portuguese squares, *St. Augustine Square* is paved with black-and-white tiles laid out in mosaic wave patterns and lined with leafy overhanging trees and lots of wooden benches. It's easy to feel as if you're in a European village, far from South China.

One of the square's main structures is the **Teatro Dom Pedro V** (⊠ *Calçada do Teatro, Downtown* ☎ *No phone*), a European-style theater with an inviting green-and-white facade built in 1859. It's an important cultural landmark for Macanese and was regularly used until World War II, when it fell into disrepair. It was renovated in 1993 by the Orient Foundation, and the 300-seat venue once again hosts concerts and recitals—especially during the annual Macau International Music Festival—as well as important public events, which is the only time you

A BIT OF HISTORY

Macau's current economic surge mirrors a long history of ebb and flow. When trading began through the Silk Road, farmers from Guangdong and Fujian settled in the area. By 1557, the Portuguese had taken Macau and made it the first European colony in East Asia. Macau was known as "A Ma Gao" in honor of the patron goddess of sailors, A-Ma. The Portuguese adapted this Chinese name to "Macau," and for more than a century, the port thrived as the main intermediary in the trade between Asia and the rest of the world. Ships from Italy, Portugal, and Spain came here to buy and sell Chinese silks and tea, Japanese crafts, Indian spices, African ivory, and Brazilian gold.

In addition to international trade, Macau became an outpost for western religions. St Francis Xavier successfully converted large numbers of Japanese and Chinese to Christianity and used Macau as a base of operations. In the 1500s and 1600s, many churches were built, including an ambitious Christian college. Today in Macau, this religious legacy can be seen in the array of well-preserved churches.

Macau's age of prosperity ended in the 1800s, when the Dutch and British gained control of most trading routes to East Asia. After the British victory over China in the 1814 Opium War, the huge, deep-water port of Hong Kong was established, and Macau was relegated to a quiet, sleepy port town. Macau did, however, remain important to Chinese refugees of World War I and World War II and the Cultural Revolution. With the widespread introduction of legalized gambling in the 1960s, Macau became a freewheeling place, where gambling, espionage, and crime reigned in the long shadow of modern, wealthy Hong Kong.

Today, textile, furniture, electronics, and other exports join a world-class tourism industry (numbers are expected to surpass even Hong Kong's in less than five years) in making Macau prosperous. Just before the 1999 handover to the Chinese government, the Portuguese administration launched a staggering number of public works. A huge international airport was built on a reclaimed island, and two new bridges were built to connect Macau's two islands. These years also saw the construction of two artificial lakes in the Outer Harbour along the Praia Grande.

Yet another phase of development is under way to transform Macau into a location of choice for casinos and luxury resorts.

can go inside. It does, however, have a garden that's open daily 10 AM to 11 PM, and admission is free.

Igreja de Santo Agostinho (*St. Augustine's Church;* ⊠*Largo de Santo Agostinho, Downtown* ☎*No phone* ☉*Daily 10–6*) dates from 1814 and has a grand, weathered exterior and a drafty interior with a high wood-beam ceiling. There's a magnificent stone altar with a statue of Christ on his knees, bearing the cross, with small crucifixes in silhouette on the hill behind him. The statue, called *Our Lord of Passos*, is carried in a procession through the streets of downtown on the first day of Lent.

Fodor'sChoice **Largo do Senado.** The charming Senado Square, Macau's hub for cen-
★ turies, is lined with neoclassical-style colonial buildings painted bright
pastels. Only pedestrians are allowed on its shiny black-and-white tiles,
and the alleys off it are packed with restaurants and shops. Take your
time wandering. There are plenty of benches on which to rest after
shopping and sightseeing. Come back at night, when locals of all ages
gather to chat and the square is beautifully lit.

The magnificent yellow **Igreja de São Domingos** (St. Dominic's Church;
⊠ *Largo de São Domingos, Downtown* ☎*No phone* ⊙*Daily 8–6*)
beckons you to take a closer look. After a restoration in 1997, it's
again among Macau's most beautiful churches, with a cream-and-white
interior that takes on a heavenly golden glow when illuminated for services. The church was originally a convent founded by Spanish Domini-
can friars in 1587. In 1822, China's first Portuguese newspaper, *The
China Bee,* was published here. The church became a repository for
sacred art in 1834 when convents were banned in Portugal.

It's hard to ignore the imposing white facade of **Santa Casa da Misericordia**
(⊠*2 Travessa da Misericordia* ☎*853/2857–3938 or 853/8399–6699*
⊠*MOP$5* ⊙*Mon.–Sat. 10–1 and 2–5:30*). Founded in 1569 by Dom
Belchior, Macau's first bishop, the Holy House of Mercy is the China
coast's oldest Christian charity, and it continues to take care of the
poor with soup kitchens and health clinics, as well as providing housing for the elderly. The exterior is neoclassical, but the interior is done
in a contrasting opulent, modern style. A reception room on the second
floor contains paintings of benefactress Marta Merop.

The neoclassical **Edifício do Leal Senado** (*Senate Building;* ⊠*163 Av. de
Almeida Ribeiro, Downtown* ☎*853/2833–7676* ⊠*Free* ⊙*Tues.–Sun.
9–9*) was built in 1784 as a municipal chamber and continues to be
used by the government today. An elegant meeting room on the first
floor opens onto a magnificent library based on one in the Mafra Convent in Portugal, with books neatly stacked on two levels of shelves
reaching to the ceiling. Art and historical exhibitions are frequently
hosted in the beautiful foyer and garden.

■ NEED A
BREAK?

Not far off the main drag but somewhat hidden down an alleyway, **Margaret's Café e Nata** (⊠*Rua Comandante Mata e Oliveira, Downtown*
☎*853/2871–0032*) offers a cool place to sit, outside under fans and
awnings, with some of the best custard tarts in town, plus fresh juices,
homemade tea blends, and pizza slices.

Look for the small cow sign marking the out-of-the-ordinary **Leitaria i Son**
(⊠*Largo do Senado 7, Downtown* ☎*853/2857–3638*) milk bar. The decor is
cafeteria-style and spartan, but the bar whips up frothy glasses of fresh milk
from its dairy and blends them with all manner of juices: papaya, coconut,
apricot, and more.

READY, SET, GO!

Grand Prix racing, which began in Macau in 1953, is the region's most glamorous annual sporting event. During the third or fourth weekend of November, the city is pierced with the sound of supercharged engines testing the 6-km (4-mi) Guia Circuit, which follows city roads along the Outer Harbour to Guia Hill and around the reservoir. The route is as challenging as that of Monaco, with rapid gear changes demanded at the right-angle Statue Corner, the Doña Maria bend, and the Melco hairpin. Cars achieve speeds of 224 kph (140 mph) on the straightaways, with the lap record approaching two minutes, 20 seconds. The premier event is the Formula Three Championship, with cars competing from around the world in what's now the official World Cup of Formula Three. Winners qualify for Formula One licenses. There are also races for motorcycles and production cars. If you plan to travel during this time, beware of the logistical disruption it causes, including rerouting of main roads and lack of hotel vacancies.

IMMERSE YOURSELF IN CULTURE

Grand Prix Museum. Inaugurated in 1993 to celebrate the 40th anniversary of the Macau Grand Prix and renovated 10 years later, this museum tells the stories of the best drivers from every year, but the highlights are the actual race cars on display. More than 20 Formula vehicles are exhibited in the hall, of which the centerpiece is the red-and-white Formula Three car driven by the late champion Aryton Senna. ✉ *431 Rua Luis Gonzaga Gomes, Downtown* ☎ *853/8798–4108* 🎟 *MOP$10, MOP$20 with Wine Museum* 🕙 *Wed.–Mon. 10–6.*

Heritage Exhibition of a Traditional Pawn Shop. This impressive re-creation documents the important role that pawnshops have played in Macau for hundreds of years. ✉ *396 Av. Almeida Ribeiro, Downtown* ☎ *No phone* 🎟 *MOP$5* 🕙 *Daily 10:30–7; closed 1st Mon. of month.*

Macao Museum of Art. The large boxy museum is as well known for its curving, rectangular framed roof as it is for its calligraphy, painting, copperware, and international film collections. It's Macau's only art museum and has five floors of eastern and western works, as well as important examples of ancient indigenous pottery found at Hác-Sá Beach. While you're there, check out the program for the rest of the **Macao Cultural Centre** (☎ *853/2870–0699* ⊕ *www.ccm.gov.mo*), which often hosts edgy music bands and theater troupes, in addition to the classic performances. ✉ *Macao Cultural Centre, Av. Xian Xing Hai, Outer Harbour* ☎ *853/8791–9814 or 853/8791–9800* ⊕*www.artmuseum. gov.mo* 🎟 *MOP$5 (free Sun.)* 🕙 *Tues.–Sun. 10–7.*

Maritime Museum. Across from the A-Ma temple, this museum is a great place to spend an interesting hour brushing up on seafaring history. The handsome white building looks like a ship, thanks to jutting white slats and porthole windows. A row of fountains out front soothes you almost as much as the calm, cool interior. Multimedia exhibits cover fishermen, merchants, and explorers from Portugal, South China, and Japan. Look

8

for compasses, telescopes, and sections of ships. There's even a small aquarium gallery with local sea life. Try your hand at astronomic navigation—which sailors have used for thousands of years—by looking up at the top floor's nifty celestial dome ceiling. ⊠ *1 Largo do Pagode da Barra, Inner Harbour* ☎ *853/2859–5481* ⊕ *www.museu maritimo.gov.mo* ✉ *MOP$10 (MOP$5 Sun.)* ⊗ *Wed.–Mon. 10–5:30.*

Quartel dos Mouros. The elegant yellow-and-white building with Moorish architectural influences built onto a slope of Barra Hill is the Moorish Barracks. It now houses the Macau Maritime Administration but was originally constructed in 1874 for Indian police regimens brought into the region, a reminder of Macau's historic relationship with the Indian city of Goa. The Barracks are not open to the public but visitors can tour the ornamented veranda. ⊠ *Barra Hill, Inner Harbour* ☎ *853/8399–6699* ✉ *Free* ⊗ *Veranda open 24 hours.*

Wine Museum. In the same building as the Grand Prix Museum, this museum has more than 1,100 wines on display; some are almost 200 years old. You'll learn about production techniques and the importance of *vinho* (wine) in Portuguese culture. More than 50 varieties are on hand for impromptu tastings. ⊠ *431 Rua Luis Gonzaga Gomes, Downtown* ☎ *853/8798–4109* ✉ *MOP$15, MOP$20 with Grand Prix Museum* ⊗ *Wed.–Mon., 10–6.*

DO SOME GARDENING

Camões Garden. Macau's most popular park is frequented from dawn to dusk by tai chi enthusiasts, lovers, students, and men huddled over Chinese chessboards with their caged songbirds nearby. The gardens, which were developed in the 18th century, are named after Luís de Camões, Portugal's greatest poet, who was banished to Macau for several years during the 16th century. A rocky niche shelters a bronze bust of the poet in the park's most famous and picturesque spot, Camões Grotto. At the grotto's entrance a bronze sculpture honors the friendship between Portugal and China. A wall of stone slabs is inscribed with poems by various contemporary writers, praising Camões and Macau.

Alongside Camões Garden is a smaller park, the **Casa Garden** (☎ *853/2855–4699* ✉ *Free* ⊗ *Weekdays 10–12:30 and 3–5:30*), originally the grounds of a merchant's estate. Today, the estate's villa, which was built in 1770, is the headquarters for the Orient Foundation, a private institution involved in community, cultural, and arts affairs. The grounds are lovingly landscaped with a variety of flora and bordered with a brick pathway. There's also a central pond stocked with

---

DISCOUNT PASS

To make Macau's museums more accessible, the Macau Government Tourist Office (MGTO) offers the Macau Museum Pass, which entitles you to a single entry into all of the following: the Grand Prix Museum, Lin Zexu Memorial Museum, Maritime Museum, Museum of Art, Museum of Macau, and Wine Museum. The five-day pass is MOP$25, and can be purchased at the MGTO or any at any participating museum.

lily pads and lotus flowers. ✉*13 Praça Luis de Camões, Downtown* ⏱*Daily 6 am–10 pm.*

Lou Lim Ieoc Gardens. These beautiful gardens were built in the 19th century by a Chinese merchant named Lou Kau. Rock formations, water, vegetation, pavilions, and sunlight were all carefully considered when planning this garden. Balanced landscapes are the hallmark of Suzhou garden style. The government took possession and restored the grounds in the late 1970s so that today you can enjoy tranquil walks among delicate flowering bushes framed with bamboo groves and artificial hills. A large auditorium frequently hosts concerts and other events, most notably recitals during the annual Macau International Music Festival. Adjacent to the gardens, a European-style edifice contains the **Macau Tea Culture House** (✉*10 Estrada de Adolfo Loureiro, Downtown* ☎*853/2882–7103* ✉*Free* ⏱*Tues.–Sun. 9–7),* a small museum with exhibits on the tea culture of Macau and China. ✉*Estrada de Adolfo Loureiro, at Av. do Conselheiro Ferreira de Almeida, Downtown* ✉*MOP$1 (free Fri.)* ⏱*Daily 8–6.*

BE AMUSED

★ **Macau Canidrome.** Asia's only greyhound track looks rundown and quaint compared to the bigger jockey club and glitzy casinos, but it offers a true taste of Macau in a more popular neighborhood near the China border crossing. The Canidrome opened in 1932 and tends to attract a steady crowd of older gamblers several times a week for the slower-pace, lower-stakes gambling rush of betting on fast dogs chasing an electronic rabbit. Check out the parade of race dogs before each race. You can sit on benches in the open-air stadium, at tables in the air-conditioned restaurant, or in an upstairs box seat. ✉*Av. do Artur Tamagnini Barbosa, at Av. General Castelo Branco, Downtown* ☎*853/2833–3399, 853/2826–1188 to place bets* ⊕*www.macauyydog. com* ✉*Public stands MOP$10, private boxes MOP$120* ⏱*Mon., Thurs., and weekends 6 PM–11 PM; first race at 7:30.*

8

☾ **Macau Fisherman's Wharf.** More of a distraction than an amusement park, this developing complex of minor attractions nonetheless has an old-world decadence. Its centerpiece is the Roman Amphitheatre, which hosts outdoor performances, but its main draws are the lively themed restaurants on the west side, such as AfriKana B.B.Q and Camões. Across from the toylike Babylon Casino, the Rocks Hotel heralds a series of themed accommodations to come. Children's rides and games, on the east end, include a role-playing war game and an underground video-game arcade. Come for the food, and stay after dark, as the Fisherman's Wharf is even more active at night. ✉*Av. da Amizade, at Av. Dr. Sun Yat-Sen, Downtown* ☎*853/8299–3300* ⊕*www.fishermanswharf.com.mo* ✉*Admission free, rides and games MOP$20–MOP$200* ⏱*Open 24 hours.*

Fodor'sChoice **Macau Tower Convention & Entertainment Centre.** Rising 1,000 feet above
★ the peaceful San Van Lake, the world's 10th-largest freestanding tower recalls a similar structure in Auckland. And it should, as both were designed by New Zealand architect Gordon Moller. The Macau Tower

offers a variety of thrills, including the Mast Climb, which challenges the daring and strong of heart and body with a two-hour climb on steel rungs 344 feet up the tower's mast for incomparable views of Macau and China. Other thrills include the Skywalk, an open-air stroll around the tower's exterior—without handrails; the SkyJump, an assisted, decelerated 765-foot descent; and the classic bungee jump. Prices range from MOP$388 for the Skywalk to MOP$1,688 for the Mast Climb, with extra charges for photos. More subdued attractions inside the tower are a mainstream movie theater and a revolving lunch and dinner buffet at the 360 Café. ⊠ *Largo da Torre de Macau, Downtown* ☎*853/8988–8656* ⊕*www.macautower.com.mo.*

TAIPA ISLAND

The island directly south of peninsular Macau was once two small islands that were, over time, joined by deposits from the Pearl River Delta. It's connected to peninsular Macau by three long bridges. The region's two universities, horse-racing track, scenic hiking trails, and its international airport are all here.

Like downtown Macau, Taipa has been greatly developed in the past few years, yet it retains a visual balance between old Macau charm and modern sleekness. Try to visit on a weekend so you can shop for clothing and crafts in the traditional flea market that's held every Sunday from morning to evening in Taipa Village.

LIVE THE VILLAGE LIFE

FodorsChoice
★

Taipa Village. Its narrow, winding streets are packed with restaurants, bakeries, shops, temples, and other buildings with traditional South Chinese and Portuguese design elements. The aptly named Rua do Cunha (Food Street) has many great Chinese, Macanese, Portuguese, and Thai restaurants. Several shops sell homemade Macanese snacks, including steamed milk pudding, almond cakes, beef jerky, and coconut candy.

Atop a small hill overlooking Taipa Village, the beautiful **Carmel Gardens** (⊠*Rua da Cunha , Taipa* ☒*Free* ⊗ *Wed.–Mon. 10–6*) have a number of palm trees that provide great shade. Within the garden stands the brilliant white-and-yellow Nossa Senhora do Carmo (Church of Our Lady of Carmel), built in 1885 and featuring a handsome single-belfry tower. Paths lead down from the Carmel Gardens to the **Taipa House Museums** (⊠*Av. da Praia, Carmo Zone* ☎*853/2882–7103* ☒*MOP$5 [free Sun.]* ⊗*Tues.–Sun. 10–6*). These five sea-green houses were originally residences of wealthy local merchants and were converted into small museums and exhibition spaces. They were all fully restored shortly before the Macau handover and are interesting examples of Porto-Chinese architecture. Official receptions are often held here as are changing art exhibitions. The Venetian Casino and the Cotai complex construction block a once marvelous view of Coloane and the South China Sea.

VEGETATE

Po Tai Un Buddhist Monastery. The region's largest temple is part of a functioning monastery with several dozen monks. The classically designed structure has an ornate main prayer hall and central pavilions with sculptures, fish ponds, and banyan trees. Monks tend the vegetable plots that supply the popular on-site vegetarian restaurant. The monastery is next to the Macau Jockey Club and nearby the Four Faces Buddha statue. ⊠ *Estrada Almirante Marques Esparteiro, Taipa* ☎ *853/2881–1007* ⬚ *Free* ⊘ *Daily noon–6.*

HORSE AROUND

Macau Jockey Club. After Dr. Stanley Ho bought the Macau Jockey Club (MJC) in 1991, he transformed what was a quiet trotting track into a lucrative high-stakes racing facility. However horse racing is now a more retro gambling option in Asia's rising casino mecca of Macau, and the local MJC pales in comparison to the truly world-class Hong Kong Jockey Club. Nonetheless the MJC continues to operate year-round, hosting an average of 100 races and entertaining a majority of local middle-aged men, as well as some younger, more curious spectators who come to see the horses close up in between races (every 30 minutes). If you're game, you can place bets at a number of stations throughout Macau and Hong Kong, as well as by phone and on the Internet. ⊠ *Estrada Governador Albano de Oliveira, Taipa* ☎ *853/2882–0868* ⊕ *www.macauhorse.com* ⬚ *Grandstand seating MOP$20.*

HEAD FOR THE HILLS

Whether you prefer a leisurely walk though a park or conquering steep hills on foot or by bike, Taipa Island has the region's best trails. The rewards for heading up Taipa Grande and Taipa Pequena, the island's two largest hills, are majestic views. The Taipa Grande trail starts at Estrada Colonel Nicolau de Mesquita, near the United Chinese Cemetery. The Taipa Pequena trail starts at Estrada Lou Lim Ieoc (Lou Lim Ieoc Gardens) behind the Regency Hotel. Be sure to wear rugged hiking shoes, use bug repellent, and, if possible, bring a mobile phone for emergency calls. The most popular place to rent bicycles is the shop at the bus stop outside the Civic and Municipal Affairs Bureau in Taipa Village on Largo Camões, where you can also find trail maps.

COLOANE ISLAND

Centuries ago, Coloane was a wild place, where pirates hid in rocky caves and coves, awaiting their chance to strike at cargo ships on the Pearl River. Early in the 20th century, the local government sponsored a huge planting program to transform Coloane from a barren place to a green one. The results were spectacular—and enduring. Today this island is idyllic, with green hills and clean sandy beaches.

Once connected to Taipa Island by a thin isthmus, Coloane is now almost completely fused with Taipa via the huge Cotai reclaimed land project, where the "Strip" is being constructed and scheduled for completion by 2010. Regardless of the recent development boom, Coloane

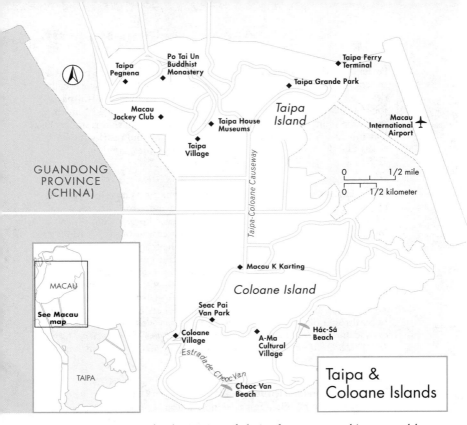

Taipa &
Coloane Islands

remains the destination of choice for anyone seeking natural beauty and tranquility.

WANDER THE TOWN

★ **Coloane Village.** Quiet, relaxed Coloane Village is home to traditional Mediterranean-style houses painted in pastels, as well as the baroque-style Chapel of St. Francis Xavier and the Taoist Tam Kung Temple. The surrounding small narrow alleys have surprises at every turn; among many things you may encounter are fishermen repairing their junks or a local baptism at the chapel.

The village's heart is a small square around a fountain with a bronze Cupid. The surrounding Macanese and Chinese open-air restaurants are among the region's best; some are the unheralded favorites of chefs visiting from Hong Kong and elsewhere in Asia.

PARK IT

A-Ma Cultural Village. A path just south of Seac Pai Van Park leads to A-Ma Cultural Village, a huge complex built in a traditional Qing Dynasty style. It pays homage to Macau's namesake, the goddess of the sea. The vibrancy and color of the details in the bell and drum towers, the tiled roofs, and the carved marble altars are truly awe-inspiring. It's as if you've been transported back to the height of the Qing Empire and

Fodor'sChoice

can now see temples in their true state of greatness. Other remarkable details include the striking rows of stairs leading to Tian Hou Palace at the entrance. Each row features painstakingly detailed marble and stone carvings of auspicious Chinese symbols: a roaring tiger, double lions, five cranes, the double phoenix, and a splendid imperial dragon. The grounds here also have a recreational fishing zone and an arboretum with more than 100 species of local and exotic flora.

Behind A-Ma Cultural Village is the 560-foot-tall **Coloane Hill**, crowned by a gleaming white-marble statue of A-Ma (commemorating the year of Macau's handover), soaring 65 feet and visible from miles away. You can make the short hike up to the top or take one of the shuttle buses that leave from the foot of the hill every 30 minutes. ⊠ *Off Estrada de Seac Pai Van Coloane Island South* ⊗ *Daily 8–6.*

> ### ASIA'S VEGAS
>
> Sheldon Anderson, CEO of the Las Vegas Sands, is spearheading a $13 billion venture to transform the Cotai area into "Asia's Las Vegas." The huge Venetian Macao-Resort-Hotel has already made its mark—and check out the list of development partners: Hilton, Conrad, Four Seasons, Sheraton, St. Regis, Shangri-La, Mandarin Oriental. In 2010 the Cotai area will have more than 20 luxury properties; more than 6,000 gaming tables; 29,000 hotel rooms; and 4,000,000 square feet of retail space.

☺ **Seac Pai Van Park** *(Coloane Park)*. This large park has extensive gardens, ponds, and waterfalls, and a large walk-in aviary with more than 200 bird species chirping and flying about. There are lots of things of interest to children, including playgrounds, a mini zoo, and an interactive museum with exhibits on nature and agriculture. ⊠ *Off Estrada de Seac Pai Van, Coloane Island West* ⊗ *Daily 8–6.*

Macau Kartodromoartodromo. Race enthusiasts and thrill-seekers alike should head to the Macau Motor Sports Club, opposite Coloane Park, the only go-kart track in both Macau and Hong Kong. Drivers must be at least 16 years old, as 200-cc-engine go-karts can speed up to 50 kmph on the 1.2 km-long, 10 meter-wide track with 10 challenging curves. Aim for a lap time under 50 seconds on a sunny day. ⊠ *Estrada de Seac Pai Van, Coloane Island West* ☎ 853/2888–2126 ⊠ *MOP$180 for 15 mins* ⊗ *Weekdays 11:30–7, weekends 10:30–8.*

WORSHIP THE SUN

Hác-Sá Beach and Cheoc Van Beach are Macau's two most accessible beaches and are usually crowded on the weekends.

Cheoc Van Beach. Perfect for romantic walks, this beach is in a sheltered cove with a nice seafood restaurant to one side, the Marine Club with kayak rentals on the other side, and a charming pousada (historic inn) overlooking the ocean. Be warned that there are lots of stray, though generally friendly, dogs on this beach. ⊠ *Off Estrada de Cheoc Van, Coloane Island South* ⊗ *Open 24 hours.*

Ⓒ **Hác-Sá.** Translated from the Chinese, hác-sá means "black sand," although the sands of the area's biggest beach are actually a deep gray. Playgrounds, picnic areas, and restaurants are all within walking distance. Even if you don't stay at the resident five-star Westin Resort, you can use the public sports complex, which is equipped with an Olympic-size swimming pool, tennis courts, and other sports facilities, for a fee. Also nearby is the Hác-Sá Reservoir BBQ park with picnic and barbecue facilities, boat rentals, and water-sports outfitters. ⊠ *Off Estrada de Hác Sá, Coloane Island South* ☺ *Open 24 hours.*

CASINOS

In February 2006, Macau surpassed Las Vegas in gambling revenue. By June 2008, Macau's casinos were turning over 2.6 times the revenue of their Vegas Strip counterparts. Small wonder that international casino groups have swarmed the region, and they continue to drive Macau's explosive double-digit growth.

From the late 1960s until 2001, Macau native Dr. Stanley Ho owned all the casinos, helping him to become one of the world's wealthiest people. One of the first steps the Chinese government took after the 1999 handover was to break up Dr. Ho's monopoly and award casino licenses to several consortiums from Las Vegas. The grand plan to transform Macau from a quiet town that offered gambling into one of the world's top gaming destinations is well underway.

THE SCENE

Gambling is lightly regulated, so there are only a few things to remember. No one under age 18 is allowed into casinos. Most casinos use Hong Kong dollars in their gaming and not Macau patacas, but you can easily exchange currencies at cashiers. High- and no-limit VIP rooms are available on request, where minimum bets range from HK$50,000 to HK$100,000 per hand. You can get cash from credit cards and ATMs 24 hours a day, and every casino has a program to extend additional credit to frequent visitors. Most casinos don't have strict dress codes outside of their VIP rooms, but men are better off not wearing shorts or sleeveless shirts. Minimum bets for most tables are higher than those in Las Vegas, but there are lower limits for slots and video gambling.

The players here may not look sophisticated, but don't be fooled. Chinese men and women have long embraced gambling, so many of Macau's gamblers are truly hard-core. Average bets are in the hundreds per hand, and many people gamble until they're completely exhausted or completely broke, usually the latter.

Macau is also famous for gambling's sister industries of pawnshops, loan sharks, seedy saunas, and prostitution. This underbelly is hidden, though. You won't encounter such things unless you seek them out.

THE GAMES

Macau's casinos are geared to Asian gamblers, so most tables are dedicated to baccarat and Asian dice games. In the past, there were few poker or roulette tables, though newer casinos such as the Galaxy, Venetian, MGM Grand, and Wynn are introducing more of these western games to the market. Similarly, slot machines, though rising in number, remain much less frequented than baccarat, the king of the Macau gambling scene.

Baccarat is by far the most popular game for Asian gamblers, so most casinos devote the majority of their floors to baccarat tables. Many Chinese gamblers believe that this is the fairest game, so they tend to make larger bets on it. You can bet on four items: the player's hand, the banker's hand, tie hand, and pair. Macau rules stipulate that you can't take the house, and there are maximum payouts, but you'll still see the biggest crowds and hear the loudest stirrings from the baccarat tables.

Big and Small (Dai-Siu) is a game based on guessing values of three dice under a covered glass canister. You can bet on values, number combinations, and most commonly, "big" value or "small" value. Hear the collective groan when three-of-a-kind turns up, and the house takes all.

Fan-tan is an ancient Chinese game largely unknown in the West. The croupier (counter) plunges an inverted silver cup into a pile of porcelain buttons on the table. He then moves the cup containing a number of buttons to one side. The trick is to guess correctly how many buttons will be left, once they are counted off in groups of four. Cash bets are placed on the table on the numerals one, two, three, or four; odds or evens; or divisions between numbers (called "corners"). This game is becoming less and less popular, though the Lisboa and Sands still have a few tables.

Pacapio is basically a Chinese version of keno. Tickets are printed with 80 Chinese characters and you select 10 characters to bet on from a computerized draw of 20 characters. There are six locations for Pacapio betting, with the most popular one being the Lisboa Betting Centre. The game operates from 10 AM to 2 AM.

Pai kao has been a popular Chinese game since the 19th century. It's played with dominoes and a revolving banker system where one player assumes the role of the house, while the casino gets a percentage of all bets. The rules are relatively complicated, and the game is offered at the Lisboa and a few other casinos.

Roulette is played using the European wheel with a single "0," giving you a slightly better chance of winning over the American wheel with both a "0" and a "00" slot. Some casinos even offer a simplified picture version, with relatively better odds. In general, roulette isn't as popular as the dice and card games, but you can still find a few live tables plus a handful of electronic tables in the larger casinos.

8

THE CASINOS

Gone are the days of Macau's dark and dingy underground gaming parlors. One is no longer bound by Stanley Ho's iron grip on the gambling scene and there's now an emerging dreamland of opportunity for the bigwigs of Las Vegas to move in and spice up the competition. Over the past few years, American-style casinos have been mushrooming like mad, primarily in Macau's NAPE (zona Nova de Aterros do Porto Exterior), or New Reclamation Area, in the Outer Harbour district between the main ferry terminal and the historic center.

But you don't have to be a hardcore gambler to enjoy browsing the glittering premises. While Dr. Ho has fought back sportingly, renovating older properties, partnering, and launching entirely new ones (e.g., the Grand Lisboa), it's the foreign exports that are most likely to please both casual tourists and serious players for their variety of gaming and other entertainment, relatively clean, well-lit atmosphere, free 24/7 accessibility, and overall glamour-resort experience. Homegrown newbie Ponte 16, however, is the one to watch.

MACAU OR MACAO?

According to the Portuguese, their heralded five-centuries-old colony is spelled "Macau," and the Macau Government Tourist Office has since adopted this spelling. However, the anglicized "Macao" is still used in some (usually) English names and titles, even within the local government.

So why is it Wynn Macau and Venetian Macao? Just as you say "tom-ay-to" and I say "tom-ah-to"—in the private sector, anything goes. Nonetheless, most new ventures here have reverted to the source: Macau.

THE PENINSULA

Casino Lisboa. Welcome to the casino that started it all. First opened in 1965 by Dr. Stanley Ho, this iconic Macau gaming den is replete with ancient jade ships in the halls, gold gilded staircases, and more baccarat tables than you can shake a craps stick at. It's great for a few rounds of HK$50 dai-siu—dice bets over cups of iced green tea. Most of the gamblers are from neighboring Guangdong province, and Cantonese is the lingua franca. Other popular pastimes at this storied casino revolve around international fine-dining venues and colorful coffee shops, if you care to wander around a maze of marbled floors and low ceilings. Make the Old Lisboa your first casino stop in Macau to get a perspective on how far this city has come since 2004, when the Sands Macao jump-started "Asia's Las Vegas." ⊠ *Av. de Lisboa, Downtown* ☎ *853/2837–5111* ⊕ *www.hotelisboa.com.*

Galaxy StarWorld. As you enter the StarWorld empire, you're greeted by tall girls in high heels, while a mariachi band serenades you from across the lobby. Up the escalator, locals typically lay it all down for baccarat, but the upstairs stud poker tables are also picking up momentum. The gaming floors are small and have a couple Chinese-style diners if you get peckish, but the cool Whisky Bar (⇨ *After Dark*) **on the 16th floor of the adjacent hotel** is an atmospheric place to either begin or wind down your evening. Opened in 2006, the neon-blue Galaxy StarWorld building is just across from the Wynn and down the block from the MGM Grand. Ironically, its live lobby entertainment and local holiday attractions bring the establishment down to earth for a kitschy, friendly feel. ✉ *Av. da Amizade, Downtown* ☎ *853/2838–3838* ⊕ *www.galaxy entertainment.com.*

Grand Lisboa. Meet the veteran Casino Lisboa's younger, more spectacular sister. Opened in February 2007 by Dr. Stanley Ho, this casino has taken Macau by storm with its giant disco ball–like orb, the "precious pearl" at the base of a spouting lotus tower of glitz. With over 300 tables and about 500 slot machines, the Grand Lisboa's main gaming floor is anchored with a glowing egg statue and a leggy Paris cabaret show every 15 minutes. For more serious spectators, the one-hour, HK$380 "Tokyo Nights" show entertains six times a day in a separate theater. The second floor features craps and sports betting and has a great bar. True to Lisboa tradition, the Grand also has a variety of dining choices, from the baroque Don Alfonso Macau 1890 to the Round the Clock Coffee Shop and a deli between the first and second gaming floors. ✉ *2–4 Av. de Lisboa, Downtown* ☎ *853/2838–5111* ⊕ *www. grandlisboa.com.*

★ **MGM Grand.** Opened in December 2007, the MGM Grand is a stylish addition to Macau's gambling scene. The lavish lounges, Dale Chihuly glass sculptures, Portuguese-inspired architecture, and fine dining of the 1,088 square meter Grande Praça arcade add to the gaming ambience. The gambling floor itself is popular with high rollers from Hong Kong, including business tycoons who are just in for a few days. One of the main owners, Pansy Ho (like her brother Lawrence Ho), is often cast as the product of her father, the "gambling godfather," Dr. Stanley Ho, but is a high-octane business professional in her own right. The glitz-and-glam energy and high-society appeal are evidence that this is the only casino in Macau with a woman's classy touch. ✉ *Av. Dr. Sun Yat Sen, Downtown* ☎ *853/8802–8888* ⊕ *www.mgmgrandmacau.com.*

Ponte 16. In the swinging seaside days of the 1950s, Macau's western port, or Ponte 16, is where all the action took place. When the eastern port opened in the mid-1960s, this area of the Macau peninsula fell into decay. The 2008 phase-one opening of Ponte 16 changed all that. Taking its cue from the good old days, Ponte 16's winning combination is gorgeous views of the Inner Harbour, with 105 gaming tables and 300 modern slot machines. Popular with Hong Kong and Taiwanese pop stars, the Macanese-owned Ponte 16 is also gaining ground with mainland mass-market gamblers and VIPs from Beijing and Shanghai. Probably because of the casino's relatively isolated location, the atmosphere tends to be casual, but that doesn't limit the minimum bet amounts on the floor. Besides, a new shopping arcade is due to replace the crumbling buildings across the street by 2009, so Ponte 16 can be credited for breathing new life into this legendary Latin Quarter. ✉ *4th fl., Rua do Visconde Paço de Arcos, Inner Harbour* ☎ *853/8861–8888* ⊕ *www.ponte16.com.mo.*

8

Sands Macao Thanks to Paul Steelman's design, the Sands Macao has one of the largest parking entrances on earth. And, until its sibling, the Venetian, stole the spotlight, this casino was the largest on earth. It's the first casino you'll see on the peninsula even before debarking from the ferry. Past the sparkling 50-ton chandelier entrance, its grand gaming floor is anchored with a live cabaret stage above an open bar and under a giant screen. Several tiers are tastefully linked with escalators leading to the high-stakes tables upstairs, just outside the 888 Buffet and food court. Its relatively friendly atmosphere and location, just across from Fisherman's Wharf and near the bar street in NAPE, is well suited as a warm-up to your night out. ✉ *203 Largo de Monte Carlo, Downtown* ☎ *853/2888–3333* ⊕ *www.sands.com.mo.*

Wynn Macau. Listen for theme songs such as "Diamonds are Forever," "Luck Be a Lady" or "Money, Money" as you watch the Wynn's outdoor Performance Lake dazzle you with flames and fountain jets of whipping water, which entrance gamblers and tourists every 15 minutes from 11 AM to midnight. Inside the "open hand" structure of Steve Wynn's Macau resort, the indoor Rotunda Tree of Prosperity also wows guests with feng shui glitz. Opened in several stages beginning in 2006, the Wynn's expansive, brightly lit gaming floor, fine dining, buffet meals, luxury shops, deluxe spa, and trendy suites make it one of the more family-friendly resorts to visit. ✉ *Rua Cidade de Sintra, Downtown* ☎ *853/2888–9966* ⊕ *www.wynnmacau.com.*

TAIPA

★ **Crown Macau.** Touting itself as Macau's first "six-star" integrated resort, the Crown is indeed stellar. Its five swank, '70s style gaming floors are decked out in browns and taupes with mod-style chandeliers. Opened in May 2007, this is the only classy casino on the island of Taipa. Facing the glow of casinos to the north on the peninsula, the strength of the Crown casino rests in its abundant selection of game play, from baccarat to straight-up slots to posh VIP gaming rooms. Its VIP resort suites and fine-dining components Aurora and Kira (⇨ *Where to Eat*), not to mention the elegantly discreet Crystal Club on the roof with outdoor seating open 24 hours, add to the overall ambience. It is equidistant from the peninsula and Cotai. ✉ *Av. de Kwong Tung, Taipa* ☎ *853/2886–8888* ⊕ *www.crown-macau.com.*

COTAI

★ **Venetian Macao-Resort-Hotel.** The opening of the Venetian in August 2007 seriously upped the ante for even Vegas-style casinos in Macau. With 10.5 million square feet of space for gambling, shopping, eating, and sleeping, it is twice the size of its sister property in Las Vegas. The faux-Renaissance decoration, built-in canals plied by crooning gondoliers, live carnival acts, and upscale luxury brands are sheer spectacle, with more than a touch of pretension. The 550,000-square-foot gaming floor has some 3,000 slot machines and more than 750 tables of casino favorites. The sprawling property also includes 3,000 suites, a 15,000-seat arena, and Cirque du Soleil's ZAIA Theater. So it's no wonder the Venetian is the must-see megacomplex that everyone's talking about. ✉*Estrada da Baía de N. Senhora da Esperança, Cotai* ☎*853/2882–8888* ⊕*www.venetianmacao.com.*

WHERE TO EAT

Macau's medley of Portuguese and Cantonese cuisine—spicy and creamy Macanese interpretations of traditional Cantonese dishes such as baked prawns, braised abalone, and seafood stews—has made it one of Asia's top fine-dining destinations for decades.

Now, thanks to the spate of new casino-hotels, Macau has also become an exciting world-class culinary frontier. Case in point: one of Asia's only sake sommeliers can be found at the Wynn's Okada Japanese restaurant, Singapore's acclaimed Wine and Gourmet Asia exhibition was held at the Venetian at the end of 2007, and the Aux Beaux Arts brasserie at the MGM Grand is bringing French panache to rival Robuchon at the Lisboa.

Long-renowned restaurants such as Fernando's and Litoral are staying the course. So, too, are Cantonese restaurants like Chiu Chow and Fat Siu Lau, particularly well known among Hong Kong residents who travel to Macau just for dim sum, weekend brunches, and seafood feasts, in search of more affordable prices and higher-quality ingredients.

But Macau dining isn't all highbrow. Near the Largo do Senado, in the villages of Taipa or Coloane, wander the back alleys for *zhu-bao-bao,* a slap of fried pork on a toasted bun served with milk tea, or the signature *pasteis de nata* (custard tart): simple and delicious, and classic Macau.

8

PLANNING

Expect to shell out MOP$90 to MOP$150 per person per meal without wine, though you can always get a boiling broth with peperoncini (pickled banana peppers) at a hole-in-the-wall noodle shop for MOP$25–MOP$30. Budget MOP$500 per person for an unforgettable dinner.

Despite the surge in upscale dining accompanying casino development in Macau, the pace is still siesta style, with serious lunches lasting a few hours. The hotels serve breakfast early, but corner coffee shops start serving ham and cheese on croissants with espresso by around 11 AM. Cocktails begin at around 6:30 PM and dinner at around 8. However, when time is of the essence, Aurora at the Crown Towers, Aux Beaux Arts at the MGM Grand, and Morton's Steakhouse at the Venetian deliver high-quality meals with fast service.

A 10% service charge is added automatically, but, depending on the service quality, it's common for customers to round up the total. While major credit cards are accepted at most restaurants, cash is preferred at the smaller eateries.

DOWNTOWN MACAU

$$ ✕**Afonso III.** After four years at the Hyatt Regency, Chef Afonso Carrao
PORTUGUESE decided to open his own place and cook the way his grandmother did.
The result is his modest café in the heart of downtown near Senado
Square, with an intimate space downstairs of dark wood and stucco,
and a more expansive upstairs. The food consists of simple, hearty,
traditional dishes served in huge portions, mostly to Portuguese expa-
triates and Macanese locals. Favorites include Afonso's Cosido à Portu-
guesa (a tangy mix of meats and vegetables), on Fridays and Saturdays
only, and the thick vegetable soups, but your best bets are the daily
specials, which invariably include *bacalhau* (Portuguese salted codfish),
braised pork, or beef stew probably better than any other you'll taste in
Macau. The wine list is extensive and comes in generous goblets or by
the bottle. ⊠*11A Rua Central, Downtown* ☎*853/2858–6272* ▭*No
credit cards* ☉*Closed Sun.*

$$$$ ✕**Aux Beaux Arts.** Styled after a 1930s Parisian brasserie, the MGM
FRENCH Grand's Aux Beaux Arts is becoming one of the trendiest restaurants in
Macau. Chinese clients are particularly fond of its fresh, catch-of-the-day
seafood—the lobster is especially choice. So, too, are the French mains,
such as steak with potatoes au gratin. Oysters and caviar are also exclu-
sive, at prices reaching MOP$7,800 for 125 grams. In-house sommeliers
are at hand to pair the latest wines with dishes. The tan wood, private
booth, and even piazza deck tables are other draws. In fact, the decor is
as much old French Concession Shanghai as it is old Paris. Either way, it's
raising the bar for Macau's restaurant reputation. ⊠*MGM Grand, Av.
Dr. Sun Yat Sen, Downtown* ☎*853/8802–3888* ▭*AE, MC, V.*

$$$$ ✕**Chiu Chow.** This sumptuous restaurant in Macau serves Chiu Chow–
CHIU CHOW style cuisine from the northeast region of south China. Many Hong
Kong and Thai Chinese have roots in Chiu Chow and revere the
thick, strong soups, chicken in hot *chinjew* sauce (made from herbs
and peppercorns), rich and crispy oyster omelets, and whole braised
crab served here. The restaurant also serves top-quality shark's fin and
abalone soup, but be prepared to pay for it. ⊠ *Hotel Lisboa, Av. da
Amizade, Downtown* ☎*853/2837–7799* ▭*AE, MC, V.*

$$$ ✕**Clube Militar de Macau (The Macau Military Club).** Founded in 1870 as a
PORTUGUESE private military club, the stately pink-and-white structure was restored
in 1995 and reopened as a restaurant. The languid old-world atmosphere perfectly complements the extensive list of traditional Portuguese dishes offered, such as *bacalhau dourado* ("golden cod," a
specialty of fried cod and potatoes), African chicken, and *arroz de
marisco* (flavored rice and seafood). Be sure to leave room for dessert—the Portuguese platter includes almond cake, sponge cake, and
egg pudding, or go for warm chestnut tart or coconut ice cream with
caramelized pineapple. For those with less of a sweet tooth, try the
Portuguese cheddar cheese. ⊠*975 Av. da Praia Grande, Downtown*
☎*853/2871–4010* ▭*AE, MC, V.*

$$ ✕**Dom Galo.** "Quirky" springs to mind when describing the colorful
PORTUGUESE decor of Dom Galo, from plastic monkey puppets to funky chicken toys
Fodor's Choice hanging from the ceilings. Located near the MGM Grand, it draws a
★ wide clientele, from graphic designers to gambling-compliance lawyers

to 10-year-old Cantonese kids celebrating birthdays. The waitstaff is from the Philippines and the owner is Portuguese—which means service is usually spot-on. And the food is good: *insalada de polvo* (octopus salad), king prawns, and steak fries served with a tangy mushroom sauce. Pitchers of sangria are essential with any meal here. So, too, are reservations, as this place becomes increasingly popular with tourists. ✉ *Av. Sir Andars Ljung Stedt, Downtown* ☎ *853/2875–1383* 🖃 *MC, V*.

$$
CANTONESE
Fodor's Choice
★

✕ **Fat Siu Lau.** Well known to both locals and Hong Kong visitors, Fat Siu Lau has kept its customers coming back since 1903 with delicious Macanese favorites and modern creations. For best results, try ordering whatever you see the chatty Cantonese stuffing themselves with on the surrounding tables, and you won't be disappointed. It will probably be whole curry crab, grilled prawns in a butter garlic sauce, and the famous roasted pigeon marinated in a secret marinade. The newer Fat Siu Lau 2 is on Macau Lan Kwai Fong Street and offers the same great food. ✉ *64 Rua da Felicidade, Downtown* ☎ *853/2857–3580* ⟁ *Reservations essential* 🖃 *MC, V*.

$$$$
ITALIAN

✕ **Il Teatro.** With its dedicated view of (and music wafting in from) the Wynn's Performance Lake show, and with the flashing glows of the Lisboa casinos providing ambience, Il Teatro is one of the most romantic restaurants in Macau, where Hong Kong pop stars and jet-setting millionaires from Malaysia hobnob. Popular among the impeccable southern Italian delights are melon-and-prosciutto starters, Parma-ham-and-lobster gnocchi, accompanied by chilled wine from an exhaustive list. Desserts range from rich chocolate cakes to homemade sorbets and ice cream imported straight from Italy. Window seats in particular are at a premium, and are best reserved three weeks in advance. The dress code is "casual elegance," which means long pants, closed-toe shoes, and no open shirts for men; it's not the place for children under five. ✉ *Wynn Macau, Rua da Sintra, Downtown* ☎ *853/8986–3648* 🖃 *AE, DC, MC, V* ⊘ *No lunch*.

$$
CANTONESE

✕ **Long Kei.** One of the oldest and most popular Cantonese restaurants in Macau, Long Kei is in busy Senado Square, in a handsome pink building a few meters from the fountain. The huge menu includes many daily specials printed only in Chinese, so ask your waiter to translate. The restaurant is noisy and chaotic and makes no attempt at glamour or sophistication. The focus is on the food, and for good reason, as it rarely disappoints. Be sure to sample the shrimp toast, congee, and the in-house roasted pork and chicken dishes. ✉ *7B Largo do Senado, Downtown* ☎ *853/2857–3970* 🖃 *MC, V*.

$$–$$$
SHANGHAINESE

✕ **Portas do Sol.** Originally a Portuguese restaurant, Portas do Sol has been transformed into a destination for exquisite dim sum and Chinese cuisine. Tiny, sweet Shanghainese pork buns, turnip cakes, steamed rice-flour crepes, and soup dumplings are some of the traditional fare, and there are some innovative new creations that look like miniature jewels on the plate. For dessert, you can choose from a wide variety of Chinese sweets, including coconut-milk sago pudding, double-boiled papaya with snow fungus (a tasteless mushroom that becomes gelatinous when cooked), and sweet red-bean porridge with ice cream. Evening diners may or may not appreciate the cabaret show and ballroom dancing.

8

Reservations are a good idea on weekends as this place fills up with Hong Kong and mainland visitors. ⊠*Hotel Lisboa, Av. da Amizade, Downtown* ☎*853/2888–3888* ▤*AE, MC, V.*

$$
PORTUGUESE
✕**Praia Grande.** This classic Portuguese restaurant retains its Mediterranean beauty inside and outside, with a gleaming white facade opening into a dining room with graceful arches, terra-cotta floors, and wrought-iron furniture. The menu is creative, with dishes ranging from Portuguese dim sum, African chicken, mussels in white wine, and pork and clams *cataplana* (in a stew of onions, tomatoes, and wine). Guitarists serenade you every night. ⊠*10A Praça Lobo d'Avila, Av. da Praia Grande, Downtown* ☎*853/2897–3022* ▤*AE, MC, V.*

$$$$
FRENCH
✕**Robuchon a Galera.** A slice of Paris in the heart of Macau, this restaurant on the third floor of the Hotel Lisboa is a must, particularly if you just hit it big in the casino. In the ornate interior with rich velvets and dark woods a Swarovski crystal star field twinkles on the ceiling. Signature dishes are a heavenly mille-feuille of tomato and crabmeat, duck breast with turnips and foie gras, and lamb served with creamy potato puree. But Robuchon's 12-course tasting menus, including two desserts, are the best way to experience the restaurant's gastronomic offerings. The wine list is as thick as an encyclopedia and includes some rare wines. ⊠*Hotel Lisboa, Av. da Amizade, Downtown* ☎*853/2888–3888* ⌂*Reservations essential* ▤*AE, MC, V.*

MACAU OUTER HARBOUR

$$
AFRICAN
✕**AfriKana B.B.Q. Restaurant.** It's one of the few places in Macau where you can eat roasted coconut chicken under thatched huts, and where Macau's historical contacts with Africa, especially Angola and Mozambique, come into sharp focus. Scores of Portuguese-speaking residents, who were born in Portugal's African colonies, come here for parties or cultural events. The eight pavilions of thatched huts feature resilient colors, from dark blues to mustard yellows to sandy reds. The all-you-can-eat evening buffets are particularly popular, with staples such as seared fish, barbecued steak, steamed carrots, and other grilled dishes. Buffet prices range from MOP$188 to MOP$268 per person, depending on the day. ⊠*Fisherman's Wharf, Outer Harbour* ☎*853/8299–3678* ▤*AE, MC, V.*

$$
PORTUGUESE
✕**Camões.** Named after the famed Portuguese poet Luis de Camões, this restaurant serves traditional Portuguese dishes in a Mediterranean ambience. The whitewashed walls are accented by dark-wood tables

and chairs and wall tiles are blue-inked with images of old schooners and Chinese junks. *Pata negra* ham (similar to prosciutto) on toasted bread, cold crab, diced pork with lime juice, and whipped potatoes are among the culinary delights. The large selection of Portuguese wines includes several labels from the famous Alentejo region of southern Portugal. Among the desserts are drunken pear and *serradura* (layers of cream and biscuits). ⊠*1st fl., Lisboan building, Fisherman's Wharf, Outer Harbour* ☎*853/2872–8818* ⊟*AE, MC, V.*

> **LOVE OF VINHO**
>
> Wine lovers should take full advantage of Macau's intimate love of *vinho*. Some restaurants have wine lists as thick as phone books. Most places list at least a couple of bottles of delicious Portuguese wine—usually a hearty red from the Dão region or a slightly sparkling *vinho verde* from the north.

$$$$
STEAK
Fodor'sChoice
★

×**Copa Steakhouse.** The first traditional American steak house in Macau, the Copa has a selection of premium quality steaks and seafood, along with a range of cigars and cocktails in an interior that looks like 1960s Las Vegas. A large fireplace pops and crackles during the winter months and blends in perfectly with the vintage chandeliers and celebrity photos hanging on the walls. Sip a cocktail at the bar near the grand piano, and get ready for huge slabs of American and Australian beef, grilled to juicy perfection before your eyes in the open kitchen. The Japanese Kagoshima beef tops the list at MOP$2,188. Other dishes include sautéed sea scallops and fresh oysters when in season. For dessert, try the sinfully rich crème brûlée. ⊠*Sands Casino, 203 Largo de Monte Carlo, Outer Harbour* ☎*853/8983–8366* ⊟*AE, MC, V* ⊘*Closed Sun. No lunch.*

$$$
THAI

×**Naam.** The Mandarin Oriental's Thai restaurant is set amid the hotel's landscaped tropical gardens. Start your meal off with a refreshing *yam som-o* (herbed pomelo salad with chicken and prawns) or aromatic *tom kha gai* (herbed coconut soup with chicken). Then move on to main courses such as the fried lobster with sweet basil and young peppercorns or the traditional favorite *moo phad bai ga praow* (spicy pork with chilies and hot basil leaves). For dessert, there's a melt-in-your-mouth *kluey thod krub bai toey* (deep-fried banana with sweet pandanus-fruit sauce). It's a popular lunch spot for local casino managers, and a hot ticket at dinnertime. ⊠*Mandarin Oriental Hotel, 956–1110 Av. da Amizade, Outer Harbour* ☎*853/8793–4818* ⚎*Reservations essential* ⊟*AE, DC, MC, V.*

$$$$
PORTUGUESE

×**Restaurante Pérola.** With its brilliant turquoise tiles, ironwork chandeliers, and dark wood, the sophisticated Pérola evokes the seafaring heritage of Portugal and Macau. The emphasis is on the freshest seafood, and there are numerous imported Portuguese ingredients in the dishes. Here you can try an excellent *cataplana,* a savory stew of fish, shellfish, and pork served in a gleaming copper pot, as well as a tangy, juicy African chicken. Rich coffees and wines complement the sublime desserts, including Portuguese serradura. ⊠*203 Largo de Monte Carlo, 3rd fl., Sands Macao, Outer Harbour* ☎*853/8983–8222* ⊟*AE, MC, V* ⊘*Closed Mon. No lunch.*

8

MACAU INNER HARBOUR

$$$
PORTUGUESE
Fodor'sChoice
★

✕ **A Lorcha.** Vastly popular A Lorcha (the name means "wooden ship") celebrates the heritage of Macau as an important port with a maritime theme for the menu. Don't miss the signature dish, Clams Lorcha Style, with tomato, beer, and garlic. Other classics include *feijoada* (Brazilian pork-and-bean stew), steamed crab, and perfectly smoky and juicy fire-roasted chicken. Remember to save room for the excellent Portuguese desserts, such as thick mango pudding and sinfully dense serradura. Watch for racers during the Grand Prix, as the Macanese owner Adriano is a fervent Formula fan. ✉*289 Rua do Almirante Sérgio, Inner Harbour* ✉*Rua do Almirate Sérgio, No. 289, AA, R/C, Macau* ☎*853/2831–3193* 🍴*Reservations essential* ▭*AE, MC, V* 🌑*Closed Tues.*

$$$$
SPANISH

✕ **La Paloma.** Specialties at this Spanish restaurant (formerly the Portuguese restaurant Os Gatos) firmly ensconced in the 17th-century Pousada de São Tiago include seafood paella, pigeon roasted or braised in three different sauces, Iberian Parma ham, pork sirloin, garoupa (grouper), and fresh sole. Don't miss the afternoon high tea, available from 3 to 6 daily, outside on the brick terrace shaded by hundred-year-old trees, in the air-conditioned interior with a view of the South China Sea, or even at the mirror-walled Paloma Bar built inside the ancient fortress. ✉*Pousada de São Tiago, Av. da República, Inner Harbour,* ☎*853/2896–8686* ▭*AE, DC, MC, V.*

$$$
MACANESE

✕ **Litoral.** One of the most popular local restaurants, Litoral serves authentic Macanese dishes that are simple, straightforward, and deliciously satisfying. Tastefully decorated with whitewashed walls and dark-wood beams, must-try dishes include the tamarind pork with shrimp paste, as well as codfish baked with potato and garlic, and a Portuguese vegetable cream soup. For dessert, try the *bebinca de leite*, a coconut-milk custard, or the traditional egg pudding, *pudim abade de priscos*. Various-priced set menus are also available, and reservations are recommended on weekends. ✉*261 Rua do Almirante Sergio, Inner Harbour* ☎*853/2896–7878* ▭*AE, MC, V.*

$$
MACANESE

✕ **O Porto Interior.** Come here for traditional Portuguese food that relies on meats, seafood, and heavy sauces, with excellent renditions of grilled prawns, African chicken, and various curries. For dinner parties, the Macanese owner Carlos will be happy to design a set-price menu on request. It's the design, however, that makes the place so special, with an elegant two-story facade, upstairs private room, brilliant white colonnades, and Iberian arches tiled with azulejos (glazed and painted Portuguese tiles) complemented by marble steps and bridges. Reservations are a good idea on weekends. ✉*259B Rua do Almirante Sergio, Inner Harbour* ☎*853/2896–7770* ▭*AE, MC, V.*

$$
ITALIAN

✕ **Pizzeria Toscana.** The Toscana's notoriety among locals sustained a move from the busy Outer Harbour to the more intimate Inner Harbour in 2005. Walk up the hill from Barra Square and look on your left for the door leading downstairs, just across from the yellow-and-white Moorish Barracks. The owners have roots in Pisa and have created a warm, rustic interior to match the refined comfort food on the menu. The *bresaola involtini* (air-cured beef with shredded Parmesan) and fresh salmon carpaccio antipasti are tasty ways to begin your meal; followed by the grilled king prawns, homemade tortellini, and, of course, the perfect wood-fired pizzas. ⊠ *Calçada da Barra, 2–A Edifício Cheong Seng, Inner Harbour* ☎ *853/2872–6637* ⚐ *Reservations essential* ▭ *AE, MC, V.*

TAIPA ISLAND

$$$$ ✕ **Aurora.** With its fine French fare and sweeping views of the Macau peninsula, Aurora is popular with high-level business clientele and those seeking modern romance. Guest chefs, such as Chris Salans of Mozaic in Bali, make frequent appearances. Sumptuous set menus begin at MOP$250, while degustation menus are also available— with or without wine pairing, in three, five, or seven courses. Cheese platters are taken seriously, as are desserts. After a main course of oven-roasted cod or truffled white polenta cake, save room for Aurora's signature crème brûlée with citrus-carrot sherbet. Buffet brunch is served from 11:30 to 4 on Sundays. ⊠ *Crown Towers, Av. de Kwong Tung, Taipa* ☎ *853/8803–6622* ⚐ *Reservations essential* ▭ *AE, MC, V* ⊘ *No lunch.*

FRENCH

A COLONIAL FEAST

The Macanese like hearty Portuguese fare. Most restaurants serve the beloved *bacalhau* (salt cod) baked, boiled, grilled, deep-fried with potato, or stewed with onion, garlic, and eggs. Other dishes include sardines, sausages, and *caldo verde* (vegetable soup). Giant prawns in a curry sauce recall the cuisine of Goa, India—another Portuguese colony. Indeed, there are dishes drawn from throughout the colonial empire, including Brazilian *feijoada* (a stew of beans, pork, and vegetables) and Mozambique chicken, baked or grilled and seasoned with piri-piri chili, tangy spices, and coconut.

8

$$$$ ✕ **Kira.** Next to Aurora and with the same stunning views of the Peninsula, Kira serves immaculate Japanese meals by chef Hiroshi Kagata. Its wasabi, for example, comes fresh and doesn't burn badly—truly sublime mustard is a sign that something fresh is taking place in the kitchen. Outdoor deck seating is nice way to enjoy Kira's carefully cut sashimi and subtle seaweed soups, if not fine cuts of Wagyu beef. There are also private booths for intimate or amorous dining. It's an excellent choice for entertaining guests and for family dining. ⊠ *Crown Towers, Av. de Kwong Tung, Taipa* ☎ *853/8803–6633* ⚐ *Reservations essential* ▭ *AE, DC, MC, V* ⊘ *No lunch.*

JAPANESE

COTAI

$$$$ ✕ **Morton's Steakhouse.** A novelty in its adopted home, Morton's draws nostalgics and newbies to its isolated outpost of Yankee rib eye and Aussie porterhouse. Dark-wood decor and low lighting add for a Godfather-like ambience. Tucked away in a corner of the Venetian's massive gambling floor, Morton's is particularly popular with convention clients and the city's casino management set—the big bosses from Vegas and Atlantic City. Hong Kong–based journalists, too, tend to haunt the bar at happy hour whenever big news happens in Macau. ⊠ *Shop 1016, Grand Canal Shoppes, The Venetian, Cotai* ☎ *853/8117–5000* ⊕ *www. mortons.com* ▭ *AE, DC, MC, V.*

STEAK

COLOANE ISLAND

$$ ✕**Fernando's.** Everyone in Hong
PORTUGUESE Kong and Macau knows about
Fodor'sChoice Fernando's, but the vine-covered
★ entrance close to Hác-Sá Beach is
difficult to spot. The open-air din-
ing pavilion and bar have attracted
beachgoers for years now, and the
enterprising Fernando has built a leg-
endary reputation for his tiny Portu-
guese restaurant. The menu focuses
on seafood paired with homegrown
vegetables, and diners choose from
among the bottles of Portuguese
reds on display rather than from a
wine list. The informal nature of the
restaurant fits in with the satisfy-
ing, home-style food such as grilled
fish, baked chicken, and huge bowl-
fuls of spicy clams, all eaten with
your fingers and washed down
with crisp Vinho Verde. ✉*Hác-
Sá Beach 9, Coloane Island South*
☎*853/2888–2531* ⚱*Reservations
not accepted* ▤*No credit cards.*

> ## KING OF TARTS
>
> Originally a modest, traditional
> bakery opened by a young Eng-
> lishman named Andrew Stow in
> 1989, **Lord Stow's Bakery** (✉*1
> Rua da Tassara, Coloane Village
> Sq.* ☎*853/2888–2534* ⊕*www.
> lordstow.com*) is now a culinary
> landmark in Coloane, just off the
> town square. Locals young and old
> sit on nearby benches munching
> the signature hot and flaky *pasteis
> de nata* (custard tarts) straight
> from the oven, enjoying the quiet
> view of Coloane's southwest coast.
> Inside the little shop, breads, muf-
> fins, cookies, flapjacks, and other
> homemade goods are on offer, but
> be sure to walk out with at least
> one tart. The neighboring Lord
> Stow's Café (☎*853/2888–2174*)
> has sit-down meals.

$$ ✕**Restaurante Espaço Lisboa.** A favorite among local Portuguese, this
PORTUGUESE Portuguese-owned restaurant with a Portuguese chef is a converted
two-story house with a small but pleasant outdoor balcony for alfresco
dining overlooking Coloane Village. Menu highlights include codfish
cakes, savory duck rice, monkfish rice, boiled bacalhau with cabbage,
sausage flambé, steak topped with ham and fried egg, and smoked ham
imported from Portugal. Take your pick from an extensive list of hearty
Portuguese wines, and finish the meal with homemade mango ice cream
with a cherry flambé. ✉*18 Rua das Gaivotas, Coloane Island West*
☎*853/2888–2226* ▤ *MC, V.*

WHERE TO STAY

The Crown Towers. The Venetian. The MGM Grand. Since late 2006,
an influx of luxury hotels has transformed Macau into a posh place to
stay, complete with Egyptian cotton sheets, hot-stone massages, and
swimming pools with underwater music. The suites at the integrated
resorts complement the likes of the Mandarin Oriental on the peninsula
and the Westin Resort on Coloane, both of which pioneered the standard of high-comfort travel in this post-colonial patch of China.

The musty three-stars are still out there, but the five-stars are generally
worth the splurge. For a true Macau experience, try staying in *pousa-
das,* restored historical buildings that have been converted into intimate
hotels with limited facilities but lots of character.

PLANNING

When choosing a hotel, consider the surroundings. In pulsating downtown Macau (or in the Outer Harbour, connected to Downtown via frequent casino shuttles), historic and cultural sites, casinos, and restaurants are all within walking distance. Hotels in more-residential Taipa, just a short bus or taxi ride away, often have incomparable sea and bright-lights views. And if you spring for the Crown Towers, you can enjoy the many top-rate facilities, within walking distance of Taipa Village.

Cotai offers one-stop sleeping, shopping, eating, and gambling. Outside the resorts, it's still a construction field, with new, glitzy hotels opening frequently. The peaceful Inner Harbour has excellent sea views, but for true otherworldly quiet, head to Coloane, where you can hit the beach and hiking trails.

For discounted rates in the grand hotels, book a package through a Hong Kong travel agency. Or, subject to availability, an agent at the Macau hydrofoil terminal can book you a room at a three- to five-star hotel for a discount price within minutes.

Macau hotels are busiest during the Grand Prix (third week of November) and all official Chinese holidays. Book at least a couple weeks in advance at these times. Year-round, weekends fill up fast and walk-ins can be prohibitively expensive. Weekday rates are often half price.

All rooms have TV, air-conditioning, telephone, and a private bathroom, unless stated otherwise.

DOWNTOWN MACAU

$$$ 🏨 **Galaxy StarWorld Hotel.** If it's good enough for China's 2008 Olympic gold medalists, it must have some appeal. And it does, at least in the luminous open "studio" suites with high ceilings, Jacuzzi tubs, and panoramic bay windows. Even the deluxe rooms, with their high-quality bedding, make you feel like you're somewhere special. At the happening Whisky Bar (⇨ *After Dark*)on the 16th floor, as well as downstairs in the lobby, StarWorld brings you flashy dancers, live bands, and even a Chaplin impersonator. The dazzling blue building was designed by Rocco Yim, also known for designing Hong Kong's towering IFC II. **Pros:** celestially designed suites, live entertainment in the lobby and lounge bar, free Internet access in every room. **Cons:** high energy at all hours, in a heavy-traffic area. ⊠ *Av. Da Amizade, Downtown* 🕾 *853/2878–1111* ⊕ *www.starworldmacau.com* 🛏 *465 rooms, 44 suites* ⚿ *In-room: safe, DVD (some), Internet. In-hotel: 4 restaurants, room service, bars, pool, gym, spa, laundry service, Internet terminal, parking (paid), no-smoking rooms.* ⊟ *AE, DC, MC, V.*

$$ 🏨 **Hotel Lisboa.** Macau's infamous landmark, with its distinctive, labyrinthine interior architecture, rumored connections to organized crime, open prostitution, and no-limit VIP rooms, now stands in the shadow of its Grand Lisboa sister. The two are connected by a bridge and share facilities, such as the Grand's modern pool, gym, and spa. The advantages to staying in the older structure are nostalgic value and lower

8

Luxury Spas

Macau is well known for its casinos and restaurants, but it's also rapidly gaining a reputation for its luxury spa and sauna facilities, offering a huge range of treatments. Almost every luxury hotel has its own spa, with special packages and offers for hotel guests. Many visitors opt for spa treatments at luxury hotels, but Macau's independent spas have become a major force in recent years, offering equally exquisite service at lower prices than hotels. All spas offer services for couples, and provide a great opportunity to relax in a peaceful space with someone special.

Treatments begin at around MOP$300 and up for 60 minutes of service. The following are some of the more impressive spa facilities available:

THE SPA AT THE MANDARIN ORIENTAL MACAU

The largest and best-known spa in town takes advantage of the Mandarin's sumptuous Mediterranean architecture and lets in lots of natural sunlight for a bright and airy spa experience. It offers numerous Chinese, European, Thai, and Japanese treatments, including its signature 2½-hour, three-part Macanese Sangría Ritual, which includes a full body scrub using fresh grapes, sangria

bath in a private outdoor Jacuzzi, and grape-seed-oil massage, for MOP$1,650. Reserve ahead. ⊠ *Mandarin Oriental Macau Hotel, 956–1110 Av. da Amizade, Outer Harbour* 🖀 *853/8793–4824, 800/968–886* ⊕ *www.mandarinoriental.com/macau/spa.*

SPA PHILOSOPHY

This Chinese-theme spa-treatment center has pollution-free, oxygenated air pumped throughout the complex. Guests are offered a variety of treatments, including a vintage-red-wine bath, as well as champagne and Godiva chocolate-liqueur skin-nourishing programs. ⊠ *327–331 Av. Xian Xing Hai, Nam On Garden, Outer Harbour* 🖀 *853/2872–8330* ⊕ *www. spaphilosophy.com.*

NIRVANA SPA

In a quiet area of town near the Nam Van Lake, the Asian-inspired Nirvana has rooms decorated in Chinese, Thai, Balinese, Indian, Macau and various other eastern themes, where therapists from Thailand and the Philippines are trained in deep-tissue, ayurvedic, herbal, shiatsu, and aromatherapy massages. ⊠ *Ground fl., China Law Bldg., 403 Av. da Praia Grande, Downtown* 🖀 *853/2833–1521.*

price. And though the Grand Lisboa opened in early 2007, the Hotel Lisboa was renovated one year later, so the rooms are just as luxurious, with hardwood floors and Jacuzzi baths. Take your time to wander through the hotel's corridors displaying jade and artworks from Dr. Stanley Ho's private collection, before running into an ostentatiously gilded staircase. Many people come to the Lisboa expressly for its restaurants: Robuchon a Galera, Portas do Sol, and Chiu Chow (⇨ *Where to Eat*). **Pros:** historical interior, central location, superior restaurants, linked to the Grand Lisboa. **Cons:** old building, low ceilings, smoky casino. ⊠ *2–4 Av. de Lisboa, Downtown* 🖀 *853/2888–3888, 800/969–130 in Hong Kong* ⊕ *www.hotelisboa.com* 🔌 *1,000 rooms, 28 suites* ⚙ *In-room: safe, DVD, Internet. In-hotel: 3 restaurants,*

room service, pool, gym, spa, laundry service, no-smoking rooms.
🖃 *AE, DC, MC, V.*

$ 🖵 **Hotel Sintra.** Just minutes away from Senado Square and right down the street from the New Yaohan department store, the Sintra is a good three-star antechamber to the Lisboan kingdom, with its own built-in Mocha minicasino accessible through the lobby. Its carpeted rooms are decorated in soothing brown-and-cream color schemes, while the staff is smartly dressed and helpful. Breakfast is an extra MOP$88 for an American buffet. **Pros:** in the heart of downtown, simple but tasteful decor. **Cons:** small rooms, small casino. ⊠ *Av. De Dom João IV, Downtown* 🕾*853/710–111, 800/969–145 in Hong Kong* ⊕*www.hotelsintra.com* 🖙*240 rooms, 11 suites* ♨*In-room: safe, refrigerator, Internet. In-hotel: restaurant, room service, Wi-Fi, no-smoking rooms.* 🖃 *AE, DC, MC, V.*

$$$ 🖵 **MGM Grand.** In Macau, the golden lion statue stands guard on the peninsula's southern coast, as guests penetrate into the MGM's spectacular Grande Praça (Grand Square), an 82-foot-tall floor-to-glass-ceiling space modeled after a Portuguese town square that serves as an inner courtyard and has fine dining under the stars. A few million Hong Kong dollars were invested in the permanent chandelier sculpture and original drawings by Dale Chihuly decorating the hotel lobby and reception. Chihuly's glassworks line the hall linking the art gallery to the patisserie, giving it a warm pink glow, while the M Bar plays soft jazz and lounge music. The rooms are everything you'd expect in the way of comfort and elegance from a luxury accommodation, but it's the classy world around them, outside the casino, that distinguishes this hotel from the rest. **Pros:** tasteful architecture, Chihuly artwork, refined dining and lounge options. **Cons:** inseparable from the casino, which can get smoky and loud; high-traffic location. ⊠ *Av. Dr. Sun Yat Sen, Downtown* 🕾*853/8802–8888* ⊕*www.mgmgrandmacau.com* 🖙*494 rooms, 99 suites* ♨*In-room: safe, refrigerator (some), DVD (some), Wi-Fi. In-hotel: 8 restaurants, room service, bars, pool, spa, laundry service, Wi-Fi, parking (paid), no-smoking rooms.* 🖃 *AE, MC, V.*

Fodor'sChoice ★

$ 🖵 **Pousada de Mong-Há.** Restored by the MGTO in 1979, this secluded pousada halfway up Mong-Há Hill was once a Portuguese military barracks, before being used to house foreign civil servants, and is now a training hotel entirely run by students of the attached Institute for Tourism Studies. Accommodation and service are exemplary, spacious rooms are delicately decorated with hand-stitched carpets, and the restaurant shows off its traditional azulejos at breakfast and teatime. Kun Iam and Lin Fung temples are nearby, as is the famous Canidrome. **Pros:** historic charm, hillside walks and views. **Cons:** half-hour walk from city center, no pool. ⊠ *Colina de Mong-Há, north of Downtown* 🕾*853/2851–5222* ⊕*www.ift.edu.mo/pousada* 🖙*16 rooms* ♨*In-room: safe, refrigerator, Internet, Wi-Fi. In-hotel: restaurant, gym, laundry service, Internet, no-smoking rooms.* 🖃 *AE, MC, V.*

$$$$ 🖵 **Wynn Macau.** If you just can't get enough of the Wynn's Performance Lake by merely admiring it at ground level, the hotel offers rooms with a plunging view of the fire-and-water spectacle, as well as of the peaceful Nam Van Lake. Alternatively, you can opt for a glittering city view

8

of the outdoor pool and neighboring Lisboa casinos, as all rooms have floor-to-ceiling windows. Hotel extras include buffet breakfast at the Café Esplanada and a daily Macau heritage tour. The Wynn resort is also home to such fine dining options as Il Teatro and Okada (☎ *853/8986–3663* ☐*AE, DC, MC, V* ⊘*No lunch*), which has one of Asia's only resident sake sommeliers. **Pros:** exclusive VIP club space, Nam Van and Performance Lake views. **Cons:** Light pollution from neighboring casinos, lowest rooms on 5th floor. ⊠*Rua Cidade de Sintra, Downtown* ☎*853/2888–9966, 800/966–963 in Hong Kong* ⊕*www. wynnmacau.com* ↪*460 rooms, 140 suites* ⋄*In-room: safe, refrigerator, Internet, Wi-Fi. In-hotel: 5 restaurants, room service, bar, pool, gym, spa, laundry service, Wi-Fi, no-smoking rooms.* ☐*AE, MC, V.*

MACAU OUTER HARBOUR

$$$ ⓒ 🏨**Mandarin Oriental.** The Mandarin Oriental is synonymous with elegance and understated opulence, and its Macau location doesn't disappoint. This hotel is also widely known for deluxe treatments in the enormous spa complex next to the gorgeous, tropical swimming pool on the landscaped grounds. You'll feel like you're in a lush rain forest as you look out from the traditional Mediterranean architecture of the hotel. It even has tennis and squash courts. The hotel's renowned restaurants include the Café Bela Vista for its endless buffet, and Naam, the exquisite Thai restaurant popular with locals and visitors alike. **Pros:** classic luxury facilities, on-site rock climbing, kid's club. **Cons:** old casino, high-traffic location. ⊠*956–1110 Av. da Amizade, Outer Harbour* ☎*853/8793–3261, 2881–1288 in Hong Kong, 800/526–6567 in U.S.* ⊕*www.mandarinoriental.com/macau* ↪*388 rooms, 28 suites* ⋄*In-room: safe, refrigerator, Internet, Wi-Fi. In-hotel: 4 restaurants, room service, bar, tennis courts, pools, gym, spa, water sports, children's programs (ages 3–12), laundry service, Internet, Wi-Fi, no-smoking rooms.* ☐*AE, DC, MC, V.*

$$ 🏨**Rocks Hotel.** Opened on Christmas Eve, 2006 as the first in a series of theme hotels to come to the east end of Fisherman's Wharf, the posh-yet-quaint five-story Rocks Hotel is modeled after the charm of 18th-century Victorian England. Each room and suite is individually decorated, with a novelty old-fashioned bathtub in addition to a modern shower stall. Balconies offer low sea views on all sides. The extensive Asian and American breakfast buffet is worth looking forward to in the morning. The foyer itself is impressive, with its grand staircase under sparkling chandeliers, although it could use some real birds in the giant gilded cage to liven up the lobby. **Pros:** distinctive decor, low-key fine dining. **Cons:** no pool or spa, located inside an amusement park. ⊠*Macau Fisherman's Wharf, Outer Harbour* ☎*853/2878–2782, 800/962–863 in Hong Kong* ⊕*www.rockshotel.com.mo* ↪*66 rooms, 6 suites* ⋄ *In-room: safe, Internet. In-hotel: restaurant, room service, bar, gym, laundry service, Internet, parking (free), no-smoking rooms.* ☐ *AE, DC, MC, V.*

$$$ 🏨**Sands Macao.** Las Vegas casino tycoon Sheldon Anderson's first venture in Macau, the Sands is nothing if not luxurious. Spacious rooms have deep, soft carpets, large beds, and huge marble bathrooms with Jacuzzis. If you opt to become a high-rolling member, you can stay in

one of the 51 deluxe or executive suites, ranging in size from 650 to 1,300 square feet, with all-in-one remote-control plasma TV, karaoke, curtains, and lighting, plus personal butler service on request. VIP members also have privileges such as private helicopter and high-limit gaming rooms at both the Sands and Venetian casinos. But all guests can enjoy the outdoor heated pool on the 6th floor, as well as the exclusive sauna, spa, and salon. **Pros:** heated outdoor pool, across the street from Fisherman's Wharf. **Cons:** not as new as the Venetian, near lots of vehicle traffic. ⊠203 *Largo de Monte Carlo, Outer Harbour* ☎*853/8983–3100* ⊕*www. sands.com.mo* ⟳ *258 rooms, 51 VIP suites* ⌂*In-room: safe, DVD, Wi-Fi. In-hotel: 7 restaurants, room service, bar, pools, gym, spa, laundry service, parking (paid).* ☱*AE, MC, V.*

MACAU INNER HARBOUR

$$$$ ▦**Pousada de São Tiago.** The spirit of the structure's past life as a 17th-
Fodor'sChoice century fortress permeates every part of this romantic and intimate
★ lodging, making it ideal for a honeymoon or wedding. Even the front entrance impressive: an ascending stone tunnel carved into the mountainside with water seeping through in quiet trickles. The pousada reopened in mid-2007 after a major renovation that consolidated accommodations into 12 modern luxury suites, each with Jacuzzi bathrooms and large balconies for room-service breakfast. Stop for high tea in the mirrored lounge, or sip a cocktail on the terrace under 100-year-old trees. **Pros:** all the modern comfort of a luxury hotel inside a 17th-century fortress, intimate, sunset views of the Inner Harbour. **Cons:** small pool, limited facilities, you'll need to call a taxi to go out. ⊠*Fortaleza de São Tiago da Barra, Av. da República, Inner Harbour* ☎*853/2837–8111, 800/969–153 in Hong Kong* ⊕*www.saotiago. com.mo* ⟳*12 suites* ⌂*In-room: Internet, Wi-Fi. In-hotel: restaurant, room service, bar, pool, laundry service, Internet, Wi-Fi, parking (free), no-smoking rooms.* ☱*AE, MC, V.*

$$ ▦**Sofitel Macau at Ponte 16.** Ever since its February 2008 opening, Ponte
Fodor'sChoice 16 has pioneered the revamp of Macau's retro western port into an
★ emerging casino and commercial pole. The neighborhood may not be there yet, but Sofitel is Ponte 16's jewel in the crown, with lush, sleek suites and a giant, curvaceous pool, complete with cocktail and juice bar, just outside the indoor buffet lounge. Adventurous and up-and-coming, it has all the edgy perks—grab it while it's hot. **Pros:** giant outdoor pool with bar serving everything from fresh fruit to fine wine, some rooms have unique views of the Inner Harbour. **Cons:** in a still-developing neighborhood, heavy traffic outside. ⊠*Rua do Visconde Paço de Arcos, Inner Harbour* ☎*853/8861–0016* ⊕*www.sofitel.com*

8

389 rooms, 19 suites ☐ *In-room: safe, DVD, Internet. In-hotel: restaurants, room service, bar, pool, gym, spa, laundry service, Internet, parking (free), no-smoking rooms.* ☐ *AE, DC, MC, V.*

TAIPA

$$ ☐ **Best Western Hotel Taipa.** In the heart of Taipa Village, the Best Western's yellow facade is classic Portuguese design and marks the front entrance to the hotel where you'll pay relatively moderate prices for rooms that are comfortable, without any luxurious bells and whistles. The Restaurante Grande and Bar Grande are serviceable, but the Rua da Cunha, known as Souvenir and Food Street, offers a range of interesting local foods, snacks, and handicrafts less than a 10-minute walk away. **Pros:** quiet, quaint location; nearby Taipa Village fair every Sunday. **Cons:** lacks personality, small pool. ☐ *822 Estrada Governador Nobre Carvalho, Taipa Island North* ☎ *853/2882–1666, 800/903–295 in Hong Kong* ⊕ *www.hoteltaipa.com* *262 rooms, 12 suites* ☐ *In-room: safe, refrigerator, Wi-Fi. In-hotel: restaurant, room service, bar, pool, gym, laundry service, Internet.* ☐ *AE, DC, MC, V.*

$$$$ ☐ **Crown Towers.** Effectively towering over northern Taipa, the Crown
Fodor'sChoice offers stunning sea views of the Macau peninsula, from each and every
★ room, suite, and villa. Even standard rooms are like suites, with a dedicated lounge, walk-in wardrobe and circular stone bath. With the second of the Crown Towers on the way, the first already has plenty to please: a panoramic-view swimming pool, a two-level spa with 12 treatment rooms, Aurora's Sunday buffet brunch, classy VIP gaming rooms, and the 24-hour Crystal Club, which provides starlight seating on the rooftop for cool cocktails in a romantic setting. The vertically designed Crown reaches high to set its own standard of chic above and beyond all the mushrooming Vegas kitsch. **Pros:** glowing sea views from every room, panoramic-view pool, open-air rooftop bar. **Cons:** may sometimes be noisy from nearby construction, still a taxi (or shuttle) ride from the peninsula. ☐ *Av. de Kwong Tung, Taipa* ☎ *853/2886–8888* ⊕ *www.crown-macau.com* *184 rooms, 24 suites, 8 villas* ☐ *In-room: safe, refrigerator (some), DVD (some), Internet, Wi-Fi. In-hotel: 6 restaurants, room service, bar, pool, gym, spa, laundry service, parking (paid), no-smoking rooms* ☐ *AE, MC, V.*

$$$$ ☐ **Four Seasons Hotel.** Opened in September 2008, the Four Seasons may be the youngest of the jet-set palaces in Macau, but its brand-name reputation is conscientiously upheld. Nestled in the southeast corner of the Venetian complex, it is independently managed, and without a casino to worry about, the focus is on providing guests with the best possible accommodation and well-being experience. Witness its comprehensive spa treatments and facilities, as well as separate pools for the kids. The Shoppes at Four Seasons luxury boutiques await you just outside the lobby, as you rejoin the tourist flow. **Pros:** focus on service, extensive spa treatments. **Cons:** attached to the Venetian, inside a shopping mall. ☐ *Estrada da Baía de N. Senhora da Esperança, Cotai* ☎ *853/2881–8888* ⊕ *www.fourseasons.com/macau* *276 rooms, 84 suites* ☐ *In-room: safe, refrigerator (some), DVD, Internet, Wi-Fi. In-hotel: 5 restaurants, room service, bar, pools, gym, spa, laundry ser-*

vice, Internet, Wi-Fi, parking (paid), no-smoking rooms. ☰ *AE, DC, MC, V.*

$$$ 🏨 **Venetian Macao-Resort-Hotel.** You either love it or you hate it. The Venetian's megalomaniac stronghold on the emerging Cotai area is both its draw and its bane. It's not everywhere you have singing gondoliers in manmade canals leading to clowns on stilts under an always-blue sky—but the other place you find it is Vegas, not Venice. Service is geared toward mainland Chinese gamblers, confirming that the Venetian is first a casino, second a shopping mall, third a convention and entertainment venue, and only last a hotel. On the upside, the Venetian's Royale, Bella, and Rialto suites are spacious enough for family-sized comfort, and the extra TV with cable in every room, variety of swimming pools, and miniature 18-hole golf course make the difference with the kids. Come for the over-the-top environment, but be prepared to share it with a round-the-clock flow of tourists. **Pros:** living rooms, comprehensive shopping and dining. **Cons:** pretentious decor, gambling and convention crowds, lack of intimacy outside the suite. ⊠*Estrada de Baía de Nossa Senhora da Esperança, Cotai* ☏*853/2882–8888* ⊕*www.venetianmacao.com* ⟿*2,531 hotel suites, 374 casino VIP suites* ⌂*In-room: safe, Wi-Fi. In-hotel: 19 restaurants, room service, bars, golf course, pools, gym, spa, laundry service, Internet, Wi-Fi, parking (paid), no-smoking rooms.* ☰ *AE, MC, V.*

COLOANE

$ 🏨 **Pousada de Coloane.** At Cheoc-Van Beach at the southernmost tip of Coloane Island, Pousada de Coloane offers a quiet, natural setting, nestled within the lush hills and mountains of Macau's south. There are ample opportunities for kayaking, hiking, and swimming. A long winding path paved with Portuguese azulejo tiles leads you to the spacious terrace overlooking the beach and is ideal for outdoor wedding receptions and other celebrations. Facilities include a pool, a fireplace, and a small bar in the restaurant. The open terrace garden and restaurant offers traditional Portuguese, Macanese, and Chinese favorites cooked in a heavy, home-style tradition, but there are also other seafood restaurants down on the beach. All 30 rooms have private hot tubs, cable TV, and balconies overlooking the beach, with the mountains of mainland China in the distance. **Pros:** intimate coastal location, sea-view balconies. **Cons:** limited facilities, no in-room Internet. ⊠*Cheoc Van Beach, Coloane Island South* ☏*853/2888–2143* ⊕*www.hotelpcoloane.com.mo* ⟿*30 rooms* ⌂*In-room: safe (some). In-hotel: restaurant, room service, bar, pool, laundry service, Internet, Wi-Fi, parking (free).* ☰ *MC, V.*

$$ 🏨 **Westin Resort.** Built into the side of a cliff, the Westin is surrounded
⟳ by the black sands of Hác-Sá Beach and lapping waves of the South
Fodor's Choice China Sea. This is where you truly get away from it all. Every room
★ faces the ocean; the place glows as much because of the sunny tropical color scheme as from the sunshine. The vast private terraces are ideal for alfresco dining and afternoon naps. Guests also receive access to Macau's renowned golf club, the PGA-standard, 18-hole Macau Golf and Country Club, which was built on the rocky cliffs and plateaus above the hotel. **Pros:** green surrounds, golf-club access, fun for kids. **Cons:** isolated location, limited access. ⊠*1918 Estrada de Hác Sá, Coloane*

8

Island South ☎*853/2887–1111, 800/228–3000 in Hong Kong* ⊕*www.westin-macau.com* ⮌*208 rooms, 20 suites* ♿*In-room: safe, Internet. In-hotel: 3 restaurants, room service, bars, golf course, tennis courts, pools, gym, spa, beachfront, bicycles, laundry service, Internet, parking (free), children's programs (ages 3–12), no-smoking rooms.* ⊟*AE, DC, MC, V.*

AFTER DARK

Old movies, countless novels, and gossip through the years have portrayed Macau's nightlife as a combustible mix of drugs, wild gambling, violent crime, and ladies of the night. Up until the 1999 handover back to mainland China, this image of Macau was mostly accurate and worked to drive away tourists.

Outside of the casinos and a few restaurants, today's Macau shuts down after 11 PM. You can slip into any dark, elegant lounge bar inside the larger hotels, and enjoy live music and expensive cocktails, but don't expect much energy or big crowds. And most late-night saunas are glorified brothels, with "workers" from China, Vietnam, Thailand, and Russia.

LOUNGES & PUBS

Because casino-hotel lounges often double as coffee shops in the morning or around midday, some "nightlife" hot spots may open as early as 7 AM.

Depending on the time of day or night, the **Whisky Bar** (⊠*StarWorld Hotel, Av. da Amizade, Downtown* ☎*853/8290–8698* ⊗*Closes 2* AM) on the 16th floor of the StarWorld Hotel provides either upbeat cabaret entertainment or a cool moment of respite from the clinking casinos all around. Happy hour is daily from 5 to 10, and the Star Band starts playing nightly at 7:30. In addition to a full selection of the usual hard stuff, the bar has 75 different kinds of whisky, including the ultra-rare Macallan 1946.

When you're finally done with the casinos and ready to look down on the rest of the world, hop over to Taipa and take the Crown Towers elevator straight up the to the lofty **Crystal Club** (⊠*38th fl., Crown Macau, Av. De Kwong Tung, Taipa* ☎*853/8803–6868* ⊕*www.crown-macau.com* ⊗*24 hours*) just around the corner from the lobby. Sip cocktails under the stars on the outdoor terrace, where tapas are served from 6 PM to 1 AM. Indoors,

---

MACAU GOLF AND COUNTRY CLUB

Macau's most famous golf course is at the **Macau Golf and Country Club,** and the only way to play there, unless you become a member, is to book a package and stay at the Westin. The beautiful 18-hole, PGA Tour–level course has breathtaking sea views from atop a plateau. ⊠*Westin Resort, 1918 Estrada de Hác-Sá, Coloane Island South* ☎*853/2887–1188* ✉*Packages around MOP$5,000* ⊗*Daily 7:30* AM*–8* PM*, call for tee times.*

the club's house DJ spins chill-out music from 8 PM to 2 AM Wednesday through Sunday.

At **McSorley's Ale House** (⊠*Shop 1038, Grand Canal Shoppes, Venetian Macao, Estrada de Baía de Nossa Senhora da Esperança, Cotai* ☎*853/2882–8198* ⊕*www.mcsorleys.com.hk* ⊙*Closes 2 am*), in the Venetian, you can catch the performers of Cirque du Soleil's ZAIA, which takes place just across the street, chilling out with a beer after a show. Its open mezzanine is a comfortable place to sit down for a pub menu of burgers and fish-and-chips, while sports fans will be watching the game around the traditional mahogany bar. A touring Irish band played here before, but occasional live music is casual and spontaneous.

For more varied dining options from an open kitchen in a more family-friendly setting, try the **Blue Frog Bar & Grill** (⊠*Shop 1037, Grand Canal Shoppes, Venetian Macao, Estrada de Baía de Nossa Senhora da Esperança, Cotai* ☎*853/2882–8281* ⊕*www.bluefrog.com.cn/macao* ⊙*Closes 2 am*), next door to McSorleys, which serves big breakfasts and buy-one-get-one burgers, and even has a children's menu. While live music is lacking from this Shanghai export, the atmosphere turns to live-broadcast sports and cocktails in the evening. Happy hour is Sunday to Friday 4–8 and two-for-one drinks begin at 8 PM every Wednesday, Ladies' Night.

Casablanca (⊠*Av. Dr. Sun Yat Sen, Outer Harbour* ☎*853/2875–1281* ⊙*Closes 4* AM) is a friendly downtown lounge where you can play a game of pool or simply sip a cocktail in its opulent interior lined with plush red-velvet curtains, while listening to music from Africa, Portugal, Spain, and beyond. Happy hour is 6–8 daily.

Macau's Lan Kwai Fong (⊠*Edifício Vista Magnífica Court Av. Dr. Sun Yat-Sen, Outer Harbour*) refers to a small collection of bars along a small stretch of street in NAPE, within sight of the huge golden Guan Yin statue in Macau's Outer Harbour. Although it takes its name from the legendary bar area in Hong Kong, in reality, it's a bunch of nice, quiet bars to meet with friends or watch sports on a big-screen TV. A large number of expats come to this area to relax and drink in the evenings, but don't expect the wild times and thumping music you might find in the original LKF in Hong Kong.

SHOWS

Cirque du Soleil pounced on the opportunity to create the first resident full-scale Vegas-style show at the Venetian in 2008. **ZAIA** (⊠*Venetian Macao, Estrada de Baía de Nossa Senhora da Esperança, Cotai* ☎ *853/2882–8818, 6333–6660 in Hong Kong* ⊕*www.cirquedusoleil. com/zaia*), staged in a meticulously engineered, cosmic-themed theater, follows the narrative of a girl traveling through space with the aid of over-the-top props—such as floating bicycles—and captivating human performances: swooping dancers, dangling equilibrists, and quick-change clown routines. Upper midrange seats offer the best view.

At this writing, Franco Dragone, former star director at Cirque du Soleil, plans to open an as-yet-untitled resident aquatic show at the City of Dreams underwater-themed casino-hotel (set to open in mid-2009) in the fall of 2009. Stay tuned for updates at *www.dragone.be.*

SHOPPING

Macau, like Hong Kong, is a free port for most items, which leads to lower prices for electronics, jewelry, and clothing than other international cities. But coming from Hong Kong's intense shopping utopia, Macau seems like a poor country cousin. There are no Hong Kong–style megamalls here, so shopping in Macau is a completely different experience, with a low-key atmosphere, small crowds, and compact areas. Commercial rents are lower, so retail shops have had a longer history and look older. Sales staff aren't as pushy and persistent; their command of English isn't as good either.

Most of Macau's shops operate year-round with a short break in late January for Chinese New Year. Opening hours vary according to the type of shop, but most retail stores are open from 10 AM to 8 PM and later on weekends. Macau's major shopping district is along its main street, Avenida Almeida Ribeiro, more commonly known by its Chinese name, **San Ma Lo**; there are also shops in **Mercadores** and its side streets; in **Cinco de Outubro**; and on the **Rua do Campo**.

Most shops accept all major credit cards, though specialty discount shops usually ask for cash. For most street vendors and some smaller stores, some friendly bargaining is expected; you should ask for the "best price," which ideally produces instant discounts of 10%–20%. The shopping mantra here, and in most of China, is "bargain hard, bargain often."

DEPARTMENT STORE & MALL

Originally a Japanese-owned department store, this failing shop was taken over by Stanley Ho several years ago and transformed into a popular shopping destination for locals. Relocated in 2008, the **New Yaohan** (⊠ *Av. Doutor Mario Soares, Downtown* ☎ *853/2872–5338*) can still call itself "Macau's only department store" with a good mix of shops selling household goods, clothing, jewelry, and beauty products. It also has an extensive food court, a well-stocked supermarket, and a large bakery on the first floor.

The Grand Canal Shoppes (⊠ *Venetian Macao, Av. Xian Xing Hai, Cotai* ☎ *853/2882–8888*) are the Venetian's vision of a gentrified megamall, complete with cobblestone walkways, arched bridges, and working waterway canals manned by singing gondoliers (rides are MOP$88). All the big-name brands and luxury shops in fashion, accessories, gifts, services and sporting goods are among its 350 retailers; it also has a spa, 19 restaurants, and an international food court. Don't be surprised to see wandering stilt walkers, violinists, and juggling jesters, especially around St. Mark's Square, which hosts four daily live performances. In 2008, the megamall extended to connect with the Shoppes at Four Seasons, adding even more exclusive luxury shops to the arcade, such as Autore which carries jewelry set with its own cultivated South Sea pearls.

SPECIALTY SHOPS

ANTIQUES & TRADITIONAL CRAFTS

It was said that in Old Macau, you could occasionally find treasures from the Ming dynasty buried among the bowls, carvings, and other old crafts in the island's many antiques shops. Those days are long gone, but Macau continues to be a thriving hub for traditional Chinese arts, crafts, and even some antiques. Try to get a professional appraisal before buying antiques, though, as Macau is also famous for high-quality reproductions of Qing and Ming dynasty items. You can see craftspeople at work making the "new antiques," particularly on the side streets of Tercena and Estalagens and the alleyways in front of the Ruins of St. Paul's. Commonly sold pieces include lacquer screens, Chinese pottery, and huge wooden chests carved from solid mahogany, camphor wood, and redwood.

Asian Artifacts (✉ *25 Rua dos Negociantes, Coloane* ☎ *853/2888–1022*) specializes in detailed restorations of authentic antiques. Every piece features "before" and "after" pictures, a personal history, and a story from the friendly British owner. **Hong Hap** (✉ *170 Cinco de Outubro, Coloane*) is a small, intimate shop where the owner, a font of information in Chinese and English, is involved with every piece on display. **Wing Tai** (✉ *1A Av. Almeida Ribeiro, Downtown*), a large, well-established antiques dealer in the heart of downtown, gives visitors a convenient introduction to Macau's variety of antique styles. A general rule of thumb when purchasing antiques is to bargain hard and bargain soft, and then bargain again.

CLOTHING

Many clothing shops offer low and discounted prices on seasonal clothing for men, women, and children. The best bargains are found in off-season clothing, athletic shoes, and factory overruns. There's the usual assortment of fake brand-name clothing sold in street stalls, but the majority of these clothes can be found in larger discount stores and tend to be genuine overruns and dead stock from major labels such as Esprit, Banana Republic, Abercrombie & Fitch, GAP, and others. Major shopping areas include the small shops on **Rua do Campo** and around **Mercadores**. There are also bustling street markets that sell clothes on **São Domingos** (off Largo do Senado), **Rua Cinco de Outubro,** and **Rua da Palha.** Credit cards are accepted at most shops, but street stalls only accept cash.

JEWELRY

Jewelry shops across from casinos in the downtown area sell luxury watches, pendants, and rings, some of which have been pawned by desperate gamblers. Prices are generally more reasonable than in Hong

Kong, and premiums for workmanship are much lower. The price of the gold fluctuates with trading on the Hong Kong Gold Exchange, and each store will have an electronic display showing the current price of gold per *tael,* which is 1.2 troy ounces. Most Asian buyers prefer 24-karat gold, and shops prominently display 24-karat coins, bars, and crafts in their windows. Trusted Hong Kong stalwarts **Chow Tai Fook** and **Chow Sang Sang** have locations throughout Macau and are known for transparent pricing and knowledgeable staff with good English-language abilities.

> BUY SMART
>
> For the best selection of traditional Chinese furniture, scroll paintings, porcelain, figurines, fans, silk robes, and lacquerware, search the area around the ruins of St. Paul's, particularly **Rua do São Antonio** and **Rua de São Paulo.** Macau has its share of phony antiques, fake name-brand watches, and other rip-offs, so buyer beware: these "gray items" have no return or warranty policies. Get receipts and signed warranties for expensive items.

WINE

In tandem with rich, hearty Portuguese cooking, Macanese have also adopted a love for wine, and little-known Portuguese wines in particular. The basement wine cellar at **Pavilions** (✉*417–425 Av. da Praia Grande, Downtown* ☎*853/2837–4026)* has a wide and varied selection, especially from Portugal and France. Although Hong Kong customs allows only one bottle per passenger, it doesn't vigorously enforce this rule, especially if you're discreet.

Side Trips to the Pearl River Delta

GUANGZHOU & SHENZEN

WORD OF MOUTH

"Da Fen Chun painting village has blocks and blocks of studios selling original and counterfeit artwork. Unfortunately, most of the artwork is now created in other, less expensive cities so you don't get to see a Monet painting in progress."

—Planner123

WELCOME TO THE PEARL RIVER DELTA

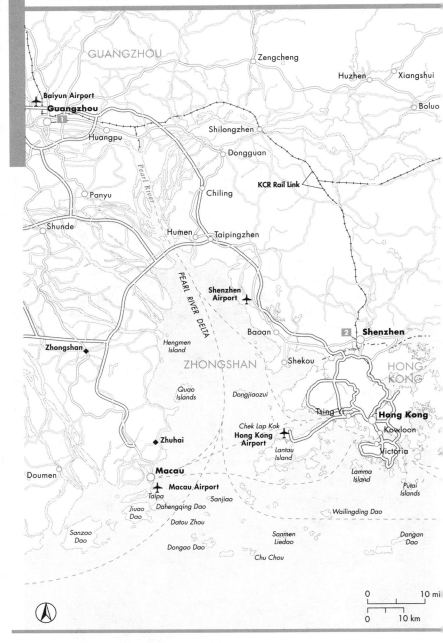

GUANGZHOU

Zengcheng

Huzhen   Xiangshui

Baiyun Airport   Boluo
Guangzhou
1
Shilongzhen
Huangpu
Dongguan

Pearl River

KCR Rail Link

Panyu   Chiling

Shunde   Humen   Taipingzhen

PEARL RIVER DELTA

**Shenzhen
Airport**

Baoan   2   **Shenzhen**

Zhongshan   HONG
                                                              KONG
                        Hengmen
                        Island
              ZHONGSHAN   Shekou

                Quao   Tsing Yi
                Islands   Dongjiaozui
                                                    Hong Kong
                        Chek Lap Kok   Kowloon
        ◆ **Zhuhai**   **Hong Kong
                        Airport**
                                    Lantau   Victoria
                                    Island
                                            Lamma
Doumen   Island
                                                        Putai
                        Macau   Islands

                        Macau Airport
                Taipa   Sanjiao
        Jiuao   Dahengqing Dao
        Dao   Datou Zhou   Wailingding Dao
    Sanzao
    Dao   Sanmen   Dangan
            Dongao Dao   Liedao   Dao
                            Chu Chou

                                    0   10 mi

                                    0   10 km

GETTING ORIENTED

The Pearl River Delta is a massive triangle. Guangzhou is at the top, Shenzhen on the east corner, and Zhuhai on the west. The area as a whole is just a bit too spread out for any one corner to make a good base of operations from which to explore the others. We recommend beginning at one corner and making your way around. Guangzhou is fairly dense, so leave yourself three days in which to soak it all in before heading down to Shenzhen. From Shenzhen's Shekou Harbor it's a one-hour ferry ride to Zhuhai, which takes less than a day to explore before returning either back to Guangzhou or into nearby Macau or Hong Kong.

1 Guangzhou. After you've recovered from the initial confusion produced by the crowds, heavy traffic, and pollution, turn to the city's unique cuisine, sights, culture, and history, such as Colonial Shamian and the nearby White Cloud Mountain.

2 Shenzhen. Come to Shenzhen for excellent shopping and dining at affordable prices. Or head to Overseas Chinese Town to take in some art and culture. For those who enjoy a round or two of golf, the city's Mission Hills Golf Club promises to blow your mind.

TOP REASONS TO GO

Feel the Buzz: This region is the undisputed engine driving China's current economic boom, and whether you're in Guangzhou or Shenzhen, you're sure to feel the buzz of this formerly Socialist nation on a serious capitalist joyride.

Explore the Ancient: Though thoroughly modern, the Pearl River Delta has by no means lost touch with its ancient roots. From the temples of Guangzhou to the Ming Dynasty–walled city of Dapeng in Shenzhen, a journey through the PRD is a journey through the centuries.

Soak Up Some Colonial Splendor: Modern Guangzhou is rife with well-preserved examples of architecture dating back to the 19th century, when European merchants amassed fortunes in the opium trade, and the buildings from which they once plied their trade still stand.

Shopping Sprees: In the mercantile capital of China, and maybe the world, it comes as no surprise that both Guangzhou and Shenzen arouse the shopaholic in all of us. Go on, indulge.

9

PEARL RIVER DELTA PLANNER

When to Go

When to go is a major question every traveler needs to ask himself, and certainly to a place like the Pearl River Delta, where summer temperatures and humidity can make the area feel like the inside of a clothes dryer halfway through the dry cycle and winter brings an all-pervading chill and dampness that sucks the joy from any endeavor no matter how well planned. The spring and autumn are good times to go, but this is complicated by a few factors. Unless you have friends in the hotel industry, don't even think about visiting Guangzhou during the annual spring trade fair, when prices of hotels skyrocket. Don't travel anywhere in China during the Golden Week holiday, which takes place annually from October 1 through 7. So what do we recommend? September, October (excluding Golden Week), and early to mid-November.

Tours & Travel Arrangements

The aptly named **China Travel Services** (☎852/2851–1700 or 852/2522–0450 ⊕www.ctshk.com/english/index.htm) is still the most trusted name in arranging tours throughout China. Its Web site has links to its many offices worldwide; it has 40 offices in Hong Kong, Kowloon, and the New Territories and can arrange just about any type of travel experience that might interest you in the Pearl River Delta. CTS can also assist with visas and booking discount hotel rooms. It's open weekdays 9 to 7, Saturday 9 to 5, and Sunday and holidays 9:30 to 12:30 and 2 to 5.

China International Travel Service Limited (*CITS* ☎8610/6522–2991 🖷8610/6522–1733 ⊕www.cits.cn/en/index.htm support-en@cits.com.cn) .Bestourchina (⊕www.bestourchina.com) is a sub-brand of CITS' online business.

Cuisine

Fresh ingredients as well prompt service are important in Cantonese cooking, so expect so your meal to be cooked to order and arrive at the table sizzling hot. Most Cantonese dishes are stir-fried or steamed, although roasted meats such as barbecued chicken and pork are also popular. Dim sum—literally meaning "touch your heart"—includes a huge selection of dumplings and pastries. Filled with meat and vegetables, they are a perfect way to start or end the day. When you go out to eat, go with as many people as you can find so that you can try as many different dishes as possible. The Cantonese are famous for their penchant for eating everything. One Cantonese saying goes "anything with its back towards the sky is edible," and the idea is so inclusive that any animal or insect, including snakes, civet cats, and locusts, make the list. The cuisine also makes use of every part of an animal's body, including feet, tongue, and entrails. Be adventurous but make sure you know what you're eating! And stick to fully cooked dishes to avoid bacterial or parasitic infections, particularly during warm weather.

Safety

Avoid giving money to beggars. Take the usual precautions against appearing conspicuously wealthy, and carry with you only the amount of cash you need. Crowded places, such as stations and clubs, often harbor pickpockets, so keep your eyes on your bags and if you see a local wearing a backpack on the front of his or her body, it's probably a good idea to do the same.

Language

The local dialect is Cantonese though almost everyone in China also speaks Mandarin or Putonghua ("common speech"), which is easier to pick up than Cantonese. Learning a few simple phrases, such as ní hǎo ("hello"), and xiè xie ("thank you"), will enrich your travel experience and make locals smile appreciatively.

Getting Around

Guangzhou's subway system is cheap, clean, and reasonably efficient. Divided into four lines that span both sides of the Pearl River, most of the areas of interest to casual visitors are found on lines 1 or 2 (the red and yellow lines on the maps). Shenzhen's brand-new metro runs from the terminus at Luohu station to the Windows of the World Station in OCT. Air-conditioned express buses crisscross most of the Pearl River Delta region several times a day. Ask at your hotel for the closest bus station.

WHAT IT COSTS IN YUAN				
¢	$	$$	$$$	$$$$
RESTAURANTS				
under Y25	Y25–Y49	Y50–Y99	Y100–Y165	over Y165
HOTELS				
under Y700	Y700–Y1,099	Y1,100–Y1,399	Y1,400–Y1,800	over Y1,800

Restaurant prices are for a main course, excluding tax and tips. Hotel prices are for a standard double room, including taxes.

Ancient Days

Don't let the *Blade Runner*–like skyline fool you. China's newest city isn't all glass and steel. Though Shenzhen City is barely three decades old, the areas outside the city are resplendent with examples of ancient Chinese culture. You'll want to take at least a day to explore the Longgang District, home to two examples modern and antique architecture existing side by side.

Like the rapidly disappearing hutong neighborhoods of Beijing, **Dapeng Fortress**—an ancient city—is a living museum. The old town contains homes, temples, shops, and courtyards that look pretty much the way they did when they were built over the course of the Ming (AD 1368–1644) and Qing (1644–1911) dynasties. For the most part, the residences are occupied, the shops are doing business, and the temples are active houses of worship. Dapeng's ancient city is surrounded by an old stone wall, and entered through a series of gates built at the cardinal points.

Likewise, the **Hakka Folk Customs Museum and Enclosures** is an amazingly well-preserved example of a walled community. Now more a museum than anything else—persecution of Hakkas went out of vogue after the collapse of the Qing Dynasty, led by Sun Yat-sen, himself a member of the clan—the enclosures still stand as an excellent example of an ancient community built with defense in mind.

9

By Joshua
Samuel Brown

The Pearl River Delta is China's workshop, its fastest-growing, ever-changing, and most affluent region. It is the industrial engine powering China's meteoric economic rise—and it shows. Earth-at-night satellite photos give a telling view of Asia. Tokyo, Seoul, and Taiwan glow brightly, but it's the boomtown cities along the Pearl River Delta that burn brightest. You will find some of the greatest shopping, a flourishing nightlife, and a culinary scene which most regions can only dream of.

The Pear River Delta is also among China's most polluted regions, and this is saying a lot. From the southern suburbs of Guangzhou city to the northern edge of Shenzhen, industry stretches in all directions. As far as the eye can see, tens of thousands of factories churn out the lion's share of the world's consumer products. This hyper-industry has polluted the entire area's soil, water, and air so badly that in Hong Kong (on the region's southern tip) pollution is an overriding public concern. On a bad day, the air quality in Guangzhou can actually be described as *abusive*. On top of all of this, much of the region is noisy and chaotic.

So with all this in mind, why would the pleasure traveler even visit Pearl River Delta? The answers are myriad. History enthusiasts head to Guangzhou, Guangdong province's ancient capital, and the historic center of both Cantonese culture and the revolution that overthrew the last dynasty. Gourmands flock to both Guangzhou and Shenzhen to indulge in some of the best examples of Chinese cuisine—and increasingly, the world—at all price ranges. Culture vultures don't mind putting up with the pollution and chaos for a chance to visit the many temples, shrines, and museums scattered throughout the region. And shopaholics? A visit to the Pearl River Delta will quickly dismiss any lingering notions that China is still a nation bound by the tenets of Marx and Mao.

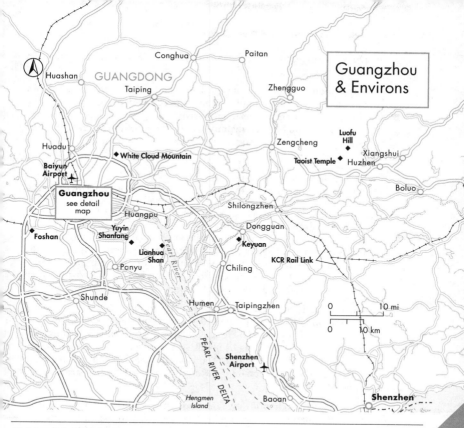

Guangzhou & Environs

GUANGZHOU

120 km (74½ mi; 1½ hrs) north of Hong Kong.

Guangzhou (also known as Canton), the capital of Guangdong province, is both a modern boomtown and an ancient port city. This metropolis of over 7 million people has all the expected accoutrements of a competitive, modern Chinese city: skyscrapers, heavy traffic, efficient metro, and serious crowds. Guangzhou is an old city with a long history. Exploring its riverfront, parks, temples, and markets, one is constantly reminded the impact its irrepressible culture, language, and cuisine has made on the world.

The city has long been considered China's gateway to the West, and the Cantonese have a reputation for being China's most savvy entertainers. From the late 18th century, western merchants set up trading houses in Guangzhou where they negotiated the purchase of tea.

In the early 20th century, Guangzhou was a hotbed of revolutionary zeal, first as the birthplace of the movement to overthrow the last dynasty (culminating in the 1911 Revolution), and then as a battleground between Nationalists and Communists in the years leading to the 1949 Communist revolution. Following the open-door policy of

Deng Xiaoping in 1979, the port city was able to resume its role as a commercial gateway to China.

Rapid modernization during the 1980s and '90s has taken its toll not just on the environment but also on the pace of city life. On bad days the clouds of building-site dust, aggressive driving, shop touts, and persistent beggars can be overwhelming. But in Guangzhou's parks, temples, winding old-quarter backstreets, restaurants, river islets, and museums, the old city and a more refined way of life is never far away.

REGIONAL TOURS

A popular tour company in Guangzhou is **GZL International Travel Service** (☎ *86020/8633 ⊕www.gzl.com.cn office@gzl.com.cn*).

GETTING HERE & AROUND

Most travelers enter Guangzhou either by train or plane. Long-distance trains pull in at the Guangzhou East Station. This station is also on the metro line, so getting to your destination right off the train is a fairly simple matter. One-way tickets to or from Hong Kong cost between Y210 and Y250, and between Y130 and Y170 to Shenzhen.

Guangzhou is connected to Shenzhen (approximately 100 km [62 mi] to the south) by the aptly named Guangzhou–Shenzhen expressway. Buses from Guangzhou to Hong Kong leave from both the Guangzhou East Station and from major hotels such as the China and the Garden hotels, and cost about Y180. You can, in a pinch, get a taxi from the station to the Shenzhen–Hong Kong border, but be prepared to pay upward of Y400.

Guangzhou is a chaotic city, famed for noise, crowds, and endless traffic jams—many a vacation hour has been wasted inside of taxicabs. Although taxis in Guangzhou are cheap and plentiful, traffic in the city is reaching nightmare proportions.

By Air Guangzhou's Baiyun Airport in Huada city established Guangzhou as a regional air hub connecting the city to major international destinations and about 100 destinations within China. The airport currently offers 10 flights per day to both Hong Kong (Y670) and Beijing (Y1,240) between 9 AM and 9 PM. It has direct flights to Paris, Los Angeles, Singapore, Bangkok, Sydney, Jakarta, and Phnom Penh and a number of cities in North America. International airport tax is Y90, domestic departure tax is Y50.

By Bus Guangzhou Provincial Passenger Bus Station is the largest bus station in Guangdong province. Buses depart here daily to the neighboring Guangxi, Hunan, Fujian, and Jiangxi Provinces. There are also deluxe buses to Shenzhen, Hong Kong, and Macau. The easiest way from Guangzhou to Hong Kong is by the deluxe bus.

By Subway Guangzhou's clean and efficient underground metro currently has two lines connecting 36 stations, including the new East and old Central railway stations. Tickets range from Y2 to Y7.

Many visitors are reluctant to ride the Guangzhou metro, perhaps fearing that without the proper linguistic skills such a journey might be fraught with confusion. That's a shame, because the Guangzhou metro is quick, convenient, and a boon to day-trippers.

If you've decided to spend a day shunning automobiles—and we hope you do—ask your hotel concierge to give you an English subway map. *See subway map later in the chapter.* For walking-tour-friendly neighborhoods, we recommend Dongshankou station. This is a lovely little area with plenty of shopping opportunities. Tree-lined streets just off the avenue are filled with enclosed gardens and old houses with traditional architecture. The area surrounding the Linhex station is the most modern part of the city. This is a good neighborhood to walk around with your head tilted skyward.

If you want to continue on an anticar trip, get off at Gongyuanqian station (where Lines 1 and 2 intersect) and walk to the Beijing Road Pedestrian Mall: the hip, trendy, and car-free heart of young consumerism in Guangzhou.

By Train Five express trains (Y234 first class, Y190 second class) depart daily for Guangzhou East Railway Station from Hong Kong's Kowloon Station. The trip takes about 1¾ hours. The last train back to Hong Kong leaves at 5:25 PM. Trains between Shenzhen's Luohu Railway Station and Guangzhou East Railway Station run every hour and cost between Y80 and Y100.

ESSENTIALS

Air Contacts **Baiyun Airport** (⊠ *Airport International Office Building, South Area of Guangzhou Baiyun International Airport* ☎ *020/3606–6999 flight information* ⊕ *www.gbiac.net/en/index.html*). **China Southern Airlines** (⊠ *181 Huanshi Lu, on left as you exit Guangzhou railway station [Guangzhou main station metro]* ☎ *020/95539 24-hr hotline* ⊕ *www.csair.com/en/index.asp*). **Zhuhai International Airport** (☎ *0756/889–5494*).

Banks **Bank of China** (⊠ *197 Dongfeng Xilu, Guangzhou 510180* ☎ *020/8333–8080* ⊕ *www.boc.cn*).**HSBC** (⊠ *G2, ground fl., Garden Hotel, No. 368 Huan Shi Dong Lu, Guangzhou, Guangdong* ☎ *020/8313–1888* ⊕ *www.hsbc.com.cn*).

Bus Contacts **Citybus** (☎ *852/2873–0818*). **Guangdong Provincial Bus Station** (⊠ *145 Huanshi Xi Lu* ☎ *020/8666–1297*). **Guangzhou Bus Station** (⊠ *158 Huanshi Xi Lu* ☎ *020/8668–4259*). **Tianhe Bus Station** (⊠ *Yuangang, Tianhe District* ☎ *020/8774–1083*).

Medical Assistance **Shenzhen People's Hospital** (⊠ *Dongmen Rd. N, Shenzhen* ☎ *0755/2553–3018 Ext. 2553, 1387 Outpatient Dept.*).

Subway Contact **Guangzhou Metro** (☎ *020/8328–9033* ⊕ *www.gzmtr.com/en*).

Train Contacts **Guangzhou East Railway Station** (⊠ *Lin Hezhong Rd., Tianhe District* ☎ *020/6134–6222*). **Guangzhou Railway Station** (⊠ *Huanshi Lu* ☎ *020/6135–7222*).

Visitor & Tour Info **China Travel Services** (⊠ *Shop 105D, 1st fl. East Wing, Timessquare, 28 Tianhebei Road, Guangzhou* ☎ *020/3882–0045* ⊕ *www.ctshk. com/english/index.htm*).

9

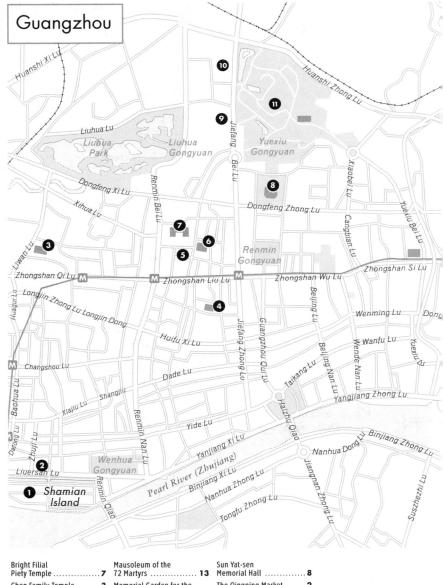

Guangzhou

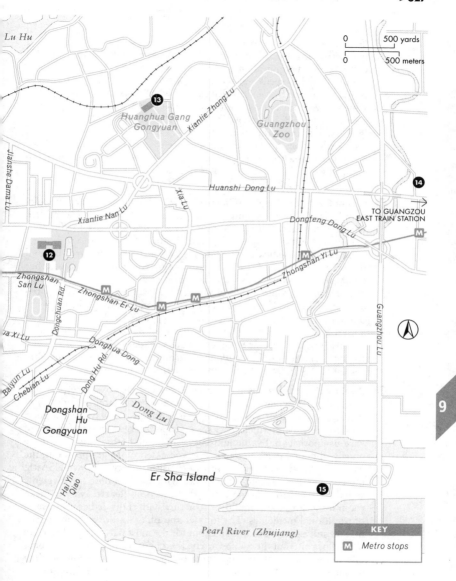

Lu Hu

13

*Huanghua Gang
Gongyuan*

Xianlie Zhong Lu

*Guangzhou
Zoo*

Huanshi Dong Lu

14

→
TO GUANGZOU
EAST TRAIN STATION

Jianshe Dama Lu

Xianlie Nan Lu

Xia Lu

Dongfeng Dong Lu

12

Ⓜ

Zhongshan Yi Lu

*Zhongshan
San Lu*

Dongchuan Rd.

Zhongshan Er Lu

Ⓜ

Ⓜ

Ⓜ

Guangzhou Lu

a Xi Lu

Dongzhua Dong

Baiyun Lu

Chebian Lu

Dong Hu Rd.

Dong Lu

*Dongshan
Hu
Gongyuan*

*Hai Yin
Qiao*

Er Sha Island

15

9

Pearl River (Zhujiang)

KEY
Ⓜ Metro stops

0 —— 500 yards
0 —— 500 meters

EXPLORING GUANGZHOU

Guangzhou is a massive, sprawling metropolis divided into several districts and many more neighborhoods. Roughly speaking, the city is divided in half by the Pearl River, which runs from east to west and separates the Haizhu District (a large island) from the districts in the north. Most of the explorations we're recommending will keep you north of the Pearl River, since this is where the majority of the more culturally edifying parts of Guangzhou lie.

> **CAUTION**
>
> Like any other urban area, Guangzhou has its fair share of pickpockets, so keep your wallet in a front pocket and your bags in front of you.

MAIN ATTRACTIONS

❼ "Bright Filial Piety Temple" *(Guangxiao Si)*. This is the oldest Buddhist temple in Guangzhou and by far the most charming. The gilded, wooden, laughing Buddha sitting at the entrance adds to the temple's warm, welcoming atmosphere. A huge, bronze incense burner, wreathed in joss-stick smoke, stands in the main courtyard. Beyond the main hall, noted for its ceiling of red-lacquer timbers, is another courtyard that contains several treasures, among them a small brick pagoda said to contain the tonsure hair of Hui-neng (the sixth patriarch of Chan Buddhism), and a couple of iron pagodas, which are the oldest of their kind in China. Above them spread the leafy branches of a myrobalan plum tree and a banyan, called Buddha's Tree because it is said Hui-neng became enlightened in its shade. ☒ *Corner of Renmin Bei and Guangxiao Lu, 2 blocks north of metro station Ximenkou, Liwan* ☎ *Y5* ⊗ *Daily 6:30–5* Ⓜ *Ximenkou.*

❷ The Qingping Market has undergone a few changes over the past few years; the sprawling cluster of stalls was once infamous for its wet market, a hotbed of animal slaughter. Though it always had a good selection of general knickknacks, as well as a large section of goods of various apothecarial value (ginseng, fungi, and herbs, as well as more cruelly obtained items like bear bile and essence of tiger prostate), the wet market scared all but the heartiest visitors away. Following SARS, the government decided to do away with the bloodier, less hygienic stalls. A large section of the old market was been cleared away to make room for a shiny, new, mall-like structure with stalls dedicated to sales of traditional medicines. The funkier and older outdoor section of the market still exists off to one side, but for the most part items on sale are of the flora and not the fauna variety. Merchants of tiger claws and bear bile still engage in their cruel trade on the base of the bridge leading to Shamian Island. Even though most of these merchants are dressed Tibetan style (perhaps to engender the sympathy of foreigners?) the majority of them are Han Chinese engaged in a despicable trade.

❶ Shamian Island. More than a century ago the Mandarins of Guangzhou designated a 44-acre sandbank outside the city walls in the Pearl River as an enclave for foreign merchants. Foreigners had previously lived and done business in a row of houses known as the Thirteen Factories, near the present Shamian, but local resentment after the Opium Wars—sometimes leading to murderous attacks—made it prudent to confine them to a protected area, which was linked to the city by two bridges that were closed at 10 every night.

The island soon became a bustling township, as trading companies from Britain, the United States, France, Holland, Italy, Germany, Portugal, and Japan built stone mansions along the waterfront. With spacious gardens and private wharves, these served as homes, offices, and warehouses. There were churches for Catholics and Protestants, banks, a yacht club, football grounds, a cricket field, and the Victory hotel.

Shamian was attacked in the 1920s but survived until the 1949 Revolution when its mansions became government offices or apartment houses and the churches were turned into factories. In recent years, however, the island has resumed much of its old character. Many colonial buildings have been restored, and both churches have been beautifully renovated and reopened to worshippers. Worth visiting is **Our Lady of Lourdes Catholic Church** (✉ *Shamian Dajie at Yijie*), with its cream-and-white neo-Gothic tower. A park with shady walks and benches has been created in the center of the island, where local residents come to chat with friends, walk around with their caged birds, or practice tai chi.

NEED A BREAK?

Have an espresso in Chinese colonial splendor at the **Shamian Island Blenz** (✉ *46 Shamian Ave.*), across from **Customs Hotel** in a building dating back to the late Qing Dynasty. Comfy couches, strong coffee, and free Internet access are available in this old building that once housed Guangzhou's U.S. Bank in the pre-revolutionary days. Right on the park, Blenz is a great place to watch people practice tai chi and traditional Chinese fan dancing.

6 **Six Banyan Temple** (*Liu Rong Si Hua Ta*). Look at any ancient scroll painting or lithograph by early western travelers, and you'll see two landmarks rising above old Guangzhou. One is the minaret of the mosque; the other is the 184-foot pagoda of the Six Banyan Temple. Still providing an excellent lookout, the pagoda appears to have nine stories, each with doorways and encircling balconies. Inside, however, there are 17 levels. Thanks to its arrangement of colored, carved roofs, it is popularly known as the Flowery Pagoda.

The temple was founded in the 5th century, but because of a series of fires, most of the existing buildings date from the 11th century. It was built by the Zen master Tanyu and is still a very active place of worship, with a community of monks and regular attendance by Zen Buddhists. It was originally called Purificatory Wisdom Temple but changed its name after a visit by the Song Dynasty poet Su Dongpo, who was so delighted by six banyan trees growing in the courtyard that he left an inscription with the characters for six banyans. ⊠ *Haizhu Bei Lu, south of Yuexiu Park, Liwan* 🚇 *Y10* ⊙ *Daily 8–5.*

IF YOU HAVE TIME

❸ **Chen Family Temple** *(Chen Jia Ci).* The Chen family is one of the Pearl River Delta's oldest and biggest clans. In the late 19th century local members, who had become rich as merchants, decided to build a memorial temple. They invited contributions from the Chens—and kindred Chans—who had emigrated overseas. Money flowed in from 72 countries, and no expense was spared. One of the temple's highlights is a huge and skillfully carved ridgepole frieze. It stretches 90 feet along the main roof and depicts scenes from the epic *Romance of Three Kingdoms,* with thousands of figures against a backdrop of ornate houses, monumental gates, and lush scenery. Elsewhere in the huge compound of pavilions and courtyards are friezes of delicately carved stone and wood, as well as fine iron castings and a dazzling altar covered with gold leaf. The temple also houses a folk-arts museum and shop. ⊠ *7 Zhongshan Qi Lu, Liwan* 🚇 *Y10* ⊙ *Daily 8:30–5* Ⓜ *Chengjia Ci.*

❺ **Guangxiao Temple** *(Guangxiao si).* This impressively restored temple and city-gate complex, also known as the Five Celestials Shrine, was once the front gate for the wall that surrounded the city. The shrine and remaining sections of the wall in Yuexiu Park are the only pieces of old Guangzhou's fortifications still standing. The complex also has an impressive model of how the city looked when the air was clean, the roads were filled with horse-drawn carts, and foreigners were confined on pain of death to one small section of the city. ⊠ *Renmin Bei Lu, 3 blocks north of the Ximenkou metro, Liwan* 🚇 *10* ⊙ *Daily 8–5* Ⓜ *Ximenkou.*

❹ **Huaisheng Mosque** *(Huaisheng Si Guang).* In the cosmopolitan era of the Tang Dynasty (618–907) a Muslim missionary named Abu Wangus, said to be an uncle of the prophet Mohammed, came to southern China. He converted many Chinese to Islam and built this mosque in Guangzhou as their house of worship. His tomb in the northern part of the city has been a place of pilgrimage for visiting Muslims, but the mosque is his best-known memorial. A high wall encloses the mosque, which is dominated by the smooth, white minaret. Rising to 108 feet, it can be climbed using an interior spiral staircase, and the views from the top—where a muezzin calls the faithful to prayer—are spectacular. Be aware that this site is only open to Muslims. ⊠ *Guangta Lu, 3 blocks southwest of the Gongyuanqian metro station, Liwan* 🚇 *Free* ⊙ *Sat.– Thurs. 8–5, except Muslim holy days* Ⓜ *Gongyuanqian.*

PARKS & MUSEUMS

⓯ **Guangdong Museum of Art** is a major cultural establishment of the "new Canton," and regularly hosts the works of painters, sculptors, and other artists from around China and the world. An excellent sculpture garden surrounds the large complex with exhibitions both large and small. Located on Ersha Island, the Web site offers a map to help you find your way—so print it out before you go. ⊠ *38 Yanyu Lu, Er Sha Island, Yuexiu* ☎ *020/8735–1468* 🚇 *Y15* ⊕ *www.GDMoA.org* ⊙ *Tues.–Sun. 9–5.*

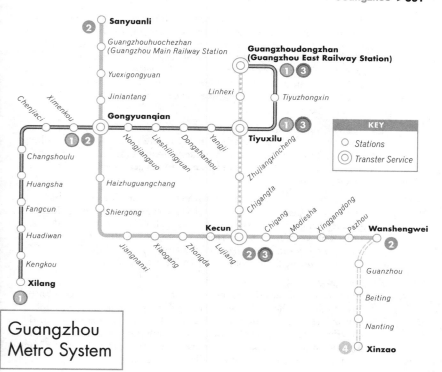

Guangzhou
Metro System

KEY
○ Stations
◎ Transfer Service

❿ Orchid Garden *(Lanpu).* This garden
★ offers a wonderfully convenient
retreat from the noise and crowds
of the city. It's spread over 20 acres,
with paths that wind through
groves of bamboo and tropical
trees to a series of classic teahouses.
Here you can sit and enjoy a wide
variety of Chinese teas, brewed the
traditional way. There are tables

WORD OF MOUTH

"There is a teahouse on a small
island in the lake and they had
the most extensive assortment of
high-end Xixing teapots I've seen
anywhere. They also had quite an
assortment of teas." —Kathie

inside and on terraces that overlook the ponds. As for the orchids,
there are 10,000 pots with more than 2,000 species of the flower, which
present a magical sight when they bloom (peak time is May and June).
✉ *Jiefang Bei Lu, Liwan* 💰 *Y5* ⏱ *Daily 8:30 AM–11 PM.*

❾ Tomb of the Southern Yue Kings. Until recently only specialist historians
★ realized that Guangzhou had once been a royal capital. In 1983 bull-
dozers clearing ground to build the China Hotel uncovered the intact
tomb of Emperor Wen Di, who ruled Nan Yue (southern China) from
137 BC to 122 BC. The tomb was faithfully restored and its treasures
placed in the adjoining **Nan Yue Museum.**

The tomb contained the skeletons of the king and 15 courtiers—guards, cooks, concubines, and a musician—who were buried alive to attend him in death. Also buried were several thousand funerary objects, clearly designed to show off the extraordinary accomplishments of the southern empire. The tomb itself—built entirely of stone slabs—is behind the museum and is remarkable for its compact size. ✉ *867 Jiefang Bei Lu, around the corner from the China Hotel, Liwan* 💵 *Y15* 🕙 *Daily 9:30–5:30.*

⑪ **Yuexiu Park** *(Yuexiu Gongyuan).* To get away from the bustle, retreat
☺ into Yuexiu Park in the heart of town. The park covers 247 rolling
★ acres and includes landscaped gardens, man-made lakes, recreational areas, and playgrounds. Children and adults get a kick out of the fish-feeding ponds.

Be sure to visit the famous **Five Rams Statue** (Wuyang Suxiang), which celebrates the legend of the five celestials who came to Guangzhou riding on goats to bring grains to the people. Guangzhou families like to take each other's photo in front of the statue before setting off to enjoy the park. ✉ *Jiefang Bei Lu, across from China Hotel, Liwan* ☎ *020/8666–1950* 🌐 *www.yuexiupark-gz.com* 💵 *Y5* 🕙 *Daily 6 AM–9 PM.*

REVOLUTIONARY MEMORIALS

In the center of the city are memorials to people who changed Chinese history during the 20th century, using Guangzhou as a base of operations. The most famous were local boy Dr. Sun Yat-sen, who led the overthrow of the Qing Dynasty, and Communist Party founders Mao Zedong and Zhou Enlai. There were many others, thousands of whom died in the struggles. All are recalled in different ways.

⑬ **Mausoleum of the 72 Martyrs** *(Huanghua Gang Qishi'er Lieshi Mu).* In a prelude to the successful revolution of 1911 a group of 88 revolutionaries staged the Guangzhou armed uprising, only to be defeated and executed by the authorities. Of those killed, 72 were buried here. Their memorial, built in 1918, incorporates a mixture of international symbols of freedom and democracy, including replicas of the Statue of Liberty. ✉ *Xianlie Zhong Lu, Yuexiu* 💵 *Y10* 🕙 *Daily 6 AM–8:30 PM.*

⑫ **Memorial Garden for the Martyrs** *(Lieshi Lingyuan).* Built in 1957, this garden has been planted around a tumulus that contains the remains of 5,000 revolutionaries killed in the 1927 destruction of the Guangzhou Commune by the Nationalists. This was the execution site of many victims. On the grounds is the **Revolutionary Museum,** which displays pictures and memorabilia of Guangdong's 20th-century rebellions. ✉ *Zhongshan San Lu, Yuexiu* 💵 *Y5* 🕙 *Daily 6 AM–9 PM.*

⑧ **Sun Yat-sen Memorial Hall** *(Zhongshan Jinian Tang.)* Dr. Sun's Memorial Hall is a handsome pavilion that stands in a garden behind a bronze statue of the leader. Built in 1929–31 with funds mostly from overseas Chinese, the building is a classic octagon, with sweeping roofs of blue tiles over carved wooden eaves and verandas of red-lacquer columns. Inside is an auditorium with seating for 5,000 and a stage for plays, concerts, and ceremonial occasions. ✉*Dongfeng Zhong Lu, Liwan* ☎*Y10* ◷*Daily 8–5:30.*

TIANHE-DISTRICT SIGHTS

⓮
☾
The Tianhe District is Guangzhou's newly designated business and upmarket residential area. It is the site of the new Guangzhou East Railway Station, the terminus for Hong Kong trains, a world-class sports stadium, and a growing number of office–apartment skyscrapers. Among the buildings is the 80-story **GITIC Plaza** which soars 1,300 feet and is China's second-tallest building. The **Guangzhou East Railway Station** (✉*Linhe Lu, Tianhe*), with its vast entrance hall is worth a peak, even if you don't have a train to catch. A hub for most of Guangzhou's sporting events, the **Tianhe Stadium Complex** (✉*Huanshi Dong Lu, East Guangzhou, Tianhe*) has two indoor and two outdoor arenas that are equipped for international soccer matches, track-and-field competitions, as well as pop concerts and large-scale ceremonies. The complex is surrounded by a pleasantly landscaped park, with outdoor cafés and tree-shaded benches. The park includes a bowling center with 38 lanes and lots of video games.

WHERE TO EAT

For centuries Guangzhou has been known as a city of gourmands, and in the last decade, it has undergone a gastronomic renaissance the likes of which few cities will ever know. At the heart of this is commerce, as business travelers bring the ingredients, spices, and culinary traditions from their homes with them. Popping up alongside venerable Cantonese restaurants are eateries specializing in flavors from around the world. Guangzhou has more excellent Indian, Italian, Thai, and Vietnamese restaurants than you can shake a joss stick at, and owing to the recent influx of Middle Eastern traders, there are some parts of town where it's easier to find a falafel than a shrimp dumpling. Of course this isn't to say that Guangzhou's traditional delicacies have been usurped. Amazing seafood dishes and braised and barbecued meats are still available in delicious variety, and succulent dim sum still rules the roost as the city's hometown favorite.

$–$$$
ECLECTIC
✕**Back Street Jazz Bar & Restaurant.** Tall bamboo groves masks a space-age interior of glass walls, sliding-metal doors, and Plexiglas walkways in this cantina attached to the Guangdong Art Museum. Food is pure world fusion, with dishes like deep-fried salmon and lotus root, Thai chicken salad, and honey-apple foie gras. The softly lit red-neon bar serves mojitos, fruit martinis, and a wide selection of wines. Back Street has an in-house jazz band playing nightly from 10 until midnight, and often hosts international bands. ✉*38 Yanyu Lu, East Gate of the Guangdong Museum of Art, Er Sha Island* ☎*020/3839–9090* ▭*AE, DC, MC, V.*

$–$$$
CHINESE
✕**Banxi Restaurant.** On the edge of Liwan Lake, this restaurant has a series of teahouse rooms and landscaped gardens interconnected by zigzag paths and bridges that give the feel of a Taoist temple. One room is built on a floating houseboat. The food is as tasty as it looks with dishes

9

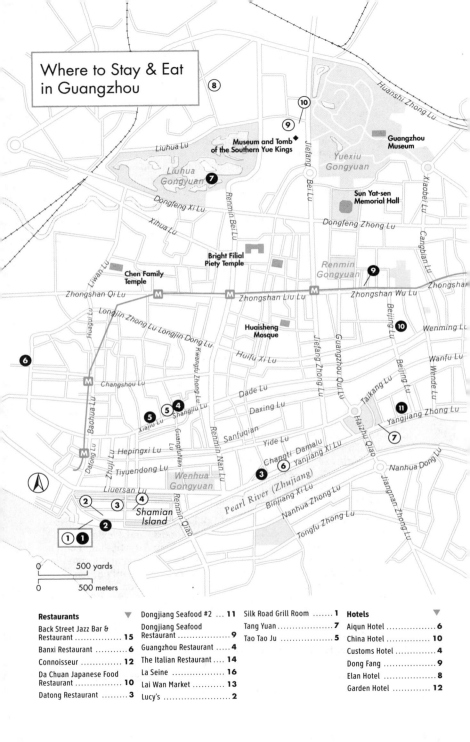

Where to Stay & Eat in Guangzhou

Huanshi Zhong Lu

Liuhua Lu

Museum and Tomb of the Southern Yue Kings

Guangzhou Museum

Jiefang Bei Lu

Liuhua Gongyuan

Yuexiu Gongyuan

Dongfeng Xi Lu

Renmin Bei Lu

Sun Yat-sen Memorial Hall

Xihua Lu

Dongfeng Zhong Lu

Xiaobei Lu

Cangbian Lu

Liwan Lu

Chen Family Temple

Bright Filial Piety Temple

Renmin Gongyuan

Zhongshan Qi Lu

Zhongshan Liu Lu

Zhongshan Wu Lu

Zhongshar

Longjin Zhong Lu Longjin Dong Lu

Huaisheng Mosque

Beijing Lu

Wenming L

Huagui Lu

Kwangfu Zhong Lu

Huifu Xi Lu

Jiefang Zhong Lu

Guangzhou Qui Lu

Wende Lu

Wanfu Lu

Changshou Lu

Dade Lu

Taikang Lu

Baohua Lu

Shangjiu Lu

Daxing Lu

Yangjiang Zhong Lu

Xiajiu Lu

Guangfuwan Lu

Sanfuqian

Haizhu Qiao

Zhuji Lu

Hepingxi Lu

Renmin Nan Lu

Yide Lu

Changti Damalu

Yanjiang Xi Lu

Nanhua Dong Lu

Tiyuendong Lu

Wenhua Gongyuan

Pearl River (Zhujiang)

Binjiang Xi Lu

Jiangnan Zhong Lu

Liuersan Lu

Renmin Qiao

Nanhua Zhong Lu

Datong Lu

Shamian Island

Tongfu Zhong Lu

0   500 yards
0   500 meters

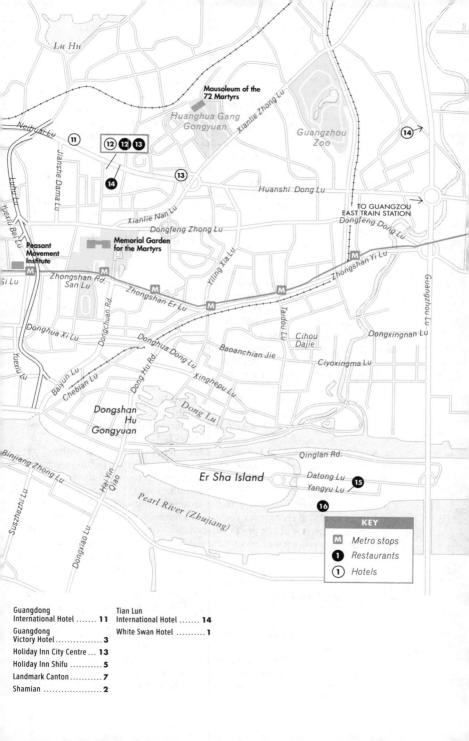

Mausoleum of the 72 Martyrs

Huanghua Gang Gongyuan

Lu Hu

Xianlie Zhong Lu

Guangzhou Zoo

Neihuai Lu

Jianshe Dama Lu

Luhu Lu

Yuexiu Bei Lu

Peasant Movement Institute

Si Lu

Zhongshan Rd. San Lu

Dongchuan Rd.

Zhongshan Er Lu

Zhongshan Yi Lu

Huanshi Dong Lu

TO GUANGZOU EAST TRAIN STATION

Dongfeng Dong Lu

Guangzhou Lu

Xianlie Nan Lu

Dongfeng Zhong Lu

Memorial Garden for the Martyrs

Yiling Xia Lu

Taidou Lu

Donghua Xi Lu

Baiyun Lu

Chebian Lu

Yuexiu Lu

Donghua Dong Lu

Dong Hu Rd.

Baoanchian Jie

Cihou Dajie

Dongxingnan Lu

Ciyoxingma Lu

Xinghepu Lu

Dongshan Hu Gongyuan

Dong Lu

Binjiang Zhong Lu

Suszhezhi Lu

Hai-Yin Qiao

Qinglan Rd.

Er Sha Island

Datong Lu

Yangyu Lu

Dongxiao Lu

Pearl River (Zhujiang)

KEY

Ⓜ Metro stops

❶ Restaurants

① Hotels

such as scallop and crab soup and quail eggs cooked with shrimp roe on a bed of green vegetables. ✉ *151 Longjin Xi Lu, Liwan Park* ☎ *020/8181–5718* 🖃 *AE, MC, V.*

$$$$
CONTINENTAL

✕ **Connoisseur.** This premier restaurant feels like regency France with its arched columns and gilded capitals, gold-framed mirrors, lustrous drapes, and immaculate table settings. The resident French chef specializes in lamb and steak dishes. ✉ *Garden Hotel, 368 Huanshi Dong Lu, 3rd fl., Huanshi Rd.* ☎ *020/3964–3962* 🖃 *AE, DC, MC, V* ⊘ *No lunch.*

> **TABLE MANNERS**
>
> When using chopsticks, do not stick them vertically into your bowl of rice—this is thought to be unlucky because it resembles the burning of joss sticks connected with death rituals. Don't be surprised to hear people slurping and burping—these are totally acceptable behaviors not only in China, but in most of Asia as well. When eating rice, bring the edge of the bowl to your mouth and use your chopsticks to push the rice in.

$
JAPANESE

✕ **Da Chuan Japanese Food Restaurant.** This local eatery is located in a busy shopping area on Beijing Road. The extensive menu includes everything from à la carte dishes plucked straight off the rotating sushi bar, to ramen, tempura, and other Japanese specialties. ✉ *294 Beijing Rd., 4th fl., Beijing Road Pedestrian Mall* ☎ *020/8319–0283* 🖃 *No credit cards.*

$–$$
CHINESE

✕ **Datong Restaurant.** Occupying all eight stories of an old riverfront building, with an open terrace on the top floor, this is one of the city's veteran dining establishments. The restaurant is popular with locals all hours of the day, so arrive early to be guaranteed a seat. The atmosphere is chaotic and noisy, but the morning and afternoon dim sum and huge menu are well worth it. Famous dishes include stewed-chicken claws (delicious, by the way), crispy-skin chicken, and roasted *Xishi* duck. Probably not the best place for vegetarians. ✉ *Nanfang Dasha, 63 Yanjiang Xi Lu, Colonial Canton* ☎ *020/8188–8988* 🖃 *AE, DC, MC, V.*

¢–$
CANTONESE

✕ **Dongjiang Seafood Restaurant.** There are two Dongjiang Seafood restaurants in Guangzhou. Both are renowned for their culinary excellence and authentic Canton decor, but we recommend the Pearl River location (on Qiao Guang and Yan Jiang roads). It features a seafood market where you can wander around and choose your own meal. The staff will try to steer you toward the most expensive items first, so make sure you check prices beforehand. Some of our favorites include the braised duck stuffed with eight delicacies and glutinous rice, stuffed giant prawns, crab in black-bean sauce, and salt-roast chicken. ✉ *No.2 Qiao Guang Rd., Pearl River* ✛ *2 blocks SE of Haizhu Shichang metro* ☎ *020/8318–4901* 🖃 *AE, DC, MC, V.*

$–$$$
CANTONESE

✕ **Guangzhou Restaurant.** One of the oldest eateries in the city, Guangzhou Restaurant was opened in 1936 and has a string of culinary awards. The setting is classic Canton, with courtyards of flowery bushes surrounded by dining rooms of various sizes. The food is reputed to be among the best in the city, with house specialties like "Eight Treasures," a mix of fowl, pork, and mushrooms served in a bowl made of winter melon. Other Cantonese dishes include duck feet stuffed with shrimp, roasted goose, and of course, dim sum. Meals here can be cheap or very expensive, depending on how exotic you're looking to get. ⊠ *2 Wenchang Nan Lu, Ancestral Guangzhou* ☎*020/8138–0388* ▤*AE, DC, MC, V.*

$
ITALIAN

✕ **The Italian Restaurant.** This aptly named restaurant is a popular hangout for western expats who work in the neighborhood. It offers a cheerful home-away-from-home feel, complete with flags from various countries hanging from the ceiling and beers from around the world. The food is inexpensive and good, with pizzas, pastas, and excellent brochette prepared by an Italian chef. The owner is an entrepreneur with a number of other restaurants and bars in the neighborhood. His reputation for catering to Western tastes is hardly undeserved. ⊠*East Tower, Pearl Building, 3rd fl., 360 Huanshi Zhong Lu., 1 block west of Garden Hotel* ☎*020/8386–6783* ▤*AE, DC, MC, V.*

$$$–$$$$
CHINESE FUSION

✕ **Lai Wan Market.** A re-creation of the old Canton waterfront, this theme restaurant has booths shaped like flower boats and small wooden stools at low counters. The Market is known for its dim sum (which is served until 5:30 PM) and two kinds of rice, one made with pork, beef, fish, and seafood, the other with fish, beef, and pork liver. ⊠*Garden Hotel, 368 Huanshi Dong Lu, 2nd fl., Huanshi Road* ☎*020/8333–8989 Ext. 3922* ▤*AE, DC, MC, V.*

$–$$
ECLECTIC

✕ **Lucy's.** With cuisines from so many cultures represented on its menu (Asian curries, mixed grills, Tex-Mex dishes, fish-and-chips, noodles, burgers, sandwiches, and much more), a UN think tank could happily share a table. A favorite among foreigners, the outdoor dining area is lovely, and even the indoor dining area has a few trees growing through the roof. Take-out service is available. ⊠*3 Shamian Nan Jie, 1 block from White Swan Hotel* ☎*020/8121–5106* ▤*No credit cards.*

$$$$
FRENCH
Fodor's Choice
★

✕ **La Seine.** This upscale restaurant on Er Sha Island offers a daily lunch buffet. Dinner highlights include classic French fare, such as beef tenderloin, escargot, and foie gras. It's an ideal place to eat before or after a show. ⊠*Xinghai Concert Hall, 33 Qing Bo Lu, Er Sha Island-Guangzhou* ✛*Close to Xinghai Concert Hall and Guangzhou Museum* ☎*020/8735–2531* ⚑*Reservations essential* ▤*AE, DC, MC, V.*

$$$$
ECLECTIC

✕ **Silk Road Grill Room.** This grill room in the White Swan Hotel is the place to see and be seen. The service is impeccable. You can choose between the set menu, which includes an appetizer, cold dish, soup, entrée, dessert, and drink (excluding wine), or à la carte. Highlight entrées include prime rib and sea-bass fillet. ⊠ *White Swan Hotel, Yi Shamian Lu, Shamian Island* ☎*020/8188–6968* ▤*AE, MC, V* ⚑*Reservations essential* ⊘*No lunch.*

$$–$$$
CANTONESE

✕ **Tang Yuan.** The location alone beats out most other restaurants in Guangzhou. It is in a faux-colonial-style mansion on an island in Liuhuahu Park. Cuisine is pure old-school Cantonese, with expensive dishes like abalone and shark's fin soup being served alongside more traditional staples like crispy fried pigeon, carbon-roasted mackerel, and stuffed garlic prawns. Naturally, there's plenty of dim sum, and the "Cantonese combo plate" features a variety of roasted meats sure to please carnivores. Although the food at Tang Yuan is excellent, most people come here for the opulence as well. Admission fee for the park is waived for guests of the restaurant, and a golf cart waits at the park's

9

entrance on Liuhua Road to whisk diners to the restaurant's palatial front door. ⊠ *Lihuahu Park, Dongfeng Xi Lu and Renmin Bei Lu, 2 blocks west of Yuexiu Gongyuan metro station* ☎ *020/3623–6993* ⊟ *AE, DC, MC, V.*

$$$$
CANTONESE

✕ **Tao Tao Ju.** Prepare yourself for the garish decor, shouted conversations of fellow diners, and a menu comprised of enough weird animal parts to send vegetarians running. Tao Tao Ju (which, roughly translated, means "house of happiness") is one of the most revered traditional Cantonese restaurants in the city. Soups are a big thing here, and the menu (available in English) has many that you're unlikely to find elsewhere. The kudzu-and-snakehead soup is delicious, and it serves more than 200 varieties of dim sum. It's open from 6:30 AM to midnight, so it's a good place to stop for a late-night meal. ⊠ *20 Dishipu Lu, Shangxiajiu* ☎ *020/8139–6111* ⊟ *AE, DC, MC, V.*

WHERE TO STAY

The purpose of your visit to Guangzhou is likely to determine where you stay. Businesspeople increasingly choose the up-and-coming Tianhe District, close to Guangzhou East Railway Station and the city's growing thicket of office skyscrapers. Visitors are more likely to choose a hotel on the oasislike Shamian Island, in the heart of the city. Though traffic is still hellish, getting around is easier now than it has been in years past. Recently completed expressways and a growing underground-train system have vastly reduced cross-city travel time.

¢   ▥ **Aiqun Hotel.** When it was built in the 1930s, this 16-story hotel was the tallest building in Pearl River Delta. Though it once hosted dignitaries of great importance during China's Republican era, these days this elegant art-deco hotel hosts visitors from around China and international travelers on a budget. Rooms are clean, comfortable, and tastefully furnished with rich mahogany, faux-colonial-era furniture. The revolving restaurant on the 16th floor of the new wing offers great views of the surrounding area. **Pros:** interesting building and decor, cozy atmosphere. **Cons:** rooms are on the small side. ⊠ *No.113 Yanjiang Rd., Pearl River District* ☎ *020/8186–6668* ⊕ *www. www.aiqunhotel. com* ➥ *330 rooms and suites* ⌂ *In-room: Internet. In-hotel: 4 restaurants* ⊟ *AE, DC, MC, V.*

$$–$$$ ▥ **China Hotel.** Managed by Marriott, this hotel is part of a complex that includes office and apartment blocks, a shopping mall big enough to get lost in, and a wide enough range of restaurants to satisfy any appetite. The hotel is favored by business travelers because it's connected to the metro and close to the Trade Fair Exhibition Hall. The business center has 16 meeting rooms, and the piano bar in the lobby offers champagne brunches. There's a walk-in humidor on the premises

and the 4th-floor gym is open around the clock. **Pros:** close to metro, newly renovated rooms. **Cons:** very much a businessperson's hotel. ⊠*Liuhua Lu, Liwan* ☎*020/8666–6888* ⊕*www.marriott.com* ☎*724 rooms, 126 suites* ⚷*In-room: Internet. In-hotel: 4 restaurants, bars, tennis court, pool, gym* ☐*AE, DC, MC, V* Ⓜ*Yuexu Gongyuan.*

¢ ⛳ **The Customs Hotel.** This clean and inexpensive hotel has character and an excellent location. The newly opened four-story establishment has an attractive colonial facade that blends well with the surrounding area. The bright interior surrounds an inner courtyard. Standard rooms are tastefully decorated with Republican-era furniture made of dark wood, though the suites seem more cluttered. If possible, get a room facing Shamian Avenue, the quiet, tree-lined street, which runs the length of the island. There is a karaoke bar and a lovely backyard garden. **Pros:** quiet neighborhood **Cons:** some people prefer their hotels characterless. ⊠*No. 35 Shamian Ave., Shamian Island, Colonial Guangzhou* ☎*20/8110–2388* ✉*customshotel@126.com* ☎*49 rooms, 7 suites* ⚷*In-room: Internet. In-hotel: 2 restaurants, bar, gym* ☐*AE, DC, MC, V.*

$–$$$ ⛳ **Dong Fang.** Across from Liuhua Park and the trade-fair headquarters, this complex is built around a 22½-acre garden with pavilions, carp-filled pools, and rock gardens. The lobby is done up in a Renaissance motif, complete with Romanesque pillars and gold-and-white floor tiling. The shopping concourse has Chinese antiques and carpets. The hotel has recently added an 86,000-square-foot convention center. Discounts of up to 30% for rooms in the off-season are not unheard of. **Pros:** spacious gardens, choice of restaurants. **Cons:** not for those who are averse to gigantic. ⊠*120 Liuhua Lu* ☎*020/8666–9900, 852/2528–0555 in Hong Kong* ⊕*www.hoteldongfang.com* ☎*699 rooms, 101 suites* ⚷*In-room: Internet. In-hotel: 6 restaurants, gym, spa* ☐*AE, DC, MC, V.*

¢–$ ⛳ **Élan Hotel.** If you like cheap, funky, and hip little hotels, this is the spot for you. Guangzhou's first attempt at a boutique hotel has compact, Ikea-inspired rooms with bold color palettes and clean lines. Celine Dion Muzak wafting through the hallways can be an annoyance, but the warm, cozy beds guarantee a restful sleep. The small 1st-floor restaurant serves cheap northeastern Chinese food that is authentic and tasty. **Pros:** basic and clean, good value. **Cons:** small rooms. ⊠*32 Zhan Qian Heng Rd.* ✛*2 blocks south of Guangzhou main railway station* ☎*020/8622–1788* ⊕*www.hotel-elan.com* ☎*76 rooms, 8 suites* ⚷*In-room: Internet. In-hotel: Restaurant* ☐*AE, DC, MC, V.*

¢–$ ⛳ **Garden Hotel.** In the northern business suburbs, this huge, aging hotel is famous for its spectacular garden that includes an artificial hill, a waterfall, and pavilions. The cavernous lobby, decorated with enormous murals, has a bar–lounge set around an ornamental pool. Though long considered the standard of luxury in Guangzhou, other hotels are now giving the Garden a run for its money. **Pros:** spacious premises and gardens, pleasant staff. **Cons:** rooms in need of renovation; not the best neighborhood. ⊠*368 Huanshi Dong Lu, Huanshi Road* ☎*020/8333–8989* ⊕*www.thegardenhotel.com.cn* ☎*828 rooms, 42 suites* ⚷*In-room: Internet. In-hotel: 7 restaurants, bar, tennis courts, pool, gym* ☐*AE, DC, MC, V.*

$–$$$ 🏨**Guangdong International Hotel.** This towering hotel in the finance district is something of an institution in Guangzhou, but it has a tired feel, as if the leap from state to private ownership hasn't been made in full. The hotel does have extensive recreation facilities and an indoor gym. For the money though, the nearby City Centre Holiday Inn is a better buy. **Pros:** friendly staff, good views from the top floors. **Cons:** uninteresting location. ⊠ *339 Huanshi Dong Lu, Huanshi Road* ☎ *020/8331–1888* ⊕ *www.gitic.com.cn* 🛏 *333 rooms, 270 suites* ♿ *In-room: Internet. In-hotel: 3 restaurants, bar, tennis court, pool, gym* ⊟ *AE, DC, MC, V.*

¢–$$$$ 🏨**Guangdong Victory Hotel.** Over the past few years, this Shamian Island hotel has undergone upgrades that have bumped it up from budget class. The two wings, both originally colonial guesthouses, have been beautifully renovated. The main building has a pink-and-white facade, an imposing portico, and twin domes on the roof, where you'll find a pool and an excellent sauna facility. Standard rooms are more than adequate, and the hotel still retains a fairly inexpensive dining room on the 1st floor. **Pros:** historic, elegant building; peaceful area; great view of the city from the rooftop pool. **Cons:** shabby fitness center. ⊠ *53 Yi Shamian Lu, Shamian Island* ☎ *020/8121–6802* ⊕ *www.vhotel.com* 🛏 *328 rooms* ♿ *In-room: Internet. In-hotel: 3 restaurants, pool, gym* ⊟ *AE, DC, MC, V.*

Fodor's Choice
★

$$–$$$ 🏨**Holiday Inn City Centre.** This centrally located hotel is bound to offer stiff competition to the Garden Hotel just down the road. The large tasteful rooms are arranged according to Chinese feng shui principles. The top three executive floors have suites and a lounge–restaurant area with stellar views of smog-shrouded Guangzhou. In addition to all of its lovely facilities, the hotel also has plenty of meeting rooms. **Pros:** good-sized rooms, central location. **Cons:** not what you'd call quaint. ⊠ *28 Guangming Rd, Overseas Chinese Village, Huanshi Dong* ☎ *020/6128–6868* ⊕ *www.guangzhou.holiday-inn.com* 🛏 *430 rooms, 38 suites* ♿ *In-room: Internet. In-hotel: Restaurant, bar, pool, gym* ⊟ *AE, DC, MC, V.*

$–$$$$ 🏨**Holiday Inn Shifu.** The newest hotel in Guangzhou, and the only four-star hotel in popular tourist area Shangxiajiu, Holiday Inn Shifu is 14 stories, with a lovely rooftop pool and an adjacent bar with views of old Guangzhou. The Shifu is also a stone's throw from the newly renovated Qingping Market, which is a must-see for first-time visitors. **Pros:** good service, friendly staff. **Cons:** beds are too hard. ⊠ *No.188 Di Shi Fu Rd., Xiangxiajiu, Liwan* ✛ *Follow signs from Changshou metro station exit* ☎ *020/8138–0088* 🛏 *278 rooms, 28 suites* ♿ *In-room: Internet. In-hotel: 2 restaurants, bar, pool, gym* ⊟ *AE, DC, MC, V* Ⓜ *Changshuo.*

¢–$ 🏨**Landmark Canton.** Towering above Haizhu Square and the main bridge across the river, this hotel is in the heart of central Guangzhou. It's managed by China Travel Service of Hong Kong, so a lot of its guests tend to be Hong Kongers on holiday, but the hotel has its fair share of foreign guests as well. There's a great chocolate shop in the lobby, and a small but very pretty Chinese garden and carp pond in the courtyard. The Landmark's location allows it to boast that most guest rooms have great views of the river and city. Pros: view of the Pearl River; decent restaurants nearby. Cons: small pool. ⊠*8 Qiao Guang Lu, Haizhu Square* ☎*020/8335–5988* ⊕*www.hotel-landmark.com.cn* ⇨*566 rooms* ⌂*In-hotel: 2 restaurants, bar, pool, gym* ⊟*AE, DC, MC, V* Ⓜ*Haizhu Guangchang.*

¢ Ⓗ**Shamian.** This is a great hotel for visitors on a budget. Its rooms are a little spartan and the lobby cramped, but it is clean and friendly and the location—right in the middle of Shamian Island—is second to none. Pros: great location. Cons: no restaurant in hotel. ⊠*52 Shamian Nan Jie, Shamian Island* ☎*020/8121–8288* ⊕*www.gdshamianhotel.com* ⇨*58 rooms, 20 suites* ⊟*AE, DC, MC, V.*

$$–$$$ Ⓗ**Tian Lun International Hotel.** A new, upscale boutique hotel located next to Guangzhou East Railway Station offers large luxury rooms with a sleek edge. The colors are kept to soft blacks, grays, and beige. The buffet in the 2nd-floor café is beautifully arranged around a centerpiece of coral, and the high ceilings lend an air of sophistication. Pros: near metro and train stations, clean and comfortable rooms. Cons: lack of English TV channels. ⊠*172 Linhe Lu Central, Tianhe District* ✛*Next to Guangzhou East Railway Station* ☎*020/8393–6388* ⊕*www.tianlun-hotel.com* ⇨*382 rooms, 23 suites* ⌂*In-room: Internet. In-hotel: 3 restaurants, pool, gym* ⊟*AE, DC, MC, V.*

¢–$$$ Ⓗ**White Swan Hotel.** Occupying a marvelous site on Shamian Island, beside the Pearl River, this huge luxury complex has landscaped gardens, two pools, a jogging track, and a separate gym and spa. Its presidential suite is just that: reserved for heads of state, it has been occupied by such luminaries as Richard Nixon and Kim Jong-il. Its restaurants are second to none; the windows of the elegant lobby bar and coffee shop frame the panorama of river traffic. Pros: quiet neighborhood, good view of Pearl River. Cons: dated decor. ⊠*Yi Shamian Lu, Shamian Island, Colonial Canton* ☎*020/8188–6968, 852/2524–0192 in Hong Kong* ⊕*www.whiteswanhotel.com* ⇨*843 rooms, 92 suites* ⌂*In-room: Internet. In-hotel: 9 restaurants, bar, pools, gym* ⊟*AE, DC, MC, V.*

9

NIGHTLIFE & THE ARTS

Though not as happening as Shanghai or Beijing, the Guangzhou nightlife scene is anything but boring. Western-style clubs vie for increasingly hip and knowledgeable crowds and invest serious money on international DJs and design. A wide variety of pubs, sports bars, coffee shops, and cafés have also sprung up. Bars tend to stay open until 2 AM; clubs continue to 5 AM.

PUBS & BARS

Bingjiang xilu (⊠*South of Shamian Island, across the Pearl River*) is *the* street for barhopping. Very popular with a younger crowd, it has great views, and if you get bored with looking north across the river you can always cross the bridge to **Yanjiang Xilu** and drink at some of the bars on that side.

Huanshi Dong Lu. Yuexiu and the area behind the Garden Hotel are popular with locals and expats (short- and long-term). Two favorites are **Gypsy** and **Cave,** both located on opposite ends of the Zhujiang Building. Cave has a distinct meat-market vibe and features nightly performances by a scantily clad woman whose specialty is dancing with snakes. Gypsy reeks of hashish and is much mellower.

The Paddy Field (⊠ *38 Huale Lu, behind Garden Hotel* ☎ *020/8360–1379*) makes you long for Ireland. There are darts, pints of Guinness and Kilkenny, and football matches on a massive screen.

Popular with foreigners and locals alike, **1920 Restaurant** (⊠ *183 Yanjiang Zhong Lu* ☎ *020/8333–6156* ⊕ *www.1920cn.com*) serves up Bavarian food and imported wheat beers on a lovely outdoor patio. Entrées start at Y60, beers at Y22.

The popular **Café Lounge** (⊠ *China Hotel, lobby* ☎ *020/8666–6888*) has a mellow vibe, big comfortable bar stools, quiet tables for two, live music on weekends, and a fine selection of cigars.

The big attraction of the **Hare & Moon** (⊠ *White Swan Hotel, Yi Shamian Lu, Shamian Island* ☎ *020/8188–6968*) is the panorama of the Pearl River as it flows past the picture windows.

DANCE CLUBS

Though normally thought of as inauspicious in Chinese culture, the number 4 is anything but at Guangzhou's newly renovated **Yes Club** (⊠ *132 Dongfeng Xi Lu, across from Liuhua Lake Park* ☎ *020 8136–8688* ☜ *Free*), which actually has four separate clubs under one roof for four distinctly different clubbing experiences. **Super Yes** has techno and electronica, whereas **Mini Yes** offers house and break beat. **Funky Yes** offers a more eclectic mixture of R&B and hip-hop, and **Club Yes** is a total chill-out zone, with softer music and lighting, and a fine selection of wine and cigars. Taken as a whole, the more than 6,000-square-foot megaclub is definitely the biggest in Guangzhou.

Deep Anger Music Power House (⊠ *183 Yanjiang Lu* ☎ *020/8317–7158* ☜ *Free* ☉ *Daily 8 PM–2 AM*) is a cool dance club located in a building that was a theater back in the days of Sun Yat-sen. Lounge lizards and history buffs will enjoy sipping a beer here.

ART & CULTURE

If you think Guangzhou's high culture begins and ends with Cantonese opera, think again, pilgrim—the art and performance scene here is vibrant, and getting more so every day. Even cynics who believe that Guangzhou's mainstream masses care more for dim sum than for dance are waking up to the fact that the city is undergoing a cultural broadening, as evidenced by the opening of small art spaces, more eclectic forms of theater, and more national attention being focused on the city's major museums. Of course, purists need not panic; the Cantonese opera has hardly disappeared.

Xinghai Concert Hall (✉*33 Qing Bo Lu, Er Sha Island* ☎*020/8735–2222 Ext. 312 for English* ⊕*www.concerthall.com.cn*) is the home of the Guangzhou Symphony Orchestra, and puts on an amazing array of concerts featuring national and international performers. Its Web site, unfortunately, is only in Chinese, but your hotel should be able to call to find out what's going on. The concert hall is surrounded by a fantastic sculpture garden, and is next door to the Guangzhou Museum of Art, making the two an excellent midafternoon to evening trip.

Guangdong Puppet Art Center (✉*21 Fenyuan St.* ☎*020/8431–0227*) hosts live puppet shows every Saturday and Sunday at 10:30 AM and 3 PM.

Guangdong Modern Dance Company (✉*13 Shuiyinhenglu, Shaheding* ☎*020/8704–9512* ⊕*www.gdmdc.com*) is mainland China's first professional modern-dance company, and the troupe is regularly praised by publications as diverse and respected as the *New York Times* and the *Toronto Sun*. This theater is its home base, so if you're a fan of dance, check out its English-language Web site for a full performance schedule.

GALLERIES & PERFORMANCE SPACES

If eclectic art is your thing, then **Vitamin Creative Space** (✉*29 Hengyi Jie, inside of Xinggang Cheng, Haizhu District* ☎*020/8429–6760* ⊕*www. vitamincreativespace.com* ⊙*Mon.–Sat. 10 AM–6 PM*) might be worth the trip. But be warned, it's located in the back of a semi-enclosed vegetable market and not easy to find even if you speak Chinese. Call first (the curator speaks English) and someone will escort you from in front of the market. Hours are somewhat erratic, but the art can be as wonderfully weird as anything you're likely to find in China.

SHOPPING

It's no surprise that the world's busiest manufacturing city offers an amazing array of shopping options. Whatever the item may be, if it's being sold chances are good that somebody's selling it in Guangzhou.

MALLS & MARKETS

Shangxiajiu (✉*Follow signs from Changshoulu metro*) is a massive warren of old buildings and shops and considered the user-friendly heart of old Guangzhou. The half-mile main street is a pedestrian mall boasting nearly 250 shops and department stores. The buildings in Shangxiajiu are old, but the stores are the same ones as in "modern Guangzhou." Even though the overall decibel level hovers around deafening, the area isn't without its charms. Our favorite shops are the small storefronts offering dried-fruit samples, which are very addictive. The area draws a big, younger crowd, but there are a few quiet back alleys that keep it from feeling too overwhelming. There's also a wide variety of street stalls selling a large selection of delicious edibles.

Beijing Road Pedestrian Mall (✉*Follow signs from Gongyuanqian metro*) offers an interesting contrast to Shangxiajiu. Shangxiajiu offers new stores in old buildings, whereas Beijing Road makes no pretense at being anything other than a fully modern, neon-draped pedestrian mall, similar to Beijing's Wangfujing Street or Shanghai's Nanjing Street. Pedestrianized and open from around 10 AM until 10 PM, this is where city teenagers buy sensible, midrange Hong Kong–style clothes and increasingly garish local brands. Noisy and fun, the street is lined with cheap food stalls, cafés, and the ubiquitous fast-food chains like KFC and McDonald's.

Haizhu Plaza (⊠*Haizhu Sq., north of Haizhu Bridge, Haizhu* Ⓜ*Guangchang* ⊘*Daily 10–6*) is a massive, two-story flea and souvenir market where casual shoppers and wholesale buyers alike bargain for kitsch—think toys, faux antiques, and Cultural Revolution–themed knickknacks. Merchants keep calculators at hand for entering figures in the heat of negotiation, and vendors sell a variety of snacks from carts located by the exits.

The **Friendship Store** (⊠*369 Huanshi Dong Lu, across from the Garden Hotel*) is an old stalwart, dating back from days of post-revolutionary China's earliest flirtation with capitalism. The Guangzhou Friendship Store occupies a five-story building with departments selling a wide range of designer wear, children's wear, luggage, and household appliances.

La Perle (⊠*367 Huanshi Dong Lu, across from the Garden Hotel* ⊘*Daily10–10*) is next to the Friendship Store, and a bit more upscale. It has genuine designer clothes at expensive rates, with shops such as Versace, Louis Vuitton, Polo, and Prada.

ANTIQUES & TRADITIONAL CRAFTS

On Shamian Island, the area between the White Swan and Victory hotels has a number of small family-owned shops that sell paintings, carvings, pottery, knickknacks, and antiques.

Guangzhou Arts Centre (⊠*698 Renmin Bei Lu* ☎*020/8667–9898*) has a fine selection of painted scrolls. The **South Jade Carving Factory** (⊠*15 Xia Jiu Lu, Shangxiajiu* ☎*020/8138–8040*) offers a wide variety of jade and jadeite products at reasonable prices. On the 2nd floor visitors can watch jade being carved. The **White Swan Arcade** (⊠*White Swan Hotel, Yi Shamian Lu, Shamian Island*) has some of the city's finest upmarket specialty shops. They sell genuine Chinese antiques, traditional craft items, works of modern and classical art, Japanese kimonos and swords, jewelry, cameras, and books published in and about China.

BOOKSTORES

Guangzhou Books Center (⊠*123 Tianhe Lu* ☎*020/3886–4208 Chinese only*) is a chain with seven floors of books on every subject, including some bargain-priced art books in English. **Xinhua Bookstore** (⊠*276 Beijing Rd.* ☎*020/8333–2636*) sells an extensive catalog of books on a wide range of subjects at very affordable prices.

GETTING HERE & AROUND

Bus 24 leaves from Dongfeng Zhonglu, just north of Renmin Gongyuan, and travels to the cable car at the bottom of the hill near Luhu Park. The

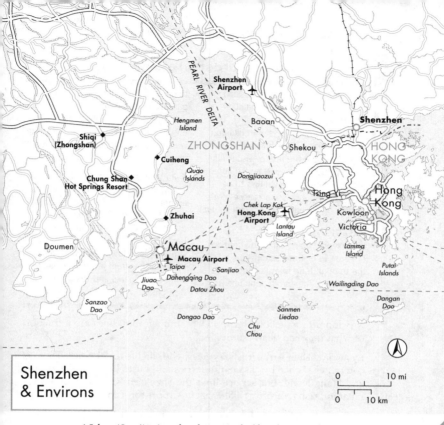

Shenzhen
& Environs

0		10 mi
0		10 km

15-km (9-mi) trip takes between half an hour and one hour, depending on traffic. A taxi shouldn't set you back more than Y100.

SHENZHEN

112 km (70 mi; 1 hr by express train, 2½ hrs by express bus) from Guangzhou. Walk across border from Hong Kong's Luohu KCR (Kowloon–Canton Railway) train station.

Shenzhen may be China's youngest city, but this is one metropolis that's definitely come of age. A small farming town until 1980, Shenzhen was chosen by Deng Xiaoping as an incubator in which the seeds of China's economic reform were to be nurtured. The results are the stuff of legend; a quarter-century later, Shenzhen is now China's richest, and, according to some, its most vibrant city.

GETTING HERE & AROUND

Tens of thousands of people cross from Hong Kong into Shenzhen (and back) daily, usually over the Luohu border crossing. Over the weekends, numbers can triple. Most visitors take the KCR train from Kowloon to the crossing and walk into Shenzhen. A more expensive—but infinitely more pleasant—way is to take the ferry from Hong Kong or

Avoid the Luohu Border-Crossing Crush

At Luohu (the main border crossing between Hong Kong and mainland China) the masses are funneled through a large three-story building. From the outside this building looks huge, but from the inside—especially when you're surrounded by a quarter million other people waiting to be processed—the crossing can be reminiscent of a scene from *Soylent Green.*

ALTERNATIVE ROUTES

If you're just going through Shenzhen en route to or from Guangzhou, take the through train from Kowloon to Guangzhou. The immigration line at the Guangzhou East station is a comparative piece of cake, even on the worst days. It's possible to buy tickets on the fly on this commuter train, but we advise booking anywhere from a few hours to a day or two in advance.

If you're heading into Shenzhen, why not trade the mad crush of Luohu for an hour-long ferry ride followed by a quick trip through the much less popular border crossing at Shekou Harbor? Although this won't bring you into downtown Shenzhen, you'll be no farther from attractions like the amusement parks and Mission Hills Golf Club.

Kowloon into Shekou Harbor. Here, immigration lines are a fraction of what they can be in Luohu.

By Air Shenzhen Airport is very busy, with flights to 50 cities. There is commuter service by catamaran ferries and buses between the airport and Hong Kong. Bus service links the Shenzhen Railway Station, via Huaren Dasha, directly to Shenzhen Airport for Y25 (one way).

By Boat & Ferry Shenzhen Party maintains an updated schedule for trains and ferries on its Web site. The Turbojet Company runs regular ferries connecting Hong Kong, Shenzhen, Macau, and Zhuhai. Check its Web site for schedules and prices.

By Bus Air-conditioned express buses crisscross most of the Pearl River Delta region several times a day. Ask at your hotel for more information. Buses for Hong Kong leave from a number of places, including the China Travel Service branches in Central and Wan Chai.

To get around, the city has a network of buses and minibuses; tickets are very inexpensive.

By Subway Shenzhen's metro, the newest in China, has two lines, and tickets range from Y2 to Y8.

By Train Shenzhen can easily be reached from Hong Kong by taking the KCR light railway from Hong Kong's Kowloon Tong KCR station to Luohu Railway Station and then crossing over to Shenzhen on foot. Trains depart from Luohu to Hong Kong every five minutes. Trains between Guangzhou East Railway Station and Shenzhen's Luohu Railway Station depart every hour and cost between Y80 and Y100.

ESSENTIALS

Air Contacts **Civil Aviation Administration of China, CAAC represented by China Southern** (✉ *181 Huanshi Lu, on left as you exit Guangzhou railway station [Guangzhou main station metro]* ☎ *020/8668–2000 24-hr hotline*). **Shenzhen Airport** (☎ *0755/2777–7821* ⊕ *www.szairport.com*).

Banks **Bank of China** (✉ *International Finance Building, 2022 Jianshe Road, Luohu District* ☎ *755/2233–8888* ⊕ *www.boc.cn*). **HSBC** (✉ *Shop No.9, Shangri-La Hotel, 1002 Jianshe Rd.* ☎ *755/8266–3228* ⊕ *www.hsbc.com.cn*).

Boat & Ferry Contacts **Macau Ferry Terminal** (✉ *Shun Tak Centre, Connaught Rd., Central* ☎ *853/2546–3528*). **Shenzhen Party** (⊕ *www.shenzhenparty.com/travel*). **The Turbojet Company** (☎ *852/2921–6688, press 3 for English* ⊕ *www.ctshk.com*).

Bus Contacts **Shenzhen Luohu Bus station** (✉ *1st–2nd fls., East Plaza, Luohu District* ☎ *755/8232–1670*).

Medical Assistance **Shenzhen People's Hospital** (✉ *Dongmen Rd. N,* ☎ *0755/2553–3018 Ext. 2553, 1387 Outpatient Dept.*).

Subway Contact **Shenzhen Metro** (☎ *020/8310–6622 for information in English,* *020/8310–6666*).

Train Contacts **The Mass Transit Rail (MTR)** (☎ *852/2881–8888* ⊕ *www.mtr.com.hk*). **Shenzhen Railway Station** (✉ *Luohu District* ☎ *020/8232–8647*).

EXPLORING SHENZHEN

Sprawling Shenzhen is composed of six districts: Luohu and Futian are the "downtown" districts; Yantian has some nice beaches and theme parks; Shekou is popular for its waterfront dining and plethora of bars and restaurants; Nanshan is Shenzhen's arts and theme-park district. Surrounding these smaller districts like a misshapen croissant are Shenzhen's two largest (and least urban) districts: Bao'an to the east and Longgang to the west.

LUOHU & FUTIAN

Though Luohu and Futian are the smallest districts in the city, for many it is this urban jungle of skyscrapers, markets, restaurants, and hotels that defines Shenzhen. Luohu (*Lo Wu* in Cantonese) is the area beginning right at the border crossing with Hong Kong. Jienshi Road is the street that ends at the border, and like many border areas, has more than just a bit of a rough feel about it. Single men walking on this road (which parallels the train tracks leading north to Guangzhou and south to Hong Kong) will be harassed by countless women shouting out "massage" and "missy" (ironically, this street also has a number of good, reputable massage parlors as well as a number of excellent restaurants).

Futian, Shenzhen's trading hub, is also where the Shenzhen's gourmands go for a night of gastronomic pleasure. The Zhenhua Road restaurant district in Futian is where scores of excellent restaurants compete for the patronage of Shenzhen's very discriminating diners.

Continued on page 354

21ST ★
CENTURY
CHINA

Since the late 1970s, China and its billion-plus population have been moving from a centrally planned socialist economy to a market-oriented consumer society on a scale and at a speed unparalleled in history.

ECONOMIC GROWTH
(GNP in billions of dollars)

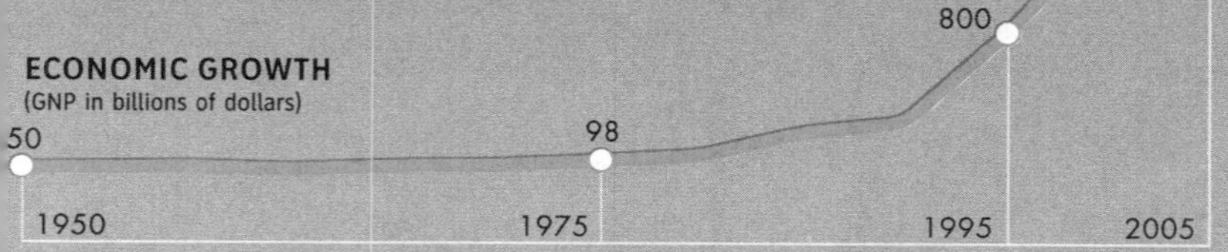

2297.4
800
50
98
1950
1975
1995
2005

Source: http://news.bbc.co.uk/

SUPER BRAND
Carrier
开利空调

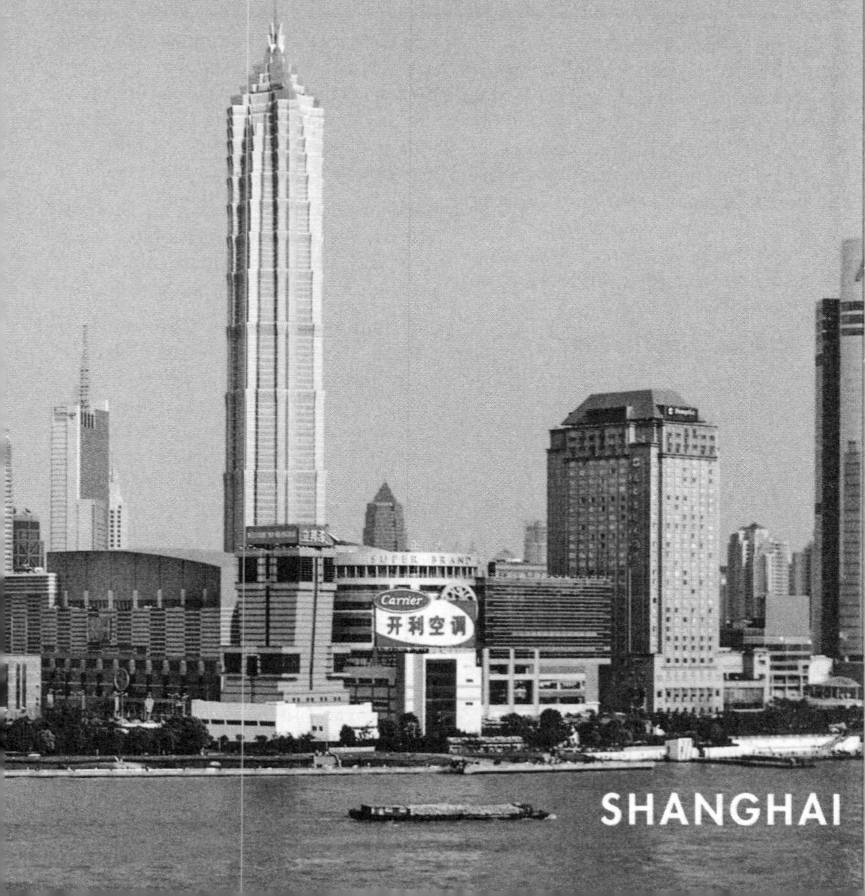

SHANGHAI

BEIJING

A Chinese Century?

The SARS hiccup aside, China's economy has been red-hot since joining the World Trade Organization in 2001. One of the engines driving the global economy, it helped revive Japan's sagging economy and the slumping international shipping industry. Worldwide commodities markets have also been boosted by China's increasing hunger for everything from copper to coffee.

The country that was long written off as just a cheap exporter is now a net importer. It's the fourth-largest economy in the world after the United States, Japan, and Germany, whose economies are growing at less than half the rate.

Such development is nothing short of remarkable, but national problems such as energy, the environment, and wealth inequality are threatening the country.

Internationally, it's how China and the United States cooperate on global issues, and how they manage their own complex relationship, that may have the greatest impact on the rest of the century. Since Nixon first opened the door in 1972, the two countries have managed to forge a working relationship. But Yuan revaluation, trade issues, energy supply (especially oil), and both countries' military role in the Asia-Pacific region are all issues that could sour this budding friendship.

GDP-ANNUAL GROWTH RATE

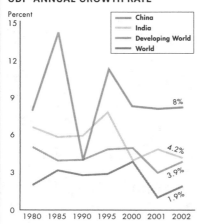

Percent

- China
- India
- Developing World
- World

15

12

9 — 8%

6 — 4.2%

3 — 3.9%

1.9%

0

1980 1985 1990 1995 2000 2001 2002

(top) Architectural stars (or starchitects) like Rem Koolhaas, Li Hu, Paul Andreu, and Jacques Herzog and Pierre de Meuron (Olympic Stadium, above) are descending on Beijing for construction of state-of-the-art Olympic venues. (right) Hong Kong skyline.

Source: World Bank/Earth Trends

HONG KONG

Fueling the Chinese Dream

China is now the number–two energy consumer in the world, after the United States. Its consumption has exploded by an average of 5% yearly since 1998. This thirst for fuel is evident on roads all over the country. The land of the bicycle is now car-crazy. Three million vehicles were recently sold, and higher sales are predicted in the coming years.

Back in 2005, the country consumed 320 million tons of crude oil, roughly one third of which was imported. It's expecting to import 500 million tons by 2020, two thirds of its projected total imports.

Where will China get this oil? Much comes from countries with troubled relations with the West such as Iran and Sudan, but it is also working on importing more from traditional U.S. suppliers such as Saudi Arabia.

There's also a growing demand for electricity, 75% of which comes from coal. In the coming 25 years, the greenhouse gases produced by China's coal burning will probably exceed that of all industrial nations combined. And the country will continue to rely on coal for electricity in the years to come, despite large hydropower projects and a plan to increase the number of nuclear power plants.

Aside from developing clean, renewable energy sources, China needs to improve its poor energy efficiency—it uses nine times the energy Japan does to produce one GDP unit. But plans are being made to improve energy efficiency by 20% by 2010.

WORLD OIL CONSUMPTION

USA 24.8%

Rest of the World 50.7%

China 7.9%

Japan 6.9%

Russia 3.5%

Germany 3.3%

India 2.9%

Source: http://www.nationmaster.com/

Can China Go Green?

A devastated environment is a major result of China's economic transformation. For example, because of deforestation around the capital, Beijing is threatened by the encroaching Gobi Desert, which dumped 300,000 tons of sand on the city in one week in 2006. Industrial carelessness and lack of regulation result in accidents such as the 50-mile benzene spill in a river near Harbin in late 2005.

Cities have been smoggy for decades because of pollution from factories, vehicles, and especially coal. But air quality is now becoming obscured by water issues. In mid-2006 the Water Resources Ministry reported that 320 million urban residents—more than the population of the United States—did not have access to clean drinking water.

Much of this is the result of a development-at-any-cost mentality, particularly in the wake of economic reform. Companies and factories, many of which are foreign-owned, have only recently had to deal with environmental laws— "scoff laws"—that are often circumvented by bribing local officials. And average citizens don't have freedom of speech or access to political tools to fight environmentally damaging projects.

Is the central government waking up? In 2006 the vice-chairman of China's increasingly outspoken State Environmental Protection Agency put it bluntly: "We will face tremendous problems if we do not change our development patterns."

Mind the Gap

China has come a long way from the days when everyone had an "iron rice bowl," or a state-appointed job that was basically guaranteed regardless of one's abilities or work performance.

Since 1980, the country has quadrupled per capita income and raised more than 220 million of its citizens out of poverty. A belt of prosperity is emerging along the coast, but hundreds of millions still live on less than $1 per day.

(left) Owning a car is the new Chinese dream. (top right) The Three Gorges Dam will be the largest in the world, supplying the hydroelectric power of 18 nuclear plants. (bottom right) China's cities are some of the most polluted in the world.

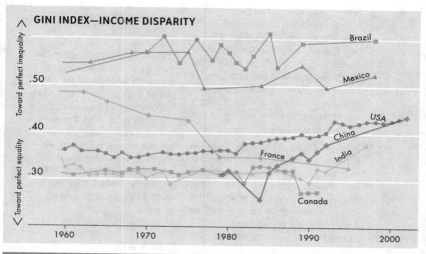

GINI INDEX—INCOME DISPARITY

Toward perfect inequality

.50

Toward perfect equality

.40

.30

Brazil

Mexico

USA

China

India

France

Canada

1960   1970   1980   1990   2000

Economists use a statistical yardstick known as the Gini coefficient to measure wealth inequality in a society, with zero being perfect equality and one being perfect inequality. The World Bank estimates that China's national Gini coefficient rose from 0.30 to 0.45 from 1982, a 50% jump in two decades. In 2006, some academics estimated China's current Gini coefficient to be closer to, or even higher, than Latin America's 0.52.

As economic inequality has grown, so has discontent, particularly in rural areas. The country recorded 87,000 public protests in 2005, an increase of 11,000 over the year before.

Many of these protests are incited by the acts of local, particularly rural, officials whose corruption policies are sometimes beyond Beijing's sphere of influence.

Most protests are focused on specific incidents or officials rather than general dissent against the government, but the growing frequency of such events is not going unnoticed by the central government. In 2005, 8,400 officials were arrested on corruption-related charges.

CHINA IN NUMBERS

	CHINA	U.S.
Area in sq km:	9,560,960	9,631,420
Population	1.3 bil	300 mil
Men (15–64 yrs)	482 mil	100 mil
Women (15–64 yrs)	456 mil	101 mil
Population growth	0.59%	0.91%
Life expectancy: men	70.8	75
Life expectancy: women	74.6	80.8
GDP per head	$1,090	$37,240
Health spending, % GDP	5.8	14.6
Doctors per 1000 pop.	1.6	3.0
Hospital beds per 1000 pop.	23.12	6.43
Infant mortality rate per 1000 births	2.1	5.7
Education spending, % GDP	95.1%	99%
Adult literacy: men	86.5%	
Adult literacy: women		99%
Internet users	111 mil	204 mil

NANSHAN & SHEKOU

Nanshan is where you'll find Shenzhen's most stylish district, Huaqiao Cheng, or Overseas Chinese Town (often called the OCT District). Shekou was the first Special Economic Zone, marking the earliest baby step of modern China's transformation from state-planned to market economy.

☺ **Splendid China.** This park features China's 74 best-known historical and geographical sights collected and miniaturized to 1:15 scale. Built in 1991 and popularized by Deng Xiaoping (who stopped in for a photo op on his famous 1992 journey south promoting free enterprise), it is still a big draw with the patriotic camera-wielding masses, and not a few westerners "doing China" in a day. The 74-acre site includes a waist-high Great Wall, a fun-size Forbidden City, and little Potala Palace. ✉ *OCT District, Shenzhen* ☎ *0755/2660–0626* ⊕ *www.cn5000.com.cn* ➢ *Y120* ⊗ *Daily 9 AM–9:30 PM* Ⓜ *Windows of the World.*

☺ **Windows of the World.** Check out the miniature makeovers of 130 of the world's most famous landmarks. This is China's biggest and busiest homegrown theme park. Divided into eight geographical areas interconnected by winding paths and a full-size monorail, it includes randomly scaled Taj Mahal, Mt. Rushmore, Sydney Harbor Opera House, and a 328-foot-high Eiffel Tower that can be seen from miles away. There is also a fireworks show at 9 PM on weekends and holidays which, for adults, is best viewed from across the street at the Crowne Plaza's rooftop V-Bar. ✉ *OCT, Nanshan District, Shenzhen* ☎ *0755/2660–8000* ⊕ *www.szwwco.com (in Chinese only)* ➢ *Y120* ⊗ *Daily 9 AM–10:30 PM* Ⓜ *Windows of the World.*

Shenzhen is a great city for art lovers. In addition to its statue-filled Overseas Chinese Town Park, the OCT neighborhood is packed with other museums.

He Xiangning Art Museum. The museum is free on Friday and features contemporary and classical art from all over China. ✉ *Shenzhen shi Huaqiaocheng Shennan Dadao 9013 hao, OCT, Nanshan District* ☎ *0755/2660–4540* ⊕ *www.hxnart.com* ⊗ *Tues.–Sun. 10–6* Ⓜ *Huaqiaocheng.*

OCT Contemporary Art Terminal. Shenzhen shi Huaqiaocheng Enping Lu is where you'll find works from the hippest artists from Beijing and beyond. ✉ *OCT, Nanshan District* ☎ *0755/2691–6199* ⊕ *www.ocat.com.cn* ➢ *Free* ⊗ *Tues.–Sun. 10–5:30* Ⓜ *Huaqiaocheng.*

YANTIAN, LONGGANG & BAO'AN

Though these three districts make up the bulk of Shenzhen's land area, most casual visitors to the city never hear of them, let alone visit them. We think this is a pity, as it's these outer regions where you'll find both the prettiest scenery and the most culturally edifying places in the Pearl River Delta, not to mention China's most famous golf course, Mission Hills.

Minsk World. When a group of Shenzhen businessmen bought a decommissioned Soviet-era aircraft carrier in the late 1990s, western intelligence agencies wondered if it was a military move by the Chinese. But the truth was revealed when these savvy entrepreneurs turned this massive warship into Minsk World, Shenzhen's most popular—and perhaps strangest—tourist attraction. Parked in perpetuity on the top deck of the ship (which is as long as three football fields placed end to end, and gets wickedly hot in the summer) are several Soviet fighter planes and helicopters. Every hour on the hour comely young ladies in military costumes perform a dance routine combining sensuality with martial flair and twirling rifles. A visit to Minsk World will be of greatest interest to military buffs. Even casual visitors should find it educational enough to warrant spending the afternoon. ⊠*Shatoujiao, Dapeng Bay, Yantian District, Shenzhen* ☎*0755/2535–5333* ⊕*www. szminsk.com (Chinese only)* ☜*Y110* ⊙*Daily 9:30–7:30.*

Dapeng Fortress. Built more than 600 years ago, the fortress is an excellent example of a Ming Dynasty military encampment (1368–1644). The fortress was originally built to resist Japanese pirates who'd been harassing the southern coastal areas of Guangdong. However, the fortress is best known as the site of the British naval attack of September 4, 1839, in which British forces attacked China in what is widely considered the beginning of the Opium Wars. As local legend goes, Chinese troops in fishing boats, led by General Lai Enjue, defeated the better-equipped enemy. Today, visitors flock to the fortress to admire the inside of the walled town, which is replete with ornately carved beams and columns, with poetic couplets painted over each door. ⊠*Pengcheng Village, Dapeng Town, Longgang District, Shenzhen* ☎*No phone* ☜*Y20* ⊙*Daily 10–9.*

Hakka Folk Customs Museum and Enclosures. This is actually a large series of concentric circular homes built inside of an exterior wall that basically turns the whole place into a large fort. Inside of the enclosure are a large number of old Hakka residences, some of which are still filled with tools and furniture left over from the Qing Dynasty. The site is somewhat feral; once you pass the ticket booth, you're pretty much on your own and free to stroll around the grounds and explore inside the residences themselves, many of which seem to have been left in a mostly natural state. Although some restoration projects pretty things up to the point of making the site look unreal, the opposite is true here. Parts of the enclosures are so real as to seem downright spooky; visitors might get the feeling that the original inhabitants may return at any moment, crossbows cocked. ⊠*Luoruihe Village, Longgang Township, Longgang District, Shenzhen* ☏*Y20* ⊙*Daily 10–6.*

OFF THE BEATEN PATH
If you're interested in watching art in the making, spend an afternoon at the **Dafen Oil Painting Village**, a small town 20 minutes by taxi from Luohu, which employs thousands of artists painting everything from originals to copies of classics. Where do all those oil paintings you find in motels come from? Visit Dafen and you'll know. Be aware, opening hours are sporadic. ⊠*Shen Hui Rd., Bu Ji St., Longgang District* ☏*0755/8473–2622* ⊙*Daily 10–6:30.*

WHERE TO EAT

Shenzhen is packed with people from other provinces, and its main culinary strength lies in this diversity. From the heavy mutton stews of Xinjiang to the spicy seafood dishes of Fujian, Shenzhen is home to thousands of restaurants existing not to please the fickle palates of visitors, but to alleviate the homesickness of people pining for native provinces left behind. Furthermore, over the past few years, Shenzhen has attracted a slew of restaurateurs from abroad, making the city a veritable culinary mecca, not merely for those with a taste for Chinese cuisine, but for international gourmands as well.

$$–$$$$
ECLECTIC
Fodor'sChoice
★
✕ **360.** The newest (and possibly brightest) star on the Shenzhen haute-cuisine scene, 360 takes up the top two floors of the Shangri-La hotel, and offers sumptuous dishes like homemade pasta with eggplant, zucchini, and pesto sauce and ginger-crusted salmon fillet with couscous and lemon-celery sauce. Ambience is chic, and the view from any table in the house is breathtaking. For food, decor, and view we can't recommend this place highly enough. ⊠*31st fl., Shangri-La hotel, 1002 Jianshi Rd., Luohu* ☏*0755/8396–1380* ⊟*AE, DC, MC, V* Ⓜ*Luohu.*

$$$–$$$$
ITALIAN
★
✕ **Blue Italian Seafood & Grill.** Arguably one of the finest Italian restaurants in China, the decor, as the name suggests, is blue—blue walls, ceilings, and mellow indigo lighting. The food is expensive but worth every penny. If you're really in the mood for decadence, try the dessert tray—chocolates, pastries, and eight different types of mousse surround a caramelized sugar statue of David. ⊠*Crowne Plaza Hotel, 3rd fl., 9026 Shen Nan Rd., OCT District* ☏*0755/2693–6888 Ext. 8022, 8023, or 8106* ⊟*AE, DC, MC, V.*

¢–$
CHINESE
✕ **Foodfeast.** This is the only place in Shekou for genuine Hakka cuisine, including rich soups made with pork and bitter melon, serious Hakka-style dumplings, stewed clay-pot dishes and roasted chicken, duck, and fatty pork. Try the durian pancake, if you're a fan of the enormously smelly "king of fruits." (Durian's odor is so strong that it is sometimes banned from subways.) Foodfeast is unpretentious, the sort of place where Sun Yet-sen might have taken tea while plotting

the revolution against the Man-chu Dynasty. ⊠*Sea World Hotel, 1st fl., Taizi Rd. #7, Shekou District* ☎*0755/2540–4730* 🖃*No credit cards.*

CONTEMPORARY ✗**Greenland Lounge.** This favorite is known for its international-style buffet and truly unique selection of Chinese teas. The glass-domed roof and smart-casual ambience make this a popular spot for Shenzhen's movers and shakers. ⊠*Lobby, Pavilion hotel, 4002 Huaqiang Rd. N, Futian District* ☎*0755/8207–8888* 🖃*AE, DC, MC, V.*

$$$ ✗**Little India.** This is definitely more
INDIAN   than your average curry house. The Nepalese chef offers cuisine from both northern India and Nepal. The restaurant is especially known for its tandoori dishes, and for its selection of baked *nan* breads. Little India is also the only restaurant in the Sea World Plaza that offers hookahs, though they'll gently ask you to smoke on the outdoor pavilion during peak hours. ⊠*Shop 73-74, Sea World Plaza, Shekou District* ☎*0755/2685–2688* 🖃*MC, V.*

$$–$$$$ ✗**Sunday Chiu Chow King.** The dim sum and other Cantonese dishes are
CHINESE   good, but what really sets this place apart is the excellent Chaozhou
FUSION   (or Chiu Chow) cuisine. The restaurant is well known on both sides of the border, and usually packed on the weekends with noisy diners from Hong Kong. Try the crispy fried tofu and steamed seafood balls, or the yin-yang soup (it's the soup that looks like a yin-and-yang symbol, made up of rice congee on one side and creamed spinach on the other—just point to the picture on the menu). All of these are Chaozhou specialty dishes. ⊠*Jen Shi Rd. 1076, 9th–10th fls., Luohu* ✛*2 blocks north of Shangri-La Hotel* ☎*0755/8231–0222* 🖃*V* Ⓜ*Luohu.*

¢   ✗**Yokohama.** Here they offer excellent sushi with amazing views of the
JAPANESE   fishing boats and ferries of Shekou Harbor to the east, and the hills of
★   Shekou to the north. Sashimi is the freshest around, and other dishes are the real deal. The clientele is mostly Japanese, which is always a good sign. Try a side dish of *oshinko* (traditional Japanese pickles)—unlike many lesser Japanese restaurants in China, Yokohama takes no shortcuts with its oshinko and offers eight different types. ⊠*Shekou Harbor, Nanhai Hotel, 10th fl., Shekou District* ☎*0755/2669–5557* 🖃*AE, DC, MC, V.*

ADVENTUROUS EATING

The Futian District's Zhen Hua Road, just two blocks north of the Hua Qiang metro station, is one of the few food streets that has not succumbed to the franchise blight of McDonald's and KFC. There are very few English menus and even less western food, so be prepared to be adventurous. Two good choices are the North Sea Fishing Village Restaurant, whose waitstaff speak a bit of English, and has live seafood in tanks out front allowing diners to point and choose, and Lao Yuan Zi, a restaurant with a definite *Crouching Tiger, Hidden Dragon* vibe.

9

WHERE TO STAY

$$–$$$$ 🛏 **Cruise Inn.** Pearlescent tiled floors and stained-glass ceilings are the first thing you'll notice in the lobby of this newly opened hotel inside the landlocked and permanently docked good ship *Minghua*, the cen-

tral feature of Shekou's Sea World Plaza. Rooms are clean, comfortable, and nautically themed. The Romantic Sea View room has a waterbed and a view of the ocean and driving range; the Captain's Suite looks out over the bar street, and has two plasma-screen televisions and a Jacuzzi. If a whimsical maritime *Alice in Wonderland*–style inn is what you're looking for, then look no farther. **Pros:** a fun, quirky place to stay. **Cons:** best if you like things nautical. ✉*Minghua Ship, Sea World, Shekou* ☎*0755/2682–5555* ⊕*www.honlux.com* ⌨*110 rooms, 1 suite* ♿*In-hotel: 3 restaurants, bars, bicycles* ☰*AE, DC, MC, V.*

$$$$ ☒ **Crowne Plaza.** This hotel holds its own among the best hotels in Asia.
Fodor's Choice The theme is pure Italian Renaissance, right down to the Venetian-gon-
★ dolier uniforms worn by the staff, and the wide spiral staircases and long hallways give the place an M. C. Escher feel. The Crowne's swimming pool is the largest in Shenzhen, and extends from an indoor pool under a domed roof to a connected outdoor pool with a swim-up bar. One regular patron told us that she comes back "because anywhere you look in this hotel there's something interesting." The Crowne also has a number of excellent restaurants. **Pros:** near metro, stylish decor. **Cons:** you may not have been thinking Italy when you came to China. ✉*OCT District,* ⚓*Across from Windows of the World metro station* ☎*0755/2693–6888* ⊕*www.crowneplaza.com cpsz@cpsz.com* ⌨*400 rooms, 47 suites* ♿*In-hotel: 4 restaurants, bars, pool, gym* ☰*AE, DC, MC, V.*

$–$$$$ ☒ **Crowne Plaza Hotel and Suites Landmark Shenzhen.** Since completing its ambitious renovation program in 2006, The Landmark has become Shenzhen's first all-suites hotel, boasting 42-inch plasma televisions and extra-large bathrooms. In addition, the hotel has three excellent restaurants, as well as a wine-and-cigar bar with a walk-in humidor. However, what makes this hotel truly unique is its personalized butler service, managed by Robert Watson, director of the Guild of Professional English Butlers and the former principal tutor at the Lady Apsley School for Butlers in London. As for amenities, this hotel basically has it all. If you're looking to experience the life of China's new elite, this is the place to do it. **Pros:** good restaurants, good amenities, personal butler service, near metro. **Cons:** not for those who like things low-key. ✉*3018 Nanhu Lu, 3 blocks NE of Shenzhen main station, Shenzhen* ☎*0755/8217–2288* ⊕*www.szlandmark.com.cn* ⌨*319 suites* ♿*In-hotel: 3 restaurants, bar, pool, gym* ☰*AE, DC, MC, V.*

¢–$ ☒ **Nan Hai.** This hotel's retro space-age exterior, featuring rounded balconies that look as if they might detach from the mother ship at any moment, is the first sight greeting visitors on the Hong Kong–Shekou ferry. Although one of Shenzhen's older luxury hotels, the Nan Hai still holds its own in the moderate-luxury class, offering a lobby piano bar, attractive rooms with balconies and sea views, and a number of excellent restaurants. **Pros:** near pier for ferries to Hong Kong International Airport. **Cons:** dated decor. ✉*1 Gongye Yilu, Shekou* ☎*0755/2669–2888* ⊕*www.nanhai-hotel.com* ⌨*396 rooms and suites* ♿*In-hotel: restaurant, bar, gym, tennis courts, pool* ☰*AE, DC, MC, V.*

$–$$$$ ⬚ **The Pavilion.** With a great location in the heart of the Futian business district, and a gorgeous interior (check out the domed-glass roof over a central piano bar–teahouse), the Pavilion is one of the top international-class hotels in Shenzhen. Service is good, especially for a locally managed hotel, and most staff members speak English. The meeting rooms have everything an international traveler could need. **Pros:** good location, and service, business elegance. **Cons:** rooms don't have much character. ⌧*4002 Huaqiang Bei Lu, Futian District,* ☎*0755/8207–8888* ⊕*www.pavilionhotel.com* ⬚*294 rooms and suites* ⟊*In-hotel: 4 restaurants, pool, gym* ▭*AE, DC, MC, V.*

¢–$ ⬚ **Seaview O City Hotel Shenzhen.** Staying in the OCT District but can't afford the Crowne Plaza? The nearby Seaview hotel is a good bet, albeit far less luxurious. Though rack prices are steep, discounts of up to 40% are usually available. The Seaview is clean, comfortable, has a water view, and thanks to its location across the street from the He Xiangning Art Museum, it is very popular with visiting artists. The 2nd-floor restaurant serves excellent western food, and the 3rd-floor Cantonese restaurant is good for dim sum. **Pros:** affordable, water views. **Cons:** pretty standard. ⌧*No. 3-5 Guangqiao St., OCT, Nanshan District, Shenzhen* ⟊*Directly in front of Huaqiao Cheng metro* ☎*0755/2660–2222* ⊕*www.octhotels.com* ⬚*436 rooms, 17 suites* ⟊*In-hotel: 2 restaurants, gym* ▭*AE, DC, MC, V.*

$$$$ ⬚ **Shangri-La Shenzhen.** The location (practically straddling the border
★ with Hong Kong) has made it a popular meeting place, and it's a city landmark. Rooms are first-class, hospitality is excellent, and the hotel features in-house wireless Internet and top-notch spa facilities. What really makes Shangri-La worth a visit is the 360 Lounge and Restaurant, which takes up the top two floors of the hotel and offers a view of Shenzhen. The Shangri-La also has a number of other excellent restaurants, making it a good choice for first-time visitors who might not want to come into contact with the neighborhood's rougher edges. **Pros:** near Lowu shopping malls. **Cons:** noisy and crowded neighborhood. ⌧*1002 Jianshe Lu, Luohu District, Shenzhen* ⟊*Luohu, east side of train station* ☎*0755/8233–0888* ⊕*www.shangri-la.com* ⬚*523 rooms, 30 suites* ⟊*In-hotel: 5 restaurants, bar, pool, gym* ▭*AE, DC, MC, V.*

¢–$$$ ⬚ **Shanshui Trends Hotel.** This budget hotel in the Futian District appeals mostly to business travelers. With a round bed and view of the interior food court, the Romance Suite is a bit musty and distinctly unromantic. However, the Japanese Suite, with its wooden tub and traditional tatami mats is much nicer. Shanshui Trends is good deal for travelers on a shoestring, located in one of Shenzhen's most happening food districts. Discounts of up to 30% are available. **Pros:** good price, good district for food. **Cons:** nothing special. ⌧*No.1 Hua Fa Bei Lu, Futian District* ⟊*2 blocks north of Hua Qiang metro station* ☎*0755/6135–8802 or 0755/6135–5555* ⬚*197 rooms, 2 suites* ⟊*In-hotel: gym, spa* ▭*AE, DC, MC, V.*

9

NIGHTLIFE & THE ARTS

Shenzhen's nightlife is so happening that it's not unusual to run into people—expats and Chinese—who've come in from Hong Kong and Guangzhou just to party. The two major nightlife centers in Shenzhen are the Luohu District and Shekou District (Luohu tends to be flashier and Shekou a bit more laid-back), but there are also a couple of cool spots in the OCT District as well. A great English-language Web site that lists the latest on what's happening in Shenzhen's ever-evolving party scene is ⊕ *www.shenzhenparty.com.*

Baby Face (⊠ *Beside Lushan Hotel, Luohu District* ☎ *0755/9234–2565* ⊕ *www.babyface.com.cn*) is the Shenzhen branch of one of China's most popular nightspots, offering imported DJs, a late-night-party scene, and extremely chic clientele (so don't show up in flip-flops).

Er Ding Mu (⊠ *Jiang Nan Chun Hotel, 3rd fl., Ai Hua Rd. No.23, Futian District* ✛ *At Nanyuan and Ai Hua Rds.* ☎ *0755/8365–1879 or 131/4883–9798*) is another popular gay club, offering a more relaxed spot for a mostly younger male crowd to unwind and hook up.

Soho Nightclub (⊠ *TaiZi Bar St, Shekou District* ☎ *0755/2669–0148 or 0755/2669–2148*) is the place in Shekou to dance, drink, and party. If you need a rest from dancing, be sure to slip out to the outdoor garden for a cocktail.

3 colors Bar (⊠ *Jing Yuan Building, 2nd fl., Song Yuan Rd., Luohu District* ☎ *0755/2588–7000*) is a lively dance club that's very in with Shenzhen's gay crowd. It's a fun place so there's often a wide mix of people.

True Colors (⊠ *3F Dongyuan Mansion, 1 Dongyuan Lu, Futian District* ☎ *0755/8212–9333*) has one of the coolest party scenes in Shenzhen and attracts top-name international DJs. Musical tastes range from trance to house, and the party usually doesn't break up until dawn.

V-Bar (⊠ *Crowne Plaza Hotel, rooftop, OCT District* ☎ *0755/2693–6888*) is without a doubt the hottest nightspot in the OCT, featuring a live band, a holographic globe hovering over a circular bar, and a fireworks show on the weekends at 9 PM courtesy of the Windows of the World theme park across the street. The V-Bar is the only bar in town with an attached swimming pool.

SHOPPING

The ever-upwardly mobile denizens of the city (not to mention bargain hunters from neighboring Hong Kong) are always looking for places to spend their hard-earned yuan, and from computer parts to fashion, shoes to cell phones, China's first city of capitalism pretty much has it all.

Dongmen Shopping Plaza (⊠ *Laojie Metro Station, Luohu District, Shenzhen* ☎ *No phone*) is Shenzhen's oldest shopping area. It's a sprawling pedestrian plaza with both large shopping centers for name-brand watches, shoes, bags, cosmetics, and clothes, and plenty of smaller outdoor shops. Foot fetishists won't want to miss the huge **Dongmen Shoes City**, close to the east side of the plaza. If you're into people-watching, grab a glass of bubble-milk tea and soak up the sights—the plaza is like a low-rent version of the fashionista youth culture in Tokyo's Ginza.

San Dao Plaza (⊠ *Jen Shi Rd. Luohu Shenzhen* ☎ *No phone* ⊗ 9 AM–8 PM Ⓜ *Luohu*) is a four-story extravaganza and the area's best market for medicinal herbs, tea, and tea-related products. The top two floors contain a series of stalls where merchants sell a wide range of Chinese teas. Visitors are generally invited to *lai, he cha,* or come drink tea. Don't worry, it isn't considered rude to have a cup without buying anything, but if you're a tea aficionado you'll find it hard to leave empty-handed. Downstairs are a large vegetable market and small shops selling traditional Chinese herbal medicines, incense, and religious items. If you speak a little Chinese, you can have your fortune told.

GOLF

Shenzhen has an abundance of golf courses, the most famous being the **Mission Hills Golf Club** (⊠ *Nan Shan, Da Wei, Sha He, Bao'an District, Shenzhen* ☎ *0755/2690–9999, 852/2826–0238 in Hong Kong* ⊕ *www.missionhillsgroup.com*). The club has 10 celebrity-designed 18-hole courses (two of which offer nighttime play), as well as a spectacular clubhouse, a tennis court, two restaurants, and an outdoor pool. There's also a five-star hotel on the premises for golfers serious about trying every course. Mission Hills offers a shuttle bus service from Hong Kong and Shenzhen (*call Shenzhen: 0755/2802–0888 or Hong Kong: 852/2973–0303 for schedule*). Greens fees: Y600 weekdays and Y1,000 weekends; caddies Y150.

The **Guangzhou Luhu Golf & Country Club** (⊠ *Lujing Rd.* ☎ *020/8350–7777*) has 18 holes spread over 180 acres of Luhu Park, 20 minutes from the Guangzhou Railway Station and 30 minutes from Baiyun Airport. The 6,820-yard, par-72 course was designed by world-renowned course-architect Dave Thomas. The club also offers a 75-bay driving range and a clubhouse with restaurants, pro shop, and a gym. Members' guests and those from affiliated clubs pay Y637 in greens fees on weekdays, Y1,274 on weekends. Nonmembers pay Y849 and Y1,486, respectively. These prices include a caddie. Clubs can be rented for Y265. The club is a member of the International Associate Club network.

9

White Swan Hotel Golf Practice Center (⊠ *White Swan Hotel, Yi Shamian Lu Shamian Island* ☎*020/8188–6968*) is a good driving range on Shamian Island if you are pressed for time or don't want to leave the city. Admission is Y70, a rental of one club is Y30, and a box of 20 balls is Y10.

The **Sand River Golf Club** (⊠*1 Baishi Lu, Nanshan District Shenzhen* ☎*0755/2690–0111* ⊙*Daily 7* AM*–9* PM) is another popular club, though not nearly as large as Mission Hills. Sand River offers two courses, one of which is designed by Gary Player and floodlighted for night playing. Other facilities include a large driving range, a lake, and various resort amenities. Greens fees: 9 holes Y330 weekdays and Y550 weekends; 18 holes Y660 weekdays and Y1,100 weekends; caddies Y160 to Y180.

The **Lakewood Golf Club** (⊠*Da'nan Mountain, Jinding District* ☎*0756/338–3666*) is about 20 minutes from the Zhuhai Ferry Terminal, and is the most popular of the city's five golf clubs. Both its Mountain Course and its Lake Course are 18 holes, and are said to be challenging. Visitor packages, including greens fees and a caddy are Y420 for weekdays and Y820 weekends. Golf carts cost Y200.

UNDERSTANDING
HONG KONG

HONG KONG THEN & NOW

With its soaring skyscrapers, futuristic fashions, and tomorrow's technology, Hong Kong may seem like it exists only in the here and now. So it may come as a surprise to hear that the area has been inhabited for thousands of years.

Hong Kong's history is inextricably linked to the sea: the original inhabitants were fisherfolk, and its strategic maritime position was what made it so attractive to the colonizing British. Even today, the newest and shiniest skyscrapers are built on land reclaimed from the harbor.

More than just a city, yet never quite a country, Hong Kong's desired and disputed territory has developed a unique character largely thanks to the great variety of people who made—and make—it their home.

Prehistory

In 2005 archaeologists uncovered 30,000-year-old stone artifacts on the Sai Kung Peninsula, evidence of Paleolithic peoples living in what is now Hong Kong. By 4,000 BC Neolithic fishing communities were scattered along the coast; by 1200–800 BC they could work bronze. Known as the Yueh, this Austro-Asiatic people were gradually assimilated by the Han Chinese settlers who trickled into the area during the first millennium AD.

Shopping & Settling

Hong Kong's reputation as a shoppers' paradise stretches back to the Tang Dynasty (618–907), when traders from China and the Middle East realized that its sheltered harbors were ideal places for boats to meet and exchange goods.

More Cantonese-speaking families from southern China began to arrive toward the end of the Song Dynasty (960–1279), notably the Tang, Hau, Pang, Liu, and Man families—known as the Five Great Clans—who built walled villages in different parts of the New Territories. Their descendants wield considerable clout in

Hong Kong to this day. Despite having only just arrived, they gave themselves the name *boon dei* (meaning "local people" and usually rendered in English as Punti), and drove the territory's previous inhabitants to living on boats.

Political Unrest

With a population of fisherfolk, farmers, and pirates, it's not surprising that Hong Kong was seen as a barbarian backwater by members of the Beijing-based imperial court. They had to bite their tongues in 1276, however, when invading Mongols forced them to flee south. Nine-year-old emperor Duan Zong and his entourage briefly set up court in Hong Kong, but went to a watery grave during a battle in the Pearl River not long after.

There was more political upheaval a few centuries later. Hong Kong's inhabitants remained loyal to the Ming Dynasty (1368–1644) during its swansong, and so were punished by the victorious Qing Dynasty (1644–1911), which ordered a forced evacuation of the coastal population inland. When the ban was lifted several generations later, another ethnic group, the Hakka, also came to live in the area.

Did You Know? Hong Kong's contemporary mafia groups, the Triads, evolved from patriotic secret societies that swore allegiance to the Ming emperor and even participated in the defeat of the Qing Dynasty in 1911, when modern China was born.

Foreign Devils

European sailors seeking to trade with China began to arrive in the Pearl River Delta in the early 16th century. The Portuguese were the trailblazers, and were allowed to set up a legal trading post on Macau in 1557. The British showed their faces within a century, and soon European merchants could do business at Guangzhou (Canton), where trade was strictly regulated. Merchants were only allowed in the city from November to May, and were forbidden from learning Chinese, leaving designated trading compounds, or bringing their families.

Foreign Mud

The Chinese initially had the upper hand in trade. Rich Europeans were desperate to get their hands on luxury goods like tea, porcelain, and silk, whereas the Chinese were unimpressed by the products European traders had to offer and insisted on payment in silver. This was problematic for the British, who used gold as their currency and had to buy their silver from Germany.

Looking for some other commodity to trade, they hit on opium, which the British East India Company could produce in large quantities in Bengal. The first shipment of what the Chinese came to call "foreign mud" was unloaded in 1773. Addiction spread so rapidly that by the mid-1830s more than 40,000 chests of the drug were being imported into China annually, despite the alarmed authorities' attempts to curb the trade.

The First Opium War

In 1839 the Chinese moved to zero-tolerance tactics. Hard-line official Lin Zexu cut off supplies of the British garrison at Guangzhou: the British were forced to hand over 20,000 chests of opium, which were publicly destroyed in Taiping. Trade was suspended, and China demanded Britain sign a treaty promising not to smuggle opium. Britain refused, and hostilities escalated rapidly into what would become known as the First Opium War. The British fleet proved itself tactically and technologically superior. They moved quickly up the coast to Shanghai, and eventually threatened Beijing, to the surprise and dismay of the emperor, who was forced to negotiate.

Did You Know? From the 15th century on, China had pretty much closed its doors to the outside world. This meant that their military and seafaring technology had stagnated while that of Europe flourished.

The British Move In

By 1841 negotiations between Britain and China were slowly ending hostilities. In January, British naval forces raised the Union Jack at Possession Point (between what are now Central and Sheung Wan), claiming Hong Kong Island as theirs. The occupation was made official with the Treaty of Nanjing, which ceded the island to Britain forever and opened five Chinese ports to foreign trade.

At the time, it took months to sail from China to Britain, so all the wheeling and dealing was done by envoys and navy officers, and the politicians got to hear about it all afterward. When British Prime Minister Lord Palmerston discovered Hong Kong was all he'd got out of the Opium War, he was distinctly unimpressed. "You have obtained a barren island with hardly a house upon it," he raged.

Did You Know? Excellent natural harbors and a source of fresh water were the reasons the British chose Hong Kong over other larger islands in the Pearl River Delta. The island's name was the result of a misunderstanding. *Heung gong*, meaning "fragrant harbor," was the name of a village near some incense mills on the island's southwest side. British sailors thought this was the name of the whole island, not just the village, and it stuck.

The Barren Rock Blooms

Merchants in Central didn't share his disdain. Traders bought lots along Queen's Road, then on the waterfront, to build stores and "godowns" (localspeak for warehouses). Meanwhile, the government was also hard at work constructing St. John's Cathedral, Central District Police Station, Government House, as well as extensive army barracks that have since been redeveloped.

Hong Kong's population began to swell: to the surprise of the British, thousands of Chinese immigrants arrived and made their homes in the areas east (Wan Chai) and west (Sheung Wan) of the colonial center. The combined sea- and land-based populations in 1841 were around 6,000; within five years they'd hit 25,000. Numbers grew steadily as mainlanders fled the Taiping Rebellion (1851–64), the first of many conflicts to drive people over the border in one direction or the other.

Did You Know? Many of Hong Kong's most powerful companies date from the beginning of the colony—onetime opium smugglers Jardine Matheson is a famous example.

Another Unequal Treaty

The new commercial big shots weren't happy with how things in the colony were working, however. Many European trade ships still headed straight for Chinese ports, leaving Hong Kong–based companies out of the loop. So Britain began to push for more liberal trade terms with China, including legalizing opium sales. China rejected these and similar demands from France and the United States.

Things came to a head in 1856, when Chinese soldiers boarded the British schooner *Arrow,* supposedly in search of pirates. This faux pas led indirectly to the Second Opium War (1856–60). France joined the British cause, with naval support from Russia and the United States. Once again, European naval technology far outstripped that of China. By 1860 European forces had occupied Beijing, which forced China to capitulate and sign the Treaty of Beijing, handing over Kowloon and allowing the British to import opium into China. Hong Kong Harbor and all its naval approaches were now in British hands.

Life with the British

Although photos from the time show colonnaded arcades, polo grounds, and idyllic lawns stretching to the sea, Hong Kong was very much a country cousin to glam Shanghai, then the center of all the commercial and cultural action in southern China. There was no doubt that Hong Kong was on the right track, however: the economy thrived, and development began on Kowloon.

By 1865 the colony's population was at 122,000 and the new residential districts clearly reflected the British colonial obsession with class and race. Breezy, servant-filled mansions on Victoria Peak housed the rich elite; the Midlevels was the domain of less affluent Portuguese, Chinese, Jewish, and Parsi businessmen; while most of the Chinese were confined to ever-growing slums in Wan Chai and Sheung Wan. When the bubonic plague struck Hong Kong in the 1890s, overcrowding and poor sanitation in these shanty towns made their inhabitants easy victims—thousands died, and half the Chinese population returned to China.

Meanwhile, more and more Chinese-owned businesses were seeing success, yet even the well-to-do were discriminated against. Despite making up 90% of the population, Hong Kong Chinese were repeatedly denied the chance to participate in the colony's government.

A Growing Colony

In 1898 those in power felt Hong Kong and Kowloon were vulnerable to overland invasion. So they set about negotiating for more land from China, which offered more than they'd hoped for: all the land south of the Shenzhen River and 235 islands, a whopping 90% increase to Hong Kong's area. There was a catch, though. This land, known as the "new territories," was only on loan to Britain for 99 years—a lease that would end on June 30, 1997.

As the new century began, the economy boomed. Work began on public services like tramways, ferries, hospitals, gas and electric power plants, and the Kowloon-Canton Railway. Despite this, the living conditions of most of Hong Kong's Chinese would remain pitiful for decades.

The 1911 Chinese Revolution and the decades of unrest and famine that followed it, however, meant that immigrants kept flooding in: by 1931 Hong Kong was home to 850,000.

Did You Know? One of Hong Kong's biggest infrastructure problems has always been fresh water. Leasing the New Territories eventually allowed several reservoirs to be built, but modern Hong Kong still relies on a pipeline from China for most of its water.

Bullets over Central

By 1938 Japanese forces controlled China's major cities, causing refugees to flood into Hong Kong in unprecedented numbers: by 1941 there were 1.6 million people in Hong Kong, half a million of them homeless. Japanese troops invaded Hong Kong eight hours after they bombed Pearl Harbor. They swept through the New Territories, taking control of Kowloon after three days of fighting.

The British government in London had long felt that defending Hong Kong against invasion was a hopeless task and thus a waste of money. Churchill ordered local forces to withstand as long as they could, but sent no reinforcements. War-scarred buildings and monuments at Central and Stanley are testament to the fighting. On Christmas Day 1941, however, Hong Kong became the first British colony to surrender to the Japanese. Governor Sir Mark Young crossed the harbor to sign the surrender in Room 336 of the Peninsula Hotel, where the Japanese had their headquarters.

Japanese Occupation

Living conditions on Hong Kong island had become horrific. Food, housing, fuel, and water shortages were massive, so the Japanese quickly sent Hong Kong's Chinese residents back to China. By the end of the war, the population was back down to 600,000. Life was grim for those left behind: thousands of local women were raped, and summary executions for treason were common. Allied civilians were sent to concentration camps at Stanley and Sham Shui Po, and a former Allied barracks at Kowloon became prisons for male POWs. Many were eventually sent to do hard labor in Japan. Hong Kong dollars were replaced by reserve-less military yen, which led to massive inflation. Most business ground to a halt, streets were renamed, and Japanese became the main language in schools.

Did You Know? Upon the Japanese surrender in 1945, the United States suggested the United Nations return Hong Kong to China. When the highest-ranking British officials were released from prison, they were unaware of this and assumed control of Hong Kong until forces arrived from Sydney, and the colony remained British.

Postwar Boomtown

It didn't take Hong Kong long to get back on its feet. People poured once more over the border from China, and numbers swelled beyond belief after Mao Zedong's communist victory in 1949. Many of the new arrivals were Shanghainese businessmen eager to invest their capital. They took advantage of the labor glut and started building the light industries (textiles, plastics, and electronics) that would make the MADE IN HONG KONG tag world-famous.

Vast shanty towns housed most of Hong Kong's population through the 1950s. The government turned a blind eye to this until Christmas Day 1953, when a fire made more than 50,000 people homeless. This eventually sparked the creation of a massive public housing program—to this day, more than 60% of Hong Kong's population live in subsidized apartment blocks, owned by the world's largest landlord, the Hong Kong Housing Authority.

Did You Know? Hong Kong was able to recover from the war so quickly partly because it used dollars and not pounds sterling, making materials from the United States much more accessible.

The Shadow of the Cultural Revolution

By the '60s, Mao's Cultural Revolution was in full swing on the other side of the border, where Red Guards were killing millions and destroying most of China's heritage. The ripple effect led first to minor events like 1966's Star Ferry Riots, supposedly the reaction to a 10¢ increase in first-class Star Ferry fares. Deep-seated dissatisfaction with the colonial government emerged as a clearer reason for protest; strikes and demonstrations followed. By 1967, riots, bombs, and arson attacks had taken more than 50 lives, but the city's residents—many of whom had fled Mao's China—got fed up with the disturbances and things slowly settled down.

Social Change

Many of the changes that transformed Hong Kong into a world-class city were due to one man: Sir Murray MacLehose, governor between 1971 and 1981. He expanded the public housing program, introduced compulsory, free, high school education, and established the Independent Commission Against Corruption (ICAC). Within a decade, Hong Kong's bribe-happy police force and public bodies were a thing of the past.

With Mao's death in 1978, China began to open up its economy. Hong Kong moved its factories over the border to cheaper Guangdong, and began to focus on the finance and service industries instead. The first skyscrapers on the Central waterfront were pointing in the direction everyone felt Hong Kong was heading: up and up.

China on Our Minds

By the early '80s, living standards had never been better, and the city's coffers never fuller. But one question had everyone in a flutter: what would happen in 1997, when the lease on the New Territories was up? After two years of behind-the-scenes political wrangling, Prime Minister Margaret Thatcher and Premier Deng Xiaoping agreed that all of Hong Kong would return to Chinese rule on July 1, 1997. Hong Kong would become a Special Administrative Region (SAR) of China, meaning its currency, economy, and legal system would remain the same for 50 years. Deng Xiaoping famously labeled this novel approach "One Country, Two Systems."

Did You Know? The 1984 Sino-British Joint Declaration provoked lots of bad feeling in Hong Kong. Residents were aggrieved about having had no say in their future. Britain's refusal to grant Hong Kong residents full British citizenship was another bone of contention.

The Demand for Democracy

Confidence in the future wavered. The economy kept growing, but so did lines outside the embassies of Canada, Australia, and the United States as many Hong Kong residents sought foreign passports, just in case. The situation exploded on June 4, 1989, when People's Liberation Army troops fired on pro-democracy protesters in Tiananmen Square. In Hong Kong, thousands filled the streets in protest, many weeping as they did. Thousands more left the country.

Hong Kong's residents had lived all their lives under the benign dictatorship of the British Government: no political parties, no elections, not even a constitution. The run-up to 1997 began to change this. A mini-constitution, the Basic Law, was drawn up in 1990; the city's first-ever elections were held the year after—but voters could only choose a third of the legislative body. One of the Basic Law's long-term aims was full democracy for Hong Kong. Britain's last governor, Chris Patten, who arrived in 1992, spent a lot of time moving and shaking the democratic cause, provoking considerable wrath from China in the process. Many complain that Britain waited far too long to get the ball rolling: at present it still seems an impossible dream.

A New Order

At midnight on June 30, 1997, the world's eyes turned to Hong Kong. With much pomp and circumstance, Britain's richest colony was handed back to China. Press and audiences alike held their breath, wondering if—or hoping that—the PLA would goose-step through Central and randomly repress crowds. In the end, the change was anticlimactic and seamless. In fact, the huge economic crisis that hit Asia at the end of 1997 made far more impact on Hong Kong than the Handover. Government intervention in the stock market meant that the Hong Kong dollar remained stable, and the SAR wasn't as hard hit as other Asian economies. The floor finally fell out of the vastly overinflated property market, though, leaving many owners bankrupt.

Troubled Times

In late 1997 the first of many avian flu outbreaks swept the region. The government reacted slowly, and was lax about tightening up public health. Many feel this contributed to the territory's next—and much deadlier—epidemic: Severe Acute Respiratory Syndrome (SARS), in 2003. Three hundred people died, no one left home without a surgical mask, and the tourist industry almost collapsed.

The city emerged from the crisis much cleaner, but incredibly angry with the inefficient action of a government it hadn't even been allowed to choose. The final straw came later that year, when the government proposed Article 23, a highly unpopular national security bill affecting freedom of the press and association. A whopping half-million people—almost 10% of the population—came out to protest. The bill was indefinitely postponed and Chief Executive Tung Chee-hwa was given a public telling-off by Beijing. He eventually resigned in 2005, and was replaced by more popular Sir Donald Tsang, financial secretary from 1995 to 2001, under both the British and the Chinese administrations, then chief secretary from 2001 on. Political reform remains a serious concern for most Hong Kongers.

Did You Know? Hong Kong's political system is a complicated patchwork of parts. A largely pro-Beijing election committee of 800 people choose the chief executive, a pseudo-presidential figure. The chief executive appoints the 21 members of the executive council, a kind of cabinet. The legislation the executive council proposes must be passed by the single-chamber legislative council (so-called LegCo), made of 60 members who serve four-year terms. Half of the members are elected directly (there's universal suffrage for those over 18). The other half are elected by "functional constituencies," largely conservative, corporate-friendly groups that represent different occupational areas.

Travel Smart
Hong Kong

WORD OF MOUTH

"Arrival into HK airport. HUGE lines at customs . . .
but I had remembered that last time we discovered
that there is another section that is to the right of
where the crowds of people are heading. The section is just on the other side of the huge columns.
And guess what? I was right (YAY for me!)"

—kooba

GETTING HERE & AROUND

Public transportation options are many and varied—all are good, too. An "Octopus" stored-value card is by far the most convenient way to get around Hong Kong. It's used on all forms of public transport: you just swipe it over the ticket-gate sensor to deduct your fare, which will be cheaper than a regular one, by the way. You can buy an Octopus card in any MTR, KCR, or Airport Express Station. They cost HK$150, of which HK$50 is a refundable deposit, and the other HK$100 is for you to use. (If you return them in less than a month, you forfeit HK$7 of your deposit as a processing fee.) You can refill the cards at any ticket counter, at speedy machines in stations, or at a 7-11 or Wellcome supermarket, where you can also use them to pay for purchases. Handy or what?

Information **Octopus Cards** (☎2266–2222 ⊕www.octopuscards.com).

▌BY AIR

Flying time to Hong Kong is around 16½ hours direct from Newark/New York, 13½ hours direct from Los Angeles, or 12¼ hours direct from San Francisco.

Airlines & Airports **Airline and Airport Links.com** (⊕www.airlineandairportlinks.com) has links to many of the world's airlines and airports.

Airline Security Issues **Transportation Security Agency** (⊕www.tsa.gov/public) has answers for almost every question that might come up.

AIRPORTS
The sleek, sophisticated Hong Kong International Airport (HKG) is never called by its official name; it's universally referred to as Chek Lap Kok, which is where it's located. At almost a mile long, the Y-shape passenger Terminal 1 is the world's second-largest terminal, while the new Terminal 2 is just as sleek and well-equipped, but smaller. Terminal 2 handles departures for selected airlines; all flights arrive at Terminal 1.

Chek Lap Kok is one of the friendliest, most efficient airports around. Walkways connect the check-in and arrival halls with nearby gates. Electric trains glide to gates at the end of the terminals. Restaurants, fast-food outlets, and bars abound—try Oliver's Super Sandwiches for snacks; Grappa's and Cafe Deco are both good bets for a bigger meal. Most eateries are open from 7 AM to 11 PM or midnight; local chain Café de Coral and Ajisen Ramen (Japanese noodles) in the east departures hall are the only outlets open 24 hours.

There's free Wi-Fi access all over the terminals after check-in. A telecom and business center, Connect Zone, is located in the Level 6 Departures Hall near Gate 24. It provides Wi-Fi and Internet access, free local phone calls, select TV programs, and other business support services. If you're going to be overnighting at Chek Lap Kok, consider buying a package from the Plaza Premium Traveler's Lounges, near Gate 60 in Terminal 1 and on level 3 in Terminal 2. The lounges have rest areas, showers, free 15-minute massages, Internet access, newspapers, and a 24-hour buffet—an overnight package costs HK$780. Note that there are no other public showers or spa or massage facilities at Chek Lap Kok.

Check in at least two hours before departing from Chek Lap Kok. If you're flying to any place but the United States and plan on taking the train to the airport, most major airlines let you use the In-Town check-in service at the Hong Kong or Kowloon Airport Express stations. You can check your bags up to 24 hours before your flight—a boon if you're flying at night and don't want to return to your hotel to look for your bags. The service is available until 1½ hours before your flight time. After September 11, 2001, carriers flying to the United States discontinued In-Town check-in indefinitely. Check with your carrier beforehand in case the rules have changed.

Airport tax is normally included in your ticket price. If it's not, hold on to HK$120 for the airport tax, payable on departure from the country. It's only levied on those 12 years and older and is waived for all transit and transfer passengers who arrive and leave on the same day. When you go through immigration, have your Hong Kong entry slip (given to you on arrival) ready to show officials along with your passport.

Airport Information **Hong Kong International Airport** (☎852/2181–8888 ⊕www. hkairport.com). **Plaza Premium Lounge** (☎852/2261–2068 ⊕www.plaza-ppl.com).

GROUND TRANSPORTATION

The Airport Express train service is the quickest and most convenient way to and from the airport. Gleaming, high-speed trains whisk you to Kowloon in 19 minutes and Central in 24 minutes. Trains run every 12 minutes between 5:50 AM and 1:15 AM daily. There's plenty of luggage space, legroom, and comfortable seating with TV screens on the backs of the passenger seats showing tourist information and the latest news. Although it's the most expensive public transport option, the speed and efficiency make it well worth the extra cost.

The Airport Express station is connected to the MTR's Tung Chung, Kowloon and Central stations—the latter is via a long, underground walkway with no luggage carts, however. One-way or same-day return fare to or from Central is HK$100; from Kowloon, HK$90. Round-trip tickets valid for one month cost HK$180 for Central and HK$160 for Kowloon. The Airport Express also runs free shuttle buses every 12 minutes between major hotels and its Hong Kong and Kowloon stations—there are seven routes. To board, you must show your ticket, boarding pass, or Airport Express ticket.

GROUND TRANSPORTATION TO CENTRAL		
Transport Mode	Time	Cost
Airport Express	24 mins	HK$100
Citybus Line A (Cityflyer)	50 mins	HK$40
Citybus Line E (Regular)	70 mins	HK$21
Limo	45 mins	HK$500
Taxi	45 mins	HK$340
Tung Chung (S1 bus) + MTR (train)	10 mins + 35 mins	HK$3.50 + HK$23

Citybus runs five buses ("A" precedes the bus number) from Chek Lap Kok to popular destinations. They have fewer stops than regular buses, which have an "E" before their number, so are more expensive. Two useful routes are the A11, serving Central, Admiralty, Wan Chai, and Causeway Bay; and the A21, going to Tsim Sha Tsui, Jordan, and Mong Kok. There's plenty of space and onboard announcements in English, so you won't miss your stop.

Several small shuttle buses with an "S" before their number run to the nearby Tung Chung MTR station, where you can get the MTR to Central and Kowloon. The trains follow the airport express route, but are a little slower and a quarter of the cost.

Taxis from the airport are reliable and plentiful and cost around HK$340 for Hong Kong Island destinations and HK$270 for Kowloon destinations, plus HK$5 per piece of luggage stored in the trunk. Two limo services in the arrivals hall, Parklane and Intercontinental, will run you into town in style. Depending on the zone and the type of car, limo rides from the airport range from HK$500 to HK$600.

GROUND TRANSPORTATION TO TSIM SHA TSUI		
Transport Mode	Time	Cost
Airport Express	19 mins	HK$90
Citybus Line A (Cityflyer)	45 mins	HK$33
Citybus Line E (Regular)	60 mins	HK$14
Limo	35 mins	HK$500
Taxi	35 mins	HK$270
Tung Chung (S1 bus) + MTR (train)	10 mins + 35 mins	HK$3.50 + HK$17

Contacts Airport Express (☎2881–8888 for MTR hotline ⊕www.mtr.com.hk). **Citybus** (☎2873–0818 ⊕www.nwstbus.com.hk). **Intercontinental Hire Car** (☎2261–2155 ⊕www.trans-island.com.hk). **Parklane Limousine Service** (☎2261–0303 ⊕www.hongkonglimo.com).

FLIGHTS

Cathay Pacific is Hong Kong's flagship carrier. It maintains high standards, with friendly service, good in-flight food, and an excellent track record for safety—all of which drive its prices higher than some of the other regional carriers. Cathay has nonstop flights from both Los Angeles and San Francisco on the west coast and from New York–JFK on the east, with connecting services to many other U.S. cities. Singapore Airlines is usually slightly less expensive and offers direct flights to San Francisco on the west coast and Newark on the east coast. Considerably less comfortable, Continental also frequently offers good-price deals, and has a nonstop flight to Hong Kong from Newark Liberty International Airport. Several other airlines offer service from the United States to Hong Kong, sometimes with connections in Asia.

If you're planning to travel to several different Asian destinations, Cathay Pacific's All Asia pass is an excellent deal. For $1,500 you get a round-trip ticket from New York (JFK), Los Angeles, or San Francisco to Hong Kong, plus 21 days of unlimited travel to four of 24 Asian cities. You can pay supplements to add on cities that aren't included and to extend the pass: $400 buys you up to 90 days. If you just want to combine Hong Kong and one other Cathay destination, though, go for a regular ticket: the airline generally allows a free Hong Kong stopover.

The One World Alliance Visit Asia Pass might work out cheaper for three or four destinations. Cities are grouped into zones, and there's a flat rate for each zone. It doesn't include flights from the United States, however. Inquire through American Airlines, Cathay Pacific, or any other One World member.

Airline Contacts All Asia Pass (Cathay Pacific, ☎800/233–2742 ⊕www.cathay-usa.com). **Cathay Pacific Airways** (☎800/233–2742 in U.S., 800/268–6868 in Canada, 2747–1888 in Hong Kong ⊕www.cathay-usa.com). **China Airlines** (☎800/227–5118, 2868–2299 in Hong Kong ⊕www.china-airlines.com/en/). **Continental Airlines** (☎800/523–3273 for U.S. and Mexico reservations, 800/231–0856 for international reservations, 852/3198–5777 in Hong Kong ⊕www.continental.com). **Singapore Airlines** (☎800/742–3333 in U.S., 852/2520–2233 in Hong Kong ⊕www.singaporeair.com). **Visit Asia Pass** (One World Alliance ⊕www.oneworld.com).

BY BOAT & FERRY

With fabulous views of both sides of Hong Kong Harbor, the Star Ferry is so much more than just a boat. It's an iconic Hong Kong landmark in its own right and has been running across the harbor since 1888. Double-bowed, green-and-white vessels connect Central and Wan Chai with Kowloon in seven minutes, daily from 6:30 AM to 11:30 PM; the ride costs HK$2.20 on the upper deck, making it the cheapest scenic tour in town.

New World First Ferry (NWFF) Services Ltd. runs nine routes from Central to the outlying islands of Lantau and Cheung Chau. Pick up printed schedules at the Hong Kong Tourist Board (HKTB) info centers at the Tsim Sha Tsui Star Ferry Concourse and in Causeway Bay MTR station; as well as through the HKTB Visitor Hot Line. Or, you can simply pick one up at the ferry ticket counters.

(For information about ferry service to Macau and locations in China, see chapter 8, Macau, and chapter 9, Pearl River Delta.)

FERRY TRAVEL			
Line/ Route	Frequency	Travel Time	Fare
DBTPL Central– Discovery Bay (Lantau)	10–30 mins	25–30 mins	HK$27
NWFF Central– Cheung Chau	30 mins	30–50 mins	HK$11.30 –HK$16.70
NWFF Central– Mui Wo (Lantau)	30 mins	30–50 mins	HK$13.- 0–HK$16.70
Star Ferry Central– Tsim Sha Tsui	6–10 mins	7 mins	HK$2.20

FERRY TRAVEL			
Star Ferry Central– Wan Chai	10–12 mins	8 mins	HK$2.20

Information **HKTB Visitor Hot Line** (☎2508–1234). **New World First Ferry** (☎2131–8181 ⊕www.nwff.com.hk). **Star Ferry** (☎2367–7065 ⊕www.starferry.com.hk). (☎2987–6128 ⊕www.discoverybay.com.hk).

▌ BY BUS

An efficient network of double-decker buses covers most of Hong Kong. Using them is a tricky business, though, as drivers don't usually speak English, and the route maps on bus shelters and company Web sites are so complex as to be off-putting. To compound this, there are several companies and no central Web site or pocket bus maps.

When determining bus direction, buses ending with the letter "L" will eventually connect to the Kowloon–Canton Railway; buses ending with the letter "M" connect to an MTR station; "A" enders go to the airport; and buses ending with the letter "X" are express.

Rattling along Hong Kong's roads at breakneck speed are numerous minibuses, which seat 16 people. They're cream with green or red roofs and prominently display the route number and the fixed price. They stop at designated spots, and you pay as you board. If you want to get off, shout *"Bah-see jam yau lok"* ("Next stop, please") to the driver and hold on tight as he screeches to a halt. There is a fine of HK$5,000 for not wearing seat belts. Though slightly more expensive than buses, minibuses are quicker and more comfortable.

FARES

Double-decker bus fares range from HK$1.20 to HK$45; minibus fares from HK$2 to HK$20. For both you must pay exact change upon entering the bus. You can also use an Octopus stored-value card on both.

Bus Information **Citybus** (☎2873–0818 ⊕www.citybus.com.hk); Hong Kong Island, cross-harbor and airport routes. **Kowloon Motor Bus** (KMB ☎2745–4466 ⊕www.kmb.com.hk); mainly serves Kowloon and New Territories. **Long Win Bus Company** (☎2261–2791 ⊕www.kmb.com.hk); serves north Lantau, including Tung Chung. **New World First Bus** (☎2136–8888 ⊕www.nwfb.com.hk); runs services on Hong Kong Island and in New Kowloon. **Octopus Cards** (☎2266–2222 ⊕www.octopuscards.com).

▮ BY CAR

Frankly, you'd be mad to rent a car on Hong Kong Island or Kowloon. Maniac drivers, traffic jams, and next to no parking make driving here severely stress-inducing, and gasoline costs up to twice what it does in the United States. So why bother, when public transportation is excellent, and taxis inexpensive? If you must have your own wheels, consider hiring a driver; most top-end hotels arrange this. The minimum rental time is two hours, which will cost you HK$-00–HK$1,000; it's HK$450–HK$500 for each subsequent hour.

If you're determined to drive yourself, your driver's license is valid in Hong Kong if you're 18 to 70 years old (those over 70 must pass a physical examination before driving). You'll need an International Driver's Permit for long stays. Check the AAA Web site for more info as well as for IDPs ($10) themselves. Rental rates begin at HK$700 per day and HK$2,900 per week for an economy car with air-conditioning, automatic transmission, and unlimited mileage. Remember that you drive on the left in Hong Kong. Take traffic regulations seriously even if other drivers don't—the police are very ticket-happy.

Information **Hawk Rent-a-Car** (☎2516–9822 ⊕www.hawkrentacar.com.

hk) has lots of models and prices; there are special rates for weekends and longer-term rentals. **Parklane Limousine** (☎2730–0662 ⊕www.hongkonglimo.com) rents Mercedes with drivers.

PARKING

There's next to no on-street parking in Central and Tsim Sha Tsui: if there isn't a sign that expressly states you *can* park (after paying a meter), assume you can't. Finding a space next to such a sign is nothing short of a miracle. Most people use multistory or mall parking garages, which cost around HK$7 per half hour. The Hong Kong traffic police are extremely vigilant and seem to take great pleasure in handing out copious parking tickets.

RULES OF THE ROAD

Cars drive on the left-hand side of the road in Hong Kong. Wearing a seat belt is obligatory in the front and back of private cars, and the standard speed limit is 50 kph (30 mph) unless road signs say otherwise. The Hong Kong Police spend a lot of time setting up photographic speed traps and handing out juicy fines for wannabe Schumachers. Likewise, using handheld cell phones while driving is forbidden. You can't make a right turn on a red light, and you should scrupulously obey lane markings regarding turns. Drunk driving is taken very seriously: the legal limit is 50 mg of alcohol per 100 ml of blood, and there are penalties of up to HK$25,000 and three years in prison for those who disobey. You can get highly detailed information on Hong Kong's road rules online, at the Transport Department's Web site.

Road Rules **Hong Kong Government Transport Department Road Safety Code** (⊕http://www.td.gov.hk/road_safety/index.htm).

▮ BY CRUISE

Star Cruises has trips through southeast Asia that start from, or call at, Hong Kong. The crème de la crème of cruisers, Cunard, docks in Hong Kong on its round-the-world trips. Princess Cruises has a wide variety of packages that call in at Hong Kong and many other Asian destinations. Holland America has short China and Japan cruises as well as round-the-world options.

Cruise Lines **Cunard** (☎800/728–6273 ⊕www.cunard.com). **Holland America** (☎877/724–5425 ⊕www.hollandamerica. com). **Princess Cruises** (☎800/774–6237 ⊕www.princess.com). **Star Cruises** (☎2317–7711 Hong Kong ⊕www.starcruises. com).

▌BY SUBWAY

By far the best way to get around Hong Kong is on the Mass Transit Railway or MTR. Since merging with the former Kowloon-Canton Railway (KCR) in late 2007, the MTR network now provides all subway and train services in Hong Kong.

There are five main MTR subway lines: the Island Line runs along the north coast of Hong Kong Island; the Tsuen Wan line goes from Central under the harbor to Tsim Sha Tsui then up to the western New Territories. Tsim Sha Tsui links to eastern New Kowloon via the Kwun Tong Line; also serving this area is the Tseung Kwan O Line, which crosses back over the harbor at Quarry Bay. Finally, the Tung Chung Line connects Central and west Kowloon with Tung Chung on Lantau, near the airport.

The MTR's highly modern, fast trains are clean and very safe, as are the stations. Platforms and exits are clearly signposted, and all MTR areas are air-conditioned. Most stations have wheelchair access, and all have convenience stores and other shops or services. Trains run every two–five minutes between 6 AM and 1 AM daily. Station entrances are marked with a dark red circle symbol containing the outline of a person with arms and legs outstretched in white.

FARES & SCHEDULES

You buy tickets from ticket machines (using coins or notes) or from English-speaking workers at the counters by the turnstile entrances. Fares are not zoned, but depend on which stations you're traveling between. There are no monthly or weekly tickets. If you're going to do more than one or two trips on the MTR (or any other form of transport), get yourself a rechargeable Octopus card. It saves you time lining up for tickets, and you get a discount on your fares, too.

Fares range from HK$3.60 to HK$23.50. The special Tourist MTR One-Day Pass (HK$50) allows you unlimited rides in a day. The three-day Airport Express Tourist Octopus pass (HK$220–HK$300) includes one journey from–to the airport, unlimited MTR travel, and HK$20 worth of trips on other transport.

Information **HKTB Visitor Hot Line** (☎2508–1234). **MTR** (☎2881–8888 ⊕www. mtr.com.hk). **Octopus Cards** (☎2266–2222 ⊕www.octopuscards.com).

▌BY TAXI

Though there are more than 18,000 taxis in Hong Kong, heavy daytime traffic in Central and Tsim Sha Tsui means they aren't the best option. Outside these areas, or after dark, they're much more useful. Drivers usually know the terrain well, but as many don't speak English, having your destination written in Chinese is a good idea. You can hail cabs on the street, provided it's a stopping area (i.e., not on double yellow lines). The white TAXI sign is lit when the cab is available. Note that it's sometimes hard to find a taxi around 4 PM when the drivers switch shifts.

Fares for the red taxis operating in urban areas start at HK$16 for the first 2 km (1½ mi), then HK$1.40 for each 2 km (.1 mi) or minute of waiting time (so fares add up fast in bumper-to-bumper traffic). There's a surcharge of HK$5 for each piece of luggage you put in the trunk, and surcharges of HK$20 for the Cross-Harbour Tunnel, HK$40 for the Eastern Harbour Tunnel, and HK$50 for the Western Harbour Tunnel. The Tsing Ma Bridge surcharge is HK$30. The Aberdeen, Lion Rock, and Junk Bay tunnels also carry small surcharges (HK$5 to HK$10).

In the New Territories taxis are green; on Lantau they're blue. Fares are slightly lower than in urban areas, but while urban taxis may travel into rural zones, rural taxis can't cross into urban zones.

Backseat passengers must wear a seat belt or face a HK$5,000 fine. Most locals don't tip; however, if you round up the fare by a few Hong Kong dollars you're sure to earn yourself a winning smile from your underpaid and overworked driver. Taxis are usually reliable, but if you have a problem, note the taxi's license number, which is usually on the dashboard, and call the Transport Complaints Unit.

In urban areas, it's as easy and safe to hail a cab on the street as to call one. There are hundreds of taxi companies, so it's usually best to get your hotel or restaurant to call a company it works with. If you need to call one yourself, try Hong Kong taxis. Note that there's a HK$5 surcharge for phone bookings.

Complaints Transport Complaints Unit (☎2889–9999). **Hong Kong taxis** (☎2574–7311).

▌ BY TRAIN

Operations of the MTR subway and former Kowloon–Canton Railway (KCR) merged in 2007 so all trains now run under the MTR name. The ultra-efficient train network connects Kowloon to the eastern and western New Territories. Trains run every 5–8 minutes, and connections to the subway are usually quick. It's a commuter service and, like the subway, has sparkling clean trains and stations—smoking and eating are forbidden in both. At this writing the train network

has three main lines, but there are all kinds of ambitious projects underway to extend its service network.

The East Rail line has 13 stops on its journey from Tsim Sha Tsui East through urban Kowloon, Sha Tin, and Tai Po on its way to Lo Wu on the Chinese boundary. East Rail is the fastest way to get to Shenzhen—it's a 40-minute trip from Tsim Sha Tsui to Lo Wu. The Tsim Sha Tsui terminus connects via a series of underground walkways with Tsim Sha Tsui subway; you can also transfer to the subway at Kowloon Tong.

The short Ma On Shan Rail service starts at Tai Wai (also on the East Rail line) and has eight stops in the northeastern New Territories. This line will one day be extended to pass through Tsim Sha Tsui.

West Rail starts at Nam Cheong (also on the subway) and stretches out through eight stops into Tuen Mun, in the western New Territories. Here West Rail connects with the weblike Light Rail Transit, an aboveground train serving mainly residential and industrial areas in the western New Territories. KCR is currently building the tracks that will extend West Rail into Tsim Sha Tsui. It's also constructing a link to connect boundary-town Lok Ma Chau with both East and West Rail.

Fares range from HK$3.70 to HK$47.50; you can pay by Octopus card or buy tickets from sales counters or ticket machines.

Train Information MTR (☎2881–8888 ⊕www.mtr.com.hk). **HKTB Visitor Hotline** (☎2508–1234). **Octopus Cards** (☎2266–2222 ⊕www.octopuscards.com).

▌ BY TRAM

PEAK TRAM

It's Hong Kong's greatest misnomer—the Peak Tram is actually a funicular railway. Since 1888 it's been rattling the 1,207 feet up the hill from Central to Victoria Peak tram terminus. As well as a sizeable adrenaline rush due to the steepness of the ascent, on a clear day it offers fabulous panoramas. Both residents and tourists use it; most passengers board at the lower terminus between Garden Road and Cotton Tree Drive. (The tram has five stations.) The fare is HK$22 one way, HK$33 round-trip, and it runs every 15 minutes between 7 AM and midnight daily. A shuttle bus runs between the lower terminus and the Star Ferry.

STREET TRAMS

Hong Kong Tramways runs old-fashioned double-decker trams along the north shore of Hong Kong Island. Routes start in Kennedy Town (in the west), and go all the way through Central, Wan Chai, Causeway Bay, North Point, and Quarry Bay to Shau Kei Wan. A branch line turns off in Wan Chai toward Happy Valley, where horse races are held in season.

Destinations are marked on the front of each tram; you board at the back and get off at the front, paying HK$2 regardless of distance (by Octopus or with exact change) as you leave. Avoid trams at rush hours, which are generally weekdays from 7:30 to 9.30 AM and 5 to 7 PM. Although trams move slowly, for short hops between Central and Western or Admiralty they can be quicker than the MTR. A leisurely top-deck ride from Western to Causeway Bay is a great city tour.

Tram Information **Hong Kong Tramways** (☎2548–7102 ⊕www.hktramways.com). **Octopus Cards** (☎2266–2222 ⊕www. octopuscards.com). **Peak Tram** (☎2849–6754 ⊕www.thepeak.com.hk).

ESSENTIALS

▌BUSINESS & TRADE SERVICES

BUSINESS CENTERS

Hong Kong has many business centers outside hotels, and some are considerably cheaper than hotel facilities. Others cost about the same but offer private desks (from HK$250 per hour for desk space to upward of HK$8,000 a month for an office). Amenities include a private address and phone-answering and forwarding services. Many centers are affiliated with accountants and lawyers who can expedite company registration. Some will even process visas and wrap gifts for you.

Harbour International Business Centre provides typing, secretarial support, and office rentals. Reservations aren't required. The Executive Centre and Regus are two international business services companies with several office locations in Hong Kong. They provide secretarial services, meeting and conference facilities, and office rentals.

The American Chamber of Commerce can arrange a Breakfast Briefing Program at your hotel for a fee based on group size. The chamber hosts luncheons and seminars, and its Young Professionals Committee holds cocktail parties at least once a month. Facilities include a library and China trade services.

Information **American Chamber of Commerce** (✉ Bank of America Tower, 12 Harcourt Rd., Room 1904, Central ☎ 2530–6900 ⊕ www.amcham.org.hk). **The Executive Centre** (☎ 2297–0222 ⊕ www.executivecentre. com). **Harbour International Business Centre** (☎ 2529–0356 ⊕ www.hibc.com). **Regus** (☎ 2166–8000 ⊕ www.regus.hk).

CONVENTION CENTER

The Hong Kong Convention & Exhibition Centre (HKCEC) is a state-of-the-art, 2.4-million-square-foot complex on Victoria Harbour. The HKCEC houses six exhibition halls, two convention halls, two theaters, and 52 meeting rooms. The center is adjacent to the Convention Plaza, which includes the 860-room Renaissance Harbour View Hotel Hong Kong, the 549-room Grand Hyatt Hong Kong, a 39-story office tower, an apartment tower, a shopping arcade, and an underground garage. Its second expansion began in July 2006 and will add 358,450 square feet upon completion, scheduled for 2009.

Information **Hong Kong Convention & Exhibition Centre** (✉ 1 Expo Dr., Wan Chai ☎ 2582–8888 ⊕ www.hkcec.com.hk).

MESSENGERS

Most business centers offer delivery service, and you can sometimes arrange a delivery through your hotel concierge. Couriers, including City-Link International, will pick up from your hotel, as will FedEx and DHL, who also have drop-off points all over Hong Kong. Price is based on weight and distance.

Information **City-Link International Courier Co. Ltd** (☎ 2382–8289 ⊕ www.citylinkexpress. com). **DHL** (☎ 2400–3388 ⊕ www.dhl.com. hk). **Federal Express** (☎ 2730–3333 ⊕ www. fedex.com/hk_english).

TRADE INFORMATION

Information **Hong Kong General Chamber of Commerce** (☎ 2529–9229 ⊕ www. chamber.org.hk). **Hong Kong Trade Development Council** (☎ 1830-668 ⊕ www. hktdc.com). **Hong Kong Trade & Industry Department** (☎ 2392–2922 ⊕ www.tid.gov. hk). **Innovation & Technology Commission** (☎ 2737–2573 ⊕ www.itc.gov.hk).

TRANSLATION SERVICES

Information **Language Line** (☎ 2511–2677 ⊕ www.languageventure.com). **Polyglot Translations** (☎ 2851–7232 ⊕ www.polyglot. com.hk). **Translation Business** (☎ 2893–5000 ⊕ www.translationbusiness.com.hk).

■ COMMUNICATIONS

INTERNET

Hong Kong is an Internet-friendly place for those bearing laptops. All mid- to high-end hotels have in-room Internet access; Wi-Fi is common both in hotels and in public places, including many cafés, bars, and restaurants. All business centers have high-speed access.

Laptops and Blackberries are so ubiquitous in Hong Kong that things can get tough if you haven't got one. Internet cafés are practically nonexistent; the only place to check e-mail on the go is at one of the many branches of the Pacific Coffee Company—you can log on to one of their free terminals if you buy a coffee (HK$20–HK$30).

Contacts Pacific Coffee Company (⊕www. pacificcoffee.com).

PHONES

The good news is that you can now make a direct-dial telephone call from virtually any point on earth. The bad news? You can't always do so cheaply. Calling from a hotel is almost always the most expensive option; hotels usually add huge surcharges to all calls, particularly international ones. In some countries you can phone from call centers or even the post office. Calling cards usually keep costs to a minimum, but only if you purchase them locally. And then there are mobile phones (⇨*below*), which are sometimes more prevalent—particularly in the developing world—than landlines; as expensive as mobile phone calls can be, they are still usually a much cheaper option than calling from your hotel.

Hong Kong was the first city in the world with a fully digitized local phone network, and the service is efficient and cheap. Even international calls are inexpensive relative to those in the United States. You can expect clear connections and helpful directory assistance. Don't hang up if you hear Cantonese when calling automated and prerecorded hotlines; English is usually the second or third language option. The country code for Hong Kong is 852; there are no local area codes.

CALLING WITHIN HONG KONG

Hong Kong phone numbers have eight digits: landline numbers usually start with a 2 (mobiles with a 9).

If you're old enough to talk in Hong Kong, you're old enough for a cell phone, which means public phones can be difficult to find. MTR stations usually have one: local calls to both land- and cell lines cost HK$1 per five minutes. If you're planning to call abroad from a pay phone, buy a phone card. Convenience stores like 7-11 sell stored-value Hello cards (only for use at pay phones) and SmartCards (a PIN-activated card you can use from any phone). Some pay phones accept credit cards.

Restaurants and shopkeepers may let you use their phone for free, as the phone company doesn't charge for individual local calls. Hotels may charge as much as HK$5 for a local call, though.

Dial 1081 for directory assistance from English-speaking operators. If a number is constantly busy and you think it might be out of order, call 109 and the operator will check the line. The operators are very helpful, if you talk slowly and clearly.

CALLING OUTSIDE HONG KONG

International rates from Hong Kong are reasonable, even more so between 9 PM and 8 AM. The international dial code is 001, then the country code.

The country code is 1 for the United States.

So to call the United States you dial 0011. You can dial direct from many hotel and business centers, but always with a hefty surcharge. Dial 10013 for international inquiries and for assistance with direct dialing. Dial 10010 for collect and operator-assisted calls to most countries, including the United States. Dial 10011 for credit-card, collect, and international conference calls.

Access Codes **AT&T Direct** (☎800/96–1111). **MCI WorldPhone** (☎800/96–1121). **Sprint International Access** (☎800/96–1877).

MOBILE PHONES

If you have a multiband phone (some countries use different frequencies than what's used in the United States) and your service provider uses the world-standard GSM network (as do T-Mobile, Cingular, and Verizon), you can probably use your phone abroad. Roaming fees can be steep, however: 99¢ a minute is considered reasonable. And overseas you normally pay the toll charges for incoming calls. It's almost always cheaper to send a text message than to make a call, since text messages have a very low set fee (often less than 5¢).

If you just want to make local calls, consider buying a new SIM card (note that your provider may have to unlock your phone for you to use a different SIM card) and a prepaid service plan in the destination. You'll then have a local number and can make local calls at local rates. If your trip is extensive, you could also simply buy a new cell phone in your destination, as the initial cost will be offset over time.

■TIP➔ **If you travel internationally frequently, save one of your old mobile phones or buy a cheap one on the Internet; ask your cell phone company to unlock it for you, and take it with you as a travel phone, buying a new SIM card with pay-as-you-go service in each destination.**

Most GSM-compatible mobile handsets work in Hong Kong. If you can unlock your phone, buying a SIM card locally is the cheapest and easiest way to make calls. Local phone company PCCW sells them from around HK$50 from their shops all over town. Local calls cost around HK$0.25 a minute.

Otherwise, you can rent handsets from CSL (HK$35 a day plus an HK$500 deposit) with prepaid SIM cards (HK$–8–HK$180). There's a stand at the airport and shops all over town. If you're only in town for a day or two, this is a good-value option.

Contacts **Cellular Abroad** (☎800/287–5072 ⊕www.cellularabroad.com) rents and sells GMS phones and sells SIM cards that work in many countries. **CSL** (☎2512–3123 on Hong Kong Island, 2393–5597 in Kowloon ⊕www.one 2free.com). **Mobal** (☎888/888–9162 ⊕www. mobalrental.com) rents mobiles and sells GSM phones (starting at $49) that will operate in 140 countries. Per-call rates vary throughout the world. **Planet Fone** (☎888/988–4777 ⊕www.planetfone.com) rents cell phones, but the per-minute rates are expensive. **PCCW** (☎2888–8888 ⊕www.pccw.com).

▌CUSTOMS & DUTIES

You're always allowed to bring goods of a certain value back home without having to pay any duty or import tax. But there's a limit on the amount of tobacco and liquor you can bring back duty-free, and some countries have separate limits for perfumes; for exact figures, check with your customs department. The values of so-called "duty-free" goods are included in these amounts. When you shop abroad, save all your receipts, as customs inspectors may ask to see them as well as the items you purchased. If the total value of your goods is more than the duty-free limit, you'll have to pay a tax (most often a flat percentage) on the value of everything beyond that limit.

Except for the usual prohibitions against narcotics, explosives, firearms, and ammunition and modest limits on alcohol, tobacco products, and perfume, you can bring anything you want into Hong Kong, including an unlimited amount of money. Nonresidents may bring in, duty-free, 60 cigarettes or 15 cigars or 75 grams of tobacco, and 1 liter of alcohol.

LOCAL DO'S & TABOOS

CUSTOMS OF THE COUNTRY

Face is ever-important. Never say anything that will make people look bad, especially in front of superiors. Having said that, Hong Kongers call it as they see it—sometimes with an honesty that westerners find brutal. You may be told how fat you're looking or that your mobile phone is a very old model. Take it in stride; it's not meant aggressively. Hong Kongers talk about money freely—how much they earn, how much their car costs—so don't be surprised to be asked about these things.

GREETINGS

Hong Kongers aren't touchy-feely. Stick to handshakes and low-key greetings.

SIGHTSEEING

By and large Hong Kongers are a rule-abiding bunch. Avoid jaywalking, eating on public transport, and feeding birds. Legislation has banned smoking in restaurants, most bars, workplaces, schools, and even public areas such as beaches, sport grounds, and parks. A whopping fine of HK$1,500 should deter even the most hardened smoker.

Hong Kong is *crowded*; pushing and nudging are common, especially on public transport.

OUT ON THE TOWN

Meals are a communal event, so food in a Chinese restaurant is always shared. You usually have a small bowl or plate to transfer food from the center platters into. Although cutlery is common in Hong Kong, it won't hurt to brush up on your use of chopsticks. Be sure not to mistake the communal serving chopsticks with your own.

It's fine to hold the bowl close to your mouth and shovel in the contents. Noisily slurping up soup and noodles is acceptable, as is belching when you're done. Covering the tablecloth in crumbs, drips, and even spat-out bones is a sign you've enjoyed your meal. Avoid leaving your chopsticks standing up in a bowl of rice—they look like the two incense sticks burned at funerals.

Hong Kongers dress quite smartly to eat out and go to the theater. Things get pretty glam at bars or clubs, too.

DOING BUSINESS

Make appointments well in advance and be punctual. Hong Kongers have a keen sense of hierarchy in the office: egalitarianism is often insulting. Let the tea lady get the tea and coffee—that's what she's there for. If you're visiting in a group, let the senior member lead proceedings.

Suits are the norm, regardless of the outside temperature. Local businesswomen are immaculately groomed. Pants are acceptable.

When entertaining, locals may insist on paying: after a slight protest, accept, as this lets them gain face.

Business cards are a big deal: not having one is like not having a personality. If possible, have yours printed in English on one side and Chinese on the other (hotels can arrange this in a few hours). Proffer your cards with both hands, receive them in the same way, then read them carefully, and make an admiring comment.

Hong Kong Customs & Excise Department (☎2815–7711 ⊕www.customs.gov.hk).

U.S. Customs and Border Protection (⊕www.cbp.gov).

▌ ELECTRICITY

The current in Hong Kong is 220 volts, 50 cycles alternating current (AC), so most American appliances can't be used without a transformer. Most plugs have three square prongs, like British plugs, though some use round prongs. You can buy adapters in just about every supermarket.

Consider making a small investment in a universal adapter, which has several types of plugs in one lightweight, compact unit. Most laptops and mobile phone chargers are dual voltage (i.e., they operate equally well on 110 and 220 volts), and thus require only an adapter. These days the same is true of small appliances such as hair dryers. Always check labels and manufacturer instructions to be sure. Don't use 110-volt outlets marked FOR SHAVERS ONLY for high-wattage appliances such as hair dryers.

Steve Kropla's Help for World Travelers (⊕www.kropla.com) has information on electrical and telephone plugs around the world. **Walkabout Travel Gear** (⊕www.walkabouttravelgear.com) has a good coverage of electricity under "adapters."

▌ EMERGENCIES

Locals and police are usually very helpful in emergencies. Most officers speak some English or will contact someone who does. For police, fire, and ambulance dial 999. There are 24-hour accident and emergency services at the Matilda, Caritas, Prince of Wales, and Queen Mary Hospitals. The Queen Mary and Adventist hospitals have 24-hour pharmacies. Local drugstore/pharmacy chain Watsons has shops throughout the city; they're

usually open until 9 PM. Most of the 12 private hospitals in Hong Kong only have primary and secondary medical services. The 46 government-run public hospitals cover all three types. Most treatments in public hospitals are heavily subsidized or free (⊕*www.ha.org.hk*).

U.S. Consulate General (✉26 Garden Rd., Central ☎2523–9011 ⊕www.usconsulate.org.hk).

Police, fire & ambulance (☎999). **Hong Kong Police & Taxi Complaint Hotline** (☎2527–7177).

Caritas Medical Centre (public) (✉111 Wing Hong St., Sham Shui Po, Kowloon ☎3408–7911 ⊕www.ha.org.hk). **Hong Kong Adventist Hospital** (private) (✉ 40 Stubbs Rd., Midlevels, Western ☎2574–6211 ⊕www.hkah.org.hk). **Hong Kong Baptist Hospital** (private) (✉223 Waterloo Rd., Kowloon ☎2229–8888 ⊕www.hkbh.org.hk). **Hong Kong Central Hospital** (private) (✉1 Lower Albert Rd., Central ☎2522–3141 ⊕www.hkch.org). **Matilda International Hospital** (private) (✉41 Mount Kellet Rd., The Peak, Central ☎2849–0111 ⊕www.matilda.org). **Prince of Wales Hospital** (public) (✉30–32 Ngan Shing St., Sha Tin, New Territories ☎2632–2211 ⊕www.ha.org.hk/pwh). **Queen Elizabeth Hospital** (public) (✉30 Gascoigne Rd., Yau Ma Tei, Kowloon ☎2958–8888). **Queen Mary Hospital** (public) (✉102 Pok Fu Lam Rd., Pok Fu Lam, Western ☎2855–3838 ⊕www.ha.org.hk/qmh).

Watsons (☎2868–4388).

GOVERNMENT ADVISORIES

As different countries have different worldviews, look at travel advisories from a range of governments to get more of a sense of what's going on out there. And be sure to parse the language carefully. For example, a warning to "avoid all travel" carries more weight than one urging you to "avoid nonessential travel," and both are much stronger than a plea to "exercise caution." A U.S. government travel warning is more permanent (though not necessarily more serious) than a so-called public announcement, which carries an expiration date.

The U.S. Department of State's Web site has more than just travel warnings and advisories. The consular information sheets issued for every country have general safety tips, entry requirements (though be sure to verify these with the country's embassy), and other useful details.

■ TIP→ Consider registering online with the State Department (https://travelregistration.state.gov), so the government will know to look for you should a crisis occur in the country you're visiting.

Hong Kong is a highly safe place as far as crime goes. The only recent safety threats were health-related: the SARS outbreak in 2003 and intermittent fears over avian flu. A massive awareness program stopped the spread of the illnesses, but it's worth checking to be sure there have been no new outbreaks.

General Information & Warnings **U.S. Department of State** (⊕www.travel.state.gov).

■ HEALTH

It's a good idea to be immunized against typhoid and Hepatitis A and B before coming to Hong Kong. In winter, a flu vaccination is also smart, especially if you're infection-prone or are a senior citizen.

Health Warnings **National Centers for Disease Control & Prevention** (CDC ☎877/394–8747 international travelers' health line ⊕www.cdc.gov/travel). **World Health Organization** (WHO ⊕www.who.int).

Water from government mains satisfies World Health Organization (WHO) standards. Expect to pay HK$10 to HK$15 for a 1½-liter bottle of purified water.

Condoms can help prevent most sexually transmitted diseases, but they aren't absolutely reliable and their quality varies from country to country. Speak with your physician and/or check the CDC or World Health Organization Web sites for

health alerts, particularly if you're pregnant, traveling with children, or have a chronic illness.

HONG KONG–SPECIFIC ISSUES

Severe Acute Respiratory Syndrome (SARS), also known as atypical pneumonia, is a respiratory illness caused by a strain of coronavirus that was first reported in parts of Asia in early 2003. Symptoms include a fever greater than 100.4°F (38°C), shortness of breath, and other flulike symptoms. The disease is thought to spread by close person-to-person contact, particularly respiratory droplets and secretions transmitted through the eyes, nose, or mouth. To prevent SARS, the Hong Kong Health Department recommends maintaining good personal hygiene, washing hands frequently, and wearing a face mask in crowded public places. SARS hasn't returned to Hong Kong, but many experts believe that it or other contagious, upper-respiratory viruses will continue to be a seasonal health concern. It is also worth noting that the World Health Organization declared Hong Kong SARS-free in 2003.

Avian influenza, commonly known as bird flu, is a form of influenza that affects birds (including poultry) but can be passed to humans. It causes initial flu symptoms, followed by respiratory and organ failure. Although rare, it's often lethal: there've been three outbreaks in Hong Kong, causing a total of seven deaths. The Hong Kong Government now exercises strict control over poultry farms and markets, and there are signs all over town warning against contact with birds. Pay heed to them, and make sure that any poultry or eggs you consume are well cooked.

Local Health Information **Department of Health Hotline** (☎2961–8989 ⊕www.dh.gov.hk). **Traveller's Health Service** (☎2150–7235 ⊕www.travelhealth.gov.hk).

OVER-THE-COUNTER REMEDIES

You can find most familiar over-the-counter medications (like aspirin and ibuprofen) easily in pharmacies such as Watsons, and often in supermarkets and convenience stores, too. Acetaminophen—or Tylenol—is often known as paracetamol locally. Oral contraceptives are also available without prescription.

■ HOURS OF OPERATION

Banks are open weekdays from 9 to 4:30 and Saturday from 9 to 12:30. Office hours are more or less the same as in the west: 9 to 5 or 6, although working longer hours is common. Some offices are open from 9 to noon on Saturday. Lunch hour is 1 PM to 2 PM; don't be surprised if offices close during lunch. Museums and sights are usually open six days a week from 9 to 5. Each site picks a different day, usually a Monday or Tuesday, to close. Pharmacies are generally open from about 10 AM until about 9 PM. For a 24-hour pharmacy you need to go to the Queen Mary or Adventist hospitals. (⇨ Emergencies, above).

HOLIDAYS

Major holidays in Hong Kong include: New Year's (first weekday in January), Chinese New Year (end of January/early February), Easter, Ching Ming (April 1), Labour Day (May 1), Dragon Boat Festival (late May/early June), Hong Kong SAR Establishment Day (July 1), Mid-Autumn Festival (late September/early October), National Day (October 1), and Christmas and Boxing Day (December 25 and 26). There are also other Chinese holidays throughout the year.

■ MAIL

Hong Kong's postal system is excellent. Airmail letters to any place in the world should take three to eight days. The Kowloon Central Post Office and the General Post Office in Central are open 8 AM to 6 PM Monday through Saturday.

Letters sent from Hong Kong are thought of as going to one of two zones. Zone 1 includes China, Japan, Taiwan, South Korea, Southeast Asia, Indonesia, and Asia. Zone 2 is everywhere else. International airmail costs HK\$2.40 or HK\$3 for a letter or postcard weighing less than 20 grams mailed to a Zone 1 or 2 address, respectively. To send a letter within Hong Kong, the cost is HK\$1.40. The post office also has an overnight express service called Speedpost.

Main Postal Branches **General Post Office** (⊠ 2 Connaught Rd., Central ☎ 2921–2222 ⊕ www.hongkongpost.com). **Kowloon Central Post Office** (⊠ 405 Nathan Road., Tsim T sa Shui).

SHIPPING PACKAGES

Packages sent airmail to the United States often take two weeks. Airmail shipments to the United Kingdom—both packages and letters—arrive within three or five days, while mail to Australia often arrives in as little as three days.

You are probably best off shipping your own parcels instead of letting shop owners do this for you, both to save money and to ensure that you are actually shipping yourself what you purchased and not a quick substitute—though most shop owners are honest and won't try to cheat you in this way. The workers at Hong Kong Post are extremely friendly and they will sell you all the packaging equipment you need, at unbelievably reasonable prices. Large international couriers in Hong Kong include DHL, Federal Express, and UPS.

Express Services **DHL** (☎ 2400–3388 ⊕ www.dhl.com.hk). **Federal Express** (☎ 2730–3333 ⊕ www.fedex.com/hk_english). **UPS** (☎ 2735–3535 ⊕ www.ups.com).

■ MONEY

Cash and plastic are the way to go. Very few shops or restaurants accept U.S. dollars, so either change in bulk or draw

Hong Kong dollars direct from an ATM. Traveler's checks aren't accepted in most shops, and can be a pain to cash—avoid them, if possible. Getting change for large bills isn't usually a problem.

SAMPLE PRICES	
Cup of Coffee/Tea	HK$30/HK$22
Glass of Wine	HK$45–HK$55
Glass of Beer	HK$45–HK$60
Sandwich	HK$25–HK$40
Fresh Juice from a Stall	HK$10
Bowl of Noodle Soup	HK$18
One-Mile Taxi Ride in Capital City	HK$16
Museum Admission	HK$10
Fake Louis Vuitton Purse	HK$100

Prices throughout this guide are given for adults. Substantially reduced fees are almost always available for children, students, and senior citizens.

■TIP➔ Banks never have every foreign currency on hand, and it may take as long as a week to order. If you're planning to exchange funds before leaving home, don't wait until the last minute.

ATMS & BANKS

Your own bank will probably charge a fee for using ATMs abroad; the foreign bank you use may also charge a fee. Nevertheless, you'll usually get a better rate of exchange at an ATM than you will at a currency-exchange office or even when changing money in a bank. And extracting funds as you need them is a safer option than carrying around a large amount of cash.

Reliable, safe ATMs are widely available throughout Hong Kong—some may carry the sign ETC instead of ATM. MTR stations are a good place to look if you're having trouble locating one. If your card was issued from a bank in an English-speaking country, the instructions on the ATM machine will appear in English.

You can withdraw cash in multiples of HK$100. ■TIP➔ PIN numbers with more than four digits are not recognized at ATMs in many countries. If yours has five or more, remember to change it before you leave.

CREDIT CARDS

Major credit cards are widely accepted in Hong Kong, though they may not be accepted at small shops, and in some shops you get better rates paying in cash. When adding tips to restaurant bills, be sure to write "HK$" and not just "$."

Throughout this guide, the following abbreviations are used: **AE**, American Express; **DC**, Diners Club; **MC**, Master-Card; and **V**, Visa.

It's a good idea to inform your credit-card company before you travel, especially if you're going abroad and don't travel internationally very often. Otherwise, the credit-card company might put a hold on your card owing to unusual activity—not a good thing halfway through your trip. Record all your credit-card numbers—as well as the phone numbers to call if your cards are lost or stolen—in a safe place, so you're prepared should something go wrong. Both MasterCard and Visa have general numbers you can call (collect if you're abroad) if your card is lost, but you're better off calling the number of your issuing bank, since Master-Card and Visa usually just transfer you to your bank; your bank's number is usually printed on your card.

If you plan to use your credit card for cash advances, you'll need to apply for a PIN at least two weeks before your trip. Although it's usually cheaper (and safer) to use a credit card abroad for large purchases (so you can cancel payments or be reimbursed if there's a problem), note that some credit-card companies *and* the banks that issue them add substantial percentages to all foreign transactions, whether they're in a foreign currency or not. Check on these fees before leaving home, so there won't be any surprises when you get the bill.

■TIP→ **Before you charge something, ask the merchant whether he or she plans to do a dynamic currency conversion (DCC). In such a transaction the credit-card** *processor* **(shop, restaurant, or hotel, not Visa or MasterCard) converts the currency and charges you in U.S. dollars. In most cases you'll pay the merchant a 3% fee for this service in addition to any credit-card company and issuing-bank foreign-transaction surcharges.**

Dynamic currency conversion programs are becoming increasingly widespread. Merchants who participate in them are supposed to ask whether you want to be charged in dollars or the local currency, but they don't always do so. And even if they do offer you a choice, they may well avoid mentioning the additional surcharges. The good news is that you *do* have a choice. And if this practice really gets your goat, you can avoid it entirely thanks to American Express; with its cards, DCC simply isn't an option.

Reporting Lost Cards **American Express** (☎800/992–3404 in U.S., 336/393–1111 collect from abroad ⊕www.americanexpress. com). **Diners Club** (☎800/234–6377 in U.S., 303/799–1504 collect from abroad ⊕www.dinersclub.com)**MasterCard** (☎800/622–7747 in U.S., 636/722–7111 collect from abroad ⊕www.mastercard.com). **Visa** (☎800/847–2911 in U.S., 410/581–9994 collect from abroad ⊕www.visa.com).

CURRENCY & EXCHANGE
The only currency used is the Hong Kong dollar, divided into 100 cents. There are bronze-color coins for 10, 20, and 50 cents; silver-color ones for 1, 2, and 5 dollars; and chunky bimetallic 10-dollar pieces. Bills can be confusing as there are a range of designs and issuing banks. There are new purple and older green 10-dollar bills, as well as bills for HK$20 (blue-green), HK$50 (purple), HK$100 (red), HK$500 (brown), and HK$1,000 (yellow). Don't be surprised if two bills of

the same value look different: three local banks (HSBC, Standard Chartered, and Bank of China) all issue bills and each has its own design. Although the image of Queen Elizabeth II doesn't appear on new coins, old ones bearing her image are still valid.

At this writing, there were approximately 7.8 Hong Kong dollars to 1 U.S. dollar. There are no currency restrictions in Hong Kong. You can exchange currency at the airport, in hotels, in banks, and through private money changers scattered through the tourist areas. Banks usually have the best rates, but as they charge a fee of up to HK$50 for nonaccount holders, it's better to change large sums infrequently. Currency exchange offices have no fees, but they offset that with poor rates. Stick to ATMs wherever you can.

■TIP→ **Even if a currency-exchange booth has a sign promising no commission, rest assured that there's some kind of huge, hidden fee. (Oh, that's right. The sign didn't say no** *fee***). And as for rates, you're almost always better off getting foreign currency at an ATM or exchanging money at a bank.**

■ PACKING

Appearances in Hong Kong are important. This is a city where suits are still de rigueur for meetings and business functions. Slop around in flip-flops and worn denims and you *will* feel there's a neon "tourist" sign over your head. Pack your nicer pairs of jeans or slacks for sightseeing—there are plenty of fake handbags around to dress them up with, come dinner.

From May through September it's seriously hot and sticky, but air-conditioning in hotels, restaurants, and museums can be arctic—keep a crushproof sweater or shawl in your day pack. Don't forget your swimsuit and sunscreen; many large hotels have pools, and you may want to spend some time on one of Hong Kong's many beaches. In October, November, March, and April, a jacket or sweater should suffice, but from December through February bring a light overcoat, preferably waterproof. No self-respecting Hong Konger leaves home each morning without a folding umbrella, nor should you.

PASSPORTS & VISAS

Citizens of the United States need only a valid passport to enter Hong Kong for stays up to three months. You need at least six months' validity on your passport before traveling to Asia. Upon arrival, officials at passport control will give you a Hong Kong entry slip. Keep this slip safe; you must present it with your passport for your return trip home. If you're planning to pop over the border into mainland China, you must first get a visa (⇨ below).

PASSPORTS

U.S. passports are valid for 10 years. You must apply in person if you're getting a passport for the first time; if your previous passport was lost, stolen, or damaged; or if your previous passport has expired and was issued more than 15 years ago or when you were under 16. All children under 18 must appear in person to apply for or renew a passport. Both parents must accompany any child under 14 (or send a notarized statement with their permission) and provide proof of their relationship to the child.

There are 13 regional passport offices, as well as 7,000 passport acceptance facilities in post offices, public libraries, and other governmental offices. If you're renewing a passport, you can do so by mail. Forms are available at passport acceptance facilities and online.

The cost to apply for a new passport is $97 for adults, $82 for children under 16; renewals are $67. Allow six weeks for processing, both for first-time passports and renewals. For an expediting fee of $60 you can reduce this time to about two weeks. If your trip is less than two

weeks away, you can get a passport even more rapidly by going to a passport office with the necessary documentation. Private expediters can get things done in as little as 48 hours, but charge hefty fees.

■**TIP**→ **Before your trip, make two copies of your passport's data page (one for someone at home and another for you to carry separately). Or scan the page and e-mail it to someone at home and/or yourself.**

VISAS

A visa is essentially formal permission to enter a country. Visas allow countries to keep track of you and other visitors—and generate revenue (from application fees). You *always* need a visa to enter a foreign country; however, many countries routinely issue tourist visas on arrival, particularly to U.S. citizens. When your passport is stamped or scanned in the immigration line, you're actually being issued a visa. Sometimes you have to stand in a separate line and pay a small fee to get your stamp before going through immigration, but you can still do this at the airport on arrival. Getting a visa isn't always that easy. Some countries require that you arrange for one in advance of your trip. There's usually—but not always—a fee involved, and said fee may be nominal ($10 or less) or substantial ($100 or more).

If you must apply for a visa in advance, you can usually do it in person or by mail. When you apply by mail, you send your passport to a designated consulate, where your passport will be examined and the visa issued. Expediters—usually the same ones who handle expedited passport applications—can do all the work of obtaining your visa for you; however, there's always an additional cost (often more than $50 per visa).

Most visas limit you to a single trip—basically during the actual dates of your planned vacation. Other visas allow you to visit as many times as you wish for a specific period of time. Remember that requirements change, sometimes at the drop of a hat, and the burden is on you to make sure that you have the appropriate visas. Otherwise, you'll be turned away at the airport or, worse, deported after you arrive in the country. No company or travel insurer gives refunds if your travel plans are disrupted because you didn't have the correct visa.

Travel agents in Hong Kong can issue visas to visit mainland China. Costs range from $130 for a visa issued within two to three working days to $160 for a same-day service. The same services cost $50 and $80 in the United States. Note: the visa application will ask your occupation. The Chinese don't look favorably on those who work in publishing or the media. People in these professions routinely state "teacher" under "occupation." Before you go, contact the embassy or consulate of the People's Republic of China to gauge the current mood.

China Visa Information **Chinese Consulate** (☎212/244-9456 ⊕www.nyconsulate.prchina. org). **Chinese Embassy** (☎202/338-6688 ⊕www.china-embassy.org). **Visa to Asia** (⊕www.visatoasia.com/china.html) provides up-to-date information on visa applications for China.

Hong Kong General Information **Hong Kong Immigration Department** (☎2824-6111 ⊕www.info.gov.hk/immd).

Hong Kong Travel Agents **China Travel Service** (☎2315-7188 ⊕www.ctshk.com) has 22 branches all over Hong Kong.**Japan Travel**

Agency (☎2368-9151 ⊕www.jta.biz) offers the quickest and most efficient visa service.

U.S. Passport Information **U.S. Department of State** (☎877/487-2778 ⊕http://travel. state.gov/passport).

U.S. Passport & Visa Expediters **A. Briggs Passport & Visa Expeditors** (☎800/806-0581 or 202/464-3000 ⊕www. abriggs.com). **American Passport Express** (☎800/455-5166 or 603/559-9888 ⊕www. americanpassport.com). **Passport Express** (☎800/362-8196 or 401/272-4612 ⊕www. passportexpress.com). **Travel Document Systems** (☎800/874-5100 or 202/638-3800 ⊕www.traveldocs.com). **Travel the World Visas** (☎866/886-8472 or 301/495-7700 ⊕www.world-visa.com).

▮ RESTROOMS

Hong Kong was once renowned for its lack of public restrooms, but things are improving. When sightseeing in the city, dip into malls or the lobby of big international hotels to use their facilities. Tipping attendants HK$2–HK$5 is the norm. Since SARS and bird flu the government has been particularly active in keeping public facilities clean, but toilet paper can be hit-and-miss: bring your own tissues in case. **Find a Loo** **The Bathroom Diaries** (⊕www.thebathroomdiaries.com) is flush with unsanitized info on restrooms the world over—each one located, reviewed, and rated.

▮ SAFETY

Hong Kong is an incredibly safe place—day and night. The police do a good job maintaining law and order, but there are still a few pickpockets about, especially in Tsim Sha Tsui. So exercise the same caution you would in any large city: be aware and avoid carrying large amounts of cash or valuables with you, and you should have no problems.

Nearly all consumer dissatisfaction in Hong Kong stems from the electronics retailers in Tsim Sha Tsui. Get some ref-

erence prices online before buying, and
always check the contents of boxed items
before you leave the shop.

**■TIP→ Distribute your cash, credit cards,
IDs, and other valuables between a deep
front pocket, an inside jacket or vest pocket,
and a hidden money pouch. Don't reach for
the money pouch once you're in public.**

■ TAXES

Hong Kong levies a 10% service charge
and a 3% government tax on hotel rooms.
There's no other sales tax or V.A.T.

■ TIME

Hong Kong is 12 hours ahead of Eastern
Standard Time and seven hours ahead
of Greenwich Mean Time. Remember
during daylight savings time to add an
hour to the time difference (so it's 13
hours ahead of EST and eight hours
ahead of GMT).

Time Zones Timeanddate.com (⊕www.time
anddate.com/worldclock) can help you figure
out the correct time anywhere in the world.

■ TIPPING

Tipping isn't a big part of Hong Kong culture. That said, hotels are one of the few
places where tips are expected. Hotels and
major restaurants usually add a 10% service charge; however, in almost all cases,
this money does not go to the waiters
and waitresses. Add on up to 10% more
for good service. Tipping restroom attendants is common, but it is generally not
the custom to leave an additional tip in
taxis and beauty salons, and unheard of
in theaters and cinemas.

TIPPING GUIDELINES FOR HONG KONG	
Bartender	HK$10–HK$20 per round of drinks, depending on the number of drinks
Bellhop	HK$5–HK$20 per bag, depending on the level of the hotel
Hotel Concierge	HK$20–HK$50, more if he or she performs a service for you
Hotel Doorman	HK$5 if he helps you get a cab
Restroom Attendants	HK$2–HK$5
Porter at Airport or Train Station	HK$2–HK$5 per bag
Waiter	5%–10% if service was good

■ VISITOR INFO

ONLINE TRAVEL TOOLS

For a guide to what's happening in Hong
Kong, check out the Hong Kong Tourist Board's (HKTB's) excellent site. For
weather info, check out the Hong Kong
Observatory. For political information
plus news and interesting business links
try the Hong Kong government site.

**All About Hong Kong Business in Hong
Kong** (⊕www.gov.hk/en/business): government-run site packed with advice. **Centamap**
(⊕www.centamap.com): online Hong Kong
street maps so detailed they give street numbers and building names. **Hong Kong Government** (⊕www.gov.hk). **Hong Kong Tourist
Board** (HKTB ⊕www.discoverhongkong.com).
Hong Kong Weather (⊕www.weather.gov.hk)

Cultural Activities HK Magazine (⊕www.
asia-city.com): online version of a quirky
weekly rag with the lowdown on just about
everything happening in town. **Hong Kong
Film** (⊕www.lovehkfilm.com): all you need
to know about Hongkollywood. **Hong Kong
Leisure and Cultural Services Department**
(⊕www.lcsd.gov.hk): access Web sites for all
of Hong Kong's museums and parks through
this government portal.

Currency Conversion **Google** (⊕www. google.com) does currency conversion. Just type in the amount you want to convert and an explanation of how you want it converted (e.g., "14 Swiss francs in dollars"), and voilà. **Oanda. com** (⊕www.oanda.com) also allows you to print out a handy table with the current day's conversion rates. **XE.com** (⊕www.xe.com) is a good currency conversion Web site.

Local Insight **Eat Drink Hong Kong** (⊕www. eatdrinkhongkong.com): excellent online guide to Hong Kong's bars and restaurants. **Gay Hong Kong** (⊕www.gayhk.com): comprehensive guide to the local scene. **Geoexpat** (⊕www.geoexpat.com): local know-how from Hong Kong's large expat community. **Hong Kong Outdoors** (⊕www.hkoutdoors.com): the authority on hiking, camping, and all things wild in Hong Kong.

Newspapers **Hong Kong Standard** (⊕www. thestandard.com.hk): free English-language paper, mainly focused on business. **South China Morning Post** (⊕www.scmp.com): leading local English-language daily.

INDEX

Color Section: Taking the tram, Victoria Peak: *Hong Kong Tourism Board.* Star Ferry: *Hong Kong Tourism.* Cantonese Opera performers, Hong Kong Heritage Museum: *Sylvain Grandadam/age fotostock.* Tai Chi practitioners, Hong Kong Park: *Hemis/Alamy.* Wan Chai shopping street: *José Fuste Raga/age fotostock.* Buddha, Po Lin Monastery, Lantau Island: *Rough Guides/Alamy.* Flagstaff Museum of Tea Ware: *Pat Behnke/Alamy.* Manpower sculpture by Rosanna Li: *Grotto Fine Art Gallery.* Trams and taxis: *Hong Kong Tourism Board.* Avenue of the Stars, Kowloon waterfront: *Brad Mitchell/Alamy.* Hakka woman: *ImageState/Alamy.* Pacific Place mall: *Hong Kong Tourism Board.* Po Lin Monastery, Lantau Island: *Werner Otto/age fotostock.* Chinese New Year Parade: *John Leung/Shutterstock.* Sai Kung Peninsula, New Territories: *Hong Kong Tourism Board.* Chow Yun-Fat in Crouching Tiger, Hidden Dragon: *Pictorial Press Ltd/Alamy.* Duk Ling junk: *Hong Kong Tourism Board.*

NOTES

NOTES

NOTES

NOTES

NOTES

NOTES

NOTES

NOTES

NOTES

NOTES

NOTES

NOTES

ABOUT OUR WRITERS

Liana Cafolla is a Hong Kong–based free-lance journalist and editor who writes for the *South China Morning Post, AsiaSpa, Business Traveller,* and other publications. Hong Kong's relentless energy and ever-changing character provide the inspiration for her articles about lifestyle, design, people, and business, as well as food and wine trends. She reviewed a mouth-watering assortment of Hong Kong restaurants for the Where to Eat chapter.

Cherise Fong, a freelance writer originally from San Francisco, currently lives in Hong Kong, where she contributes regularly to CNN.com International's Digital Biz special and writes copy for the design studio and publisher AllRightsReserved. Her previous stints and sojourns include polishing English for local media in Beijing, Web scripting for startups in London, Monaco, and New York, technical translating in Paris, webmastering while living in a chateau in the small French village of Herimoncourt. Cherise updated the Experience, Neighborhoods, Cultural Sights, and Side Trip to Macau chapters of this book.

Helen Luk is a veteran journalist, globetrotter, and fervent food lover. She has traveled to 26 countries and shows no sign of slowing down. Her favorite destinations include Siem Reap, Kyoto, Xinjiang in western China, Prague, and Seville. She previously worked for the *South China Morning Post* and the Associated Press in Hong Kong and now runs a business and accounting magazine. Helen contributed to the Where to Eat chapter in this book.

Zoe Mak was born in Hong Kong and studied in Toronto, where she began her journalism career at *Ming Pao Daily News.* She moved back to Hong Kong in 2007 and now writes a weekly beauty column for the *South China Morning Post.* In both Toronto and Hong Kong, as well as Japan, Taiwan, and the United States, Zoe learned that shopping is a wonderful way to get to know a new culture. She considers herself a full-time bargain hunter and she never stops searching for the best shops and the best deals on her travels. She updated the shopping chapter of this edition of *Fodor's Hong Kong.*

Dominique Rowe attended a record number of English boarding schools before abandoning London's drizzle for sunny Hong Kong, the land of her birth. Her meteorological obsession led her to a stint as a weather reporter on TVB Pearl, where her repartée and unusual wardrobe garnered a not-insubstantial fan club. After working as chief editor of *JUICE,* a trendy Hong Kong fashion and nightlife magazine, Dominique is now a freelance writer, contributing to *AsiaSpa* and *TIME* in addition to the nightlife and shopping chapters of *Fodor's Hong Kong, 21st edition.*

We'd also like to thank writers Joshua Samuel Brown ("Spirituality in China" article, the Pearl River Delta chapter); Elyse Singleton ("Markets" article); Chris Horton ("21st Century China" article); Hannah Lee (the Pearl River Delta chapter); and Albert Wong (Where to Stay chapter).